DPT

3 1833 05200 9278

P9-EEN-849

Advanced Microsoft® Office Documents 2007 Edition Inside Out

NOTICE: If any part of these contents is lost or damaged, the Patron will be charged for the total cost of all items.

_____ Disk   _____ Video

_____ Cassette   ___/___ CD

___/___ Text   _____ Other

Stephanie Krieger

PUBLISHED BY
Microsoft Press
A Division of Microsoft Corporation
One Microsoft Way
Redmond, Washington 98052-6399

Copyright © 2007 by Stephanie Krieger

All rights reserved. No part of the contents of this book may be reproduced or transmitted in any form
or by any means without the written permission of the publisher.

Library of Congress Control Number: 2006939803

Printed and bound in the United States of America.

1 2 3 4 5 6 7 8 9 QWE 2 1 0 9 8 7

Distributed in Canada by H.B. Fenn and Company Ltd.

A CIP catalogue record for this book is available from the British Library.

Microsoft Press books are available through booksellers and distributors worldwide. For further infor-
mation about international editions, contact your local Microsoft Corporation office or contact Microsoft
Press International directly at fax (425) 936-7329. Visit our Web site at www.microsoft.com/mspress.
Send comments to mspinput@microsoft.com.

Microsoft, Microsoft Press, Excel, Groove, Internet Explorer, OneNote, PowerPoint, SharePoint, Visio,
Visual Basic, Windows, Windows Server and Windows Vista are either registered trademarks or
trademarks of Microsoft Corporation in the United States and/or other countries. Other product and
company names mentioned herein may be the trademarks of their respective owners.

The example companies, organizations, products, domain names, e-mail addresses, logos, people, places,
and events depicted herein are fictitious. No association with any real company, organization, product,
domain name, e-mail address, logo, person, place, or event is intended or should be inferred.

This book expresses the author's views and opinions. The information contained in this book is provided
without any express, statutory, or implied warranties. Neither the authors, Microsoft Corporation, nor its
resellers, or distributors will be held liable for any damages caused or alleged to be caused either directly
or indirectly by this book.

Acquisitions Editor: Juliana Aldous Atkinson
Developmental Editor: Sandra Haynes
Project Editor: Jenny Moss Benson
Editorial Production Services: Custom Editorial Productions, Inc.
Technical Reviewer: Beth Melton

Body Part No. X13-24131

For those two beautiful little blessings who share my desk but refuse to do any of the writing—my Finster and Janie.

"'Aha!' he said, 'I have caught nature in the act.'
But he was deceived by appearances, which happens only too often,
whether one uses a microscope or not."

–Voltaire, Micromegas

Contents at a Glance

Table of Contents

What do you think of this book? We want to hear from you!

Microsoft is interested in hearing your feedback so we can continually improve our books and learning resources for you. To participate in a brief online survey, please visit:

www.microsoft.com/learning/booksurvey/

Part 5 Templates, Automation, and Customization

What do you think of this book? We want to hear from you!

Microsoft is interested in hearing your feedback so we can continually improve our books and learning resources for you. To participate in a brief online survey, please visit:

www.microsoft.com/learning/booksurvey/

Acknowledgments

When I've mentioned that I'm working on this large book, people have often asked if I have a co-author or if I'm writing it by myself. What they don't realize is that a book like this is anything but a sole effort simply because it has a sole author. So, thank you...

- To my family—Mom, Dad, Elise, Michael, Ari, and Jared—for believing in me even when you hardly ever see me. I love you all. And special thanks to Mom, who worked overtime throughout this project as my unofficial shrink and sounding board.

- To everyone at MS Press and CEP who contributed to this project. In particular, thank you Lucinda Rowley, Sandra Haynes, and Jenny Moss Benson for your confidence in this book.

- To Beth Melton, technical reviewer extraordinaire, for your marvelous contributions to this project. The book and I are both better for knowing you.

- To Jan Clavey, for jumping in to catch the Hail Mary pass.

- To Stuart Stuple, for allowing me to randomize when I know you didn't have the time for it; to Tristan Davis, for responding to emails from the other side of the world; to Roberto Taboada for reading my novel-length emails; and to the many other members of the 2007 Office release product team whose knowledge, insights, and generosity have helped make this a better book, including Jessica Arnold, Jon Bailor, Krista Bendig, Savraj Dhanjal, Joe Friend, Mike Maxey, Margaret Plumley, Scott Rockfeld, Alex Simmons, and Brandon Taylor. And, the thanks extend as well to the patient support engineers who worked as test engineers throughout the beta, especially Jagadeesh Parameswaran and Irfan Parwez.

- To the wonderful people I have the pleasure to work with both at Microsoft and among my other clients (with thanks for many reasons, not the least of which has often been your patience and understanding in the face of book deadlines), including Nathalie Alfred, Cameron Anderson, Gonzalo Arellano, Roger Baerwolf, Alex Blanton, Sue Cahill, Otto Cate, Tawni Christensen, Danielle Damasius, Sheila Davis, John Donnarumma, Tish Gilvey, Lynn Haller, Lisa Holland Smith, Jessica Iben, Kari Jackson-Klönther, Mark Johnson, Angela Johnson, Sheridan Jones, Tess Kander, Amilcar Kaufman, Dan Klinglesmith, Jason Kozleski, Amanda Lefebvre, Pam Mauseth, Krista McClimans, Blanka Michalski, Charlie Montgomery, Lisa Pere, Jessica Reading, Becca Robinson, Elsa Rosenberg, and John Smithwick.

- To the Microsoft MVP program that I am so privileged to be a part of, and that association that's made me better at what I do by enabling me to be part of a community of generous and talented experts, with special thanks to my MVP Lead, Ed Hickey.

- To David Rubin and Jeff Bucari for technical support and photography (respectively) above and beyond the call of friendship.

- And, to Gayle Madeira, the lazy operator herself.

About the CD

The companion CD that ships with this book contains many tools and resources to help you get the most out of your Inside Out book.

What's On the CD

Your Inside Out CD includes the following:

- **Sample files.** Click the Install Sample Files button on the CD's Welcome tab to install the documents, templates, code samples, and other exercise-related resources referenced in the book.

- Articles and additional documentation on a variety of document production and customization topics.

- Recorded webcasts from the author demonstrating many of the tasks covered throughout this book.

- Links to a wide range of free online resources, including articles, community and support Web sites, downloadable tools, and trial software.

- Links to expert blogs and other Web sites directly from members of the 2007 Office release product team as well as several Microsoft MVPs.

- **Additional eBooks.** In this section you'll find the fully searchable electronic version of this book along with the following resources:
    - *Microsoft Computer Dictionary*, Fifth Edition
    - *First Look 2007 Microsoft Office System* (Katherine Murray, 2006)
    - Sample chapter and poster from *Look Both Ways: Help Protect Your Family on the Internet* (Linda Criddle, 2007)
    - Windows Vista Product Guide

System Requirements

Following are the minimum system requirements necessary to run the CD:

- Microsoft Windows Vista, Windows XP with Service Pack (SP) 2, Windows Server 2003 with SP1, or later operating system

- 500 megahertz (MHz) processor or higher

- 2 gigabyte (GB) storage space; a portion of this disk space will be freed after installation if the original download package is removed from the hard drive.

- 256 megabytes (MB) RAM

- CD-ROM or DVD-ROM drive
- 1024x768 or higher resolution monitor
- Microsoft Windows or Windows Vista–compatible sound card and speakers
- Microsoft Internet Explorer 6 or higher
- Microsoft Mouse or compatible pointing device

> **Note**
> An Internet connection is necessary to access the hyperlinks on the CD. Connect time charges may apply.

Support Information

Every effort has been made to ensure the accuracy of the contents of the book and of this CD. As corrections or changes are collected, they will be added to a Microsoft Knowledge Base article. Microsoft Press provides support for books and companion CDs at the following Web site:

http://www.microsoft.com/learning/support/books/

If you have comments, questions, or ideas regarding the book or this CD, or questions that are not answered by visiting the site above, please send them via e-mail to:

mspinput@microsoft.com

You can also click the Feedback or CD Support links on the Welcome page. Please note that Microsoft software product support is not offered through the above addresses.

If your question is about the software, and not about the content of this book, please visit the Microsoft Help and Support page or the Microsoft Knowledge Base at:

http://support.microsoft.com

In the United States, Microsoft software product support issues not covered by the Microsoft Knowledge Base are addressed by Microsoft Product Support Services. Location-specific software support options are available from:

http://support.microsoft.com/gp/selfoverview/

Microsoft Press provides corrections for books through the World Wide Web at *http://www.microsoft.com/mspress/support/*. To connect directly to the Microsoft Press Knowledge Base and enter a query regarding a question or issue that you may have, go to *http://www.microsoft.com/mspress/support/search.htm*.

Conventions and Features Used in This Book

This book uses special text and design conventions to make it easier for you to find the information you need.

Text Conventions

Convention	Meaning
Abbreviated commands for navigating the Ribbon	For your convenience, this book uses abbreviated commands. For example, "Click Home, Insert, Insert Cells" means that you should click the Home tab on the Ribbon, then click the Insert button, and finally click the Insert Cells command.
Boldface type	**Boldface** type is used to indicate text that you type.
Initial Capital Letters	The first letters of the names of tabs, dialog boxes, dialog box elements, and commands are capitalized. Example: the Save As dialog box.
Italicized type	*Italicized* type is used to indicate new terms.
Plus sign (+) in text	Keyboard shortcuts are indicated by a plus sign (+) separating two key names. For example, CTRL+ALT+DELETE means that you press the Ctrl, Alt, and Delete keys at the same time.

Design Conventions

INSIDE OUT

These are the book's signature tips. In these tips, you'll get the straight scoop on what's going on with the software—inside information about why a feature works the way it does. You'll also find handy workarounds to deal with software problems.

TROUBLESHOOTING

Look for these sidebars to find solutions to common problems you might encounter. Troubleshooting sidebars appear next to related information in the chapters.

Cross-references point you to other locations in the book that offer additional information about the topic being discussed.

CAUTION!

Cautions identify potential problems that you should look out for when you're completing a task or problems that you must address before you can complete a task.

Note

Notes offer additional information related to the task being discussed.

Introduction

Each time a new version of Microsoft Office is released, a flurry of books, training courses, and other resources quickly follow. Almost always—whether those resources are identified as being for beginner, intermediate, or advanced users—they expect that you need to learn everything again from the ground up. But, just because there's a new version of Microsoft Office, doesn't mean that Microsoft Office is new to you.

As a trainer and document consultant, I've often been frustrated by the lack of available resources that move beyond 'click here' or 'point there' to explain *why* things work the way they do, which best practices can make a real difference to your work, and what tools you may be missing that could simplify your work and expand your possibilities. So, I decided that was exactly the book I wanted to write for the 2007 Microsoft Office system.

With the release of the 2007 Office system, the programs you know have become more powerful, more flexible, and easier to use than ever before. If ever there was a time for experienced Microsoft Office users to take their work to a new level and learn to get more out of these incredible programs, this is it.

Throughout this book, you'll learn about new features across the 2007 release. You'll also learn how to put what you already know together with both new and existing methods and concepts to work the way the experts do, how to create the kind of documents and templates you've always wanted, and how to take full advantage of the capabilities in these programs to find the simple solutions you've often wondered about. It's all about doing less work, getting better results, and expanding your possibilities.

Who Will Benefit Most from This Book

You're an experienced Microsoft Office user and you don't need to start from scratch. This book takes you at your word, so the basics you already know are not repeated here. Though a few chapters that are specific to advanced tasks (such as Microsoft Office Excel 2007 PivotTables) do start from the beginning and move at an advanced pace, you'll find far more lists of key tips, hands-on concepts, and advanced timesaving or troubleshooting methods in most chapters than step-by-step instructions for using the basics of a feature. Following are just a few examples of what you'll find here.

- The Microsoft Office Word 2007 chapter on styles (Chapter 5, "Styles") does not walk you through steps for how to use the New Style dialog box. Instead, the chapter addresses the way that styles are structured, how to create effective style sets, and how to manage styles in documents and templates. It introduces the new Themes feature with everything you need to make use of this powerful new formatting tool and provides guidance for more advanced tasks, such as how to simplify your work with the often overcomplicated list styles feature (outline numbered lists).

- The Office Excel 2007 chapter on charts (Chapter 15, "Charts") does not step you through creating a basic chart or explain basics such as what an axis is. Instead, the chapter gives you the direction you need to use the new charting engine efficiently; timesaving tips for creating effective charts; help for more advanced tasks such as managing data, combining chart types, and working with secondary axes; and step by step instructions and troubleshooting for creating complex chart types such as price/volume charts and bubble charts.

- The Microsoft Office PowerPoint 2007 chapter on creating presentations (Chapter 19, "Slides and Presentations") does not step you through the basics of applying a layout or explain the difference between adding your logo to a master or an individual slide. Instead, this chapter explains how to set up either a presentation or a slide show so that it will behave the way you want it to; how to work effectively with masters, layouts, and designs; how to manage various content types (such as charts or embedded Office Word 2007 tables) in your presentation; and how to take advantage of new features such as custom slide layouts and the unique benefits of Themes that you get when working in Office PowerPoint 2007.

- Assuming that you are an experienced Microsoft Office user looking for new ways to both simplify and expand on your use of Word, Excel, and PowerPoint, this book also provides extensive introductions to using Microsoft Visual Basic for Applications (VBA) (Chapter 21, "VBA Primer") and the new Office Open XML Formats (Chapter 22, "Office Open XML Essentials").

  I strongly believe that the programming capabilities built-in to the 2007 Office release programs can greatly simplify your work and save you time. You absolutely don't need to be a programmer to make use of this powerful functionality. That said, an understanding of core features and experience working with the 2007 release programs is essential to being able to capitalize on the available programmability and customization options in Word, Excel, and PowerPoint. So, those who have mastered the essentials of complex document production (covered in Parts 1 through 4 of this book) will get the most from Part 5 of this book, titled "Templates, Automation, and Customization."

Additional Resources for Reviewing the Basics

At the beginning of most feature-specific chapters throughout this book, I've referenced this introduction as the place to find recommendations of additional resources for those who want more basic information on a given topic. The *Step by Step* book series is a good place to start for core basics.

- *Microsoft Office Word 2007 Step by Step*, by Joyce Cox and Joan Preppernau

- *Microsoft Office Excel 2007 Step by Step*, by Curtis D. Frye

- *Microsoft Office PowerPoint 2007 Step by Step*, by Joyce Cox and Joan Preppernau

For detailed coverage that starts from the beginning, you may also want to check out the program-specific books of the *Inside Out* series, including *Microsoft Office Excel 2007 Inside Out* and *Microsoft Office Word 2007 Inside Out.*

 For additional resources at all levels, including links to blogs and other Web sites from some of the members of the 2007 Office release product team as well as several Microsoft MVPs, see the Expert Tips tab of this book's CD.

What You Can Expect from This Book

This book is a comprehensive guide to advanced document and template production, troubleshooting, and customization using Word, Excel, and PowerPoint.

Approximately 30 percent of this book's content covers Word topics, and about 15 percent each is devoted to topics within Excel, PowerPoint, and big-picture concepts that cross multiple programs (such as managing electronic documents or creating templates). Approximately 20 percent of this book's content is devoted to programmability topics (VBA and XML). And, the remaining 5 percent covers other programs in the 2007 Office system, including Microsoft Office Visio 2007, Microsoft Office OneNote 2007, Microsoft Office Groove 2007, and Microsoft Windows SharePoint Services, which are introduced where appropriate to complement the work you do with documents.

The most important distinction I want to make for those venturing into this book is that it's not a general guide to the 2007 Office system. For example, you will learn how to lay out complex pages, create professional graphics, customize the Ribbon, and troubleshoot documents more easily, but you won't learn how to configure email settings or create a database here.

So, if you're ready to take your work with Microsoft Office documents to the next level, read on, and welcome to the 2007 Office system.

PART 1
Document Essentials

Introducing the 2007 Microsoft Office System

Reading this book, chances are that you are an experienced Microsoft Office user looking to take your work to a new level. So, when you first saw the 2007 Microsoft Office release, your reaction might have been very much like mine.

It looks cool. The XML file formats sound interesting. There are some great new features that enable people to build documents in a few clicks, and most of the basics are easier to access. But, wait! I need more than the basics. I need to create professional, flexible, complex documents. Did the Microsoft Office program designers forget about me, the advanced user? I can't sacrifice flexibility for ease of use!

Sound familiar? If so, you're likely to be as pleasantly surprised as I was.

No, they didn't forget about us. In fact, you might be amazed at the documents and templates you can create, and how much easier it can be to get them done.

In this first chapter, I'll provide you with introductions to some of the key changes for document production in the 2007 Office release programs Word, Excel, and PowerPoint and help you settle in and get comfortable with the new programs, the new interface, and the new file formats. I'll also introduce you to some core concepts for advanced document production.

Redefining Documents for Today's Business Demands

As recently as a few years ago, the word *document* might have conjured images of typewriters, steno pads, or that white correction fluid we all used constantly to paint over typos. Today, if you work a lot with documents, you probably think of anything from the typical interoffice memo, to a budget planning workbook, a marketing pitch book full of complex financials and graphics, a slide presentation, or a set of automated forms and templates created for use across an organization.

The days of slide carrousels are long gone. Documents no longer need to be outsourced to a printer or a desktop publishing company because they include graphics or a complex page layout. What's more, it's much more likely that the recipient of your document will access the document from their e-mail inbox rather than by the use of a letter opener.

So, it makes sense that the time has come for the way we create documents to change as well. The 2007 Office suite takes full advantage of new technologies like XML to create entirely new, integrated, seamless solutions.

Creating Documents Across the Office System

When you think of documents, do you automatically think of Microsoft Word? Word is certainly the best home for most documents that are predominantly text, usually regardless of the complexity of the layout or graphic elements you might need to include. But, do you consider all of your options when you prepare to create a document?

When you use the best program for the task (whether the task is a document such as a report or presentation, or just one element of that document, such as a chart or a diagram), you usually get the best results with the least amount of work. This book will take you to the next level of document production—giving you the keys to the great documents and templates you need to create in Microsoft Office Word 2007 as well as in Microsoft Office Excel 2007 and Microsoft Office PowerPoint 2007. We'll also look at how you can take advantage of the benefits available when you use those programs together and how you can incorporate elements from Microsoft Office Visio 2007 and Microsoft Office OneNote 2007 into your documents for even more power and flexibility.

What's New for Your Documents in the 2007 Office Suite

Recently, one of the program managers working on the Office Word 2007 team asked me what I think of the 2007 Office system. My answer was that I'm overjoyed with 75 percent of it, I like 85 percent, I'm okay with 95 percent, and I will learn to live with the other 5 percent. He thought this sounded just about right.

You see, there are 400 million users of Microsoft Office worldwide. So, when the folks on the product teams design a new version, they have to try to consider all 400 million of us. No easy task, to say the least. It stands to reason that I might not like a feature that's an absolute lifesaver to someone else. I might also have come to depend on a feature that only a handful of us out of the 400 million ever used, so it was dropped from the program.

That said, complex document production is what I do and have done for years. So, you'll read a lot of enthusiasm in this book, because the 2007 Office suite presents many incredible advances. But, do not expect me to be a cheerleader.

Just like you, as an experienced Microsoft Office user, I've come to depend on features and methods that might have changed or, in a few cases, even disappeared. The more experienced you are, the more frustrating it can be to find and acclimate to the best new method available for a given task. So, I have made it my business to provide help throughout the book for coping with and adapting to such changes as they arise.

This overview introduces key changes and important new features. You can also expect much additional new or changed functionality to be addressed throughout the book, where applicable.

Word, Excel, and PowerPoint

The most talked about stories of what's new across the 2007 Office system programs Word, Excel, and PowerPoint are the new user interface and the new file formats–both of which are discussed later in this chapter. Additionally, there's quite a bit of new cross-program functionality, such as Document Themes and Quick Styles (also introduced later in this chapter), which are designed to help you to create better looking, more effective documents more easily across all three programs.

But, before we get there, let's take a quick look at the methodology behind the sweeping changes in this version of Microsoft Office. Virtually all of the changes across the 2007 Office release, as well as within each program, are designed along one or more of a few key concepts.

Ease of Use

The new user interface, for example, is intended to make commands more easily accessible, expose functionality you might not be aware of, and generally provide a more streamlined experience for creating and editing content.

Transparency

The new file formats, for example, are based on XML. These XML-based formats enable you to easily access literally all of the document content, including document metadata–helping to alleviate security concerns over potentially private hidden content. The XML formats can also dramatically reduce file sizes and greatly enhance the integration and automation capabilities of your documents, which you'll learn about in this book.

Enhanced Capabilities for More Dynamic Documents

Following are just a few of my favorite new features in Word, Excel, and PowerPoint that exemplify the tremendous document production capabilities of the 2007 Office suite.

Favorite Feature	Why You Will Want to Use It
Document Themes	Apply coordinated sets of colors, fonts, and graphic effects to the entire document in one click. If that sounds a bit too formulaic for you as an advanced user, have no fear. You can customize Themes, create your own, and save them for sharing across computers or with other people.
Quick Styles	Quick Styles enable you to apply several types of formatting at once to everything from text or tables to slide backgrounds, diagrams, or charts. Quick Styles are available from galleries that provide previews of each available option. As with Themes, many types of Quick Styles can be customized. Some can also be saved as templates and shared with others. See Figure 1-1 for an example of a Quick Style gallery.
Live Previews	Just point to a formatting option (such as a Theme or a Quick Style), to see exactly how that formatting will look when applied to your document. Move your pointer away without making a selection and your document is unchanged. This is a terrific, timesaving advance—particularly for those of us who regularly design documents and templates.

Favorite Feature	Why You Will Want to Use It
SmartArt	The hapless Diagram And Organizational Chart tool has been replaced with phenomenally flexible SmartArt—a far more interesting, powerful, and professional approach to creating customized business diagrams quickly and easily. See Figure 1-2.

Figure 1-1 The Picture Styles gallery is one of the many types of Quick Styles available.

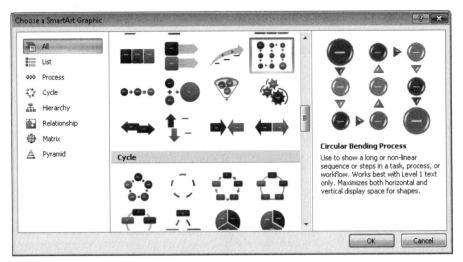

Figure 1-2 SmartArt diagrams are available in the 2007 Office release programs Word, Excel, PowerPoint, and parts of Outlook.

Word

Most core concepts about document construction have not changed—such as using styles to simplify formatting and keep document appearance consistent, or inserting a section break where you need page layout formatting to change for just part of a document. What has changed is the way you access and manage some features, as well as the addition of several new, highly integrated features, and a few that have been redesigned very much for the better.

In addition to the features already mentioned as being common to the 2007 Office release programs Word, Excel, and PowerPoint, the following table lists my top picks for the new or changed features that will have the biggest impact in your daily work with Word.

Favorite Feature	Why You Will Want to Use It
Styles	The addition of a Manage Styles dialog box provides much more control and flexibility over the way styles are handled in your documents and templates. See Figure 1-3. The ability to save complete sets of paragraph and character styles as Quick Style Sets for instant application to any document adds an easy and powerful new dimension to document and template design.
Document Building Blocks	Building Blocks provide quick access to precreated chunks of formatted document content ranging from headers and footers, to complete cover pages, to most any type of content that you need to use repeatedly. You can save your own custom Building Blocks to any template, so they can be easily shared with others.
Content Controls	Content Controls are a new generation of form controls. At their simplest, they're more powerful and easier to use than earlier form controls. But, Content Controls can also be bound to XML data so that they populate with information stored in sources ranging from Document Properties to a SharePoint server.
Compare Documents	Finally! Word has full document blacklining capability without compromises, to help you collaborate more effectively. See Figure 1-4.

Figure 1-3 In the new Manage Styles dialog box, you can edit styles, recommend and prioritize styles, restrict the use of certain styles or formatting, and set formatting defaults.

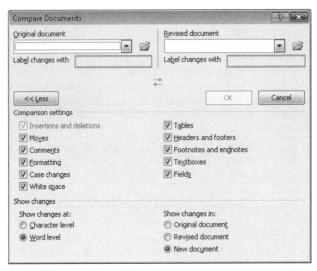

Figure 1-4 The new Compare Documents dialog box provides robust document blacklining capabilities.

Excel

Whether, like me, you cherish the power and flexibility of Excel with the giddy delight of a school kid's first crush, or you are one of those people I used to be who avoids Excel because you don't like math, you might not be able to hold back your joy when you see some of the program's new functionality.

As with Word, the same Excel you already know is still very much alive and well. But, you'll find a tremendous amount of new functionality that will simplify and add punch to several of the things you need Excel to do.

Following are a few of my picks for the new or changed functionality that will have the biggest impact on the documents and document content that you use Excel to create.

Favorite Feature	Why You Will Want to Use It
Tables	You can now identify any worksheet range as a table, for better formatting and much easier data management.
Conditional Formatting	The Conditional Formatting tool has been revamped and expanded, including a new dialog box that enables you to view and manage conditional formatting rules across your workbook. Additionally, the revised feature includes a host of impressive data visualization options, such as displaying data bars in worksheet cells for the appearance of a formatted bar chart, no chart required. See Figure 1-5.

Favorite Feature	Why You Will Want to Use It
Charts	Charting has been redesigned. If this doesn't strike you as good news, I urge you to give it a chance. The new charting tools are designed for improved formatting capabilities and, on that, they surely deliver. The charting tools also take tremendous advantage of the new user interface to provide easier access to a great deal of chart functionality, as shown in Figure 1-6.
PivotTables and PivotCharts	If you're already a fan of PivotTables, you will love the changes to this feature in terms of flexibility and ease of use. If you have not yet made your peace with PivotTables, now is the time to try it.

Figure 1-5 The Conditional Formatting options include much new functionality, such as the new data visualization tools and a tool for managing formatting rules.

Figure 1-6 The three Chart Tools contextual tabs provide quick access to a tremendous number of chart formatting commands, including direct access to most chart elements.

> **Note**
>
> Fans of PivotTables will also be excited to learn about the new PivotDiagram feature in Microsoft Office Visio 2007. It's so easy and powerful, it's almost magical—no exaggeration here. Learn about PivotDiagrams in Chapter 17, "The Excel-Visio Connection."

If you need information on some of the other exceptional advances in Microsoft Excel outside of document production, such as Excel Services, find a thorough look at Office Excel 2007 from top to bottom in the Microsoft Press book *Microsoft Office Excel 2007 Inside Out*.

PowerPoint

I am so delighted with some of the new functionality in Office PowerPoint 2007 that I am almost willing to forgive the PowerPoint team for removing one of my longtime favorite features, Recolor Picture for embedded objects (see Chapter 19, "Slides and Presentations," for workarounds on this issue, particularly related to embedded Word tables).

Having led with the bad news, the good news is quite good. Here are my picks for the top new features that will offer the biggest benefits to the documents and document content you create in PowerPoint.

Favorite Feature	Why You Will Want to Use It
Custom Slide Layouts	Finally! Each slide layout is now a separate, customizable entity attached to the slide master. You can also add your own custom layouts and additional placeholders (such as text, content, or picture placeholders) to any layout. See Figure 1-7.
Custom Shapes	You can now convert most AutoShapes to freeform objects and then use the Edit Points feature to turn those shapes into just about anything you need them to be. See Figure 1-8.
Selection Pane	The new Selection And Visibility pane enables you to easily select any object on the slide (regardless of layers). You can also use this pane to hide objects on a slide and to rename shapes.
WordArt	I've long been a supporter of this undervalued feature that enables you to format text the way you do shapes. Now, you can apply WordArt formatting to any text box.

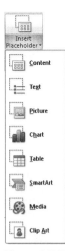

Figure 1-7 Use Insert Placeholders to add custom elements to slide layouts.

3 1833 05200 9278

Figure 1-8 Convert an AutoShape to a freeform object to design your own custom shapes.

Introducing the Office Open XML File Formats

The new XML file formats provide a number of benefits, including easier management of hidden data, reduced file size, and improved customization and programmability options. So, what do you need to know to start using these new file formats? The answer is much easier than you might think.

The File Types

The new file types use four character file name extensions instead of the three character extensions used by most software programs. These new file types add either the letter *x* to the end of the extension to indicate a macro-free file, or they add the letter *m* to the end of the extension to indicate a macro-enabled file (that is, a file in which you can store macros written in Microsoft Visual Basic for Applications [VBA]). For example, the default file format for Word documents is docx.

Note that when you save a file in the legacy format (that is, the format used by Microsoft Office versions 97 through 2003), the original three character extensions are still used.

Choosing Your Format

By default, new documents are saved in the applicable new macro-free file format for that program. To change this default, or just to view all available file formats for the program, see the Options dialog box for that program.

1. Click the Microsoft Office Button, shown here, and then click <Program> Options.

2. On the Save tab of the applicable Options dialog box, see the drop-down list labeled Save Files In This Format.

INSIDE OUT   Moving forward with the new file formats

If your first response to the new XML file formats is to set your default to save in the legacy formats, you might want to reconsider. Here are two good reasons to take a deep breath and go with the flow of change.

- Users of earlier versions of Microsoft Office will be able to use the files you save in the new XML file formats. Microsoft has included a Compatibility Pack for Microsoft Office 2003 and Microsoft Office XP, available on the Microsoft Update Web site. Users of these earlier versions of Microsoft Office will automatically get the Compatibility Pack the first time they run Microsoft Update subsequent to the release of the 2007 Office system.

- The new file formats opened the door for the Microsoft Office designers to add quite a bit of the new functionality in the 2007 Office release. So, if you choose to stick with the legacy file formats, some of the best new functionality—such as

   Document Themes and their related formatting capabilities, or the new SmartArt capability—won't be available in your documents. In some cases, when you try to access the new option in a legacy document, you get the equivalent feature from earlier versions. For example, when you click to insert SmartArt in a legacy document, you get the unfortunate Diagram And Organizational Chart tool.

Note that you can easily tell when you're working in a legacy document, because [Compatibility Mode] appears after the file name in the title bar.

What Else Do I Need to Know About These File Formats?

The new file formats are actually .zip files in disguise. This means that if you change the file extension of a document in the new file format to .zip, you can actually open the zipped folder to access and edit the XML content of the file.

So, why should you care? Although you never need see the XML content of your files if you prefer to avoid it, you might be amazed at how easily you can do so much without any programming knowledge at all. For example, say that your company logo changes. You could open each file and then insert, place, and size the logo each time it is needed. Or, you could just open the file in .zip format and replace the new picture file as-is, in the correct folder. The placement and sizing information is retained from the previously inserted version of the logo.

To learn how to take advantage of the new file format capabilities, as well as to take that knowledge to the next level, see Chapter 22, "Office Open XML Essentials."

The New User Interface: Ribbons and Then Some

There are no more menus (well, almost) and no more toolbars (well, sort of) in the 2007 Office release programs Word, Excel, and PowerPoint (as well as Access and parts of Outlook). But, you will not miss them for long.

The traditional menu and toolbar organization has been replaced with a more interactive, accessible command layout known as the Ribbon. Each of the programs that use the new interface has a Ribbon. The Ribbon exposes more functionality, so you have easier access to common formatting features and are more likely to find functionality you would not otherwise have known about. Figure 1-9 introduces basic Ribbon organization and terminology.

Microsoft Office Button

Quick Access Toolbar   Tabs   Contextual Tabs

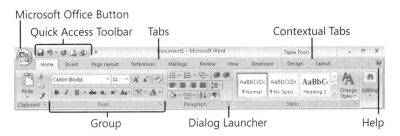

Group   Dialog Launcher   Help

Figure 1-9 The Ribbon is a key element of the new interface in the 2007 release programs Word, Excel, PowerPoint, Access, and parts of Outlook. The example used here is from Word.

INSIDE OUT   The Developer Tab

Whether or not you're a developer, if you're an advanced user, you will want to enable the Developer tab of the Ribbon. In addition to VBA and XML options, this tab includes such features as Content Controls for form design, document protection options, Document Information Panel options, and (in Word) options for managing attached templates (the Templates And Add-Ins dialog box). To find this option, in the <Program> Options dialog box, click Personalize and then click Show Developer Tab In The Ribbon. As with several options on the Personalize tab, once you enable this setting in one program, it becomes available in all programs that share the new interface.

Microsoft Office Online Training has created Interactive Command Reference Guides for Word, Excel, and PowerPoint. These guides enable you to click a command in a facsimile of the applicable Office 2003 interface to see the steps for accessing the command in the 2007 version of the program. Find links to these freely available command reference guides on the Resources tab of this book's CD. Also on the Resources tab, find Ribbon Mapping Workbooks for Word, Excel, and PowerPoint. These workbooks, also provided by Office Online Training, list the commands on the menus and toolbars in the 2003 version of the program you select, and indicate where to find the command in the 2007 version.

Getting Comfortable in Your Workspace

One of the most important first steps I take when working in a new program, or a new version of a program, is to settle in to the environment and get comfortable. And, while the Ribbon is big news, there is more to know about your new workspace, as well as many customizable options.

The Quick Access Toolbar

To customize a Ribbon, you need to use Office Open XML (learn the basics of how to customize the Ribbon in Chapter 22). However, that does not mean that any customization requires programming knowledge.

A Quick Access Toolbar, shown in Figure 1-9, is available in each program that uses the new interface, and is designed precisely to enable users to keep their most frequently used commands always accessible.

In addition to the Quick Access Toolbar for each program, you can save a unique Quick Access Toolbar for any document or template, as shown in Figure 1-10.

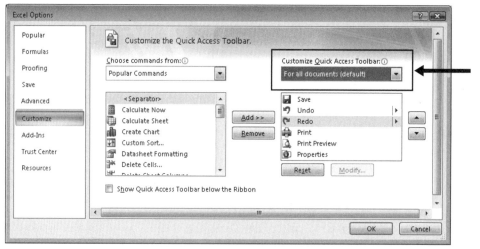

Figure 1-10 On the Customization tab of the <Program> Options dialog box (Excel is shown), you can customize a unique Quick Access Toolbar for an individual document.

The Customizable Status Bar

The updated status bar is a power user's best friend. Just right-click the status bar to add or remove items. For example, the image that follows shows the options offered when you right-click the status bar in Word.

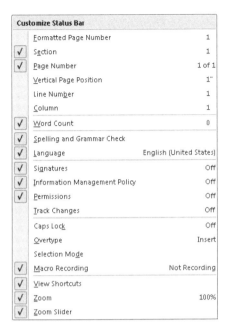

Note that most items on the status bar are active, so clicking an item will perform an action. For example, click the word count on the status bar to open the Word Count dialog box for more information. Or, click the percent value shown at the end of the Zoom slider in the following image to open the Zoom dialog box for options such as Page Width and Full Page.

The Mini Toolbar

The Mini Toolbar appears, by default, when you select text in Word, Excel, or Power-Point. It provides shortcuts to common text formatting options. This toolbar is initially transparent. If you click an option, the toolbar becomes solid. If not, it will disappear after a few seconds.

If you do not want the Mini Toolbar to appear, you can disable it from the Popular tab of the <Program> Options dialog box.

New Keyboard Options

Like many advanced users, I tend to be a bit keyboard-centric. So, I'm delighted with the new version of accelerator keys (the underscored character in menus and dialog boxes) known as KeyTips.

When you press the Alt key, KeyTips appear as pop-ups instead of underscored characters, indicating the key to press to access a Ribbon tab or Quick Access Toolbar option, as shown here.

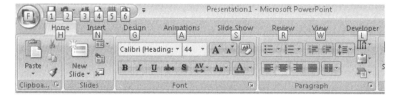

Once you press the key to enable a Ribbon tab, KeyTips appear for each option on that tab. So, you can drill down to the feature you need, just as you could with traditional accelerator keys (which are still available in dialog boxes). But, because so many more features are immediately accessible on the Ribbon, you now have keyboard access to almost all functionality.

You may notice that the keys associated with some Ribbon tab names are not what you would expect (the Insert tab, for example, uses *N* for its KeyTip instead of *I*.) This is so that users who, like myself, memorized accelerator key combinations in Office 2003 can still use those shortcuts in the 2007 Office release programs.

INSIDE OUT   Using keyboard shortcuts to manage your environment

To find a pretty thorough list of keyboard shortcuts for any 2007 Office release program, just search for the topic *keyboard shortcuts* through the Help pane in that program. However, here are a few important keyboard options to help you manage your new environment more easily: Ctrl+F1 minimizes or restores the Ribbon. F6 (or Shift+F6 in reverse) cycles keyboard focus between the document, an open pane (such as the Style pane), the status bar, and the Ribbon and Quick Access Toolbar. As with menus and galleries, you can also use the arrow keys on the keyboard to move through an active pane, status bar options, or even all commands on a Ribbon tab.

Documents 101: Understanding How the Office Programs "Think"

As you settle in and get comfortable with the programs, take a look at the way you work on documents in general. The 2007 Office release is designed, more than ever, to help you accomplish more in less time. But, the core concepts that have always worked for advanced Microsoft Office document production are unchanged.

Think about the way you approach documents and consider some key concepts that might be able to save you time and effort as well as improve your results.

The Benefits of Being Lazy

The best document production professional I know is a woman by the name of Gayle. The first time I watched Gayle work, she was churning out pages for a Word presentation document. She spent just 15 or 20 minutes on each page, including financial tables, Excel charts, and even PowerPoint and Visio diagrams. Not only did they look great in print, but every one of these pages was literally perfect on the screen.

When I asked how she managed to create flawless, complex pages so quickly, Gayle said it's because she's lazy. She doesn't like to do any more work than absolutely necessary, so she never puts anything in a document that doesn't need to be there. That, she says, is why she gets along so well with Microsoft Office, and with Word in particular.

The key to creating complex documents that Gayle knows so well is actually quite simple. When you understand a bit about how the programs "think"—that is, the reasons behind the way software features behave—everything you need to create becomes much easier.

Less Work In = Better Results Out

The most common mistake I see people make when working on documents is this.

1. Something unexpected and unwanted happens in your document.

2. You don't understand what happened and don't have time to figure it out, so you just keep going.

3. You're frustrated because the program isn't doing what you want it to do, so you use whatever workaround you can think of to keep going forward because you have to meet a deadline.

Sound familiar? If so, you're in good company. Most people do the very same thing. The problem with this process, however, is that it can cause you to dig yourself continually deeper until your document stops working properly, its appearance is less than stellar, and you have a good chance of missing that deadline.

If this has ever happened to you, ask yourself this: How long did it take you to fix or find workarounds for the problems in your document? Things often become cliché because they're universally true—doing it right the first time really is faster and easier than doing it over.

No matter what your timeline or the pressure to get the document done, taking the time to stay in control will always save you time. When something unwanted occurs on screen, undo actions until you're comfortable with what you see and then proceed again. The Undo command (press Ctrl+Z or click Undo on the Quick Access Toolbar) may just be the most important feature in any Microsoft Office program. In the 2007 Office suite, you can undo up to your last 1,000 actions in Word, 150 actions in PowerPoint, and 100 actions in Excel.

INSIDE OUT   Maximizing the power of Undo

The undo cache is (thankfully!) no longer cleared in Excel and PowerPoint when you save —so you can now undo actions that occurred before a save in any of the three programs.

Of course, you still can't undo some actions (such as deleting a sheet from an Excel workbook). But, you do still get a separate undo cache for each open document in a given program. For example, if you have two workbooks open in Excel at the same time, you can undo up to the last 100 actions in each.

Note also that you automatically get the maximum number of undos in Word and Excel, but the number of undos allowed by default in PowerPoint is 20. To change this number, click the Office button and then click PowerPoint Options. You'll find the option Maximum Number Of Undos on the Advanced tab in the PowerPoint Options dialog box.

Planning Your Documents

One of the most important document-related lessons you can teach yourself is how to plan and maintain control of your document. Considering the document as a whole, and taking a bit of time to plan, can save you an enormous amount of time and stress later.

When teaching advanced document production, train-the-trainer, or document troubleshooting, one of my favorite class exercises to illustrate this point is to ask people to approach their document as they would a golf game. What is the fewest number of steps you can take to get the job done?

When you approach the tee to begin a game of golf, you wouldn't hit the ball without first looking to see where the green is located or planning the best way to get there. Approaching a document without any planning is as ineffective as thinking about only your next stroke in a golf game.

Think, for example, about how you approach a Word document. If you create a style whenever the need arises without thought to how it will be used or how it will interact with other styles, you're likely to end up with too many styles, inconsistent styles, or the constant need to double-back and fix formatting. Instead, take a few minutes upfront to think about what formatting will be needed and how styles will be used, and you can create a set of styles that work together effortlessly. That small amount of planning enables you to format the bulk of your document with literally a few clicks. And, if formatting does need to change later, the styles have been designed to work together, so making those changes is quick, simple, and seamless.

> **Note**
>
> For specific best practices on creating effective style sets in Word, see Chapter 5, "Styles." See the section titled "Formatting Financial Tables" in Chapter 6, "Tables," for a troubleshooting exercise you can try for yourself (using files on the CD) on how to simplify your document work by planning.

Finding the Simple Solution

Rule number one in Microsoft Office document production: If a task seems cumbersome, there probably is an easier way. When most people run into a software task they don't know how to do, they usually assume the solution is complicated. In fact, people typically overlook the best solution because it seems too easy to possibly work. Here's a quick look at a few examples with common cumbersome workarounds as well as the simple, effective solution. Has this happened to you?

Issue	Common Workarounds That Don't Work	The Simple Solution—Works Every Time
In Word, a section break type changes from Next Page to Continuous for no apparent reason.	You insert a new Next Page section break and then delete the Continuous break, but the new break changes as well. So, you insert several Next Page section breaks on either side of the original break and remove one at a time, like pick-up sticks. But, still you can't retain the Next Page formatting. So, you insert a page break after the Continuous section break.	Place your insertion point after the break. In the Page Setup dialog box, on the Layout tab, select New Page from the Section Start drop-down list and then click OK. See the section titled "Understanding Section Break Types" in Chapter 8, "Sections."
Data label leader lines do not appear on an pie chart when you copy it from Excel to Word.	You try moving the label to make the leader line appear, and that doesn't work. So, you delete the labels and then reinsert and reposition them, but still no leader lines. Finally, you draw lines on the chart to approximate the appearance of leader lines.	Zoom in tighter on the chart in Excel before copying it. Accuracy of what you copy increases with your zoom in Excel. See the section titled "Creating Charts for Use in Other Programs" in Chapter 15, "Charts."
Font size in text placeholders shrinks or is inconsistent from slide to slide, regardless of slide and slide master settings.	Instead of using the appropriate slide layouts, you change the layout to blank for affected slides and format every text box manually.	In the AutoCorrect dialog box, turn off the options to AutoFit text to placeholders. See the section titled "Effective Document Setup" in Chapter 19, "Slides and Presentations."

For each of the examples provided in the preceding table, taking just a moment to understand why the behavior occurs will lead you to the simple solution and save you the time and frustration of ineffective workarounds.

Using the 2007 Office Suite Effectively: Never Do the Same Work Twice

When looking for the simple solution, you can save even more time and effort by using the programs of the 2007 Office system together effectively. Sure, you can create charts and diagrams and even do some calculations in Word, or create text-heavy documents in PowerPoint or Excel. But, even though there is some overlap between the programs, each program has its forte.

Even though much has changed in the 2007 Office release, one key concept (and much of the functionality that supports it) remains very much the same. When you let the programs do what they do best, you will always do the least work for the best results.

Word: The Organizer

"A place for everything and everything in its place." That 19th-century maxim is more true for 21st century Word than perhaps anything to come before it. Word "likes" things to be as simple and organized as possible. In fact, if you do more work than necessary, Word just might rebel.

To "get along" with Word and keep your documents easy to manage, always use the simplest option for any task. For example, don't use a table when a paragraph indent will do; don't use a floating object or add a new section when a table will do. Learn more about finding the simple solution for your Word documents throughout Part 2 of this book, beginning with understanding how Word organizes formatting in Chapter 4, "Building Easy-to-Manage, Robust Documents."

Excel: The Logician

Whenever I've ever said that Excel can't do something, I've been wrong. You don't have to be an mathematician or an engineer to get more from Excel than you probably expect. Personally, I wouldn't know what to do with an inverse hyperbolic cosine if it walked up to me and gave me a hug. But, I have found functions, formulas, and assorted features that have saved me more times than I could possibly calculate. For example, here's one of my favorite timesaving, troubleshooting miracles.

If a complex chart with hundreds of rows of data (such as a price\volume chart) gets disconnected from its data source, there's no way to reconstruct that data from the chart itself, right? Wrong. If the chart is displaying the data, the chart still knows the data. A simple macro will extract that data in no time. In fact, it's so commonly used, that a macro is available with step-by-step instructions in a Microsoft Knowledge Base article—no programming experience required. Just search for KB300643 at *www.microsoft.com*. (Find more information about this knowledge base article in the troubleshooting tip titled "How can I retrieve lost chart data?" in Chapter 15.)

That said, you don't even need a macro for so much of what you can do with Excel. From conditional statements, to concatenation, to interpolation, things that might sound complicated are surprisingly quick and easy. Learn more about how to harness the power, logic, and simplicity of Excel in Part 3 of this book.

PowerPoint: The Efficiency Expert

If you think of PowerPoint as a graphic design program, you probably don't like it very much. Though you can surely get creative with PowerPoint, it's not about graphic design at all. PowerPoint is a presentation program—it's about precision, efficiency, and displaying your important information professionally. My favorite thing about PowerPoint, in fact, is that getting things perfect is always faster and easier than getting them "close enough."

For example, use the Change Shape feature to change all shapes in your diagram at once. No resizing, reformatting, or retyping needed. And what about the drawing guides? The Align and Distribute tools can help you position objects perfectly with a few precise clicks. But, when those tools won't do what you need, use drawing guides to align with no trial and error, measure distance, or help lay out a slide. Learn more about PowerPoint precision as well as its newfound flexibility in Part 4 of this book.

Putting It All Together

More than ever, the "personalities" of the 2007 Office release programs are designed to complement and support each other. If I could share only one thing about what's new in the 2007 Office system, it would be the way that everything works together.

The most important advance is not the interface, or the file formats, or any individual feature—but the way in which features and programs integrate more effectively. As you learn about new features in the chapters to come, consider how a feature builds on or works along with others. For example, in Word 2007, pay attention to how styles and Themes work together or the ways in which Building Blocks use and interact with both Themes and Content Controls.

These interactions and the power you can get when you take advantage of them will be particularly important when you get to later chapters such as "Planning Your Documents" (Chapter 12), or "The Many Faces of Microsoft Office Templates" (Chapter 20).

After all, the goal is not to use as many cool, new features as you can. The goal is to create better documents with less work.

Understanding Electronic Documents

In the age of typewriters, it didn't much matter how we went about creating documents. All the recipient ever saw was the paper result.

Today, most documents are shared electronically both when we collaborate with others and when we deliver the final product, so much more information is actually shared than the text, graphics, and formatting we add to the page. With the powerful tools at our disposal today, we can also create far more professional, impactful, and complex documents than ever before, and share them much more easily.

However, in the immortal words of Spiderman (or, more accurately, Uncle Ben), "With great power comes great responsibility." Although building great documents is surely less difficult than battling arch villains, the power to create and share documents the way we do today does carry some important considerations.

In this chapter, we'll look at the differences to consider when sharing documents electronically—from those that affect the professionalism of your finished product to those that affect the security of your private information—and explore some simple solutions.

Differences to Consider When Sharing Documents Electronically

Keep two principal areas in mind when creating a document that you will share electronically—the way you construct the document and the document content. The method of document construction is an important consideration because it can affect the message you convey as well as the success of your collaboration with others. Considering the content of your document is also important because you might be sharing more content than you intended.

Document Construction

You may already know that using the simplest method for the task will usually give you better results with less work. But, when it comes to sharing documents electronically, the way a document is crafted can also substantially affect the way your document content is perceived.

Consider a basic example. The pages shown in Figures 2-1 and 2-2 contain the same information and similar formatting choices. In fact, the only difference between the two pages is the way they are constructed. Formatting marks, often called non-printing characters, are visible in both figures. Which document would you prefer to claim as your own?

Using the best features for each task—such as styles, Themes, tables, and SmartArt graphics—the well-crafted page shown in Figure 2-1 took much less time to create than the page created with workarounds, shown in Figure 2-2. Even more important, consider the impact of the information conveyed. Clearly, the version shown in Figure 2-1 makes a more professional statement. What's more, construction choices in Figure 2-1 help ensure that what the recipients see on their screen, and what they print out, is exactly what the author of the document intended.

Making a Professional Impression

If you're thinking that the way the document looks with formatting marks doesn't apply to you because you don't turn on formatting marks in your documents, think again. You can learn about the value of using formatting marks in Chapter 4, "Building Easy-to-Manage, Robust Documents," but just because you don't turn them on doesn't mean the recipient of your document does not. Anyone who opens your Microsoft Word document might do so with formatting marks visible. Imagine the work that went into both writing and creating the document in Figure 2-2. Isn't it a shame that the reader's eye has to muddle through the mess of formatting to get to the point?

But, formatting marks are just one element of what makes Figure 2-1 so much more professional looking than Figure 2-2. Something as simple as paragraph indents that don't line up perfectly or a sloppy diagram that looks "close enough" to what you wanted can detract from your document's content and diminish the weight of your important information. Keep in mind that the point of formatting, layout, and any number of capabilities across Microsoft Office is to help your document's content shine.

Ensuring That What You Send Is What They See

When your documents are shared electronically, good construction isn't just about a professional-looking result. It's also about knowing what the recipient will see when they receive your document. When you send a document as an e-mail message, it is sent over the Internet in HTML. Documents created in the Microsoft Office programs are designed to be able to translate well to and from HTML. But, if you're fudging the layout and using workarounds for formatting, neither Microsoft Office Outlook 2007 nor any messaging program you might use will know how to translate it. For example, when you fake the appearance of bullets or a table, as in Figure 2-2, the translator has no way of knowing that you were trying to approximate bulleted text or a table, so the layout could be distorted when the document reaches the recipient.

Introduction¶

This·report·examines·overall·company·performance·for·the·most·recent·fiscal·year,·both·globally·and·regionally,·and·provides·a·look·at·our·competitive·standing·geographically,·demographically,·and·by·product·line.¶

Executive·Summary¶

➤→ North·America·and·Asia·Pacific·continue·to·lag·behind·EMEA·in·growth,·while·still·remaining·ahead·of·competitive·averages·and·market·expectations.¶

➤→ Consider·the·following·product·growth·figures·(in·000's)·by·region:¶

¤	Q1¤	Q2¤	Q3¤	Q4¤	¤
North·America¤	321¤	350¤	312¤	375¤	¤
EMEA¤	432¤	425¤	398¤	412¤	¤
Asia·Pacific¤	341¤	368¤	306¤	333¤	¤

This·paper·examines·the·growth·that·can·be·retained·by·achieving·better·cooperation·between·our·regional·business·and·more·unified·business·approach.¶

Figure 2-1 Even with formatting marks visible, the content shown here is clean, professional, and readable.

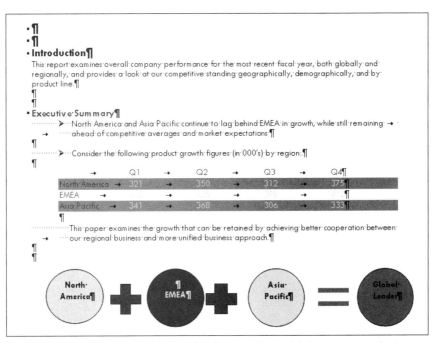

Figure 2-2 This content is the same as that shown in Figure 2-1, but constructed using formatting workarounds.

Understanding How Font Choices Can Impact What Recipients See

In addition to sharing documents as e-mail messages, one of the simplest components of formatting documents in any program is also often one of the most problematic: fonts. You can choose beautiful, creative, and interesting fonts. But, if they are not standard fonts and do not exist on the recipient's computer, your document might look entirely different to the recipient. When a font does not exist on a computer, the program in which you open a document (such as Microsoft Word or Microsoft Excel) will substitute what it believes to be the closest font available. Often, the closest font is a larger font that can cause alterations in alignment of complex layouts, change pagination, or distort graphics.

Embedding a font in your document is not a complete solution either, because this will only affect the way recipients view the document on screen. If the recipient chooses to print the document from a computer where the font is not installed, a standard font will be substituted in the printed version, potentially causing the same issues as mentioned in the preceding paragraph. Note also that several hundred kilobytes (KB) are typically added to your document size for embedding a single font. This is the same for both the Office Open XML file formats and the legacy file formats used by earlier versions of Office. Also note that fonts can be embedded in Microsoft Office Word 2007 and Microsoft Office PowerPoint 2007, but not in Microsoft Office Excel 2007.

INSIDE OUT   Get more information about your fonts

When you download custom fonts, keep in mind that not all fonts have the same rights and properties. Some fonts might not be True Type fonts, in which case their appearance can change based on printer font definitions. Additionally, your rights to some fonts may be limited, such as fonts that disallow embedding or render documents read-only.

You can learn much more about fonts in general, such as understanding True Type fonts, at the Microsoft Typography site, *www.microsoft.com/typography*. In addition, you'll find free tools there including the Font Properties Extension tool. After you download and install this add-in, just right-click a font in the Windows Control Panel and then select Properties to see the usual font properties as well as information such as font copyright and whether the font can be embedded.

Thanks very much to this book's talented technical reviewer, Microsoft Office System MVP Beth Melton, for the lead on this cool tool.

The default fonts used in the 2007 Office system programs Word, Excel, and PowerPoint (Calibri and Cambria), as well as many new standard fonts available in these programs, were not available in earlier versions of Microsoft Office. However, they are included in the Microsoft Office Compatibility Pack (for Microsoft Office versions 2003, XP, and 2000), which is designed to enable users of earlier versions to open and work with documents that use the new Office Open XML file formats. The Compatibility Pack is distributed as part of Automatic Updates for users of these two earlier Microsoft

Office versions, and it is available for download from the Microsoft Web site as well, for users who choose not to receive automatic updates. Keep this in mind when selecting fonts for your documents.

Document Content

Do you know what information your document contains? Are you certain about that? When you share documents electronically, you might be sharing much more than the content you intended to share. Document metadata, defined in the following section, as well as hidden data that you and other document editors can inadvertently add to documents, can result in sharing private information. Fortunately, these issues are much easier to manage than you might expect. An explanation of the issues and options for managing them follow.

Securing the Private Information in Your Documents

In a nutshell: There is no reason to fear your documents, and anyone who says otherwise is selling something.

Document metadata (the term most commonly used to refer to hidden data in your documents) has become such a hot topic in recent years that the amount of misinformation available on the subject is downright rampant. The truth is that this is an extremely important issue, but one that can be easy to manage. The best way to stay in control of your documents and help ensure that you do not share potentially private information is simply to be aware of the types of hidden content that can exist in your document and the steps you can take to resolve them.

The Simple Truth About Document Metadata and Hidden Content

Most of the potentially private hidden data in your documents is not actually metadata at all, but content you or other document editors have added to the document at some point. So, what then is metadata?

Metadata Defined

Metadata, in computer terms, is information that a software program automatically stores in a file to enable some functionality. Virtually all software programs store some type of metadata in their files, the great majority of which is not a privacy risk at all. For example, the version of software used to create a document may be stored in the document as metadata.

The more powerful a software program, the more metadata it is likely to store. Office Word 2007, Office Excel 2007, and Office PowerPoint 2007 store metadata such as the date the file was created and name of the author. Most metadata is not visible in the document window, but can be found through a dialog box. For example, the create date is listed in the Document Properties dialog box.

Hidden Data Defined

Unlike document metadata, hidden data refers to content that you add to a document but might not see in the document window. Examples of hidden data include text in Word that is formatted with the hidden font attribute, unresolved tracked changes in Word or Excel, or comments in Word, Excel, or PowerPoint. Content added to commonly used document parts such as headers, footers, and footnotes can also be hidden data, depending on the way you view your documents.

Options for Managing Hidden Data in the 2007 Office System

One of the most common misconceptions about document metadata and hidden data is that the number of potentially private hidden content types is infinite or somehow unmanageable. In fact, a discrete list of things are commonly thought of as document metadata or hidden data, and you can remove virtually all of them from your 2007 Office release documents by yourself, quickly and easily. What's more, just because something is a potential privacy risk to someone, doesn't mean it will be to you. Review the list of possible hidden data types and decide for yourself what content types you want to check for and remove from your documents.

 Find a Hidden Data Checklist on this book's CD, along with links to additional resources on the Microsoft Web site for learning about document metadata and hidden data, including how to manage this content in earlier versions of Microsoft Office. The Hidden Data Checklist lists common types of hidden data and is created in an Excel template so that you can easily edit and share it.

In the 2007 Office release, options for removing metadata and other hidden content have become much better than ever before. One of the most important new tools for managing this content is the Document Inspector.

Using the Document Inspector

The Document Inspector searches for a wide range of potentially hidden content types, including both metadata and hidden data, and gives you the option to remove them from your document. See the Document Inspector options for Word in Figure 2-3.

Figure 2-3 To access the Document Inspector in Word, Excel, or PowerPoint, click the Microsoft Office Button, point to Prepare, and then click Inspect Document.

The Document Inspector, like any tool that automatically removes hidden data, can be a bit heavy-handed. That is, it will remove either all or nothing of the content types it finds. So, when using any tool for removing hidden data, the most important thing to remember is that just because something can potentially be private information doesn't mean it is. Be aware of the content types you want to check for and the circumstances in which you consider content to be private information that you want to remove.

For example, headers and footers are usually intentional content that you want to share. However, if you add content to a header or footer in a Word document and then disable that header and footer (such as adding content to a Different First Page header and then turning off the Different First Page feature), the content you added is still saved with the document unless you remove it. So, while it is unlikely that you would want to delete all header and footer content in your document, you might want to check to ensure that no private information is saved in disabled or otherwise unused headers and footers.

When you use the Document Inspector, in addition to simply being aware of what it is you might be choosing to remove, keep in mind the following additional information when reviewing some of the data types searched for by the Document Inspector.

Chapter 2

Option	What You Need To Know
In Word, Excel, and PowerPoint	
Document Properties and Personal Information	In addition to Document Properties such as author name and create date, any custom document properties saved in your document will be removed when you select Remove All for this option in the Document Inspector. This is important because many companies use custom document properties for a number of reasons, such as to enable functionality in add-in programs like document management systems.
Custom XML Data	Custom XML data can be additional functionality that your document requires. It's a good idea to know what the custom XML data in your document is before removing it. Or, as when removing any hidden data, just make a copy of the document first before removing this content to be sure that you retain a fully functional copy of your file.
Headers and Footers	As mentioned earlier, header and footer content is most often intentional and meant to be shared. Instead of removing all header and footer content, you can take a few quick steps to ensure that you have no inadvertent content in your document headers and footers. ● In Excel, view each sheet in Page Layout view or Print Preview to view all header and footer content in the file. The only header and footer content you would not view in this case would be content on hidden sheets or objects formatted to be invisible, both of which are separately addressed in the Document Inspector. ● In Word (where headers and footers also incorporate watermarks), if there is a possibility that the Different Odd And Even or Different First Page settings were used at some point in the document, turn these features on (or off, as applicable) to check for content in unused headers and footers. Find these options on the Header & Footer Tools Design tab when your insertion point is in the header and footer layer of the document. ● Additionally, check for sections that contain fewer pages than would be necessary to show all headers and footers—such as sections of less than one page or sections of one page where Different First Page is enabled. The easiest way to do this is to simply add page breaks in short sections and delete them after checking for hidden header and footer content. ● Though the Document Inspector in PowerPoint does not check for header and footer content, you might want to do this yourself. If you add header or footer content to any master, slide, or handouts and notes pages and then disable that content from appearing, the content may be retained in the Header and Footer dialog box unless you delete it. Find this dialog box on the Insert tab.
In Excel and PowerPoint	
Invisible Content	Invisible Content in Excel and Invisible On-Slide Content in PowerPoint both refer to objects that have been hidden using the Selection And Visibility Pane. To access this pane, select an object and then, on the Drawing Tools Format tab, in the Arrange group, click Selection Pane. Keep in mind, however, that this option will not find potentially invisible text or objects that are formatted as white on a white background or otherwise formatted to be obscured.

Option	What You Need To Know
In Word	
Hidden Text	It's important to note that this option only searches for text formatted with the hidden font attribute. It will not find text formatted as white on a white background or otherwise formatted to be obscured.

INSIDE OUT   More to embedded Excel objects than meets the eye

One feature in particular that is not addressed by the Document Inspector warrants noting here. As you most likely know, when you paste any content from one program to another as an embedded object, recipients of your document can simply double-click to access the original object. However, when the object you embed originates in an Excel workbook, you actually embed the *entire workbook* from which the object originated.

For example, say you have an Excel workbook containing tables with sales summaries for each of your customers. If you copy just the table relating to one customer and paste it as an embedded object into a Word document you are sending to that customer, the recipient can double-click that object to open the originating workbook—where they will see the content related to your other customers as well.

To protect your privacy, it's a good idea to paste Excel objects into other programs as pictures unless you want to share all content in the originating workbook. If you have an existing embedded Excel object in a Word document, you can easily convert it to a picture because embedded objects are stored in Word as fields. To do this, just select the object and press Ctrl+Shift+F9. This keyboard shortcut strips any field result of its code, in this case leaving only a picture. Before you convert the object to a picture, it is a good idea to ensure that you have a live copy of the originating workbook saved in case of future editing needs. (Note, however, that this shortcut won't work if you use the option named Excel Chart (Entire Workbook), available from the paste SmartTag when you paste a chart from an Excel 2007 document to a Word 2007 document. See Chapter 15, "Charts" for more information about pasting Excel charts successfully and securely in Word.)

 If you're a Microsoft Visual Studio developer or have access to a developer with that skill set, keep in mind that the Document Inspector is extensible. You can add modules to the Document Inspector to search for and manage exactly the content types you want. Find links to developer resources on the Resources and Expert Tips tabs of this book's CD.

Saving to the PDF or XPS File Formats

When you need a quick and easy solution to help ensure that your document contains no hidden content that could be a privacy risk, and the recipient of your document will not need to edit it, you might want to use the new functionality available across many of the 2007 Office system programs to save your document to either the Portable Document Format (PDF) or the new XML Paper Specification (XPS) format.

Chapter 2

This capability is available as a free download to anyone who owns 2007 Office system programs. Once installed, the option to publish a copy of your file in one of these formats will appear as a Save As command under the Microsoft Office Button in Word, Excel, or PowerPoint, and on the File menu in some of the other programs across the 2007 Office system, such as Microsoft Office OneNote 2007 and Microsoft Office Visio 2007. (The option to access the download appears in the referenced menu location if you haven't yet installed this tool.)

When you take just a few minutes to ensure that you are aware of all the content in your document, there is no reason to be concerned about sharing your document in its original format. But, for those occasions when you just want a quick solution and the recipient won't need to edit the file, PDF and XPS file formats can be a nice, simple alternative.

XPS and PDF file formats do not carry over many types of metadata and hidden content, making them a good option for sharing files. However, when you save a copy of your document in one of these formats, file properties information will be saved by default. To ensure that you are not sharing private information from File Properties, disable this command in the Options dialog box when you publish to one of these file formats. To do this in Word, Excel, or PowerPoint, take the following steps.

1. Click the Microsoft Office Button, point to Save As, and then click PDF Or XPS.

2. In the Publish To PDF Or XPS dialog box, select your preferred file type from the Save As Type list.

3. Click Options to open the dialog box where you can exclude document properties from the published copy, specify a page range to publish, or select from other options (options for XPS and PDF differ slightly). See Figure 2-4.

Figure 2-4 This dialog box shows the options available when you publish a copy of your document in the PDF file format.

   4. Click OK and then click Publish.

Note that your original document will not be affected when you publish a copy in one of these file formats.

 If you have not yet installed the Publish To PDF Or XPS capability for the 2007 Office system, you can also find the link to this download on the Resources tab of this book's CD.

Using the New File Formats to Manage Hidden Data

One of the key benefits of the new Office Open XML file formats is that all content, including metadata, is more transparent—easier to access and to remove. To learn about options for using the file formats to manage metadata and document content in general, see Chapter 22, "Office Open XML Essentials."

Using Options in Windows Vista to Manage Personal Information

If you're using Windows Vista, you have an additional method for removing personal information that's stored in file properties before you share a document.

   1. To use the Windows Vista tool, first browse to your file in Windows Explorer (press Windows+E to open Explorer).

   2. Right-click your file and then click Properties.

   3. In the Properties dialog box that opens, on the Details tab, click Remove Properties And Personal Information to open the Remove Properties dialog box. See Figure 2-5.

Chapter 2

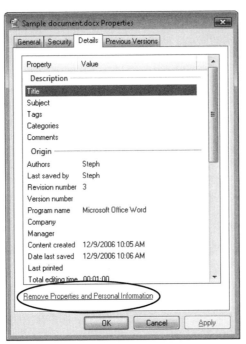

Figure 2-5 Access the Remove Properties dialog box from the Details tab of the Properties dialog box for a file selected in Windows Vista Explorer.

In the Remove Properties dialog box, you can choose to remove any properties saved by the program in which the file was created as well as information saved with the file by Windows (such as text you add using the new Tags feature in Windows Vista). You can also choose the option to save the cleaned version of the document as a copy to retain a fully functional version of your document for your own use.

> **Note**
>
> Tools for removing hidden data are available in other programs across the 2007 Office system as well. For example, to remove hidden data from your Visio files, on the File menu in Visio, click Remove Hidden Information.

Securing Documents

In addition to managing hidden data, you might have documents to which you want to control access or editing rights.

Although you can, as always, save a Microsoft Office document with a password or set a document as read-only, security options today are far more sophisticated, with better protection and more options. Following is a brief summary of options available to help secure your content in Word, Excel, and PowerPoint.

Restricting Permission to Your Documents

Depending on which of the 2007 Office release edition you own, you may be able to use Information Rights Management (IRM) to allow only specified individuals to access a document. Using IRM, you can assign unique rights to each user, including restricting the ability to copy, print, forward, modify, or fax a document. You can even set an expiration date after which users can not access a document.

> **Note**
>
> While a document protected with IRM is open, the Microsoft Windows print screen capability and the Microsoft Office OneNote screen clipping feature are disabled for all open windows, if the user does not have permission to copy the document. However, users may be able to take a screen capture of a restricted document using third-party screen capture programs or even a digital camera.

IRM is available in Microsoft Office 2007 Ultimate, Professional Plus, and Enterprise editions, and requires installation of the Windows Rights Management client. When being used throughout a company, this can be set up and installed by a system administrator. For individual use, you will be prompted to install and set up the client the first time you attempt to restrict a document or open a restricted document to which you have been granted permission.

To restrict permission to a document, do the following.

1. Click the Microsoft Office Button, point to Prepare, Restrict Permission, and then click Restricted Access.

> **Note**
>
> You can also find Restricted Access by clicking Protect Document on either the Review or the Developer tab. Remember that you must be running an edition of the 2007 release that supports IRM or you won't see these options.

2. In the Permission dialog box, click Restrict Permission To This Document.

Chapter 2

3. In the Read and Change boxes, add e-mail addresses for those to whom you want to grant permission. Note that you can click Read or Change to select user names from your Address Book.

    Enter addresses of users to whom you want to grant full control of a document in either the Read or Change box. You will have the opportunity to change permission in the next step.

4. To customize permissions, click More Options. In this dialog box, you can change permission levels (see Figure 2-6) and add further options to permissions—such as setting an expiration date or allowing printing. Note that items listed under the heading Additional Permissions are granted for all authorized users of a document and can't be set by an individual.

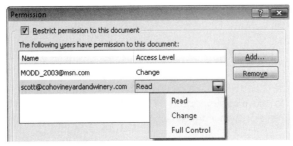

Figure 2-6 To change permission level for a specific user, use the drop-down list beside the selected user address, as shown here.

> **Note**
>
> When IRM is applied to a document, the document content is encrypted. So, if a recipient attempts to open the file in a text editor (such as Microsoft Notepad) to view or extract content, they might see some file properties information (such as the author's name), but the document content will be unreadable.

Protecting Documents from Editing

Using protection features in Word and Excel, you can protect all or part of a document from editing.

Protecting a Word Document

On the Review tab, click Protect Document, and then click Restrict Formatting And Editing to open the Protect Document task pane. Here you can restrict formatting as well as editing of the document, and apply password protection to either. Additionally, when you select No Changes or Comments as the type of editing restriction, you can allow all or just specified users to freely edit selected portions of the document.

Learn more about using document protection in Chapter 20, "The Many Faces of Microsoft Office Templates."

Protecting an Excel Document

On the Review tab, you have options to Protect Sheet, Protect Workbook, and Allow Users To Edit Ranges, including password protection for each of these options.

- When you select the Protect Sheet option, you are protecting the active sheet only. In the Protect Sheet dialog box, you can specify a range of permissions, such as selecting cells, editing cells, or inserting or deleting rows or columns.

> **Note**
>
> To enable editing for certain cells when a sheet is protected, unlock the cells in which you want to allow editing. To do this, select the cells to unlock, then on the Home tab, in the Cells group, click Format and then click Lock Cell. Note that this command toggles on and off. Notice that Protect Sheet is also available from the Format options on the Home tab.

- When you select Protect Workbook and then select Protect Structure And Windows, you restrict the ability to make changes to the workbook, such as hiding or renaming sheets. The Protect Structure And Windows dialog box gives you the option to protect either or both structure and windows.

> **Note**
>
> Similar to the Protect Document options in Word, if you're running a 2007 release edition that supports IRM you'll notice that the other options available when you click Protect Workbook are IRM options.

- With Allow Users To Edit Ranges, you can assign editing permission for just part of a worksheet to specific users, or apply a unique password for editing cells in the selected range.

Chapter 2

INSIDE OUT **Using the New Mark As Final feature**

The new Mark As Final feature available in Word, Excel, and PowerPoint sets the Status document property value to Final and protects the document from any type of editing. Note, however, that this is intended for use by those collaborating on a document and not as a security feature. Password protection is not available for Mark As Final, so any recipient of your document can turn off this feature. To turn on Mark As Final, under the Microsoft Office Button point to Prepare and then click Mark As Final.

Signing Documents and Using the Trust Center

Word, Excel, and PowerPoint have improved options for digitally signing both documents and macro projects. Additionally, the new Trust Center available in these programs gives you significant control over both how you save and how you open documents for greater security. Learn more about both of these features in Chapter 23, "Using VBA and XML Together to Create Add-Ins."

Collaborating and Sharing with Others

The phrase *effective collaboration* strikes me as one of those corporate-speak terms, like *synergy* or *think outside the box*. They're terms that became popular because they meant something important, but are now used so much for so many different reasons that you might begin to wonder if they really mean anything at all.

So, what does *effective collaboration* mean in the real world in which you live? Literally, of course, it just means working productively with others. But, for this chapter on collaborating and sharing with others, effective collaboration means much more than that. It means:

- Sharing ideas and content more easily.

- Having more dynamic ways to communicate about projects.

- Getting better results with less work.

- Managing and tracking content more easily.

Why is an advanced book about documents addressing this topic? Collaboration in business so often takes the form of documents—from project management to budget planning, business pitches, or legal matters—that not introducing at least some of the improved collaboration solutions in the 2007 Office system would be neglectful. This chapter will introduce key solutions for more effective document collaboration and provide a quick reference for getting started with the method of your choice.

Understanding and Using the 2007 Office System Collaboration Environments

Document collaboration tools are evident throughout the 2007 Office system programs. Surely features like enhanced document reviewing tools and content integration between Microsoft Office Word 2007, Microsoft Office Excel 2007, and Microsoft Office PowerPoint 2007 all support collaboration. But, what about dedicated collaboration tools? That is, programs that enable you to share and collaborate on documents across your team—whether that team is within your department, across your company, on a client site, or anywhere at all.

The dedicated collaboration tools in the 2007 Office system are Microsoft Windows SharePoint Services (WSS) and Microsoft Office Groove 2007. Both of these technologies enable you to share and manage documents across a team and track related tasks, schedules, and resources. Although the capabilities of WSS and Office Groove 2007 overlap, both have their individual strengths.

- WSS shared workspaces are where you can share content and information with any size group inside your computer network. This is a powerful and customizable technology that can be used on its own or with other Microsoft SharePoint technologies. If your company runs a Microsoft Office SharePoint Server 2007, for example, WSS can integrate even more powerfully with your 2007 Office release programs—such as by managing Office PowerPoint 2007 slide libraries where users can efficiently reuse content from decks created across your team or organization.

  WSS provides productivity tools like task management and discussion boards, but it is also an ideal place to share and manage completed documents because they're stored in a central, secure, and easily accessible location.

- Groove is where you and your team get the work done. Groove workspaces are designed for smaller groups (up to 30) but can be used by any size group. And, they can be automatically accessed by anyone you designate both inside and outside of your computer network, such as consultants with whom you need to collaborate. You can also access your Groove workspace from anywhere, whether or not you are connected to your network. Groove is designed for working together throughout your project, with productivity features such as a meetings tool that enables you to both plan and hold team meetings, and a chat tool for instant messaging with members of your workspace.

> **Note**
>
> Although both WSS and Groove workspaces can be accessed by approved users outside of your network, doing this in WSS requires additional steps (such as creation of an extranet).

In the 2007 Office system, Groove and WSS also work effectively together, because you can easily publish completed documents from a Groove workspace to a WSS shared workspace, where it can be securely stored and indexed for easy access. So, if you have access to both Groove and WSS, when should you use each? Although your requirements might differ from project to project, here is my recommendation in a nutshell.

- If you need to be able to work on a project easily from anywhere with a team that does not share the same network, you want a Groove workspace.

- If a large number of people on your network or extranet need to easily access a wide range of content, you want a WSS shared workspace.

Use the overviews that follow to help you determine the best workspace for your work style and your particular project.

> **Small Business or Individual? Go Live.**
>
> If you think you can't use SharePoint or Groove because you're not part of a large company, think again. You have a number of options, but one of the best and least expensive ways to go is to subscribe to one of the new Microsoft Office Live services.
>
> Office Live Collaboration and Office Live Essentials are subscription options offering a mix of programs and tools, and both include your own secure, fully hosted SharePoint site.
>
> For home and small business users who buy software through retail outlets rather than through the volume licensing agreements that larger companies use, Groove is available in the new retail suite Microsoft Office Ultimate 2007. But, if you don't need all the programs in the Ultimate suite, you might want to try the new Office Live Groove subscription service that offers the same functionality as Office Groove 2007.
>
> Find links to more information about these Microsoft Office Live services on the Resources tab of this book's CD.

Creating and Using Shared Workspaces with Windows SharePoint Services

After you sign in to WSS, you can go in several directions.

- Jump into a document library to grab the content you need
- Add content to an existing library
- Navigate to a project workspace to check task lists, schedules, and agenda items
- Create or edit your own site or workspace

> **Note**
>
> Keep in mind that WSS provides administrators a great deal of flexibility to assign and limit rights. So, you might have rights to add and edit pages or even create new workspaces on one site, but just read-only access to documents on another.

Understanding the Workspace

A WSS shared workspace (such as the example shown in Figure 3-1) can consist of any combination of document libraries, lists (such as calendars, links, or tasks), discussion boards, surveys, general Web pages, and additional sites and workspaces (such as a meeting workspace) that reside within the main workspace.

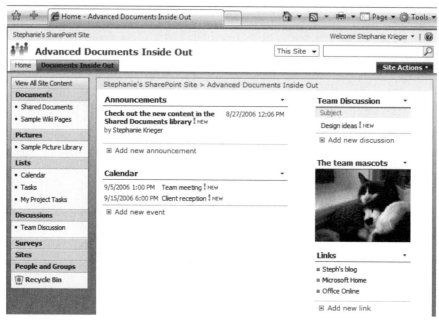

Figure 3-1   The page shown here is a home page for a sample WSS shared workspace.

Libraries

A WSS workspace has four types of libraries, including document, form, wiki page, and picture libraries.

- Document, form, and picture library types are similar in structure, and are to some extent interchangeable. For example, you can upload pictures or forms to a document library. In fact, you might encounter some online help content or other sources that refer to all of these as document libraries. However, certain library types also have tools specific to their content types, such as a slide show tool for viewing pictures in a picture library.

- Wiki pages (see Figure 3-2 for an example) are, essentially, collaborative blogs. That is, they are designed for unstructured contributions by multiple authors. WSS wiki pages support rich text formatting, including tables and pictures, and do not require authors to know any HTML to publish or edit content. Wiki pages automatically create new versions each time someone edits the page, so that you can track changes from one session to the next. To see changes, click History in the bar at the top of a wiki page.

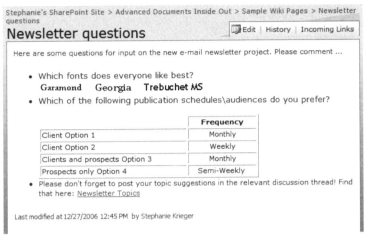

Figure 3-2 The page shown here is a sample wiki page in a WSS shared workspace.

Lists and Other Communication Tools

A WSS workspace can include a variety of lists and other tools, depending on the type of workspace. A collaboration workspace typically includes an announcement board, a discussion board (discussions work similarly to newsgroups, where individual users add posts to a given topic), a contact list, and a links list. A meeting workspace might include a project task list, a meeting agenda, a list of objectives, and a list of attendees.

Each of these lists or communication tools includes a link at the bottom of the existing list where you can add new content, such as Add New Link or Add New Announcement. Simply click the option for a step-by-step guide to adding the item you need.

> **Note**
>
> WSS sites can include two different types of task lists—a classic task list for managing a group of work items and a project task list that displays your tasks in a Gantt chart, so you can visually track tasks against a project timeline.

Accessing or Adding Content in a WSS Document Library

You can access content from a WSS library in a few ways. To open an item, you can simply point to the item and click. When you do this, depending on your permissions for the item, it may open automatically in a read-only state within its originating program or give you the option to open it for editing or read-only.

You can also point to an item in a document library and then click the arrow that appears for a list of options including editing the document, checking out the document so that others can't edit it, and viewing the document, as well as options to view file properties and manage permissions to the document. Note that if you do not set specific permissions from this list of options, the individual item will take on the default permissions for the site.

TROUBLESHOOTING

I don't see workspace options when working in a workspace document

When you open a 2007 Office system document directly from a WSS workspace, you can access several document management tools directly from the program in which you're editing the document.

In the Document Management task pane, access related documents, tasks, and links from the active workspace, as well as view a list of workspace members along with their online status. You can also click Options at the bottom of this task pane to set Document Management preferences, such as when to automatically show the Document Management task pane.

In programs that use the new Microsoft Office interface, such as Word, Excel, and Power-Point, when a workspace document is open, you will see an additional Server option under the Microsoft Office Button. Point to Server for several options, including Document Management Information, which opens the task pane.

In the programs that have the new Microsoft Office Button, you can also find Document Management preferences in the Options dialog box. To do this, click the Microsoft Office Button and then click <Program> Options. At the bottom of the Advanced tab, click Service Options.

INSIDE OUT   Review WSS libraries or lists using Excel queries

Under the Actions button on the toolbar at the top of any workspace index page, such as a library or list, try the option Export To Spreadsheet. This option creates a Web query file that you can open in Office Excel 2007.

For libraries, this query provides a list of content along with information about each item from the columns that appear on the library index page (such as date modified or author). For lists such as tasks and calendars, this option can be a great way to get an editable list of upcoming events or tasks (including pertinent information such as due dates) for quick reference. When you open the query file in Excel, you get the option to open it as a table, a PivotTable report, or a PivotChart report.

Adding Content to a Library or List

From the command bar at the top of a document library, you can either create a new document based on templates stored in the workspace, or upload one or more existing documents. Additionally, you can publish existing documents to a shared workspace directly from Word, Excel, or PowerPoint. To do the latter, click the Microsoft Office Button, point to Publish, and then click Document Management Server.

> **Note**
>
> Notice that you can also create a new workspace from the Publish options available through the Microsoft Office Button.

For all other types of workspace content, such as wiki page libraries, calendars, and task lists, just click New in the command bar at the top of the relevant page to add a new item.

Creating or Editing a WSS Shared Workspace

Provided that you have rights to edit or add to the structure of a WSS shared workspace, you can do quite a bit with surprisingly little work.

Adding Sites, Pages, or Lists

To add a new page or group of pages to your workspace (such as a document library, task list, survey, or meeting workspace), do the following.

1. At the top-right of the active page in your workspace, click Site Actions, as shown in the following graphic, and then click Create.

2. On the Create Page site, point to a content type to see its description and then click to select the type of content you want to create. Step-by-step instructions and options are provided for every type of space you can create from this location.

Understanding and Using Web Parts

Each visual component on a page in your workspace is a Web Part that you can edit. For example, announcements, calendar, team discussion, picture, and links are each separate Web Parts in the page image shown earlier in Figure 3-1.

You can edit existing Web Parts (such as changing the title of a Web Part or adding a picture to an image Web Part) or add new Web Parts to an existing page. All existing content types on your site (such as libraries and lists) are automatically available as Web Parts that can be viewed from any site page. Additionally, you can select Web Parts from online services as well as custom Web Parts created for use in your organization.

To edit or add Web Parts for the active page, on the Site Actions menu, click Edit Page. When you do, you will open the shared version of the page for editing.

- To edit an existing Web Part, click the Edit menu on that Web Part and then click Modify Shared Web Part, as shown here.

- To add a Web Part to the page, at the top of the column where you want the new part to appear, click Add A Web Part. Then, to view additional Web Part options beyond the existing site components, in the Add Web Parts dialog box, click Advanced Web Part Gallery And Options.

> **Note**
>
> As an alternative to using the Site Actions menu to enter Edit Mode for a given page, you can also click the Web Part menu that appears as an arrow at the top-right corner of any existing Web Part on a page and then click Modify Shared Web Part.

Managing Site Settings and Permissions

To edit settings and user permissions for the active site, on the Site Actions menu, click Site Settings. To edit settings and permissions for all sites within your workspace, from the Site Settings page, under Site Collection Administration, click Go To Top Level Site Settings.

Creating and Using Groove Workspaces

When you start Groove, the Launchbar (shown in the image that follows) opens by default. From the Launchbar, you can access your existing workspaces, create a new workspace, or communicate with other workspace members who are currently online.

Chapter 3

If you do not see the Launchbar when you start Groove, you can access your Launchbar, existing workspaces, and a variety of program preferences from the Groove icon in the Windows system tray.

Understanding Your Workspace

A workspace is comprised of tools, each managing a different type of content, such as files, discussions, or meetings. Each tool is identified and accessed by a page tab at the bottom of the Groove window, similar to sheets in an Excel workbook, as you see in Figure 3-3.

Figure 3-3 Each tab in a Groove workspace accesses a unique tool, such as the files, discussions, and meetings that are shown here.

At the top of the page for any tool is a command bar with options for the actions that you can take within that tool, such as adding new content.

While you're in a workspace, it will update automatically whenever a change occurs, such as when members move between tools, enter or leave a workspace, add or change content in a workspace, or add or modify tools. For example, the number you see beside the Discussion tool in Figure 3-3 indicates how many workspace members are currently in that tool. A number appears on the tab for any tool whenever it is occupied by at least one workspace member.

When a change occurs in a workspace, your screen might simply update to reflect the change, or you might see an alert, depending on your settings. To change your alert level, on the Options menu, click Preferences and then click Alerts. Alerts most often appear as a screen tip in the system tray that you can click to perform an action, such as accepting an invitation to join a workspace.

Managing Files in a Workspace

All files for a Groove workspace are stored locally on each workspace member's computer, and they are kept in sync automatically. When you add files or folders to the Files tool in a standard Groove workspace, you are adding copies of those files. Only the copy of a file that is added to your workspace will be affected whenever the file is accessed from the workspace.

When a new member accepts an invitation to join a workspace, the workspace is actually sent to the new member so that copies of all files reside on each member's computer. It is because files reside locally that members can access a workspace from anywhere. However, this is also the reason that Groove recommends not exceeding 2GB total size for a single workspace. Groove is unable to send workspaces to new members if they exceed this size limit.

Creating a Workspace

To create a new workspace, on the Launchbar, click New Workspace. Then select the type of workspace you need and click OK.

- The workspace type referred to as Standard in the New Workspace dialog box is what most people think of as a Groove workspace, and (except where otherwise specified) it is the workspace type referred to throughout this section. Standard workspaces are created with Files and Discussion tools by default. You can then add additional tools as needed, after the workspace is created.

- A File Sharing workspace is a mechanism for sharing the contents of a folder with other computers or other people. File Sharing workspaces do not appear on the Workspaces menu. You can access File Sharing workspaces from the Launchbar. Or, on the Options menu, click Workspace Manager. When you open a file sharing workspace, it opens as a folder in a Windows Explorer dialog box.

- Workspaces based on templates are commonly Standard workspaces to which additional tools and custom settings have already been applied. You can create your own workspace templates or select from templates available online. To select from online templates, in the New Workspace dialog box, click Browse Templates. To create your own workspace template based on an active workspace, on the File menu, click Save Workspace As and then click Template.

> **Note**
>
> When you create a template, it includes all tools in the active workspace on which the template is based (such as Files, Discussion, and Meetings). While saving your template, you get the options to also include existing content in all tools as well as the list of workspace members.

Adding Tools to Your Workspace

To add a tool to the workspace, click the Add Tools icon at the bottom of the workspace window and then select the tool to add. Groove will generate the tool automatically and add the applicable tab to your workspace. In addition to the list of tools you see when you click Add Tools, your company may have custom tools available or you can access additional tools online.

Most tools are designed for multiple pieces of content. So, for example, you can add details for each new meeting to the same Meetings tool. However, you can also add more than one of the same tool type to the workspace when necessary, such as when you want a separate Meetings tool for tracking meetings only attended by managers.

You can rename a tool or customize your alert levels for a particular tool. To take either of these actions, right-click the tab for the applicable tool and then select the command you need.

Inviting Others to Join a Workspace

You can invite anyone to join a Groove workspace. However, those you invite must have Groove 2007 installed on their computer (or have an Office Live Groove account) to access workspaces. Note also that Groove 2007 workspaces are not backward compatible to Groove Virtual Office (the previous version of Groove).

When you invite someone to the workspace, if the recipient has a known Groove account, the invitation will appear in their system tray as a Groove alert. If the recipient does not have a known Groove account, the invitation will be sent by e-mail. If an e-mail recipient has Groove 2007 installed, they can double-click the attached Groove invitation file to open and respond.

To send a workspace invitation, at the bottom of the Workspace Members pane, type the name or e-mail address of the recipient and then click Go. Or, click the More option beside the Invite To Workspace heading to list several recipients at once or to search for a recipient in contacts folders as well as the Groove public directory.

Setting Roles and Permissions

Notice that you set the role for recipients (Manager, Participant, or Guest) in the Send Invitation dialog box shown here.

Roles controls a recipient's rights in the workspace. For the easiest workspace management, invite users in the same invitation only when you want to give them the same rights. However, workspace managers can change a member's role at any time through the Workspace Properties dialog box. Find Workspace Properties where you see the Common Tasks list in your workspace or on the Launchbar.

> **Note**
>
> If you send a workspace invitation to someone who is already a member of that workspace, the recipient will see an alert saying that you request them to come to that workspace. You can also send this type of request to members who are online by right-clicking their name in the Workspace Members list and selecting Send Alert To Come Here.

Permissions are controlled by assigned role rather than by individual member. To customize permissions for roles in your workspace, in the Workspace Properties dialog box, click the Permissions tab.

Using Office OneNote 2007 as a Collaboration Tool

No discussion of document collaboration tools in the 2007 Office system is complete without a mention of Microsoft Office OneNote 2007 shared notebooks and live sharing sessions.

Shared Notebooks and Live Sharing Sessions

In the previous version of Microsoft OneNote, it was possible to create a shared note-taking session, now called a live sharing session. In these sessions, you can invite others on your network or over the Internet to share specified pages of your notebook in real time. During a live sharing session, participants can edit the same pages from their own computers and see notes from all participants as they're taken.

> **Note**
>
> Any type of note that you can take in Office OneNote 2007 on your computer can be taken during a live sharing session, such as typed notes, handwritten (inked) notes, audio notes, or screen clippings.

In OneNote 2007, it is now also possible to create shared notebooks. You can share a notebook with your other computers as well as with other users, such as when you want to keep a team notebook for a project. Shared notebooks can be accessed and edited by multiple participants simultaneously and automatically remain in sync.

Creating a Live Sharing Session

To create a live sharing session in OneNote, on the Share menu, point to Live Sharing Session and then click Start Sharing Current Session for a task pane that will guide you through the necessary steps. Or, from any open task pane, click the name of the active task pane and then click Start Live Session from the task pane list.

Creating a Shared Notebook

To create a shared notebook, on the Share menu, click Create Shared Notebook. This opens a wizard that walks you through the steps to create and share the notebook. Shared notebooks can use any OneNote template and have all the same capabilities of regular OneNote notebooks.

You can save your shared notebook to a WSS site, a network drive, or any shared drive location. Note, however, that to share a notebook, you must have rights to share files and folders on your computer.

 If you don't already use OneNote 2007, find a link through which you can download a free, fully functional trial of this or any 2007 Office system program, on the Extending Office tab of this book's CD.

PART 2

Word

You want documents that remain easy to use and easy to share regardless of content or editing needs. Should you consider playing the lottery instead, for better odds?

Actually, you might be surprised at just how much document-related stress you can easily avoid, and how solid your documents can be. There is a reason for everything that happens in a Microsoft Word document. You might not always like the reason, but when you take the time to understand it, the pieces can come together nicely and much more simply than you might expect.

The difference between good, healthy documents that can stand up to editing and frustrating documents that continually let you down is the difference between understanding *why* versus just knowing *how*.

What You Can Really Do with Word

The document shown here contains 12 graphics and 14 tables. The file size is just 430KB. What's more, it took just two hours to create everything you see on these pages. Sound too good to be true? Check it out for yourself. You can edit this document, share it, do as you like with it. This document will not let you down.

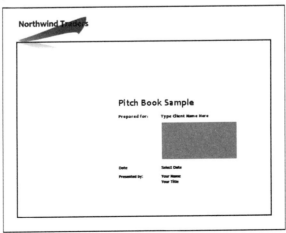

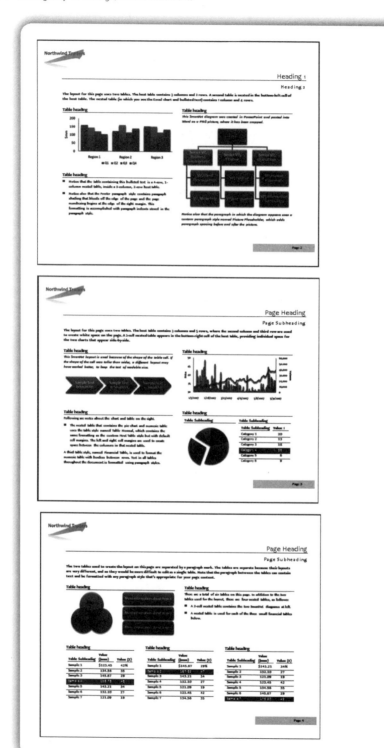

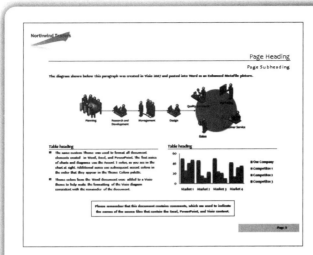

This is what you can really do with Microsoft Office Word 2007.

Find this document, Fearless.docx, as well as the accompanying files containing the original graphics you see in this document (Fearless.xlsx, Fearless.pptx, and Fearless. vsd), in the sample files you can install from the Welcome tab of this book's CD.

Staying in Control: Be the Boss of Your Documents

As introduced in Chapter 1, "Welcome to the 2007 Microsoft Office System," Microsoft Word "likes" things to be as simple and as organized as possible. That doesn't mean that you have to sacrifice design or complex layouts. On the contrary, the simpler and more organized your choices, the more complex your document can be without losing stability or complicating your efforts.

The Three Levels of Word Formatting

The best place to start to understand why things work the way they do in Office Word 2007 is with the three levels of formatting. Word organizes most of the formatting you can apply in your document into these three levels—font, paragraph, and section—with font being the simplest of the three and section being the most complex.

Here's a quick introduction to each of the three levels of formatting, including how they're stored in your document.

Chapter 4

Font Formatting

Font formatting is anything you can apply to as little as one character, such as font face (for example, Times New Roman, Arial, Calibri) or font size. Any formatting available from the Font group on a Ribbon tab or the Font dialog box, as well as language setting, text borders, and text shading, are all types of font formatting.

When you apply font formatting in your document, it is stored directly in the character to which you apply it.

Paragraph Formatting

Paragraph formatting includes anything you can apply to as little as one paragraph, such as paragraph alignment or indents. Any formatting available from the Paragraph group on a Ribbon tab (such as bullets, numbering, and paragraph borders and shading), or from the Paragraph dialog box, are types of paragraph formatting.

When you apply paragraph formatting in your document, it is stored in the paragraph mark at the end of the paragraph where the formatting appears.

INSIDE OUT   Formatting vs. tools to manage formatting

If you think of styles as formatting, think again. Neither styles nor the new Themes feature are actually formatting. Rather, both of these features are tools for organizing, storing, and applying several types of formatting at once. For example, a paragraph style can store a range of paragraph formatting settings and font formatting settings together, to easily access and apply them together.

Section Formatting

Section formatting is often thought of as page setup formatting. Any formatting that can be applied from the Page Setup group on the Page Layout tab or from the Page Setup dialog box, as well as text columns, page and footnote number formatting, and information about which header and footer appears on a page, are all types of section formatting.

To change any type of section formatting for just part of the document, a section break is required. That's because all section formatting is stored in the section break at the end of the section. Note that for single-section documents, section formatting is stored in the last paragraph mark in the document.

> **Note**
>
> There are a few settings in the Page Setup dialog box that are not really section format-
> ting, because you can't change them for just part of the document. These include the
> Different Odd And Even header and footer setting on the Layout tab, as well as the
> Multiple Pages settings on the Margin tab. Conversely, settings in that dialog box that
> you might not think of as formatting at all (such as Paper Source) are indeed section
> formatting, stored in a section break when you change the setting for just part of the
> document.

For more on how section formatting is stored, when section breaks are required, and
how to manage section formatting, see Chapter 8, "Sections."

Managing the Three Levels with the Reveal Formatting Task Pane

The Reveal Formatting task pane is a great tool for troubleshooting document formatting because you can see all formatting for a selection at a glance. But, Reveal Formatting can also help to bring into focus the concept of the three levels of formatting and
how Word organizes formatting in a document.

As you see in the image that follows, a look at the Reveal Formatting task pane clearly
demonstrates how formatting is organized along the three levels being discussed here.

To view formatting for your current selection, press SHIFT+F1. When using Reveal Formatting, keep the following in mind.

- Blue, underlined text in the Reveal Formatting task pane is linked to a dialog box where you can change the referenced type of formatting for your selection.

- The option Compare To Another Selection enables you to select any other content in the document to see an instant comparison of formatting for both selections.

- If your selection includes a table or paragraphs that contain bullets or numbering, you will see additional categories in the Reveal Formatting task pane. These are not additional levels of formatting. Bullets and numbering are paragraph-level formatting, as explained earlier. Tables are not formatting at all, as explained in the next section of this chapter. Breaking out these items simply helps you to quickly see formatting for a selection, because bullets, numbering, and tables can each contain quite a bit of unique formatting.

Understanding Objects and Stories

A document consists of a range of content types (or objects) and formatting, both of which can be added to the body area of the document or to other areas, such as a header, a footnote, or a comment. These areas are known in Word as stories.

The Story Behind Word Stories

Although the concept of stories in Word is most often addressed when using code (such as VBA) to interact with your document, it's an important part of the way Word organizes content. Understanding stories can help you stay in control of any document you need to create.

A story is simply a distinct component of the document that can contain its own content and formatting, similar to the concept of layers in a graphics program. In fact, stories are layers in some ways, as follows.

- Headers and footers (which also comprise watermarks), as well as footnote separators, are all story types that sit behind the main document story.

- Comments, as well as the text areas within text boxes or shapes, are story types that sit on top or in front of the main document story.

Stories, Objects, and Formatting

A text box is a type of object (content type) that you can insert into your document. Wait a minute. Didn't I just tell you that text boxes are stories? Not exactly.

A text box is an object. The text area within that object is a discrete location, separate from the main document, into which you can add text and other content—that is, a story. (Note that there is just one of each story type in a document. So, for example, the text within the collection of all text boxes in a document belongs to the same story.)

So, what about tables? If the content area within text boxes is a separate story, is the area within tables a separate story as well? No. Unlike text boxes, tables become a part of the story into which they're inserted. A table sits in a paragraph mark, just like text. So, Word treats the content you add within a table very much like any other content in the applicable story. It is because of this that tables are often the simplest solution for creating complex layouts in Word.

In a nutshell, here are the simple definitions of formatting, objects, and stories.

- Stories are the locations in your document where you can add content and formatting.

- Objects are the content types you add to your document.

- Formatting is an attribute applied to an object or story.

Finding the Simple Approach to Any Task

The reason that you as an advanced Word user will benefit from taking the time to distinguish between formatting, objects, and stories, is that it can help you find the simplest solution for whatever you need to do in a document.

My rule of thumb for the simplest approach to a document task is the method that will add the least information to the document and require the least work. For example:

- Anything that can be stored in a style (that is, paragraph and font formatting, or table structure formatting in the case of table styles) is the simplest way to apply formatting to text and objects, because styles consolidate several types of formatting into a single container—less work for you to apply, less information for Word to manage. See Chapter 5, "Styles," to learn more about creating styles that simplify documents.

- As discussed earlier, tables are the simplest solution in most cases for organizing complex layouts, because they don't require adding a new layer (such as is required by text boxes). They also don't require adding additional sets of formatting information to the document, such as the section breaks you need when using text columns to lay out a page. Learn more about the logic behind using tables as a layout tool and how to make them work for you, in Chapter 6, "Tables."

Chapter 4

> **Note**
>
> Understanding stories, objects, and formatting in your document can help you not just with the documents you create today, but can be a great help when you begin to venture into working with your documents programmatically. Learn more in Chapter 21, "VBA Primer."

Document Logic: Bringing Yourself to the Document

One of the easiest things you can do to stay in control of your documents is to remember what you already knew before you ever sat down at a computer. The two most important skills for simplifying complex document production have nothing to do with software features. They're skills you've been developing and using since childhood—planning and organization.

People often learn software programs by memorizing the set of steps necessary to execute tasks. When it comes to Word, that approach just won't get you as far as you might want to go. Using Word effectively at an advanced level requires that you take time to think and understand what's happening in your document. If that sounds like more of a commitment than you want to make to a software program, consider this: The time you spend planning, organizing, and thinking about your document is a fraction of the time most people spend on the point, click, and tear-your-hair-out method.

Staying in control of your document can be as simple as understanding what's happening on screen at all times. And that can be much simpler to do than you might think. Using tools such as the Reveal Formatting task pane, along with formatting marks (often referred to as nonprinting characters) and the available options for viewing your document, everything you need to manage your document effectively is right in front of you.

Working with Formatting Marks

The issue of whether to work with formatting marks visible in your document is very simple: You simply can't know what's going on in your document without them.

They're annoying, they get in your way, it's hard to see what the document looks like when formatting marks are visible. Although I don't agree with those statements—I've used formatting marks for so long that they've become like background noise—I know that many of you feel that way. Well, sorry, there's no easy way around this one. Formatting marks tell you a great deal about how your document is formatted. You'll never be fully in control of a complex document without them.

For example, in the image shown here, why don't the right edges of the paragraph borders on the two heading paragraphs line up?

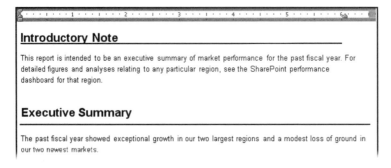

If you're looking at the ruler in the preceding image, assuming that your insertion point is in the first paragraph, you'll say it's because there's a right indent on the first paragraph. But, if you move the right indent in this case, it won't make any difference at all. Why not? With formatting marks visible, you can see the answer immediately. That's no border, as you can see in the following image. It's the old-fashioned, rudimentary workaround of underlining tabs.

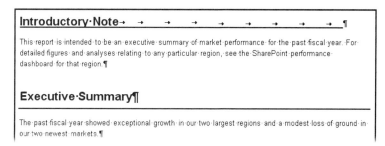

Not only do formatting marks enable you to see the problem immediately, but you can also correct it quickly without trial and error, because you can see exactly what content you need to alter.

Take another example. Have you ever copied content from one part of a document only to have the formatting change when you paste that content? That happened because you pasted the content into a paragraph mark containing a different set of formatting.

As discussed earlier, paragraph marks store formatting. When you press ENTER twice to create a new paragraph, as you would on a typewriter, you're adding an extra, unnecessary set of formatting to your document.

So, not only is it less precise and, ultimately, more work to press ENTER twice after every paragraph than to add formatting for space before or after the paragraph to your paragraph styles, you're also adding an unnecessary set of content to the document that can get in your way later.

When you view formatting marks, you see spaces, tab characters, object anchors, page breaks, and other marks that inform you about how your document is constructed. But, you also see the paragraph marks, cell and row markers, and section breaks that store formatting, which means you have more information about the formatting in your document without having to look for it.

To view formatting marks, press the Show\Hide ¶ icon in the Paragraph group on the Home tab or press CTRL+SHIFT+8. The option Show All Formatting Marks is also available at the bottom of the Reveal Formatting task pane.

You can also customize, to some degree, which formatting marks appear on screen. To do this:

1. Click the Microsoft Office Button and then click Word Options.

Chapter 4

2. On the Display tab of the Word Options dialog box, select the formatting marks you want to view.

> **Note**
>
> When you turn on individual formatting marks using the steps provided here, they will remain on even if you turn off formatting marks using Show\Hide ¶ (CTRL+SHIFT+8).

Using Views Effectively

Is it better to work in Print Layout view, Draft view (formerly called Normal view), Outline view, or Print Preview? The best answer to that question is all of the above. If you work in one view all the time, you might be doing yourself a disservice. Changing views based on the task at hand can save a lot of time and effort. Following is a summary of the benefits of each of these Word views.

View	When to Use It
Print Layout	Print Layout is the best view to use when creating complex documents, because you need to be able to see page layout to manage page layout. Print Layout view enables you to see exactly what your document will look like when printed, with the addition of formatting marks to help you stay in control.
Draft	Draft view doesn't show headers, footers, footnotes, or page layout, so it's not the best view to use for complex document creation. But, because of what you don't see in this view, it also uses less memory—so it can be faster to work in Draft view when simply editing text in a large document. Draft view always shows section and page breaks fully across the page, and it has an optional style area that shows the paragraph styles applied throughout the document. To turn on the style area in Draft view, in the Word Options dialog box, on the Advanced tab, find the Draft option under the Display heading.
Outline	When using Heading styles 1 through 9, or any styles with Outline Level formatting applied, this view is a great tool for quickly reorganizing content in your document. For example, click the plus sign that appears beside any top-level heading when in this view to automatically select it and all content that falls below it. Then, just drag and drop the entire selection to a new location. When you select Outline on the View tab in Word 2007, you see a new contextual Outlining tab that helps you manage the outline (similar to the Outline toolbar that appears in this view in previous versions). To return to your previous view, on the Outlining tab click Close Outline View.
Print Preview	Print Preview is a great way to quickly see your finished product without having to toggle formatting marks and table gridlines on and off. You can also disable the Magnifier on the Print Preview tab to click into the document and edit while in Print Preview. Note that editing in Print Preview is a bit more limited in Word 2007 than in previous versions. Only the Print Preview tab and contextual tabs will appear on the Ribbon when in this view. However, many formatting features will still work in Print Preview. To access those that you often use in this view, add them to your Quick Access Toolbar.

Monitoring the Health of Your Document

You plan, you organize, you stay in control of your document, but still something goes wrong. Perhaps you inherited a document from someone else or added content to a document from another source. What do you do when the document refuses to behave?

Giving your document a time-out probably isn't an effective way to resolve the issue, but there's usually an easy solution.

What Is Document Corruption?

Actually, let's begin with what corruption is not. *Corrupt* is, without a doubt, the most frequently misused word in document production. Yes, documents and content can become corrupt. But, just because something has gone wrong in your document doesn't mean it's corrupt.

The majority of problem documents I've seen across law firms, investment banks, and major corporations, have not been corrupt at all. Formatting errors or misunderstood formatting account for more than their share of documents labeled as corrupt.

- An outline numbered list incorrectly numbers paragraphs.

- A table falls off the edge of the page and ignores formatting commands to reset its size.

- Shaded paragraphs overlap in the printed document.

All of these are examples of common formatting errors often mistaken for document corruption. The problem, of course, is that when someone assumes a document is corrupt, they look for the wrong type of solution. In instances like the formatting error examples provided here, diagnosing and fixing the individual formatting problem is what you need to do. Extreme troubleshooting solutions are not only unnecessary, they won't get the job done. So, what are the most common solutions for the examples provided here?

- When paragraph numbering in an outline doesn't adjust to accommodate changes in the outline, check to see if the Start At value (also called the Set Numbering Value) has been set for some paragraphs. This value forces the paragraph to always show the specified number and not adjust for changes to the outline.

- When a table exceeds the width of the page or any desired width and won't respond to commands to adjust it (such as AutoFit To Window), check to see if the table contains more content than can fit within the desired width. For example, you might select the table and then press CTRL+SHIFT+< repeatedly, as needed, to reduce font size to see if this reduces table size as well.

- When shaded paragraphs look fine on screen but overlap in Print Preview or when printed, check to see the type of shading applied. Using Fill Color to shade paragraphs works fine in just about any scenario. But, using Pattern fills is another story. Patterns include a background and a foreground—information that some printers (as well as some e-mail clients) don't know how to handle.

Chapter 4

In contrast to these simple solutions, the troubleshooting workarounds and extreme solution attempts I've seen for such formatting issues include stripping a 300-page document to plain text and reformatting it from scratch or converting all tables in the document to text and reformatting them with a variety of workarounds.

Poorly formatted documents can sometimes lead to corruption when content is mismanaged or content is added to the document from an incompatible source. But, the fact remains that corruption is not the same as problematic formatting.

TROUBLESHOOTING

How can I clean up bad formatting quickly throughout the document?

The Replace feature in Word is, of course, great for global corrections to text. But, Replace is also a fantastic troubleshooting tool for repairing problem formatting.

For example, if two paragraph marks are used to create vertical space between each paragraph in your document, you can replace all instances of two consecutive paragraph marks with one paragraph mark containing formatting for space after the paragraph.

To replace formatting marks as well as some content types (such as fields), select the item from the Special menu within the Replace dialog box. Or, if you know the character code for the item you want, you can type it directly into the Find or Replace box. The Format menu in the Replace dialog box gives you the option to find or replace a wide range of font and paragraph formatting as well as paragraph, character, or list styles.

In the Replace dialog box shown here, I'm searching for two consecutive paragraph marks and replacing them with one paragraph mark containing formatting for 12 points after the paragraph.

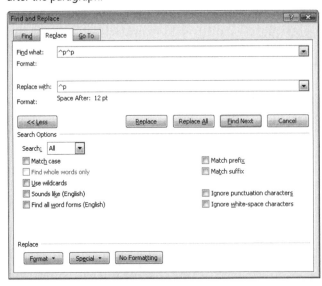

Corruption is when something happens in a document or element of a document that Word doesn't understand. For example, if a table becomes corrupt, Word might lose the ability to properly manage content in that table. So, pasting content into that table could cause the document to crash.

So, how do you distinguish between a formatting error and corruption? If an issue isn't obviously a formatting error, the easiest place to start is with Open And Repair.

Using Open And Repair

Open And Repair has been around since Word 2002, but it continues to improve with age. Essentially, Open And Repair diagnoses and, in many cases, repairs genuine document corruption. It's a great place to start because, if Open And Repair doesn't find corruption in your document, it's likely that the problem you need to be looking for is a formatting issue and not corruption at all.

When Open And Repair finds corruption in your document, a Show Repairs dialog box opens with a list of the corruption types found in your document (such as corrupt tables or styles). In many cases, you can select an error in the list and click Go To in order to be taken directly to the source of the problem. For those who remember the dreaded error message "A Table in this document has become corrupt" before the advent of Open And Repair–when you had to figure out for yourself which table was the trouble-maker–you can see how this feature is an enormous timesaver.

To use Open And Repair, do the following.

1. Click the Microsoft Office Button and then click Open (or press CTRL+O).

2. In the Open dialog box, browse to and select your file.

3. Instead of clicking the Open button, click the arrow to the right of the Open button, as shown here, and then click Open And Repair.

When the document opens, if the Show Repairs dialog box does not appear, Word found no corruption in your document. If the dialog box does appear, take note of the errors and then click Close. To make the repairs permanent, save the document.

CAUTION!

In repairing some types of corruption, such as tables or numbered styles, Word might alter your formatting or even, in rare cases, your document content. Because of this, notice that documents opened with Open And Repair in Word 2007 always open as an unsaved copy of the original. It's a good idea to page through the document completely after closing the Show Repairs dialog box but before saving the document (especially if replacing the original), to ensure that no content or formatting has been changed.

Open And Repair can also be an excellent tool for ensuring the integrity of a complex document or template as you create it. I often open a healthy document or template with Open And Repair as I'm working on it, to ensure that no problems arise during construction.

INSIDE OUT Using the new file formats to repair corruption

The new Office Open XML Formats provide additional options for addressing document problems. Because Office Open XML files are actually a collection of files, errors are more easily compartmentalized and so they can be more easily rectified. See Chapter 22, "Office Open XML Essentials," to learn more about fixing document problems through the file formats.

The Five Tools You Need to Create Any Word Document

People often think that, because Word is so powerful, it would take far too much time to learn everything they need to create complex documents effectively. The fact is that, for all the power of Word, the list of what you need to learn to create most documents is much shorter than most people realize.

If you look through the Word content in a book like this one, you might pass over some things, believing them to be details you don't need. Well, some features are certainly more applicable to some people than others. For example, you might never need to include mathematical equations in your document; someone else might never need an index or a bibliography.

However, some things that might seem like details are actually essential components that can make all the difference in the world. When you know the right details, everything comes together. In Word, those details are the five tools you need to create any complex document.

- Styles
- Tables
- Graphics
- Sections
- Quick Parts

If the last item in that list looks foreign to you, it's because Quick Parts are new functionality in Word 2007. That last item in this list used to be fields—which have now been absorbed by the much broader and more powerful Quick Parts.

When you understand how these five features work together most effectively, no document is out of your reach. The next five chapters will give you the tools you need to bring the right details together and create great Word documents.

To say that styles are important to Microsoft Word documents is a bit like saying that electricity is important to air conditioning.

Without electricity, you could use a paper fan and a block of ice to keep cool—though that wouldn't be very easy or a particularly good long-term solution. Of course, making that ice and keeping it cold would be no picnic either, but people have found ways to get it done since the days of ancient Rome.

Similarly, you have always been able to create Word documents without styles, and you still can in Microsoft Office Word 2007. But, I for one wouldn't want to try. So much Microsoft Word functionality is built around styles. What's more, styles exist to save you time, make formatting easier, and help keep documents consistent. So, why would you ever create a document without them?

Chapter Assumptions

As an advanced Microsoft Office user, I'm assuming you know what a style is and the basics of how to apply, create, and edit styles. This chapter will focus instead both on what's new for styles in Office Word 2007 and advanced tasks such as creating effective sets of styles for use by yourself and others, creating custom Themes, and managing styles effectively.

In the introduction to this book you can find a list of resources for those who want more basic-level information, under the heading "Who Will Benefit Most from This Book".

What's New for Styles in Word 2007

The concept of styles in Word is the same as ever—a named collection of formatting commands that you can apply all at once, as needed, throughout your document. Word still has four types of styles—character, paragraph, list, and table—as well as a Styles pane for accessing styles, and New Style and Modify Style dialog boxes. Once you get past the basics, however, there's a lot that's new and it's very good news.

- New tools for managing styles, including additions to the Styles pane (formerly called the Styles And Formatting task pane), as well as the Manage Styles dialog box and the Style Inspector, can simplify your work significantly.

- The new Quick Styles and Themes features add new dimensions to what you can do with styles.

- Revisions to the way you interact with list styles and multilevel lists help to reveal the logic behind these often misunderstood features.

Paragraph and Character Quick Styles

On the Home tab, in the Styles group, the gallery you see is the new Styles gallery for paragraph and character Quick Styles. Quick Styles, as introduced earlier in this book, are available for many features across Word, Microsoft Office Excel 2007, and Microsoft Office PowerPoint 2007. But, the Styles gallery on the Home tab in Word, shown here, is where the new Quick Styles capabilities and Word styles meet.

Word gives you the option to add any paragraph or character style in your document to the Quick Style list for that document, which means that the style appears in the Styles gallery on the Home tab. And, you can remove any style from the Quick Style list without deleting it from the document.

Because the contents of the Styles gallery can be easily customized for any document or template, the gallery can be a very handy tool when creating documents to be used by others, or templates that you will reuse frequently. For example, customize the Styles gallery to contain only the styles that you want users to apply in the document.

When you create a new paragraph style on screen—that is, without using the New Style dialog box—the style is added to the Styles gallery by default. When you create or edit a paragraph or character style through the New Style or Modify Style dialog boxes, you can turn off the Add To Quick Style List option, which appears at the bottom of both dialog boxes.

INSIDE OUT   Creating Quick Styles on screen

The Apply Styles pane, shown here, contains the Style Name box (formerly called the Style box) that was available on the Formatting toolbar in previous versions. The familiar shortcut CTRL+SHIFT+S opens and activates this pane. Once open, use the X at the top of the pane to close it. This pane can float or dock, and it contains options to reapply the active style, access the Modify Style dialog box, or open the Styles pane, discussed in the section of this chapter titled "The Styles Pane."

As in previous versions, you can create a style on screen by adding your desired formatting to a paragraph, typing a name for the style in the Style Name box, and then pressing ENTER.

However, the addition of Quick Styles functionality now offers an additional option for creating a paragraph style on screen. Instead of clicking in the Apply Styles pane to type a style name, right-click in the paragraph, point to Styles, and then select Save Selection As A New Quick Style to open a dialog box in which you can type the style name. A new Quick Style in this case is nothing more than a new paragraph style that is included in the Styles gallery.

(Note that the Styles option is not available when you right-click text inside tables. However, when you do see this option, notice that you now also have the option there to update the style to match the selected paragraph.)

For those who like to use the Style list that now appears in the Apply Styles pane, but don't want to relinquish the real estate, you can add the Style list on its own to the Quick Access Toolbar. To do this, on the Customize tab of the Word Options dialog box, in the Choose Commands From list select Commands Not In The Ribbon. This option is named Style and appears in the list with an i-beam cursor icon.

To remove a style from the Quick Style list, you can also right-click the style name in the Styles gallery and then select the option Remove From Quick Style Gallery, as you see here.

The Styles Pane

The Styles pane was formerly called the Styles And Formatting task pane. Open the Styles pane from the dialog launch icon in the Styles group on the Home tab, or with the new keyboard shortcut CTRL+SHIFT+ALT+S. Note that this shortcut toggles the pane open and closed.

Though very similar to its predecessor task pane, the Styles pane has some new features that are worth noting, particularly for advanced users who create templates or trouble-shoot documents.

As always, just click a style name in this pane to apply it to the selection. Or, to expand a menu of options, click the arrow that appears beside a style name when you hover the pointer on the name. These options include updating the style to match the selection, selecting all instances of the style in the document, modifying the style, and deleting the style.

TROUBLESHOOTING

How can I quickly see where styles are obscured by direct formatting?

At first glance, the option to Select All <#> Instances of a style might seem a bit useless, because changing the definition of a style automatically updates all instances of that style in a document. However, when troubleshooting poorly formatted documents, this option can be a terrific timesaver.

If you edit a style and the formatting of seemingly unrelated paragraphs changes, direct formatting is a likely culprit. That's because, when someone applies direct formatting on top of a paragraph style, the appearance of that paragraph can be so completely changed that you could never tell what style is applied without using a diagnostic tool (such as Distinguish Style Source in the Reveal Formatting task pane, the Style Area Width in Draft view, or the new Style Inspector).

With Select All <#> Instances, you can quickly scan through the document to see where the style is applied, even on paragraphs that no longer bear a resemblance to their ap-plied style because of direct formatting. That can save a great deal of time clearing un-wanted direct formatting, so that you don't have to resort to clearing direct formatting for large portions of the document where some of it might need to be reapplied later.

Additionally, this option is useful if you are cleaning up the document by deleting unnec-essary styles. If the style is unused in the document, the option will read Select All: Not Currently Used.

Following are new features you'll find on the menu of options available for each style in the Styles pane.

- The first new option is Clear Formatting Of <#> Instances. This option enables you to quickly clear all instances of a style in the document, without deleting the style.

- The next new option here is Revert To <Base Style Name>. If you create a new style based on anything other than Normal, the option to delete the style is replaced with the option Revert To <Base Style Name>. When you select this option, you are prompted to delete the style in order to complete the action. The difference between this option and simply deleting the style is that paragraphs with the deleted style will revert to the base style instead of reverting to Normal.

- At the bottom of this menu is also another access point for adding a style to the Styles gallery or removing it from that gallery.

The most important additions to the Styles pane are the new options at the bottom of the pane, which are discussed as relevant topics arise later in this chapter. Note, however, that the Show Preview option at the bottom of the Styles pane enables you to toggle formatted style previews in the Styles pane with a simple listing of style names.

> **Note**
> There's a small bug in the new Styles pane that's worth noting. If you apply a style through the Apply Styles box, you won't see the style change reflected in the Styles pane until you change your selection (just moving your insertion point within the paragraph will do the trick).

Creating Effective Style Sets

For styles to do their job properly, the styles in the document need to be created as a set. That is, design styles in your document to work together. As discussed in Chapter 1, "Welcome to the 2007 Microsoft Office System"" in the section titled "Planning Your Documents," creating a style without any thought to how it will be used or how it will interact with other styles is quite likely to do more harm than good.

TROUBLESHOOTING

How do I know what styles are okay to use in my organization?

One of the most common errors I see made by software trainers and tech support staff is failing to explain the reasons behind restrictions or limitations in the company's policy on software use. This action (or lack of action) often causes the restriction to be misinterpreted as a software limitation and can lead to misdiagnosis of document problems. Some of the most common examples of this are a few very popular style myths.

Many companies don't like users to edit Normal style because changes to that style will affect all styles based on Normal. Additionally, companies may prefer that users only use custom styles created by the firm to help keep the look of documents consistent throughout the company.

The problem is that users are told to never edit Normal style, use built-in Word styles, or use any styles other than those created by the firm, but not told why. So, the misinterpretations grow and circulate, and myths begin to be taken as truths. These myths include the common fallacies that editing Normal style, using built-in Word styles, or including custom styles from outside the company in a document can cause document corruption.

When to edit Normal style and when to use built-in or custom styles are discussed in this chapter. For information on what document corruption really is and how to diagnose it, see the section titled "Monitoring the Health of Your Document" in Chapter 4, " Building Easy-to-Manage, Robust Documents."

Consider Built-In vs. Custom Styles

Built-in styles are those that are available to a new Word document by default, before any custom styles have been created. A new, default Word document contains a whopping 264 styles before you even get started, between those actually stored in the document and those that are added as you use applicable features (such as a header or a footnote).

As you can imagine, 264 styles on its own is a good reason to use built-in styles when they will work for your needs. After all, why add additional styles to a document when you can just edit the existing styles? In the spirit of the 'lazy operator' introduced in Chapter 1, you'll get along best with Word when you don't add anything to a document that doesn't need to be there.

Let's take a closer look at those 264 built-in styles. That number breaks down as follows.

- 93 paragraph styles
- 24 character styles
- 4 list styles
- 143 table styles

For those familiar with the fact that in Office Word 2003, a default Word document had an available 154 built-in styles, note that 98 of the 110 additional built-in styles in Word 2007 are table styles, 6 are character styles, and 6 are paragraph styles.

However, before you start screaming that this is crazy and you don't want 264 styles in your documents, consider the following.

- You and anyone for whom you create documents never need to see or interact with any styles other than those you want to use.

- The built-in styles that exist in the documents have been designed into the program—their existence does no harm.

- A great many built-in styles work with features you just might want to use one day, such as reference tables or captions.

- Some built-in styles have unique properties that can save you time, such as generating a table of contents, cross-references, or a multilevel outline list from the Heading 1–9 styles.

- In Word 2007, only character and paragraph styles appear in the Styles pane, so you don't have to worry at all about those 98 extra table styles. List styles appear only in the Multilevel List gallery and table styles in the Table Styles gallery. The only negative there is that you might occasionally miss the ability to have the list or table styles you want to use handy in the Styles pane—but if you know the style name, you can still type it in the Apply Styles pane to apply it in your document.

So, am I telling you to always use built-in styles rather than create your own? Of course not. There will be times when creating your own styles makes sense. The best practice is to first consider whether you can modify built-in styles for your needs, particularly when it comes to paragraph and character styles.

- Because many built-in paragraph styles have additional properties for working with Word features, as discussed earlier, there's an important added benefit to sticking with built-in paragraph styles. Common built-in paragraph styles are also named intuitively, such as Body Text, Heading 1–9, Header, Footer, or Footnote Text.

  The most common reason to create your own styles is when a unique style naming convention is the most logical for those using the document or template you're creating. However, using style aliases can be a good alternative to adding additional styles to the document. See the Inside Out tip "Creating Style Aliases" in this section for more on style aliases.

- Word provides more character styles than you probably need, such as the new styles that have names evocative of perfume marketing (Intense Reference or Subtle Reference, for example).

  Some character styles that might seem to not be named intuitively—such as Strong for bold or Emphasis for italics—take on those less direct names to make them more easily editable. For example, if you wanted to change all instances of bolded text in your document to underlined, your Strong style would still make sense

Chapter 5

if you changed the formatting contained in that style to be underline instead of bold. If that character style were named Bold, however, and you changed the formatting to underline, that would hardly be logical for other users of your document. Also remember that many character styles, such as Hyperlink, Page Number, and Footnote Reference, are required by Word features.

- Despite the 143 table styles, I usually create my own custom table styles rather than editing built-in styles. This is because most of the built-in table styles contain more formatting than I would include in a table style, and it's more work to undo existing formatting in these styles than to create my own, clean table styles. Learn more about table styles later in this chapter.

- There are so few list styles, that it often makes sense to create your own. Of course, if an existing list contains much of the formatting you need, there's certainly more sense in customizing it than creating your own. The goal of all styles, after all, is to save you work. Learn more about working with list styles and multi-level lists later in this chapter.

INSIDE OUT   Creating style aliases

If you've ever tried to rename a built-in style and your effort resulted in your new style name being appended to the existing style name following a comma, what you did was create an alias for your style. A style alias is an alternate style name you can type in the Apply Style pane then press ENTER to apply the style.

Built-in styles can't be renamed, but you can create an alias for any style (built-in or custom) in the Modify Style dialog box. To do this, just type a comma at the end of the style name, followed by the alias you want. With built-in styles, replacing the style name in the Modify Style dialog box will have the same effect as appending an alias to the existing name. The replacement name becomes the alias.

Using style aliases can be a good timesaver when you want to create shortcuts for applying common styles but don't want to use up keyboard shortcuts. Style aliases are also a good alternative to adding custom styles when the only reason to do so is to use a unique naming convention for the styles in a document or template.

Benefits of Using Character Styles

As discussed in this chapter, some character styles are necessary because they work with Word features, such as the Footnote Reference or Page Number style. But, if you just want to bold occasional words, for example, why use a character style rather than direct formatting?

The fact is that it's often not necessary to use character styles in these cases and doing so won't win you any benefits. Character styles used to offer different behavior from direct character formatting and could be retained more consistently when changes were made to underlying paragraph styles. However, in recent versions of Word, this has become a nonissue, because direct character formatting and character styles have the same retention behavior.

However, using character styles for that occasional bold word can be helpful in some cases, simply because they have a name and can be edited. For example, if you bold every instance of the client's name throughout a long document and later decide that you want those to be underlined instead of bold, that change is much easier with a character style. If you used the Replace feature in that case to search for all bold text and replace with underline, you would also catch any bolded text where bold is part of the paragraph style, such as headings. However, if you have a character style for bold that you use in those cases, you can simply edit the style to make that change.

INSIDE OUT **What determines whether font formatting is retained when I change styles?**

Have you ever wondered why font formatting is sometimes kept and sometimes not when you apply a new paragraph style to a selection? The answer is simple percentages. If you apply direct font formatting to up to 50 percent of a paragraph, the formatting will be retained. However, direct font formatting applied to 51 percent or more will not.

The idea is that, if you apply font formatting directly to just part of a paragraph (such as changing the color of a single word), you probably want to keep that text unique so that it stands out from the paragraph. But, if you've applied font formatting directly to most or all of the paragraph, it's more likely that you want the formatting of all text to change when you apply a new style.

To retain unique font formatting on more than half the paragraph regardless of paragraph style changes, use a character style.

Thanks to Stuart Stuple, a member of the Word 2007 design team and unparalleled style guru, for insight into this issue and several others in this chapter.

Making Effective Use of Base and Following Styles

There is more to consider when creating styles than what the formatting will look like applied in your document. If the styles are not intuitive and easy to use, it doesn't much matter how they would look in the document. The more you consider ease of use, the more likely styles will be used properly in your documents, so the more likely your documents will look consistent and remain healthy in the long-term.

Two of the most important components for keeping styles easy-to-manage in documents are also two of the most often overlooked: base styles and style for the following paragraph.

Chapter 5

Base Styles

Most styles have another style upon which they are based. A style that uses a base style contains all the formatting settings in the base style (other than those you specify not to include) as well as its own settings. The importance of a base style is that whenever a base style is changed, any styles based upon that style change as well.

The advantage of using a base style is that it saves time when editing document formatting and keeps styles consistent. For this reason, Normal style is usually considered the best base style for most of your styles.

- Normal is based on document defaults, not a base style, so it will only change when you change it explicitly or when you change the default font or paragraph formatting for the document or attached template.

- When you have a consistent base style, such as Normal, you simply change the one base style to distribute the change automatically throughout the document styles.

   For example, if your body text size is 12 points and you want to make it 10 points, simply make that change in Normal style. Any styles based on Normal style (that do not have the font size defined in their style definition) will automatically change to reflect the new font size of their base style.

Normal is provided to be a base style, which is the only reason it's better than any other style for this purpose. And, since Normal is based on document defaults, it's easy to edit.

I've never found a reason to create a custom style to act as a base style. But, if you prefer to create your own base style, there's not likely to be any harm in it. The most important thing is that your base style not have a base style of its own, to avoid unwanted chain reactions when you edit formatting.

To create a paragraph style that has no base style, do the following.

1. From the Styles pane, open the New Style dialog box.

2. After you select Paragraph or Linked as the Style Type, you can select No Style from the top of the Style Based On list, as shown here.

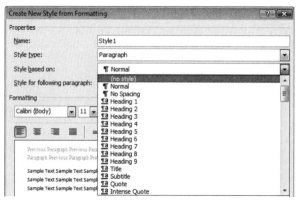

CAUTION !

Keep in mind that base styles are designed to help simplify your work when you need to edit formatting. It's not a good idea to create an entire set of styles without base styles. When you do this, you rob yourself of a key ease-of-use benefit of styles functionality.

For style types other than paragraph and linked styles, base styles are a bit different.

- Character styles can use base styles. These styles are typically based on a character style named Default Paragraph Font, which essentially means that any properties not explicitly set in the character style will match the formatting of the underlying paragraph. The alternative to using a base style for character styles is the Underlying Properties option at the top of the Style Based On list in the New Style or Modify Style dialog box. However, this option has the same effect as using Default Paragraph Font, so nothing is gained by taking the time to change this setting.

- All table styles have base styles. Table Normal is the default base style for table styles and the best to use, unless you have a specific reason to base one style on another. Similar to Normal paragraph style, Table Normal is based on default table formatting (that is, no borders or shading, cells top aligned, left and right cell margins of 0.08 inches [1.9 millimeters]). All other built-in table styles are based on Table Normal.

- All list styles are based on the style named No List. However, unlike other style types, list styles do not give you the option to change the base style. When you create custom list styles, they are automatically based on No List. For the logic behind this, see the list styles sections later in this chapter.

Note

The default base styles for character, table, and list styles—that is, Default Paragraph Font, Table Normal, and No List—are the only three built-in styles in Word that can't be customized.

You may occasionally want to base one style on another, but tread carefully. For example, you might want to base a subheading style on the heading style, so that a change to the properties of the heading style (such as font) would be updated automatically in the related subheading style. I say to tread carefully, because basing one style on another is the quickest route to the "circular based on list" error, discussed in the Troubleshooting tip that follows.

TROUBLESHOOTING

Why do I get an error stating that a style has a circular based on list?

When you create a paragraph style on screen, remember that the base style is the original style applied to the paragraph from which you create your new style. So, if the paragraph was formatted with Normal style before you added formatting and created your new style, Normal will be the base style. Similarly, if the paragraph was formatting with Heading 1 style or List Bullet style before you made your changes and created a new style, that will be the base style. Paying attention to the original paragraph style before you add formatting to create a new style is probably the most important step you can take in creating a style. Keep in mind that if you change the base style later, any formatting in your style that came from the base style will be changed as well—so you'll have to do extra work to reset the formatting you want.

Creating styles without attention to the base style can lead you to think the formatting has a mind of its own, because changes you make to one style automatically make uninvited changes to others based on that style. The most common cause of this problem is when someone creates several styles on screen from the same paragraph. For example, you format the paragraph and create one style; change the formatting and create a second style; and so on. Each style you've created is now based on the style before that. It creates a chain of base styles so that when you make changes to the first, the change ripples through all subsequent styles in your based-on chain.

Doing this also often leads to the error message "This style has a circular based on list," which occurs when the base style chain leads back to the style itself, so that two styles are based on one another. Most often, the warning occurs when you attempt to create a circular relationship, so you can avoid it. However, if you get this error message on existing style settings, set the base style to Normal to break the cycle. Before you make this change to a style, however, take note of the formatting contained in the style so that you can replace any formatting lost by changing the base style.

Style for the Following Paragraph

This paragraph style feature is one of my favorites, and it amazes me how often it's ignored. Style for the following paragraph means the style you get when you press ENTER to start a new paragraph.

By default for most styles, consistent with the underlying concepts of paragraph formatting in Word, when you press ENTER, you get the same style as you had in the preceding paragraph. (Some styles, such as Heading 1–9, are followed by Normal style by default.) However, when you create or edit styles, you can change the Style For Following Paragraph setting as appropriate to simplify workflow.

For example, if every page in your presentation template starts with a Heading 1 paragraph, followed by a Heading 2 paragraph, followed by a Heading 3 paragraph—why not set that up to be automatic?

You can customize this setting when you create a style through the New Style dialog box, or change this setting for any paragraph style through the Modify Style dialog box. To do the latter, take the following steps.

1. In the Styles pane, click the arrow beside the style you want to change and then click Modify.

2. In the Modify Style dialog box, select the style you want to follow your style from the list labeled Style For Following Paragraph.

The page heading example given earlier is the most common use I've seen for this feature. Another good example can be seen in the template I'm using to write this book, created by Microsoft Press. When I apply the style that's a placeholder for a numbered figure that will appear in the chapter and then press ENTER, I get the figure number style. Press ENTER again and I get the figure caption style. That's a nice timesaver and a perfect use for this feature, because—as you see wherever numbered figures appear in this book—those three styles are consistently used together.

As with any feature, take the time to customize this setting only in examples like these, where it will simplify something for the users of the document. A common mistake with this setting is to overuse it, adding confusion and complication rather than simplifying workflow. The most common example of misuse for this feature is to set each lower level of a multilevel list to follow the previous level. That doesn't simplify anything—in fact, it can complicate use of the outline-numbered styles—because you won't always want the lower level style to follow the higher level. It's common in outlines to have body text between numbered paragraphs, or consecutive paragraphs on the same level.

Change the style for the following paragraph only where styles will be consistently used in succession.

Understanding Linked Styles

For the first time, linked styles are referred to in several places in Word—such as in the Styles pane and as a style type option in the New Style dialog box. But, linked styles are not new to Word 2007.

Have you ever selected just a few words in a paragraph and then applied a paragraph style only to have the style apply as if it were a character style, only to the selected text? You were using a linked style.

A linked style can be applied as a paragraph or a character style. Nearly half of all built-in paragraph styles in Word 2007 are actually linked styles.

The main difference for linked styles in Word 2007 is that, for the first time, linked styles are explicit in Word 2007 and you can choose to create paragraph styles as linked styles.

Chapter 5

TROUBLESHOOTING

Why does my document contain Char and Para styles that I didn't create?

When a style named for an existing document style, plus a *Char* or *Para* suffix, appears in the document, a linked style has become unlinked. This is a bug that most often occurs in documents with problematic formatting, but it is not indicative of document or style corruption.

If content is inserted into the document that causes a conflict in the definition of a linked style, the style can become unlinked, generating this additional Char or Para style. For example, if you have a linked style in Document A that is applied as a paragraph style, and the same style name with different formatting in Document B, where it's applied as a character style, copying the content from Document B into Document A can cause this conflict to occur.

It's a good idea to resolve these excess styles when they occur in the document to avoid user confusion, as well as to take their appearance as a sign that you might need to review and clean up the document's styles and formatting in general. When you delete a Char or Para style, however, its companion style might also be deleted.

To avoid losing formatting, replace instances of that style with another style before deleting styles. When the style to be deleted is linked to a style you need, just replace instances of the style with any other style as a placeholder. Once you've cleaned up the Char or Para styles you don't need, you can re-create your good style if it was also deleted, and then replace the placeholder style with your intended style. For information on using the Replace feature with formatting and special characters, see the Troubleshooting tip "How can I clean up bad formatting quickly throughout the document?" in Chapter 4.

Styles that Make User-Friendly Documents

When you plan the styles for a document or template, the following basic best practices are good to keep in mind for helping to ensure ease of use.

- Use styles, like any other Word feature, only when doing so will simplify your work and the document. The majority of documents and document content do benefit from styles, but creating a mass of styles just to avoid the use of any direct formatting is overcomplicating the purpose of styles and is likely to lead to overburdened documents that are difficult to edit and manage.

- Keep the set of styles as simple as possible. For example, don't create three identical styles with different names, just for content in separate parts of the document. The existence of too many styles confuses users and is as likely to result in inconsistent formatting as not using styles at all.

- Use intuitive style names that will make sense to document users. When creating your own custom styles, use a consistent naming convention.

- Consider base styles, style for the following paragraph, and linked styles in developing your style set and check your completed set of styles for proper use of these three features.

- Include only those paragraph and character styles you want users to access in the Quick Style list. Additionally, see the "Managing Styles" section later in this chapter to learn about using the new Recommend features for controlling which styles users see.

Using Quick Style Sets

Once you have customized the Styles gallery to contain only the styles you want users to access, you can save the styles in that gallery as a Quick Style Set for use in other documents.

A Quick Style Set is a type of template that contains only paragraph and character styles. You can apply a Quick Style Set to any document without changing the attached template. A Quick Style Set changes nothing but the makeup of paragraph and character styles in the document.

Word comes with some built-in style sets as well, and you can find both built-in and your custom style sets in the same location. To access Quick Style Sets, on the Home tab, in the Styles group, click Change Styles and then click Style Set. Then, just click a Quick Style Set to apply it in your document.

To save the contents of your active Quick Style list as a new Quick Style Set, do the following.

1. On the Home tab, in the Styles group, click Change Styles and then click Style Set.

2. At the bottom of the Style Set gallery, click Save As Quick Style Set.

3. Name your new style set and then click Save. The new style set name will automatically appear in the Quick Style Set gallery.

At the bottom of the Quick Style Set gallery, note that you also have the option to reset the Quick Styles in your document to the defaults for the attached template.

Quick Style Sets are a clean and simple option for when you need to provide consistent sets of styles for a group of users, without dictating layout or other template elements. Quick Style Sets can also be great for people who create content for multiple clients.

For example, I often write for different Microsoft Web sites, many of which have their own style requirements. Instead of saving several document templates when all I need is a set of styles, I have separate Quick Style Sets to apply to blank documents when I'm writing content for Microsoft Work Essentials, Office Online Training, Microsoft Office Webcasts, or other sites.

Because Quick Style Sets are saved as Word templates, you can edit them easily. To learn more about editing and managing Quick Style Set templates and other types of Word 2007 templates, see Chapter 20, "The Many Faces of Microsoft Office Templates."

Chapter 5

Working with Themes

As introduced in Chapter 1, a Document Theme is a set of fonts, colors, and graphic effects, which you can apply to your document with a single click. The same Themes (both built-in and those you create or customize) are available in Word, Office Excel 2007, and Office PowerPoint 2007.

> **Note**
>
> These same Themes are also available in any part of Microsoft Office Outlook 2007 that has formatting options similar to Word (such as in e-mail messages and tasks). Additionally, Theme Fonts and Theme Colors are available in the Calendar Printing Assistant for Office Outlook 2007—a new Microsoft Office Tools program for when you need formatted versions of your Outlook calendars. The new Theme Fonts and Theme Effects features in Microsoft Office Visio 2007, however, are unrelated to Document Themes in Word, Excel, and PowerPoint, though the concepts are similar.

> **Note**
>
> The Calendar Printing Assistant for Outlook is available to all licensed owners of Outlook 2007, as part of the new Office Genuine Advantage program that provides great free add-ins and extras to anyone with legitimate copies of Microsoft Office programs or suites. Find links to information about the Office Genuine Advantage program and the download site for the Calendar Printing Assistant on the Resources page of this book's CD.

If Themes sound similar to PowerPoint design templates, it's because PowerPoint design templates are very much the inspiration for Themes. In fact, though Themes are available in Word, Excel, and PowerPoint, additional characteristics are uniquely available to Themes when created or applied in PowerPoint, including elements of Slide Master, Slide Layout, and Slide Background formatting. For this reason, custom Themes that you want to use in multiple programs are best created in PowerPoint. For more information on creating Themes in PowerPoint, see Chapter 19, "Slides and Presentations."

Before discussing how to create or even apply Themes, however, it's important to note that Themes are only available to documents saved in the new Office Open XML Formats. Theme components are saved in your documents as XML, so they are not available to documents saved in the legacy file formats.

INSIDE OUT   Themes and legacy documents

If you apply a Theme in a document and then save the document down to a legacy file format (such as the Word 97 - 2003 Document file format, .doc), your formatting will be retained, with the exception of any graphic effects not available in earlier version of Microsoft Office. However, the Theme characteristics of that formatting (the ability to swap automatically with new formatting choices) will not be available to the document.

Note also that if the document is once again converted to an Open XML Format (such as the Word 2007 default format, .docx), the formatting will not automatically be Theme-ready. The document will behave as if it had been created as a legacy document, and will need to be reformatted to work with Themes.

New documents created in the new file formats are automatically Theme-ready. However, to make any document Theme-ready after converting it to an Open XML Format, you first need to apply Theme components to your document content. Learn how to do this easily in the next section of this chapter.

In Word and Excel, Themes are available on the Page Layout tab. In PowerPoint, Themes are available on the Design tab. You can apply a Theme in its entirety, or cherry-pick sets of Theme Colors, Theme Fonts, or Theme Effects.

To apply a Theme or Theme element in your Word document, do the following.

1. On the Page Layout tab, in the Themes group shown in the following image, click to expand the Themes gallery or the Colors, Fonts, or Effects galleries, as desired.

2. The Live Preview feature works with Themes, so you can point to options in the gallery to see how each looks in your document.

3. When you find the option you want, click to apply it to the document.

The Style–Theme Relationship

The most important thing to understand about Themes is that they are designed to swap. That is, when you select a new Theme, all fonts, colors, and graphic effects in your document that belong to the Theme will automatically change to match your new Theme.

> **Note**
>
> One of my favorite details in the 2007 release is the fact that the entries in galleries, such as various Quick Style galleries or Building Block galleries in Word, automatically adjust to reflect the colors, fonts, and effects (as applicable) of the active Theme.

However, for fonts and colors to swap when Themes are changed, the Theme-specific options must be applied in your document, as follows.

Theme Fonts

Each Theme includes a heading font and a body font. By default in Word 2007, documents use the body font for styles such as Normal and Body Text, and the heading font for styles such as Heading 1–9.

When you look at any font list, such as you see here, notice that you see Theme Fonts at the top of the list. Beside the font names in this section, you see the labels (Headings) and (Body). You may also notice that the same fonts exist lower in the same list without these labels.

When you apply Theme fonts, you aren't actually applying the specific font. Instead, you're telling the style or the content to use whatever is the active Heading or Body font. So, for example, if I apply Calibri (Body) to one paragraph and apply Calibri without the body label to another, only the first will swap to new Theme Fonts if the Theme is changed in the document.

Theme Colors

If you have changed colors in the Excel palette or a PowerPoint color scheme in an earlier version of Microsoft Office, you're already at least somewhat familiar with the way Theme Colors work.

A set of Theme Colors is comprised of 12 colors, as you see in the Create New Theme Colors dialog box, shown here. Ten of these are available to be applied anywhere in your documents; the 11th and 12th are for Hyperlink and Followed Hyperlink formatting, respectively. Notice that, similar to the PowerPoint color scheme concept, some of these colors are designed for use with text and backgrounds, and others are accent colors.

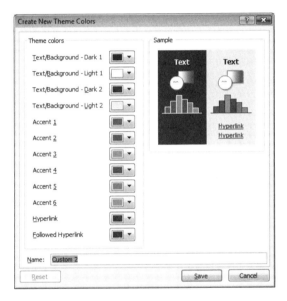

When you apply a Theme, each of the 10 Theme colors generally available to your document are provided as solid colors, as well as in five shades of that color, for a total of 60 coordinated colors in the palette. For colors in your document to swap when Themes are changed, they must be applied from the Theme Colors portion of the color palette, shown here.

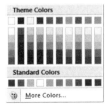

Similar to Theme Fonts, when you apply a color from the Theme Colors palette, you aren't actually applying that specific color. Instead, you're applying whatever color is located in that position in the color palette. For this reason, if you apply the exact same color as one of your Theme colors, but don't select it from the Theme Colors portion of the palette (for example, if you apply the color by specifying the RGB values), the color will not swap when Themes are changed.

Making Your Documents Theme-Ready

In a new Word document, by default, Heading 1 style uses Cambria font and a blue font color. Notice, however, when you look at the ScreenTip shown here containing the description of the Heading 1 style, that the font is specified as +Heading and the font color as Accent 1.

This style definition is Theme-ready—designed to swap automatically when the Theme is changed. If the heading font for the new Theme is, for example, Century Gothic, the appearance of paragraphs formatted with Heading 1 style will change to use the Century Gothic font, but the style definition will remain exactly the same.

As already mentioned, new Word documents are Theme-ready by default. However, to make a document Theme-ready, all you need is to use the Theme Fonts and Theme Colors as described earlier in this section. Of course, be sure not to use Theme Fonts or Theme Colors in any instances where you don't want the formatting to swap with a new Theme.

For documents converted from the legacy file formats, apply Theme Fonts or Theme Colors to the document (for example, by adding them to the document styles) to make the document Theme-ready. One easy way to do this in Word documents is to apply a Quick Style Set that uses Theme-ready styles. If the Quick Style Set includes the same style names as your document, the formatting will change automatically to match the new style definitions, making them Theme-ready.

Following up on the built-in versus custom style discussion earlier in this chapter, this shortcut for easily adding Theme components to converted legacy documents is another good reason to use built-in style names in your documents.

Customizing Themes

As mentioned earlier, if you want to use the same custom Theme in all of your Microsoft Office documents, create your Theme in PowerPoint to have all Theme elements available. However, you can also create a Theme in Word (or Excel), when appropriate.

Note that if you create a Theme in Word or Excel and later need to add additional elements to that Theme for PowerPoint, you can edit the custom Theme. See the Inside Out tip in this section, titled "Editing Custom Themes," for more information.

To create your own custom Theme, take the following steps.

1. On the Page Layout tab, in the Themes group, apply the Theme that is closest to the formatting you want, or the combination of Theme Colors, Theme Fonts, and Theme Effects that is closest to what you want to include in your new Theme.

2. At the bottom of the Theme Colors gallery, click Create New Theme Colors.

3. In the dialog box that opens, you will see the currently applied Theme Colors. Click any of these colors for the option to customize it.

   When customizing a color in this dialog box, you can select from Theme Colors or Standard Colors, or click More Colors to specify a custom color.

   When you have customized all colors you want to change, name your custom color set and then click Save. For ease of use, it's a good idea to give your custom Theme Colors the same name as you plan to give your custom Theme.

4. In the Theme Fonts gallery, select Create New Theme Fonts.

5. Select the heading and body font you want to include in your new Theme. Then, name your new Theme Fonts and click Save.

6. When you're happy with the appearance of your custom Theme, in the Themes gallery click Save Current Theme. Then, just name your new Theme and click OK.

   The new Theme will be added to the Themes gallery in Word, Excel, and Power-Point, under the Custom heading.

INSIDE OUT   Editing custom Themes

Once you have created a custom Theme Colors set, you can right-click the set where it appears in the Theme Colors gallery and select Edit to change your custom colors. The same is true for custom Theme Fonts.

To edit a custom Theme, apply that Theme in your document, customize it as needed, and then save the Theme, giving it the same name as your existing custom Theme. When you do so, you will be prompted to replace the existing custom Theme.

Sharing Themes

So, you've created your custom Theme. Ready to share it with others or with your other computers? There are two principal ways to get this done.

- Copy the actual Theme files from one computer to another.

- Share a document that contains the custom Theme.

Chapter 5

Sharing Themes by Copying Theme Files

A complete Theme consists of four files, including the .thmx file that contains the overall Theme settings, and three XML files—one each for Theme fonts, colors, and effects.

You can copy any of these four files independently, or copy them as a group. For example, if you just want to share a set of custom Theme colors, copy just the XML file containing the name you gave your custom Theme Colors set, from the Theme Colors folder. When you do this, the destination machine will have the new Theme Colors set but will not have the related elements of the custom Theme. Similarly, if you copy just the .thmx file but not the colors, fonts, or effects files, the custom Theme will appear in the Themes gallery and can be applied with all of its elements intact—but you won't see individual options for the theme fonts, colors, or effects in their respective galleries if the files storing those settings don't exist on the destination machine.

> **Note**
>
> Unless you've had custom graphic effects created for you, it's not usually necessary to copy those files. Since graphic effects can't be customized through the user interface, it's the norm to include a selection from the built-in Theme Effects gallery options in a custom Theme.

Custom Theme files are located in the Document Themes folder, which resides in your main Templates folder. This is the folder identified as your User Templates folder on the Trusted Locations tab of the Word Options dialog box. For more information about default template folder locations, see Chapter 20.

In the Document Themes folder, you'll see any custom .thmx files you've saved, as well as three subfolders named Theme Colors, Theme Effects, and Theme Fonts. Inside each of those folders are the XML files for any custom color, font, or effect sets you've saved. (Note that, if your custom Theme uses a built-in set for any of these elements, no file will appear in the corresponding folder.) Also note that, because it's likely that you'll name the Theme Fonts and Theme Colors for a custom Theme with the same name, the XML file names may be identical. If that's the case, be sure to note the location of the file, so that you place it in the correct destination folder.

Once a custom Theme or any custom Theme element is added to a new computer, it automatically becomes available in the applicable galleries in Word, Excel, and Power-Point.

Sharing Themes by Applying the Theme from an Existing Document

If you want to share a Theme, but don't want the recipient to need to worry about what files go where, just share any document in which that Theme is applied.

To apply a custom Theme to the active document from a Theme contained in another document, at the bottom of the Themes gallery click Browse For Themes. Using the dialog box that opens, locate the file containing the Theme you want to apply and then click Open. Notice that you can apply a Theme from any Theme-ready Word, Excel, or PowerPoint file, or from a .thmx file.

Once the Theme is applied to the active document, you must save it as a custom Theme in order to have it available to other Word, Excel, and PowerPoint documents on the active computer.

Mastering Lists

Do you believe bullets and numbering to be buggy or simply bewitched? Are you amazed (or, perhaps, appalled) at the ability of the lists in your documents to morph at will into unexpected forms? If so, you've come to the right place.

First things first: Bullets and numbering in Word can be easy, manageable, and down-right pleasant to use. Okay, perhaps you don't believe me yet, but give it a chance. If you use the guidelines and best practices provided here, you just might be convinced.

> **Note**
>
> For law firms, legal departments, or any company that has relied on numbering add-in programs in the past, note that List Styles in Word 2007 can do everything you're likely to need from outline numbering, including the ability to save and share numbering schemes, and to use multiple numbering schemes in the same document. Learn how later in this chapter.

What's New for Single-Level Lists

In previous versions of Word, text and number position settings, which control first line and hanging indents in bulleted and numbered paragraphs, are set in the Bullets And Numbering dialog box. This often causes confusion because, if you change the indents on the ruler or through the paragraph style, they will be overridden by the Bullets And Numbering setting whenever you return to the Bullets And Numbering dialog box.

In Word 2007, the dialog boxes for bullets and numbering have been simplified. Yip-pee! On the Home tab, in the Paragraph group, click the Bullets icon or Numbering icon to view its gallery. Select a preset option or click the Define New... option to open a dialog box where you can customize the bullet or number format.

You see familiar options in the Define New Bullet and Define New Number Format dialog boxes shown here, including the option to select the bullet or number style, to set font attributes for the bullet or number (such as specifying a font color that applies just to the bullet or number), and to set the alignment of the bullet or number. That's all there is—and that's all you need, because any other formatting in your bulleted or numbered paragraph can be set through the paragraph style.

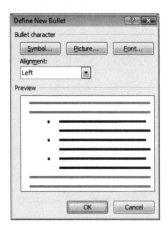 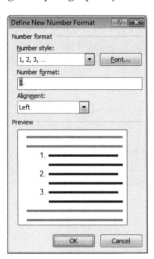

Note

The reference to alignment in any bullets or numbering dialog box refers to the alignment of the bullet or number itself, and does not relate to the paragraph alignment. For example, the numbering shown here is right-aligned.

8. Sample paragraph text.
9. Sample paragraph text.
10. Sample paragraph text.
11. Sample paragraph text.

That is, the numbers continue to align along their right edge, as the number of digits increases. For bullets, changing alignment in the Define New Bullet dialog box simply changes whether the bullet ends to the left, center, or right of the first line indent. For more on number alignment in list paragraphs, see the Troubleshooting tip titled "When I use center paragraph alignment, automatic numbering is not correctly aligned" later in this chapter.

The other significant change in single-level lists is that if you apply bullets or numbering to text formatted with the Normal paragraph style, the paragraph style for your numbered or bulleted paragraphs will be changed to List Paragraph style. Unfortunately, however, your bullet or number formatting doesn't automatically get updated in the style, so if you apply that style later in the document, no bullet or number.

This behavior is intentional. The purpose is that if you have several different lists that all need the same paragraph formatting other than the bullet or numbering, you can use one style for the rest of the formatting. However, for long or complex documents, or any document that will be edited by others, this is not the best practice. Whenever multiple formatting alternatives are used with the same style, you risk confusing users or making the document more complex to edit. Consider, for example, that a user trying to be conscientious will update the style to include the bullet or number formatting they're using, not realizing that it will change all paragraphs that use that style to be part of the active list.

For best practice and ease of editing in long, complex, or shared documents, attach each unique number or bullet format in your document to its own paragraph style.

> **Note**
>
> The setting Don't Add Space Between Paragraphs Of The Same Style is on by default in the built-in bullet and number styles, including when you use bullets or numbering in an Outlook 2007 e-mail message. To turn off this setting, find it in the Paragraph dialog box, which is available either through the Format menu in the New Style or Modify Style dialog box, or through the dialog launcher in the Paragraph group on the Home or Page Layout tabs (or the Format Text tab in Outlook).

Differentiating List Styles and Multilevel Lists

Multilevel lists, in earlier versions called Outline Numbered lists, have changed only by some minor reorganization of the dialog box (now called Define New Multilevel List), which includes the very nice addition to set stepping indents for all levels of the list at once, as you see here.

A multilevel list contains nine levels of numbering that work together to form an outline. Numbering updates automatically when you add or remove numbered paragraphs, or when you change the list level of existing paragraphs.

Each level of a multilevel list can (and usually should) be attached to its own paragraph style, which makes the outline easier to apply and the related paragraph formatting easier to edit.

Chapter 5

A list style is, essentially, packaging for a multilevel list. That is, it's a multilevel list that's given a name, so that it can be accessed and edited more easily. List styles can contain all of the same functionality as multilevel lists. The main difference is that a list style is named, so you can save it, share it, and modify it.

A multilevel list that is not part of a list style can't be modified. When you modify a multilevel list, you're actually creating a new list based on the existing list formatting.

Simply put, all list styles are multilevel lists, but not all multilevel lists are list styles. A list style enables you to save, share, and modify multilevel lists. There is no downside to using list styles instead of multilevel lists, and quite a bit to be gained, so the remainder of the list-related content in this chapter will focus on list styles.

TROUBLESHOOTING

Is it true that too many list templates cause document corruption?

As mentioned earlier in this chapter, you can't actually edit a multilevel list. Whenever you do, you really create a new list definition based on the active list. Each list is stored in your document as a List Template.

Just as with any document formatting, however, best practice in Word is to never add anything to the document that doesn't need to be there. A handful or two of list templates in one document is not likely to be a problem. But, consider that every time you make any edit whatsoever to an existing multilevel list, you actually add another list template to the document. So, a long document edited by many people over an extended period of time could end up with hundreds, if not thousands of list templates. When the number of list templates starts to get high, bad things can happen. That is, document behavior can become unstable.

When you use a list style, you give a name to the multilevel list that enables Word to identify your list, so the list template can be modified. This is the reason that you will find the Modify Multilevel List dialog box through the List Styles dialog box, but a Define New Multilevel List dialog box only available directly through the Multilevel List gallery (though both dialog boxes actually contain the same options).

Note that list templates can be easily accessed and managed through the Object Model [that is, through Microsoft Visual Basic for Applications (VBA)], but not from the Word user interface. To learn the basics of working in Word VBA, see Chapter 21, "VBA Primer."

Creating and Using List Styles

To create a new list style, you can access the New Style dialog box from the Multilevel List gallery or from the Styles pane. If you start from the Multilevel List gallery, be sure to choose the option Define New List Style and not the option to define a new multilevel list. If you start from the Styles pane, in the Create New Style From Formatting dialog box, you will first need to select List as the Style Type. Then, do the following.

> **Note**
>
> Notice that the name of this dialog box changes based on how you access it—either Define New List Style or Create New Style From Formatting—but the behavior and result are identical.

1. On the Format menu, select Numbering to open the Modify Multilevel List dialog box. Then, click More to view all options in this dialog box.

   The Modify Multilevel List dialog box is where you will customize all formatting for all numbers of your list. Though some of this can be done directly in the Define New List Style dialog box, setting all of the formatting in one location saves work and reduces the possibility of error.

2. Format each list level as shown in the following graphic.

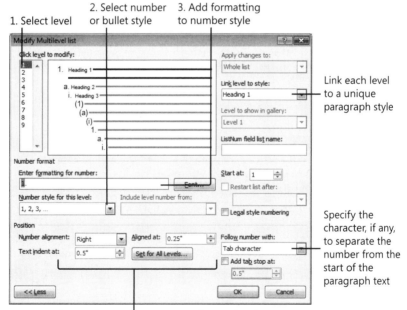

Set the number and text positions for one level at a time or for all levels in your outline at once

Notice in this graphic that, after you select a level in step 1, you can then select a number style and add any formatting (such as a period or close parenthesis) to the numbering for that level. You can, however, attach a style to the list level,

change the Follow Number With character, or change the Restart List After setting at any point while formatting a given level.

CAUTION !

Two common errors derail many multilevel lists.

- Do not set the Start At value for any level of your list, unless you have a specific requirement in your document to do so. When you set the Start At value, that number is no longer dynamic, so it will not change to accommodate changes in your list.

- Do not type numbering into the box labeled Enter Formatting For Number. When you select a number style from the list labeled Number Style For This Level, it is added to the Formatting box as a field, so it will update dynamically. Any text you type into the Enter Formatting For Number box is static (such as a period) and thus will always be the same for each new paragraph on that level.

3. When you are happy with the settings in the Preview pane within the Modify Multilevel List dialog box, click OK to return to the Style dialog box. Then, just name your style and click OK.

Once you have created a list style, it will appear in the Multilevel List gallery. List styles do not appear in the Styles pane, but the paragraph styles associated with them can appear in this pane. To start using a list style, you can click the gallery entry for the list style or apply any paragraph style attached to the list.

Note

You may already know that, for any multilevel list or list style, you can change the out-line level of the active paragraph using the Increase Indent and Decrease Indent buttons in the Paragraph group on the Home tab; TAB and SHIFT+TAB on your keyboard, or ALT+SHIFT+ the left or right arrow keys.

But, did you know that the key combinations ALT+SHIFT+ left or right arrow will switch between Heading 1–9 styles when your insertion point isn't in a bulleted or numbered list? In a tangential note, you can also use ALT+SHIFT+ the up and down arrow keys to move the entire active paragraph up or down in the document.

To modify a list style, right-click the list style in the Multilevel List gallery and then click Modify to open the Modify Style dialog box. You can also modify your list style through the Manage Styles dialog box discussed later in this chapter.

INSIDE OUT   Understanding number alignment and text indent

In the Modify Multilevel List dialog box, three settings under the heading Position, as shown here, affect the position of the active level's number or bullet relative to the paragraph text.

Alignment, as discussed earlier for single-level lists, refers to the alignment of the numbers or bullets themselves and does not affect paragraph alignment. The Aligned At setting corresponds to the paragraph's first line indent. The Text Indent At setting refers to the paragraph's hanging indent (that is, the left indent for all lines of the paragraph except the first).

Don't be concerned if you look at the definition for an associated paragraph style for a level in a list—or in the Paragraph dialog box—and see settings instead for left indent plus either hanging indent (most common) or first line indent. This is because first line and hanging indents are, technically, mutually exclusive. When you set both a first line and a hanging indent through the Multilevel list dialog box, whichever of those indents is smaller is actually seen by Word as the left indent, because it is the left-most edge of the paragraph.

TROUBLESHOOTING

My multilevel lists are not behaving as they should

To keep your lists playing nicely, keep one rule in mind: Any formatting that can be done in the Define New Multilevel List (or Modify Multilevel List) dialog box, should always be done there. Unlike the single-level lists discussed earlier, the multilevel list dialog boxes contain many formatting options that affect the paragraph format.

For example, don't change the indents in a paragraph that's part of a multilevel list or list style by changing them on the ruler or through the Paragraph dialog box. If you do, they're likely to revert at some point to the formatting saved with the numbering.

Notice that the Multilevel list dialog box is no longer available through the New Style or Modify Style dialog boxes for paragraph styles. This is a terrific change, because it reduces the urge to try to control the list with the paragraph style, which just won't work.

Attach paragraph styles to list levels, set indents, and apply any other numbering-related formatting through the Multilevel list dialog boxes only, and your outlines will consistently behave better than you ever imagined.

TROUBLESHOOTING

When I use center paragraph alignment, automatic numbering is not correctly aligned

When the paragraph style attached to a list level uses center paragraph alignment, such as when you want the number to appear on its own line above the paragraph text, as shown here, you need to check four settings to ensure that your numbering is correctly centered.

> **Article I.**
> **Sample paragraph text**

In the Modify Multilevel List dialog box:

- Set Number Alignment to Left
- Set Aligned At to 0
- Set Text Indent At to 0
- Set Follow Number With to Nothing

Left number alignment actually means no alignment, because the number alignment is then left to match the paragraph alignment. The Aligned At and Text Indent At settings need to be zero, because you don't want to indent the number when the paragraph is already centered. Following the number with nothing allows you to type one or two manual line breaks (SHIFT+ENTER) after the number, if needed, to perfectly center the number over the paragraph text.

Sharing Lists Between Documents and Templates

To copy a list style to another document or template, you must do so through the Organizer, as follows.

1. In the Styles pane, click Manage Styles.

2. At the bottom of the Manage Styles dialog box, click Import\Export to open the Organizer.

   On the Styles tab of the Organizer, style contents of your active document appear on the left and those of Normal.dotm appear on the right.

3. Click Close beneath Normal.dotm and then click the Open button that appears in its place.

4. Browse to and select the document or template to which you want to copy your list style.

    To select a document rather than a template, in the list that appears beside the File Name box, change the file type being accessed.

5. On the left side of the document where your active document's styles appear, select the list style and *all* associated paragraph styles. To select these all at once, hold the CTRL key while selecting.

6. Click the Copy button to copy the styles to the destination document or template.

7. Close the Organizer. When you do, you will be prompted to save the document or template to which you copied your list style.

Notice in the Organizer that you can select any document or template for both the left and right sides of the dialog box. So, you can actually copy the styles without having either document open, or when the destination document is open instead of the source document.

Once you have copied a list style, it will appear in the Multilevel List gallery whenever the destination document or template is open. As long as you copy all associated paragraph styles along with the list style, the relationship between the list style and its paragraph styles, as well as all list style formatting, will remain intact.

Working with Table Styles

In Word 2007, table styles are visible only when your insertion point is in a table. They do not appear in the Styles pane.

When a table is active, you will find available table styles on the Table Tools Design tab, in the Table Styles group, as you see here.

In this gallery, you'll find 99 table styles, including the default style, Table Grid, as well as the 98 new table styles mentioned earlier. The new table styles shown in the gallery

Chapter 5

are part of Quick Style formatting options that were introduced in Chapter 1. These are all Theme-ready styles that will adjust to changes in the applied Theme.

The remaining styles that complete the set of 143 available table styles are legacy styles carried over from the previous version of Word. These styles remain hidden until they are used. If you apply one of these remaining styles by typing the style name in the Apply Styles pane, that style will then become visible for the active document in the Table Styles gallery.

Creating Table Styles

To create a new table style, either click the New Style button at the bottom of the Styles pane, or click New Table Style at the bottom of the Table Styles gallery. If you start from the Styles pane, when the Create New Style From Formatting dialog box opens, you will first need to select Table as the Style Type.

When you add formatting to your style, notice the list labeled Apply Formatting To. Be sure to change this setting as needed to specify formatting for the entire table, a heading row, first column, or other table element.

TROUBLESHOOTING

Table style formatting doesn't work correctly

Two common problems when working with table styles are that formatting you apply doesn't seem to "take" when you create the style, and that table styles conflict with paragraph styles when applied to tables. The following best practices address these issues.

- When you create a table style, unique settings for different parts of the table can be lost when set at the same time. So, when a table style requires unique formatting for certain parts of the table, it's a good idea to confirm the formatting as you go. For example, apply the formatting you want to include in the entire table and then click OK to create the style. If the formatting looks correct on your active table, right-click the style in the Table Styles gallery and then click Modify Table Style. In the Modify Style dialog box, select the part of the table that needs unique formatting from the Apply Formatting To list and then specify the formatting you need. Click OK again to check that this formatting has been applied correctly. Repeat this step for each part of the table that requires unique formatting.

- When you include font or paragraph formatting in a table style, that formatting can conflict with paragraph styles you apply to content in your tables, causing inconsistent results. To avoid this, use table styles for table structure formatting only (such as cell borders and shading, or cell margins) and use paragraphs styles for the formatting of text inside your tables.

Setting a Default Table Style

By default, new tables are formatted with Table Grid style, which is the Table Normal base style introduced earlier, plus a half-point width grid of borders on all cells. Depending on the way you use tables, however, that grid might not be appropriate for most tables.

For example, I use tables frequently for laying out pages, as discussed in the next chapter. When a table is used for layout, it's not usually appropriate for the grid to appear. For this reason, I set Table Normal to be the default for all new tables I create.

A default table style can be set by document or by template, so that if you have a particular table style designed for the tables in your document, you can set that style as the default to save time and help ensure consistent formatting.

To set a table style as the default, do the following.

1. Right-click the style where it appears in the Table Styles gallery and then click Set As Default.

2. In the Default Table Style dialog box that opens, specify whether to make the selected style the default for the active document only or for all new documents based on the active template and then click OK.

Managing Styles

When you are responsible for a document's formatting or when you are creating documents and templates for yourself and others to use, managing styles is a big part of the job. In Word 2007, two new features have been added that make the job easier and give you a great deal more control.

The Wonderful New World of the Manage Styles Dialog Box

The Manage Styles dialog box is one of the nicest new features available for styles in Word. This dialog box combines the Style dialog box functionality of earlier versions (an access point to create, modify, or delete styles, as well as to access the Organizer) with new capabilities including the ability to prioritize, restrict, and show or hide styles, as well as to set font and paragraph defaults.

Chapter 5

- The Edit tab of the Manage Styles dialog box offers the equivalent of the Style dialog box in the previous version of Word.

- On the Recommend tab of this dialog box, you can prioritize the order in which styles appear (referred to as the Recommended order) and specify whether a style is visible, hidden, or hidden until used.

  - To prioritize styles, you can click the Move Up, Move Down, or Make Last buttons, or click Assign Value to prioritize the style by assigning it a numeric value. This last option is a timesaver because, as you can see by the list of styles assigned the value of 1 in the screen shot shown here, styles with the same numeric value are automatically alphabetized.

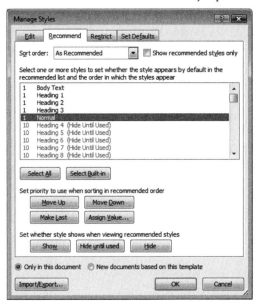

  - To set the document to show only recommended styles, or to set styles to appear in recommended order in the Styles pane, at the bottom of the Styles pane, click Options.

  - Though the option to Show, Hide, or Hide Until Used can be handy, be careful with these when considering the usability of your document. For example, Hide Until Used is an excellent setting for built-in styles that apply only to certain parts of the document, such as Header or Footer, because they will remain out of the user's way until needed. However, don't use this setting for the styles you create or customize for use in the body of your document. After all, user can't use a style unless they know it exists.

> **Note**
>
> To apply a hidden style, type the style name in the Apply Styles pane and then press ENTER.

- On the Restrict tab, you can permit or restrict the use of specified styles, as well as block styles from changing formatting if another Theme or Quick Style Set is applied in the document. Note that when you set a style to be restricted, a lock icon appears next to the style name on this tab and Locked will appear as an attribute in the style description where it appears on the Edit tab.

  Setting restrictions on this tab will prompt you to enable document protection when you close the Manage Styles dialog box. Note also that locked styles are automatically hidden, regardless of their Show or Hide setting on the Recommend tab.

- On the Set Defaults tab, you can set defaults for font, font color, and font size, as well as paragraph indents and spacing. Any styles based on document defaults, such as Normal style, will take on these settings.

Notice that for all tabs in the Manage Styles dialog box, you can apply your settings to the active document or to all new documents based on the active template.

Introducing The Style Inspector

 At the bottom of the Styles pane, click the Style Inspector icon to open the new Style Inspector dialog box, shown here.

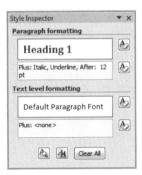

The Style Inspector is a simple but invaluable pane that enables you to distinguish styled from direct formatting in selected text. This tool is great for use when troubleshooting document formatting because you can both distinguish what formatting belongs to the style and quickly clear either direct or styled formatting at both the font and paragraph levels.

Chapter 5

Microsoft Word tables make me happy. Tables are the great document organizer, the complex document simplifier, and the layout expert.

If this is not your experience, or even if you suspect that I need professional help, stick around. There is a secret to making friends with Microsoft Word tables and, in this chapter, I'm going to show you how to put that secret to work for any type of table you need.

So, what's the secret? It's quite simple—literally. If you want tables to simplify your documents, do the same for your tables. Keeping table structure clean and simple, and understanding how to format content effectively inside tables, is all you need to know to soothe this often misunderstood beast. You see, there's nothing at all savage about Microsoft Word tables.

Chapter Assumptions

As advanced users, I'm assuming that you're familiar with what a table is, and that you understand basic structure such as rows, columns, and cells. I'm also assuming that you've created tables before, have seen the Table Properties dialog box, and that terminology such as *AutoFit* or *cell margins* is at least somewhat familiar to you, even if you've not used these features in the past.

This chapter will provide background on the core concepts of how tables work and what can make them work for you. We'll also look at creating tables for uses ranging from basic text tables, to formatting financials, to complex document layout.

In the introduction to this book you can find a list of resources for those who want more basic information, in the section titled "Who Will Benefit Most from This Book."

What's New for Tables in Word 2007

The main difference in tables for Microsoft Office Word 2007 is simply how to access the features you need for working with tables. The underlying functionality and range of table capabilities is largely unchanged, with a couple of exceptions, as follows.

- New Quick Styles capabilities are available for formatting tables. Those were introduced in Chapter 5, "Styles," and are also addressed later in this chapter.

- The Quick Tables gallery, where you can save your own tables for later use, is discussed in Chapter 9, "Quick Parts."

When you insert a table into an Office Word 2007 document, or place your insertion point in any existing table, you get two contextual tabs that include most of the tools you need for working with tables.

On the Table Tools Design tab, shown here, you get new Table Style Options for adding features such as banded columns or a total row, as well as the new Table Styles gallery, introduced in Chapter 5.

You also see the Draw Borders group, which provides Draw Table options that are generally as impractical and inefficient as they ever were. However, Draw Table can be useful for table editing, so look for tips on that later in this chapter.

In the Draw Borders group, however, you do have some handy tools. Line Style, Line Weight, and Pen Color (which actually just refers to line color) all work with the Borders option in the Table Styles group as well, to save you a trip to the Borders And Shading dialog box.

The Table Tools Layout tab, as you see it in the next image, is where the bulk of table tools reside. Common table structure formatting options are nicely exposed here, with the notable exception that a few features are oddly placed, as follows.

- AutoFit is located in the Cell Size group, but changing the AutoFit setting affects the entire table as always. See more on AutoFit in the section titled "Using Tables to Create Page Layout" later in this chapter.

- The Cell Margins option in the Alignment group opens the Table Options dialog box, where you can set default cell margins for the table. It's important to note because this setting affects the entire table whereas the other options in the group are selection-specific.

- If you're looking for a couple of features you'd expect to find in the Rows & Columns group, just look left or right on the same tab. Options to select table, column, row, or cell are in the Tables group on that tab, and the option to repeat heading rows is in the Data group.

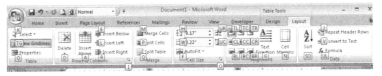

If, like me, you've memorized keyboard accelerators for working with tables because few table tasks have keyboard shortcuts, you might be a bit frustrated at first with the new organization. But, table structure formatting is actually more accessible in Word 2007 for keyboard users as well. If you're looking for easier keyboard access, try one of these options.

- ALT+JL accesses the Table Tools Layout tab when your insertion point is in a table. From there, you're just a keystroke away from most table structure formatting options—including access to the Table Properties dialog box. As introduced in Chapter 1, "Welcome to the 2007 Microsoft Office System," these new accelerator keys, called KeyTips, provide easy keyboard access to any feature on the Ribbon. The following image shows the KeyTips exposed for the Table Tools Layout tab after pressing ALT+CL.

- As always, SHIFT+F10 opens the shortcut menus you otherwise get when you right-click. The shortcut menu options for tables in Word 2007 are largely unchanged, with access to features including Table Properties, Borders And Shading, Cell Alignment, AutoFit options, and several settings that vary based on your active selection.

The Great Document Organizer

I often compare tables to a closet organizer or that tray in your silverware drawer. Whatever your specific reason for using a table, a table is a container, designed to help you fit more on the page while keeping that content organized and easy to manage. Similar to a closet or drawer organizer, tables provide a separate compartment (a cell) for each piece of content.

If you think of a table relative to the three levels of formatting—those levels are explained in Chapter 4, "Building Easy-to-Manage, Robust Documents"—tables are objects in which you can place content and apply almost any of the same font or paragraph formatting that you can apply in the body of a document.

So, the cells of a table are very much like a collection of related, miniature pages—only they're simpler, because they don't require section breaks to arrange the pages. You can

Chapter 6

add text, graphics, and even other tables inside table cells, just as you can in the body of the document.

TROUBLESHOOTING

How are tables related to section breaks, paragraph marks, and paragraph styles?

There are many common misconceptions about creating and formatting tables. Three of the most common, all of which can cause unnecessary document complications, are addressed in the list that follows.

- Tables never require section breaks. A table is an object, it is not a type of formatting. Section breaks are only required to change page layout *formatting* for part of a document. One of the benefits of using a table as a page layout tool is that it obviates the need for using section breaks to effect a complex page layout (such as when part of the page requires content in multiple columns).

- There is no need for, and no benefit gained from, placing empty paragraph marks around tables. A table sits in a paragraph mark, just like any other type of inline document content (such as text, or a graphic formatted with the In Line With Text graphic layout), and it can be treated exactly the same. Paragraph marks that do not apply to any content are never a good idea; they simply add extra sets of formatting to the document, which can get in your way and complicate editing. Though a paragraph mark is required to separate two consecutive tables, that paragraph doesn't need to be empty.

- Any paragraph style that can be applied in the body of your document can be applied inside a table, including heading styles and those that contain bullets or numbering. Paragraph styles have no ill effect on tables and are the best way to format most table content. The only exceptions to this statement are if the style contains a frame (and you should avoid frames at all costs anyway, as explained in Chapter 7, "Managing Graphics") or if the style contains line and page break options, such as Keep Text Together or Page Break Before formatting.

  Line and page break options are fine to use in tables, as long as they are used only where needed and not in all cells of the table.

Key Practices for Creating Tables That Work

The following best practices apply to creating Word tables for any purpose.

- To create a table, drag your pointer across and down the table grid available on the Insert tab in the Tables group. You might notice that the grid no longer expands to larger than ten columns by eight rows. So, if you need a larger table, click Insert Table below the grid for the dialog box where you can enter the number of columns and rows you need. Of course, you can always add columns and rows later, if required.

Do not use Draw Table to create a table. Doing so will always take longer and never be as precise as the other methods discussed here. Even if what you need is a creative layout, Draw Table isn't the way to get there. Word is not a drawing program and tables are not art. If you want tables to work effectively, approach them methodically and with order.

- Maintain the table grid structure as much as possible, particularly when using tables for page layout.

  For example, using merged headings—such as for a top-level heading over several columns in a financial table—is the simplest solution for that formatting. (Get help for managing merged heading cells in the section titled "Formatting Financial Tables" later in this chapter.) But, merging and splitting cells to contort the table into the layout you want will cause you more work in the long run than just about any other layout method. Nested tables are a much simpler solution to complex page layouts than merging and splitting the cells of a single table. Learn more about this in the section titled "Using Tables to Create Page Layout" later in this chapter.

- Avoid using the Text Wrap Around setting for tables. This setting places the table in an invisible frame, which can be cumbersome to manage. Nesting tables, discussed later in this chapter, will enable you to easily create just about any layout you need without having to position and manage floating objects. Learn more about possible issues with the Text Wrap Around setting in the section of this chapter titled "Using Nested Tables vs. Text Wrap Around Tables."

Choosing Between Paragraph Formatting and Table Formatting

For formatting purposes, a table has two distinct parts: the table structure—which is the actual table object—and the table content, such as the text and graphics you place in the table.

For formatting the table structure, you have settings such as column width, row height, cell margins, and AutoFit options. For formatting the table content, you have font and paragraph formatting. Often, however, the lines between the two get blurred, because formatting table content can also change the appearance of the table structure.

Use the following best practice guidelines to keep your table formatting as simple and effective as possible.

Paragraph Spacing vs. Row Height

When you need vertical space in a table row, the reason is most often to make your table easier to read and make the layout more attractive, just as with setting space between paragraphs. When this is your reason for adding vertical space in table rows, setting spacing before or after the paragraph is a simpler and more flexible solution than setting row height.

- Paragraph spacing is always relative to paragraph content, so spacing between the paragraph content and the top and bottom edges of the cell remains constant even when you add or remove content. In the example shown here, paragraph spacing of six points both before and after the paragraph is used. No row height is set. Notice how the spacing remains constant when a new line of text is added.

| This·is·a·sample·line·of·text·inside·a·table·cell.¤ | ¤ |

| This·is·a·sample·line·of·text·inside·a·table·cell.·The·same·table·cell·with·a·second·line·of·text·added.¤ | ¤ |

- In contrast, when you set row height, that height is a minimum (unless you specify that the height is to remain exact regardless of content). So, row height will expand as you add content, but it won't continue to maintain consistent space between the content and the edges of the cell, as you see in the example shown here. Notice what happens in the image on the right, when a second line of text is added.

| This·is·a·sample·line·of·text·inside·a·table·cell.¤ | ¤ |

| This·is·a·sample·line·of·text·inside·a·table·cell.·The·same·table·cell·with·a·second·line·of·text·added.¤ | ¤ |

Setting an exact row height is a further complication, because content that exceeds the height of the row is cut off, as shown in the parallel images below.

| This·is·a·sample·line·of·text·inside·a·table·cell.¤ | ¤ |

| This·is·a·sample·line·of·text·inside·a·table·cell.·The·same·table·cell·with·a·second·line·of·text·added.¤ | ¤ |

The time to set row height is when using the table for page layout, in situations where you want to apportion a certain amount of the page for specific content. Learn more about how and when to do this in the section titled "Using Tables to Create Page Layout" later in this chapter.

Paragraph Spacing vs. Cell Margins

When you want constant space between cell content and the top and bottom edges of the cell, adding space before and after the paragraph is an easy solution, as discussed earlier. Though you can add top and bottom cell margins to accomplish this, it's less flexible, so it ends up being more work for you and other editors of the document.

Space before and after the paragraph can be included in paragraph styles for easy editing. Additionally, if you change the type of content in the cell, a different paragraph style can provide different spacing as needed without any editing of the table structure. Instead, if you set top and bottom cell margins, you need to return to the Table Options or Cell Options dialog box whenever a change needs to be made.

> **Note**
>
> In Word 2007, you can still access spacing before and after the paragraph through the Paragraph dialog box, which is now accessible from the dialog launcher on the Home tab, in the Paragraph group. You can also set Spacing Before And After the paragraph directly from the Ribbon, on the Page Layout tab, in the Paragraph group.

However, top and bottom cell margins are a good thing to keep in mind for occasions when you might need consistent space between content and cell boundaries regardless of what content ends up in the cell. As mentioned earlier, default cell margins for the entire table are available on the Table Tools Layout tab, in the Alignment group. The Cell Margins button opens the Table Options dialog box. To set cell margins for selected cells only, in the Table Properties dialog box, click Cell and then click Options.

INSIDE OUT   Spacing between cells and the HTML revolution that never was

Tables in Word changed dramatically for the better back in Microsoft Office 2000, with the introduction of options such as cell margins and support for nested tables. That was also the Microsoft Office version when the default paste method for text and tables changed to HTML.

As you probably know, HTML is the language in which Web pages are written. Back in the olden-days of the late 20th century, when the Web was the big, new thing, the folks who design Microsoft Office saw a need to support HTML document creation. Many of the new table features that were introduced in Word 2000 were intended to support HTML tables.

The table setting to allow spacing between cells is known in HTML as cell padding. You'll find this setting in the Table Options dialog box shown here, but it's more important to note for troubleshooting purposes than for intentional use.

There's nothing wrong with using this feature to create space between cell content and cell boundaries, other than the fact that it's not as intuitive to most users as paragraph spacing or cell margins, because it's simply not as well known. So, if document trouble-shooting is part of what you do, you're more likely to run into this setting when a user doesn't know what's going on in the table.

Tables with spacing between cells (cell padding) enabled used to look like they had a thick border, but the border didn't print. Now, with the change to dashed table gridlines, it's easier to tell when spacing between cells is enabled because that thick border will be dashed, as you see in the following image.

Depending upon the amount of spacing between cells, the border may simply appear to be thick or it may look like a double dashed line. (Note that the color of gridlines changes depending upon your selected Microsoft Office color scheme. When you use the default (blue) color scheme, gridlines are blue.)

Because HTML is still the default paste type for text and tables pasted into Word documents, tables pasted from the Web will retain this formatting. To turn off spacing between cells, on the Table Tools Layout tab, in the Alignment group, click Cell Margins to open the Table Options dialog box. Turn off Allow Spacing Between Cells and click OK.

The Relationship Between Paragraph Spacing and Vertical Cell Alignment

When you apply spacing before or after the paragraph for content inside tables, that spacing can affect the appearance of row height, discussed previously, as well as vertical cell alignment. For example, applying an equal amount of spacing both before and after the paragraph will center the text vertically in the cell and add height to the row, without setting row height or changing cell alignment.

Take a look at the following images. The image on the left uses spacing of 10 points before and after the paragraph. The image on the right looks exactly the same with row height set to at least 0.5 inches and vertical cell alignment set to center.

However, as discussed earlier, if more content is added to the cell that uses paragraph spacing to set height and alignment, the space between the content and cell boundaries is maintained, while the cell with both row height and cell alignment set will close up around the content as more content is added. Clearly, the paragraph formatting option is less work and produces better results.

However, when using paragraph spacing, also consider its effect on vertical cell alignment. For example, if you bottom-align cells, but the content sits higher than the bottom of the cell, it's likely that space after the paragraph was applied to the cell content.

INSIDE OUT   ### Cell alignment vs. paragraph alignment

Vertical cell alignment is table structure formatting. However, horizontal cell alignment is actually paragraph alignment.

When you set cell alignment using the options shown in the following image (available on either the Table Tools Layout tab or the right-click shortcut menu) you set both vertical and horizontal alignment at once.

So, if you're using paragraph styles to format the content in your table and you change the horizontal alignment using the options shown in the preceding image, you actually apply direct formatting on top of your paragraph style. While it will look the same, it may complicate future changes to the table formatting since the alignment will no longer be part of the paragraph style.

Instead, to set vertical cell alignment without affecting paragraph alignment, do so through the Table Properties dialog box. To do this, first select the cells to format and then, on the Table Tools Layout tab, in the Tables group, click Properties. Find vertical cell alignment options on the Cell tab of the Table Properties dialog box. Note that you can also access the Table Properties dialog box from the ruler. To do this, just double-click any column margin icon on the ruler (such as the one you see beside this paragraph).

Paragraph Indents vs. Cell Margins

Paragraph indents control the left and right edges of a paragraph, regardless of where that paragraph is located in your document. So, paragraph indents can be applied as easily to text in table cells as they can to text in the document body.

Paragraph indents relate to left and right cell margins just as they relate to left and right page margins. You can add a paragraph indent to move text further away from the cell margin, or add a negative paragraph indent to move text beyond a cell margin.

Just as with page margins and paragraph indents, when you need to change indents for just a few cells, setting paragraph indents is usually less work and easier to manage than customizing cell margins for just some cells in your table.

The primary reason that this is the easier solution is that paragraph indents can be included in paragraph styles, so they're easy to change for all applicable cells whenever needed. If this strikes you as a minor point, consider that you might have the same style applied to some of the cells in several tables throughout the document, so paragraph styles can be a much faster editing solution.

Chapter 6

Paragraph Borders vs. Cell Borders

Cell borders are printable lines that show the cell boundary. Paragraph borders are lines that border a paragraph of text. For example, the headings in the image on the left use cell borders and the headings in the image on the right use paragraph borders.

Q1	Q2	Q3	Q4
123.1	134.2	121.0	124.6
132.5	120.6	118.9	129.4

Q1	Q2	Q3	Q4
123.1	134.2	121.0	124.6
132.5	120.6	118.9	129.4

When applied to content in table cells, paragraph borders do the exact same thing they do in the body of the document. That is, they extend from the left indent to the right indent of the paragraph. When both left and right indents are zero, the border is actually extending from the left margin to the right margin. In the document body, this refers to page margins; in a table cell, it refers to cell margins.

Because left and right cell margins in Word are 0.08 inches (1.9 millimeters) by default, a paragraph border applied in a table cell automatically creates space between columns as you see in the earlier image showing paragraph borders on table headings. If cell margins are removed, space between those paragraph borders will be removed as well.

The best practice in this case is simply to understand the differences between cell borders and paragraph borders, so that you can use the option that best suits the formatting you need.

INSIDE OUT   Using paragraph borders to create space between columns

When I look at complex tables in documents, I commonly see tables that have small, blank columns between every column of data. This is frustrating, because it can make it more difficult to format data. For example, you can't set a decimal tab on the ruler to create decimal paragraph alignment when noncontiguous columns are selected.

Instead of creating extra work for yourself by adding extra columns to your table to make space between columns of data, use paragraph borders on the headings (and subtotal or total cells, if applicable) to effect the appearance of space between columns. In the following image, for example, the table has just three columns. Left and right paragraph indents applied to the bordered paragraphs create the appearance of space between the columns.

	2006	2007E
North America	$44.2	$56.7
Asia Pacific	78.5	56.2
Europe	34.6	42.7
Latin America	12.6	16.8

To accomplish the formatting shown here, simply apply bottom paragraph borders to the text in the heading cells and then add equal left and right paragraph indents to the same cells.

CAUTION !

In table cells, only cell borders can be applied from the border button options on either the Table Tools Design tab or the Home tab. Paragraph borders in table cells must be set through the Borders And Shading dialog box, which can be accessed from the shortcut menu when you right-click in a table, or from the bottom of any Borders pop-up menu on the Ribbon, such as you see here.

In the Borders And Shading dialog box, pay careful attention to the Apply To options. Depending on your selection in a table, the Apply To default will be either Table or Cell. To apply a paragraph border, change the Apply To setting to Paragraph. Note also that you can only apply borders and shading to one Apply To setting any time the Borders And Shading dialog box is opened.

Paragraph Styles vs. Table Styles

Use table styles to format table structure only, unless you can include *all* font and paragraph formatting you'll need in the table style. When you include font and paragraph formatting in your table style, that formatting can conflict with the paragraph styles you apply to table content, causing inconsistent results. (For more on table styles, see Chapter 5.) Notice that many built-in table styles include some font formatting and take that into consideration when using them.

Because most tables require some formatting customization or at least the flexibility to customize, the best practice is to use table styles for table structure formatting only and paragraph styles to format table content.

Chapter 6

Which Paragraph Formatting Option Is Best?

For questions on the best paragraph formatting options to use in tables, such as whether to use indents or tabs, follow the same best practices as for text in the document body. That is, the simplest solution is always best.

For example, indents are always a simpler solution than tabs where both will work, because indents are stored in the paragraph mark and require no additional characters. So, an indent can be entirely contained in a paragraph style for easy application and editing. Don't ever place a tab character in a table cell if an indent (or paragraph alignment) can do what you need. More specifically, consider the following.

- When decimal alignment is correctly created, there is no need to type tab characters before the number.

- Left, first-line, or hanging indents can accomplish virtually any indents required for table row headings.

- One of the few instances when tabs are the best solution for table content formatting is when you need to align the currency symbols of decimally-aligned numbers in a table column.

Learn more about the examples addressed in the preceding list in the section titled "Formatting Financial Tables," later in this chapter.

Using Table Properties to Simplify Table Setup

Although many settings from the Table Properties dialog box are now available directly on the Table Tools Layout tab, a few of the most useful settings can still only be accessed through the dialog box.

Setting Column and Table Widths as a Percentage of the Whole

Instead of calculating the precise column and table width measurements you need, you can set column width to be a percentage of the table width or table width to be a percentage of the width of the active window. Setting column and table widths as a percentage of the whole is also handy to keep the table size relative to the page width—so that table size automatically adjusts if page margins or orientation change, and column widths remain relative to their original settings.

> **Note**
>
> *Active window* refers to the distance between the left and right margins where content resides. This is most commonly the left and right page margins. However, if content is inside a table cell (including one table nested inside another), the active window is the distance between the left and right cell margins. When content is in a text column, the active window is the distance between the left and right column margins.

For example, if you're creating a pleading caption to fall at the top of a legal document, you need left and right columns of equal width and a small center column to hold the dividing characters (the close parentheses in this case), as shown here.

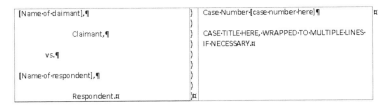

Not only does it take longer to calculate what the specific width of each of those columns needs to be, but your table won't adjust if page margins or paper size changes.

Try the preceding example for yourself. To do so, create a single-row, three-column table. Place your insertion point in the first column and then do the following.

1. Right-click and then select Table Properties from the shortcut menu. In the Table Properties dialog box, select the Column tab.

2. Change the Measure In setting to Percent.

3. Set the Preferred Width for the first column to 49%. Then, click Next Column.

4. Set the middle column to 2% and click Next Column again.

5. Set the right column to 49% and click Next Column again.

   Note that when you click Next Column after setting the last column, you see the changes applied to the entire table.

6. Click the Table tab of the Table Properties dialog box.

7. Set the Measure In setting on this tab to Percent as well.

8. Set the Preferred Width for the table to 100%. Then, click OK.

If you skip the last step and don't set the preferred width of the table, an empty table might shrink to minimal width (that is, AutoFit To Contents) when you click OK.

 If you work in legal and need to create pleading captions, see the document named Pleading Caption.docx on the CD for a completed example of the caption started in the preceding steps.

Though the example used is a very simple table type, it's easy to see how using percent width instead of calculating specific measurements can make table setup both easier and more flexible for any table that requires column and table widths to be set.

Indenting Tables

The most precise way to indent the table from the left margin is to use the Table Properties dialog box. Though you can drag the left edge of the left column to indent the table,

Chapter 6

that can cause you to need to fix the widths of many columns. Instead, in the Table Properties dialog box, on the Table tab, you can set a precise Indent From Left with no trial, error, or reformatting.

Keep in mind that you can add a negative indent here, just as you can with paragraph indents, for when you need the table to exceed the left margin of the page. This can be particularly handy, for example, when you need a graphic to sit outside of the page margin and don't want to mess with the complicated positioning required for floating graphics. Learn more about using tables to help simplify graphic layout both in the section of this chapter titled "Using Tables to Create Page Layout" and in Chapter 7.

> **Note**
>
> There is a benefit to setting Indent From Left through the Table Properties dialog box, as shown in this section. But, there is a faster way to set the horizontal alignment of the table than using this dialog box. When the entire table is selected, paragraph alignment works as table alignment instead. For example, to center a table on the page, first select the entire table and then press CTRL+E or, on the Home tab, in the Paragraph group, click the Center icon.
>
> Note that there are several ways to select the entire table, including using the Select options on the Table Tools Layout tab or clicking the Table Move Handle that appears at the top-left corner of a table when you position your pointer over the table. When an entire table is selected, the end-of-row markers are included in the selection. If end-of-row markers are not selected, the entire table is not selected and this shortcut won't work.

Setting Cell Options

In the Table Options dialog box, discussed earlier, you can change cell margins for the entire table and adjust the setting to allow spacing (padding) between cells. To set unique margins for just some cells in the table, use the Cell Options dialog box instead. The Cell Options dialog box also contains the option to Wrap Text in table cells, which is on by default for tables created in Word. However, Wrap Text can be an important setting when formatting tables pasted from other sources, particularly from Microsoft Office Excel 2007, as discussed later in this chapter.

To access the Cell Options dialog box, in the Table Properties dialog box, on the Cell tab, click Options. Note that all settings in the Cell Options dialog box apply only to selected cells.

What You Need to Know About AutoFit

As mentioned earlier, AutoFit, despite its placement in the Cell Size group on the Table Tools Layout tab, affects the entire active table regardless of your selection. AutoFit is also an easy and important tool for managing table layout. The table that follows explains key behaviors of each AutoFit option.

Setting	When to Use It
AutoFit To Window	This setting causes the table to always fit 100 percent of the width of the active window in which the table resides. When this setting is active, if you insert content into cells that exceeds the width of the cell, the column width will expand to accommodate the content, but the table will not exceed the width of the active window unless the table contains too much content to possibly fit the active window.
AutoFit To Contents	This setting shrinks column widths to fit their content. Though this is the least useful of the AutoFit settings because it will cause columns in your table to have differing widths and therefore look less precise, AutoFit To Contents can be a good troubleshooting tool for tables that exceed the width of the page. On occasions when a table has so much content that applying AutoFit To Window can't condense the table to fit in the active window, AutoFit To Contents can often do the trick. When you apply this setting in such instances, text might be wrapped oddly to make the content fit. However, it's a nice tool to help you quickly see all contents of an oversized table, when you need to determine the best way to fix table formatting.
Fixed Column Width	This setting will keep column widths from automatically adjusting to accommodate their contents. It also turns off the ability of the table to automatically adjust to changes in margins or page orientation. Fixed Column Width is the best AutoFit setting to use when using tables to create page layout (as discussed in the next section of this chapter) because it keeps the layout as you set it, regardless of content added to cells.

TROUBLESHOOTING

I change margins or page orientation, but the table width won't change to match

By default, new tables created in Word for the past several versions have been set to Automatically Resize To Fit Contents. This setting is found in the Table Options dialog box. When the Fixed Column Width AutoFit setting is applied, Automatically Resize To Fit Contents toggles off; when either of the other two AutoFit settings are applied, Automatically Resize To Fit Contents toggles on. However, Automatically Resize To Fit Contents is not the same as any AutoFit setting.

When a table is first created in Word, if you change margins or page orientation, the table width won't change to match. You must apply the AutoFit setting AutoFit To Window for tables to automatically adjust to margin and orientation changes.

This setting can be particularly handy for tables in headers and footers that need to adjust automatically to page layout changes for page numbering or other header and footer content to be properly centered or right-aligned. The ability to use AutoFit for this purpose, in fact, is one reason tables are a much better option for centering or right-aligning header or footer content than the old-fashioned tab settings that are still resident in default header and footer paragraph styles. (If you're wondering where the new Insert Alignment Tab feature fits into this question, see Chapter 8, "Sections.")

Chapter 6

Using Tables to Create Page Layout

Tables are usually the simplest solution to creating a complex page layout, because they allow you to place text, graphics, and even other tables side-by-side without the need for complex positioning settings or section breaks. For example, the layout for the pitch book page shown here is accomplished with a simple table of five rows by three columns, as you can see with table gridlines visible in the second image.

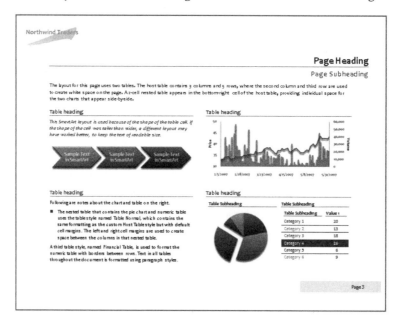

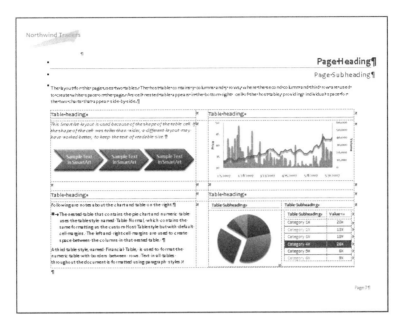

Note that the small chart and table that appear side-by-side in the bottom right corner of the page are in nested tables. Learn about using nested tables later in this section.

The page shown above is page three of the document Fearless.docx, introduced in Chapter 4. To open this document and examine it for yourself, find it in the sample files that you can install from the Welcome tab of this book's CD.

Creating an Effective Host Table

Tables used to create page layout are often called host tables. To create an effective host table, use the following best practices.

- As introduced earlier in this chapter, maintain the table grid structure. This is particularly important for tables used to create a complex page layout. If your layout seems to require splitting or merging cells, consider inserting a nested table instead to keep the layout clean and simple to edit. For example, notice on the preceding sample page that the two small objects in the bottom-right of the page are in nested tables. That table was inserted to allow for the flexibility needed in the layout without causing unnecessary complications in the host table.

  If, instead, the bottom-right cell of the table had been split to allow separate cells for each object, then an edit as simple as moving those items to another part of the page would have become far more cumbersome. Learn how to create and use nested tables effectively later in this section.

- Provide a cell for each logically separate piece of content.
  - Though you can put text in the same cell with a nested table or a graphic, tables or graphics will usually be easier to manage if each gets its own cell. Additionally, when you use a table cell as a placeholder for a graphic object, you can use the dimensions of the table cell to easily size the graphic. Learn how to do this in Chapter 7.
  - Multiple related paragraphs of text can be placed in the same cell. Even multiple paragraphs that take different paragraph styles, such as subheadings and bulleted text, can sit in the same cell. A single table cell can contain as many paragraphs as you reasonably need, as long as they're well formatted, and anything that you've heard to the contrary is another one of those popular but untrue fables about the misbehavior of Word.
  - However, if you have text that needs to align vertically with text in other table columns, each item to align across the page should go in its own row. For example, if each item in a bulleted list in the first column needs to align with descriptive text in the second column, then each bulleted paragraph should get its own row of the table.

  Keep in mind that a table is there to do the layout for you. Putting lots of text into one cell and then faking alignment (such as with excess paragraph marks between pieces of text) defeats the purpose of using a table and is likely to make your work more complicated rather than less.

  - Headings that are part of the page layout, such as the four quadrant headings on the sample page shown earlier in this section, logically belong in their own cells. Placing headings in their own cells enables you to keep headings aligned automatically to keep the page layout looking precise and professional.

- If you size table columns using your default unit of measure rather than a percentage of the window's width, as recommended earlier in this chapter, keep in mind that the measurement you see on the ruler does not include the width of cell margins. However, the column width measurement in the Table Properties dialog box does include cell margins.

INSIDE OUT   Sizing precisely using the rulers

To view column width on the ruler as well as to resize column width more precisely than $1/16$th of an inch, hold the ALT key while clicking or dragging the right edge of the column, or hold both mouse buttons simultaneously while clicking or dragging.

Note that the ALT and double-button shortcuts for viewing or precisely changing measurements on the ruler can be used with any ruler measurement, including paragraph indents, tab stops, page margins, and the width of text columns. These shortcuts also work for settings changed on the vertical ruler, including table row height as well as top and bottom page margins.

- Once you have sized the columns to the widths you need for your layout, apply the AutoFit setting Fixed Column Width, explained in the preceding section. This is the only AutoFit setting that will keep column widths from changing to accommodate the width of content added to the table. For example, when you insert a picture into a table cell through the Picture option on the Insert tab, the picture will automatically size to fit the table cell if Fixed Column Width is the applied AutoFit setting.

- Set row height only where you want to apportion a certain amount of the page to specific content. A layout table might have multiple columns where content can flow as needed, in which case setting row height is unnecessary. But, when you are using table cells as placeholders for graphics, or you want to limit certain content to a specific portion of the page, setting row height can make that easier. Like any other setting, only take the step of setting row height if it will save you work—such as enabling you to use the cell dimensions to size a graphic with no trial and error.

- Consider if your host table needs cell margins. Leaving the default left and right cell margins provides an automatic space buffer between content in neighboring cells. However, if you have divider columns and rows in a host table, this buffer is unnecessary. Additionally, without cell margins, graphics and nested tables inserted into table cells will fit more snugly for a clean layout.

- If you often use tables to create page layout, add a host table style to your global template or whatever template you use for complex documents. A table style that contains no borders and no cell margins can be handy for quickly creating host tables. See Chapter 5 to learn about creating table styles, saving styles to templates in Word, and setting a default table style for the active document or template.

Using Nested Tables vs. Text Wrap Around Tables

As introduced earlier in this chapter, and discussed further in the Troubleshooting tip in this section, avoid using text wrap around tables. Instead, when you need content beside a table, nested tables are the perfect, simple solution.

A nested table is simply one table inside another. You can nest a complete, formatted table in a host table, or you can insert a new table directly into a cell of a host table and then format the nested table.

To create one table inside another, do the following.

1. Click in the cell where you want the nested table to appear.

2. On the Insert tab, click Table and then move your pointer across and down the grid to indicate the columns and rows you want in your nested table, just as you would when creating any table in Word. Click to insert the nested table.

3. Format the nested table exactly as you would any table. Just be sure that you know whether your insertion point is in the nested table or host table before making changes.

To paste an existing table into a host table, do the following.

1. Select and then cut or copy the table from its original location.

2. Click in the cell of the host table where you want to paste the nested table. When a table is in the Clipboard and your insertion point is inside a table, the default paste method is Paste As Nested Table. Find this option on the Home tab, in the Clipboard group, under the Paste options. Or, simply press CTRL+V to paste.

CAUTION !

Though this issue is largely resolved in Word 2007, there might be instances when you will paste intending to nest the table and your table will be appended to the host table instead. If this happens, simply undo the action (CTRL+Z), then type a space in the host cell where you want to nest the table and paste again. The addition of the space will indicate to Word that your intention is to place content inside that cell and then pasting as a nested table (just using CTRL+V for the default paste method) will work fine. That space will cause an excess paragraph mark to be inserted before your nested table. You can delete that paragraph mark and excess space as soon as the table is pasted.

Nested tables are typically used in three ways.

- Nested tables enable you to easily add flexibility to a page's layout while leaving the host table clean and simple to manage, as in the example of the two objects in the bottom right corner of the page, shown earlier in this chapter.

- When you need rows to grow independently of one another, use nested tables. For example, if you have a layout with two columns of text or other content, where you need the height in one of the columns to grow as content is added, without affecting the row height in the other column, start with a two-column host table and nest tables as needed in either column. For example, the page shown here has a two-row, three-column host table. The top row is for the headings and the center column is used as a divider. The second cell in the left column uses a nested table to divide the text and graphic, in order not to be affected by the height of the graphic in the same cell of the right-hand column.

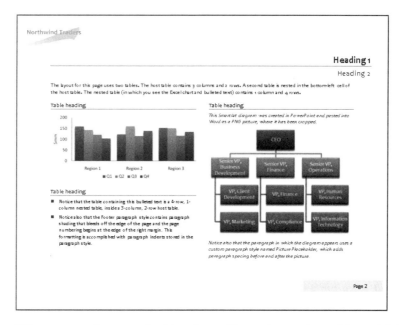

- When you need content beside a data table, such as a chart of financial data beside a table of the same financial data, nest the data table inside a host table cell.

TROUBLESHOOTING

I received the error "A table in this document has become corrupted"

When the error "A table in this document has become corrupted" appears, as you see here, the text written in that error message does provide the best recommendation. That is, close the document and open it using Open And Repair. However, keep a few things in mind before using this utility with corrupt tables.

When you open a document using this utility, Word attempts to repair it automatically. A Show Repairs dialog box will appear, listing any corruption errors in the document that Open And Repair has corrected. You can select the item in the Show Repairs list and then click Go To to be taken directly to the source of the problem. For those who had to contend with this error message in versions of Word before Open And Repair existed, you know what a timesaver it can be when Word takes you to the table in question.

However, note that when repairing corruption, Word might need to remove or change parts of the document. For example, you might lose table formatting or even table content in some circumstances.

Following are a few best practice guidelines to help reduce instances of table corruption.

- Do not use the Text Wrap Around tables feature.

- Do not place floating graphics (that is, any graphic with a Text Wrapping setting other than In Line With Text) in, on, or behind tables.

- When pasting tables from Web sites, paste them as Formatted Text (RTF) using the Paste Special dialog box instead of the default paste, which is HTML. To access this dialog box, on the Home tab, in the Clipboard group, click Paste and then click Paste Special, or press the new keyboard shortcut CTRL+ALT+V.

- Avoid contorting the table structure. That is, don't delete individual cells of a row or column, or excessively split or merge cells to accommodate content.

- When nesting tables, avoid adding excess layers. Nested tables are extremely stable when used correctly, but adding an unnecessary volume of extra layers can cause instability. If the corruption error refers to a nested table, removing the outermost layer (that is, placing all content and nested tables into a new host table) will almost always resolve the issue.

Managing Nested Tables

Use the following best practices to work effectively with nested tables.

- If you're unsure of whether your insertion point is in the nested table or the host table, select the table to confirm before performing any formatting task.

- To place your insertion point in the host cell containing a nested table, click in the last cell of the nested table, at the end of any content in the cell, and then press the right arrow key twice. Note that when your insertion point is in the host cell containing a nested table, the cell might appear expanded to make room for your insertion point. When you move your insertion point out of the cell, the cell will return to its normal size.

- Apply the AutoFit To Window setting to any nested table to fit it snugly within its host cell. (This assumes that you have set the host table to Fixed Column Width.)

- Remember to remove the cell margins from the host cell, as discussed earlier in this chapter, if you want the nested table to use the entire host cell.

- If you want to copy or move a nested table outside of the host table, apply the AutoFit setting Fixed Column Width before moving the table, to maintain its proportions. If you leave the setting to AutoFit To Window, the table size will change to use 100 percent of the width of its new window.

- Remember that a table is an inline object, so paragraph formatting in the host cell can affect the positioning of the nested table. For example, if you apply space before the paragraph to the host cell, the nested table in that cell will have space above it.

- Keep in mind that the host cell is the nested table's window. So, for example, if the nested table has an indent from left applied, that will be an indent from the left of the host cell.

- As mentioned in the preceding Troubleshooting tip, do not add excess layers of nested tables. Nesting tables are an excellent alternative to contorting table structure, and an easy way to create complex layouts. But, overuse of any objects or formatting in Word documents can cause unnecessary complications.

TROUBLESHOOTING

I need to understand table cell and end-of-row markers

Similar to paragraph marks and section breaks, the formatting marks in a table store information.

The cell marker in each cell stores cell formatting information, but also acts as the last paragraph mark in the cell. So, for example, if you have a bulleted list in the cell and the last bullet in the list is smaller than the others, the reason is most likely that a smaller font size was applied in the cell before the bulleted list was added, so the last paragraph mark (that is, the cell marker) still contains the smaller font size. To correct such instances, select the entire cell (rather than just cell contents) to reapply the formatting or applicable style.

The row marker stores information about table formatting. This is the reason that vertically merging cells in a table can sometimes cause the table to become more difficult to manage. This is also the reason that including row markers in your selection when selecting a table can make a difference in the results of several actions (such as when using paragraph alignment shortcuts to align a table on the page, as discussed earlier).

Formatting Financial Tables

Though all tables are, to an extent, used for laying out content on a page, tables used to organize text or data are different from layout tables in a few ways. Primarily, whereas content that you add to layout tables needs to fit the page layout you design, tables used to lay out text or data need to fit your content.

Chapter 6

Most of what you need to know to effectively format financial tables has already been introduced in this chapter. In fact, formatting a financial table in Word is much the same as formatting the simplest text tables. The only difference is that financial tables often have some specific formatting requirements that make them look more complicated than they actually are. Use the following best practices to format flawless financials every time.

- Take steps to help you work precisely, to avoid spending time on trial and error. For example, set all data columns to equal width, when possible, before applying decimal alignment. That way, you can select all columns that will require the same alignment

  To set columns to equal width, select the columns to format and then, on the Table Tools Design tab, click Distribute Columns. Or, right-click and select Distribute Columns Evenly from the shortcut menu.

- Work in a logical order, when possible, to keep your effort to a minimum. For example, wait until all column widths are the correct size before merging heading cells.

- Remember that the same paragraph and font formatting can be used in a table as in the body of a document. So, row headings, column headings, decimal number alignment, and so on, can all be accomplished with font and paragraph formatting.

  For help with much of this, see the sections on paragraph formatting versus table formatting earlier in this chapter, specifically those sections titled "Paragraph Indents vs. Cell Margins," "Paragraph Borders vs. Cell Borders," and "Which Paragraph Formatting Option Is Best?" Notice tips such as using paragraph borders to create the appearance of space between columns without having to use spacer columns, which can help save time when formatting financials. And, as with any document task, keep in mind that your table will be easier to manage if you only apply formatting where needed. For example, only add the indents needed to create the appearance of space between columns in those cells that contain paragraph borders. That way, if a data cell needs to exceed the indent slightly, you'll encounter no unnecessary complications.

- If your table requires calculations, consider calculating the data in Excel and then pasting the table content into Word as a Word table. Though Word provides a handful of common formulas, Excel is the far more powerful number cruncher. Formulas in Word have a significant limitation for formatting financials, in particular that only the content in the field can get automatic number formatting, potentially making your number format appear different in that cell than in cells where the text is typed. Setting up your data in Excel also enables you to more easily add or edit number formats as needed, and getting that table into Word when you're ready can be quick and painless, as explained later in this chapter.

  For data that will continue to update while the document is being edited, consider pasting the table in Word as a Word table, but link it to the Excel data. You can then break the link when the data is final, before sharing your document. If you do this, wait to do detailed table formatting or change table content until after the link is broken, to avoid losing your work when links are updated. See the Troubleshooting tip that follows for help linking and unlinking tables.

TROUBLESHOOTING

I lose information in my table when updating links or my document indicates more links than I have

When you paste an Excel table into Word as a linked Word table, keep in mind that the entire table is linked, not just the data inside that table. Use the following best practices to link and unlink tables from Excel to Word, and to troubleshoot common issues related to linked tables.

- To paste a table copied from Excel into Word as a linked table, in Word press CTRL+ALT+V to open the Paste Special dialog box. Select Paste Link, confirm that the paste type is HTML, and then click OK. Note that HTML retains much more of the source formatting than Formatted Text (RTF), but either of these options will paste the content as a Word table, linked to the source Excel data.

- A linked table in Word is stored as a field. If you press ALT+F9 to toggle field codes, you can see that the table is actually contained in a LINK field. So, you can apply paragraph or table styles to the content in the table, or even direct font or paragraph formatting, and that formatting will be retained when you update the link. (To update the link, either right-click and then click Update Link or press F9). However, if you change content (such as typing currency symbols on the data, or adding a tab character), that information will be deleted when you update the link, because the link refers to all content within the table.

- When the data is final and you no longer need the link, you can break the link in order to finish editing the table without losing your work. To break the link, click in the table and press CTRL+SHIFT+F9. Or, click the Microsoft Office Button, point to Prepare, and then click Edit Links to Files. In the Links dialog box, select the link to break and then click Break Link.

- If the Links dialog box shows more links than you believe to be in the document, one reason may be the way you deleted a linked table. The table is contained within the link, rather than the other way around. So, if you delete just the table, the field may be left behind. When you press ALT+F9 to toggle all field codes in the document, you'll see the field code if it's still in your document. If the field code still exists, select the document and then press F9 to update fields. The table will reappear. To ensure that you've deleted a linked table, toggle field codes and then delete the entire field instead of deleting the table.

For more on working with fields, see Chapter 9, "Quick Parts."

Chapter 6

Decimally Align Numbers and Currency Symbols

Though you use a decimal tab stop to create decimal alignment in Word, the formatting behaves like true alignment and does not require the use of any tab characters when created correctly. For decimal alignment to work correctly in table cells, first confirm the following.

- Set paragraph alignment to Left for all cells that will be decimally aligned.

- Clear any tab stops that exist in the cells to be decimally aligned. To do this, first select the cells and then do the following.

1. On the Home tab or the Page Layout tab, in the Paragraph group, click the dialog launcher icon to open the Paragraph dialog box. Then, click the Tabs button to open the Tabs dialog box. Or, use the legacy accelerator key combination ALT+O, T.

2. Click Clear All and then click OK.

Once you've confirmed the preceding settings, follow these steps to set decimal alignment.

CAUTION

The steps provided here to decimally align multiple table columns at once may not work correctly if text wrap is enabled on your table.

1. Select all cells that will need similar decimal alignment. That is, if you have four contiguous columns of similar width, containing similar data, you can select them all at once to set the decimal alignment. Note that if columns are significantly different in width, or if data is significantly different in neighboring columns (such as two-digit numbers in one column and eight-digit numbers in another), set decimal alignment separately for each column.

2. Click the tab selection icon at the left of the ruler until the decimal tab icon appears, as shown here. Then, click on the ruler between the margins of the first column in your selection where you want the decimal alignment to appear (that is, where the decimal point for the aligned numbers should appear). The setting will be placed at the same position in all selected columns.

   Note that this action won't work if you have selected noncontiguous columns. To place the decimal tab stop for non-contiguous columns, you can use the Tabs dialog box. This isn't recommended, however, because finding the correct setting without use of the ruler can take some trial and error.

3. To move the decimal alignment once you've placed the tab stop, simply drag the decimal tab stop to the new position. As mentioned earlier in the chapter, hold the ALT key while dragging to move precisely. To keep formatting consistent

across all columns, be sure to select all columns that have the same alignment before making the change.

To be sure that your decimal alignment works correctly and remains easy to manage, keep the following in mind.

- When decimal alignment is correctly set, the text in the cells will automatically move to the alignment, as they would if you applied center or right paragraph alignment. Typing tab characters in the cells to push the text over should never be necessary to accomplish decimal alignment. If this is necessary in your table, other tab stops remain in the cells. To keep your table easy to manage, take the time to remove excess tab stops instead of adding extra tab characters.

- If decimals don't align correctly in your cells, either paragraph alignment isn't set to Left or the column doesn't have sufficient width to accommodate all numbers.

- Aligning currency symbols in a financial table is the only common exception to when you might need a tab character in a table cell. When currency symbols need to be aligned in decimally aligned cells, add an additional left tab stop for the currency symbol. Then, place one tab character before the currency symbol and another before the number to be decimally aligned (use CTRL+TAB to place a tab character in a table cell). Once you add this additional tab stop, the decimal tab no longer behaves like alignment and instead behaves like a tab, which is the reason the tab character will be required. Your setting should look something like the following graphic.

As you can see in the image, the additional tab stop is only placed in cells where the currency symbol is present.

CAUTION !

Only place the additional tab to align currency symbols in cells that contain currency symbols. For example, if only the first cell and cells in subtotal and total rows contain currency symbols, those are the only cells that should get the additional tab stop. Placing this additional tab stop in cells without currency symbols will require two tab characters in every data cell, which can make editing the table tremendously more complicated than necessary.

When formatting financial tables, keep in mind shortcuts available to save you time, such as using Replace, selecting noncontiguous cells, and the keyboard shortcuts for

Chapter 6

the Format Painter (explained in the Inside Out tip in this section). Using the Replace feature, for example, you can search for all instances of a currency symbol in your table and replace it with tab characters surrounding that currency symbol as well as the additional tab stop needed to align the currency symbol. Try the best practices provided here for formatting financials, as well as these suggested formatting shortcuts, in the Troubleshooting exercise explained in this section.

INSIDE OUT   The underexposed formatting clipboard

You probably know that you can click the Format Painter icon on the Home tab to copy formatting from one selection to another, or double-click that icon to paste the copied formatting to several places. However, you might not know about the keyboard shortcuts for the Format Painter, which provide additional benefits.

Instead of clicking the Format Painter icon, press CTRL+SHIFT+C to copy the paragraph and font formatting of your selection. Doing so places the formatting into its own clipboard, so that you can then paste that formatting to any other selection in that document or any Word document, until you either copy another set of formatting or end your Word session. To paste copied formatting, press CTRL+SHIFT+V.

In addition to the clipboard-style benefit of the keyboard shortcuts, using the keyboard shortcut can be particularly useful for copying formatting from one table cell to another, because it can be difficult to click precisely between cells to use the Format Painter icon, especially in small tables.

Note that the keyboard options provided here also work in Microsoft Office PowerPoint 2007, but they are not available in Excel.

TROUBLESHOOTING

How can I learn to troubleshoot documents more easily?

Learning to troubleshoot documents is a bit like learning auto mechanics. Before you can effectively diagnose and correct problems, you have to know how the pieces fit together. If you or anyone you know has taken an auto mechanics class, chances are that they had to either take apart or put together a car's engine. Once you know how the pieces work together, troubleshooting a problem is all about process of elimination, which is simply a matter of logic and organization.

When I teach document troubleshooting or advanced document production, one of my favorite exercises to help develop troubleshooting skills in Word is to format a complex financial table in 15 steps or less. More specifically, it's to list the steps required to format that table. This exercise helps you learn how to save time by planning your approach to a complex document task, as well as how the components of a complex table fit together to help you more easily diagnose table formatting problems.

To try this exercise for yourself, find the document Table Exercise.docx in the sample files you can install from the Welcome tab of the CD. That document contains the unformatted table along with guidelines for the exercise. Though your steps might differ from those I've chosen and still be just as correct, you can check your results against mine by opening the file Completed Table.docx, also in the sample files available on the book's CD.

Managing Tables from Other Sources

The best practices introduced throughout this chapter will provide most of what you need to know to effectively format most tables. However, when tables originate in other sources, some additional considerations may be required. The two most common sources of tables pasted into Word documents from other programs are those that originate in Excel and those that originate on Web sites.

Considerations for Tables That Originate in Excel

When you paste a table from Excel 2007 into Word 2007, you get better translation than in earlier versions of Word. However, consider the following suggestions to help you avoid excess cleanup work later.

- Before copying your Excel table, expand all columns to fit their contents. Keep in mind that content can cross cells in an Excel worksheet without merging cells, but not in a Word table. As discussed throughout this chapter, excessive merged cells in a Word table can make the table more difficult to edit.

- If you have divider columns in the Excel table through which some headings or other content pass, delete them before copying the table to avoid unnecessary merged cells, as mentioned in the preceding bullet.

- If numeric data uses Accounting number format or a custom number format that decimally aligns data in Excel, excess leading or trailing spaces will appear in the table cells after they're pasted in Word. You can either change the number format to Number or Currency before copying the table, or use an easy shortcut provided in the Troubleshooting tip in this section to remove the spaces after the table is pasted into Word.

Before making any of the preceding recommended changes to your Excel table, consider making a copy of the sheet on which the table resides, so that you can avoid changing the original Excel table. To do this quickly in the Excel workbook, simply hold the CTRL key while dragging the sheet tab to the right. When you see an arrow appear to the right of the existing sheet tab, release the pointer and then release the CTRL key.

Chapter 6

Considerations for Tables That Originate On the Web

Similar to tables that originate in Excel, tables that originate on Web pages are generally cleaner when pasted into Word 2007 than in earlier versions. However, some cleanup can still be required. Use the following guidelines to help keep Word tables easy-to-manage when they originate on the Web.

- To paste content that originates on the Web into Word , use the Formatted Text (RTF) option in the Paste Special dialog box (CTRL+ALT+V). Because the default paste method for text and tables in Word is HTML, and Web pages are created in HTML, using the default paste can leave some content that is not compatible with Word, potentially causing formatting complications.

  Note that when you paste as Formatted Text, you are likely to lose some formatting, but reformatting the table is likely to be much less work than fixing a document that becomes unstable because of misinterpreted content.

- If a table is pasted from the Web using the default (HTML) paste, use the following steps to clean up any residual formatting issues.

1. Select the table and press CTRL+SPACEBAR. As you may know, this keyboard shortcut clears direct font formatting from a selection. Some HTML information that can remain resident in content pasted into Word is retained as direct font formatting that you don't see in the document.

2. Unless you need to retain some of the original table structure formatting, such as borders and shading, apply Table Normal table style to clear out any potentially incompatible table structure formatting stored in the cell or row markers. Even if you want to use some of the original formatting, taking this step can often save you much more time in fixing the table than you'll spend reapplying the formatting.

3. Delete any excess columns that contain no content. Because of the way HTML tables are constructed, it's common to find tables with several excess columns, usually very narrow.

4. Turn off spacing between cells, as explained earlier in this chapter.

5. Occasionally, Web tables contain content that translates in Word as empty, invisible graphic objects. If cells appear to be empty but are wide enough to contain content, click in the cells to see if invisible graphic objects are present. If so, simply delete them.

6. Web tables are very often nested. So, if you clear formatting, such as by applying Table Normal style, using the CTRL+SPACEBAR shortcut, or applying paragraph styles, and some formatting is retained, check to see if the table is nested. To do this easily, select and then cut the table. If the table was nested, a host table will remain. You can delete the unnecessary host table and then just paste to replace the table you cut.

Managing Graphics

Whether you need pictures, charts, diagrams, or text boxes, graphics are an impor-tant part of most complex documents you create in Microsoft Word. Why then, you might be wondering, isn't this chapter about *creating* graphics?

In this chapter, we're looking at *managing* graphics, including such topics as under-standing picture types and simplifying layout. Although you can create some of the newly designed Microsoft Office graphic types in Microsoft Office Word 2007, you can get additional benefits and do less work when you use the best program for any task, such as using Microsoft Office Excel 2007 for charts or Microsoft Office PowerPoint 2007 for diagrams. So, you'll find help for creating graphics later in this book. An ex-planation of what programs are best for creating each graphic type, along with cross-references to the chapters in this book where you can get help for getting them done, is included in this chapter in the section titled "Using the Best Program for the Graphic Task."

Meanwhile, this chapter will give you everything you need to know to easily and ef-fectively manage graphic objects in Office Word 2007. Getting exactly the graphic you need, exactly where you need it, can be much easier than you might think.

Chapter Assumptions

As advanced Microsoft Office users, I'm assuming that you're familiar with terms like *text wrapping* and *cropping*, even if you haven't used them, and that you've worked with at least some type of graphics in Word documents in the past.

This chapter primarily focuses on best practices for working with graphics in Word and how to simplify your work to help you get the perfect result every time.

In the introduction to this book, you can find a list of resources for those who want more basic-level information, in the section titled "Who Will Benefit Most from This Book."

What's New for Graphics in Office Word 2007

Because of the new graphics engine in the 2007 Office release, and the truly beautiful charts and diagrams you can create, you might think that just about everything related to working with graphics is new.

The best news about the new graphics engine, for your use when creating documents, is the shared functionality across the 2007 release programs. For example, whether you choose to create a diagram in Word or Office PowerPoint 2007, you have access to the same formatting effects. That formatting also integrates automatically with Themes in either program (discussed in Chapter 5, "Styles"), to keep your colors and fonts consistent with the rest of your document content.

However, when it comes to the best practices for managing graphics in Word, most of what's new are simply additional design options and easier ways to access the features you need. Working with graphics in Word has never been easier, but you might be surprised to find out how much you already know.

In terms of ease of access, most graphic types have one or more of their own contextual tabs. When you insert a picture, for example, you get the Picture Tools Format tab, shown here.

A number of features that you see in this image—such as Text Wrapping options—apply to several types of objects, so you can find those options on other contextual tabs as well as the Page Layout tab, in addition to the Picture Tools Format tab. However, there's more to the tools you see here than just a new organization. See the section of this chapter titled "Graphic Layout Simplified" for more on this topic.

> **Note**
>
> The presence of the Arrange options on the Page Layout tab can be helpful for objects such as embedded or linked diagram objects from Microsoft Office Visio 2007. These objects are not associated with a contextual tab, but can make use of the Arrange features when needed.

Outside of what you see in the Word interface, one of my favorite new features for working with graphics is actually related to working with the new Office Open XML Formats. Say, for example, that your company gets a new logo. So, you have two dozen templates in which you need to replace the logo that appears in the document headers. Instead of opening each document, opening the header (or headers), and then inserting, sizing, and positioning the logo in each, you can just replace the picture file in the XML for each template. Sizing, positioning, and placement information is automatically kept in the XML, so you don't even need to open the templates in Word to get the job done perfectly.

The ability to replace images in this way is the functionality used for the new Change Picture feature that you see on the Picture Tools Format tab. This feature enables you to swap a picture while working in the document, retaining positioning as well as some sizing information. The behavior of the Change Picture feature is different in a couple of ways from what you get when you swap the image file in the XML, so learn more about this feature and when you might want to use one method or the other, under the heading "Formatting Pictures" later in this chapter.

To learn how to interact with the new Office Open XML Formats for tasks such as the one described here, see Chapter 22, "Office Open XML Essentials." To learn everything else you need to know for managing graphics in Word, read on.

Using the Best Program for the Graphic Task

Provided that Office Excel 2007 is installed on your computer, you can create Excel charts directly in Word (or PowerPoint). You can also create powerful new SmartArt diagrams in Word, Excel, or PowerPoint. However, if you have access to all three of these 2007 release programs, there are some good reasons not to use Word for these tasks.

Essentially, there's nothing wrong with creating graphics right in your Word documents, and much of the direction that you'll find in other chapters for creating these graphic types will apply just as well if you choose to create them in Word. However, you always get added benefits when you use the best program for the task at hand, and graphics provide some of the best examples of this. Additionally, when you create your graphics in another program and paste them into Word as pictures, your work gets even easier, as follows.

- Pasting graphics into Word as pictures can help to minimize file size in complex documents, make the document easier to manage, and help ensure the appearance of your graphics on recipients' computers.

- Though Word has an Edit Picture feature, the original, live graphic isn't editable when pasted as a picture. So, when you paste your graphic into Word as a picture, you can be confident that your chart or diagram content remains intact, regardless of where your document goes.

- Pasting as a picture can also help protect sensitive information. For example, just because you want to share a certain chart with recipients of your document doesn't mean you want them to have access to your source data.

> **Note**
>
> Considering the reasons provided here, you can see why pasting graphics into Word as pictures is the standard in most large document production centers (such as those at many global investments banks, where dozens of graphic-heavy pitch books are produced daily).

TROUBLESHOOTING

What happens if I use 2007 release graphics in legacy file format documents?

When you create documents in the legacy file formats (such as .doc), you don't have the option to create the new graphic types (such as SmartArt). Clicking an option for a new graphic type will provide legacy graphic tools (such as the unfortunate Microsoft Office 2003 Diagram And Organizational Chart tool).

When you save a document in one of the legacy file formats after adding 2007 release graphics to the document, new graphic types such as SmartArt become pictures. Charts become embedded chart objects, and will revert to the legacy charting tools if the embedded object is edited while the document is open in Word 2003.

If you share a Word 2007 document with users of earlier versions of Microsoft Office, they can open and edit the file because of the compatibility pack available for earlier Microsoft Office versions. However, graphics—including both charts and SmartArt diagrams that you created with tools in the new 2007 Office release—will convert to pictures when the file is opened.

When these graphics are automatically converted to pictures, whether it's by saving the file down to the legacy format or by opening the file in an earlier version of Word, file size grows tremendously. For example, a sample single-page Word 2007 document that contains one live SmartArt diagram and one live Excel 2007 chart is 24 kilobytes (KB). When saved down to the legacy file format, it becomes 393 KB (with the diagram as a bitmap and the chart as an embedded object). Similarly, if the Word 2007 version is opened and then saved in Word 2003, the file size of the sample document becomes 156 KB.

In addition to the increased file size, the picture file type that Word uses when converting objects automatically to pictures (typically the .png file format), while usually the best choice for 2007 release graphics, doesn't always provide the best resolution.

Instead of letting this automatic conversion control how your graphics look or the size of your files, create your charts and diagrams in Excel 2007 and PowerPoint 2007. Then, paste them into either your Word 2007 or legacy documents as pictures, where you can control the picture type and, therefore, control both the image quality and the file size of the documents you share, regardless of where those documents end up.

Further to the benefits you get when you use the best program for the graphics task, following is a list of the principal Microsoft Office graphic types available in the 2007 release, along with an explanation of which program to use and why.

The Graphic	The Best Program for the Task
Charts	Use Excel. Though you can create Excel charts directly in Word, when you create the charts for your document in Excel, you can keep all charts related to a given document in one workbook for easy access, archiving, editing, and data management. See Chapter 15, "Charts," for an advanced look at creating the chart types you need with the new Excel charting engine, as well as how to get those charts into Word.
SmartArt diagrams	Use PowerPoint. The new SmartArt capability is a technology shared by the 2007 release programs Word, Excel, and PowerPoint. However, when you use PowerPoint to create these diagrams, you get two key additional benefits. You can: ● Generate a diagram from an existing PowerPoint bulleted list ● Use PowerPoint drawing guides to help align content easily when customizing SmartArt diagrams The Align Or Distribute tools available to many Microsoft Office graphics are not available in SmartArt diagrams, so the drawing guides can be an important timesaver. See Chapter 18, "Creating Professional Presentation Graphics" for help creating and customizing SmartArt diagrams.
Drawings created with Microsoft Office shapes	Use PowerPoint. You can insert shapes directly into a Word document, but PowerPoint offers many additional features for working with these types of objects. ● PowerPoint offers new shapes and new formatting effects that are not available in Word. ● The Selection And Visibility Pane enables you to select, hide, or name any drawing object on a slide. ● Drawing guides provide additional tools to simplify layout. ● Shapes are faster to create in PowerPoint, with shortcuts such as the ability to add text to any AutoShape just by selecting the shape and beginning to type. ● PowerPoint offers greater flexibility for working with shapes, including the ability to convert Shapes to freeform objects that you can customize with the Edit Points feature. Several of these features, such as the Selection And Visibility pane and the ability to convert Shapes to freeform objects, are also available in Excel 2007 but are not in Word. Find all the information you need for creating presentation graphics with PowerPoint, and getting those graphics into Word, in Chapter 18.
WordArt	Use PowerPoint. WordArt in PowerPoint (and Excel) offers the ability to apply formatting and effects to text in any text box, and offers a variety of new formatting effects similar to those for Shapes. This new version of WordArt is not available in Word. As with the other PowerPoint graphics referenced above, find help for using WordArt in Chapter 18.

In addition to the graphic types you can create for your Word documents in Excel and PowerPoint, read Chapter 17, "The Excel–Visio Connection," to learn about using Office Visio 2007 to generate diagrams from Excel data, and for tips on creating Visio diagrams for use in other 2007 release programs.

Objects vs. Pictures

The term *objects* as used here refers to objects created directly in your document as well as to those embedded as objects from other programs. The benefits of using pictures instead of objects has already been introduced in the preceding section. However, understanding the difference between pictures and objects is an important part of being able to effectively manage the graphics in your documents.

The difference between an object and a picture is similar to the difference between your computer and a picture of your computer. A picture is an image of an object. Just as you can't type or search the Internet using a picture of a computer, you can't edit data in a picture of a chart—the picture has no data.

The most common reason for creating graphics directly in Word or pasting graphics from other programs (such as Visio) as embedded objects, is to be able to edit those graphics right in your document. On the surface, it sounds both easier and faster than having to go to another file to edit your graphic. But, when you need to update the graphics you create in other programs, it takes just a minute to get them into Word flawlessly. And, because the same Themes are available in Excel and PowerPoint, it takes literally one click to coordinate graphics created in those programs with the design of your Word document.

Linked and Embedded Objects

When you paste most graphics from other Microsoft Office programs into Word using the default paste method (CTRL+V or Home, Paste), they remain editable graphics by default. You also get a paste SmartTag at the bottom-right corner of the pasted graphic, providing different paste options that vary based on the type of content.

For best results, it's a good idea to use Paste Special to paste graphics into your document, so that you can see all available paste options (including available picture format types) and stay in control of how content is placed in your document. To access Paste Special, press CTRL+ALT+V or, on the Home tab, click to expand Paste options, and then click Paste Special.

However, it's good to know what the default paste types are as well as the paste SmartTag options for common Microsoft Office graphic types. Those are detailed in the list that follows. (However, if you use the default paste method, keep in mind that the paste SmartTag disappears after you make any edit to the pasted graphic.)

- An Excel chart pastes as a live chart, linked to the source workbook. The paste SmartTag options include embedding the source workbook in the chart or pasting the chart as a picture.

  In Word, when a chart is pasted as a linked or embedded object, the chart is editable in Word as if it had been created in that program. You see Chart Tools contextual tabs on the Ribbon when you select any portion of the chart, and chart formatting responds to changes in your Word document theme. However, the entire source workbook is either linked to the chart or embedded in the chart. So, when you select the option to edit the chart data, the originating workbook opens, if it is available.

> **Note**
>
> If the source data workbook for a linked chart becomes unavailable, the chart will still seem to be a live, dynamic chart, but the ability to access or edit the data will be lost. If this happens, you can copy the chart back to an Excel worksheet and use an Excel macro to retrieve the lost data. For help getting this done, see the Troubleshooting tip "How can I retrieve lost chart data?" in Chapter 15.

- A SmartArt graphic pastes as a live, editable graphic. The paste SmartTag options include pasting the diagram as a picture.

- Drawings created with shapes paste as Microsoft Office graphic objects. However, because shape functionality has been updated to the new graphics engine in other 2007 release programs and not in Word, those objects won't be editable and you won't get a contextual tab. In fact, if you use new graphic effects not available in Word (such as reflection options), you're likely to get some distortion when you paste. However, the paste SmartTag options include pasting as a picture, which will retain formatting correctly and provide access to the Picture Tools Format contextual tab.

- A Visio diagram pastes as an embedded Visio object, with no paste SmartTag options. To paste a Visio diagram as a picture, you must use Paste Special.

When most object types are linked or embedded in a Word document, they're stored in the Word document as fields. This is good news, because it makes the objects easy to convert to pictures, as discussed later in this section. However, Excel charts are an exception. Because Excel charts can be created directly from Word, linking or embedding the chart (when using the default paste or the paste SmartTag options) only links or embeds the data. Otherwise, the chart behaves like a chart created directly in your document, and it can't be easily converted to a picture.

> **Note**
>
> If you use Paste Special to paste an Excel chart as a linked or embedded object, it will paste as traditional embedded or linked object (that is, stored in a field code so that it's editable through the Chart Object options when you right-click the object and able to be converted to a picture using the CTRL+SHIFT+F9 shortcut). However, this option provides unnecessary complications beyond those discussed in this chapter for embedded objects, such as possible sizing distortion if the chart is on its own sheet in the source workbook.

Embedding objects in your documents enables you to edit the object directly from your document, provided the source program is available. So, if you share a document containing an embedded object, anyone who opens the document can potentially edit your graphic. Keep in mind that embedded objects are not limited to graphics and may be other object types, such as entire documents.

Linking objects requires not just the source program, but access to the source file. If you share a document containing a linked object, recipients of your document can see the image of the object but will get an error message if their computer doesn't have access to the source file location. Clearly, it's not a good idea to share documents outside of your organization that contain links to other files, both because of the inconvenience of error messages and because of the potential loss of information once the document is no longer in your control.

> **Note**
>
> Linked content in your document is not limited to graphics, and may include tables pasted from Excel as well, as discussed in Chapter 6, "Tables."

TROUBLESHOOTING

Do embedded Excel objects pose a privacy risk?

If you embed any Excel object into a file in another program (including Word), you embed not just the object, but the entire source workbook. So, recipients of your document can access all content on all sheets of that source workbook just by opening or editing the embedded object.

For example, if you have a workbook containing PivotTable reports for your top five clients and you embed a chart related to one client in a Word report for that client, the data in the source workbook relating to your other four top clients will be equally accessible to anyone who receives that Word report.

When you embed an Excel table or other worksheet content into Word, the object is stored in the document as a field, so you can simply select the object and then press CTRL+SHIFT+F9 to convert it to a picture. However, this option doesn't work when you paste an Excel chart into a Word document and use the paste SmartTag option to select embedded object, because (even though the entire source workbook is embedded when you do this) the object remains live.

To protect sensitive information in your Excel workbooks, always paste content of any kind from Excel into other programs as pictures.

To paste an object with a link to its source file, use Paste Special (CTRL+ALT+V). In the Paste Special dialog box, shown here after a Visio object was copied, click Paste Link to see the paste options. Paste As options often change after selecting Paste Link, because linking is not available for all options. Note that linking is not an available option in the Paste Special dialog box for pasting some graphic types that are able to be created in Word, such as SmartArt diagrams.

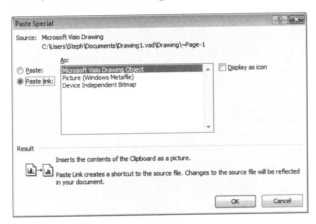

As always, the Paste As options in the Paste Special dialog box differ based on the type of content that you've copied to the clipboard.

Converting Embedded or Linked Objects to Pictures

With the exception of Excel charts, embedded or linked objects are stored in Word as fields. Because of this, you can simply remove the field code to leave just the image of the linked or embedded object—that is, to convert the object to a picture. To do this, select the object and press CTRL+SHIFT+F9. This keyboard shortcut removes any field code, leaving only its result.

Chapter 7

CAUTION !

After you convert a linked or embedded object to a picture, the original object is no longer editable and any dynamic data is lost. For this reason, before converting any object to a picture that might require editing later, first save a copy of the source object in its originating program. Find instructions for how to get this done under the heading "Editing Linked and Embedded Objects" later in this section.

In the case of most types of fields, including EMBED fields, the keyboard shortcut is the only way to remove the field code. Learn more about editing field codes in Chapter 9, "Quick Parts." However, in the case of linked objects, links can also be broken or edited through the Links dialog box, shown here. To access this dialog box, click the Microsoft Office Button, point to Prepare, and then click Edit Links To Files. This option will only be an available Prepare option if links to other files exist in your document.

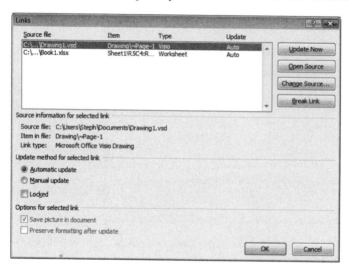

It's important to note that, even though you can't break the link for an Excel chart using the keyboard shortcut to disconnect a field result from the field code, the links for charts pasted from Excel into Word using the default paste method are available and can be broken through the dialog box shown in the preceding image. If you break the link to chart data in this way, you can still select and edit formatting of chart elements (such as changing the color or effects applied to data series) but any access to source data will be lost.

> **Note**
>
> Hyperlinks, even to other files, are not the same as linked objects, and are not accessible through the Links dialog box. A HYPERLINK is a field type in Word, but is not related to the LINK field.

Editing Linked and Embedded Objects

For any linked or embedded object that can't be edited directly on the Word document page (this includes all embedded objects other than Word tables linked to Excel data and most Excel charts pasted into Word as anything other than pictures), the steps for editing the object are very similar.

1. Right-click the object and then point to <Type> Object. Notice that the options provided include Edit and Open.

> **Note**
>
> The Convert option that you see on the same menu as Edit and Open doesn't do what you might expect. That is, it may offer options to convert to other object types, but does not convert the object to a picture. For example, an embedded Excel worksheet object will offer Convert options to change the object to a different type of Excel workbook (such as a legacy workbook or a macro-enabled workbook). For others, Convert doesn't really offer any options at all. In the case of Visio objects, for example, the only option for an embedded Visio drawing is to convert to an embedded Visio drawing. Breaking the link to convert the object to a picture, or copying the object and pasting it as the picture type of your choice, is usually a more effective approach to converting the object type.

2. If you need to change the dimensions of the pasted object itself (such as if part of your graphic is cut off in the object) select Edit. Otherwise, for any changes to the object itself, select Open.

   When you select Edit, the object window opens only as large as the space allotted to the embedded object. The Ribbon (or menu and toolbars, as applicable) from the source program becomes available. However, because you're working within the space of the object, it's a bit more difficult to manage. When you select Open, the object is opened in a separate window in the source program, so that you can edit it as you would any object in that program.

CAUTION !

When you select Edit for a linked or embedded Visio object, the File menu is not correct—it primarily reflects options from the Microsoft Office Button menu. (This is also true for Visio objects in PowerPoint.) To access Visio File menu options, such as Page Setup, you must select Open from the Visio Object options available when you right-click the object.

3. Depending upon the option you select, do the following.

a. If you select the Edit option, drag the black, thatched edge (shown here in the cross section of an embedded Visio object) to resize the object boundaries.

When you've finished working in Edit mode, just click in the Word document, outside of the object, to close the object.

b. If you select the Open option, when you finish making changes, you can simply click the X in the top-right corner of the source program window to close the object and return to the document (you might need to manually switch your window back to the document if you use this method). Or, on the Microsoft Office Button menu (or the File menu, depending upon the program) select the option to close the object and return to Word.

Determining the Best Picture Type for Your Graphic

To this point in the chapter, I've given you many reasons to paste graphics into your Word documents as pictures. But, what type of picture is best for your particular graphic?

Getting the best picture quality for the smallest file size is easy when you use Paste Special to paste graphics into Word as pictures. But, the best picture type to select in the Paste Special dialog box varies based on the source program for the particular graphic. The table that follows summarizes the common picture types that might be available when you use Paste Special to paste a graphic into Word, along with the best practices for using each.

> **Note**
>
> When determining the best type of picture for your particular graphic, consider how the document will be used. If the document is likely to be used both on screen and printed, you might want to print a sample graphic to make sure the selected picture type is as clear in print as on screen.

Picture Type	When to Use It
Picture (PNG)	This is the best picture type to use when pasting any content from PowerPoint or (in some cases) Excel into Word as a picture. (Note that for content between previous versions of Word, PowerPoint, and Excel, Enhanced Metafile was the better choice.) The .png file extension, which stands for Portable Network Graphic, is an Internet-compatible picture type similar to JPG (.jpg) or GIF (.gif), both referenced below. Like the other Internet-compatible picture types, PNG pictures are a type of bitmap. PNG pictures can occasionally appear a bit less crisp than some other picture types in the Microsoft Office programs, but that is less so in the 2007 release than it was previously. This is a good format to try for most graphic types when the results you get pasting in other picture formats are not as good as expected. This file format is also an excellent choice when pasting any type of graphic that you'll be sharing with users of Microsoft Office for Mac. > **Note** > .png is an available picture file format in the Paint accessory program available in Microsoft Windows (Both Windows XP and Windows Vista), and it often provides excellent clarity for screen shots with much smaller file sizes than Windows Bitmaps.
Picture (Enhanced Metafile)	This is the best picture type to use when pasting any content from Visio into Word as a picture. Additionally, this is a good option to try when pasting an Excel chart into Word, if the PNG format doesn't provide optimal results. As mentioned earlier, this format used to be the best choice for graphics originating in PowerPoint, but that is no longer the case in the 2007 release. > **Note** > If you want to paste a Visio diagram with a link to the source file during document editing to save time and then break that link for security reasons before sending out the file, choose Microsoft Visio Drawing Object along with the Paste Link option in the Paste Special dialog box. When you break the link, Word converts the object to an Enhanced Metafile Picture.

Device Independent Bitmap	This picture type usually adds the most file size to your document, but it's usually an excellent choice for the best quality when graphics originate in vector drawing programs such as Adobe Illustrator. *Device independent* means that graphic contents won't be affected by settings in the program where the bitmap is placed. For example, if you have a logo created in a vector graphics program and that logo contains text, the font definition might be different in Word than in the source program, potentially changing the appearance of your logo. With a Device Independent Bitmap, that doesn't happen, because the graphic is independent of the program where it's placed.
Bitmap	When you see Bitmap in the Paste Special dialog box, this refers to a Windows Bitmap. Similar to a Device Independent Bitmap, a Windows Bitmap is likely to be a large file but historically provides excellent quality. The main difference is that a Windows Bitmap is not necessarily independent of the destination program. Although Windows Bitmaps are known to be a good choice for quality, this is not the case for graphics originating in the 2007 Office release programs. PNG pictures usually offer smaller file sizes with better quality for graphics created in the 2007 release.
Picture (JPG) or Picture (GIF)	Most people are familiar with the .jpg file format, because it's the most common file format used by digital cameras. Both JPG and GIF are good choices when pasting pictures that were already picture files when copied. JPG and, especially, GIF can also be good choices when pasting graphics originating in programs outside of Microsoft Office. These picture file types, along with PNG, are also good choices for users of Office for the Mac when their documents will be shared with users of Windows versions of Microsoft Office.
Picture (TIF)	Though TIF is not an available option for many types of graphics, pasting a picture using the .tif file format when available can often provide an excellent alternative for high quality graphics. In particular, when the graphic (such as a company logo designed in a vector graphics program) contains text, TIF will often provide the best picture quality both in print and on screen.

TROUBLESHOOTING

I need to convert a graphic to another picture type

If the perfect picture type for your graphic isn't available in the Paste Special dialog box, or if you need to reduce file size without losing quality, two utility programs—Microsoft Windows Paint and Microsoft Office Picture Manager—can come in very handy.

For example, if you take a screen shot using any method and then attempt to paste it into Word using Paste Special, Bitmap and Device Independent Bitmap are your only options. However, if you first paste that screen shot into the Paint accessory program and then copy it again, Windows Metafile becomes an option when you use Paste Special in Word. To access Paint, click the Windows Start button and then click Accessories.

Or, if you have a large image file, such as a high resolution .jpg image that's several megabytes in size, and would like to reduce the file size without significantly reducing quality, you can use Picture Manager to export that picture to another format (such as

.gif) that might be a fraction of the file size. Note that you can also compress pictures, often very effectively, using Picture Manager.

To access Picture Manager, on the Windows Start menu, click All Programs, Microsoft Office, and then Microsoft Office Tools. To export a picture to another file type using Picture Manager, on the File menu, click Export. To compress a picture, on the Picture menu, click Compress Pictures. The Export and Compress features, like most tasks in Picture Manager, provide a pane of options, including file types for exporting pictures or usage requirements (such as document or e-mail) for compressing pictures.

INSIDE OUT   **Referencing source files for your graphics**

Naturally, Murphy's Law dictates that as soon as you get rid of a graphic source file, or even think that you won't need to edit the graphic again, you are guaranteed not only to need to edit it, but to do so urgently.

So, when pasting graphics into Word as pictures, make sure that you can always find the source file when the time comes to edit that graphic. To do this easily, place a comment with the name and location of the source file on the page in the Word document where the graphic appears. To save even more time, consider including the source file path in the comment as a hyperlink (CTRL+K).

Some time ago, a developer friend recommended another solution for storing the source file information instead of using comments. He uses the Alternate Text area provided for pictures that will appear on Web pages. I'm not a great fan of this solution under most circumstances, because comments are easier to remove when you're ready to share the document outside of your organization and quicker to access when you need the source file name, but it might come in handy if you have a document where comments aren't an option. To access the Alternative Text area, on the Picture Tools Format tab, in the Size group, click the dialog launcher to open the Size dialog box and then click the Alt Text tab.

Graphic Layout Simplified

When you're ready to paste a graphic into your Word document, first ask yourself the following question: Would you prefer to spend the next 20 minutes of your life struggling to position that graphic, only to give up and decide it's close enough when you simply can take no more, or do you have something better to do with that time?

If you have something better to do, and I hope that you do, just remember the following four words: *in line with text.*

It might seem as though text wrapping options such as Tight or Square, shown here, are the easiest way to get the layout you want. But, positioning and anchoring can be complicated and documents can become much more difficult to manage.

Instead, when you use the In Line With Text option at the top of the options shown here, you're actually turning off text wrapping. When you do this, your graphic sits on the same document layer as text or tables. So, you can position and format that graphic as easily as you do a paragraph of text. Additionally, when your graphics are formatted to be in line with text, you can place them in table cells for simplified solutions to complex page layouts.

To learn about the concept of layers in Word, see Chapter 4, "Building Easy-to-Manage, Robust Documents." To learn how to use tables to simplify complex page layouts, see Chapter 6.

CAUTION !

Never place floating graphics (that is, graphics that use text wrapping settings other than In Line With Text) on, in, or behind tables, especially nested tables. Doing so can lead to the table corruption error message and might require repairing the table. For help with that error message, see the Troubleshooting tip titled "I Received the error 'A table in This Document Has Become Corrupted'" in Chapter 6.

Using the In Line With Text Layout

By default, most picture types are automatically positioned in line with text when you paste or insert them into your document. To set this default, click the Microsoft Office Button and then click Word Options. On the Advanced tab of the Word Options dialog box, confirm that the Insert/Paste Pictures As option is set to In Line With Text, as you see here.

To set a graphic to the In Line With Text layout, first select the graphic. Then, on the Picture Tools Format tab (or the applicable contextual Format tab for the selected graphic), click Text Wrapping and then click In Line With Text. Note that text wrapping options are also available from the shortcut menu when you right-click a graphic.

As mentioned earlier, graphics that use this layout option can be formatted as easily as text. For example, apply center or right paragraph alignment to move the graphic horizontally on the page. Paragraph indents and spacing before or after the paragraph can also come in handy when positioning graphics. In fact, if you have a lot of graphics in your document and want them all formatted consistently, it's a good idea to create a paragraph style for your graphics just as you would for text that you want to keep consistent throughout the document.

> **Note**
>
> In addition to paragraph formatting, when you have a graphic in the body of a paragraph, you can use character spacing position (raised or lowered) to adjust the selected graphic vertically on the line of text. To access character spacing position, on the Home tab, in the Font group, click the dialog launcher to open the Font dialog box and then click the Character Spacing tab.

Recognizing Graphic Layout

In recent versions of Word, it was easy to distinguish a graphic formatted to be in line with text from a floating graphic, either by the handles when the graphic is selected or by the mouse pointer when hovering over the graphic. That's no longer the case, but there are still visual cues you can use to quickly identify whether a graphic is floating or sitting in line with text.

If you're viewing all formatting marks, you can see the object anchor (shown beside this paragraph) that appears for any floating object other than a frame. The anchor may appear in the margin to the left of a paragraph, or it may appear inside the perimeter of the object, usually in the top-right corner. If you're not viewing all formatting marks, or you're not comfortable with this method, remember that Text Wrapping is an option when you right-click most types of graphics, so you can just right-click and then point to Text Wrapping to see the setting.

- Though the handles of selected object no longer differ based on layout (except in legacy documents), it's still good to know what you can learn about a graphic from the handles you see when the object is selected. Any 2007 release drawing object that uses the new graphics engine, such as charts, SmartArt graphics, or shapes pasted into Word from PowerPoint using the default paste method, have a new type of border and handles when selected, as you see in the following image.

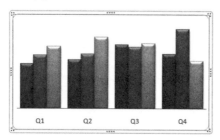

This border is pale blue regardless of your color scheme, and the handles are the series of dots on each side of the object as well as at its corners.

- Pictures have round handles at the corners and square handles on each side, as you see in the following image, with the green rotation handle attached to the top picture handle.

Despite the fact that these handles look very similar to floating objects in the previous version of Word, they are now the same for pictures formatted to sit in line with text, including the rotation handle.

- Graphics created directly in Word that don't use the new graphics engine, such as shapes and WordArt, have handles very similar to the previous version. Shapes have similar handles to pictures, but they're blue. WordArt is formatted as in line with text by default, and has similar handles to graphics in earlier versions of Word that were formatted to be in line with text, as you see here.

Your Text Here

- Legacy Word documents provide similar handles to the previous version, with floating graphics using the blue handles now used by shapes in Word, and graphics formatted to be in line with text using the same handles you see for WordArt in the preceding image.

> **Note**
> Embedded or linked objects from some programs, such as Visio, use the same handles as legacy documents even in Word documents created using the new file formats.

One of the most useful things about knowing what type of handles belong to certain object types is that it enables you to know at a glance whether a graphic is a picture or an object.

Using Table Cells as Graphic Placeholders

As discussed in Chapter 6, tables are the perfect layout tool for complex page layouts, such as when you need graphics beside text, tables, or other graphics. When you use a table cell as a placeholder for a graphic, you can also save time and avoid trial and error by using the dimensions of that cell to size your graphic perfectly before you even paste it into Word.

For example, if you have a cell that is 4 inches wide by 2 inches tall, you can precisely size a chart in Excel before copying it. In Excel, on the Chart Tools Format tab, just type the Word table cell dimensions in the Size group, as you see here.

SmartArt diagrams offer the same sizing option, so it's easy to get that diagram into Word when you create it in PowerPoint.

Though the Format contextual tab for any graphic type provides this Size group, keep in mind that many graphic types don't adjust automatically when resized (as charts or SmartArt diagrams do) and may distort when resized (such as a group of shapes). In such cases, either constrain proportions before resizing or use the Word table cell size to set drawing guides on the PowerPoint slide within which you can create your graphic to size. Learn about working with drawing guides in Chapter 18, "Creating Professional Presentation Graphics."

CAUTION

Using the Size group to resize objects is a nice timesaver. However, double-check the size after pasting in Word, as minor corrections might need to be made. There appears to be a small glitch in this new functionality, and size settings may not always hold perfectly. However, it still pays to resize the graphics in the originating program, because this bug will only cause a minor shift in size if any.

Note

To constrain proportions in PowerPoint before resizing a drawing object, launch the Size And Position dialog box from the Size group of the Drawing Tools Format tab, and then select Lock Aspect Ratio.

Formatting Pictures

Use the following best practice guidelines to tweak the pictures you insert into your Word documents to perfection, using the groups available on the Picture Tools Format tab. Then, learn more about formatting graphics, including some of the features available on the Picture Tools Format tab, in Chapter 18.

- The Adjust group, shown in the preceding image, includes many feature that might be familiar from the Picture toolbar in previous versions of Word.
  - Use Brightness and Contrast options to adjust picture tone and clarity (such as lightening a dark image).
  - Though Compress Pictures can sometimes save you a bit of file size, for better compression results, see the Troubleshooting tip earlier in this chapter titled "I Need to Convert a Graphic to Another Picture Type."
  - Reset Picture can be a handy tool, because it resets the picture to its original state when inserted or pasted into Word, before you applied any customizations. For example, sizing, cropping, and recoloring information added after pasting the picture will be removed.

Note

Reset is also an available option in the Size dialog box, available from the Size group. When you use the Reset option in the dialog box, only size and cropping information is reset; picture formatting (such as Picture Styles) is retained.

In addition to features you are likely to have used before in Word, Recolor Picture is an option that was previously only available in PowerPoint. In the 2007 Office release programs, it's available for all pictures, but the feature has been signifi-cantly simplified. You can no longer select specific color changes for each color in the picture. Instead, this feature now incorporates previous color changes (such as grayscale and washout) that were available to all pictures in earlier versions, and includes the option to set a single hue to be used throughout the picture (cre-ating a color wash over the image). Note also that the Set Transparent Color op-tion is now located under Recolor Picture options.

Early in this chapter, I mentioned the Change Picture feature as well as the ability to swap a picture in the XML, both of which retain some size, positioning, and formatting information for the new picture. Change Picture is available from the Adjust group, or when you right-click a Picture. To use this feature, with the pic-ture selected, click Change Picture, and then select a different image.

When you use Change Picture, the image is swapped, but position and picture style formatting are retained, as well as some sizing information. Because picture sizing is proportional by default, when you switch the picture for one of a differ-ent size, it will be resized to match the height or the width of the original picture.

If you use the XML instead to swap the file (as explained in Chapter 22), there are some differences in behavior. First, exact size is retained by default, so images with different proportions might distort (you can change the size settings in the XML as well to avoid this, or correct the new image once you open the document). Also, if the same image is used multiple times in the same document (such as a logo in the header as well as on the cover page of a report), replacing the file once in the XML replaces all instances of the image that appear in the document. The Change Picture feature, however, only replaces the selected instance of an image.

- The Picture Styles group shown in the preceding image includes Quick Styles for picture formatting that can be very interesting. These styles can be used with graphics formatted to be in line with text, which gives you more design flexibil-ity without compromising ease of use. Note also that you can use Picture Border and Picture Effects tools on their own or in conjunction with a style, and that the dialog launcher in this group opens the Format Picture dialog box, for additional formatting options.

One of the most fun new features, however, is the Picture Shape tool, which enables you to choose from the collection of drawing shapes to apply a shape to the picture, as you see in the following example.

It's important to note here that the graphic remains a picture when you do this and does not become a drawing shape.

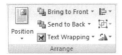

- The Arrange group (shown in the preceding image) appears in similar form on several tabs, as mentioned earlier. When you format pictures to be in line with text, most of these options are not available. Therefore, Arrange tools will be covered in more detail in Chapter 18, when we address how to use drawing tools effectively.

Note

If you must overlap a graphic with other content, the best text wrapping choice is Behind Text. This keeps the graphic relatively easy to manage because you are less likely to accidentally select it. Behind Text is also the setting to use when placing a graphic in the header and footer layer to act as a watermark, as discussed in Chapter 8, "Sections."

However, when you use this text wrapping option, the graphic might be difficult to select. To easily select a graphic formatted to sit behind text, on the Home tab, in the Editing group, click Select, and then click Select Object. This action changes your mouse pointer so that it will ignore content on the text layer and enable you to easily select any object with text wrapping enabled.

- When you use the Size group, shown in the preceding image and introduced earlier for sizing other graphic types, pictures are proportionally resized by default. So, you can apply either a height or a width setting and the other setting will adjust automatically to constrain proportions. To resize pictures without constraining proportions, click the dialog launcher in this group for the Size dialog box, which provides additional options.

- To use the Crop tool, click Crop and then drag any handle to crop from whatever direction you need. When finished cropping, either click Crop again to turn off the tool, or press ESC. To set specific crop measurements instead of dragging to crop, click the dialog launcher in this group and add cropping measurements in the Size dialog box.

INSIDE OUT   Use the Crop tool to add space around a graphic

You've probably used the Crop tool to crop parts of a picture, but how about to add to a picture? Cropping out from a graphic adds space around the graphic. To do this, just drag away from the picture from any crop handle, or type negative crop values in the Size dialog box.

Using Text Boxes

Text boxes, because they're always a floating graphic, are something I recommend avoiding in Word documents to keep your work as simple as possible. However, though they can be more complicated to manage than graphics formatted to be in line with text, text boxes are also the least likely floating graphic type to cause complications in your document.

As mentioned earlier, never put a floating graphic behind or in front of a table. However, other than that limitation, if you need text to float because it needs to overlap or wrap around other content, text boxes in Word 2007 are easier than ever to use and manage. Several types of text boxes are available for uses such as page sidebars in the Text Box Quick Parts gallery, available on the Insert tab. Learn more about these and other Quick Parts galleries in Chapter 9.

Keep in mind, however, that paragraph formatting and tables are both simpler solutions than floating graphics whenever it's possible to use them for the formatting you need. So, for example, if you simply need formatting such as a border around text, or a formatted block of text between columns of text, be sure that you're using the simplest option available.

TROUBLESHOOTING

Why should I avoid using frames?

When you must have content that wraps around or overlaps text, a text box is a better solution than a text frame. Frames are used for a number of features, such as Drop Cap or text wrap around tables, and they are also available to be included in paragraph styles. However, it's common for documents containing frames to be more difficult to manage.

Fortunately, frames are less prevalent in Word 2007 than in previous versions. However, if you experience unidentified trouble in a document, check for content in frames and delete the frame where possible. You can then place content in table cells for layout, or in text boxes if the layout requires a floating object.

A frame is easy to recognize when you click inside it or select it, because of its unique border and handles, as shown here.

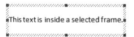

When you click inside a frame, the border appears thatched and with no handles. When the frame is selected, the border is still thatched, but with square handles at the sides and corners.

To remove a frame, right-click the frame border, select Format Frame, and then click Remove Frame. Note, however, that frames embedded in some features—such as Drop Caps—can't be accessed in this way. To remove the frame in these cases, turn off the feature that includes the frame.

Note that when used with text wrap around tables, the frame is invisible. However, the frame often becomes visible after the table corrupts. In these cases, you can use the preceding instructions to remove the frame.

Sections

Need a landscape page in the middle of a portrait document? Want automatically updating information in your headers and footers? Perhaps you'd like footnotes to restart numbering for each new topic?

From page borders, to watermarks, to text columns, to page orientation, section formatting can be one of the easiest components to manage in Microsoft Word documents. Ironically, it's also one of the most common areas where people get frustrated.

If you're among the many Microsoft Word users who has ever experienced stress from section breaks, headers and footers that appeared to change against your will, page orientation that refused to change at all, or any section formatting frustration, now would be a good time to take a deep, cleansing breath. There's a reason, and a simple solution, for just about any of the above.

Chapter Assumptions

As advanced users, I assume you know how to apply basic section formatting features, such as changing page margins or orientation, or inserting a footnote. I also assume you know the basics of what section breaks are and that you have used them before.

Instead of spending time on these basics, this chapter will focus on understanding how section formatting works so that you can manage all types of section formatting more easily. In addition to best practices, we'll look at common section formatting trouble spots, such as changing section break type and managing the Link To Previous feature in headers and footers.

In the introduction to this book, you can find a list of resources for those who want more basic-level information, in the section titled "Who Will Benefit Most from This Book."

What's New For Section Formatting in Word 2007

The essentials of section formatting are unchanged from earlier versions of Microsoft Word. You still insert a section break wherever you need to change page layout formatting for just part of the document. Section breaks still store formatting for the section that precedes the break, and the types of formatting stored in a section break (detailed in the next part of this chapter) are the same as in recent versions.

The primary changes for section formatting, like many features in the 2007 Microsoft Office release, are the methods by which you can access features as well as new options for some features. In the case of section formatting, these changes are particularly significant with the addition of several timesaving galleries and integration with the powerful new Building Blocks functionality, introduced in the list that follows.

- You'll now find common section formatting commands, as well as access to section breaks, in the Page Setup group on the Page Layout tab, shown here. Click the dialog launcher in that group to open the Page Setup dialog box, which is largely unchanged from the previous version.

> **Note**
>
> Notice the inclusion of Hyphenation, which is not section formatting, in the Page Setup group on the Page Layout tab. Hyphenation can only be applied to the entire document and is not affected by section breaks.
>
> The ability to exempt paragraphs from hyphenation, however, is paragraph level formatting and can be included in paragraph styles. To exclude paragraphs or paragraph styles from hyphenation, in the Paragraph dialog box, on the Line And Page Breaks tab, click Don't Hyphenate.

- When your insertion point is in a header, footer, or watermark, you get the Header & Footer Tools Design contextual tab, shown here.

    Notice the Insert Alignment Tab option in the Position group. This option is addressed in the Troubleshooting tip titled "I have trouble aligning content in the header or footer," later in this chapter.

- There's one small but quite nice new timesaver available for accessing headers and footers. From Print Layout view, you can still double-click in the header or footer area to open the header or footer layer. Unlike in previous versions, this method will work in Microsoft Office Word 2007 whether or not content already exists in the header or footer being accessed.

Additionally, you can now also right-click the header or footer area when working in Print Layout view for the option to edit the header or footer.

- Many of the settings in the Page Setup group provide quick-access galleries, such as the Margins gallery shown here. Clicking Custom Margins here, or the customization option at the bottom of any similar gallery, will open the applicable dialog box for the feature.

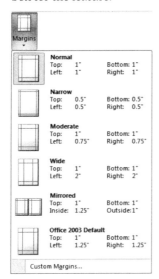

- Building Block galleries for section-level formatting include Header, Footer, Page Numbering, and Watermark. Find the Header & Footer group, shown here, on the Insert tab. The Page Background group (containing the Watermark gallery), also shown here, is on the Page Layout tab.

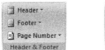

Additionally, the new Cover Page gallery, shown in the following image, appears on the Insert tab. Cover Page Building Blocks interact with the Different First Page header and footer for the first section of your document.

Chapter 8

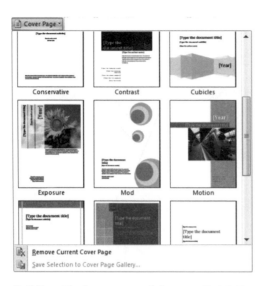

Building Blocks are part of the new Quick Parts technology, a broad new capability in Office Word 2007 that's discussed in detail in Chapter 9, "Quick Parts." When you use Building Blocks, you can change the entire design of a document element (such as a header, footer, or cover page) instantly, while leaving your content intact. In addition to section-related Building Block galleries, Building Blocks are available for many document components. Learn more about this new capability, including how to save and share custom Building Blocks, in Chapter 9.

> **Note**
>
> In the Page Background tab, Watermarks (which reside in the header and footer layer) and Page Borders are both section formatting, but Page Color is not. Page Color is a setting primarily intended for Web pages. Formatting applied from this option (previously known as Page Background) applies to the entire document and does not print by default.
>
> To print a document with the Page Color formatting visible, on the Display tab of the Word Options dialog box, under the heading Print Options, select Print Background Colors And Images. You can access this option either through the Word Options dialog box or through the Options button in the Print dialog box. Keep in mind that this setting is not document-specific. If you enable it to print just one document, disable it after printing to avoid printing page color settings for other documents.

Are You Sure You Need a Section Break?

One of the quickest and most common ways to overcomplicate your document formatting is to use too many section breaks. Remember, a section break stores the formatting for the section that precedes it. So, every break you insert is another set of formatting you add to the document.

That's not to say that using section breaks is bad at all. Like many features, section breaks are a useful, simple, and stable solution when used properly. After all, the ability to change page layout formatting for just part of the document is an essential component of most complex documents and even some that aren't so complex. So, don't hesitate to use section breaks in any instance where you know they're the simplest solution for the task.

Formatting Changes That Require a Section Break

So, when is a section break necessary? The table that follows tells you when a section break is required to change the formatting for just part of the document.

A section break is required	A section break might be required
Page margins	Headers, footers, and watermarks
Page orientation	Restarting footnote, endnote, and line numbering
Paper size	
Paper source (that is, printer tray)	
Vertical alignment of the entire page	
Page borders	
Page, footnote, or endnote number format	
Text columns	

The items in the second column of the preceding table are most definitely section formatting, but they offer some options that don't require a section break, as follows.

- There are four types of headers and footers, and each section can display as many as three of those. Note also that watermarks are included in the preceding table reference because watermarks are inserted on the header and footer layer, so they're part of headers and footers. To figure out when to use a different type of header or footer instead of adding a new section, see "Using Headers and Footers" later in this chapter.

- Footnote, endnote, and line numbering can all be restarted either by page or by section. Note, however, that suppressing line numbering for a portion of the document does require a section break.

Chapter 8

> **Note**
>
> Those who have used footnotes and endnotes quite a bit in previous versions will likely have noticed that if you restart footnotes in one section, you can't have them continue that numbering in the next section. When you set Continue for the new section, it continues counting from the total number of footnotes or endnotes in the document, not just the preceding section. Well, that nasty little bug has been fixed, and footnote or endnote numbering set to be continuous will now continue correctly from the previous section, even if the previous section restarted numbering.

When Not to Use a Section Break

If it isn't listed in the preceding table, it doesn't require a section break in Word. Some common examples of unnecessary section break use follow.

- When you just need to start a new page, do not use a section break. Use a page break (CTRL+ENTER) or Page Break Before paragraph formatting. Page breaks and section breaks are never interchangeable. A section break adds a set of formatting to the document, a page break is nothing but a nonprinting character and stores no formatting.

- Starting a new multilevel list or list style doesn't ever require a section break. This is paragraph-level formatting.

- Inserting a table or a graphic object never requires a section break.

- Inserting reference tables, such as tables of contents or indexes, never requires a section break. The reason it's common to see section breaks before or after reference tables is that it's common to use unique page number formatting for pages containing reference tables (such as lowercase roman numerals). It's the page number format change, and not the reference table, that requires the section break.

> **Note**
>
> In versions of Word prior to 2003, a section break was required to change document protection settings for just part of the document, but that is no longer the case.

In addition to the preceding examples, people often use section formatting where a simpler solution exists. Consider the following examples.

- If you need text in multiple columns on a portion of the page, but the text does not need to wrap from one column to the next, a table is a much simpler solution than text columns, because a table requires no section breaks.

- If you need to change margins for just a few paragraphs, changing paragraph indents is much simpler than changing page margins. Indents are paragraph formatting, so they can be stored in a style. And, paragraph formatting never requires a section break.

In a contrasting example, say that a table is too wide for a portrait page. In that case, using a section break to change page orientation for the page containing the table is most likely the best solution (unless the content of the table can be reduced in size without affecting readability). If instead, for example, you took a screen shot of the table and then pasted it back into the document as a picture so that you could rotate it on its side, that would be a far more complicated solution than a simple section break.

INSIDE OUT Page breaks vs. page break before formatting

If you have a paragraph style that is always used as a page heading (for example, this is a common use of the Heading 1 style), apply Page Break Before formatting to the style instead of inserting page break formatting marks.

Keep in mind that a formatting mark such as a page break, even though it doesn't store formatting like a section break does, is in fact a character. It's not formatting. When you can create the same effect with paragraph formatting that can be stored in a style (such as Page Break Before formatting), you help keep your document easy to edit. If, for example, you decide later not to have a page break before each instance of the Heading 1 style, removing Page Break Before formatting is easier and faster than finding each page break and deleting it, even if you use the Replace feature to do so.

To apply Page Break Before formatting, on the Home tab or Page Layout tab, in the Paragraph group, click the dialog launcher to open the Paragraph dialog box. On the Line And Page Breaks tab, click Page Break Before. Notice that when you apply Page Break Before formatting (or any pagination options from the Line And Page Breaks tab), a small black square appears outside the left margin on any paragraph to which this formatting is applied. This is a nonprinting character, or formatting mark, that indicates pagination formatting is applied.

As introduced in Chapter 1, "Welcome to the 2007 Microsoft Office System," and discussed in detail in Chapter 4, "Building Easy-to-Manage, Robust Documents," the simplest solution is always best. Though you should never put anything in the document that doesn't need to be there (such as an unnecessary section break), don't be afraid to use the capabilities of the software. For more on how to determine the simplest solution for any task, see Chapter 4.

Keeping Sections Simple

Rule number one: When you're working with section breaks, work with formatting marks visible. If you can't see section breaks, you can't manage them effectively. To turn on formatting marks, press CTRL+*. (Note that the asterisk on the number keypad does not work for this shortcut.)

When viewing formatting marks, a complete section break looks like the image that follows.

==Section Break (Next Page)==

Note that because there are different types of section breaks (discussed later in this section), the break type (such as Next Page, shown in the preceding graphic) might vary, but your section breaks will otherwise look like this.

I've often heard people say that they tried to change page orientation, paper size, or other section formatting for part of the document, but the formatting they changed was applied to the wrong part of the document. This is not a bug. If this has happened to you, your insertion point was simply in the wrong section of the document.

> **Note**
>
> It's also helpful to keep track of which section you're currently working in by viewing the section number on the Status bar. If you don't see Section: # toward the left side of the status bar, right-click the Status bar and then click Section to add this option.

Keep in mind that section breaks can be partly or entirely hidden after a paragraph mark when viewing the document in Print Layout view. A partially hidden section break might look something like the image shown here. The section break in this case is the double line that follows the paragraph mark.

¶············

If you can't see section breaks easily, view the document in Draft view. Section breaks (as well as page and column breaks) always appear fully across the page in Draft view. When working with section formatting, it can be helpful to switch back and forth between Draft view and Print Layout view, so that you can see section breaks (in Draft view) and the page layout formatting those breaks enable (in Print Layout view) as needed. In addition to using the View tab or the view shortcuts on the Status bar to switch between these views, the keyboard shortcut CTRL+ALT+P changes your view to Print Layout, and CTRL+ALT+N changes your view to Draft.

Keeping an eye on your section breaks, however, is just one component of keeping section formatting simple. The key to managing sections easily is to understand how section formatting is stored.

Understanding How Section Formatting Is Stored

A section break stores the formatting for the section that precedes it. So, if a section break is deleted, section formatting applied to the section that preceded that break will change to match whatever section formatting is stored in the next available break. Note that in a single-section document, section formatting is stored in the last paragraph mark. Learn more about the significance of the last paragraph mark in the Troubleshooting tip in this section, titled "What do I need to know about the Last Paragraph Mark?"

Take the following sample pages, for example. As you can see in this two-section document, section one uses portrait orientation and section two uses landscape orientation. If the section break between these sections is removed, will the entire document become portrait or landscape?

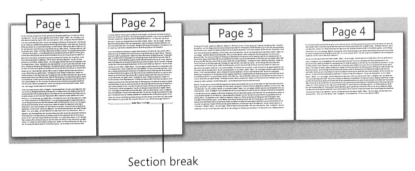

Section break

If you answered landscape, you're correct. When you delete the section break that follows the portrait section, you delete the portrait orientation setting that was stored in that section break. The pages that were in the section before the break become part of the next section (the only remaining section, in this case) when the break is deleted.

CAUTION!

Before deleting any section break, take note of all differences in section formatting between the sections before and after the break. Remember that, after you delete a break, *all* section formatting in the section that preceded the break will revert to the formatting saved in the section that followed the break.

TROUBLESHOOTING

What do I need to know about the last paragraph mark?

The last paragraph mark in the document stores section formatting for a single-section document or for the last section of a multi-section document.

If you copy the last section of the document and paste it into another document, you can see that the results vary significantly depending on whether that last paragraph mark is included in your selection. If you copy the section including that paragraph mark, section formatting (such as headers and footers) is retained. Without that paragraph mark, it's not.

That paragraph mark also stores some information for the overall document, which has led over the years to a common misunderstanding about how to remove corruption from a document. The widely-held perception that copying the document without that last paragraph mark removes document integrity corruption is incorrect. Unless the corruption is related to something stored in that paragraph mark, all you do by leaving the paragraph mark out of the document when copying is to blind Word to the fact that the corruption exists. That paragraph mark might have stored the information that the document was aware of an error, but it didn't necessarily contain the error. So, you can bet that error will resurface.

As explained in Chapter 4, use Open And Repair for far quicker, easier, and effective results when endeavoring to repair integrity errors in a document.

To change any section formatting, simply place your insertion point directly before the location where you want the change to start and then do the following.

1. On the Page Layout tab, in the Page Setup group, click Break and then click the section break type that you need. Because most section formatting changes require a new page (such as page orientation or headers and footers), Next Page is the most frequently used section break type.

2. Place your insertion point anywhere after the section break. Then, change the section formatting you need to change.

INSIDE OUT   Choosing where to apply section formatting

Pay attention to the Apply To list that appears in most dialog boxes used for section formatting commands, such as Page Setup or the Page Borders tab of the Borders And Shading dialog box. If you have content selected, instead of a blinking insertion point, the default Apply To option might be different.

Whether or not you're using a dialog box to apply section formatting, your selection can affect the result. For example, if you have text selected when you apply text columns, section breaks will be inserted before and after your selection and the new text column setting will only be applied to the selected content. Notice that, in such a situation, you don't have to add a section break before changing the formatting. Word does this for you.

In dialog boxes that offer an Apply To list, you can also let Word add section breaks for you. Instead of inserting a section break and then changing formatting, open the dialog box for the formatting you want to change. For example, open the Page Setup dialog box to change page orientation. When you do, change the Apply To setting to This Point Forward, change page orientation, and click OK. A Next Page section break will be inserted and your page orientation will be changed following the break. Alternatively, if you select a portion of the document before opening the dialog box, you can change the Apply To setting to Selected Text. When you do that, similar to the text columns change, section breaks will be added both before and after your selection and only the content between the breaks will take on the new formatting.

Note that text columns are the only feature for which section breaks are automatically added around your selection when you choose a new setting from the gallery. For other section formatting features, you can only have Word insert your section break automatically when you use the Apply To setting in the applicable dialog box.

Understanding Section Break Types

There are four types of section breaks, as listed in the portion of the Breaks gallery shown here. Further information about each of these section break types is provided in the list that follows.

- A Next Page section break, as mentioned earlier, is the most common type of section break. This break starts the new section on a new page.

- A Continuous section break starts the new section immediately after the break. Though section formatting that requires a new page will still start on the next page when this break type is used, for best results use Next Page section breaks for this type of formatting. If, for example, you use a Continuous section break when you need a new header, if the document uses Different First Page headers and footers, those will not appear for the new section because the first page of the new section is not a complete page. Continuous section breaks are most often used with the text columns feature.

- Odd Page and Even Page section breaks start the new section on a new page, but they force that section to start on either an odd or an even page, respectively. These options are designed primarily for book-style formatting, such as where you might want each new chapter to begin on a right-hand (odd) page. To learn more about creating book-style formatting, see the last section in this chapter.

As explained earlier, a section break stores formatting for the section that precedes the break. However, information about the type of section break is stored in the section that follows the break. This is because the type of section break actually refers to the way the section after the break starts, known in Word as Section Start type.

So, to change the section break type for an existing section break in your document, do the following.

1. Place your insertion point after the break you want to change. It can be anywhere in the section that follows the break.

2. On the Page Layout tab, in the Page Setup group, click the dialog launcher to open the Page Setup dialog box, and then click the Layout tab.

3. In the Section Start list, change the setting to the break type you want. For example, to change a Continuous break to a Next Page break, select New Page as the Section Start type and then click OK.

TROUBLESHOOTING

Why does Word change section break type for existing breaks?

You inserted a Next Page section break, you know you did. So, why is that break now a Continuous section break? Well, you might be surprised to know that you told Word to do this. Section Start type, as explained earlier in this section, is managed in the section that follows the break. So, if the break following the break in question is deleted, the section takes on the start type of the next section. For example, if you delete a Continuous section break, the Next Page section break that preceded it will become a Continuous break.

When this happens, just use the steps given in this chapter for changing section break type. Note that, if the section break ignores the change, it's most likely because formatting in the section that follows the break will not allow the change. For example, if a Continuous break becomes a Next Page section break and you then change the page orientation of the section that follows the break, Word will not allow you to change that section break back to a continuous break. This is because you cannot change page orientation in the middle of a page.

Using Headers and Footers

As introduced earlier, a Word document contains four types of headers and footers. In addition to the regular header and footer, First Page, Odd Page, and Even Page headers and footers are available to your document.

> **Note**
>
> Unique first-page formatting is also available for page borders, as you can see in the Apply To list available on the Page Borders tab of the Borders And Shading dialog box, shown here.
>
>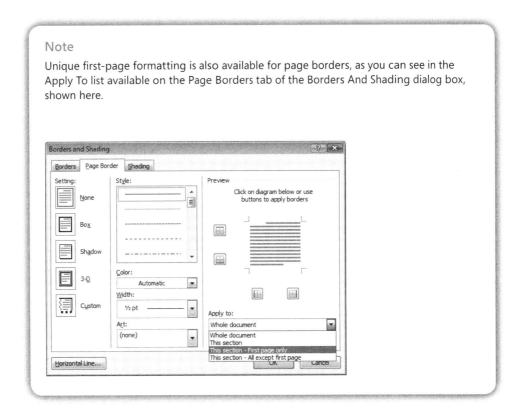

To add a header or footer to your Word document, on the Insert tab, click Header or Footer as applicable, and then either click to insert one of the available Building Block designs or click Edit Header (or Edit Footer) to open the header and footer layer, where you can add a custom header or footer. As discussed earlier, to edit the header or footer, you can also double-click (or right-click) in the header or footer area from Print Layout view. Note that, if you insert a Building Block, the header or footer will open automatically so that you can add content or edit the design.

TROUBLESHOOTING

I have trouble aligning content in the header or footer

When your insertion point is in a header or footer, notice that the Header and Footer paragraph styles still contain the antiquated center and right tab stops. The problem with these tab stops is that, if margins or page orientation change, the tabs do not move. So, for example, a center tab that's placed in the center of the page for default margins is no longer in the center of the page when the margins are changed. To keep your formatting as clean and easy as possible, remove these tab stops from the styles in the document template, so that you don't have to fuss with them in new documents. Get help for doing this in Chapter 5, "Styles."

The Header & Footer Tools Design tab has a new option called Insert Alignment Tab, which enables you to use tab characters to center and right align text. These characters keep the text centered or right-aligned when margins or orientation change. When you use alignment tabs, you see no tab stop on the ruler or in the Style Inspector. Even if you update the paragraph style after applying an alignment tab, you still see no information related to this tab. That's because alignment tabs are nonprinting characters and not formatting at all. (Note that the ScreenTip for the Insert Alignment Tab feature incorrectly states that the feature adds a tab stop.)

The upside to using alignment tabs is that, if you have sections with different margins or orientation that include headers or footers using Link To Previous, the content will be correctly aligned for each section without turning off Link To Previous and independently aligning content. The downside is that, because alignment tabs aren't stored in a paragraph style like formatting or visible on the ruler, they might be a bit confusing to document editors.

To insert an alignment tab, click Insert Alignment Tab, select your preferences from the options shown here, and then click OK. A tab character will be added at your insertion point. When using alignment tabs, it's particularly important to remove the default center and right tabs to avoid user confusion.

If you don't need to link headers and footers between sections with different orientation or page margins, using a simple table to left, center, and right-align content on the same line in a header or footer is still the simplest and best solution. In a table, you can position content in left, center, and right cells independently both horizontally and vertically, for more flexibility. A table is also a well-known object type that users can easily edit. Learn about how to set up a table for use in headers and footers in Chapter 6, "Tables."

Many components within Header, Footer, or Page Number Building Blocks are contained in Content Controls, a new type of object available to Word documents. Content Controls are similar to, but tremendously more powerful and flexible than, form controls. For example, the placeholder for the document title, as shown here, is inside a Content Control.

Title
[Type·the·document·title]

When you point to the field, the control appears as a blue box surrounding the field. When your insertion point is inside the Content Control, you can also see the name of the control, as you do in the preceding image. Learn more about the role of Content Controls in various Building Blocks in Chapter 9, and get the full scoop on Content Controls in Chapter 11, "Content Controls: Creating Forms and Then Some."

Many built-in header and footer Building Blocks also use text boxes or floating graphic objects (that is, graphic objects that use Text Wrapping settings other than In Line With Text). Do not confuse floating graphics with Content Controls. Whereas Content Controls are beneficial to your documents, floating graphic objects can make your document more difficult to manage. Consider if the formatting you want can be accomplished with a table or with graphics formatted in line with text, before using one of these built-in options that contains floating graphics. To learn more about reasons to avoid floating objects in your documents, see Chapter 7, "Managing Graphics."

TROUBLESHOOTING

What pitfalls can I avoid when adding page numbers?

Though there is a Page Number gallery available, both from the Insert tab and from the Header & Footer Tools Design contextual tab, be careful which options you select from this gallery.

In previous versions of Word, the Page Numbers option on the Insert menu was to be avoided, because page numbers were inserted inside text frames. (Find a Troubleshooting tip in Chapter 7 that addresses key issues with frames.) In Word, frames are fortunately no longer used for page numbers. However, several built-in page number Building Blocks, just like many of the header and footer Building Blocks discussed earlier, insert the page number inside a text box or other floating shape. Although not as diabolical as frames by any means, a text box is still a floating object that your document probably doesn't need. If your intent is to place the page number in the header or footer, there is unlikely to be a reason to use a text box. So, unless you need to take advantage of the page number Building Blocks options that add the page numbering outside of the page margins, avoid built-in options that insert the page number inside a floating object. Remember that if your page number field is *not* inside a floating object, you can format it just like any document text—such as by centering or right aligning the page number by changing paragraph alignment.

Chapter 8

To add a page number at your insertion point (such as in an open header or footer), you can insert one of the simple page number options from the Page Number gallery (or any option that doesn't use floating objects to position the page number), or you can create the field yourself. To create the field, type the word **PAGE** and then select it. Press CTRL+F9, followed by F9. The first keyboard shortcut turns the text into a field and the second updates that field to show the correct result.

Regardless of how you insert page numbers, customize page number formatting through the Page Number Format dialog box. At the bottom of the Page Number gallery, click Format Page Numbers to open this dialog box, where you can change number format, set numbering to restart or continue with each new section, or set a specific Start At value for the active section.

Managing Different First Page and Different Odd & Even Headers and Footers

When you need a unique header or footer just for the first page of a document or section of a document, you usually don't need to add a section break. On the Header & Footer Tools Design contextual tab, in the Options group, just click Different First Page. This option will enable you to have an additional header and footer for just the first page of the active section.

Note

Though it's not technically necessary to add a section break when you need a unique header or footer for just the first page of a document or section, consider your content. If the first page of the section is clearly separate content (such as a single-page chapter of a book), it might be more logical to use a section break rather than the Different First Page option. In the example given here, that single-page chapter could grow longer, in which case the first page header and footer would no longer be a good solution. Additionally, if you have section breaks between most chapters, you might prefer to put one here as well for consistency, to make the formatting more intuitive to other editors.

Similarly, when you need different headers and footers for odd and even pages (such as book-style formatting that requires headers and footers to appear on the outside of all pages), find the Different Odd & Even Pages option directly below Different First Page in the Options group on the Header & Footer Tools Design tab. Unlike Different First Page, however, Different Odd & Even Pages can only be enabled or disabled for the document, not for individual sections.

Note that the Odd Page header and footer and the regular header and footer are actually one and the same. When Different Odd & Even Pages is enabled, the regular header and footer content becomes Odd Page header and footer content. If this option is disabled, Odd Page header and footer content becomes the regular header and footer content.

You can recognize the type of header or footer that's active by the name of the header or footer on the tabs that appear at the bottom of headers and the top of footers in Word. For example, in the image that follows, my insertion point is inside a First Page header.

Notice that the tab indicates the type of header or footer as well as the section number.

> **Note**
>
> There's a labeling error on the Header & Footer Tools Design contextual tab that warrants noting. In the Navigation group on that tab, the Next Section and Previous Section buttons actually mean next or previous header or footer. These buttons are the same as the Next and Previous buttons on the Header And Footer toolbar in previous versions, moving one header or footer at a time through the document.

TROUBLESHOOTING

What happens to header and footer content when I disable that header or footer?

If you add content to a header or footer and then disable it in the document, that content remains stored in the document. So, if you later enable that header and footer again, the content will once again appear.

Although in some ways, this is a good thing, there are important issues to consider.

- If the header or footer contains sensitive information, you might want to delete the content before sharing the document.

- If the document is copied and changed for another use, the original headers and footers that were disabled are still stored. If users of the new document are not aware of this, inappropriate content can be left in the document. For example, if the header contained a client's logo and you then copied the document for use on another client's project, leaving the previous client's logo in the hidden headers and footers could prove embarrassing when the document is shared.

- When errors occur in the document, it's common to forget that hidden header and footer content might exist. For example, say that your document crashes, and so you open it using the Open And Repair feature. The Show Repairs dialog box tells you that there's a text box or other error caused by a floating object, but you see no floating objects in your document. The first thing to check is whether the document has hidden headers and footers.

Headers and footers can be disabled in several ways. You might turn off the Different First Page or Different Odd & Even Pages settings. Or, if a section with these settings enabled is only a page (or less) in length, some or all of the headers or footers for the section will be hidden. For example, if a section is less than a page long, its headers and footers don't appear on screen in any view, but they are still resident in the document. When pages are added to the section, the appropriate header or footer then appears.

Understanding Link To Previous

The Link To Previous feature, which also appears on header and footer tabs as Same As Previous, has been the scourge of many a document. As it happens, this feature has no bugs; nothing at all wrong with it. But, if you don't understand what it's doing, it is quite likely to drive you mad.

Here's the theory: Just because you start a new section doesn't mean you want a new header or footer. It's common to need the same header and footer throughout a document that contains several section breaks for reasons such as page orientation or page border changes. So, to save you work, headers and footers default to be linked. That way, if you change the header in one section, it automatically changes in every connected section where Link To Previous is enabled.

Here's the reality: You forget that Link To Previous is enabled, and you change the header or footer for the new section. So, the change is also made in the previous section, and you might not even realize it until later, when all of your headers and footers are a mess.

So, what do you do? It's just a matter of making a habit to check for the Same As Previous tab on the right side of headers or footers, as you see in the header example shown here.

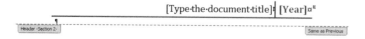

But, there's a catch. You can see that the active header or footer doesn't show the Same As Previous tab, but that doesn't mean that the next header or footer isn't linked to the one you're about to change. Before making changes, make it a habit to scroll through headers and footers both before and after the existing header and footer to check for Same As Previous.

Also note that newly added sections or newly added headers and footers within sections will always have Link To Previous enabled. So, if you turn off Link To Previous throughout your document and later add a new section, be sure to once again check for Link To Previous before making header or footer changes.

> **Note**
>
> Keep in mind that Link To Previous is managed separately for each header and each footer. If you turn off Link To Previous for a given header, the corresponding footer is not changed.

INSIDE OUT **Undo unwanted changes in headers and footers without excess work**

When you do accidentally change headers and footers that are linked, you don't have to undo and then recreate everything you just changed. Just copy the changed content before you undo the changes (press CTRL+Z to undo). Then, after you turn off Link To Previous, you can just paste the copied content into only that header or footer where you want it to appear.

The clipboard is not cleared when you undo actions, so the content you copied before undoing the change remains in the clipboard to be pasted when you need it.

> **Note**
>
> When working on a long document that requires unique headers and footers for most sections, a macro to turn off Link To Previous throughout the document can be a nice timesaver. This macro and others are provided in the sample files you can install from the Wecome tab of this book's CD as sample document production timesavers to accompany Chapter 21, "VBA Primer."

Simplifying Book-Style Page Layout

Managing book-style page layout often seems more complex than it is simply because Word offers more than one option that serve the same or similar purposes. The main differences between book-style and standard page layout are allowances for binding and two-sided printing. Specifically, pages that are printed on two sides and bound may require additional space between the margin and the binding edge, and they may have unique header and footer requirements for facing pages.

The unique header and footer requirements can be resolved using the Different Odd & Even setting discussed earlier in this chapter. The table that follows explains each of the options available to accommodate binding.

To access the dialog box shown in Figure 8-1, on the Page Layout tab, in the Page Setup group, click the dialog launcher.

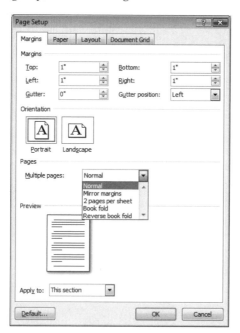

Figure 8-1 The binding options discussed in this section can be found on the Margins tab of the Page Setup dialog box, shown here.

Option	When and How to Use It
Gutter	When a document is bound, additional space beyond the margin might be required on either the left or top edge to accommodate the binding. This space is the gutter. Word provides Gutter and Gutter Position options where you can set the width of the gutter and specify its position to be the left or top edge of the page.
	Note that there is no difference in resulting behavior between increasing the left or top page margin and adding a gutter.
Mirror Margins	This option changes your left and right page margins to inside and outside margins, so that facing pages have equal margins inside (by the binding) and at their outside edges.
	Note that using a gutter with facing pages will automatically position the gutter at the inside page edge.
	Mirror Margins is an option on the Multiple Pages drop-down list, shown in Figure 8-1. Though the majority of options in the Page Setup dialog box can be changed for individual sections, options on the Multiple Pages list apply to the entire document.

| Book Fold | Similar to Mirror Margins, Book Fold is an option in the Multiple Pages list and can only be set for the entire document. Book Fold also changes margins from left and right to inside and outside. |
| | However, this option reorders pages for printing based on a folded booklet binding. When you select Book Fold, you must specify the number of pages in the booklet. Word then reorders the pages as needed to print correctly for folded binding. |

Creating Watermarks

As mentioned earlier, watermarks reside on the header and footer layer. A watermark usually uses the space between the header and footer, though it can use the entire space of the header and footer layer.

Watermark options have changed in Word 2007 with the introduction of the Watermarks gallery. You now have the option to insert a preset option from the gallery or to click More Watermarks at the bottom of the gallery for the familiar Printed Watermark dialog box .

If you have only one header and footer in the document, a watermark is no problem. To add a watermark, on the Page Layout tab, in the Page Background group, click Watermarks. Then, either click to insert a preset option or click More Watermarks to open the Printed Watermark dialog box, where you can specify a custom picture or text watermark. Insert the watermark from the gallery or the dialog box and it's applied to the entire document, because it's part of that single header and footer.

However, if you have multiple headers or footers in the document (note that this may include sections with no header or footer content, but for which the Link To Previous command is disabled), the behavior of the gallery options will differ from that of the dialog box options.

- When you apply a watermark from the Printed Watermark dialog box, it's always applied to the entire document.

  If you add a second watermark from the Printed Watermark dialog box, the earlier watermark added from the dialog box is removed.

- When you apply a watermark from the Watermark gallery, it's only applied to the active header.

  If you add a different watermark from the gallery to the same header for which you previously added a watermark from the gallery, the new watermark replaces the existing one.

Chapter 8

CAUTION

Watermarks inserted from the Watermark gallery or the Printed Watermark dialog box are not interchangeable. If you insert a watermark from the dialog box, any watermarks in the document that you added from the gallery are ignored, so you'll end up with two watermarks in that section. However, if you use the Remove Watermark feature in the gallery, all watermarks in the document (from both sources) are removed.

TROUBLESHOOTING

When I insert a new watermark, the existing watermark is left behind

As mentioned in the preceding cautionary note, watermarks inserted from the Watermark gallery and the Printed Watermark dialog box aren't interchangeable.

You can see some of why these features work independently when you're working in any Word document saved in one of the 2007 release file formats (such as the default .docx format). Just enable Design Mode (on the Developer tab) and then open any header in which a watermark exists that you added from the gallery. An XML tag for that watermark appears in the header, as you see here.

No XML tag is visible in legacy documents, or in any documents for watermarks inserted from the Printed Watermark dialog box.

That XML tag can save you time and work if you end up with duplicate watermarks or need a watermark you added from the gallery to appear in multiple headers. Just delete the XML tag to remove the watermark from the active header. Or, copy the XML tag just as you would copy text, and paste it in any additional headers where you want that watermark to appear.

Alternatively, if you want a watermark other than those available through the Watermark gallery or the Printed Watermark dialog box, remember that the watermark is just content on the header and footer layer. So, you can edit watermarks just like any content in your document or create your own from scratch.

If you insert the custom watermark through the Printed Watermark dialog box, Word will recognize it as a watermark, so it will swap automatically if you choose to replace it with another. If you instead manually create a text box or insert and format a picture for your watermark, you can still format it to do the job of a watermark. But, if you want to replace it with another watermark, you will need to manually delete it first. To get the best of both worlds, consider inserting your custom watermark through the Printed Watermark dialog box and then editing the watermark as needed.

For example, notice that text watermarks are inserted as WordArt. If you want a text watermark other than the options available through the gallery or the Printed Watermark dialog box, just insert a preset option and then edit the WordArt text.

Note, however, that as with any WordArt shape, when you change the text, the original size will be retained. Adjusting the size of the WordArt shape will adjust the size of the text within that shape. Just drag the handles to resize the object or, on the WordArt Tools Format tab, adjust height and width in the Size group.

Note

Though Microsoft Office PowerPoint 2007 and Microsoft Office Excel 2007 have new WordArt tools, Word does not. You use a contextual tab for formatting WordArt in Word, but you'll probably recognize the tools available there as being very similar to the Office 2003 version of WordArt. If you want to take advantage of the newer formatting options, create the WordArt for your watermark in Office PowerPoint 2007 and then save it as a picture that you can insert into Word. To save an object as a picture in PowerPoint, right-click the object and then select Save As Picture. That feature will usually select the best picture file type option for your selected object. In this case, the best picture file type will be .png. See Chapter 7 for help with selecting picture formats for use in Word.

Quick Parts are the evolution of AutoText, a new way to work with fields, and a new way to create template content. Then again, they're really so much more than that.

Quick Parts—in particular, the elements of Quick Parts called Building Blocks—are a new approach to generating documents. Wherever you see a gallery on the Ribbon with the option to insert preformatted sets of content—such as the Cover Page, Header, Footer, or Table Of Contents galleries—those are Building Blocks.

If you've seen these new options, and the hair on the back of your neck stood up in revolt against cookie-cutter document content, tell it to relax. I will be the first to say that there are some entries in just about all of those galleries that you'd be wise to avoid, and I'll tell you why as this chapter progresses. But don't give the movie a bad review just because you don't like some of the costumes. This feature is a blockbuster for anyone who creates templates or frequently reuses similar pieces of custom content, and this chapter will show you how Building Blocks can make a difference for you.

Though you can use any of the built-in entries if they work for your needs, they're just examples to show you the kinds of things you can do. Building Blocks are designed for your custom content.

In addition to Building Blocks, fields (one of my longtime favorite features) are now considered part of the Quick Parts family of functionality. As introduced in Chapter 4, "Building Easy-to-Manage, Robust Documents," fields are one of five key components for building any complex document. They're also easier to use, more important, and more flexible than you might realize. So, this chapter will show you both what's new for fields and how to make friends with this unassuming powerhouse of a feature.

Chapter Assumptions

Though the Building Block component of Quick Parts is new functionality, I'm making some assumptions in this chapter. As advanced Microsoft Word users, I assume that you have some familiarity with the AutoText feature available in earlier versions, as well as at least the basics of common features for which there are Building Block galleries, such as headers, tables of contents, and tables. As for fields, I'm assuming that you know what a field is and have at least a general idea of when they're used and how to recognize them.

This chapter will take you through what you need to know as advanced users to make the most of Quick Parts, from Building Blocks to fields.

In the introduction to this book, you can find a list of resources for those who want more basic-level information, in the section titled "Who Will Benefit Most from This Book."

Understanding Building Blocks: The Evolution of Documents

The Building Blocks feature takes the concept of AutoText and makes it smarter. Some types of Building Blocks just insert formatted content at the insertion point, but others do quite a bit more.

For example, insert an entry from the Cover Page gallery, and it will insert as the first page of your document by default, adding a first page header and footer if one isn't already active for the first section of your document. If you later select a new cover page option for the front of your document, the existing page gets swapped automatically for the new one, but much of the content you added to the cover page remains intact and is automatically formatted to match the new design.

Many Building Blocks include content stored in Content Controls, which is a new feature that, among other functionality, enables your content to be retained when the design is swapped. A Content Control appears as a blue highlight when you point to content stored in a control or as a blue highlight with the control visible around it when you select placeholder text inside a control. Once you add your own content to a control, just the blue outline of the control is visible when your insertion point is inside the control. (Note, however, that only the content within a Content Control, and not the control itself, is not visible when working in Draft view.)

In the examples shown here, placeholder text for the document title is stored in a Content Control. The image on the left shows what that control looks like when you point to it, and the image on the right shows the way it looks when you click in the control. (Notice that clicking inside a control that contains placeholder text automatically selects that text.)

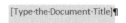   

As mentioned in earlier chapters, Content Controls are the new generation of form controls. They're sleek and much more flexible than previous form capabilities in Microsoft Word. For example, one of the most powerful components of Content Controls is that they can easily be bound to external data, such as document properties or custom XML data. Content Controls are explained in detail in Chapter 11, "Content Controls: Creating Forms and Then Some," and will be addressed as appropriate as we look at Building Blocks in this chapter.

> **Note**
>
> Because Content Controls are not available to legacy documents, Content Controls contained in Building Block entries will be converted to static text (or to images, depending on the type of content) when saved in a legacy document.

When a Building Blocks entry is saved, it's assigned to a gallery, and to a category within that gallery. Note that many built-in gallery names differ slightly in dialog boxes related to Building Blocks from the way they appear in their corresponding gallery. Built-in Building Block galleries include AutoText, Cover Pages, Headers, Footers, Page Numbers, Tables, Table Of Contents, Bibliography, Text Boxes, Watermarks, Equations, and Quick Parts.

Within each gallery, there are pre-created categories (such as Built-In or General) in which entry previews are organized, and you can create your own categories as well. Notice, for example, the custom Client Presentations category in the Table Of Contents gallery shown here.

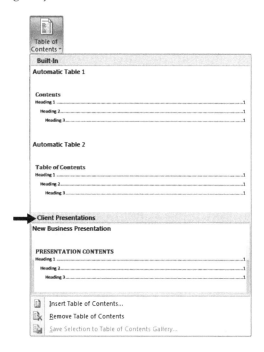

Building Block entries can be saved to a master Building Blocks template (or other global template) for availability to all documents. Or, you can save unique Building Blocks entries in any Microsoft Office Word 2007 template.

> **Note**
>
> As mentioned in Chapter 5, "Styles," notice that previews in the Building Blocks galleries update to match the current theme in your document. This is a very nice touch, particularly because some designs work better with certain colors or fonts. This capability applies to both built-in and custom Building Blocks, but will only apply to your custom entries if they're Theme-ready. To learn about making Word content Theme-ready, see Chapter 5.

TROUBLESHOOTING

What happened to my legacy AutoText?

If a template created in an earlier version of Microsoft Word contains AutoText entries, those will become Building Block entries assigned to the category named AutoText.

You can still type a unique entry name and press F3 to insert it (you can do that with any Building Block entry in Office Word 2007). Like AutoText entries, Building Blocks can be inserted into documents or templates, but the entry definitions can only be stored in templates.

Note that the feature to auto-complete AutoText entries by pressing Enter is no longer available. But, you do get a nice alternative method of accessing entries through galleries. The downside to AutoText Building Blocks is that the AutoText gallery doesn't appear on any built-in Ribbon tab. You can add that (or any) Building Block gallery to the Quick Access Toolbar, as discussed later in this chapter. Or, to give users another easy way to access those entries, change the properties of your AutoText Building Block entries to assign them to the Quick Parts gallery instead. You can still use F3 to insert them, but they will appear in the Quick Parts gallery on the Insert tab, so that users can easily insert them from a preview of the entry. Learn how to edit Building Block properties later in this section.

INSIDE OUT   ### Using the new Equation tools

As mentioned earlier in this section, Equations are now a type of Building Block. Built-in support for equations replaces Microsoft Equation 3.0 (also known as Equation Editor) that you may know from earlier versions of Word.

If you've used Equation Editor in the past, you can see just by looking at the Equation Tools Design contextual tab (shown here) that the new built-in equation tools are much more flexible.

Use the Equation button in the Tools group on this tab (or in the Symbols group on the Insert tab) to access the Equation gallery. Also note that the dialog launcher in the Tools group on the tab shown here opens the Equation Options dialog box, where you'll find a host of options sure to bring joy to the mathematically inclined.

The new equation functionality uses the Office Open XML capabilities of the new file formats, so it's not available in legacy documents. If you copy an equation created with these new tools and paste it into a legacy document, the equation will be converted to a picture when the document is saved.

For legacy documents, Equation 3.0 is available through the Object dialog box. Find Object in the Text group on the Insert tab. Also note that, if you have existing Equation 3.0 objects in documents when you upgrade them to the new file formats, you'll still need to edit them in Equation Editor or replace them with new equations using the new tools. Equation 3.0 objects do not convert to the new equation format.

Chapter 9

Creating Your Own Building Blocks

To save any content as a Building Block entry, start by selecting the content you want to save. This content can include a combination of text, tables, fields, graphics, and Content Controls. With the content selected, use one of the following methods to open the Create New Building Block dialog box.

- Press ALT+F3.

- At the bottom of the gallery to which you want to add your new entry, click Save Selection To <Name> Gallery.

When you use the keyboard shortcut in the preceding options, the assigned gallery in the dialog box (shown here) will default to Quick Parts. Otherwise, the gallery will default to the gallery from which you opened the dialog box. Regardless, you can change the gallery assignment at any time when this dialog box is open.

Additionally, keep the following in mind when saving new entries.

- When you type a description for your new entry, that description appears in the ScreenTip when users point to the entry preview in the gallery.

> **Note**
>
> If ScreenTip descriptions don't appear when you point to a gallery entry, check your settings for this functionality. Click the Microsoft Office Button and then click Word Options. On the Popular tab, in the ScreenTip Style list, select Show Feature Descriptions In ScreenTips.

- Just as with the AutoText feature from earlier versions, Building Block entries can be saved to any loaded global template or to the active template. Select any available template from the Save In list in the Create New Building Block dialog box. To learn about global templates, see Chapter 20, "The Many Faces of Microsoft Office Templates."

  Note that with Building Blocks, you can move an entry from one template to another without resaving the entry or using the Organizer (which you may have used in previous versions to move or copy AutoText entries between templates). Building Block entries aren't, in fact, available through the Organizer. See the next part of this chapter to learn how to move Building Block entries between templates.

- Finally, notice that you have the option in the Create New Building Block dialog box to set each entry to be inserted on its own, in its own paragraph, or on its own page.

Each of the options available in the Create New Building Block dialog box is also available from the Modify Building Block dialog box, discussed later in this chapter.

Once you click OK in the Create New Building Block dialog box, your new entry appears in the relevant gallery, if that gallery is exposed in your Word window. See the Troubleshooting tip in this section for more on accessing custom galleries. However, the entry is not saved until you save the template to which this entry was added. If you do not have occasion to save the template before exiting your current Word session, you'll be prompted to save the template when you exit Word.

Note

There is an exception to the rule that you'll be prompted to save the template before exiting Word. Word saves changes to Normal.dotm automatically when you exit the program. You can, however, enable the option to be prompted when you've made changes to Normal.dotm. To do this, in the Word Options dialog box, on the Advanced tab, select Prompt Before Saving Normal Template, which appears under the Save options.

INSIDE OUT   Saving to Normal.dotm or BuildingBlocks.dotx

Normal.dotm is, for most purposes, the equivalent of Normal.dot in previous versions of Word. This is where your global user settings are saved for Word and where recorded macros are saved by default.

However, although you can save Building Block entries to Normal.dotm, Building Blocks have their own global template, Building Blocks.dotx.

Similar to Quick Style Sets, discussed in Chapter 5, Building Blocks templates are .dotx files (that is, regular macro-free Word templates) and have a specific folder assigned specifically for this content type. If you create a custom template (saved in any Word template file format) that consists just of Building Block entries, or for which those entries are the only content you want to access, you can save it to the Document Building Blocks folder to make those entries globally available to all your Word documents.

Similar to Normal.dotm, if you move, rename, or delete the existing BuildingBlocks.dotx template, a new one will be generated containing the default entries. In fact, because Building Block entries from any template become globally available just by saving the template in your Document Building Blocks folder, renaming the template won't stop the unwanted entries from appearing. So, if you do not want to see the built-in entries for any gallery, delete them from BuildingBlocks.dotx rather than deleting that template. You can do this easily through the Building Blocks Organizer, discussed in the section titled "Managing Building Blocks" later in this chapter.

For information on where to find your Document Building Blocks folder, as well as where to find the master version of BuildingBlocks.dotx, see Chapter 20.

Chapter 9

TROUBLESHOOTING

Where are my custom Building Block galleries?

First of all, it's important to clarify that custom categories and custom galleries are not the same thing. That is, a gallery can contain multiple categories. You can create custom categories for any existing Building Block gallery.

For example, you can assign a new Cover Page entry to the Custom *category*, and it will appear in the Cover Page gallery, under the heading Custom. But, the Custom Cover Pages *gallery* is a separate gallery that doesn't appear on the Ribbon by default.

Word comes with several custom galleries available through the Create New Building Block or Modify Building Block dialog boxes. Though you can assign an entry to one of these custom galleries, the galleries don't automatically appear anywhere.

You can add any gallery to the Quick Access Toolbar. Additionally, Content Controls include a type of control designed to make any gallery you specify available at the insertion point. Learn more about Building Block Gallery controls in Chapter 11.

However, to make a custom gallery appear on the Ribbon (or any gallery that doesn't appear on the Ribbon by default), you need to use XML. Learn the basics of how to customize the Ribbon in Chapter 22, "Office Open XML Essentials."

Inserting Building Block Entries

With many types of Building Block entries, such as Quick Parts, you can insert them where needed, as often as needed. However, some types of Building Blocks have additional properties, as mentioned earlier, that enable them to automatically swap in your document when you select a different entry from one currently in the document. Additionally, those Building Block types that swap when you select a new entry may in fact delete some of your content, so it's important to understand how they work. All Building Block types that swap when a new entry is selected are explained in the list that follows.

- Cover Page, Table Of Contents, and Bibliography galleries are designed with the idea that you usually need only one of any of these in a given document, but Word does provide ways in which you can include several. Right-click an entry in any of these galleries for the option to insert the Building Block at the beginning or end of the document, beginning or end of the section, or at the current document position.

  If you just click to insert a cover page, rather than using a right-click option, it's inserted at the front of your document. If you click to insert a table of contents or bibliography, it's inserted at your current document location. When you use the default setting, inserting a new entry just by clicking will replace the first entry of that same type. However, when you use the right-click options to insert more than one of any of these content types in a document, existing entries of the same type are not replaced. Note that if you later just click to insert an entry, any existing cover page at the front of your document, or the first table of contents or bibliography in your document, will be replaced.

In the case of cover pages, content you've added or edited inside Content Controls is retained when you swap to a new design (provided the same Content Controls appear in the new design), but formatting customizations are not saved. Similarly, customizations made to tables of contents and bibliographies are not retained when you select a different gallery entry.

> **Note**
>
> Though you can add several tables of contents to the document at once using Building Blocks, these tables will all contain identical entries by default. To learn how to include different content in each table of contents within a document, see Chapter 10, "Reference Tables and Tools." Also in that chapter, learn about options for the new bibliography feature. While this new feature doesn't offer the same flexibility as a table of contents, you can have unique bibliographies in a document for references in a given language.

- Header, Footer, Page Number, and Watermark Building Block entries also swap, but do so according to header and footer rules. That is, the active header, footer, or page number at your insertion point is swapped when you select an entry from one of these galleries.

  For example, if your insertion point is on a page that uses a first page header, only the first page header (and any other first page headers linked to this one) is changed when you select a new option from the Header gallery.

  However, it's important to note that any header or footer option you select from the Header and Footer galleries is placed in the header or footer on the active page. Odd Page and Even Page gallery entries are provided for cases where you enable Different Odd & Even Pages in your document and need that type of formatting, but they can be added to any active header or footer and using those options does *not* enable the Different Odd & Even Pages setting.

CAUTION!

Any content in the active header or footer is replaced when you select an entry from one of these galleries, whether or not it was created from a Building Block. The only content automatically retained is content inside Content Controls that also exist in the new header or footer. To retain other content when you select a new header or footer, first copy the content and then select the new header or footer. Because that copied content is in your clipboard, you can paste it as needed into the new header or footer.

Note

As discussed in Chapter 8, "Sections," keep in mind that only watermarks for which you see previews in the Watermark gallery are Building Block entries. Watermarks applied from the Printed Watermark dialog box always apply to the entire document and do not swap with those applied to individual headers.

- Building block entries assigned to the custom versions of the galleries mentioned in this list, such as cover pages, have the same behavior as entries in the relevant built-in gallery. For example, if you click to insert a cover page from the built-in Cover Page gallery and later click to insert a cover page from the Custom Cover Page gallery into the same document, the new cover page will replace the first.

  Word can make these types of connections either because of the Building Block location (such as in headers or footers) or because of XML tags surrounding the Building Block entry, such as in cover pages and watermarks. To see the XML tags in your document, turn on Design Mode. You'll find this option on the Developer tab.

Note

If you don't see the Developer tab, click the Microsoft Office Button and then click Word Options. Find the setting to show the Developer tab on the Popular tab of that dialog box. Note that most settings made on the Popular tab apply to all programs that use a Ribbon in place of traditional menus and toolbars.

XML tags are used for several types of content, including all Content Controls and some Building Block types. For example, notice the XML tag named Watermarks in the header shown here.

XML tags are always paired, consisting of start and end tags, as you see here. XML tags surround the content to which they refer. In the case of this watermark tag, it appears empty but is not. The watermark is a floating graphic object anchored to the tag. See the Troubleshooting tip "When I insert a new watermark, the existing watermark is left behind." in Chapter 8, to learn about using the tag to simplify your work with watermarks. To learn tips for using the XML tags in Content Controls, see Chapter 11.

Managing Building Blocks

The Building Blocks Organizer has got to be one of the most efficient new Word features. From this one location, you can manage all Building Block entries in all available templates. Note that "available templates" refers to BuildingBlocks.dotx, Normal.dotm, any other global templates, and any active template (that is, the active document if it is a template, or the active document's attached template). Using the Building Blocks Organizer, you can do any of the following.

- Edit the properties of any Building Block entry, such as renaming it, changing its assigned gallery or category, or even moving it to another template just by changing the entry's Save In property.

- Delete Building Block entries.

- Insert an entry from any available template, and any gallery (whether or not the gallery appears on the Ribbon), into your document.

- View all available Building Blocks sorted by name, gallery, category, or source template.

To access the Building Blocks Organizer, on the Insert tab, click Quick Parts and then click Building Blocks Organizer. Or, right-click any entry in a Building Blocks gallery and then select Organize And Delete to open the Building Blocks Organizer and automatically locate the entry in the same step.

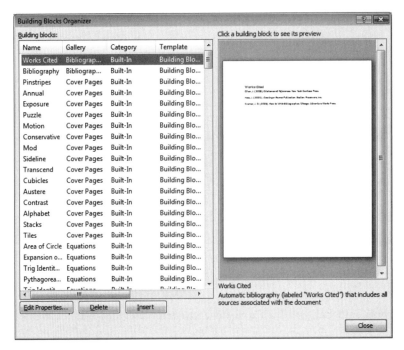

In the Building Blocks Organizer, shown here, just select an entry and then select Edit Properties, Delete, or Insert, as need. The Edit Properties option opens the Modify Building Block dialog box, which contains exactly the same options as the Create New Building Block dialog box. Notice in the preceding dialog box that the description of the selected entry appears below the preview. This description is the same one discussed earlier that appears in the ScreenTip when you point to the entry in its gallery. Add or edit descriptions in the Create New or Modify Building Block dialog boxes.

> **Note**
>
> Notice that the Building Blocks Organizer has no relationship to the Organizer dialog box that you may know from earlier versions of Word. That Organizer dialog box is still available, however, for moving or copying styles or VBA modules between documents and templates. For help using the Organizer to manage styles, see Chapter 5.

Document Property Quick Parts

In previous versions of Word, you might have used fields to add information to your document, such as Title or Author. In Word 2007, Document Property Quick Parts replace and substantially expand on this functionality.

When you insert any of the Document Property Quick Parts shown here into the document, they appear inside a Content Control. Each of these controls is bound to data stored in your document. You can add or edit some of this data through the Document Properties dialog box or the new Document Information Panel, discussed later. Others, including Abstract and the various company information options, are linked to custom XML data that Word automatically generates when you insert and then add content to one of these Quick Parts.

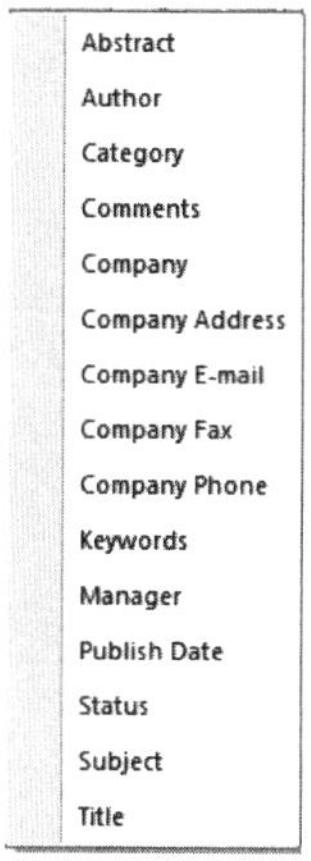

Abstract

Author

Category

Comments

Company

Company Address

Company E-mail

Company Fax

Company Phone

Keywords

Manager

Publish Date

Status

Subject

Title

Chapter 9

Custom XML data is data stored in the Open XML formats, and it adds functionality to your documents. Some types of custom XML data are available to your documents through built-in functionality such as the Document Property Quick Parts discussed here. You can also create your own custom XML data for binding to Content Controls.

> **Note**
> The concept of binding Content Controls to data is addressed in more detail in Chapter 11. You can also learn the basics of how to bind controls to your own custom data in Chapter 22.

Regardless of what data is bound to Document Property Quick Parts, the major benefit here is that you can edit the data at the source (whether that's in the Document Information Panel, in the file's XML, or perhaps on a server) or in any instance of the relevant Quick Part in your document, and it will update in all locations. For example, if a Title Quick Part appears on the cover page and in the footer of your document, you can edit the title in Document Properties or in either of those Quick Parts, and it will update in all three places automatically.

> **Note**
>
> The Document Property menu in the Quick Parts gallery is unavailable when you're working in a legacy document because Content Controls and data binding are not available functionality for legacy documents.

INSIDE OUT   What do I need to know about the Document Information Panel?

To access the Document Information Panel, click the Microsoft Office Button, point to Prepare, and then click Properties. The default Document Information Panel, shown in the image that follows, contains many common Document Properties Summary fields.

The idea is to provide quick access to common document information when you need it. To access the Document Properties dialog box once the Document Information Panel is open, at the top of the panel click Document Properties and then click Advanced Properties.

If Microsoft Office InfoPath 2007 is installed on your computer, you can also access the Document Information Panel from the Document Panel button in the Templates group on the Developer tab. When you use the Developer tab option, you get the Document Information Panel dialog box, from which you can set the panel to appear automatically when documents are opened and on initial save, or select a custom panel from a template you've created.

Templates for custom Document Information Panels are not typical Microsoft Office templates. Custom Information Panel templates can be created from Office InfoPath 2007 forms or from within Microsoft Office SharePoint Server 2007. To learn how to do this, find links to related MSDN Library articles on this book's CD.

Working with Fields

So, you no longer need fields for adding document property information to your document. Document Property Quick Parts handle these tasks much more effectively. In fact, document property fields only still exist for use in legacy documents where such Quick Parts are not available.

But, fields in general are still present throughout your Word documents, and they're as important as ever. A field is, essentially, dynamic text. It's information stored in your document that displays a result. Fields are used for many built-in features—from tables of contents to page numbers to embedded objects—and can be used to expand the capabilities of other features, such as with the LISTNUM fields and STYLEREF fields discussed later in this chapter. Many fields can be customized to display just the information you need in exactly the format you need it. You can even nest fields inside one another as an easy alternative to some types of automation, or to simplify formatting options, such as when the information that the field displays is conditional.

As an advanced user, you probably recognize that the Field dialog box (shown in the image that follows) remains the same as it was in the previous version of Word. To find this dialog box in Word 2007, on the Insert tab, click Quick Parts and then click Field.

You can select a field from the Field Names list and customize it through settings shown automatically when you select the field name. Or, after selecting the field name, click Field Codes at the bottom of the dialog box for an Options button that you can click to open the Field Options dialog box.

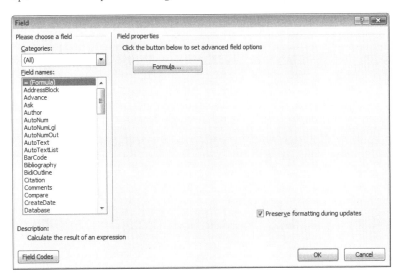

However, as an advanced user, this dialog box is not usually the fastest or easiest way for you to create, or especially to edit, a field. Most fields can be created and edited directly on screen.

So, why should you really care about fields or how to create or edit field codes on screen? First, because an understanding of fields enables you to easily automate many things you might not know Word can do—from something as simple as a field to display the number of pages in the active section, to a customized cross-reference field to suppress non-delimiter characters in a paragraph number (such as when you want a cross-reference to "Article II" to display as "II.")

> **Note**
>
> In case you're curious, the field name for the first example in the preceding paragraph is SECTIONPAGES. The switch for suppressing non-delimiter characters is "\t."

Understanding Field Construction

A field code consists of a field name and, where applicable, information used to customize the field. This custom information can be information from the document, such as a bookmark or style name, or options you can specify that are known as switches. A switch is an option that customizes the information or formatting of information displayed by the field.

For example, look at the codes for a few common types of fields.

- The page number field shown here is a default page number field. This field displays the page number in arabic numerals.

  { PAGE }

- The page number field in the image that follows is customized using a formatting switch. A switch always starts with a backslash followed by an identifying character. Some switches, such as the one shown here, also require more information. In this case, the format is specified as uppercase roman numerals by typing the word *roman* in uppercase letters.

  { PAGE * ROMAN }

- The hyperlink field shown in the following image is a default hyperlink to the Microsoft home page. It contains only the field name and the target location.

  { HYPERLINK "www.microsoft.com" }

- The hyperlink field in the next image is customized with two switches. The \n switch doesn't require additional information. This switch simply indicates that the target location be opened in a new window. The \o switch requires text after it in quotation marks, as you see here, because it's used to specify the ScreenTip text that appears when you point to the link.

  { HYPERLINK "www.microsoft.com" \n \o "Sample ScreenTip Text" }

Creating Fields

If you know the name of the field you want to create, along with any specific syntax it requires, you can create that field right on screen with just a few keystrokes. To try this, start by creating a basic page number field, as follows.

1. Type the word **PAGE** and then select it.

    Though field names are not case sensitive, I always type field names in uppercase letters to match the way field codes are generated by Word.

2. Press CTRL+F9 to convert the selected text to a field and then press F9 to update the field so that the result displays.

    Be careful about what's selected when you convert the text to the field. If any extra characters are included, such as punctuation, you'll get an error result.

3. To toggle between viewing the selected field and its result, press SHIFT+F9. Or, press ALT+F9 to toggle between the code and result for all fields in the document at once.

> **Note**
>
> Using ALT+F9 to toggle field codes is the same as changing the Word setting to display field codes instead of their values, an option available on the Advanced tab of the Word Options dialog box.

If you don't know the name of the field you need, you can find it in the Field dialog box. To access this dialog box, on the Insert tab, click Quick Parts and then click Field. As you scroll through the Field Names list, see the description for the selected field directly below that list.

Customizing Fields

For fields that require more information than the field name, such as a HYPERLINK field that requires a target address or a STYLEREF field that requires a style name, simply type that information in quotation marks after the field name and then select all of that text to convert the text to a field, as outlined in the steps in the preceding section.

For example, to create the HYPERLINK field with a target of the Microsoft home page, as shown earlier, type **HYPERLINK "www.microsoft.com"**, select everything from the H in HYPERLINK to the end quotation mark, and then follow the steps provided earlier for converting this to a field and displaying its result.

Chapter 9

TROUBLESHOOTING

My hyperlink to a network file path doesn't work

When you create a hyperlink by typing the text for the field and converting it to a field code, hyperlinks to network locations have a unique requirement. You need to type two backslashes between each folder in the path, rather than the one backslash that typically appears.

For example, if I want to link to Book1.xlsx, located in my default Documents folder, I type **HYPERLINK "C:\\Users\\Steph\\Documents\\Book1.xlsx"**. I then select everything from the H in HYPERLINK through the end quotation mark and then press CTRL+F9 followed by F9. If you put just a single backslash between folders in the path, the target displayed when you display the field result may be a distortion of the path you typed, and the link will not work.

Note also that you can't edit the display text for a hyperlink in the field code, and if you edit the target in an existing hyperlink field, the display text won't update. But, you can edit the display text directly from the field result without affecting the target or anything else about the field code. To avoid deleting the code and leaving only the display text result, don't delete the last character in the existing display text until after you type the new display text. And, if you ever have difficulty editing a field code or its result, with your insertion point in the field, just press CTRL+K to make the changes you need through the Hyperlink dialog box.

If you want to add switches to any field, just type all of the information you want to include as it would appear in the field code once created, and then select all of that text to convert it to a field. For example, to create a table of contents generated from outline levels one and two, with hyperlinks from the table entries to their corresponding headings in the document, do the following:

1. Type TOC \o "1-2" \h.

   The \o switch indicates to generate the TOC from outline levels, the levels in quotation marks indicate the top and bottom levels you want to include (three levels are used by default if you don't specify levels), and the \h switch adds hyperlinks from each entry to its corresponding location in the document.

2. Select all of that text and then press CTRL+F9 followed by F9 to convert to a field and update the result.

If you don't know the available field options or correct syntax for a particular field type, there are two easy ways to find it. First, in the Field dialog box, select the field in the Field Names list, click Field Codes, and then click Options for the Field Options dialog box. In this dialog box, you see a list of available switches and/or formatting customizations, along with descriptions and an example of the correct syntax. For an even easier source of help, click the Help button on the right edge of the Ribbon, and in the help search box, type **Field Code:** followed by the field code name. Office Online help provides detailed help for almost every field code, including a complete description of syntax and available switches.

TROUBLESHOOTING

Why doesn't my field update correctly?

If you have a field that stops updating correctly when changes are made in the document, the most likely cause is a field switch. Field switches exist to provide customization options when the defaults won't work. But, when you specify some types of switches, you take away part of the dynamic nature of the field.

Think of this in another way. If you specify the start at value for footnotes or endnotes in a given document section, that value won't automatically adjust if you change the number of footnotes in a preceding section. Similarly, if you specify a value or a format in a field code, that code will no longer update that value or format automatically. So, if you get the result you want with default settings, don't add switches that keep settings from being dynamic unless that is your intention. You can delete switches from existing field codes as easily as adding them when you create new codes, as discussed in the next part of this chapter.

See a common example of this issue, and how to avoid it, in the section titled "LISTNUM Fields" that follows.

For further examples of creating custom fields, two field types are specified in this chapter, LISTNUM fields and STYLEREF fields. I'm using these examples because of how frequently they can be helpful, how generally little-known they are, and the fact that they're good examples of useful fields that aren't available through a built-in feature other than the Fields dialog box.

LISTNUM Fields

A LISTNUM field is, literally, an outline list stored inside a field code. Practically speaking, a LISTNUM field is designed for occasions where you need a paragraph number within an outline that doesn't constrain to the formatting requirements of your list style or multilevel list. For example, when you need to have multiple outline numbers appear in the same paragraph, as shown with bolded text in the sample here, do this with a LISTNUM field.

1) Sample level 1 text.

2) Sample level 1 text.

3) **For example:**   a)   **Sample level 2 text.**

                  b)   Sample level 2 text.

                  c)   Sample level 2 text.

When you add a LISTNUM field in an existing outline list, it will automatically take on the formatting of the active list. For this reason, it's a good idea not to do too much customization to your LISTNUM fields unless you need to do so, as discussed in the Troubleshooting tip "Why doesn't my field update correctly?" earlier in this chapter.

For example, to add the a) in the preceding image, use a LISTNUM field. To do this, simply apply the correct paragraph style for your list level for the paragraph numbered 3, and then type the text of that paragraph as you normally would. Except, instead of typing a), type LISTNUM, select it, convert it to a field, and then update its result. By default, a LISTNUM field will take on the correct number, one list level lower than the list number that precedes it. The paragraph number 3 represents the first level in the list, so the LISTNUM field automatically displays the correct number (a letter in this case) for the second level in the list. When you then use the style for your second list level in the next paragraph, it numbers automatically to b), because the LISTNUM field became an automatic part of your outline.

LISTNUM field switches include the ability to set the specific level in the list (\l) or the specific start at value to display (\s). For each of those switches, specify a number after the switch.

Additionally, you can specify a LISTNUM Field List Name, to give your LISTNUM field a particular list format. To create a name for any existing list style or multilevel list, just type a name in the LISTNUM Field List Name box shown here in the Modify Multilevel List dialog box, available through the List Style dialog box. Learn how to create and modify list styles, including how to access this dialog box, in Chapter 5.

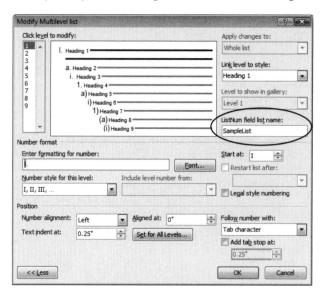

Once you create a list name, you can specify the name in a LISTNUM field. To do this, type the name in quotation marks after the field name, and then type any switches. Note that the order isn't important, as long as the field name comes first. If you type another switch before the list name, the field will work as well. This flexibility in field syntax is common to most fields.

For example, using the LISTNUM Field List Name shown in the preceding dialog box, I could create a LISTNUM field that would automatically take on the formatting of that list regardless of where I place the field in the active document. To create that field, type **LISTNUM "SampleList"**, select the text you just typed, and then convert it to a field.

CAUTION!

Just as with using switches, be careful about overusing LISTNUM Field List Names. If you're going to place the LISTNUM field in an existing list, it will automatically take on that list's formatting. If you don't specify a list name, and you change the formatting of the list in which the field appears, the field will automatically change formatting to match. If you've specified a list name, the formatting in your field will continue to reflect the named list, regardless of how the active list changes.

STYLEREF Fields

STYLEREF fields are quite simple to use, but not as well-known as they deserve to be, which is the reason for the mention here.

A STYLEREF field can be a great way to format headers in a long document, when you want the topic on any given page to be reflected in the headers. By default, STYLEREF fields show the text of the first instance of the field to appear on a given page. So, without any section breaks or new headers, you can have the most recent top-level heading, for example, appear in the header on every page. Assuming that your top-level headings use Heading 1 paragraph style, the field code for this example would be STYLEREF "Heading 1."

This field type also has several switches, including those that enable you to display the paragraph numbers in or out of context with your outline or to suppress any nondelimited characters in the paragraph number. Find a complete list of available switches for the STYLEREF field, along with descriptions of each, in the Field Options dialog box mentioned earlier. To get to the Field Options dialog box for this specific field, do the following.

1. On the Insert tab, click Quick Parts and then click Fields.

2. In the Style Names list, select STYLEREF.

3. Click Field Codes and then click Options. The Field Options dialog box that opens displays options for the selected field.

INSIDE OUT   **Using Reference Fields**

Reference fields—from TOC or INDEX to the new and unique CITATION fields for bibli-ographies or TC and XE table entry fields—have qualities and behaviors that are different from those mentioned in this chapter's general discussion about creating and editing fields. Additionally, the ability to create and edit fields on screen, demonstrated in this chapter, is particularly useful when it comes to working with reference fields.

Once you're comfortable with the preceding content in this chapter about working with fields, find more information specifically about working with reference fields in Chapter 10.

Chapter 9

Editing Fields

Just as you can create field codes right on screen with a few keystrokes, you can edit field codes directly as well, whether you created them on screen or through a built-in feature, such as Table Of Contents.

To edit a field code, toggle the field so that you can see its code (SHIFT+F9 to toggle the selected field, or ALT+F9 to toggle all fields in the document), and then simply edit the code as if you were creating it.

For example, when you create an automatic table of contents in Word from one of the built-in options in the Table Of Contents gallery, or from the Index And Tables dialog box, it's created from outline levels one through three and includes hyperlinks from each entry to its referenced location, as well as other options. To change the number of levels and remove the hyperlinks, just press ALT+F9 to toggle all field codes, and then edit the code as if you were creating it. That is, change the levels to what you want them to be and delete the \h switch that controls the hyperlink.

CAUTION

When a reference table uses the \h switch for hyperlinks, a separate hyperlink field code is added to each entry. Because of this, if you press SHIFT+F9 to display the selected TOC field code, you might get odd results. When working with reference fields, always use ALT+F9 to display field codes. Learn more about working with reference fields in the next chapter.

When you've finished editing, just press F9 to update the selected field and then ALT+F9 to toggle field codes back so they display their results. This is a simple example of how editing field codes on screen can be an enormous timesaver and help you avoid re-creating or reformatting content.

Converting Fields to Static Results

If you want to remove a field code and leave only its result, such as to convert an embedded object to a picture (discussed in Chapter 7, "Managing Graphics"), select the field code (or its result) and press CTRL+SHIFT+F9. Whatever the displayed result of the field is (whether it's text or an image) it remains and the field code is removed, so that the content is no longer dynamic.

Nesting Fields

It won't happen often, but it's good to know that you have the option to nest one field inside another when you need it.

If you've ever nested functions in Microsoft Excel, nesting fields is a very similar concept. A nested field is just a field whose arguments are other fields. There are many reasons for nesting one field inside another, but the most common is when you need to display different information based on a given condition. In these cases, you would start with an IF field, and then use other fields to specify arguments of that conditional statement, as demonstrated later in this section.

I want to share a note of caution before proceeding with the steps to create a nested field. I've had occasion to see Word users, even very talented and experienced Word developers, get carried away with nested fields. So, if your nested field begins to look like an essay, ask yourself if you're overcomplicating things before you do more work than is necessary. Remember that the idea behind any field is to provide a simple approach when you need dynamic content. If your field looks like a complex computer program, a macro or another solution may be able to do the job more easily.

But, when you have good reason for your nested field, and it is the simplest solution, you might be surprised at how truly simple it can be to create.

For example, say that you want to use a STYLEREF field in the document header, as introduced earlier in this chapter. Perhaps the first part of your document needs to display the top-level heading in the header, and the second part needs to show more detail, such as by showing the second-level headings throughout the chapter. If you have no other reason to add a section break between those document portions, don't do it for the STYLEREF field—just use a nested field. That is, if the heading text is the name of the first chapter, display the text of the Heading 1 style; if not, display the text of the Heading 2 style. That field code, when complete, would look like the code shown here.

```
{ IF { STYLEREF "Heading 1" } = "My first section" { STYLEREF "Heading 1" } { STYLEREF "Heading 2" } }
```

To create this field, do the following.

1. Type all of the text that will be included in your field code. For this example, type **IF STYLEREF "Heading 1" = "My first section" STYLEREF "Heading 1" STYLEREF "Heading 2"**.

2. Convert the inside content to field codes where needed first, one at a time. That is, select the first instance of STYLEREF "Heading 1" in that text and convert it

Chapter 9

to a field code (CTRL+F9). Then, select the second instance of that same text and convert it. Then, select STYLEREF "Heading 2" and convert that.

3. Select the entire text of what will be the nested field code, from the I in IF to the close quotation mark after Heading 2, and then press CTRL+F9 to convert it to a field, followed by F9 to update the results for the entire nested field.

> **Note**
>
> If you're trying this nested field example for yourself, it will work best in a document containing several Heading 1 and Heading 2 paragraphs, with one of the Heading 1 paragraphs matching the text in the field. You can find a sample document with a completed example of this nested field, named Nested Field Sample.docx, in the sample documents you can install from the Welcome tab of this book's CD.

I f you need a default table of contents, generated from the top three outline levels, you're fine. Otherwise, watch out. Need an index? No problem, but do you have the necessary years to devote to the task?

Prepare yourself. If you're among the many who hold these and other common misconceptions about working with reference tables in Microsoft Word, your documents are about to get easier. Reference tables in Microsoft Word have long been more flexible and easier to use than they might seem at first glance. But, in Microsoft Office Word 2007, there's even more to the story.

Chapter Assumptions

As advanced users, you don't need me to tell you how to insert a table of contents, an index, or a cross-reference (other than, perhaps, where to find it in the new interface). And, you probably don't want me to take your time discussing how to create or format a footnote or endnote.

Instead of spending time on the basics you already know, this chapter focuses on customizing reference tables and tools and introduces the new Office Word 2007 reference component, bibliographies. We'll also look at timesaving techniques for everything from indexes to cross-references, to help you get exactly the result you need without extra work.

Note that many of the concepts and tips in this chapter are based on creating and editing field codes, and some require an understanding of the integration between reference tables and the new Building Blocks functionality. If you're not already familiar with these tasks and features, you'll get the most out of this chapter if you review Chapter 9, "Quick Parts," before continuing here.

In the introduction to this book, you can find a list of resources for those who want more basic-level information, in the section titled "Who Will Benefit Most from This Book."

What's New for Reference Tools in Word 2007

In Chapter 9, you've already seen the Table Of Contents and Bibliography Building Block galleries. And, although the new bibliography feature stands out as the biggest story for what's new with reference tools, there are other advances of note as well.

First, as with most features, how you access reference and research tools has changed. Most reference tools are on the References tab, shown here.

However, Cross-References (shown in the preceding graphic) are also available on the Insert tab, in the Links group, as shown on the left in the graphics that follow. Additionally, the Research pane is available from the Review tab, in the Proofing group, as shown on the right in the graphics that follow.

Notice, in the Proofing group, a new feature named Translation ScreenTip. For those working in multi-language documents, this tool is a nice timesaver. Once you enable this feature, you can just point to a word to see a ScreenTip that provides a complete cross-language dictionary reference.

To enable Translation ScreenTips, on the Review tab, in the Proofing group, click Translation ScreenTip and then click the language for which you want to see ScreenTips, as shown here.

Translation ScreenTips are available in the same languages for which you have the appropriate dictionaries installed. The languages you see by default in the Translation ScreenTip list vary by Microsoft Office language version. However, keep in mind that you can't necessarily use ScreenTip translations between all of the languages listed. For example, I'm able to translate between English and French or Spanish. However, I can only translate Arabic to or from French using the ScreenTip tool. To view the language pairs for which you have dictionaries installed, on the Research pane, click Research Options and then click Update\Remove. Also keep in mind that you may have more translation options available to you through the Research pane, using online translation dictionaries.

Editing Reference Fields

Nowhere in Word is the ability to directly edit field codes, introduced in Chapter 9, more important than when working with reference fields.

Reference fields such as TOC and INDEX offer many more customization options than are available through their respective dialog boxes. And, editing table entry fields on screen can save tremendous time over working with the Mark <Feature> Entry dialog boxes. Many of the instructions provided in this chapter are for editing field codes directly either because it is the only way to accomplish the task, or because it is the faster method.

Remember that, if you don't know if the customization you need for a field is available, or you're not sure of the syntax, you can get that information from the Field dialog box. Access this dialog box from the Quick Parts gallery on the Insert tab. Or, right-click a field and then select Edit Field.

As you work through this chapter, remember the following commands for working with field codes.

Command	Action
CTRL+F9	Converts selected text to a field. Or, if no text is selected, inserts empty field braces. To become a valid field, the selected text must include a field name and any required syntax for that field. As needed, field switches and other customization can also be included. This command is only available as a keyboard shortcut.
F9	Updates selected fields. This option is also available when you right-click a field. Note that, to display the field result, it's often necessary to update the field after converting text to a field. Additionally, you can update specific reference field types from relevant groups on the References tab, or from the Content Control headings for tables of contents and bibliographies.
CTRL+SHIFT+F9	Removes the selected field code and leaves only its result. Note that this shortcut does not work with table entry fields, because their result is not displayed in the same field. This command is only available as a keyboard shortcut, except when working with LINK fields, as introduced in Chapter 7, "Managing Graphics."
SHIFT+F9	Toggles the selected field between its code and its result. This command is also available from the shortcut menu that appears when you right-click a field. When working with reference tables that contain hyperlinks, use ALT+F9 (discussed in the next row of this table), instead, to easily access the reference table field code instead of the field codes for individual entry hyperlinks.
ALT+F9	Toggles all fields between their codes and results. This command toggles the setting Show Field Codes Instead Of Their Values, available on the Advanced tab of the Word Options dialog box. The setting you enable when using this command will apply to all documents you open until you use the toggle command again.

Chapter 10

My favorite thing about working with reference field codes is that they give you the ability to customize so much that you might not expect. For example, do you want to preserve line breaks in headings that appear in the table of contents? Just add the \x switch. If that detail is addressed, there's a good chance the one you need is as well. The Field dialog box shows 16 available switches for the TOC field, 15 switches for the INDEX field, and 8 switches plus formatting options for the REF field (cross-reference). Many of the most commonly used switches for these fields are addressed as this chapter progresses.

INSIDE OUT   Suppress text associated with paragraph numbers in cross-references

Cross-references offer a great example of how easy it can be to customize field codes.

On a number of occasions, I've run into documents where many cross-references to paragraph numbers were required, but the owner of the document didn't want the cross-references to include the text associated with the paragraph number (such as words like *Article*, *Section*, or *Appendix*).

The cross reference (REF) field offers a \t switch that suppresses all nondelimited characters. So, for example, if you have a cross-reference to *Article I* and add the \t switch, the reference will appear just as *I*.

So, what do you do when you have hundreds of cross-references throughout the document that need the same switch? Use the Replace feature. When you toggle all fields to display field codes (ALT+F9), the Replace feature will search field code content as text.

A cross-reference to a paragraph number uses either the \r, \n, or \w switch (depending upon which paragraph number style you use). So, you can simply search for instances of the applicable paragraph number switch and replace it with that same switch plus the \t switch (remember to type a space between the two switches in the Replace box). Then, select the entire document (CTRL+A), press F9 to update all selected fields, and then press ALT+F9 again to display field results.

Managing Tables of Contents

When you insert one of the built-in tables of contents from the Table Of Contents Building Block gallery, you get a table of contents built from text formatted with the first three outline levels. Keep in mind that this includes both the built-in heading styles Heading 1 through Heading 3, and any other paragraphs formatted to levels one through three using the Outline Level paragraph formatting options available in the Paragraph dialog box, as shown here.

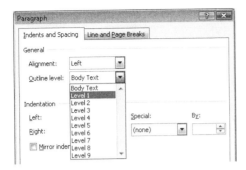

You can open the Table Of Contents dialog box to edit the options for what content is used to generate your table of contents, or edit the field code directly. To access the dialog box, on the References tab, click Table Of Contents and then click Insert Table Of Contents.

INSIDE OUT   Benefits of Using Table of Contents Building Blocks

Although you can go directly to the Table Of Contents dialog box to insert your table of contents instead of using the Building Block options, remember that you can customize table of contents Building Block entries and save your customizations to the Table Of Contents gallery. The benefits offered by using Building Block entries, including the ability to swap designs or update the table of contents directly from the Content Control, make it worthwhile to start with the Building Block options rather than trying to circumvent them. For that matter, you can simply create a TOC field on screen as well, but editing the field inside the Content Control gives you the same flexibility without losing any functionality.

Additionally, when you need to remove a table of contents from the document, use the Remove Table Of Contents option at the bottom of the Table Of Contents gallery, whether or not you inserted your table of contents using Building Blocks. This option removes the TOC field, the Content Control (if applicable), and all hidden bookmarks added by the table of contents. The fact that this option removes hidden bookmarks resolves a longstanding issue, because hidden bookmarks left behind by deleted tables of contents can become a source of document instability if the number of bookmarks becomes excessive.

To view the hidden bookmarks added to your document by a table of contents, on the Insert tab, click Bookmarks and then select the Hidden Bookmarks check box. Note that you may need to turn the Hidden Bookmarks option off and then on again to reveal the bookmarks. Hidden bookmarks added by your table of contents begin with the characters "_Toc."

Editing the field code can be faster and gives you more flexibility than using the dialog box. The following list explains how to edit the field code for some common customizations.

- To generate the table of contents from Heading styles but not other text formatted with Outline Level formatting, delete the \u switch from the default TOC field code.

- To generate the table of contents from table entry fields (TC entries) instead of outline levels or styles, add the \f switch and delete both the \u switch and the \o switch (along with the "1-3" level indicators that follow the \o switch by default).

- To specify additional styles from which to generate the table of contents, add the \t switch, followed by the style name and level number, each separated by commas and all contained inside a single set of quotation marks. The example field code shown here is for a table of contents generated from heading styles Heading 1 through Heading 3, along with level one entries from a style named Page Heading and level three entries from a style named Table Heading.

{ TOC·\o·"1-3"·\u·\t·"Page Heading,·1,·Table Heading,·3" }

> **Note**
>
> After you add, edit, or delete any content from a field code, remember to press F9 to update the result.

TROUBLESHOOTING

My table of contents or index formatting changed unexpectedly

If you apply direct formatting to an entry in your table of contents or index and other entries change as well, that's because the paragraph styles used in table of contents and indexes are all set, by default, to update automatically.

So, for example, if you select a first-level entry in a table of contents and format it to be bold, all other entries on the same level will become bold as well, because TOC 1 paragraph style uses the Automatically Update setting.

You can disable Automatically Update through the Modify Style dialog box. To access this dialog box for TOC or Index styles, either go through the Manage Styles dialog box (get more information on using the new Manage Styles feature in Chapter 5, "Styles") or click the Modify button in the Table Of Contents or Index dialog box, as applicable.

Using TC Entry Fields

When you need to generate a table of contents from pieces of text that comprise just part of a paragraph—such as run-in headings—the most reliable way to accomplish this is with TC entry fields. You can create these field codes directly, but this is one case where the dialog box might save you time.

The Mark Table Of Contents Entry dialog box is only available through the keyboard shortcut ALT+SHIFT+O (unless you add the command to your Quick Access Toolbar). One of the nicest things about the dialog box shown here is that it's modeless, meaning that you can click between the dialog box and the document as much as you need without closing the dialog box.

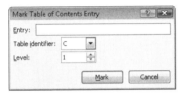

If you select the text to appear in the table of contents before you open or click in the dialog box, the Entry text box will automatically populate with your selected text. Then, just select the table of contents level and click Mark.

Note that you only need to specify a Table Identifier when you need multiple table of contents in the same document. Learn how to work with this option later in this chapter.

The significant drawback to using TC entry fields is that automatic paragraph numbers don't get included with entries. See the Inside Out tip in this section for a nice alternative (other than the Style Separator) for when you need to include paragraph numbers for run-in headings in your table of contents.

TROUBLESHOOTING

I'm having trouble with Style Separators

For those who need to generate a table of contents from run-in headings, the Style Separator has long been a popular option. This feature is available in Word 2007 only from the Customize tab of the Word Options dialog box. But, if you haven't used it yet, now is not the time to start.

Essentially, this feature adds a hidden paragraph mark at the end of the run-in heading, so that the text that appears after the separator looks as if it's in the same paragraph, but it's really in its own paragraph formatted with a different style. The hidden paragraph workaround for tables of contents dates back to the first Windows-based version of Word, and it really is as antiquated an option as that sounds. A few common problems occur with style separators.

- When you make global changes to paragraph marks, such as by using the Replace feature to change formatting in paragraph marks, the style separator is seen as a paragraph mark and will be affected by the change. So, if paragraph formatting is added to the style separator (such as paragraph spacing) and recipients have hidden text enabled to view or print, the text after the separator won't appear as if it's in the same paragraph.

- Because style separators are formatted with hidden text, they will only appear when hidden text is being viewed. Hidden text is considered a formatting mark and becomes visible when you set hidden text to be visible (on the Display tab of the Word Options dialog box) or set all formatting marks to be visible (CTRL+ *).

- Also because of the hidden text attribute of Style Separators, they're recognized as hidden text by the Document Inspector as well as by third-party hidden data removal tools. Removing Style Separators can affect the formatting of your document as well as the content of your table of contents. When the style separator is deleted, the run-in heading takes on the formatting that appeared after the separator, because the heading formatting was stored in the deleted separator.

For a simple alternative to the Style Separator, see the Inside Out tip that follows.

INSIDE OUT   Using linked styles as an alternative to TC entry fields

If you need to generate a table of contents from run-in headings but don't want to use TC entry fields, is there a good alternative? Though Style Separators have long been available for this task, they have their issues, as discussed in the preceding Troubleshooting tip.

However, with the new style functionality that enables you to explicitly create and show linked styles, you now have a simple alternative. (For information on linked styles, see Chapter 5.) Similar to the Style Separator, using linked styles for this task will include automatic paragraph numbers for the run-in headings you add to the table of contents.

To generate a table of contents from text formatted with linked styles, do the following.

1. Create a linked style for each level of your table of contents that will be generated from run-in headings. Include any font formatting in your linked style that's unique to the heading portion of the run-in heading paragraph.

2. In the TOC field code, add the \t switch discussed earlier in this chapter, along with the styles names created in the preceding step and the level number you want to assign to each linked style.

3. Apply the linked styles to the run-in headings where needed throughout the document. Be sure to select only the heading portion of the run-in heading paragraph before applying your style. The text to which you apply the linked style will be the text that appears in your table of contents.

Although you technically were able to use this method in earlier versions of Word, it was not a particularly clean workaround, because linked styles weren't explicitly visible.   The reason linked styles works for this task is that you can only specify paragraph styles in the TOC field code, and you can apply character styles to just part of a paragraph. Linked styles are both paragraph and character styles by design, so you can apply them to your run-in headings and include them in the table of contents.

Note, however, that this technique will only work with run-in headings (just as with the Style Separator). If the first typed character in the paragraph isn't included in your selection, the entry won't appear in the table of contents.

Creating Multiple Tables of Contents in One Document

Although many formatting customization options are available for tables of contents, most TOC field options relate to specifying which document content is used to generate the table of contents. Some of these options have already been addressed in this chapter; those that have not yet been introduced are options to use when you need to create more than one table of contents in a single document. These are as follows.

- Use the \f (Table Identifier) switch with TC entry fields to assign specified entries to a specific table of contents.

- Use the \l (Level) switch with TC entry fields to generate separate tables of contents for different levels of entries.

- Use the bookmark switch to generate a table of contents for just a portion of the document at a time.

- Generate tables of contents from different specified styles.

CAUTION

With any of the options provided here, keep in mind that adding a particular switch might not be all you need to do to get the desired result. You might also need to delete switches that add content you don't want. For example, if generating a table of contents only from TC entry fields that use a specific table identifier, be sure that the \o, \u, or \t switches are not included, or you might get other content in your table of contents as well. When editing any field code directly, it's important to understand all the existing switches that appear in the field code as well as those you choose to add.

Using the Table Identifier Switch

When you generate a table of contents from TC entry fields, you can specify a Table Identifier, mentioned earlier. This option is inserted into the TC entry field as the

\f switch, followed by an identifying letter. To generate a table of contents from just those entries labeled with a specific Table Identifier, add the same \f switch, with the same identifying letter, to the TOC field code. For example, if you have a TC entry field that uses E as its identifier, as you see here,

`{ TC·"Sample·Entry"·\f·E·\l·"1" }`

use the same identifier in the TOC field code to generate a table of contents only from TC entries that have the E identifier, like so:

`{ TOC·\f·E }`

Using the Level Switch

Like the Table Identifier switch, the Level switch only affects tables of contents generated from TC entry fields. Each TC entry field contains a Level switch, indicating the level of the table of contents on which the entry needs to appear. To generate a table of contents for just TC entry fields that specify a given level, add that same Level switch to the TOC field.

Using Bookmarks

To generate a table of contents from just a portion of the document, first add a bookmark around the desired portion of the document. Then, add the \b switch, along with the bookmark name in quotation marks, to the TOC field. In the example shown here, part of the document is contained within a bookmark named Sample. The table of contents will be generated from only content within that bookmark.

`{ TOC·\b·"Sample" }`

This is a particularly nice option because it enables you to generate multiple tables of contents in a document, but still use any available content option (such as outline levels or styles) for generating each table of contents.

Using Specified Styles

As discussed earlier, the \t switch enables you to include styled text in your table of contents other than text formatted with built-in heading styles or Outline Level formatting. Remember to delete the \o and \u switches to avoid using those built-in heading and outline options when you want to generate the table of contents only with styles specified using the \t switch.

INSIDE OUT   **Suppressing page numbers for just some table of contents levels**

One of the most commonly needed table of contents customizations, other than those for selecting the content used to generate the table of contents, is the ability to suppress page numbers. Though you can use the Table Of Contents dialog box to do this for all levels, the only way to suppress page number for just some table of contents levels is through the field code.

To do this, use the \n switch. By itself, the \n switch suppresses numbers for all table of contents entries. To specify levels, indicate the range to suppress as highest level through lowest level, just as when using the \o switch to specify which outline levels to include.

For example, to suppress page numbers for level three, but show them on any other levels, add **\n "3-3"** to your field code. To suppress page numbers for levels two through four, add **\n "2-4"** to your field code.

TROUBLESHOOTING

The TOC field doesn't offer the options I need

If you've reviewed all of the available TOC field switches and still can't find the option you need for your particular formatting requirements, consider some possible easy options before you start typing that table of contents manually and spending your day searching for page numbers.

First of all, the table of contents you need is probably at least close to an available TOC field option. For example, do you need the table of contents to show page numbering in a format that's not possible with a TOC field? If so, generate the table of contents automatically to be as close as possible, then convert the field to text (CTRL+SHIFT+F9) and make your remaining customizations.

Or, you can take that one step further and try using a macro either to generate the manual table of contents you need automatically whenever you need to update it, or to complete the automatic table of contents that you converted to text. Find an example of this that you can use and customize in the sample file named Sample Macros.dotm that accompanies Chapter 21, "VBA Primer."

Creating a Table of Figures

A table of figures is actually just a TOC field with a unique switch. The \c switch indicates that the table is a table of figures, and it requires that you specify a caption label. For example, the field code for a table of figures generated for a set of objects labeled *Figure* looks like this:

```
{ TOC \c "Figure" }
```

Because tables of figures use the TOC field code, some field options such as adding hyperlinks between entries and their referenced text, or suppressing page numbers, can be used in tables of figures as well.

TROUBLESHOOTING

AutoCaption doesn't work on my equations

As always, a table of figures is generated from sequence fields that are identified with a caption label. These labeled sequence fields are created and formatted automatically using the Insert Caption feature on the References tab.

When you click Insert Caption, the Caption dialog box opens. In that dialog box, you can select AutoCaption, through which you can specify certain types of objects to be automatically captioned when created or inserted. Note that once you enable AutoCaption for an object type, it remains on for all documents you edit until you disable the option.

The list of items available to AutoCaption can vary based on the programs installed on your computer. For example, Microsoft Visio Drawing Object will only appear in the list of AutoCaption options if Microsoft Visio is installed.

However, if you're accustomed to being able to use AutoCaption for equations and that no longer works, here's the reason. The AutoCaption equation option works with Microsoft Equation 3.0, the equation generating program used in previous versions of Word (and still available to legacy documents).

The new equation-building functionality for Word 2007 is built-in functionality. As mentioned in Chapter 9, the new functionality is much improved over Equation 3.0. However, the new equation tools don't work with AutoCaption.

Of course, that doesn't mean you can't automatically caption your equations. To do this, just format a placeholder from the Equation gallery as you want it to appear and add a caption to it. Then, select the equation and caption and add them to your Equation gallery as a single entry. When you create new equations from that gallery entry, they'll include the caption. Because the caption contains a sequence field, it will automatically number just as if AutoCaption had inserted it. For help saving custom Building Block entries, see Chapter 9.

Working with Indexes

No matter what you've heard or experienced in the past, creating an index really doesn't need to consume the better part of your youth. Here's the secret: There are two efficient ways to mark entries for your index, and neither one relies solely on the Mark Index Entry dialog box.

Using Index Entry Fields

If you want to manually work through your document and mark entries as you find them, creating and editing field codes can help you save significant time and reduce errors. All you need to know is the correct syntax for index entry (XE) field codes.

An index can have up to nine levels. Where entry names are specified in the INDEX field, each level is separated by a colon. So, for example, an index entry in this book that provides information about the INDEX field code might be a third-level entry, like so:

{PAGE * ROMAN}

The XE field code for this reference would look like this:

{XE "Fields:Reference:Index"}

Entries often need to specify a page range instead of a page number. Do this by first bookmarking the text to reference and then adding the \r switch, along with the bookmark name, to the XE field code. If you surround the text for the preceding entry with a bookmark named **testentry**, the XE field code to reference that bookmark for a page range will look like this:

{XE "Fields:Reference:Index" \r "testentry"}

To type a cross-reference to be used in place of page numbers for an entry, use the \t switch followed by the reference text, like so:

{XE "Fields:Reference:Index" \t "See Building Blocks"}

Note that switches for bold or italic formatting on specified entries (the \b and \i switches, respectively) are also common.

As mentioned earlier, many switches are available for the INDEX field code, but these are the most common. Once you understand this syntax, you can use your knowledge of this field code along with the Mark Index Entry dialog box, to save tremendous time when marking your document for an index.

Marking an Index

Start with the Mark Index Entry dialog box. To access this dialog box, on the References tab, in the Index group, click Mark Entry. Or, press ALT+SHIFT+X.

The dialog box has the substantial benefit that it will mark all instances of an entry automatically. However, using the Mark All option assumes that the text you want to mark uses the same word(s) as the index entry. It also assumes that you've got great attention to detail, because index entries are very sensitive. That is, misspell a word or differ capitalization for your entry name, and you get a separate entry.

So, depending on your particular needs, you might want to create your XE fields directly, or insert an XE field through the Mark Index Entry dialog box and then copy and edit it as needed.

When using the dialog box, shown here, keep a few things in mind.

- To mark entries with more than two levels, add all subsequent levels together in the Subentry box, each level separated by a colon.

- Selected document text will only populate the Main Entry box, not the Subentry. Be very careful when typing entry text, because entries are both spelling and case sensitive.

- To reference a range of pages, you must create the bookmark for the page range before it will be accessible in this dialog box.

Creating An Index from an AutoMark File

If you know the list of entries you want to appear in your index and you know what text needs to be marked to create that index, you don't need to use either the dialog box or create XE fields yourself. Just create an AutoMark file.

> **Note**
>
> If you've searched Word help on the topic of indexes, you might also see the AutoMark option referred to as using a "concordance" file.

To create an AutoMark file, start with a blank Word document and insert a two-column table. Your table should not have headers and does not require formatting, but it must be a genuine Word table (as opposed to creating the appearance of a table with tabs or embedding a Microsoft Excel table).

- Use one row per each piece of text to be marked. If you're marking more than one piece of text for a given entry, create a separate row for each.

- Type the text to be marked in the left column and the entry name in the right column.

- To type entry names that include subentries, just add a colon between each level.

When you're ready to mark your index, save and close the AutoMark file. Note also that, if you later need to add entries, you can add them to the same AutoMark file and run the procedure that follows again without duplicating entries.

To mark your document using this file, in the document to be marked, do the following.

1. On the References tab in the Index group, click Insert Index and then click AutoMark.

2. In the AutoMark dialog box, browse to your AutoMark file.

    Notice that the files of type defaults to the legacy Word document format. You can use any Word document format as an AutoMark file, so change the files of type accordingly to find your .docx or other Word 2007 file.

3. When you select the file you need, click Open. The destination document will automatically be marked with all entries from your AutoMark file.

Once your document is marked, go ahead and insert or update your index. Keep in mind that you can insert an index from the References tab or by creating an INDEX field directly. Either way, if you need additional customizations for your index, check out the available INDEX field switches before considering complicated workarounds.

Creating a Bibliography

The bibliography feature is a welcome addition to Word reference tools, and it works quite nicely.

You can save sources to be available to any document where you need to cite them, and you can add sources just for particular documents as well. You can even generate a unique bibliography just for sources in a given language.

Creating and Managing Sources

To create a new source, on the References tab, in the Citations & Bibliography group, click Insert Citation and then click Add New Source. Or, click Manages Sources and then click New.

In the Create Source dialog box, shown in the following image, complete the fields you want to include for your source. Note that you can add\edit information for a saved source at any time.

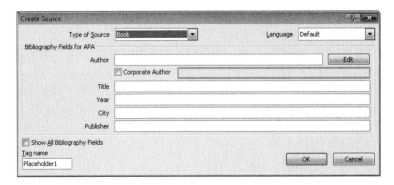

Notice the option Show All Bibliography Fields at the bottom of the dialog box, which greatly expands the number of fields available to your sources. Also notice the Edit options for the *Author, Editor,* and *Translator* fields. This opens the Edit Name dialog box, where you can easily create a list of names. Finally, notice Tag Name at the bottom of the dialog box. This tag name is used in the CITATION field codes to uniquely identify the referenced source.

When you create a new source, it's automatically added to your master source list and available to your active document as well. In the Source Manager, you can copy sources between the master list and active document, as well as add, edit, or delete sources, or even add sources from a new source list. Source lists are saved as XML files. To access the Source Manager, on the References tab, in the Citations & Bibliography group, click Manage Sources.

> **Note**
>
> Because source lists are saved as XML files, you can add or edit sources directly in the XML, and easily share source lists with others. Learn how to edit Office Open XML files in Chapter 22, "Office Open XML Essentials."

Working with Citations

Once a source is available to your active document, you can insert a citation to that source. To do this, on the References tab, click Insert Citation and then click the source name to reference. If the source name you need doesn't appear here, the source has not been made available to your active document. To make existing sources available to the active document, use the Source Manager introduced earlier to copy them from the master source list.

If you haven't yet added a source for the citation you need, click Add New Placeholder under the Insert Citation options. This will enable you to add a new Tag Name, as mentioned earlier, for a source to be edited later.

When a citation is added to your document through the Insert Citation options, it's contained within a Content Control, which provides additional functionality. From the citation control, as shown here, you can edit the citation to specify pages or to suppress the author, year, or title in the citation. You can also edit the source or convert the citation to static text.

CAUTION

The keyboard shortcut CTRL+SHIFT+F9 doesn't work to convert a citation to text. If you use this keyboard shortcut, the citation will be deleted. To remove the citation functionality and leave just the citation text, use the option provided in the Content Control.

Creating a Bibliography

Once you've inserted at least one citation in your document, you can generate a bibliography. Note that bibliographies can only be inserted from the Bibliography gallery, though you can, of course, save your own customized bibliographies to the gallery. Once you insert a bibliography, notice that the Bibliography gallery is also available from the heading of the Content Control that contains the bibliography.

INSIDE OUT   Create a unique bibliography for sources in a specified language

If you have multiple languages enabled, you can assign any source to a specific language and then create separate bibliographies for sources in each language.

To enable additional languages for use in the 2007 Office release, on the Start menu point to All Programs, click Microsoft Office, click Microsoft Office Tools, and then click Microsoft Office 2007 Language Settings. Select a language from the Available Editing Languages list and then click Add. Newly added languages become available the next time you open a given 2007 release program.

To generate unique bibliographies for sources in different languages, start by assigning sources to the appropriate language. Once multiple languages are enabled, you'll find the Language option at the top-right of the Create Source or Edit Source dialog box.

After you insert a bibliography, click the Content Control heading and then click Filter Languages, as shown here.

Chapter 10

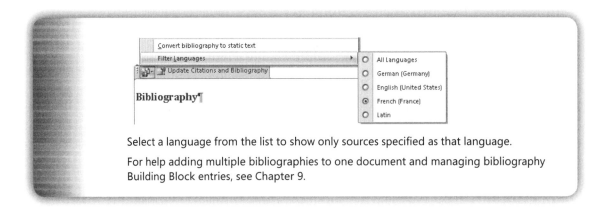

Select a language from the list to show only sources specified as that language.

For help adding multiple bibliographies to one document and managing bibliography Building Block entries, see Chapter 9.

A Footnote About Footnotes and Endnotes

As advanced users, you probably know how to insert, format, and convert between footnotes and endnotes. But, a couple of items still warrant mentioning here.

The majority of issues that even advanced users run into with footnotes and endnotes are either related to the separators, which are addressed in the Troubleshooting tip in this section, or to numbering, which is addressed in Chapter 8, "Sections."

In addition to these issues, note the Next Footnote options in the Footnotes group on the References tab (shown here), which you can use to scroll through all footnotes and endnotes in your document.

Also note that the Footnote And Endnote dialog box, where you access format settings including number format and numbering options, is available from the dialog launcher at the bottom-right corner of the Footnotes group.

TROUBLESHOOTING

I can't access that line above my footnotes or endnotes

The line that appears by default above footnotes and endnotes is not in the body of the document or the document footer. It's a Footnote (or Endnote) Separator. The default separator is a short line, approximately 2 inches (5.08 cm), that begins at the left margin. When a separator line extends from the left to the right margin, that's the Footnote (or Endnote) Continuation Separator. It occurs when a footnote runs onto a second page. Similarly inaccessible text might also appear at the bottom of footnotes that extend to additional pages. This is the Footnote (or Endnote) Continuation Notice.

You can edit the separators and notices from the Notes pane, accessible from Draft, Outline, or Web Layout view by clicking Show Notes on the References tab, or by double-clicking a footnote or endnote reference where it appears in the text. Select the separator or notice you need from the drop-down list at the top of the Notes pane.

Separators and notices sit in paragraph marks just like text. You can delete the existing separators, add other content to act as separators, add text or other content to the notices, and use font and paragraph formatting (including styles) to format any of these. Additionally, the separators have a Reset option at the top of the Notes pane that will replace whatever content you add or edit with the default separator. The Reset option will not, however, remove formatting customizations you make. So, to reset the formatting of a separator (formatted with Normal style by default), press CTRL+SHIFT+N.

Content Controls: Creating Forms and Then Some

M icrosoft Word form controls have changed. In fact, they're not just for forms any-more. Although the legacy form controls still exist for anyone adverse to saving time and getting better results, the new Content Controls functionality in Microsoft Office Word 2007 offers very good news for the rest of us.

As you might have gathered from that introduction, this isn't the place to learn about the legacy form controls that you know from the past several versions. They're still there because the new Content Controls aren't available to legacy documents. But this book is about the 2007 Microsoft Office release, and so this chapter focuses on understanding and working with the new, and outrageously improved, Content Controls capability.

That said, keep in mind that Content Controls are a new type of functionality—not intended to be a direct replacement of the legacy controls. You'll notice, for example that there are no check boxes. However, if you look at Content Controls and think they don't have what you need for a particular project, consider automating the document input using a dialog box instead of resigning yourself to legacy form controls.

With all the Microsoft Office template automation I do, I've never once used the legacy form controls in a document unless a client absolutely insisted, because they're cumber-some to create and to use and, frankly, they're ugly. When I've needed to automate tem-plates for user input in the past, I've always created dialog boxes using Microsoft Visual Basic for Applications (VBA).

Creating and automating dialog boxes is pretty quick and easy to do, and you can learn the basics of how to do this in Chapter 21, "VBA Primer." But, the new XML-based Con-tent Controls further simplify quite a bit of that work. So, there will be times when a dialog box is no longer needed. Content Controls are so user-friendly that they've been integrated with several built-in features of Office Word 2007. And, you can create your own for forms and many document uses. If you create just about any type of Word doc-uments and templates for others to use, or that you frequently reuse, you need to know about Content Controls.

Chapter Assumptions

This chapter assumes that you have some familiarity with form control terminology (such as *drop-down list* and *date picker*), as well as at least a basic understanding of docu-ment properties and document protection.

Additionally, this chapter makes several references to Document Building Blocks and other types of Quick Parts functionality that are integrated with Content Control functionality. If you're not familiar with these new capabilities, you'll get more out of this chapter if you review Chapter 9, "Quick Parts," before continuing here.

Although Content Controls are new functionality, you're not new users of Microsoft Word. So, I'm approaching this feature, like all topics throughout this book, from an advanced perspective. This chapter covers the use of Content Controls from the user interface, and it explains the types of automation available with Content Controls. However, coverage of how to work with Content Controls using XML is addressed primarily in Chapter 22, "Office Open XML Essentials." If you're new to Content Controls, consider this chapter a prerequisite for working with this feature in Chapter 22.

In the introduction to this book, you can find a list of resources for those who want more basic-level information, in the section titled "Who Will Benefit Most from This Book."

Working with Content Controls

A Content Control is, essentially, a container that enables you to store and act on different types of document content. Some of these controls are simply placeholders for text or other content, some enable your users to select from choices of content that you specify, and some provide additional types of functionality to help you do more with the content they contain. All Content Controls are XML-based, so they enable you to take advantage of XML data storage and sharing capabilities to get more done in your documents with less work.

As shown in Chapter 9, you can recognize a Content Control in a couple of ways. When you hover over any Content Control, it appears shaded (blue in most color schemes), as shown here on the left. When you click in or otherwise activate a control, you either see a tag at the top that contains a title, such as Name in the example shown here on the right, or a similar tag on the left of the control that contains no text. The tag that appears at the top may have additional icons that provide other functionality for the content within the control. (When working in Draft view, however, only the content within the control is visible and not the control itself.)

Most controls contain placeholder text or other placeholder content until user content is added. If a control contains placeholder content, that content will be selected when you click in the control. If the control has already been edited by a user, you see the border of the control when you click in it, but text won't automatically be selected.

Types of Content Controls

Seven types of Content Controls are available, as follows.

Control	Description
Rich Text	A Rich Text control can contain text, tables, graphics, and most formatting that you can apply in the body of the document. A single Rich Text control can also contain multiple paragraphs.
Plain Text	A Plain Text control can contain text as well as common font and paragraph formatting. These controls can't take tables or graphics and can only contain a single paragraph. (Note that Plain Text Properties in the Content Control Properties dialog box include an option to allow multiple paragraphs. The label on that option is incorrect, as explained later in this chapter.)
	Text Wrapping breaks can be inserted into Plain Text controls from the Breaks options on the Page Layout tab. Depending on the settings for the individual controls, however, manual line breaks (SHIFT+ENTER) may not be available in Plain Text controls.
	If you press the TAB key from a Plain Text control, your insertion point moves to the next Content Control. To add a tab character inside a Plain Text control, press CTRL+TAB.
Picture	A Picture control lets you click the placeholder to add a picture from your saved picture files. Once a Picture control contains a picture, click the picture icon on the tab containing the control name to change the picture, or right-click the image and select Change Picture. See Chapter 7, "Managing Graphics," to learn more about the Change Picture command, which is available to all pictures in your Word 2007 documents. (Note that when a Picture control in a header or footer contains a placeholder, you can click the placeholder to add your image when working in Print Layout view without having to open the header or footer.)
Drop-Down List	A Drop-Down List control gives you the ability to add multiple content choices from which users can select. With this control type, users can only select from the options provided and can't type text directly into the control. Click the arrow on the right side of the control to access the list of options.
Combo Box	Like a Drop-Down list, a Combo Box control gives you the ability to add multiple content choices from which users can select. However, with a Combo Box, users can type text directly in the control or select from the options provided. Click the arrow on the right side of the control to select from the list of options.
	Similar to a Plain Text control, a Combo Box control can't accept tables or graphics. Combo Box controls are designed to only allow a single line of text, but you can insert a Text Wrapping Break from the Breaks options on the Page Layout tab.
Date Picker	Similar to a Combo Box control, a Date Picker enables you to add text to a control or select from options. In this case, click the arrow on the right side of the control for a calendar from which you can select a date.
Building Block Gallery	The Building Block Gallery Content Control enables you to select a Building Block gallery to be accessible from the Content Control. This control type has the same behavior as Rich Text controls in addition to the ability to select a gallery option. Once you assign a gallery to a control, that gallery is accessible at a click from an icon on the tab at the top of the control.
	Note that not all built-in galleries are available to Building Block Gallery controls, but all custom galleries are.

Built-In Features That Use Content Controls

The new Quick Parts functionality is heavily integrated with Content Controls. Many built-in Building Block entries include Content Controls, such as cover pages, headers, and footers. Some other types of built-in Building Block entries (such as tables of contents, bibliographies, and equations) are wholly contained in Content Controls. Additionally, Document Property Quick Parts are all created using Content Controls.

Notice that, in instances where an entire Building Block entry is stored within a control, the control provides additional functionality, such as the ability to update a table of contents or bibliography, or formatting and layout options for equations.

See Chapter 9 to learn about how Quick Parts work with Content Controls.

> **Note**
>
> In addition to Quick Parts, Content Controls are used in most of the built-in Word templates.

INSIDE OUT DATE fields vs. Date Pickers

If you insert a DATE field by any method (using the Date And Time dialog box, using the Field dialog box, or creating the field on screen), it appears to be inside a Content Control. In fact, this will happen whether you're working in a Word 2007 document or a legacy document, the latter of which is not even compatible with Content Controls.

This is simply an anomaly. Call it an undocumented feature, if you will. The DATE field does no harm in its slightly odd condition, and it has a nice little bonus of an Update icon on the tag at the top of the control, which does the same thing as pressing F9 to update a selected field.

However, if you're working in a Word 2007 document, take advantage of the added functionality available to some types of controls and consider if a Date Picker control can possibly do the job more effectively.

Using Content Controls

When you use Content Controls that already exist in a document, such as in the built-in Word templates, you might notice that some disappear when you type in them while others can't be deleted at all.

Some controls can be set to be removed when their content is edited. All controls can be set to not allow deletion or even to not allow editing. Note also that several types of Content Controls can be used with the Document Protection feature, discussed later, for documents in which you want to completely manage document layout and allow users to only edit within designated controls.

You can apply styles and formatting to content inside controls just as you can in the body of the document. However, controls can also be formatted to automatically use a particular style or formatting when you add content.

Note that placeholder content does print, but the Content Control itself does not.

Creating Controls

To create a new Content Control, on the Developer tab, in the Controls group (shown here), just click the type of control you want.

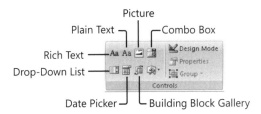

When you do, the control will be added at your insertion point and will take on default settings for that control. These settings, all of which you can edit for the individual controls you create, are as follows.

- Content controls take on the same formatting as the paragraph into which they're inserted.

- Plain Text controls do not allow line breaks (other than the Text Wrapping Break mentioned earlier).

- Every type of control you can create contains placeholder content. For picture controls, this is a graphic that you can click to open the Insert Picture dialog box. For all other control types, this is text, such as "Click here to enter text" for Rich Text and Plain Text controls. This text is formatted with a character style named Placeholder Text that applies gray font color by default. Placeholder text formatting is separate from the formatting for content you add to controls, so that you can easily tell the difference between placeholder text and user-edited text.

- Controls are not deleted when their placeholder content is edited.

- Users can edit and delete controls.

- Building Blocks Gallery controls default to showing the Quick Parts gallery.

- Date Picker controls default to displaying selected dates using the Windows System Short Date setting.

> **Note**
>
> The System Short Date setting for Windows is available through the Windows Control Panel, under Regional And Language options.

- Combo Box controls have no functionality beyond that of Plain Text controls until you add a list of options to them.

- Drop-Down List controls have no functionality until you add a list of options to them.

Formatting Controls and Editing Properties

Once you've added a control to your document, you can name the control, customize the options provided in the preceding list, and format both the placeholder content and the user-edited content within the control.

To edit controls, start by turning on Design Mode. Note that you can access control properties without being in Design Mode, but because of additional options that are limited to Design Mode, your best bet is to go there whenever you need to edit Content Control settings. To turn on Design Mode, on the Developer tab, in the Controls group, click Design Mode.

> **Note**
>
> If you don't see the Developer tab, click the Microsoft Office Button and then click Word Options. On the Popular tab, click Show Developer Tab In The Ribbon. Note that this setting is available from the <Program Name> Options dialog box in any program where you see the Ribbon. As with many settings on the Popular tab, enabling this setting in any of these programs will show the Developer tab in all of them.

When you turn on Design Mode, the tags inside Content Controls become visible, as in this example. The tags are the shapes that wrap around the text and sit inside the control.

These are XML tags, used to identify the particular control when you want to act on it programmatically. XML tags are always paired, as you see here, wrapping around the content to which they refer.

> **Note**
> By default, tags on Content Controls have the same name as the title of the control, but you can customize this when creating your own controls.

As mentioned in Chapter 9, XML tags are also visible for many types of Quick Parts when Design Mode is enabled. These can be very handy for identifying the start and end points of various content types when you need to do advanced editing. XML tags surrounding Quick Part use the type of Quick Part as the name of the XML tag, such as Cover Pages, to make them easy to recognize. This is particularly good to keep in mind when working in Design Mode because not all XML tags you see indicate the presence of Content Controls.

Editing Control Properties

To edit the settings for a control, click in that control and then, on the Developer tab, in the Controls group, click Properties to open the Content Control Properties dialog box. When Design Mode is active, Properties is also available from the shortcut menu you get when you right-click in a Content Control.

The Content Control Properties dialog box has the same name regardless of the control type you're editing, but the options available in the dialog box change depending on the type of control, as detailed in the list that follows.

> **Note**
> If you click Properties and a Properties pane opens that shows "**ThisDocument** Document" at the top of the pane, your insertion point is either not inside a Content Control, or not inside a control for which you can edit properties (such as the DATE field control mentioned earlier or the control surrounding a built-in Table Of Contents Building Block entry). Just click the X at the top of that pane to close it, make sure your insertion point is inside the control for which you want to edit properties, and then click Properties again.

- General options, shown in the image that follows, are the same for all controls except Picture controls, which don't offer the Style option. See the Inside Out tip in this section for how to apply font and paragraph formatting to user-edited content in Picture controls.

- Locking options, shown here, are the same for all controls. Note that, if you set a control to not allow editing, that control can't be formatted outside of Design Mode. Also note that, because the placeholder content (that is, content added or edited while in Design Mode) has its own formatting and doesn't take on formatting you set for user-edited content in the control, formatting needs to be applied directly to placeholder content while in Design Mode for that formatting to be reflected in the document.

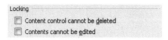

> **Note**
>
> When setting controls to not be edited or deleted, remember that any user of the document has the ability to edit those settings. To keep users from removing or altering controls where you need to control layout or content, use Document Protection along with your Content Controls, as discussed later in this chapter.

- With the exception of Picture controls, each control also has control-specific properties available in this dialog box. As mentioned earlier, these include the option to have the control automatically removed when its content is edited. And, for Plain Text controls, this also includes the option to allow line breaks. Find more information about line breaks in Plain Text controls in a Troubleshooting tip within this section.

  The control-specific properties within this dialog box are where you'll find the option to select a gallery and related category for a Building Block Gallery control, or add list items for a Drop-Down List control.

  Notice, in the Drop-Down List Properties shown here, that you can add, edit, delete, or reorder list entries.

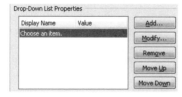

Note

Drop-Down List Properties looks identical in the Content Control Properties dialog box for both Drop-Down List and Combo Box controls.

TROUBLESHOOTING

I can't create multiple paragraphs in a Plain Text control

The Content Control Properties dialog box for Plain Text controls explicitly states that the option to allow carriage returns means to allow multiple paragraphs. If you've enabled that option but still can't get multiple paragraphs in that control, you're not wrong. The information in that dialog box is wrong.

Allowing "carriage returns" in Plain Text Content Controls doesn't enable multiple paragraphs. It enables line breaks (SHIFT+ENTER) only. In fact, if you copy multiple paragraphs and paste them into a Plain Text control, the paragraph marks will be converted automatically to line breaks.

To get multiple paragraphs in a single Content Control, use the Rich Text control.

INSIDE OUT   Use the XML tags to format user-edited content

The left side of the XML tag inside any Content Control stores the formatting for the user-edited content in that control. So, to apply a style or formatting, just select the left side of the control and apply the formatting you need as if you had selected text. The formatting will not appear on placeholder text, but it will automatically be used when the content of the control is edited.

Formatting the left tag is interchangeable with the option Use A Style To Format Contents, which appears in the Content Control Properties dialog box. However, it's a bit more flexible because, in addition to being able to apply linked or character styles, you can also apply direct formatting.

Thanks for this very cool tip go to Tristan Davis, a Program Manager at Microsoft in charge of Content Controls and other programmability issues for the 2007 release, who also provided other insights used in this chapter and in Part 5 of this book, "Templates, Automation, and Customization."

Note that this tip is particularly handy for Picture controls that don't offer the style option in the Content Control Properties dialog box. For example, you might want to apply a style to the Content Control that provides space before or after the paragraph, paragraph alignment, or even character spacing and positioning, depending on the placement of the Picture control. Keep in mind that paragraph and font formatting only applies to graphics formatted with the In Line With Text graphic layout, which is the default for Picture Content Controls. See Chapter 7 for more on using font and paragraph formatting to format graphics.

Chapter 11

TROUBLESHOOTING

I can't get out of Design Mode

If you turn on Design Mode in a document that contains Content Controls and are then unable to turn it off, you should see a message box explaining that Design Mode can't be turned off because placeholder text in a control contains invalid items. Additionally, when you click OK in that message box, the offending control should be selected.

When this happens, the most likely culprit is usually a floating graphic object included in the placeholder text, though this can also happen when all placeholder content is removed or when one control is placed inside another while in Design Mode.

See Chapter 7 for alternatives to using floating objects in your documents and reasons you might want to consider them. However, if you must include floating objects or other invalid items in the placeholder text, save and close the document and then reopen it. Design Mode will no longer be active.

Note that floating graphics in Content Controls can also make the control look quite odd, because controls wrap around their content.

It's also worth noting that the issues mentioned here occur in some of the built-in templates available from the New Document dialog box, in case you're using those as jumping-off points for creating your own.

Formatting Placeholder and User-Edited Control Content

You must be in Design Mode to add, edit, or format most placeholder content. Any content you add to the control while in Design Mode automatically becomes placeholder content.

To edit the formatting of placeholder text inside a control, the easiest option is to edit the Placeholder Text character style. When you do that, new controls you create will take on the formatting of your edited style. For help editing styles, see Chapter 5, "Styles." Of course, when your Rich Text controls need to contain more complex formatting in placeholder text, such as different styles on different paragraphs, you can use any styles or formatting that you need and apply them directly to the placeholder content.

As discussed earlier in this chapter, using the Style option in the Content Control Properties dialog box, or formatting the left tag inside a control, applies font and paragraph formatting to user-edited content in the control. Keep in mind, however, that when you make changes to the formatting in a control after the control contains user-edited content, your changes won't be reflected automatically on existing content. If a user adds new content at the beginning of the control, it will take on your new formatting. However, from within existing content, formatting will follow Word formatting rules. That is, new content takes on the formatting at the insertion point.

For best results when changing the formatting of controls that already contain some user-edited content, apply the style or formatting you need directly to the existing content and update the formatting for the control either by selecting the left tag or through the Content Control Properties dialog box. That way, you update the formatting on existing content and you're ensured that future editing will result in the formatting you want.

For Picture controls, in addition to using the left tag to apply font and paragraph formatting for user-edited content, you can format the picture placeholder to take on the formatting you need for the user-added picture. When you select the picture placeholder within the Picture control, you get the Picture Tools Format contextual tab. So, you can format attributes—such as changing picture size or applying a grayscale effect—and that formatting will be retained when the placeholder is replaced with a picture. Note that, because picture sizing is proportional by default, if the user-added picture has different proportions from the placeholder, the smaller of the dimensions set in the placeholder is kept and the user-added picture is resized proportionally.

INSIDE OUT   Reset placeholder text or convert user-edited content to placeholder text

If you add text as placeholder text and later want to reset that placeholder text to the default text for that control type, simply delete all placeholder content while in Design Mode. When you click outside the control, the default placeholder text will appear. Do not, however, cut the entire contents of the user-edited text while in Design Mode because this will delete the control as well.

Note that applying the Placeholder Text character style only changes the formatting of placeholder content and not its properties. That is, you can't convert user-edited text to placeholder text while in Design Mode just by applying the Placeholder Text style.

To convert user-edited text to placeholder text, do the following.

1. With Design Mode turned off, select the text you want to convert to placeholder text and cut it (CTRL+X).

   Do not select the entire contents of the control because this will delete the control as well. If you want to use the entire contents as placeholder text, leave out the last paragraph mark when selecting the content to cut.

2. Turn on Design Mode. Delete (do not cut) the remaining user-edited text and then click outside the control. This will reset placeholder text to the default. Note that you can take this step before turning on Design Mode, if you prefer, but the step that follows must be done in Design Mode.

3. Paste the content you cut earlier inside the control (CTRL+V). From the Paste SmartTag that appears, select the option to match destination formatting.

4. Turn off Design Mode. The text you pasted in Design Mode should now be placeholder text.

Chapter 11

Nesting Controls

You can nest controls in the user-edited content of a control, but not in placeholder content.

The only situation where you're likely to find this useful is when you want to contain a large part of a formatted document inside a control. In that case, add the placeholder content for the host control as regular user-edited content (that is, not as placeholder content at all). Remember that placeholder content can't be edited outside of Design Mode, so when a user clicks in a control that has placeholder content, they either replace all of it or none of it. In a case where you want to include a large part of document content as placeholder text, it's likely that you'll want the user to be able to retain some of it, so it should be saved as user-edited text in any case.

If you need to nest controls inside a host control, start with a Rich Text control and add the text content you need outside of Design Mode so that the user can edit it. Then, while still outside of Design Mode, insert each of the nested controls you need. You can later edit any of the controls in Design Mode as needed.

When you click into placeholder text in a control while Design Mode is active, you'll notice that you don't have the ability to nest new controls within placeholder text. You can use a workaround by inserting them separately and then pasting them into your placeholder text, but Word will let you know it doesn't want you to do that, because you'll be unable to exit Design Mode. As with other causes of Design Mode being forced to remain on, you can save, close, and reopen the document to turn it off. But, for best results, heed Word's warning here. You can experience usability problems if you try to add nested controls as placeholder text within a control. Remember that placeholder text is not designed to be edited by the user.

Understanding Document Protection Options

The same document protection options are available from both the Review tab and the Developer tab. When you click Protect Document, as shown here, Restrict Reviewing Options refers to what you most likely think of as document protection. The Restrict Permission options refer to Information Rights Management (IRM), discussed in Chapter 2, "Understanding Electronic Documents." As mentioned in Chapter 2, depending on your edition of the 2007 release, you may or may not see the Restrict Permission options.

When you click Restrict Formatting And Editing from the Protect Document options, the Restrict Formatting And Editing pane opens. The first option in that pane, shown here, addresses formatting restrictions, which can also be accomplished from the Manage Styles dialog box introduced in Chapter 5.

The options you need for protecting documents so that users can only edit content inside controls are under Editing Restrictions.

Four options are available under the Editing Restrictions heading, described as follows.

- The Tracked Changes restriction forces Tracked Changes to remain on, but allows any type of editing. This option can only be enabled for the entire document.

- The Comments restriction allows no content editing, but it does allow users to add or edit comments. This option has an Exceptions setting that allows you to select portions of the document to keep freely editable, and to assign editing rights for those exceptions to everyone or just to specified users.

- The Filling In Forms option is one of the options to consider for use with Content Controls. This option can be enabled for the entire document or by section. (Note that you will only see the option to select sections when multiple sections exist in the document.) When you enable forms protection, users can only access or edit content inside controls. More specifically, users can only add or edit text within controls, because formatting and the ability to insert or paste objects is prohibited. The exception to this is Picture controls, to which users can add a picture while forms protection is active. However, once a picture is added in a Picture control, it can't be replaced while Filling In Forms protection is active.

Chapter 11

CAUTION!

Do not enable Filling In Forms protection mode when using Building Block Gallery controls. These controls are not available to users when the document is protected for forms. In these cases, or when you want users to be able to format and edit any type of content inside controls, consider protecting part of the document in No Changes (Read Only) protection mode instead.

- The No Changes (Read Only) option does not allow any editing of the document. However, as with the Comments option, you can select portions of the document to make them freely available to all or just specified users.

  When you need users to access Building Block Gallery controls, or to format and work with objects inside Content Controls, consider using the No Changes (Read Only) option with each of the Content Controls selected as exception areas that users can edit. To allow editing of Content Controls while in No Changes (Read Only) mode, select controls one at a time and click Everyone or select users to permit under the Exceptions section in the Restrict Formatting And Editing Pane. If you use this option, however, keep two things in mind.

  - If the entire control is selected as an exception to the protection setting, users can still enable Design Mode and can still delete or edit the control (unless the options to restrict editing or deletion are enabled in the Content Control Properties dialog box).

  - When a control is selected as an exception in this protection mode, placeholder text does not behave like placeholder text. It behaves like user-edited text, which means that users can click in and edit placeholder text without being in Design Mode.

Once you've set the options you need, click Yes, Start Enforcing Protection. The dialog box that opens gives you the option to include a password. You're not required to add a password. However, if you don't add a password, or if users have access to the password, any user can unprotect the document.

Content Controls and Automation

As discussed briefly in Chapter 9, the primary method of automation designed for use with Content Controls is the new Word data binding capability. This is XML functionality that enables you to automatically populate controls with content from other sources. Document Property Quick Parts, discussed in Chapter 9, are examples of controls that are dynamically bound to data.

When a control is bound to data, the content in the control automatically updates when the bound data changes. Bound controls are bound in both directions, meaning that you can change data inside the control or inside the source data, and it updates in both locations. Controls can be bound to data in document properties or other custom XML that you add to the document, or to data in other locations, such as on a Microsoft Windows SharePoint Services site.

Note, however, that only data suitable for controls with plain text properties (such as Plain Text controls, Date Pickers, and Drop-Down Lists) can be bound to Content Controls. Rich text content (such as tables or graphics) is not supported for data binding in the 2007 release.

Learn how to bind controls to custom XML data in Chapter 22.

As with most new Word features, Content Controls are also available as an object in the Word VBA object model, so that you can use macros when appropriate to act on them.

Note

For SharePoint developers and those who use Visual Studio Tools for Office to create managed code for the programs of the 2007 release, note that these platforms are not addressed in the automation components of this book. The automation-related content in this book provides a thorough introduction to the programming platforms for the 2007 Office release that don't require the use of professional development platforms. Office Open XML and VBA are covered because advanced users can use them to take documents and templates further without having to be professional developers and without having to purchase additional software beyond the Microsoft Office programs.

However, for those who want to take their Microsoft Office programming to the next level, find additional resources and recommended references at the end of Chapters 21, 22, and 23, "Using VBA and XML Together to Create Add-Ins."

Y ou understand the core concepts of Microsoft Word and the unique factors to consider when delivering documents electronically. You know what makes a robust, easy-to-manage document, and you've mastered styles, tables, graphics, sections, and Quick Parts—the five key components for creating any Microsoft Office Word 2007 document. You know how to use those components together effectively and how to determine the simplest solution for the document task. You can even run circles around reference tables when the need arises, and your forms have never been in better form. So, are you done? Is that everything you need for creating effective documents?

If you've been given the content, been told how to display that content, and been provided with a document design, then yes, you're good to go for creating that document in Office Word 2007. But, if the company, career, job, responsibility, or task affected by that document is yours, then you're now ready to begin.

Planning effective documents is about more than solid construction. An effective document also uses design and layout choices that get your content noticed. And, of course, there's that tiny little detail of the content. After all, you create documents to share important information, not to share important formatting.

This chapter provides key considerations to address when planning your documents, from design choices, to delivery method, to layout, to the content itself. Additionally, the last part of this chapter looks at features in Microsoft Office OneNote 2007 that can save you time and simplify your work at several stages of document planning.

Chapter Assumptions

Much of the information in this chapter is in the form of concepts that apply regardless of the program in which you're working, though I do assume that you're familiar with the content in all preceding chapters that cover Word documents.

However, though I take an advanced approach to all content in this book, the coverage of Office OneNote 2007 features in this chapter does not assume that you have prior experience with any version of OneNote.

In the introduction to this book, you can find a list of resources for those who want more basic-level information, in the section titled "Who Will Benefit Most from This Book."

Design Considerations

Dress sharply and they notice the dress. Dress impeccably and they notice the woman.
– Coco Chanel

If you read my first book or you've ever attended an advanced training session with me, you've probably seen or heard me use this Coco Chanel quote. That's because, as much as this quotation can apply equally well to women or men, it also applies perfectly to your documents.

The purpose of layout and formatting is to get your content noticed. Using graphics, color, or complex layouts for any other reason is a waste of your time and quite likely to be nothing more than a distraction to your reader. At the same time, when your content gets noticed, you want to be sure it makes the statement you want it to make.

For example, if you're delivering a business pitch to a client whose style is so formal that he wears a navy pinstripe suit to the company picnic, would you wear jeans and a baseball cap and carry your presentation in a backpack? Probably not. To make sure that your document makes the right statement to its recipient, consider the following four questions.

- How are you delivering it?

    There are several items for you to consider based on whether the recipient will see the document in print or on screen.

- Why are you sending it?

    For example, is it a business pitch, a resume, or a report?

- To whom are you sending it?

    Determine what type of presentation will resonate best with the particular recipients.

- Who is sending it?

    That is, decide what you want the document to express about you or your business.

How Will Your Document Be Delivered?

As examined in Chapter 2, "Understanding Electronic Documents," there are unique construction decisions to make when you're delivering a document electronically. For example, someone who opens your document in Word can see exactly how you created it—whether it's clean and professional or sloppy and difficult to manage. Additionally, when you include live graphic objects or embedded objects in your document, any recipient can edit those objects, giving you less control over your content. Find the simplest solutions to address these and other electronic document issues in Chapter 2.

However, you'll need to consider another set of issues related to how your document will be shared, and they fall under the heading of design. Does your design travel well?

When you're delivering a printed document, meaning that the recipient sees the same pieces of paper that come out of your printer, you know whether your design works well as soon as the pages are printed.

For other delivery methods, however, there might be a number of things to consider, as addressed in the list that follows. For example, when creating the sample documents for this book's CD that also appear as images in some chapters (such as *Fearless.docx*, shown in Chapter 4, "Building Easy-to-Manage, Robust Documents"), I selected design colors that are still clear when the page is shown in grayscale.

- Gradient or pattern fills can look different based on display drivers or printer drivers. A beautiful gradient fill that looks perfect on your machine might look pixilated or washed out on a recipient's machine that has an inferior display driver. Also, as mentioned in Chapter 4, some printer drivers can't manage pattern fills, and will oddly space or overlap text that uses this formatting.

- Tone and color saturation can look different with some on-screen projectors. Though this issue is more commonly encountered with Microsoft PowerPoint presentations, it applies to any document you open while projecting your screen. If you'll be using an unfamiliar projector to share your document, and you won't have the opportunity to check and adjust the projection quality before giving the presentation, consider using subtle colors that don't risk extremes when projected.

- Similar to the previous issue, sharing your screen using any Web meeting software, such as Microsoft Office Live Meeting, can affect the way some colors, fill types, and graphic objects look on screen. Gradient fills and intricate graphics can differ greatly in both general appearance and image quality. To help ensure that your presentation design has the desired effect on your audience, view your document from another computer when in the screen-sharing environment, before presenting it to others.

  For an example of what *not* to do when formatting documents for Web meetings, check out the recorded webcasts included on the Expert Tips tab of this book's CD. As you'll see, I learned this tip from making the mistake myself. For example, in the Microsoft Office Excel 2007 webcast, you'll see a couple of charts with gradient formatting that look just awful in LiveMeeting. (Thanks to Excel MVP Jon Peltier for pointing out the error after viewing one of my webcasts.)

- Pale colors, small fonts, and complex graphics often become difficult to read when a document is sent by fax. So, for example, if your branding includes a complex logo with either very light or very dark elements, you might want to consider designing a separate version of your logo for use with fax documents.

- People read e-mail messages and Web pages differently than they do a traditional document, partly because page breaks are not usually seen on screen for e-mail and Web pages, and view and zoom options differ from traditional document environments. Consider sending the e-mail message to yourself first or viewing the document as a Web page before sharing it, to make sure that what you send is the same as what the recipient sees.

Two issues in particular that are addressed in Chapter 2 also cross into design considerations.

- If the recipient doesn't have the fonts you use, your document layout and pagination might look very different on the recipient's computer.

- When sending documents over the Internet as the body of an e-mail message, remember that formatted documents are transmitted over the Internet using HTML. To help ensure that image resolution is retained, use Web-friendly picture types for any graphics, such as JPG, GIF, or PNG.

Focus On the Content

Who is the recipient and why are they reading your document?

Thinking about these questions together, you can select the key points in your content and determine the most effective way to display them. Check out a few examples.

- Do you want your recipient to notice financial results? Consider charting data so that the impressive numbers pop, rather than explaining them in bullet points.

- Is the recipient a no-nonsense, facts-and-figures type? If so, provide a table beside the chart so that they can compare the impressive visual to the equally impressive raw data.

- Do you need to convey the importance of specific deadlines? Try a workflow diagram that shows how each deadline impacts next steps, instead of just bolding those deadlines in paragraph text.

Your document doesn't have to be a career-changing report to warrant a chart, a table, or a diagram. Take the new SmartArt diagramming feature, for example. You can actually create a great-looking, professional-quality diagram just about as easily as typing a bulleted list—so why not demonstrate the workflow process you're proposing, for example, by adding a diagram to your interoffice memo instead of writing paragraphs of text? See Chapter 18, "Creating Professional Presentation Graphics," for help getting that done.

Once you determine which points to emphasize and what content types to use, consider what you know about the recipient's business style and how can you mirror that in your document design.

Whether it's a report for your boss, a letter to your staff explaining new policies, a new business pitch, or your resume, it's important to remember that most documents are marketing documents in one sense or another. That is, whether you're selling your company's services, demonstrating your professional abilities or job performance, or just conveying your opinion, you're still using that document to sell something. And, one of the first things every good salesperson or marketer learns is to tailor the pitch to the prospective client. Just keep in mind that the recipient of your document is your target market for whatever that document is selling.

Where this concept applies to design, consider simple touches such as selecting a heading text color or a font that suits the recipient's style. It doesn't take much. No matter what the client's style, the design details you add should help your document be appealing to read, not make the document about the design. A design concept that suits your client's style won't ever sell a bad idea, but it can help to get a good idea noticed.

Making the Right Statement About You and Your Business

As important as the recipient's style can be to the effectiveness of your document, your own style is even more so. You don't have to be on the *Fortune 500* list to benefit from developing a brand identity and presenting a consistent, professional appearance.

- Choose one or two fonts that suit your professional style, and use them for all of your everyday business documents.

- Create a set of core styles for text, tables, and lists that incorporates a few carefully chosen colors as well as spacing and layout that's easy to read, and that consistently uses the fonts you've selected.

- Use graphic effects (such as bevels, shadows, or gradients) sparingly and consistently to make great-looking graphics that emphasize your information but don't overpower it.

> **Note**
> If you have a logo, consider font, color, and effect choices that complement your logo. If you don't yet have a logo but want one, considering creating your own using Microsoft Office PowerPoint 2007, and incorporating key font, color, or effect elements from your chosen design. See Chapter 18 for more on the tools that can help you get this done.

Did you notice that three of the key components for basic branding—font, color, and graphic effects—just happen to be the three components of Document Themes? See Chapter 5, "Styles," to learn about saving your own custom Themes.

Once you have your Theme and a corresponding set of styles, consider the page layouts and document types that you need to use regularly. That's where templates come in. See Chapter 20, "The Many Faces of Microsoft Office Templates," to learn about templates options in Word as well as in Office Excel 2007 and Office PowerPoint 2007.

That's really all there is to creating some simple branding for your documents. Of course, you can take these concepts further and many larger companies and brands do just that. In fact, many professional design firms specialize in developing brand identities. Naturally, these go well beyond creating basic branding elements for your documents.

But, when it comes to developing basic branding for your documents, you don't need to be a professional graphic designer. An eye for color and a knack for layout surely help.

If you're not confident in those particular skills and don't have someone who can help you, start with one of the built-in Themes that you like and customize it a bit to suit your style.

If you find yourself agonizing over color or fonts choices, remember that the most important thing in the design of business documents is to keep it clean, consistent, and professional. Solid document construction that still looks good when the recipient turns on formatting marks says at least as much about your professionalism as the colors and fonts you select.

Content Planning

Deciding how any document should look ultimately begins, of course, with what information that document needs to contain. Once you know what you want to convey to the recipient, you can better utilize design and layout choices to help that information hit its mark.

Making Choices About Content

The secret to being boring is to tell everything.
—Voltaire

Here we arrive at the subject that demands my other favorite quotation for discussing effective documents. Voltaire is a hero of mine, and so I quote him often on just about any topic. Still, I don't believe there's a better way to simply say that making choices makes for more effective documents.

For example, everyone knows the one-page resume rule, but people often ignore it. You might think your accomplishments require several pages, but the stranger receiving that resume probably doesn't want to read them all and surely won't find every detail to be relevant. A one-page resume in a readable font size is more likely to be thoroughly reviewed and its key points remembered than a four-page monster in eight-point font.

The same holds true for just about any type of important document. Across the various document production centers in which I've worked or consulted over the years, I can't tell you how many documents I've seen that require a magnifying glass. Worst of all, most of these were marketing documents—documents used to sell the company's services. One global investment bank, for example, where dozens of pitch books are produced daily, has a standard that allows text on the page to be as small as three points. Try applying three point font size to some text to see just how ridiculous that would look to the recipient of your document.

Having to reduce the font substantially, widen the margins, or reduce line or paragraph spacing to make the information fit, usually means you're including more information than the recipient is likely to take the time to read. You're also greatly increasing chances that the information you really need them to notice will be lost in the crowd.

If you must give every bit of information, consider splitting a crowded page onto multiple pages so that each page remains approachable to your reader and important points can still shine through. But, before you do, consider the document content from the recipient's point of view. If you were the recipient, would you really need or want to read every detail? And, would you bother wading through pages of details to find a few key important points?

To conclude this topic, I'll leave you with one more of my favorite quotes on the subject.

Fillet the fish. Throw the rest away.
      —Kurt Vonnegut

Using Layout and Design to Organize Your Content

As already discussed in this chapter, design elements should help your content stand out. Good design and layout organizes and emphasizes your content. So, how do you make choices about what design and layout elements will effectively organize your important points? Following are a few suggestions to help you get started.

- Choose one or two complementary colors to use in heading text and for highlighting key pieces of information, such as shading table cells or bordering a paragraph. Adding small details, such as using one of your highlight colors for the color of bullets or numbering (not the paragraph text, just the bullet or number), can help lend organization and style to the page without overpowering the content.

- Use basic formatting, such as a border beneath top-level heading text or a left indent on body text, to help organize the content on the page. Highlight colors, discussed in the preceding bullet, can also help to organize the page when used for things such as heading text and borders.

- Use graphics only when they help convey information more effectively. A picture is only worth 10,000 words if it conveys the particular 10,000 words that matter. For example, a chart of key data or a relationship or process diagram can convey much more than text. But, using a piece of Clip Art just to add an image to the page doesn't emphasize your content, it detracts from it.

- Similarly, avoid graphics that talk down to recipients, such as block arrows on the page that do nothing but point to pieces of content. If the recipient doesn't know how to read a document all by themselves, creating the document is a waste of your time.

- Remember that tables are natural organizers. When you need a complex layout, it's essential to keep it organized or your important information is likely to get lost in the confusion. Using a table to lay out the page can help you do that with far less work and far better results than fussing with text columns or floating graphics. See Chapter 6, "Tables," to learn about using tables to create page layout.

INSIDE OUT   Simple, creative solutions to difficult layout requirements

When you need a layout that seems improbable if not impossible, remember to consider the simple solutions.

Much as I recommend in this chapter to avoid overcrowding a page, there will be times when something just has to fit. That doesn't mean, however, that the solution needs to be a complicated one. The more you know technically about good document construction, the better you can incorporate construction into effective design and layout without doing unnecessary work. Something as simple as a slight margin or character spacing change might be unnoticeable to document recipients, but allow for the fit you need.

Remember, for example, that you can condense or expand character spacing by as little as one-tenth of a point at a time. You can also adjust character positioning above or below the baseline. (To find these options, on the Home tab, in the Font group, click the dialog launcher and then click the Character Spacing tab of the Font dialog box.) Similarly, reducing left and right cell margins by a few hundredths of an inch (or a few tenths of a millimeter) might allow your content to fit without reducing font size, and still leave some spacing between the content of your cells.

Getting creative with your document layout doesn't have to mean getting complicated. In fact, the simpler your solution, the better the result is likely to be.

Using OneNote for Document Planning and Outlines

So, what is a section on OneNote doing at the end of the Word part in a book about advanced document production?

Since the day I started using OneNote a couple of years ago, few work days have passed when I haven't used it for one reason or another. The program has become indispensible for me for planning and organization, and so a chapter about planning effective documents seemed the perfect place to give you an introduction to some of the OneNote tools I use regularly when planning and developing documents.

In addition to the OneNote features covered here, if you're working with others to plan your document, see the end of Chapter 3, "Collaborating and Sharing with Others." That chapter provides information about two additional OneNote tools—Shared Notebooks and Live Sharing Sessions—that are enormously useful when working with a team.

For those who are not familiar with OneNote, it's essentially an electronic notebook, but its capabilities go well beyond what that definition might convey. First of all, many people think of OneNote as being just for Tablet PCs because it's common to think of hand writing notes. However, that's not the case at all. I use OneNote more often on my desktop computer than I do on my Tablet PC.

The notes you keep in OneNote can include typewritten notes, notes written with an ink input device like a Tablet PC pen, documents from other programs, graphics, screen clippings, audio and video notes, and Microsoft Office Outlook 2007 items (such as meeting information). For me, OneNote is a notebook that I never lose, that never runs out of pages, and in which I can always easily find the notes I took on a particular topic.

So, although Word is unquestionably the best home for most documents, I use OneNote to help me prepare long or complex documents more easily. For example, for a recent white paper that I was assigned to write, I took notes in OneNote during a planning meeting with the client. I then applied outline formatting to those notes, so that I could organize them easily, and used them to build out the outline for my document. When I was happy with the outline, I sent it to Word to save some work as I began writing the document.

Could I have done the same in Word? Yes, but OneNote is all about note-taking, so it offers additional benefits that save time because they're designed for brainstorming and helping to organize thoughts and tasks.

Notes are automatically saved in OneNote—I don't need to save a bunch of documents for the notes from each meeting. So, if I have multiple meetings on the same subject, I can access all relevant notes together without having to search through multiple files. And, because a OneNote page isn't restricted to linear content, as discussed later in this chapter, it's easy to take notes on my notes—that is, to use the OneNote page as a working tool or a virtual whiteboard.

Setting Up a OneNote Outline

To start a new OneNote page, click New Page at the top of the page tabs, use the New options on the Standard toolbar, or press CTRL+N. When you do this, your insertion point is placed in the title area at the top of the page. Type a title if you want one, and then press ENTER to move your insertion point onto the body of the page.

> **Note**
> Keep in mind when working in OneNote that pages don't have to be linear. Click anywhere on the page—vertically or horizontally from other content—to start typing other notes.

Most of the formatting you can apply to OneNote text is available through task panes, including Font, Bullets, Numbering, and Lists. To start a single-level bulleted or numbered list, click the Bullets or Numbering icon on the Formatting toolbar. You can also click the arrow beside either of these icons to select from additional options or to select More in order to open the relevant task pane.

> **Note**
>
> You can press CTRL+F1 in OneNote in order to view a task pane, and then select the specific pane you want from the pop-up menu at the top of the task pane.

To create a multilevel outline list, press ENTER from a bulleted or numbered paragraph and then press TAB to move to a new level. A different bullet or number will appear for that level. To change the bullet or number for the new level, open the relevant task pane and just click to apply the bullet or number formatting you want. That change will apply to all new paragraphs on that level. You can continue to add levels as needed, in the same manner. To change the number or bullet style for existing paragraphs in a list level, see the Troubleshooting tip in this section.

Indents for each new list level as well as vertical spacing between levels of the list are controlled in the List task pane shown here.

- To change Indent From Previous List Level for a single level in the list, just click into any instance of that level. Select the entire outline to change this for all levels at once.

- If you click into a single paragraph to change vertical spacing, only that paragraph will be affected by the Between List Items setting, and the paragraphs on that level between previous and next higher levels will be affected by the Above The List and Below The List settings. To change vertical spacing for the entire list, select the list before making changes.

 To reorganize content in your outline, notice that when you point to any content on a OneNote page, a selection icon appears to the left of that content, as you see here. In the case of notes in an outline, click that icon to select the active paragraph and any lower-level paragraphs that fall under that item. You can simply select and drag text to a new location in your outline and the outline will renumber.

To change the level of the active outline paragraph, your options are very similar to those in Word. At the beginning of the paragraph, press TAB or SHIFT+TAB to demote or promote the level, respectively. You can also press the Increase and Decrease Indent icons on the Formatting toolbar, or press ALT+SHIFT+ left or right arrow keys.

> **Note**
>
> If you press the TAB key at the end of text on a line in OneNote, a table will automatically be added. You can continue to tab after each new set of text to add additional columns and then press ENTER to add new rows. Although tables in OneNote have limited formatting options, when you use the Send To Microsoft Office Word command addressed in the next part of this chapter, the table will automatically convert to a genuine Word table.

TROUBLESHOOTING

Changing the bullet or number style in a OneNote outline only changes the active paragraph

When you set up an outline in OneNote, the bullet or number style selected will apply to all future paragraphs that you add to that level of that outline. However, when you want to change the bullet or number style for an existing outline level, you first need to select the entire outline.

To select the entire outline easily, click the top of the note container, such as in the example shown here.

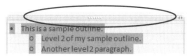

If you don't see the note container, on the Tools menu, click Options and then click Display. Check the option Show Note Containers On Pages. Or, if you don't want to show note containers, point to the first paragraph in your outline to show the selection icon (as shown earlier). Then, click that icon to select the entire outline.

Once the outline is selected, the Change Numbers (or Bullets) On list in the relevant task pane will become available. Select the level for which you want to change the bullet or number style and then select the new style, as you see here.

Also note the Customize Numbering option at the bottom of the Numbering task pane. This option opens a new pane, where you can customize the format for a selected numbering style, including a starting value for the list, indent from text, and text to follow the number, such as a close parenthesis or a period.

From OneNote Page to Word Document Without Hardly Typing

Once you've outlined your document in OneNote, you don't have to start typing all over again. You can send all contents of the active page, or selected pages, to Word in just a couple of clicks.

To do this, on the File menu, point to Send To and then click Microsoft Office Word. This will create a new Word document that contains all content of your OneNote page. If you selected multiple OneNote pages to send to Word, they will appear successively in the same Word document. The page title, as well as the time and date, will be copied along with your notes from each page.

> **Note**
>
> If a note container is selected when you use the Send To Microsoft Office Word command, only the content of the selected container will appear in the new Word document.

Outline lists are sent to Word as what is known as a hybrid list. That is, the outline remains intact with genuine automatic numbering, but each level is perceived by Word to be a separate list. If you add new items to the list by adding a new paragraph and changing the list level, the formatting might not match the formatting you need.

For best results once that outline gets into Word, select the entire outline and apply a multilevel list or list style. Word will recognize the correct outline levels when you do this, so you can convert the entire outline to a Word outline, essentially, in just a click. In fact, if paragraph styles are attached to your list style, they will be applied to the correct levels when you do this. For help working with multilevel lists and list styles in Word, see Chapter 5.

When Should a Document Live in OneNote?

When you need to deliver a document that's a finished product, that looks great, and is professionally formatted, you know that document belongs in Word. But, if a document will remain a working tool after it's delivered—such as when you're delivering a document as a reference for the recipient—sharing that document directly in OneNote may be a highly effective alternative.

For example, I recently delivered OneNote training sessions to a group of market researchers. When they deliver research results to clients, they often do so in large Word documents they call notebooks. These notebooks contain little formatting, they're simply extensive lists of focus group or survey responses, scattered with the occasional graph of quantifiable results, and they contain extensive indexes of key words from throughout the results. Those indexes take the researchers literally days to compile.

If they instead deliver those *notebook* documents in OneNote, provided the client has OneNote installed on their computers, they can organize the results easily by placing each set of feedback on its own page or each group of feedback in its own section. Then, the client can use the incredible search tools in OneNote to find any key word they need—no index required. OneNote searches a section, group of sections, the active notebook, or all of your notebooks at once, and then provides a task pane displaying the results, such as you see in Figure 12-1. It's an instant, automatic, endless index.

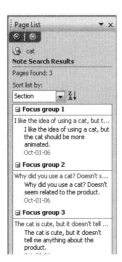

Figure 12-1 In this example, the word *cat* was the keyword searched throughout the notebook. Each focus group heading indicates a separate OneNote section.

Additionally, using the Note Tags feature, you can tag notes for different types of follow-up, such as those you see here.

View all tagged notes from throughout your notebook (or in individual sections) instantly in the Tags Summary task pane, which organizes results similarly to those shown in the Page List task pane for search results. And, when the document is a work-in-progress for a project team, keep in mind that tags are also available that automatically create Office Outlook 2007 tasks.

Other Document Assists from OneNote

When creating the documents you usually create—those that will live in Word, or perhaps in Excel or PowerPoint—the following two additional OneNote features can be tremendously useful.

Using the Screen Clipping Feature for Technical Documents

The OneNote Screen Clipping feature lets you capture all or part of your screen in any program open on your computer. Though many people find this handy for things such as grabbing news or other information off of the Web to add to their notes, it can also be particularly useful when creating technical documents that require screen shots from a software program.

With OneNote Screen Clippings, you have more control than you do when you use the print screen key on your keyboard, because you can drag to select a specific portion of the screen. When you do this, the screen clipping is inserted onto a blank page in your OneNote notebook and also copied to your clipboard. The page in OneNote where your clipping appears includes a time and date stamp for when that clipping was taken, for later reference. And, if the clipping was taken from a Web page, the URL is also included as a hyperlink below the screen clipping.

To take a screen clipping of the active window, press WINDOWS+S. This action freezes the active window and changes your pointer to a cross hair. Then, just drag to select the portion of the screen you want to clip and release the pointer to take the screen shot.

> **Note**
>
> If you take a screen clipping to use in your notes, you can also set that clipping as a background to take notes directly on it. To turn a clipping or any picture on a OneNote page into a background, right-click the picture and then select Set Picture As Background.

Reviewing Documents Directly from Your Notes

Want to review a document and make notes about changes without having to add notes (such as in comments) directly to the document? You can insert your document into OneNote, where the pages will appear successively on a OneNote page. The document pages are set behind the OneNote text area, so that you can take notes directly on the image of the document.

Chapter 12

To do this, on the Insert menu, click Files As Printouts. Then, just select the file to insert and click Open. A virtual printer is used to insert the file. When OneNote is installed on your computer, this virtual printer is also available as a printer option from your other 2007 Office release programs. For example, the image shown here is the Print dialog box in Word, where Send To OneNote 2007 is the selected printer.

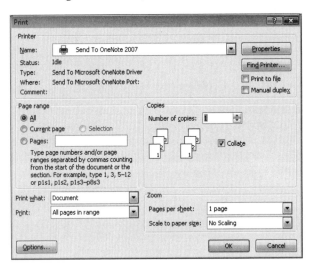

Note

The features introduced here are those that I believe are most applicable to helping you plan documents. To learn about other OneNote capabilities or to try the program, find more information at *http://office.microsoft.com/onenote* or find a link on this book's CD to the Microsoft Office downloads page where you can download a free, fully functional trial of OneNote.

Data-Based Documents: Formatting and Managing Worksheets

D o you think of your Microsoft Excel files as documents? If not, you might be selling them short. Text-based documents, such as reports that require complex formatting with text, tables, and graphics, surely belong in Microsoft Word. But, when you share a Microsoft Excel file containing worksheets data, charts, or maybe even Pivot-Table reports, you are absolutely sharing a document.

So, in the first of this book's chapters on Microsoft Office Excel 2007, we're looking at formatting documents. From cells, rows, and columns to worksheets and workbooks, this chapter is all about letting your Office Excel 2007 files shine like the documents they are. Of course, because much of your Excel document content is dynamic, much of the formatting is as well. That is, there's more to formatting your Excel worksheet content than a well chosen font or color. Formatting Excel documents effectively can mean making your data do more for you.

If the idea of formatting worksheet content isn't exhilarating, and you're tempted to run along to the sexier topics of charts or PivotTables, give it a minute. Among many interesting advances in the new version of Excel, some of those that you're likely to use most often are addressed in this chapter: native Excel tables, cell styles, and a whole new world of conditional formatting.

Chapter Assumptions

Although this chapter addresses core, essential features, it does so from the perspective of an advanced user. I assume that you have experience with some version of Excel, and are already familiar with basics like understanding the structure of a worksheet. So, instead of spending time on such basics, this chapter focuses on helping you capitalize on the improved formatting capabilities for Excel worksheet content.

This chapter also assumes you're familiar with Document Themes, introduced in Chapter 5, "Styles," as well as the existence of Quick Styles, mentioned in a number of earlier chapters.

In the introduction to this book, you can find a list of resources for those who want more basic-level information, in the section titled "Who Will Benefit Most from This Book."

What's New for Worksheets in Excel 2007

The core concepts of Excel are unchanged. It is still the best home for your data, lord of the number crunchers, and master of logic. When it comes to formatting worksheet content, the news in a nutshell is simply that your worksheets can be better-looking and more dynamic than ever before.

The big stories for worksheet formatting are tables and conditional formatting, but there are other key new features as well, including cell styles, mentioned earlier, and the long overdue Page Layout view. Additionally, a great many formatting options are nicely exposed on the Home, Page Layout, and View tabs, giving you easy access to some handy tools that you might have missed in the past.

It's also important to note that, with the introduction of Themes for the 2007 Office release programs Word, Excel, and PowerPoint, the 56-color swapping palette you know from earlier versions of Excel has been replaced with a palette that offers much greater flexibility. Learn more about working with Themes in Excel later in this chapter.

> **Note**
>
> When you open a workbook in an earlier version of Excel, remember that 16 of the colors in the 56-color palette are chart colors. So, for example, if you open the palette for applying font color, you'll only see 40 available colors.

- Excel tables are the evolution of the List feature that was in the two previous two versions of Excel, and quite an impressive evolution it is. When you format a range as a table, you get additional functionality, much of which is shown in the following image of the Table Tools Design contextual tab. Learn to format Excel tables in the section titled "Formatting Ranges and Tables" later in this chapter, and get more information about the data-management capabilities of tables in Chapter 14, "Working with Data."

- Conditional formatting (shown in the following image) is tremendously improved, both with dramatic new data visualization options and with the ability to manage formatting rules throughout the workbook from a single dialog box. See the section titled "Increasing Your Options with Conditional Formatting" later in this chapter.

- Cell Styles, shown below, are a type of Quick Style that you can customize and even copy between workbooks. Get the details in this chapter, in the section titled "Using Cell Styles."

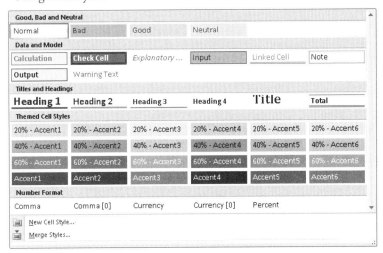

- Page Layout view, shown in the image that follows, is accessible from the View tab or the view shortcuts on the Status bar. In Page Layout view, similar in concept to the Print Layout view in Microsoft Word, you see the complete page layout as it will print, but with elements that don't print by default (such as gridlines and column/row headings). You can change sheet margins on the rulers, as in Word, and can edit headers and footers directly on the sheet, with the help of the Header And Footer Tools Design contextual tab.

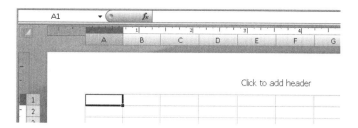

When Your Document Lives in Excel

Unlike Microsoft Office Word 2007, where document formatting is about a robust, professional finished product that gets your content noticed, Excel has always been about function rather than form. However, you don't have to sacrifice one for the other.

Much of the available formatting in Excel is tied to the functionality, such as tables or conditional formatting. So, when you make your documents look better, you also have the opportunity to make them perform better.

For this reason, when you work in Excel, it's essential to think about what you need the content of your worksheets to do while you're addressing how you want them to look. Consider the following examples.

- When formatting a range of cells, instead of just applying borders, shading, or font color individually, think about the reasons you're formatting that range as a unit. Can you format that range as a table instead, and then take advantage of the additional functionality that Excel tables offer?

- If your workbook includes several sheets, do you format related ranges or related sheets consistently? When data from one sheet to the next is related, applying related formatting can do more than help your workbook look professional. You can also use consistent formatting across ranges or worksheets to make the logic of your workbook more intuitive for recipients.

Just as when you're working in Office Word 2007, avoid getting carried away with formatting in Excel. Remember, the purpose of formatting is to help make your information shine through.

In Excel, this concept goes a step further because your Excel documents are often dynamic work products that need to continue to change after you've delivered them. Overly formatted worksheets can be difficult to read and make it harder to understand the logic in your data. Always consider the workbook as a whole and choose consistent formatting that, where appropriate, can add functionality to your worksheets. Also think about the effective design and layout issues addressed for Word documents in Chapter 12, "Planning Your Documents," because many of these (from considerations for electronic documents to design and branding best practices) can apply equally to your documents that live in Excel.

> **Note**
>
> For help and best practices when creating Excel worksheet content for use in Word documents, see Chapter 6, "Tables," in the Word portion of this book.

Streamlining Worksheet Formatting

Formatting worksheet content has been a source of stress for many in the past, because doing so has been quite inflexible relative to formatting documents in Word or even in Microsoft PowerPoint. If you combine the new formatting capabilities in Excel with a methodical approach to worksheet formatting, that stress can be a thing of the past.

Taking a methodical approach in this case means to remember that, regardless of what part of a workbook you're using, the entire workbook is a single unit. The workbook is comprised of sheets, which are comprised of rows and columns, which are in turn comprised of cells.

Why am I stating what seems to be so obvious? Because, if you're like most Excel users, you don't usually think about this and it can show in your formatting. More importantly, it can also show in your frustration when workbooks need to be edited. To work more effectively in Excel with less stress, keep the following concepts in mind.

- Just as when creating documents in Word, to do the least work possible, start by formatting the largest possible portions of the document (workbook) first.

    1. Do whatever you can do to the entire workbook (such as applying a Theme and setting workbook defaults).

> **Note**
>
> One of the easiest things you can do to save time when formatting workbooks is to set your formatting defaults for new workbooks. To do this, click the Microsoft Office Button and then click Excel Options. On the Popular tab, in addition to settings that apply throughout several of the 2007 release programs, you'll see the options presented here for use when creating new workbooks.
>
>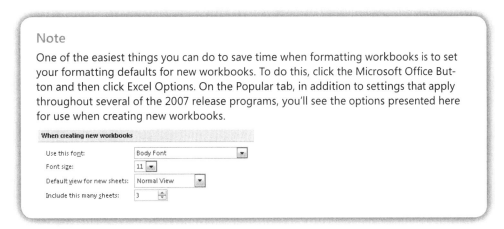

2. Set formatting that applies to one or more sheets at a time (such as setting row height or applying headers and footers).

3. Format specific ranges or tables.

4. Format individual cells that require formatting that's unique from the applicable range or table.

● Remember that formatting applied to individual cells takes priority over the formatting of ranges, tables, or worksheets. This is similar to the way character formatting takes precedence over paragraph formatting in Word. So, for example, if you format a table and then apply unique formatting to a few cells in the table, that unique cell formatting will remain intact when you apply a new table style.

● When you copy or move cells, rows, or columns, the formatting travels along by default. Use Paste options, addressed in the Inside Out tip in this section, to get the result you need and avoid having to fix unwanted formatting later.

As you can see from the preceding list, working methodically in Excel is very similar to working methodically in Word, or for that matter, in any software program. That's because, though much of what goes into creating effective documents is about knowing the features of the program and how to use them, the other key ingredient has nothing to do with software. Creating effective Microsoft Office documents requires paying attention to what's happening in your documents so that you can stay in control of their content. It requires a bit of planning and organization so that you can keep things as simple as possible, and focus on the product rather than the process.

Note

The simplest tools can sometimes be the most useful when you're looking for ways to format documents effectively. For example, use simple keyboard shortcuts to get exactly what you need with less work. Two that I regularly use for Excel worksheet formatting are ALT+ENTER, to wrap text to a new line within the same cell, and CTRL+ENTER, for filling all cells in a selected range with the same content. To use CTRL+ENTER, select the range to fill, type the content you need as if you were working in a single cell, and then press CTRL+ENTER (instead of ENTER alone) to fill all cells in the selected range.

INSIDE OUT   Making use of Paste options

If you've only used Paste in Excel to paste content that you cut or copied from another location, you're missing out on a powerful tool. Paste Special has long given you the ability to paste only individual components of your selection, such as values or formatting, or combinations of components, such as pasting values and number formats but no other formatting. To access Paste Special, use the new keyboard shortcut CTRL+ALT+V that works in Word, Excel, and PowerPoint. Or, on the Home tab, click to expand Paste options and then click Paste Special.

In addition to these options that can help you avoid many formatting fiascos, the Paste Special shortcuts that used to be available from a pop-up menu on the Standard toolbar are now right in front of you when you click Paste on the Home tab. These options include two of my favorite timesavers, Paste Values and No Borders, the second of which pastes everything but any borders on the source content, leaving the destination borders alone.

Also notice that the Paste options and the Paste Special dialog box offer the Transpose option, which pastes copied columns of data as rows and vice versa, and Operations. With Operations, you copy a value, select the range to which you'd like to apply the value, and then select the option to Add, Subtract, Multiply, or Divide by the copied value for each cell in the destination range.

TROUBLESHOOTING

How can I clear unique cell formatting without clearing all formatting?

When you format a range on a worksheet and have unique formatting applied to some cells, you can either turn off one setting at a time to get rid of only unwanted formatting elements, or use Clear Formats to remove all formatting and then start over, right?

Not exactly, at least, not anymore. When you format a range as a table and then apply unique formatting to just some cells of that table, you can remove just the unique formatting and leave table formatting intact. To do this, select just the cells for which you want to clear unique formatting (if you select the entire table, the action that follows will remove the table style), and then on the Home tab, in the Editing group, click Clear and then click Clear Formats. Keep in mind that this is a benefit of using table styles and will not work with formatting on a range that isn't specified as a table. Learn about additional benefits of formatting ranges as tables later in this chapter.

Working with Themes in Excel

Themes, introduced in Chapter 5, work much the same in Excel as they do in Word. So, for Theme basics, including understanding the components of Themes (fonts, colors, and effects), how to apply them, and how to save a custom Theme, see Chapter 5.

When applying formatting to your worksheets, remember to apply Theme-ready formatting by selecting from options specified as applicable to Themes. That is, select fonts from the Theme Fonts options at the top of font drop-down lists, such as you see in the image that follows on the left, and select colors from the Theme Colors portion of the color palette, shown in the following image on the right.

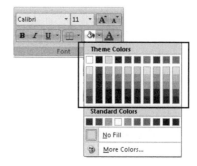

Remember that, if you select a font or specify a color that's used in the active Theme, but don't select it from the Theme options, your formatting won't be Theme-ready—meaning that it won't swap to take on new formatting when you change the active Theme.

New workbooks are set to take on the active Theme's body font by default. As shown earlier, to access defaults for new workbooks, click the Microsoft Office Button and then click Excel Options. On the Popular tab, you'll find default settings including font, font size, number of sheets, and default view.

> **Note**
>
> If you hover over the list of available options in the Theme Fonts gallery, Live Preview shows a small change in the appearance of your workbook even if the workbook is blank. That's because one of the nice little details of Themes in Excel is that row and column headings automatically take on the body font of the active Theme.

As mentioned earlier, the old 56-color Excel palette has been replaced by Theme colors. So, you no longer go into Options to change a color in the palette, or to copy colors from one workbook to another. Instead, for easy application to any workbook, save a custom Theme or custom Theme Colors for the set of colors you need.

> **Note**
>
> When you need to use a Theme that was created on another computer, remember (as discussed in Chapter 5) that you can also copy a custom Theme from any document. To do this, on the Page Layout tab, click Themes and then click Browse For Themes. Select the file from which you want to copy the active Theme and then click Open. Because you have the same Themes available in Word, Excel, and PowerPoint, you can copy the Theme from a Theme-ready document created in any of these programs.

It's worth noting here that Theme Effects apply to Excel charts much as they do to other graphics, such as SmartArt diagrams. When you first create a chart, changing Theme Effects will have no visual impact on your chart, unless your chart is based on a saved template that had a Chart Style applied. To use Theme Effects with charts, first apply a Chart Style that uses graphic effects. Then, when you hover over the various options in the Theme Effects galleries, you'll see different variations on the Chart Style for each set of Theme Effects. Learn about formatting Excel charts, including more about how Excel charts interact with Themes, in Chapter 15, "Charts."

To keep worksheet formatting streamlined, consider using styles in Excel much the way you do in Word. Between the new cell styles and table styles, you can save time, keep your formatting more consistent, and create Theme-ready workbooks more easily. In the next two sections of this chapter, learn about cell and table styles and how they interact with Themes.

Using Cell Styles

Cell styles are the new incarnation of the extremely limited Styles feature that appeared on the Format menu in earlier versions of Excel. Cell styles are now part of Quick Styles functionality that you see for many features across the 2007 release.

Notice that the Cell Styles gallery, shown here, includes a few categories of built-in styles.

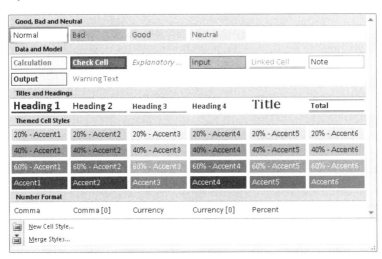

Take note of the following when using built-in cell styles from this gallery.

- Styles in the Good, Bad, And Neutral and Data And Model categories are not entirely Theme-ready, meaning that although they use the active Theme body font, they don't use Theme-ready colors. This is intentional so that a certain color can take on a specific meaning (such as green for good or red for bad) that will apply regardless of your applied theme.

- In the same categories mentioned in the preceding bullet, style names might give you the impression that they have added functionality beyond formatting. They don't. Those style names are just suggestions of the ways in which you might use cell styles to indicate certain types of results. However, in those cases, I recommend using conditional formatting instead, so that the formatting will change based on criteria, to always reflect the intended sentiment.

- Though the styles in the Titles And Headings category look very much like some built-in Word paragraph styles, remember that you are still working in Excel. The borders used on some of those styles, for example, are cell borders. So, if your text is going to exceed the cell in which you type it, be sure to apply the appropriate style to all cells across which the text stretches, if you want the border to appear throughout the heading.

- Even though there is a category called Themed Cell Styles, styles under the Titles And Headings category are also entirely Theme-ready.

- Number Format styles are carry-overs from the old Styles feature, and they apply only number formatting by default. The benefit of using these styles over using a number format directly from the Number options on the Home tab or the Format Cells dialog box comes when you need to update the formatting. After you apply a style to cells, whenever you modify the style, the formatting of cells that use that style updates automatically.

You can create your own styles, modify built-in styles, duplicate built-in styles to create your own variations, or delete any unwanted styles. Any of these modifications are made for the active workbook only. Of course, you can save any workbook as a template to use for creating future workbooks. See Chapter 20, "The Many Faces of Microsoft Office Templates," for options related to working with Excel templates.

TROUBLESHOOTING

Why does one cell style sit on top of another?

A cell can only contain one cell style at a time, but it's common for cells to appear as if the first style remains when the new style is applied. This is because each cell style has the ability to include any of six unique sets of attributes (Number, Alignment, Font, Border, Fill, and Protection), as you see in the following image. Notice that these categories correspond to the six tabs of the Format Cells dialog box.

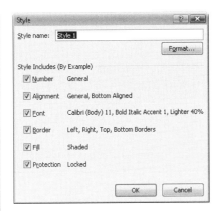

Some styles have settings for all six of these categories. But, many of the built-in styles use only certain categories (such as the Number Format styles). When you apply a new style that doesn't use all categories to a selection of cells, formatting from unused categories remains unchanged, regardless of whether that formatting was part of a style. However, the new style becomes the recognized style for those selected cells. By "recognized" style, I mean that if you edit the most recently applied style, cell appearance will change, whereas modifying a style that was applied earlier will not affect cells that still contain some attributes of that style, but have since had a new style applied.

This behavior makes cell styles far more practical, because you might often want to change font, fill, or alignment formatting, for example, where you don't want to change number format or borders. However, to keep your custom cell styles intuitive for all users and to avoid confusion, you might want to develop a naming convention that indicates what categories are used.

You can create cell styles based on the formatting in a selected cell (referred to as By Example) or based on an existing cell style. To create a style by example, select the cell to use as the basis for your style before proceeding.

1. On the Home tab, click Cell Styles and then either click New Cell Style (to create a style by example) or right-click an existing style and then click Duplicate.

    In the Style dialog box, you'll see the existing formatting for your new style under the heading Style Includes. If you create the style based on formatting in a selected cell, that heading reads Style Includes (By Example).

2. Select the categories you want to include in your new style. When you create a style by example, all categories are selected by default. When you duplicate a style, the selected categories will match the duplicated style.

> **Note**
>
> The Format Cells category formerly called Patterns is now called Fill, and the options have expanded to include gradient fill shading. This option is available on the Fill tab of the Format Cells dialog box wherever you access that dialog box, including Cell Styles and Table Styles.

3. Click the Format button to access the Format Cells dialog box. Remember that the tabs in this dialog box correspond to the cell style categories. Select each tab you need, customize desired attributes, and then click OK.

4. Confirm that the settings you customized in the Format Cells dialog box appear by each category name, as applicable, in the Style dialog box. Name your style and then click OK. Your new style will appear in the Cell Style gallery under a Custom category heading.

TROUBLESHOOTING

> **Spacing prints incorrectly on worksheets with shaded cells**
>
> Note that this issue is also addressed for Word documents in Chapter 4, "Building Easy-to-Manage, Robust Documents."
>
> Some printer drivers are not capable of managing pattern cell fills, because those fills have multiple layers (a foreground and a background). When unsupported pattern fills are applied, whether directly through the Format Cells dialog box or through a cell or table style, printers can misinterpret the foreground and background formatting and skew spacing to either overlap worksheet content or leave large gaps between pieces of content.
>
> To avoid this issue, use any of the options under Background Colors (including the new Fill Effects) on the Fill tab of the Format Cells dialog box, instead of using the Pattern Color and Pattern Style options.

To modify a cell style, right-click the style name in the gallery and then click Modify to access the Style dialog box. Notice that you can also delete styles from the shortcut menu that appears when you right-click. You can delete any cell style other than Normal. However, note that built-in styles are only deleted from the active workbook. (Also note that, if you delete a style, relevant formatting is removed from any cells in the workbook to which the style was applied.)

To copy all cell styles from another workbook, start by opening the workbook containing the style definitions you want. Then do the following.

1. On the Home tab, click Cell Styles and then click Merge Styles.

2. Select the workbook containing the desired style definitions from the Merge Style dialog box. Only open workbooks will appear in this list.

This action will import your own custom styles from the selected workbook and give you the option to update the formatting of styles that exist in both workbooks (including built-in styles).

Formatting Ranges as Tables

When you format a range as a table, you get the benefit of table styles, enabling you to apply several formatting attributes at once. But that's just the beginning of what you can do with Excel tables. Following are additional formatting-related capabilities of tables.

- The table automatically expands when you add adjacent data in rows or columns, so the newly added data is formatted to match your table without any extra work.

- Drag the icon shown here, which appears at the bottom-right corner of all tables, to resize the table range. You can drag left, right, up, or down.

- Simply drag selected table rows or columns to reorder them. As you drag, a gray bar appears. This bar indicates where the selected column or row will fall when you release the pointer.

> **Note**
>
> If you drag just a few cells from a row or column, Excel will assume that you want to replace the destination cells, as it does when you drag cells on a worksheet outside of a table, and will prompt you accordingly. You can only drag to reorder complete rows or columns in a table.

- Just right-click for the options to insert, delete, or select table rows and columns.

Beyond the formatting capabilities of tables are powerful data-management tools, which enable you, for example, to quickly create calculated columns, use structured references in formulas, and export table data for other uses such as a Microsoft Office Visio 2007 PivotDiagram. For working with the data-management capabilities of tables, see Chapter 14. For formatting tables and managing table structure, you're in the right place.

To format a range of data as a table, first click in or select the range to use as your table. Your range does not need to contain data prior to creating your table. Notice that, when you start with an existing contiguous data range, you don't have to select the range first—just click somewhere in the range and Excel will recognize it automatically. Then, do the following.

1. On the Home tab, click Format As Table and then click the table style that you want to apply. Or, on the Insert tab, click Table.

2. In the Format As Table dialog box that opens, Excel will confirm what it believes to be the correct range for your table. If this is not the correct range, you can simply drag to select the correct range without closing the dialog box. (The dialog box has a range selection icon, but you don't need to use it to access the worksheet.)

3. With the Format As Table dialog box still open, if your selected range includes table headers, check the box labeled My Table Has Headers. If not, leave that box blank and a header row will be added. Click OK to format the table.

    If you started with the Table option on the Insert tab, the default table style for the active workbook will be applied to the new table.

Once the table style has been applied, simply click anywhere inside the table to apply a new table style either from the Format As Table gallery on the Home tab or from the Table Styles gallery on the Table Tools Design tab.

In addition to the built-in table styles that you see in the gallery, you can further customize table formatting with the Table Style Options on the Table Tools Design tab shown earlier. Notice that, when you check options such as Banded Rows or Banded Columns, the previews in the Table Style gallery update to reflect the change. This is because several table styles include attributes for the various Table Style Options that only appear in the previews when those options are in use.

You can't modify built-in table styles, but you can duplicate them to create your own table styles based on built-in styles. To create your own custom table styles, do the following.

1. On the Home tab, click Format As Table or, on the Table Tools Design tab, click Table Styles. From either of these galleries, either click New Table Style or right-click an existing style and then click Duplicate.

2. In the New Table Quick Style dialog box, shown here, select the table element to customize and then click Format. The Format Cells dialog box will open with Font, Border, and Fill options available. Set the options you want to format for the selected table element and then click OK. Repeat this action for each part of the table that you want to customize.

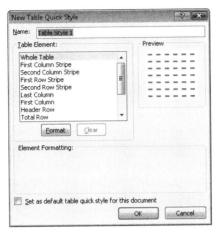

Once you've added formatting for an element, you can see a description of the element formatting below the Table Element list. Also notice that you can undo any formatting applied to an individual element. Once you've customized a table element, the Clear option becomes available for that element in the New Table Quick Style dialog box.

3. If you want to use the new table style as the default for all tables in the active workbook, check the option Set As Default Table Quick Style For This Document. Then, click OK to create your new style.

4. The style will appear under the heading Custom at the top of the Table Style and Format As Table galleries.

Note

You can set any table style as the document default at any time. To do this, right-click the style in either the Table Styles or Format As Table gallery and then click Set As Default.

To modify a custom style, right-click the style and then click Modify. You can also delete a custom style from the shortcut options provided when you right-click. Built-in table styles can't be deleted.

INSIDE OUT   Copy table styles between workbooks

Excel doesn't provide a mechanism for copying your custom table styles between workbooks. Of course, you can create a template that contains table styles and those will be available in any workbooks you create based on that template. However, there are two easy workarounds for when you just need to get custom table styles into your active workbook. For either of the following options, note that a table formatted with each style you want to copy must exist in the source workbook.

First, to copy table styles from one workbook to another, open the workbook that contains the styles you want and copy the sheet(s) containing the tables formatted with those custom styles to the destination workbook. To do this, right-click the sheet tab containing the table styles you need (you can select several sheets at once, if needed) and then click Move Or Copy. In the dialog box that opens, select the destination workbook from the To Book list, check the Create A Copy option, and then click OK. The destination workbook containing your copied sheet(s) will become the active workbook. Once you confirm that you're working in the destination workbook, delete the sheets you just copied and the custom table styles will stay behind.

Or, if you often want the same custom table styles, but don't want to base your workbooks on a custom template, create a template just for table styles. To do this, create a single-sheet workbook that contains a table formatted with each of your custom styles, save it as an Excel template (an .xltx file), and then close it. Excel saves new templates, by default, to the Templates folder. Whenever you need those table styles in a workbook, right-click a sheet tab in the destination workbook and then click Insert. From the dialog box that opens, select your table style template. The sheet you created in that template will be added to your destination workbook. Confirm that your custom table styles are now in the destination workbook and then just delete the unnecessary sheet.

Increasing Your Options with Conditional Formatting

The underlying concept of conditional formatting is unchanged. That is, conditional formatting enables you to set criteria for when specified formatting should appear. For example, change the color of a cell when its value exceeds a specified amount.

However, that's just about the only thing that's still the same for conditional formatting, and that is extremely good news. This feature has changed very much for the better.

When you view the Conditional Formatting options on the Home tab, shown earlier in this chapter, you see the option to select from several common rules that highlight cells based on specific criteria. When you select a preset option from the Highlight Cell Rules or the Top/Bottom Rules, you're prompted to enter the criteria and specify the formatting you need.

In addition to these commonly used rules, the Conditional Formatting options now include three entirely new types of formatting, known as the data visualization options.

These options, including Data Bars, Color Scales, and Icon Sets, add formatting that enables you to visually compare a set of values. For example, when you apply data bars to a column of numbers, you get the appearance of a bar chart directly in your cells, as you see in the Average column in the following example.

Column1	Q1	Q2	Q3	Q4	Average
Region 1	23	22	43	44	33.0
Region 2	22	44	37	30	33.3
Region 3	35	26	50	41	38.0
Region 4	25	48	24	9	26.5
Region 5	31	6	11	50	24.5

> **Note**
>
> From the perspective of a clean document design that effectively displays your data, think about what you want the formatting to accomplish before using data visualization tools. Data bars are likely to provide effective emphasis in most cases. However, when using color scales, consider light colors that won't overshadow your data with dense formatting. And, when using icon sets, make sure they highlight something you want to say about your data rather than distracting attention from the data.

In addition to the preset options, find the More Rules option at the bottom of each rule category, which is essentially the same as the New Rule option that appears on the Conditional Formatting menu. Selecting any of these opens the New Formatting Rule dialog box, shown here. The only difference is that, when you open the dialog box from the More Rules option in one of these categories, the dialog box defaults to the active rule category.

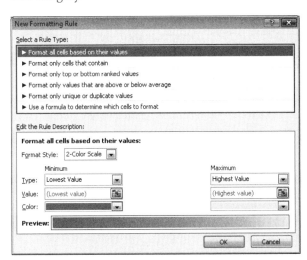

There are six types of rules, as you see in the preceding image. All data visualization categories fall under the first type, Format All Cells Based On Their Values.

To apply any type of conditional formatting rule, start by selecting the cells to format and then do the following.

1. On the Home tab, click Conditional Formatting. Either select a preset option, or select More Rules or New Rule to open the New Formatting Rule dialog box.

   All preset options will set criteria based on your values, if selected cells contain values, and apply default formatting. However, options in the Highlight Cell Rules and Top/Bottom Rules categories will prompt you to confirm or change criteria and formatting; the data visualization categories will not.

2. If you open the New Formatting Rule dialog box, select the type of rule you need, and then specify criteria and formatting.

   Notice that you can use Theme colors for any type of conditional formatting rules.

> **Note**
>
> When you apply conditional formatting in an Excel table and then add rows or columns to that table, the conditional formatting will automatically extend to new rows but not to new columns.

TROUBLESHOOTING

Cells using conditional formatting don't match the formatting specified

When the formatting you specify for conditional formatting rules looks different in the selected cells, those cells most likely contain multiple formatting rules. Applying multiple conditional formatting rules to the same cells can be useful at times. For example, you might want to highlight the top or bottom values in a range while using data bars to compare all values in that range.

However, because you can apply multiple rules to the same cells, when a new formatting rule is applied to cells that already contain conditional formatting, the earlier rule always remains intact. This can cause cell appearance to look different from what you expect.

To remove one conditional formatting rule before applying another, select the cells and then, on the Conditional Formatting menu of options, point to Clear Rules and then click Clear Rules From Selected Cells. To remove earlier rules after new conditional formatting has been applied, without removing the new rule, use the Conditional Formatting Rules Manager dialog box discussed in this section.

Note that, in that dialog box, you can also format some types of rules to stop being applied if the criteria for a given rule is true, so that multiple rules appear under specified conditions.

Managing the Rules in Your Workbook

The most important advance in conditional formatting is the addition of the Conditional Formatting Rules Manager, shown in the image that follows. You can edit, reorder, or delete rules throughout your workbook from this one location, and you can even add additional rules to ranges that already have formatting rules applied.

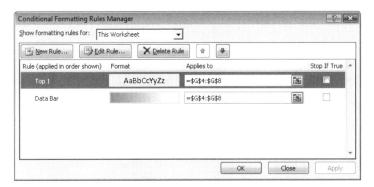

- From the Show Formatting Rules For list, choose to view existing rules for the Current Selection, This Worksheet, or any sheet in the active workbook.

- After you select a rule from the list, click New Rule to add an additional rule for the same range or click Edit Rule to change the criteria or formatting for that rule.

- Notice that you can edit the applied data range for a rule directly in this dialog box.

- Use the arrow buttons to the right of the Delete Rule option to reorder multiple rules applied to the same range. This changes the order in which rules are applied to the range, which can change the formatting that's visible in the cell.

- You can also order rules on the same range for use with the Stop If True option. When you check this option for a given rule, Excel will not apply lower rules to the same range if the criteria for the selected rule is true in a given cell. This helps ensure that the most important conditional formatting information appears in your data. Note, however, that this option isn't available for data visualization rules because they compare a range of values rather than specifying criteria as true or false.

Managing Page Layout Effectively

The Page Layout tab, shown here, is nicely organized to display most functionality you need for organized and effective worksheet formatting.

Though, as advanced users, you're most likely familiar with the options on this tab, take note of a few particular items.

- The Page Setup group is arranged much like the Page Setup group on the Page Layout tab in Word, with Margins, Orientation, Paper Size, and even Breaks.

- Notice the drop-down lists for the Width and Height settings in the Scale To Fit group. Clicking the More Pages option at the bottom of either list opens the Page Setup dialog box to the Page tab, just as if you clicked the dialog launcher in the Scale To Fit group.

- One of my favorite features on this tab is the Sheet Options group. It's so common to forget that you can show, hide, or even print gridlines and headings.

- When you have graphic objects on your worksheets, note the Selection Pane option in the Arrange group. The Selection And Visibility pane shows each graphic (such as pictures or drawing objects) on the active sheet and gives you easy access to select each or even to choose to hide certain graphics, such as if you want to print a worksheet without displaying only certain graphics.

> **Note**
>
> To avoid sharing a workbook with inadvertently hidden graphics, use the Document Inspector, introduced in Chapter 2, "Understanding Electronic Documents," before sharing your workbook electronically.

Note that this pane won't recognize individual drawing objects created directly in Excel charts.

- Unlike in Word, the Background feature in Excel is for on-screen backgrounds only and can't be printed. To print a watermark image on a worksheet, insert a picture into the header or footer that exceeds the height of the header or footer by the amount of the page that you want to watermark. Pictures that exceed the header or footer height automatically fall behind the page. And, once you insert a picture into the header or footer, the Format Picture option on the Header & Footer Tools Design tab becomes available, where you can set the image color to Washout.

When working on page layout formatting, try the new Page Layout view discussed earlier in this chapter. Just as in Word, when you can actually see the page layout, it's much easier to edit.

For example, to change margins using the rulers in Page Layout, point to any margin on the horizontal or vertical ruler and your insertion point will turn into a double-backed black arrow. When it does, simply drag to change the margins. You can change margins by as little as 1/100th of an inch at a time using this method (unlike in Word, no additional key is required for this precise resizing in Excel), and the measurement will appear in a ScreenTip as you drag.

Headers and Footers

In Page Layout view, the headers and footers are also automatically visible. In fact, if you click Header & Footer on the Insert menu, your view will be changed to Page Layout view.

> **Note**
> Though you can still access the Header/Footer tab of the Page Setup dialog box, don't do it. The Header & Footer Tools Design contextual tab, shown here, is an enormous improvement over the functionality available in that dialog box.

You can now click into the left, center, or right areas of the header or footer directly on the sheet to edit the header or footer. You can also break the left, center, and right section barriers and create a header or footer that extends across the page. To do this, just start typing in one section. When your content exceeds the width of the active header or footer portion, the header or footer automatically becomes a single area. Some readers might recognize this functionality from similar capabilities in Microsoft Excel for Mac.

> **Note**
> To wrap text within the left, center, or right area of a header or footer, press ALT+ENTER.

Note that, although you can add and edit text in the header or footer directly on the sheet, you can add other items, such as Pictures, from the Header & Footer Elements group on the Header & Footer Tools Design tab. Even though the Font group on the Home tab is available to your content in headers and footers, many options, such as Picture on the Insert tab, are not.

> **Note**
>
> A single header or footer is limited to a maximum of 255 characters, including formatting marks (such as spaces) and special characters.

The most exciting new elements for headers and footers, however, are available in the Options group on the Header & Footer Tools Design tab. Welcome new options, such as the Different First Page or Different Odd And Even Pages settings that you know from Word, are available along with the handy new setting to scale header and footer content with the document.

> **Note**
>
> As in Word, the Odd Page header and footer contains the same content as the regular header and footer. However, you can enable Different Odd & Even Pages for only selected sheets in Excel, whereas this option in Word can only be set for the entire document.

Notice that the name of the active header or footer type appears at the top-left of the header area or bottom-left of the Footer area so that you know whether you're working in the regular, first page, odd page, or even page header or footers.

INSIDE OUT   Keep your workbook consistent by applying formatting to multiple sheets at once

If you select multiple worksheets at once, formatting you change—from margins to headers and footers, to row height or column width, even to font formatting or applying styles—will change for all selected sheets.

To select contiguous sheets, hold the SHIFT key while clicking the sheet tabs you want to select. To select noncontiguous sheets, hold the CTRL key while clicking sheet tabs to select them. Also remember that, to quickly select an entire worksheet for making changes such as column width or row height, click the icon in the top-left corner of the sheet that appears between the column and row headings.

Note that, if you have multiple sheets selected when you format just a specified range on a sheet, the same range will be identically formatted on all selected sheets. However, be careful when editing worksheets with multiple sheets selected, because any data you add when multiple sheets are selected is added to all selected sheets as well.

Treat Your Workbooks Like the Documents They Are

The many comparisons to Word formatting throughout this chapter, such as with Themes, styles, the Page Setup group on the Page Layout tab, the new Page Layout view, or the new header and footer capabilities, help to make one point crystal clear: your Excel workbooks are just as much documents as the files you create in Word.

To manage your Excel documents effectively, consider not only the concepts and best practices provided in this chapter, but also review Chapter 2 and Chapter 12, to help you create and share complex workbooks with confidence.

For those of you who hesitate to delve into the world of Microsoft Excel because you don't like math, I'd like to start this chapter with a little story.

I dropped pre-calculus twice during high school. Yes, I used to be a ranking member of the math phobic society. Ironically, by some odd stroke of luck, I placed out on the math achievement test in my senior year. So, I wasn't required to take math in college. It was a dream come true, until I went to graduate school for business and discovered that linear calculus was required for my first economics class. I was terrified. Thankfully, my economics professor did something I never thought anyone could do—the wonderful Dr. G. helped me understand the relevance of the math needed for his class. I then found, much to my astonishment, that I actually enjoy math.

This newfound appreciation for the beauty of mathematical logic enabled me a few years later to embrace Microsoft Excel, and I learned something I like even more. That is, Excel is actually the ideal program for anyone suffering from a math phobia, because Excel does the math for you.

With this story in mind, I want to welcome all math lovers and math phobics alike to this chapter on working with data in Microsoft Office Excel 2007. Though I hope you'll discover more useful math-related tools than you knew before, as well as find tips and best practices for getting more from the number crunching powers of Office Excel 2007, very little knowledge of math or affection for the subject is actually required here.

Chapter Assumptions

I don't assume you're a math whiz for purposes of this chapter. However, I do assume that, as advanced Microsoft Office users, you have some experience with at least basic Excel functions and some familiarity with simple data tools such as sorts, filters, and named ranges.

This chapter covers working with data from a general business perspective. Call it an advanced layperson's look at Excel data. I give you information here that I believe most pertinent to professionals who are advanced Microsoft Office users and can benefit from the many capabilities of Excel, but who don't need the technical insight into Excel that math-specific professions might require. If you're an engineer, scientist, financial analyst, or CIA code-breaker, you will probably find valid tips here—but you might also want to check out a resource that takes a more technical and detailed dive into Excel data, such as one that explores specific advanced functions or discusses using the new Excel Services capabilities with Microsoft Office SharePoint Server 2007.

Find links to some good, highly technical Excel resources on the Expert Tips tab of this book's CD, including Web sites from members of the Excel product team and from some Excel MVPs.

In the introduction to this book, you can find a list of resources for those who want more basic-level information, in the section titled "Who Will Benefit Most from This Book."

What's New for Number Crunching in Excel 2007

The most important advance for the features and concepts addressed in this chapter is simply the way you access functions and data tools. And, though that might sound too basic to spark your interest, it's rather terrific in this case. From the organization and availability of features on the Formulas and Data tabs, shown in the following images, to some marvelously simple timesavers outlined in the list that follows, the beauty of the Excel advances addressed in this chapter is that doing just about anything you need to do with data can be truly and undeniably easy.

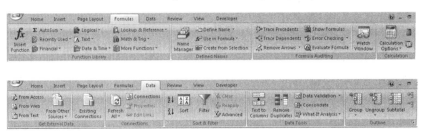

- Creating and formatting Excel tables was addressed in Chapter 13, "Data-Based Documents." This chapter takes that information a step further to show you the built-in data management capabilities of this great new feature, such as creating calculated columns in one step or swappable total-row functions, shown in the following image.

- AutoComplete for functions is my favorite new feature for working with data in Excel, and one that I use every time I open the program. Just begin to type a function, and a list appears of all possible functions that fit the spelling, as you see in the SUM example that follows. You can continue to type to complete the function, scroll through the list, or click an option in the list.

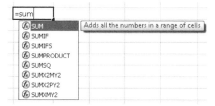

Point or scroll to any option in the AutoComplete list, and a ScreenTip appears showing a brief description of the selected function. When you want to use a selected function from the AutoComplete list, just press the TAB key and then add the necessary arguments.

> **Note**
>
> After you press the TAB key to select a function, or if you type the open parenthesis that follows the function name, the AutoComplete list disappears and the argument list for the active function appears to help you complete the function.

- In previous versions of Excel, you can view your choice of six calculations for selected data on the Status bar, for quick reference when you don't need to save a formula result in the workbook. Now, with the help of the customizable Status bar, you can show all six at once. Just right-click the Status bar and select as many as you like from among Average, Count, Numerical Count, Minimum, Maximum, and Sum. The results will appear on the Status bar automatically, as shown here, whenever appropriate data is selected.

Average: 158.75   Count: 4   Numerical Count: 4   Min: 112   Max: 192   Sum: 635

> **Note**
>
> Of the calculations available on the Status bar, the Count option acts on any selected cells other than empty cells, and all other available Status bar calculations only act on selections containing numeric values (non-numeric cells included in the selection are ignored). Results for any Status bar calculation only appear when two or more cells are selected. Also note that Count on the Status bar is the equivalent of the COUNTA function, and Numerical Count is the equivalent of the COUNT function.

Using Tables as a Data Tool

When you format a range in Excel as a table, you get a working set of data instead of a simple worksheet of values. To learn how to format a range as a table, see Chapter 13. Once you've created that table, take advantage of the following data-management capabilities.

- When you need a column of formulas for your data range, such as sums or averages for each row, you'll save time if you add those formulas after your range has been formatted as a table. Tables provide a feature called Calculated Columns that enables you to add a column of formulas to the table just by adding a formula into any cell of an empty table column. When you do, the entire column populates with the same formula. In fact, if you then change that formula in any cell of the calculated column, all other cells in that column automatically update to match.

  To add a calculated column to the right of existing table columns, just create a single formula in any cell of the column adjacent to the right edge of the table. The table will automatically expand and create the calculated column at the same time. Additionally, when you expand the table to add additional rows, the calculated column will continue to fill new cells with the same formula.

- When you add a total row to a table, the functions you place in that row are interchangeable. To do this, on the Table Tools Design contextual tab in the Table Options group, click Total Row to add a total row to the bottom of the table. Or, right-click in the table, point to Table, and then click Totals Row.

  The total row appears with a formula in the total row cell for the last column. If the data in the last column is numeric, a sum of visible cells appears in the last cell in the total row. Otherwise, a count of visible cells appears in that cell.

  You can drag the fill handle (the box at the bottom-right corner of a selected cell) to the left to fill the same formula into other cells in that row, if appropriate. However, each cell in the total row has an available drop-down list of function options, as you saw in the preceding section of this chapter. Just click in any cell of the total row to add or change the function for that cell, as you see here.

Note that, when you choose one of the eight shortcut options available from this drop-down list, the function is actually inserted as an option of the SUBTOTAL function that performs your selected calculation type on only visible cells. The Troubleshooting tip in this section titled "How can I sum only the visible cells in my range?" will help you learn more about SUBTOTAL functions and how they translate to the eight calculation types shown in the preceding image.

> **Note**
>
> If you add a formula in the row directly beneath a table that doesn't have a total row, one will automatically be added. However, if it doesn't already use a SUBTOTAL option, the formula you entered won't be changed to one of the SUBTOTAL function options automatically. To use a SUBTOTAL option for acting on only visible cells, select the function from the drop-down list once the total row is added.

- Tables, much like named ranges, enable you to use structured references in formulas that automatically adjust to accommodate changes in the data range. For example, when PivotTable data refers to a table name instead of a cell range, and the table range expands, the PivotTable data range updates automatically when you refresh data.

  Tables also take structured references quite a bit further than typical defined names. When you use a table, you can use structured references to specified portions of content within that table, both in formulas you create within the table as well as those you create in the workbook outside of that table.

  For example, if you create a formula anywhere in your workbook to sum the second column of the first table in the workbook, you might do so by typing **=SUM(** and selecting the range to sum. However, when that range is a table column, the cell references won't appear in your formula. Instead, your formula will look something like this: =SUM(Table1[Column2]). Learn how to work with this capability in the section of this chapter titled "Defining Names and Using Structured References."

- The first half of the Table Tools Design contextual tab, shown in the image that follows, offers a handful of data-related features, some more significant than others.

  - If you intend to reference the table in formulas or with other functionality (such as macros), it's a good idea to change the table name to something more intuitive that describes the data in the table. Otherwise, there's nothing wrong with leaving the default name.

  - Resize Table enables you to redefine the cell range for the table. Note, however, that it's usually quicker and easier to drag from the bottom-right corner of the table to do this, as explained in Chapter 13.

  - Though it's nice to have Summarize With Pivot in the Tools group on this tab, that option does the same thing as selecting PivotTable from the Insert tab. See Chapter 16, "Powerful Reporting, Easier Than You Think," for details.

○ Remove Duplicates, available in the Tools group, does exactly what it sounds like. In the Remove Duplicates dialog box, shown in the following image, you see a list of column headings. Select only those columns in which you want to check for duplicate values. When duplicates are found, the entire applicable row will be deleted. Note that you can find this option on the Data tab as well, where it can also be used with worksheet ranges not formatted as tables.

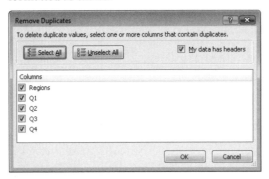

○ Convert To Range, the last option in the Tools group, is unlikely to be something you need often, but it's nice to have it there when you do. This option strips all table functionality. Formatting from the table style remains, but it becomes direct cell formatting. For help with table formatting if you choose to turn that range back into a table, see this section's Troubleshooting tip on the subject of table styles.

○ The External Table Data group primarily provides options discussed in the last section of this chapter. However, it's worth noting here a nice shortcut for exporting the table to a Microsoft Office Visio 2007 PivotDiagram, available under the Export options. See Chapter 17, "The Excel–Visio Connection," for details on the outrageously cool new PivotDiagram feature.

TROUBLESHOOTING

Table style isn't visible after converting a range to a table

If you convert a range to a table, any direct cell formatting remains intact and takes precedence over the table style.

To clear the direct formatting so that the new table style is visible, select part of the table and then, on the Home tab, click Clear and then click Clear Formats. You can select as much of the table at once as you like, but not the entire table. If the entire table is selected, both the direct formatting and the table style will be stripped. For example, try selecting all headings at once and then all data cells at once.

Note that outside borders included in direct cell formatting might be left behind when you do this. If so, select the entire table (even if an outside border only appears on part of the table), right-click, and then click Format Cells. On the Border tab, click None and then click OK. Only the borders included in the direct formatting will be cleared when you do this; any borders that belong to the table style will remain. See Chapter 13 for more on formatting tables.

INSIDE OUT   Create sample data in a snap

If you're a software trainer creating samples for class, or if you just want to create quick sample data with which to try some of the features discussed in this chapter, check out the RANDBETWEEN function. This function was previously available only if you installed the Analysis Tool Pack add-in, but it's now a built-in Excel function.

To use RANDBETWEEN, choose a minimum and a maximum value and Excel provides a random whole number result. For example, =RANDBETWEEN(100,200) provides a random whole number between 100 and 200.

To quickly create sample data using this function, start by adding a RANDBETWEEN formula in one cell and then drag the fill handle at the bottom-right corner of the cell down and across as many rows and columns of data as needed. (Alternatively, you can select the range you want to fill with that formula, add the formula once, and press CTRL+ENTER instead of ENTER to fill the entire range at once.)

Note, however, that RANDBETWEEN function results automatically change whenever the workbook calculates, so to get static data, take one further step. Once you've filled the range you want, the range is already selected. While it's still selected, do the following: Copy the selection (CTRL+C) and then, on the Home tab, click Paste options, and then click Paste Values. Press ENTER at the end of the sequence to deactivate copy mode. Or, for keyboard lovers like myself, the following keyboard sequence does all of this for you: CTRL+C, ALT, H, V, V, ENTER.

TROUBLESHOOTING

How can I sum only the visible cells in my range?

When you have hidden rows or columns within a data range, functions can be frustrating because most of them include hidden cells when calculated. In fact, for earlier versions of Excel (specifically, Excel 2002 or earlier), the Microsoft Knowledge Base contains an article that provides a macro for summing only visible cells.

However, this has become much easier to do in recent versions by using the function number argument of the SUBTOTAL function. You can use the SUBTOTAL function to perform 11 different common functions on a specified data range, either with or without hidden cells included.

For example, the function number to sum only visible cells is 109. So, the formula **=SUBTOTAL(109,A1:A25)** provides a sum of visible cells in the range A1:A25. After you select the SUBTOTAL function from the function AutoComplete list, you get a subsequent list of function numbers from which to select, as shown here.

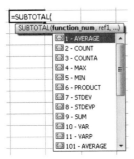

Numbers ranging from 1 to 11 include hidden cells, and those ranging from 101 to 111 exclude hidden cells. Note that the SUBTOTAL options that exclude visible cells are automatically used when you select one of the eight available function shortcuts from the drop-down list in a table total row.

However, note that the function numbers from 1 to 11 and from 101 to 111 in a table total row will exclude both hidden cells and those that don't appear because of a filter. However, when working in a range that is not a table, you must use the function numbers 101 to 111 to exclude hidden cells.

Creating Formulas—Working with Functions

Ever wonder what the difference is between a function and a formula? It might appear that Excel uses the terms interchangeably, but it really doesn't. A function is an action that you want to perform. A formula is the entire expression you create, including the function and the related arguments that you supply.

For example, **SUM** is a function, **=SUM(A1:A25)** is a formula.

This section looks at Excel functions in general, from accessing the function you need to referencing data, nesting functions, or auditing formulas.

If There's Logic to It, Excel Functions Can Do It

There's very little that Excel can't do when it comes to working with data. More than 300 built-in functions are available from the Formulas tab, providing a much broader range of actions than most Excel users realize, including many functions that aren't mathematical calculations at all. The Function Library group on the Formulas tab does a nice job of exposing them all, and making it easy to figure out which function you need.

When you point to an option under any of the headings in this group, you get a Screen-Tip showing a description of the selected function, such as with the CONCATENATE function shown here.

CONCATENATE is a good example of the fact that there's also much more you can do with many functions than you might expect at first glance. The description you see in the ScreenTip for the preceding image gives you a basic idea of when you might want to use that function. Then, click the function you want to open the Function Arguments dialog box, which helps you to complete the formula by providing space for each required argument. In the case of CONCATENATE, the dialog box provides space for text strings to combine and adds space for more strings as you need it. But, this dialog box also provides more information about the function, such as the fact that you can use CONCATENATE to join up to 255 strings.

Even so, that dialog box doesn't tell you everything you might need to know to get the most out of the function. Sticking with the CONCATENATE example, you might want to know that you can use other functions in your formula as individual strings or that you can use an ampersand (&) as an operator to join text strings instead of using the CONCATENATE function name. If you click Help On This Function in the Function Arguments dialog box, you get much of this information, including examples. Help on Excel functions is hands-down the best built-in help available in any of the Microsoft Office programs, and there are a few easy ways to access it in addition to the Function Arguments dialog box.

If you're typing your function or selecting it from the AutoComplete options instead of using the Function Arguments dialog box to complete it, the fastest method for getting help is to use the hyperlink in the function argument ScreenTip. You won't know the hyperlink is there until you point to the function name in the tip, when the name will appear underlined as you see in the image that follows.

Of course, you can also press F1 at any time for help, and then type the function name into the Search box. Detailed help exists for most functions, including explanations of each argument and, in many cases, examples that you can copy and paste into a worksheet. Note that, if you press F1 when pointing to a function in the Function Library group, you'll get a help article that provides a complete list of built-in worksheet functions by category, with descriptions and hyperlinks to the help articles for each.

> **Note**
>
> If the hundreds of built-in functions and the various ways in which you can use many of them don't give you what you need, you can find even more or write your own custom functions using Microsoft Visual Basic for Applications (VBA). (Check out the Worksheet-Function object in Excel VBA for a few built-in functions that don't appear on the Formulas tab.) See Chapter 21, "VBA Primer," to learn how to get started working with VBA.

The only limitation to the ease of using functions is that you have to understand enough about what the function is intended to do to be able to complete it effectively. When you aren't completely clear on a particular argument required by a function, use the Function Arguments dialog box to complete the formula.

If you've started to type the function, or selected it from the AutoComplete list, click Insert Function on the Formulas tab to open the Function Arguments dialog box. When your insertion point is in a cell that contains a function, this dialog box will automatically be set up for that function. Click into the box for any argument to see descriptive information, such as the required format for the active argument.

Nesting Formulas

If you remember that a function is just an action and a formula is what you use functions to create, it's easy to see how you might expand the capabilities of your work with functions by using multiple functions together within a single formula.

To use a function as an argument of another function, the following two points are all you need to know.

- Type the function name and its arguments—do not put an equal sign before the name of the nested formula. Only the outermost formula starts with an equal sign.

- Depending on the syntax of your formula, you might need to place parentheses around the nested formula, just as you would place parentheses around an individual operation in any formula in order to control the way the formula calculates. Other characters, however, such as quotation marks, are never used around a nested formula.

Following is a simple example of a nested formula.

```
=IF(SUM(A19:A20)>=AVERAGE(A21:A22),"True","False")
```

To confirm the logic in your nested formula—that is, to confirm that the formula is calculating nested formulas in the order you want—use the Evaluate Formula tool in the Formula Auditing group on the Formulas toolbar. To do this, select the cell you want to evaluate and then click Evaluate Formula.

In the Evaluate Formula dialog box, shown below for the sample nested formula given in the preceding example, click Evaluate to see the results of the underlined portion of the formula. Continue to click Evaluate to view the order in which Excel completes the calculation.

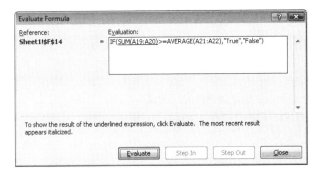

> **Note**
>
> When defined names or structured references are used (discussed in the following section of this chapter), Evaluate will first show the cell range indicated by the reference and then show the result of the applicable calculation.

Defining Names and Using Structured References

The Defined Names group on the Formulas tab refers to naming cell ranges for use as structured references. As introduced in the tables section earlier in this chapter, a structured reference is a reference to a named range rather than a cell range. The purpose of using names is so that you can simply update the cell range included in the defined name, and any references to that name throughout the workbook automatically update.

Creating and Using Defined Names

For example, say that you name the range C1:C10 as C_range and use that in several formulas, such as =Average(C_range). If you later need to include more data in that range and you redefine C_range to include C1:C18, all formulas that reference that range will update accordingly.

To quickly name a cell range, start by selecting the range. Then, in the Name Box on the Formula bar, shown in the following image, type the name you want to use for the range and press ENTER. Names can only contain letters and numbers, and can't contain spaces.

By default, a new name will be recognized throughout the workbook, so that you can reference a range on one sheet from a formula on another sheet, without having to specify the source worksheet. However, to make the named range local only to the active worksheet, so that you can use the same name for ranges on more than one sheet in the same workbook, type the sheet name, followed by an exclamation point, before the range name.

For example, type **myrange** as a range name that will be recognized throughout the workbook, or **Sheet1!myrange** to have the same range name only recognized on Sheet 1. However, except in cases where the duplication of range names would be intuitive to all users of the workbook, avoid duplicating range names to avoid confusion in your formulas.

Instead of creating ranges using the Name Box, you can use the New Name dialog box, where you can select the scope for the reference (workbook or active worksheet) and add comments about the range. To access this dialog box, on the Formulas tab, in the Defined Names group, click Define Name.

You can also click Name Manager in that same tab group, to open the new Name Manager dialog box. In that dialog box, shown here, you can see all defined names and table names throughout your workbook.

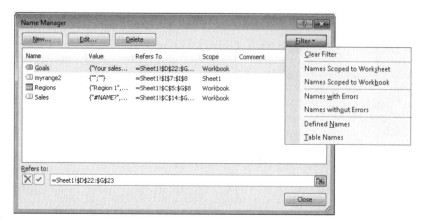

- Just select a defined name to edit its range in the Refers To box at the bottom of the dialog box shown here. When you've finished making changes, click the check icon to accept the changes.

- You can also select a name and then click Edit to change the name, comments, or cell range of a defined name, or the name of a table. Note that the scope of a defined name can't be edited.

> **Note**
>
> If you change the name of a range or a table, any references to that range or table will automatically update with the new name. However, references to those named items in other workbooks will only update if both workbooks are open at the same time. If the workbook containing the reference isn't open when you change the referenced name, an error may occur when you next open the workbook in which the reference resides.

- Click Filter to limit your view by local or global name, table or defined name, or names containing errors.

Notice the Create From Selection option in the Defined Names group, which provides a nice tool for naming several ranges at once. Use this tool when you want to name ranges such as rows or columns in tables, because the new defined names will be taken from your choice of the left or right columns, or top or bottom rows of your selection.

For example, if you want to create defined names for individual table rows, start by selecting the data to include in the range along with the row headings, as you see in the following image on the left. When you click Create From Selection, select Left Column as the source from which to create the names. When you do this, the resulting names and their respective ranges are shown, as you see in the following image on the right. Notice that the cells used for the defined names are not included in the ranges.

Regions	Q1	Q2	Q3	Q4
Region 1	141	158	144	174
Region 2	192	133	149	141
Region 3	182	112	192	149
Region 4	155	145	159	119
Total	670	548	644	583

Using Structured References to Table Content

As introduced earlier in this chapter, when you create a formula that references certain parts of a table, such as an entire column of data, the totals row, or all data in the table, you can use structured references to that table content. Structured references enable formulas to automatically adjust for changes in the table data range.

Following are the portions of the table that you can reference in this way, along with the correct reference. Syntax for using these references is discussed following the table.

Chapter 14

Table Component	Reference
The entire table	Table name
Any column	Column heading name surrounded by brackets, such as [Q1] if the first column name is Q1
All data	[#Data]
Column headings	[#Headers]
The total row	[#Totals]
The active row	[#ThisRow]
All contents of the specified table or column, including header and total cells if they contain applicable values	[#All]

For the examples of structured references that follow, refer to the table in the following image. The name of this table is Regions. SUM formulas are used for all examples.

Regions	Q1	Q2	Q3	Q4
Region 1	141	158	144	174
Region 2	192	133	149	141
Region 3	182	112	192	149
Region 4	155	145	159	119
Total	670	548	644	583

Sample Formula	Result
=SUM([Q2],[Q4])	Sums the combination of all values in columns Q2 and Q4. This reference is used inside the table because it doesn't specify the table name.
=SUM(Regions)	Sums all numeric cells in the entire table, excluding the total row but including calculated columns.
=SUM(Regions[#Totals])	Sums all values in the total row. Returns a #Ref! error if the table has no total row.
=SUM(Regions[[#Totals],[Q1]],E5)	Sums the total row cell in column Q1 with the value of cell E5. Notice the double brackets around the totals and column references. Each reference to a portion of the table gets its own brackets, and the entire reference to a portion of the table is surrounded by an outer set of brackets.
=SUM(Regions[[#Totals],[Q1]:[Q3]])	Sums the total cells of columns Q1 through Q3. Notice the colon used between column references to indicate a range.

Keep the following rules in mind to help create structured references.

- When using references inside the table, such as in calculated columns, you don't need to specify the table name. Outside of the table, always specify the table name.

- Type brackets around each element of a structured reference other than the table name, as well as brackets around an entire expression that refers to a single specific portion of the table.

- Use a comma between any of the five special item identifiers (those options that start with the pound sign) and the range to which they refer.

- Use formula operators as you would in standard ranges, such as [Q1]:[Q3] to refer to columns Q1 *through* Q3. Use [Q1],[Q3] to refer to columns Q1 *and* Q3. Note, however, that only contiguous ranges (those that use a colon) can be qualified by a single special item identifier.

- [#ThisRow] doesn't do exactly what you might think, because table rows can't actually be specified as structured references. This option can only apply to specified cells in the active row, so it always must be used with column identifiers. For example, =Regions[[#ThisRow],[Q1]] refers to the cell in the active row in column Q1.

So, what do you really have to know among all of the structured reference options discussed in this section? Not as much as you'd think. In fact, the preceding bullet points are pretty much all you need to remember, because AutoComplete for formulas offers help for working with structured table references. When you start to create the reference either directly in a cell or in the Formula bar, you'll see the available AutoComplete options.

For example, using the sample table shown earlier, the following steps use AutoComplete to add a structured reference as the range for a SUM function.

1. Type **=SUM(R** and you'll see AutoComplete with function names that start with the letter *R*, as well as the table name.

2. Scroll to Regions in the AutoComplete list and press the TAB key to apply it to your formula.

3. Next, type a single open bracket after the table name if you just want to reference a portion of the table, or type two consecutive open brackets if you're going to use a special item identifier along with a specified portion of the table. AutoComplete will again show you available options for the specified table and specified syntax, such as you see in the image that follows.

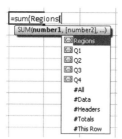

If the option you want isn't available, check your syntax (for example, you might need an additional bracket or a comma between references).

Managing Formulas

You have a complex workbook with multiple tables on multiple worksheets and many formulas throughout. When one calculation leads to the next, which leads to the next, the last thing you need to see is an error result. You have nested formulas, array formulas, structured references—and one small error in just one of those can cause a domino effect of errors to ripple throughout your workbook. How do you even begin to track down the culprit? Better yet, how do you put controls into your formulas to avoid those error messages in the first place? Let's take these two questions one at a time.

Tracking Down Errors—Formula Auditing

When an error occurs in a cell, you have several options to help you quickly resolve the issue, as follows.

- When you select a cell containing an error result, an error SmartTag appears. When you point to this icon, you can click the arrow that appears beside it for information on the type of error, a shortcut to the online help topic for that error type, the option Show Calculation Steps that opens the Evaluate Formula dialog box discussed earlier in this chapter, and other options.

- Determining the source of the error might be as easy as clicking in the Formula bar when the error cell is selected, as you will see all referenced cells or ranges highlighted on the active sheet. If you understand the type of error, this might be enough information to quickly get you to the result you need. Of course, if some references are to ranges outside of the active sheet, those won't be highlighted on screen.

- When you have more than one error on the sheet, on the Formulas tab in the Formula Auditing group, click Error Checking. The dialog box that opens provides similar options to an error SmartTag, as well as Previous and Next buttons to let you move through all errors on the sheet.

- To trace the source of the error for the selected cell, click the arrow beside Error Checking and then click Trace Error. Precedent arrows showing all available referenced cells in the error formula will appear. When using precedent or dependent arrows, notice that precedent arrows for off-screen references (such as source data on other sheets or in other workbooks), appear as a dashed line leading to a worksheet icon. Double-click the dashed arrow to open the Go To dialog, in which you'll see the location of the source range. Note, however, that if the source range is in a separate workbook, that workbook must be opened to access it using this method.

- When the answer isn't obvious to you, Evaluate Formula is the easiest way to see the source of the error, because each time you click the Evaluate button, you see the next step in the formula, until the error occurs. So, you can quickly and clearly see which argument is the cause of the error.

Avoiding Errors and Managing Data with Data Validation

Of course, avoiding errors before they happen is an even better solution than troubleshooting the problem later. It's certainly not always possible to control the worksheet to that extent, and not necessarily even appropriate in all cases, but using the Data Validation tool can be a great help.

Say, for example, that data entered into certain cells must be whole numbers between 50 and 80, or an error will result in formulas that are dependent on those cells. You can select the cells that require those values and set up data validation that informs users of the type of values required. You can even stop them from entering other types of values.

To do this, start by selecting all cells that require the same validation. Noncontiguous ranges can be used (to include noncontiguous cells, hold the CTRL key while selecting). Then, do the following.

1. On the Data tab in the Data Tools group, click Data Validation.

2. In the dialog box that appears, complete the settings you want on the Settings, Input Message, and Error Alert tabs. The example shown in Figures 14-1 through 14-3 uses the preceding scenario that required whole numbers between 50 and 80.

Figure 14-1 On the Settings tab, specify criteria for data entered into selected cells. Actions on the other two tabs of this dialog box are ignored if no criteria are set on this tab.

Figure 14-2 On the Input Message tab, specify a message, if any, that you want to display when a user clicks in a selected cell. The title is not required.

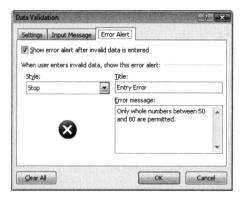

Figure 14-3 On the Error Alert tab, specify what you want to happen, if anything, when an error occurs.

Notice, as referenced in Figures 14-1 through 14-3, that you can't add an input message or an error alert without specifying data validation criteria. However, you are not required to use both an input message and an error alert action when you use data validation. So, you might choose to use this feature to prevent errors or just to provide guidance to users on preferred types of data.

> **Note**
>
> When you turn off the Ignore Blanks option on the Settings tab, you have some control over blank cells but not complete control. If the user clicks in a cell and deletes all content, any error action will be taken. However, if a user selects the cell and presses Delete, the content of the cell will be deleted.

> **CAUTION !**
>
> When you use the fill handle or otherwise copy content from one cell to another, data validation settings are copied as well. So, if you fill a cell for which validation is active with invalid data from another cell that has no validation, data validation will be removed from the destination cell.

Simplifying Data Organization

When you use Excel, you're working in an environment designed for logic and clarity. Excel is a spreadsheet after all—no matter what kind of great formatting you use in your workbooks, the concepts of Excel remain black and white. So, for best results whenever you create Excel documents or use Excel to create content for other documents, let the logic of Excel work for you.

Keep in mind that something as simple as the Freeze Panes feature on the View tab can help you review your worksheet data more effectively. Or, when you need to keep an eye on a few specific, important cells in any open workbook, regardless of which open workbook is active at the time, use the Watch Window (available from the Formula Auditing group on the Formulas tab).

> **Note**
>
> When your data range is formatted as an Excel table, you have an organization tool that is even easier to use than Freeze Panes. Notice that if you scroll down in the table so that the table headings move past the top of the screen, the sheet column headings automatically take on the table column heading names.

Also look for friendly solutions that can streamline your work while still being intuitive to other users of the workbook. For example, before you hide columns or rows, consider if the Outline feature wouldn't be more effective. Using the Outline options on the Data tab, you can group selected cells so that you can expand or collapse portions of your workbook as needed. When you group cells using the Outline feature, a pane appears at the left or at the top of your worksheet (depending on whether you have grouped rows or columns) with guidelines showing the grouped range and a minus icon that you can click to collapse that range. When collapsed, the icon becomes a plus sign that you can click to again expand that range. Using this feature can allow you to easily hide cells when you don't want to view them, but the pane that shows the outline makes it clear to any user that the worksheet includes hidden cells.

> **Note**
>
> The Subtotal tool in the Outline group on the Data tab is not available for ranges format-ted as tables. However, when you hide cells (or collapse grouped cells), remember that the total row, by default, uses SUBTOTAL formulas that only include visible values. See the section on working with table data earlier in this chapter for an explanation of SUB-TOTAL function behavior and options.

Also remember that tasks that might sound complex don't always need to be. For exam-ple, though I'll be the first person to tell you that PivotTables are simpler than you may think, you might need just an AutoFilter for the information you want from your data.

Filters and sorts have in fact become more flexible, with new features such as the ability to sort cells by color. Sort & Filter options are available on the Data tab or on the Home tab.

- To create a custom sort, such as sorting by cell or font color, on the Home tab, in the Editing group, click Sort & Filter and then click Custom Sort. Or, on the Data tab, in the Sort & Filter group, click Sort. Use the Sort dialog box, shown here, to add the sorting rules you need.

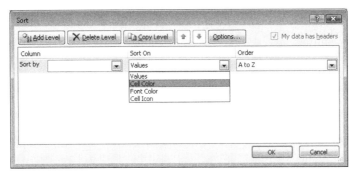

Depending on the sort type you select, you'll get different options. When you sort on Cell Color, for example, you can select which color out of those available in the range to sort at the top or bottom of the list. Notice also that you can copy a sort level to duplicate the settings and then change just what you need. This is particularly handy when you want to sort by color or icon and specify the order for more than just the first or last values in the list. Remember that sorts will execute in the order in which the sort levels appear in this dialog box.

● To apply a filter, on the Home tab, in the Editing group, click Sort & Filter and then click Filter. Or, on the Data tab, in the Sort & Filter group, click Filter. Either of these actions applies an AutoFilter arrow to the column headings in your selected range. (When working in a range that's formatted as an Excel table, remember that the AutoFilter arrows are automatically applied to your column headings by default.) When you click an AutoFilter arrow, you get filter options as well as another access point for sort options, as you see here.

The Sort By Color and Filter By Color options include fill color, font color, or icons, as applicable to the selected range. Note that colors that are part of a table style do not appear as available options to sort or filter by color, as those are applied automatically based on content position in the table rather than the content itself.

INSIDE OUT New Excel limits

Personally, I've never run out of available space on an Excel worksheet or needed more arguments in a function than Excel could handle, but I know that many of you have. For those of you who run into these limits more often than you'd like, you're much less likely to than you were in the past. Following are a few examples of the changes in Excel limitations.

- Excel now allows 1,048,576 rows by 16,384 columns in a single worksheet, up from 65,536 rows by 256 columns in the previous version.

- You can now include up to 255 arguments in a single formula, up from 30 in the previous version.

- From 56 colors in a workbook in previous versions, as discussed in Chapter 13, Excel can now handle 16 million colors.

- From 4,000 cell styles and 250 custom number formats in the previous version, Excel now allows up to 64,000 unique cell styles and number formats combined. (Note that 250 remains the limit for custom number formats in a workbook.)

To see a thorough list of Excel limits, press F1 to open the Help pane and then type **Excel specifications and limits**.

TROUBLESHOOTING

The active range on the worksheet exceeds the range in use

Pressing CTRL+END on an Excel worksheet takes you to the last cell on the worksheet that contains data. At least, that's what it's supposed to do. However, CTRL+END often moves you to a point on the sheet well beyond the last cell currently in use.

When Excel sees the range in use as being greater than it actually is, that's because of content that previously existed on the worksheet. But, it takes just a second to reset this using the Visual Basic Editor.

For any VBA-based solutions, I'm generally referring you to the VBA primer chapter later in the book. However, this issue warrants an exception because of how common an issue it is and how easy it is to fix. Take the following steps.

1. With the sheet you want to reset in your active view, on the Developer tab, click Visual Basic, or press ALT+F11.

2. In the Visual Basic Editor, you should see a pane at the bottom of the screen named Immediate. If you don't, on the View menu, click Immediate Window, or press CTRL+G.

3. Click in the Immediate Window and then type the following exactly as it appears (no spaces):

```
ActiveSheet.UsedRange
```

4. Press ENTER. It will appear as if nothing has happened. Press ALT+F11 to return to your sheet and try CTRL+END again. The range in use should have been reset to the correct range in use. You can close the Visual Basic Editor without further action, once you no longer need it.

To learn about the many timesavers you can accomplish in one line of code by using the Immediate Window, see Chapter 21.

When You Need to Use External Data

When your source data isn't in an Excel workbook, have no fear. It's quite easy to import data from a number of sources, and even in many cases to keep that data linked to a dynamic source, so that it updates automatically when needed. Following is a summary overview of common data types you may want to import and related options. Find all of these options on the Data tab, in the Get External Data group.

- When you import data from a Microsoft Office Access 2007 database, you select the database that contains your source data and Excel prompts you to select a table within that database, if it contains multiple tables. Once you select the data source, you get the option to import the data into a table, PivotTable, or PivotTable and PivotChart. Even if you want to create a PivotTable, it's a good idea to import the data as a table. You can create a PivotTable or PivotChart from the table in just a click, and you get quicker access to the source data.

- When you choose the option to import data from the Web, you get a window in which you can browse to the Web page you need. Excel can import table content from a Web site, so an arrow will appear beside each table on the selected page that can be imported. You can select as many as you need. Just click the yellow arrows to place a check box by each table you want to import. After you click Import and choose the location for your content, you'll see a line of text indicating that Excel is getting the data, and it will populate as many cells as needed to provide the data you requested.

> **Note**
>
> When selecting a location for imported data, be sure to leave enough room between the imported content and any other existing data on the sheet. If the imported data would overwrite an existing range, Excel may attempt to move the data but might copy unwanted formatting when it does. Alternately, Excel might refuse the operation. If the operation is refused, but a single cell is available where you indicated to place the imported data, the text string that indicates what data is being imported will appear. Though it looks like static text, it's not. Move that string to a location on the sheet with ample space for the imported data and then, on the Data tab, click Refresh All to finish importing the data.

- When you import data from text, your source file can be a.txt or .csv file type. (Note that the .prn file format is listed as an available format as well, but this refers to space-delimited text files and not to printer files.) Data imported from a text source (such as text delimited with commas between fields in a record) will be imported into an unformatted range. Like other data types, data from a text source will remain linked to its originating file by default. However, you will be prompted to select the file from which to get data whenever you click Refresh. For this reason, when you have multiple imported text ranges, refresh them one at a time rather than refreshing all data connections at once, to ensure that the correct data is refreshed to the correct range. To refresh the selected range instead of all connections at once, right-click in the range and then click Refresh. Or, on the Data tab, click the arrow below Refresh All and then click Refresh.

Importing data from other sources, such as SQL or XML data, is accessible through the From Other Sources list in the Get External Data group.

For any imported data type, note that you can set several custom properties, such as how and when the data refreshes. To access these options, click in the external data range and then, on the Data tab, in the Connections group, click Properties. Available options vary based on the type of data source.

The following are additional notes to keep in mind when working with data connections.

- With the exception of external data types that can be imported as Excel tables, such as Access tables, if you format an imported range as a table, you will be prompted to break the link to external data.

- The Connections option in the Connections group on the Data tab shows all active connections in the current workbook and gives you options to add connections as well as to refresh, remove, or edit the properties of active connections. When you remove a connection, you don't remove the imported range from your workbook, only its link to the external data.

> **Note**
>
> The Existing Connections option in the Get External Data group on the Data tab shows available connection sources on your computer.

- Notice that links are also managed from the Connections group on the Data tab. The Edit Links option enables you to view and manage data linked between Excel workbooks.

Charts

O kay, it's time to have some fun. Microsoft Excel charts are among my favorite features in any program, and that hasn't changed with the introduction of a brand new charting engine for Microsoft Office Excel 2007.

To me, fun with software is when content looks so great or works so well in a document that you assume it must be difficult to create, but it's actually easy. That's charting in Microsoft Excel, and that's what we're going to look at in this chapter.

Creating and formatting high-quality, complex charts can be positively, absolutely easy. And, despite the loss of a few familiar shortcuts with the introduction of the new Office Excel 2007 charts, the gains outweigh the losses on the changes to this major piece of Excel functionality. There's a lot to be said for giving charts the formatting flexibility they now have. There are also enough new timesavers that you aren't likely to miss those few retired favorites for very long.

Chapter Assumptions

I'm not going to take your time in this chapter to show the difference between a plot area and a chart area, or explain what a data label is. I won't step you through the process of creating a chart or tell you when to use a column chart or a line chart.

Instead, skipping quickly through some basics you already know with quick tips and best practices, this chapter focuses on making effective use of the new charting tools. Everything in this chapter is based on the assumption that you knew charting basics before you got here and have confidently created at least basic charts in a recent version of Excel.

Similar to the preceding chapter on working with data in Excel, this chapter takes an advanced layperson's approach. Though I go into detail on the idiosyncrasies of various chart elements and provide troubleshooting directions for a number of issues, I don't cover scientific or technical charting, such as engineers might require.

 So, if you're a scientist, engineer, or in another math-centric profession that requires technical charting, you are still likely to find new information in this chapter. However, you might also want to explore some more technical charting resources, and so I've provided links to some of those on this book's CD.

Note, however, that this chapter does address two specific advanced chart types that are worth exploring regardless of the chart types you usually need. Price/volume charts and bubble charts have a number of formatting peculiarities, the details of which can help you better understand and manage custom requirements for a wide range of complex chart types. So, I highly recommend sticking around for those parts of the chapter even if your only possible need for a price/volume or bubble chart would be if you decide to dress up as an investment banker for Halloween and find yourself in need of props.

In the introduction to this book, you can find a list of resources for those who want more basic-level information, in the section titled "Who Will Benefit Most from This Book."

What's New for Charts in Excel 2007

This section is quite different from the "what's new" section in many chapters because the answer in this case is both everything and nothing. The charting engine is entirely new, which means that charts look different, have different formatting capabilities, and offer different methods for editing and managing chart elements.

However, whatever chart types you knew how to create before, you still know. Most of the customizations you've made to charts in the past you can still make. We'll be looking at new features, new capabilities and limitations, and new methods throughout this chapter. But, it's important to know that most of what you already know about Excel charting is still valid.

As mentioned earlier, a few shortcuts are gone, but in place of some are new and even easier options. For example, you can no longer double-click a chart element to open its format dialog box, but you can still right-click or press Ctrl+1. And, most chart elements are now exposed on the Chart Tools Layout tab for much quicker access than in the past.

The shortcut I miss the most is the ability to drag a data point along the value axis in order to change data directly on the chart. But, I'm willing to forgive that loss for my favorite new timesaver–you might not believe how easy it is to size Excel charts for use in other programs.

The preceding examples notwithstanding, attempting to outline every new element of an entirely refurbished major feature in one little upfront section just won't do it justice. Instead, please consider this entire chapter the answer to "what's new for Excel charts."

> **Note**
> For information on the new Chart templates, see Chapter 20, "The Many Faces of Microsoft Office Templates."

The New Essentials for Creating Charts

Before diving into more advanced topics, following is a quick summary of some charting essentials that have changed as well as confirmation of a few things that remain the same.

- To create a chart on its own sheet, you can still use the shortcut F11–which creates the default chart type. This is now the only method for creating a chart directly on its own sheet. You can, however, move any chart to its own sheet after creating it, as discussed later in this list.

- Initially, the default chart type is a clustered column chart. However, to set a different chart type as your default, on the Insert tab, in the Charts group, click the dialog launcher to open the Insert Chart dialog box. Then, just select the chart type that you want to use as your default and click Set As Default Chart. Nothing will appear to happen, but your default chart type will change. To confirm this, close and reopen the Insert Chart dialog box. The chart you set as your default should be selected.

- If the data range for your chart is contiguous, you can simply click in the data range and then create your chart. The entire range does not need to be selected.

- If your source data is in a table, the chart sees the table as the data range. What this means is that if the table cell range is increased or reduced, the chart will automatically update to reflect the revised data range. See Chapter 14, "Working with Data," to learn about structured references to tables.

> **Note**
>
> If you delete a row or column from an Excel table being used as a chart's source data, you may get an error message when you next access the chart. However, after you click OK to dismiss the error message, the chart should update correctly to recognize the change in the data range.

- If you create a chart from the Chart group on the Insert tab, including using the Insert Chart dialog box, it will be created as an object on the active data sheet. The new charting engine doesn't offer a Chart Wizard. Just select your data (remember that to use noncontiguous data, you need to hold the CTRL key while selecting) and then either press F11 for a chart on its own sheet, or use the Chart group on the Insert tab to create a chart object on the active sheet.

Chapter 15

CAUTION !

When using the CTRL key to select noncontiguous data, it's important to drag to select any contiguous areas within the data, just as you would for a single contiguous data source. Individually selecting cells that you intend to be part of the same series can cause undesired results.

- To change the type of chart after it's created, select the chart and then, on the Chart Tools Design tab, click Change Chart Type. Or, right-click the chart and then choose Change Chart Type.

- To move a chart between its own sheet and a worksheet, on the Chart Tools Design tab, click Move Chart, or right-click the chart and then click Move Chart.

- Not all chart types, of course, are appropriate for all data—and different chart types may be more or less effective depending on both the data and what you want the data to express. In the Insert Chart dialog box (or the Change Chart Type dialog box—which contains the same options), you no longer see descriptions of chart types, as you do in earlier versions. However, they're not gone. When you point to any chart type in the Chart group galleries on the Insert tab, a ScreenTip gives you a description of what the chart type displays and, in many cases, when to use it. For example, see the ScreenTip for a Clustered Bar Chart in the image that follows.

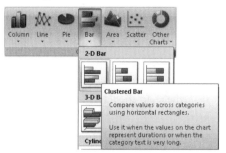

If you're not positive about the most effective chart type for your data, use the Change Chart Type option on the Chart Tools Design tab to try out a few before you spend time customizing formatting. Also keep in mind that simple customizations, such as changing the axis scale to more snugly fit your data range, can have a substantial effect on the statement you make.

For example, the following charts use the same data. The only difference between them is that the minimum and maximum values on the vertical (value) axis for the chart on the right have been customized to fit the data.

Fighter-Pilot Cool Chart Formatting   **317**

Finally, if you're not sure of your data's best side, consider using a PivotTable to find it. PivotTables are easier than the great majority of Excel users think they are, and they're designed to be Excel's very own spin doctors. See Chapter 16, "Powerful Reporting, Easier Than You Think," to learn how to create and use PivotTables.

Fighter-Pilot Cool Chart Formatting

This is where you garner the benefits of change. The new charting engine is part of the overall new graphics engine for the 2007 release. So, charts now have formatting capabilities very similar to drawing objects, such as SmartArt diagrams or shapes.

In addition to fancy formatting, this section looks at customization options from individual chart elements to the overall chart layout, as well as considerations for unique chart types.

Using Chart Quick Styles

Just because you want charts to look customized doesn't mean you have to do it all yourself. Charts offer two types of Quick Styles that are designed to work together—Chart Styles and Chart Layouts, both of which are available on the Chart Tools Design tab, as shown here.

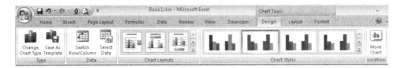

Like any set of Quick Styles, each choice within these two sets applies several formatting attributes at once. So, you can apply a Chart Layout that's close to what you want, for example, and then further customize individual chart elements as needed, such as deleting gridlines or adding data labels. Or, select a Chart Style that includes a bevel effect on the data series, and then change the type of bevel or add a custom shadow.

> **Note**
>
> Unlike most types of Quick Styles, note that Live Preview doesn't work with Chart Styles or Chart Layouts. However, Live Preview does work in charts that are objects on a worksheet for formatting options in the Shape Styles and WordArt Styles groups of the Chart Tools Format tab.

A key change to remember for chart formatting is that charts are now drawing objects. You can select a data series or a data point, for example, and then on the Chart Tools Format tab, shown in the following image, customize the formatting by using options in the Shape Styles group. You can also use the new WordArt Styles (also on the Chart Tools Format tab) to enhance the formatting of chart text.

Note that, if you customize formatting for individual chart elements after applying a Chart Style, you can reset the formatting of just that element of the style without affecting other customizations. To do this, select the element to reset and then, on either the Chart Tools Format tab or the Chart Tools Layout tab, in the Current Selection group, click Reset To Match Style. To reset multiple elements at once, select the Chart Area and then click Reset To Match Style.

INSIDE OUT Use Theme Effects with Chart Styles

The various types of Quick Styles for graphics, from Chart Styles to SmartArt Styles to Shape Styles, are the places where you see Theme Effects really go to work.

Though you will see different defaults for graphic formatting options (such as shape borders) depending on your active Theme, apply a Quick Style that contains some type of 3-D formatting, and then point to various Theme Effects (in the Themes group on the Page Layout tab) to see live previews of what Theme Effects can really do for your graphics.

In the case of charts, try changing Theme Effects after applying a Chart Style that includes Bevel formatting for the data series.

> **Note**
>
> Notice that you now have 3-D Format settings, such as Bevel options, for two-dimensional (2-D) charts. These are very different effects from using a 3-D chart type. Though 3-D chart types can change the perspective from which you look at the chart, 3-D Format settings simply add depth to individual chart elements.

Customizing Chart Elements

The Chart Options dialog box is no more. In its place is the Chart Tools Layout tab, shown in the following image, where you can access any chart element.

Before you begin to work with the Chart Tools Layout tab, however, keep one important shortcut in mind. As you might already know from previous versions, to delete any chart element—from gridlines to data series—just select that element on the chart and then press the DELETE key. (Note that, for charts on their own sheet, if you paste data back on the chart after deleting it, you will no longer be able to delete elements just by pressing the DELETE key. You can, however, right-click and then click Delete.)

With the exception of deleted data series or data points, deleted chart elements aren't actually gone. They're simply not shown. So, you can select the chart element you need from the Chart Tools Layout tab at any time, such as with the Axes options that you see here.

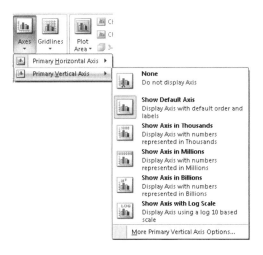

In fact, if you customize a chart element and then delete it, you can later restore it from the Chart Tools Layout options and your customizations will be intact. For help replacing deleted chart data, see the section of this chapter titled "Timesaving Techniques for Adding or Editing Chart Data."

> **Note**
>
> If you select the plot area and then press DELETE, any formatting applied to the plot area disappears, but the plot area itself always remains.

At the bottom of each menu of options for the various chart elements shown on the Chart Tools Layout tab, click More <Chart Element> Options to open the Format dialog box for that chart element. You can also access the same Format dialog box from the shortcut menu that appears when you right-click a chart element.

Additionally, if a chart element is difficult to select, select it from the drop-down list in the Current Selection group on either the Chart Tools Layout or Chart Tools Format tabs. In that same tab group, you can then click Format Selection (if needed) to open the appropriate dialog box for your selection.

When you get into those Format dialog boxes, you'll find several new options, such as Shadow options and new Fill, Line Color, and Line Style options that are available to many chart elements. For details on how to set specific options, such as the new Stop settings for gradient lines or fill, see Chapter 18, "Creating Professional Presentation Graphics." Though that chapter is in the Microsoft Office PowerPoint 2007 portion of this book, the details of these settings apply to all drawing objects that have the capabilities of the new graphics engine.

> **Note**
>
> One of the nicest new features of the Format dialog boxes is that they're modeless. That is, you can open a Format dialog box for any chart element and then leave it open as you select different chart elements for which to make changes. As your selection changes, the options in the dialog box change to match. This new functionality helps to explain why there's no Cancel button in the Format dialog box—formatting is applied as soon as you set it, so that you can move on to something new. However, you can undo actions even while a Format dialog box is open. Just click on the sheet and then either click Undo on the Quick Access Toolbar or press CTRL+Z. Then, select a chart element and click back into the dialog box to continue formatting.

In addition to the new graphic formatting options, the following subsections address key points to keep in mind about some other new formatting options as well as a few old standards.

Chart Text

Rule number one for formatting text in charts: the Chart Area is the container for all chart elements. When you want your font formatting—whether it's traditional font formatting or WordArt formatting—to apply to all text in all elements of the chart, select the Chart Area before applying the settings you need.

- Font settings are not available from the Format dialog boxes for any chart element. Instead, use the Font group on the Home tab for most settings (or find Font on the shortcut menu when you right-click a chart element that contains text). You can also use the Alignment group on the Home tab for text alignment and orientation (angles), though some of these settings are available from the Format dialog boxes. Additionally, click the dialog launcher at the bottom-right of the Font group for a pleasant surprise.

  In the Font dialog box available to charts, notice several welcome formatting additions, including Small Caps, All Caps, Equalize Character Height, and Offset percentage for the Superscript and Subscript settings. You also get a wide range of underline styles and the ability to change the color of underlines. Even more fun is the Character Spacing tab, shown here, where you can expand and condense spacing for chart text.

  These font improvements are a benefit of the new graphics engine. So, in Excel, they're only available to charts and other drawing objects, and not to worksheet cells. You'll find these same font formatting improvements available to any text content in Office PowerPoint 2007.

> **Note**
> Among all of the additions to the Font dialog box for chart text, one deletion is worth noting. The often frustrating Auto Scale setting for text is, thankfully, gone. So, your chart text will no longer shrink to oblivion when you resize the chart.

Chapter 15

- As mentioned earlier, also remember that text in charts can now be formatted as WordArt. Using the WordArt Styles group on the Chart Tools Format tab (see the following image), you can select a preset style or customize fill, line, and effects with very similar options to shapes.

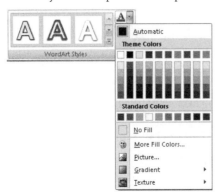

In the WordArt Styles group, notice that fill options include picture, gradient, and texture fills. Keep in mind that these options refer to the fill of the actual text characters themselves (such as the text of axis labels). In contrast, if you select a fill style from the Format Axis dialog box, the text area that contains each axis label is formatted with that fill.

> **Note**
>
> To wrap text within any label automatically generated from source data (such as an axis label or data label), the text must use line breaks in the source data. To do this, in the cell where the source data appears, press ALT+ENTER to insert a line break wherever you want the text to break to a new line in the chart. However, in an axis title, data label, or text box that you edit by clicking in the box and typing, press SHIFT+ENTER to create a line break.

Axes

Understanding different types of axes is one of the easiest ways to understand different chart types. There are, essentially, two types of axes—category and value—explained as follows.

- A category axis can be either a date axis or text axis (known as time-scale axis and category axis in earlier versions). Category axes are typically used by charts containing two or more axes, which track values across categories—such as tracking sales for the past four quarters, which you might do with a column, line, or bar chart. These are often referred to as category-value charts and they include the majority of built-in chart types available in Excel, including column, line, bar, area, stock, and surface charts.

- A value axis enables you to plot a range of values. Values can be plotted across categories, such as in the chart types referenced in the preceding bullet. Or, values can be plotted relative to other values—such as to compare salary increases relative to length of employment, as you can do with a scatter chart. Built-in Excel value-value chart types include scatter and bubble charts.

Similar to a value-value chart, a radar chart contains just one value axis, plotting all values relative to a center point to show variance from the center value. Though this chart type has just one axis, that axis appears separately for each data series, radiating out from the center, as you see in the following image. The axis labels can only appear once, but the line running from the center point to each category label (Q1 through Q4) is the same value axis.

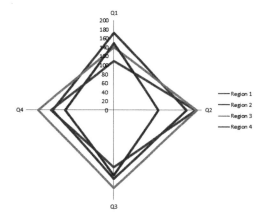

Note

Pie charts and donut charts don't plot values along an axis. Rather, they show contributions to a whole. A donut chart is used when you need to show the type of relationship you would with a pie chart, but using multiple data series.

In the Axes options on the Chart Tools Layout tab, shown in the following image, notice that Excel refers to axes as vertical and horizontal, indicating where they appear on the chart rather than the axis type.

However, if you point to an axis, a ScreenTip specifies horizontal or vertical as well as category or value.

> **Note**
>
> The terms *horizontal axis* and *x-axis* are used somewhat interchangeably in this chapter because x-axis is a common charting reference that generally refers to the same chart element being referred to by Excel as the horizontal axis. Keep in mind that horizontal/vertical, x-axis/y-axis, and category/value aren't necessarily synonymous. For example, a bar chart is a category/value chart, but its value axis is the horizontal axis. Similarly, both the x-axis and y-axis for a scatter chart are value axes.

The quick-access options on the Chart Tools Layout tab for displaying a given axis vary by axis type (category or value). For additional axis customizations, open the Format Axis dialog box.

On the Axis Options tab of the Format Axis dialog box, shown in the following image for a value axis, you have virtually the same options as are available from the Scale tab of the Format Axis dialog box in the previous version, as well as some options available on the Patterns tab in earlier versions.

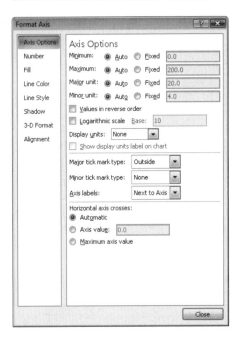

CAUTION!

> Though it's common to need to customize the scale—the maximum and minimum values—on an axis (and this can often be a good idea, as mentioned earlier), remember that those values become static once you customize them. Axis Options set to Auto change automatically when content in your data requires it; those set to Fixed remain static regardless of changes to the source data. So, for example, say that you have values ranging from 50 to 100, and you customize your value axis accordingly with 100 as the maximum value. If you then add data to your chart and new values exceed 100, those values won't be visible on your chart.
>
> Customizing axes is often an important step in displaying your data effectively. Just remember to update a customized axis scale if changes to the data require it.

In addition to Axis Options, notice some new formatting capabilities for axes, including the following.

- Fill options refer to the fill of the text box area around each axis label.

- Shadow settings affect the line itself. If you apply a fill to the axis labels, the shadow setting is applied individually to each axis label area as well.

As you format any chart element, remember (as mentioned earlier) that these objects are now seen as drawing objects by Excel. So, you can also format line and fill settings for the axis or its labels by using the Shape Fill, Shape Outline, and Shape Effects settings on the Chart Tools Format tab. You can also use the WordArt styles settings on the same tab to format axis label text.

With all of the great new formatting capabilities, however, it's worth noting that a couple of settings in the Format Axis dialog box (as well as the Format dialog boxes for some other chart elements, as indicated) have simply been misplaced.

- A 3-D Format tab appears in the Format Axis dialog box, but the options available on that tab are unlikely to have any visible effect on the selected axis.

- A Vertical Alignment option is available on the Alignment tab of the Format Axis dialog box as well as the Format dialog boxes for several chart elements containing text (Vertical Alignment changes to Horizontal Alignment if you rotate or stack the label text.) Though this option appears to be a new addition that enables you to align multiline labels within the text area, it doesn't work as expected. This option works with text boxes and other text-enabled drawing shapes that you can add to a chart, but it doesn't work for text within chart elements.

INSIDE OUT   Group a category axis

You can visually group categories together on any category axis just by adding a second row or column of axis labels in your data.

For example, say that you want to look at revenue by salesperson. You might want to group those salespeople by region, as you see on the category axis in this simple example.

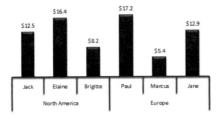

Total Revenue (U.S. $mm)

The groups in the preceding image (North America and Europe) are created by adding a column to the left of your category axis labels (or a row above your category axis labels, if data is in rows), where the category name appears before the first axis label to which it applies. For example, the data below corresponds to the preceding chart example.

Column1	Column2	Total Revenue (U.S. $mm)
North America	Jack	12.5
	Elaine	16.4
	Brigitte	8.2
Europe	Paul	17.2
	Marcus	5.4
	Jane	12.9

TROUBLESHOOTING

The last date doesn't appear on my line chart x-axis

When you need the last date to appear as the last axis label on a line chart, you can usually do that with some trial and error. To remove the trial and error, you just need to change that line chart to a scatter line and then specify a few values in the Axis Options. But, let me first give you a bit of background and explain your choices.

A line chart's horizontal axis is a category axis. So, whether you use the Date Axis or Text Axis option in the Format Axis dialog box, you need to change the number of data points between each label to manipulate which labels appear on the axis. In the case of a Date Axis, change the Major Unit; for a Text Axis, change the settings for Intervals Between Labels.

There is, however, a simple calculation you can use to remove the guesswork. The problem with a line chart is that the result will only work if it's a whole number. But, stick with me—this formula will help you regardless.

To calculate the Major Unit or Interval Between Labels, type the following formula, substituting your own values: **=(last date – first date)/one less than the number of axis labels you want**. Remember that the first and last dates, even if formatted as dates, are still numbers. For example, if you take the publication date of this book (2/1/2007) and change the number format in Excel to Number, that value would appear as 39114.

If the result of the formula is a whole number, then the easiest solution is to select Text Axis and use that formula result as the values for both Intervals Between Tick Marks and Intervals Between Labels. You can also use it with a Date Axis as the Major Unit, setting the unit of measure to Days. However, if the formula result is not a whole number, your resulting axis is likely to be off and you won't get the last axis label you need. So, you can continue trying different numbers of axis labels for the last argument in the formula, or you can change your line chart to a scatter line, and do this without issue.

When you change your line chart (or line series in a combination chart) to an XY Scatter Chart With Straight Lines (with or without markers), the line might change dramatically, covering only a portion of the plot area. Don't be concerned, that's just because you need to set up the horizontal axis—which is now a value axis.

To do this, use the first date and last date in your data, in number formats (as mentioned above) as the Minimum Value and Maximum Value. Then, use the result of the formula given earlier in this tip as the Major Unit. If the formula result exceeds seven decimal places, make sure that you're seeing all decimal places before you use the result as the Major Unit value. (General number format, for example, rounds results to eight decimal places, which may provide an inaccurate result as the Major Unit.) With no trial and error, you'll then have exactly the line chart you need, with an axis that shows the exact dates you want and with the exact number of axis labels you need.

Check out the Webcast titled "Advanced Tips and Tricks for Fast and Fabulous Excel 2007 Charts" on the Expert Tips tab of this book's CD for a live demo of these steps as well as many other tasks discussed in this chapter.

Gridlines

The new line style options available to other chart elements, such as axes, are available to gridlines as well. However, if you choose Gradient Line on the Line Color tab of the Format Gridlines dialog box, the gradient will progress from the top gridline to the bottom gridline (or the left gridline to the right gridline) rather than gradient changes taking place within each individual line.

Chart and Axis Titles

The most notable change for titles is simply that there is no longer a dialog box in which to edit their text. Otherwise, their behavior is much the same with some improved formatting options discussed in the section titled "Chart Text" earlier in this chapter.

Titles are now always inserted with placeholder text, which you can click in and edit like any text box, or select and then click in the Formula bar to link the title to a cell value.

You can link the text boxes for titles, data labels, or custom text boxes inserted on a chart to cell values in the workbook. To do this, select the title, label, or text box, and then click in the Formula bar. Type **=Your Cell Address**, remembering to specify the sheet name if the reference is on a different sheet. Rather than worrying about syntax, the easiest way to link the selected box to a cell value is to type the equal sign in the Formula bar and then browse to the cell, select it, and press ENTER to apply the link.

Combining Chart Types

Combining chart types, such as when you want to display some chart series as columns and others as lines, is very easy to do. You just start with the chart type you want for the majority of series, and then select each series you want to change to another chart type and select the new chart type you need. For example, if you want a chart with two column series and one line series, do the following.

1. Create a column chart.

2. Select the data series that you want to display as a line chart and then, on the Chart Tools Design tab, click Change Chart Type.

3. Select the chart type for the selected series and then click OK.

   If a single data series is selected when you open the Change Chart Type dialog box, only the selected series will be affected.

Where things get a bit more complicated is when different chart types require different types of axes. An excellent example of this is a price/volume chart, where the volume is displayed in columns and the price as a scatter line. A scatter line is used instead of a line chart for the price series to control the appearance of the last date on the horizontal axis, as discussed in the Troubleshooting tip titled "The last date doesn't appear on my line chart x-axis" earlier in this chapter. Review the detailed instructions for creating this chart type in the section of this chapter titled "Price/Volume Charts" and apply the techniques discussed there for working with mixed axes requirements to any chart type where this issue presents itself.

Using Secondary Axes

When different chart series have extremely different values—such as when one series shows sales volume and the other shows year-over-year percentage change in sales—you are likely to need to show those series on different value axes to be able to see them both effectively at the same time.

To assign a series to a secondary value axis, right-click the series and then select Format Data Series. On the Series Options tab, select Secondary Axis from the Plot Series On options. If you have many series in your chart, assign each to the most appropriate value axis.

Note

When different series require different types of x-axes (category or value), you can't mix their vertical (value) axis assignments. That is, if you have two scatter series, for example, and one column series, both scatter series will need to be plotted on the same axes because scatter charts and column charts require different types of x-axes.

Note that, if you change the chart type of a series to one that requires a different type of x-axis (such as changing a line series to a scatter line so you can get a value x-axis, as discussed earlier), the series with the unique x-axis type requirement is automatically plotted on a secondary value axis, and a secondary x-axis (be it value or category, as needed) appears on the chart. Secondary x-axes usually appear, by default, across the top of a chart. To see a detailed example of options for dealing with the appearance and placement of multiple axes, see the section of this chapter on price/volume charts.

TROUBLESHOOTING

One column or bar series is hidden behind another

When you add a secondary value axis for one or more series of a column or bar chart, some series might become hidden behind others. This is because each value axis plots its series independently, so Excel sees the series on each of those axes as being independent of the others—as if they were separate charts.

Changing Gap Width settings on the Series Options tab of the Format Data Series dialog box can enable you to see hidden series by making those in front appear narrower than those in back, but the Overlap setting on the Series Options tab doesn't apply to series plotted on separate axes. To see the series side by side, you need to use a workaround—and though it isn't the neatest workaround you'll ever see for a feature, it will get the job done. To see the series side by side, follow these steps.

1. Add two series to the chart containing all zero values—we'll call them space series. (Note that just one space series might be required in some cases, but I find it usually takes less trial and error when you use two.)

2. If you're showing the legend, right-click each space series label in the legend and then click DELETE. Notice that you now have separate options when you right-click here for Delete or Delete Series, so you don't need to worry about deleting a series when you delete its label from the legend.

3. Move one of the space series to the secondary axis. If this doesn't move your visible series side by side and centered between tick marks, reorder the series until you get the effect you need.

4. To reorder data series, on the Chart Tools Design tab, click Select Data. In the box labeled Legend Entries (Series), select the series to move and then click the Move Up or Move Down arrows. Notice that settings in this dialog box don't update until you close the dialog box. So, you might need to revisit this dialog box a couple of times to get the exact result you want.

TROUBLESHOOTING

The axis assignment shown in the Format Data Series dialog box is incorrect

If you assign a series to a secondary axis and later open the Format Data Series dialog box to find that the Plot Series On options are set to Primary Axis and unavailable, you might be encountering a bug.

As of press time for this book, a bug was present that would cause the incorrect value axis assignment to appear in the Format Data Series dialog box and make that assignment unavailable. This issue only occurs when chart types that require different types of x-axes (that is, mixed category and value x-axes) are combined.

As long as you can see by looking at the chart that the series is plotted on the axis you need it to be, don't worry about an incorrect axis assignment being indicated in the dialog box. It won't affect the behavior of your chart.

Adding Drawing Objects to Charts

When you need a shape, a text box, or an image on your chart (such as a text box to annotate a particular date in the chart), just select the drawing object you need from the Insert group on the Chart Tools Layout tab or the Illustrations group of the Insert tab.

Simply insert the shape or picture you need as you would on a worksheet. You can then select a shape and just begin typing to add text, or just click into a text box to begin editing it. As mentioned earlier, remember that you can link a text box to the value in a cell on a worksheet. You can do the same with a shape. To do this, start by selecting the text box or shape and then do the following.

1. Click in the Formula bar.

2. Type =.

3. Browse to and select the cell you want to link, and then press ENTER.

You can format a linked text box as needed with one exception—numeric values in your linked cell will always display the same number format in the linked text box. There is no way to format numbers separately in the text box. Even if the text box you link is a chart element (such as a data label), the Number format options in the Format Data Labels dialog box won't apply to values linked using this method.

For other picture, shape, and text box formatting, see Chapter 18. However, one point warrants noting here. If you open the Selection And Visibility pane on a chart sheet or on a worksheet that contains a chart, the pane recognizes the chart as an object. It does not, however, recognize separate shapes or other drawing objects created on your chart. This is because your chart itself is a drawing object. Objects created on your chart become a part of the chart. That's good news, because if you copy your chart to another program, for example, you'll want those objects to come along automatically.

Note that, if you instead paste or drag a graphic onto a chart, it does appear as a separate object in the Selection And Visibility pane. Watch out for this because, if it appears as a separate object in that pane, it's not part of the chart—so it won't come along for the ride when you copy that chart to paste it in another location.

INSIDE OUT   Paste pictures as data points

With all the great new formatting options, it's nice to know that one of the coolest formatting shortcuts from earlier versions of Excel is still available.

Though you can now use a picture as the fill for any chart element that has fill options, you can also paste a picture on just selected data series or individual data points to apply the picture as the fill for your selection.

Just select and then copy a picture in its source program (the picture itself, *not* the picture file). Then, in Excel, select the data series or data point you want to fill with the picture and paste. For example, copy an image of your company logo from the header of a Microsoft Office Word 2007 document and then paste it on the data point that represents your company in a scatter chart.

This shortcut isn't limited just to pictures. You can also copy any Office Art object (such as a group of shapes or a Clip Art drawing) and paste it as data point fill. Not that you'd ever want to do so, but you can even paste a SmartArt diagram as data point fill.

To use pictures as the fill for chart elements other than data series or data points, or to customize the appearance of picture fills for data, use the Fill options in the applicable Format dialog box.

Timesaving Techniques for Adding or Editing Chart Data

As mentioned earlier, when you format your source data as a table, you gain benefits for the chart, such as the chart automatically updating to reflect changes in the source data range. So, you probably won't need to make as much use of shortcuts for adding data to your chart as you might have in the past. However, using a table in this way isn't always practical—such as when your chart needs to be created from noncontiguous data or your table organization doesn't lend itself to being in a table. With this in mind, following are two helpful methods for adding data to a chart.

- When your data is not in an Excel table and the new series you want to add has exactly the same configuration as existing series (that is, it uses the same cells within its row or column as all other existing series), you can simply copy the new series data and paste it onto the chart. For example, say that your original chart takes the data for Regions 1 through 4 from the following range.

Region	Q1	Q2	Q3	Q4
Region 1	109	187	127	143
Region 2	173	166	153	139
Region 3	140	189	174	173
Region 4	150	102	146	111
Region 5	106	108	156	138
Region 6	106	108	156	138
Region 7	150	102	146	111

To add one or more of the other regions in that data, just select and copy it. Then, select the chart where you want to add the data and just paste (CTRL+V). Your new series will appear exactly as if it had always been there.

> **Note**
>
> Though pasting data series works in earlier versions, the new series won't consistently take on existing customized chart formatting. This is, fortunately, not the case in Excel 2007. Your new data will take on whatever applicable formatting is active when the series is pasted.

This method, however, isn't necessarily as easy when adding data points to existing series or adding new series in a different configuration than existing series. It can also be inconsistent when source data is in an Excel table. In those cases, edit the data range using the Select Data Source dialog box.

- When you open the Select Data Source dialog box (through the Chart Tools Layout tab or the shortcut menu available when you right-click the chart), you see an option to add data. Don't use it. Instead, notice that the existing data range is highlighted on the worksheet.

  You can simply click in the worksheet while the Select Data Source dialog box is open. Just select the revised data range and then press ENTER to apply it. (Remember to hold the CTRL key when selecting noncontiguous data.)

- As an alternative to either of the preceding options for adding a data series, try using the SERIES function. When you select a data series, a formula is created with the SERIES function in the Formula bar. That formula has four parts, as shown in the following image.

f_x =SERIES(Sheet1!$E$1,Sheet1!$A$2:$B$7,Sheet1!$E$2:$E$7,2)

1. The first argument is for the series name.

2. The second argument is for the category labels in a category-value chart or the x-values in a value-value chart.

3. The third argument is for the values in a category-value chart or the y-values in a value-value chart.

4. The last argument indicates the position in the series order.

   To add a new series using this formula, first copy the formula for any existing chart series. To do this, select a series, click into the Formula bar, select the contents of the formula, and then copy (CTRL+C). Then, do the following.

1. Press ESC twice, so that no series is selected. Then select the Chart Area. Be careful not to leave a series selected, or you'll replace the selected series instead of adding a new one.

2. Click in the Formula bar and then paste (CTRL+V).

3. Edit the cell references in the appropriate arguments of the SERIES formula to represent the values of the data in your new series.

4. Press ENTER to add the new series. Don't press ENTER until after you've edited the values for the new series (as indicated in the preceding step), or no new series will be added.

TROUBLESHOOTING

How can I retrieve lost chart data?

You created a chart with complex data linked to an external source and that data source has now disappeared. Of course, if you're like most people, you probably need to edit that source data twenty minutes before an urgent deadline. Fortunately, this isn't at all the disaster you probably expect.

If the chart still displays the data, the chart still knows the data. So, you can use a Microsoft Visual Basic for Applications (VBA) macro to extract that data from the chart. I wish I had come up with this one, but alas I did not. You'll find the answer in a Microsoft Knowledge Base article that's been around for several Microsoft Office versions.

The article isn't yet updated (as of this book's press time) for Excel 2007, but the version of the article for Excel 2003 still works without a hitch. The article provides the complete macro and detailed instructions for using that macro to extract your data, so you don't

Chapter 15

need to know VBA to use this solution. The article even provides help for linking your chart to the new source data.

The Knowledge Base article ID is 300643. To access this article, go to http://support.microsoft.com and search for the article ID number. You can use either the Search Support (KB) option on the Help And Support home page or the Search Microsoft.com For box that appears at the top of most microsoft.com pages.

Reorder Data Series and Set Data Display Options

As mentioned in an earlier Troubleshooting tip, the Select Data Source dialog box is the place to go to change the order in which series appear on the chart as well as in the chart legend. To change series order, select the series to move from the Legend Entries (Series) box in the Select Data Source dialog box and then click the Move Up or Move Down arrows as needed.

> **Note**
>
> You can also reorder data series using the SERIES formula that was introduced under the preceding heading. Change the value of the fourth argument in the SERIES formula for whatever series you want to reorder, and the series numbers for the other chart series will automatically adjust to accommodate the change.

In the Select Data Source dialog box, also notice the option Hidden And Empty Cells. When you click that option, you get a dialog box where you can opt to show data on the chart from hidden rows and columns included in your source data, and you can set options for how to plot empty cells. To learn how to use these options to connect data gaps in a line chart, see the Troubleshooting tip that follows.

TROUBLESHOOTING

I need to connect data gaps in a line chart

Excel gives you options for how you want to plot empty cells in the active chart. So, when you want a line series to be continuous even when the data includes empty cells, you just need to set the option for how you want to plot blank cells (and yes, there is a catch, but read on for the solution).

With the chart active, on the Chart Tools Design tab, click Select Data and then click Hidden And Empty Cells. The option you want is Connect Data Points With Line. (Note that, in previous versions, these settings are available from the Options dialog box on the Tools menu, and this option is called Interpolated.) The aforementioned catch is that, if any of your data series are not line or similar chart types, this option will be unavailable.

If Connect Data Points With Line is unavailable in the Hidden And Empty Cell Settings dialog box, but at least one series in your chart is a line or similar, you can set this property using the Immediate Window in the Visual Basic Editor. As mentioned in Chapter 14, in the Troubleshooting tip about resetting the used range, most of my references to using VBA refer you to Chapter 21, "VBA Primer." However, you don't need to learn your VBA ABCs just to use the occasional quick and easy solution.

To set Connect Data Points With Line for the line series in a combination chart, press ALT+F11 to open the Visual Basic Editor. Then, if you don't see the Immediate Window at the bottom of your screen, press CTRL+G to open it. Click in the Immediate Window and then type the following:

```
ActiveWorkbook.Charts("Chart Name").DisplayBlanksAs = xlinterpolated
```

With your insertion point in the line of code you just typed, press ENTER to apply this setting. Note that at least one series in your chart must have the ability to use this setting (such as a line, scatter line, or radar chart), or an error message will appear.

Creating Advanced Chart Types

Most complex charts are easy to create. It's just that the more complex the chart type, the more likely it is to require some specific choices along the way. Once you understand the concepts behind these choices, you can apply them as needed to a variety of chart types.

With that in mind, this section takes you step-by-step through creating two complex chart types. I've chosen these two chart types because they so often trip up even confident, experienced Excel users. The first of these, bubble charts, are a built-in chart type. The second, price/volume charts, are combination column and line charts often used in the securities industry.

Bubble Charts

A bubble chart is really just a scatter chart with an extra value per data point, so let's first take a look at how you construct a scatter chart.

When you create a scatter chart, each data point is the intersection of two values. For example, take a look at the following data.

Column1	# years with firm	% Salary increase
Robert	13	10
Ron	9	10
Phineas	7	9
Alan	6	8
Jane	5	8
Charlotte	4	6
Mae	1	4

The scatter chart shown in the following image is created from the preceding data table. Notice that the first column of data becomes the horizontal axis and the second becomes the vertical axis.

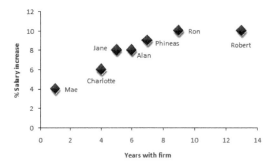

When you create a scatter chart, don't select the data labels or series labels—Excel won't understand them. Just select the x and y values. The data labels in the preceding chart are created by linking each label to the correct cell—something you'll see how to do for the upcoming bubble chart.

Use a bubble chart when you need to include a third value for each data point. That third value appears as the size of the bubble. Following along with the same salary example, the bubble might be used to represent each person's current salary. To do that, add a third column of data, as you see in the following graphic, and then *sort the data table so that the largest bubble value is on top*. That sort enables the smaller bubbles to sit in front when data overlaps. So, for the previous example, the bubble chart data should look like this:

Column1	# years with firm	% Salary increase	Current Salary ($m)
Ron	9	10	120
Jane	5	8	120
Charlotte	4	6	100
Robert	13	10	80
Alan	6	8	70
Phineas	7	9	60
Mae	1	4	45

That data results in a bubble chart that looks like the following image.

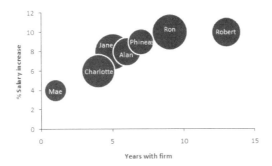

Chapter 15

> **Note**
>
> If you work in securities and you need a bubble chart for the common use of comparing deals across a market segment, set up your data as follows: Use *Days Trading Volume* as your x-values, *% Market Cap* as your y-values, and *Deal Size* as your bubble sizes.

Though you can't add category data labels automatically as part of the chart, you can do the following to get that done.

1. To easily identify each data point, add data labels to the chart that show both the x-value and the y-value. To do this, right-click the Data Series and select Add Data Labels. Then, right-click the labels and select Format Data Labels. Select the data to show on the Label Options tab.

2. If the amount of overlap between bubbles makes it ineffective to use the Label Position setting found on the Label Options tab of the Format Data Labels dialog box, move each data label to sit on or beside the corresponding bubble. They're easy to identify because the ScreenTip for each bubble provides its x and y values, as well as the bubble size. To move individual data labels, select the data labels and then click once on the individual label you want to select. You can then drag labels to new positions as needed.

3. Select the first label to link. In the Formula Bar, type = and then browse to your data. Select the cell containing the label for the applicable data point (because you can see the x and y values in the label, finding the cell's label should be quick and easy) and then press ENTER. Repeat this action for each label as needed.

Price/Volume Charts

A price/volume chart, as advertised earlier in this chapter, is a common chart in the securities industry, used to show the daily price and trading volume of a security over a period of time.

For those readers not in the securities field, the value of this chart type is that it's a combination chart requiring secondary axes, using series that require different types of x-axes—so you can see several complex types of chart customization managed in a single chart.

> **Note**
>
> Find the completed price/volume chart used in the example that follows in the file named Price Volume.xlsx, available in the sample files you can install from the Welcome tab of this book's CD. You can open, examine, or edit that chart for yourself—or use the source data to try to duplicate the completed chart on your own. Additionally, the Excel webcast available on the Expert Tips tab of the CD (as mentioned earlier in this chapter) includes demonstrations of both price/volume and bubble charts.

A price/volume chart commonly contains hundreds of data points—for example, if you're tracking stock performance over an entire year. The sample I'm using tracks performance of our fictional sample stock from the beginning of March through the end of November. Set up the data just as you might for any category-value chart, with the x-axis labels (the dates in this case) in the first column, followed by the data series in columns, with the series names at the top of each column. Following is a snippet from that data—the full data range is 195 rows long in this case.

Date	Price	Volume
3/5/2007	34.00	27,000
3/6/2007	34.38	38,000
3/7/2007	34.13	10,000
3/8/2007	34.20	7,000
3/9/2007	34.35	29,000
3/12/2007	33.10	11,000
3/13/2007	33.00	24,000
3/14/2007	32.88	35,000
3/15/2007	33.50	44,000
3/16/2007	34.00	56,000
3/19/2007	34.13	22,000

> **Note**
>
> You might notice that the data is very much sample data, in that you may see data points for dates (such as holidays) when the market is not open.

To create the chart, do the following.

1. Select the data, including x-axis labels and series titles, and then press F11 to create the default chart type on its own sheet. If your default chart type isn't a clustered column chart, change the chart type to a clustered column chart. (As mentioned earlier, access the Change Chart Type dialog box on the Chart Tools Design tab.)

2. Select the volume series and then open the Format Data Series dialog box. Change the Plot Series On setting to Secondary Axis.

   If the series is difficult to select, remember that you can select the series using the drop-down list in the Current Selection group on the Chart Tools Layout or Format tabs, and then open the dialog box from that same group. (Or, select the series name in the legend and then right-click for the Format Data Series option.) You need to place the volume series on the secondary axis because the x-axis for the price series is the one you'll want to display on the chart—so plotting the price series on the primary axis makes that quicker and easier to do.

3. Select the price series (because the price series won't be easy to see as yet, you'll most likely need to use the Current Selection group to do this). Then, on the Chart Tools Design tab, click Change Chart Type and select Scatter With Straight Lines as the chart type for the selected series. You'll then be able to see the price series as a line, but it most likely won't stretch across the entire plot area. This is because you need to customize the x-axis values.

> **Note**
>
> When creating a chart of this type, selecting a scatter line instead of a typical line chart enables you to ensure that the last date in your data appears on the x-axis without trial and error, as explained in the Troubleshooting tip referenced in the next step.

4. Set the Minimum, Maximum, and Major Unit values for the primary x-axis so that the last date in your data appears as the last axis label. The Minimum and Maximum values are the first and last dates in your data, respectively, expressed as numbers. The Major Unit is the result of the calculation provided in the Troubleshooting tip titled "The last date doesn't appear on my line chart x-axis" earlier in this chapter.

   It's worth noting that, when you use this method to show the last date on the x-axis, all dates in the data range are included in the x-axis and not just those for which the market is open. This isn't typically considered a problem because the dates did occur in the time period being displayed. But, it's good to be aware that your x-axis labels might include dates for which there are no corresponding price or volume values.

Chapter 15

5. Customize the y-axes as needed. For example, in the sample chart, all price data ranges between 30 and 55, so I fix the Minimum value at 30 and the Maximum at 55.

6. To remove any unwanted gaps in the volume data that might occur because all dates aren't included in true stock data (which usually excludes weekends and holidays), you'll need to change the category axis type for the volume series to a Text Axis. To do this, on the Chart Tools Layout tab, click Axes, point to Secondary Horizontal Axis, and then click Show Left To Right Axis. The axis will appear across the top of the chart, and your volume series will flip upside down. *Don't panic!* Open the Format Axis dialog box for this axis and then select Text Axis as the Axis Type. While you're in this dialog box, set all tick mark and axis label type options to None, and on the Line Color tab, select No Line. Close the dialog box.

7. Open the Format Axis dialog box for the secondary y-axis (the one on which the volume series is plotted). On the Axis Options tab, under the heading Horizontal Axis Crosses, click Axis Value and then type a zero. Click OK. Your volume series should now be right-side up once again.

8. You can now apply any Chart Style or other formatting you want to perfect your chart. That's all there is to it. Your completed chart, if you're using the sample data available on the CD, should look something like the image that follows.

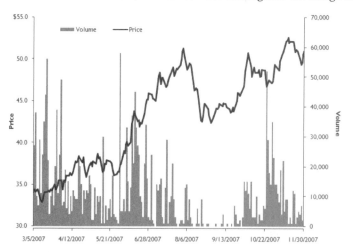

See the following Inside Out tip to learn how to get the currency symbol on the top label for the primary vertical axis.

INSIDE OUT   **Create a custom number format for specific values on a chart axis**

When you want to customize the number format of individual value axis labels, such as the currency symbol on the top label of the primary vertical axis in the price/volume chart shown in this section, do the following.

1. Select the axis to customize and then open the Format Axis dialog box.

2. On the Number tab of that dialog box, select Custom.

3. In the Format Code text box, type the custom format you want. To specify a format for just one value, start by typing that value inside brackets, following an equal sign. After the closing bracket, type the format for that value followed by a semicolon. After the semicolon, type the format for all other values. For example, the custom number format used in the sample price/volume chart's primary vertical axis looks like this:

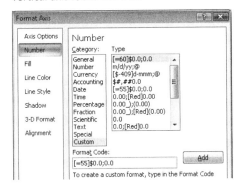

You can examine this example for yourself in the sample file Price Volume.xlsx mentioned earlier.

Note that, for custom number formats, a zero is used when you want to ensure that the digit will appear—use a pound sign when you only want a digit to appear if used by the number. For example, if you set up a number format as 0,000, the number 325 would appear as 0,325. If you set up the format as #,##0, the number will appear as 325.

You can have more arguments than the two used in this example. For each value for which you want to specify a format, start with the number in brackets after an equal sign and follow the close bracket with the format. Separate each argument with a semicolon. Where you see two arguments in a number format but no specified values, the second argument refers to negative values.

4. Click Add once you've finished typing in the custom format and then click OK. Click OK when done.

To apply the format to your axis, you must take the step to add it to the custom list. Remember that this custom format is static to the specific value you indicate. So, if the scale for the applicable axis changes, you might need to change the specified value. Notice that, once you've added a custom format, it becomes part of the list in the active workbook so that you can use it again. Custom number formats that you save for chart formatting are available for use by any chart in any open workbook, as long as the workbook containing that format is open.

Creating Charts for Use in Other Programs

Though you can now create Excel charts directly in Office Word 2007 or PowerPoint, you might still want to create and manage them in Excel in order to keep all data and charts related to one document or presentation together in a single workbook.

Also, as discussed in the Word part of this book, in Chapter 7, "Managing Graphics," creating graphics in their originating program and then pasting them into Word as pictures (instead of leaving live graphics in your document) can help you keep private source data private and help you ensure that the chart you send is the chart all recipients see.

Because you can create Excel charts in Word or PowerPoint, when you paste an Excel chart into either of those programs using the default paste method (CTRL+V), it remains a live chart linked to the source data. To embed the entire workbook (watch out for private data in the source workbook if you do this) or to paste as a picture, you can choose from the paste SmartTag that appears after you paste the chart. However, for best results when you want to paste as a picture, use Paste Special instead (as described later in this chapter) so that you can control the picture type.

Because pasting as a picture is the most secure way to go, particularly for your Word documents, that's the method that I discuss in the sections that follow. You can use the resizing and copy steps, however, regardless of what paste method you prefer.

Resizing Charts

Resizing charts wasn't ever as difficult as people often assumed, but it's never been this easy. On the Chart Tools Format tab, just specify the height and width for the chart. Some reformatting might be required for substantial reductions in chart size—most of which can be quickly accomplished by just reducing font size throughout the chart.

> **Note**
>
> If the legend disappears when you resize a chart, on the Chart Tools Layout tab, click Legend and then click an option to show the legend at a specific position on the chart. The legend will pop back into place on your resized chart, and you can then move or customize it as needed.

When a chart is on its own sheet, the sheet size will remain the same and the chart area will reduce when you resize the chart. If the chart itself becomes too small within the chart area, select the plot area and drag to expand its size so that the plot area uses the maximum available space within the chart area. Also remember to zoom in on charts after you resize them to be smaller, so that you can see all elements as accurately as possible. Object appearance in Excel does become more accurate when you zoom in.

Getting Your Chart into Word

If that chart is destined for a Word document, it's likely that you've used a table cell as the placeholder for the chart. If you aren't familiar with how and why to use tables as page layouts, see Chapter 6, "Tables."

1. If you are using a table cell as a placeholder, click in the placeholder cell in your Word document and then, on the Table Tools Layout tab, note the width and height of the cell.

2. Back in Excel, select the chart and then, on the Chart Tools Format tab, enter the placeholder table cell's height and width measurements as the chart height and width. Then, as mentioned in the preceding section of this chapter, adjust formatting if needed.

3. Select the chart area and then copy (CTRL+C).

4. In Word, click in the placeholder table cell and press CTRL+ALT+V to open the Paste Special dialog box. Select either Picture (PNG) or Picture (Enhanced Metafile) as the picture type and then click OK.

   As discussed in Chapter 7, PNG and Enhanced Metafile are usually the best picture formats when pasting Excel content into Word. If you aren't happy with your results with one of these picture types, try the other, as results with these picture formats can vary depending on the particular chart's formatting. Also as noted in Chapter 7, the chart size you set in Excel may be altered very slightly after you paste the chart into Word. If so, you can make the adjustment in the Size group on the Picture Tools Format tab.

5. If your default paste format for pictures in Word is not In Line With Text, right-click the picture, point to Text Wrapping, and then click In Line With Text. The picture will fall perfectly into place.

Note

If you want to paste your picture as an Enhanced Metafile, you can use the Copy As Picture tool in Excel in place of step 3 in the preceding steps. Using Copy As Picture instead of just copying your chart with CTRL+C ensures that you won't risk pasting an unwanted embedded or linked object. The downside to Copy As Picture is that PNG is not an available paste format in the destination 2007 release program when you use this method.

To use Copy As Picture, select the chart and then, on the Home tab, click to expand Paste options, point to As Picture, and then click Copy As Picture. In the Copy As Picture dialog box, shown here, the Appearance option As Shown On Screen usually provides the better results. Use the Picture option for Picture (Enhanced Metafile) to be an available Paste Special option in the destination program.

Getting Your Chart into PowerPoint

You can use the same copy and paste steps for Word when you want to get your Excel chart into PowerPoint as a picture. If you want to know the size available on your slide in order to resize the chart before copying it, create a rectangle on the slide in the size you want the chart and take its measurements from the Drawing Tools Format tab.

However, because PowerPoint and Excel have similar graphics capabilities, there's not quite as much reason to paste Excel charts into PowerPoint as pictures as there is when using those charts in Word. Unless you want to keep all data for your presentation in one workbook (which is a nice idea for efficient editing) or you will be sharing the PowerPoint file with others who should not edit the chart or see the source data, go ahead and create those charts directly in PowerPoint—you'll get all the same capabilities as if you created the chart in Excel, with no drawbacks.

Powerful Reporting, Easier Than You Think: A PivotTable Primer

PivotTable and PivotChart reports have a bad reputation, but don't believe everything you hear. Though you can get more complex if you want to, PivotTables don't have to be any more challenging to create and use than a typical bar or column chart. However, simple as your PivotTable may be, it's likely to be a powerful analytical tool that can do more for you than you probably expect.

This chapter on PivotTable and PivotChart reports is quite a bit different from most chapters to this point. That is, it covers basics—because basic PivotTables, by popular opinion at least, are an advanced skill. You also get sample data on the CD to use for all steps throughout this chapter, so you can follow along step-by-step if you'd like to do so, to try each new task for yourself.

The only assumptions for this chapter are that you're an advanced Microsoft Office user and you're comfortable with some Microsoft Office Excel 2007 data and chart functionality—including creating and formatting at least basic charts, and the essentials of working with worksheet data, such as formatting a range as a table and creating simple formulas. If you're not confident with these Office Excel 2007 skills, check out Chapter 14, "Working with Data" and Chapter 15, "Charts," before continuing here.

As for what's new with PivotTables and PivotCharts, for those of you who have used them before, the surprises are all good. The new capabilities for PivotTables and Pivot-Charts are primarily organization, ease-of-access, and enhanced formatting options—with more flexibility at a number of points in the process. Essentially, the changes here are consistent with the type of changes throughout the 2007 release, and they're sure to be highly intuitive to an experienced PivotTable user. So, instead of detailing changes up front for this feature, if you're experienced with PivotTables and PivotCharts, breeze through this chapter and you'll find what's new as you progress. For everyone else, let's start from the beginning.

Why Use a PivotTable?

A PivotTable report is a table that shows you values across categories—much like a column, bar, or line chart—but that also enables you to easily look at the same set of data from different angles. You might use a PivotTable as an analytical tool for reporting—such as for preparing budgets or periodic management reports. Or, you might use it as a spin doctor to help you find the best face to put on your data, such as when trying to decide which data to include in a chart or what chart type to use.

You can pivot any data that can be quantified, ranging from currency or other numeric values to qualitative data that can be counted. For example, if I need to report on training courses attended in the past year by vice presidents across the company, I could create a PivotTable to look at total cost per person, cost per business area, or cost per type or instance of a course—as well as the number of hours spent in class or the type of classes attended by each person.

Creating a PivotTable

> **Note**
> If you want to use the sample data shown in this chapter to try these tasks for yourself, open the file named Pivot Data.xlsx that you'll find in the sample files you can install from the Welcome tab of this book's CD. To see a few completed PivotTable and Pivot-Chart reports using that data, open the PivotTables.xlsx file from the same CD tab.

You can create a PivotTable from any of several data sources, from a basic Excel worksheet to external data sources such as a Microsoft Office Access 2007 database or a Microsoft Windows SharePoint Services list. A valid data source needs to be set up like a database table—with field names and a value for each record in each field.

For this chapter, we're going to stick with using an Excel worksheet as your data source. The three subsections that follow will walk you through setting up your data, creating a basic PivotTable, and beginning to use pivot fields.

Setting Up Your Data

Set up your data in columns, with a single row of headings. For best results, if you're typing your data in manually, type your headings and the first couple of rows of data, and then format the range as a table. Using a table, you can take advantage of table features such as calculated columns that help you set up the data throughout the table with the least work possible.

Be sure to type a value in each cell on each row, unless you expressly want to include blank values in your PivotTable analysis. So, for example, if more than one row that you need in your data has the same values for some columns, repeat those values on each row where they're required. As you're probably noticing, what you're setting up is the equivalent of a very simple database, where each row represents a record, and each column represents a field.

For example, take a look at the sample data used for the PivotTable and PivotChart examples throughout this chapter.

	A	B	C	D	E	F	G
						Number of	Cost this
1	Name	Business Area	Course	Date Completed	Total Course Cost	Attendees	Person
2	Alex M.	Business Development	Effective Interviewing	03-01-07	$3,000	5	$600
3	Alex M.	Business Development	Leadership Skills Development	04-15-07	$4,500	5	$900
4	Andrea H.	Administration	Effective Interviewing	03-01-07	$3,000	5	$600
5	Andrea H.	Administration	Leadership Skills Development	04-15-07	$4,500	5	$900
6	Anita L.	Business Development	Leadership Skills Development	04-15-07	$4,500	5	$900
7	James A.	Administration	Effective Interviewing	03-01-07	$3,000	5	$600
8	Jeff B.	Administration	Six Sigma Train-the-Trainer	03-10-07	$5,000	4	$1,250
9	Phillipe W.	Information Technology	Six Sigma Train-the-Trainer	03-10-07	$5,000	4	$1,250
10	Phillipe W.	Information Technology	Effective Interviewing	03-01-07	$3,000	5	$600
11	Scott R.	Finance	Leadership Skills Development	04-15-07	$4,500	5	$900
12	Stacy R.	Finance	Six Sigma Train-the-Trainer	03-10-07	$5,000	4	$1,250
13	Stacy R.	Finance	Effective Interviewing	03-01-07	$3,000	5	$600
14	Valerie B.	Information Technology	Leadership Skills Development	04-15-07	$4,500	5	$900
15	Dominic P.	Business Development	Six Sigma Train-the-Trainer	03-10-07	$5,000	4	$1,250

> **Note**
>
> Another benefit to using a table for your source data is that, if you add or remove data rows, the source data range will automatically update. However, changes to data are not automatically reflected in existing PivotTables and PivotCharts. To refresh data, on the PivotTable Tools Options tab or the PivotChart Tools Analyze tab, click Refresh. (Refresh is also available from the shortcut menu when you right-click anywhere inside a Pivot-Table.)
>
> Note that you can set the table to automatically refresh data when the workbook is opened. To do this, on the PivotTable Tools Options tab, in the PivotTable group, click Options and then click Data. Select the setting Refresh Data When Opening The File. This setting will affect all tables in the workbook that are based on the same data.

Creating the Table

To begin creating the PivotTable, click in the data table and then, on the Insert tab, click PivotTable. Or, on the Table Tools Design tab, click Summarize With Pivot. The following dialog box will appear.

> **Note**
>
> Notice in the Create Pivot Table dialog box that, if you wanted to use an external data source, this would be the place to select it. If you do want to use external data, you don't need to select anything in your workbook before accessing the dialog box.

Leave the defaults and just click OK. It's a good idea to place your PivotTable on a separate sheet from the source data (as is the default), just to make a clear distinction between the source data and the PivotTable. You might also want multiple PivotTables or PivotCharts in the same workbook, based on the same data—so keeping the data on its own sheet can help to keep your workbook more organized.

When the PivotTable is first created, it's empty—you need to select the fields to include in the table. What you'll initially see is an empty area on a worksheet for your PivotTable along with the PivotTable Field List pane, both shown in the following image. (The PivotTable Field List pane is docked by default, and appears only when your insertion point is inside the PivotTable area on the worksheet.)

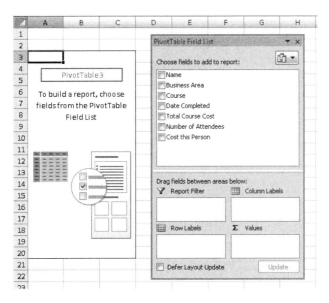

- Notice that the PivotTable Field List pane includes a list of the column headings from your source data as possible fields for use in your PivotTable.

- Additionally, there are four PivotTable areas including Column Labels, Row Labels, Values, and Report Filter. (For those with prior experience using Pivot Tables, notice that Report Filter is the field area that used to be called the Page area.)

- If you prefer to arrange the pane in a different layout, use the button that appears next to the heading Choose Fields To Add To Report. You can stack fields and table areas (as they are in the preceding image), place them side by side, or choose to show just one or the other.

Just click a field in the field list portion of the pane to select it as a field that you want to include in your table. Think of this step as if you were creating a column chart. For example, perhaps you want to look at cost per person using our sample data. Just click to select Name and Cost This Person. Excel adds the fields to what it believes to be the correct PivotTable area—either Row Labels or Values—as you see here.

The corresponding PivotTable, with no additional formatting added, looks like this.

Row Labels	Sum of Cost this Person
Alex M.	1500
Andrea H.	1500
Anita L.	900
Dominic P.	1250
James A.	600
Jeff B.	1250
Phillipe W.	1850
Scott R.	900
Stacy R.	1850
Valerie B.	900
Grand Total	**12500**

If you then want to further categorize the row field to see people grouped within their business area, click Business Area to add that field to your table. Initially, you might not get what you want—fields are prioritized in the order added, so the first row field chosen in the example that follows (Name) remains the highest-level row field.

Row Labels	Sum of Cost this Person
⊟ **Alex M.**	**1500**
Business Development	1500
⊟ **Andrea H.**	**1500**
Administration	1500
⊟ **Anita L.**	**900**
Business Development	900
⊟ **Dominic P.**	**1250**
Business Development	1250
⊟ lamoc A	600

To group the people by their business area, just reorder the fields in the Row Labels area. That is, drag the Business Area field above the Name field where they appear in the Row Labels area of the PivotTable Field List pane, as you see here.

This is very much like grouping the labels in a category axis for a column or similar chart (see the Inside Out tip "Group a category axis" in Chapter 15 for details). Now, that PivotTable looks like this.

Row Labels	Sum of Cost this Person
⊟ **Administration**	**3350**
Andrea H.	1500
James A.	600
Jeff B.	1250
⊟ **Business Development**	**3650**
Alex M.	1500
Anita L.	900
Dominic P.	1250
⊟ **Finance**	**2750**
Scott R.	900
Stacy R.	1850
⊟ **Information Technology**	**2750**
Phillipe W.	1850
Valerie B.	900
Grand Total	**12500**

For comparison, if this was a column chart instead of a PivotTable, it would look something like this.

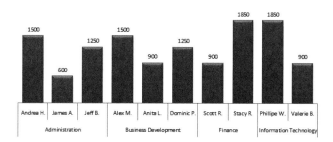

Whenever you add fields to the PivotTable by clicking to select them in the PivotTable Field List pane, they're added to either the Row Labels or Values area, based on whether Excel recognizes the data as numeric values. You can, however, move any field to any other area just by dragging it. You can also add fields to the various areas directly by dragging them from the field portion to the table area portion of the pane, instead of clicking to select the field.

INSIDE OUT   Drag fields on or off the table itself

For those who used PivotTables in earlier versions, you might notice that in Excel 2007, you can't drag fields on or off the PivotTable itself by default. You can, however, remove a field from the table or move it to another area of the table from the shortcut menu available when you right-click a field in the PivotTable.

If you prefer to drag fields directly on or off the PivotTable, you can change that setting in the PivotTable Options dialog box. To do this, on the PivotTable Tools Options tab, in the PivotTable group, click Options and then click Display. Select Classic PivotTable Layout and then click OK. The downside is that you lose the clean, updated layout of PivotTables, reverting to the legacy PivotTable layout—which is a benefit I'm not willing to give up for this small convenience. But, for those who disagree and prefer the legacy layout options, you won't lose any other new functionality when you change this setting.

Note

If you add a field to the Values area, and Excel doesn't recognize that field as numeric values, Excel will show those values in the PivotTable report as a count of records in that field.

If dragging isn't your cup of tea, click to add fields to the areas where they fall by default, and then click the arrow at the right of the field name where it appears in the table area portion of the pane. The options in that pop-up menu, shown in the following image, include the ability to move that field to any other area in the PivotTable, to move fields up or down in priority within a given PivotTable area, or to access Field Settings (discussed later in this chapter).

TROUBLESHOOTING

Can I still use a PivotTable to consolidate ranges from multiple worksheets?

If you've created PivotTables in the past using the Multiple Consolidation Ranges option in the PivotTable And PivotChart Wizard, don't despair, you still can. To access this option, use the wizard in place of the new options for creating your PivotTable or Pivot-Chart. You can access the wizard in two ways, as follows.

- Use the legacy accelerator key combination ALT+D,P.

- Add the wizard to your Quick Access Toolbar. To do this, find PivotTable And Pivot-Chart Wizard on the All Commands list (or the Commands Not In The Ribbon list) under Choose Commands From on the Customize tab of the Excel Options dialog box.

For those not familiar with this option, it doesn't work quite the same as the PivotTable and PivotChart reports being addressed in this chapter. This option requires both row and column headings—consistently applied in all ranges—and essentially consolidates them into a single range by quantifying record values to combine them.

If you're new to PivotTable functionality, I urge you to wait until you're comfortable creating the classic PivotTables discussed in this chapter before venturing here, if in fact you choose to check out this option at all. Excel doesn't interpret the data quite as seamlessly with Multiple Consolidation Ranges as it does with class PivotTable and PivotChart reports, and choosing this option might lead you to that popular misconception that PivotTable functionality is unfriendly (to say the least). Keep in mind that you're only accessing the consolidation option through legacy tools—so it isn't as intuitive as the new PivotTable tools.

Also, because the consolidation option is a legacy feature, it doesn't understand Excel tables as well as you might hope. If you're using this option with data formatted as a table, convert that table to a range before using Multiple Consolidation Ranges.

Understanding PivotTable Field Areas

Understanding the four PivotTable field areas is the key to being able to use PivotTable reports effectively. Following are nutshell definitions of each, followed by an example from the sample data being used in this chapter.

- Use the Values area for the fields that represent the data you want to analyze. Each value field is the equivalent of a data series in a column chart.

  For example, in a PivotTable showing training cost per person, the cost is the Values field.

- The Row Labels and Column Labels are the categories for which you want to view data. These areas are the equivalent of the category axis labels or series names on a column chart.

  For example, when analyzing cost per person, the list of people's names would be a row field. The person's business area or the name of the course might be either an additional row field or a column field. Though column fields (or subsequent row fields) are typically used to break out data for the categories in the primary row field, row and column fields can be used interchangeably, as suits your data.

- The Report Filter area is for fields by which you can filter your Row Label or Column Label entries, to show only row or column entries that match the filter criteria.

  For example, Business Area or Course might be an effective Report Filter, if you want to view cost per person for just certain business areas or certain courses at once.

INSIDE OUT Filter fields before or after adding them to your PivotTable report

One of the nicest new features of the PivotTable Field List pane is the ability to filter a field from the PivotTable Field List pane. You can filter a field at any time, whether or not you've added it to a table area. If you filter a field before adding it to a table area, you can still remove the filter once the field is part of the PivotTable.

When you hover over a field name in the area of the PivotTable Field List pane from which you select fields to include in your report, you see an arrow to the right. Click that arrow for a pop-up menu of sort and filter options, shown here using the Business Area field from the sample data.

Separate filter options are available based on whether the field is used as a label (that is, a row or column field) or as a value field. Notice also that sort and label filter options are available from the drop-down menu accessible from either the Row Labels or Column Labels headings in the PivotTable itself.

Note that, if you move a filtered field between the Row Labels and Column Labels areas, the filter remains intact. However, if you move a field from Row or Column Labels to Report Filter, the existing filter is cleared automatically.

Once you set a filter, a funnel icon appears beside the field name in the field list as well on the field heading in the PivotTable. To remove the filter, click the arrow beside either funnel icon or right-click any value of the filtered field that appears in the table and then point to Filter. Click the option Clear Filters From <Field Name>. You can also clear filters using the Clear Filters command that appears in the Clear options in the Actions group on the PivotTable Tools Options tab.

If you have prior experience with PivotTables, you might recognize the sort options available to PivotTables from the PivotTable Field Advanced Options dialog box available in the previous version (through the Field Settings dialog box). Many of the filter options, however, are new.

Managing PivotTables

So, you now have a basic PivotTable report. You can move fields around and examine your data in as many ways as you can logically combine the fields from your source data. But, chances are that you may want to customize things a bit more. The subsections that follow provide an overview of capabilities along with key tips for customizing field settings and table settings.

Field Settings

You can reorganize the layout of your table, customize field names, manage subtotal options, select formulas by which to present or summarize value fields, and sort or filter field results. You can do any of this through the Field Settings dialog box for the appropriate field type—but you don't actually need a dialog box for most of it.

Between the PivotTable Tools contextual tabs and the shortcut menu options available when you right-click a field in the table, you can customize a great many field settings, some with just a click. Following are instructions for how to accomplish some of the most useful field customizations.

- On the PivotTable Tools Design tab, in the Layout group shown in the following image, you can change the Report Layout between Compact, Outline, and Tabular formats—or add blank rows between each group of row labels for a layout that's easier to read.

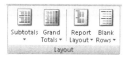

Chapter 16

Note that Report Layout options affect all levels of row headings—meaning that you can have only one layout setting per table. Adding blank rows will affect each row field that has a lower-level field grouped beneath it.

- Expand and collapse (+/-) buttons are on by default for any row or column field that has a lower-level field grouped beneath it. To hide these buttons, on the PivotTable Tools Options tab, in the Show/Hide Group, click +/- Buttons.

- To hide subtotals for any row or column field that has a lower-level field grouped beneath it, right-click any instance of the field and then click Subtotal "<Field Name>". To hide all subtotals in the table at once, turn them off from the Layout group on the PivotTable Tools Design tab. Learn more about showing or hiding subtotals in the Troubleshooting tip in this section.

- To change the name of a field as it appears in the table, click in any instance of that field in the table and then, on the PivotTable Tools Options tab, in the Active Field group, edit the name as needed and then press ENTER. This does not affect the name of the field in your source data.

> **Note**
> Use the Expand and Collapse options in the Active Field group to expand or collapse all visible instances of the active field. To expand or collapse individual entries, use the +/- buttons. You can also expand or collapse one entry or the entire field from the shortcut menu available when you right-click any entry in the field.

- As mentioned earlier, when Excel recognizes a field you add to the Value area as numeric, it sums the values by default; otherwise, it counts them. However, you can change that function as needed, with quite a bit of flexibility. For common functions, just right-click in any instance of the value field, point to Summarize Data By, and then click the function you want from the six options provided or click More Options for the Value Field Settings dialog box.

- To change the number format for all instances of a value field, right-click any instance and then click Number Format.

> **Note**
>
> For both label and value fields, the options when you right-click include Format Cells. Unlike the Number Format option for value fields, Format Cells affects only selected cells, just as if you were selecting cells in a typical worksheet. Formatting applied through the Format Cells dialog box in this way is direct formatting and will not be removed when you apply a PivotTable style. Depending on your PivotTable settings, however, cell formatting may not be retained when you refresh table data. To retain cell formatting when the table is updated, in the PivotTable Options dialog box, on the Layout & Format tab, click Preserve Cell Formatting On Update.

- If you need to extract a portion of data from the current PivotTable organization, just right-click a value field and then click Show Details. Excel will create a table on a new sheet containing all details from your source data for the portion of the table you requested. For example, I can right-click the value beside Business Development, as shown in the following image, and then click Show Details.

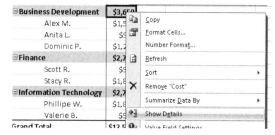

Excel then creates the following table on a new sheet.

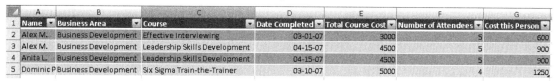

> **Note**
>
> If Show Details is disabled for your table, in the PivotTable Options dialog box, on the Data tab, click Enable Show Details.

Chapter 16

TROUBLESHOOTING

I can't get rid of subtotals in a PivotTable row or column field

If you turn off subtotals for a field and nothing seems to happen, you're just running into a common misunderstanding. You need to turn off the subtotal from the field that displays the subtotal, not from the field that contributes the values for the subtotal.

For example, say you have three row fields, as shown in the following PivotTable.

Row Labels	Sum of Cost this Person
⊟ Administration	3350
⊟ Andrea H.	1500
Effective Interviewing	600
Leadership Skills Development	900
⊟ James A.	600
Effective Interviewing	600
⊟ Jeff B.	1250
Six Sigma Train-the-Trainer	1250
⊟ Business Development	3650
⊟ Alex M.	1500
Effective Interviewing	600
Leadership Skills Development	900

If you don't want the subtotals that appear on each row where you see a name, you have to turn off subtotals for the Name field. Even though those subtotals are combining the values from the lower Course Name field, it's not the Course Name subtotal you're seeing.

Every row or column field has subtotals turned on by default. But, those subtotals only become visible when you give them a lower-level field by which to subtotal.

You can turn off subtotals for a single field at any time from the options available when you right-click in the field. Just click Subtotal "<Field Name>". If nothing happens, be sure you selected the correct field when you turned off subtotals. To turn off all subtotals in the PivotTable at once, on the PivotTable Tools Design tab, click Subtotals, and then click Do Not Show Subtotals.

Using the Field Settings Dialog Boxes

For fields in the Row Label, Column Label, or Report Filter areas, you need the Field Settings dialog box for just two tasks—customizing the function used for subtotals and placing page breaks between items when printing.

For fields in the Values area, open the Value Field Settings dialog box, as mentioned earlier, to access additional functions beyond those available from the shortcut options when you right-click the field. This is also the only place to access the Show Values As options, which enable you to display a value field with a number of types of calculations that add flexibility to the limited number of functions you can use to summarize a value field. For example, you can choose to display values as the difference from or percentage of a specific value from another field, as you see in the following image.

Create Calculated Fields

In addition to the fields in your source data, you can add a field that is a calculation based on the values in one or more of your source data fields. Calculated fields can only be used in the Values area of the table.

- To create a calculated field, on the PivotTable Tools Options tab, in the Tools group, click Formulas and then click Calculated Field. In the Insert Calculated Field dialog box, shown in the following image, name your field and then create your formula, inserting fields into the formula as needed from the list provided. Click Add when done to add the new field to the field list in the PivotTable Field List pane. The field will be added to the Values area in your table. You can remove it from the PivotTable just as you would any field.

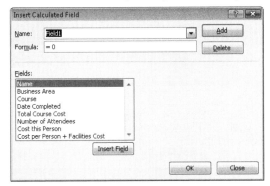

- To delete a calculated field from the field list, or to modify it, use the Insert Calculated Field dialog box. When you open that dialog box, select the field you want to delete from the drop-down list labeled Name and then click Delete. Notice that Modify also becomes an option when you select an existing calculated field name from this list.

Table Options

You can rename a PivotTable from the PivotTable Tools Options tab, and you can add or remove grand total rows and columns from the PivotTable Tools Design tab. You can also remove an individual grand total row or column from the options available when you right-click the cell containing that grand total's label.

However, when you venture into the Options dialog box for PivotTables, you get a great deal more flexibility. To access this dialog box, on the PivotTable Tools Options tab, in the PivotTable group, click Options. Or, right-click anywhere in the table and then click PivotTable Options.

I recommend that you take a gander through this dialog box the first time you create a PivotTable just to take stock of the details you can manage here. In addition to those PivotTable Options settings mentioned earlier in the chapter, here are a few of my favorites.

- On the Layout & Format tab, you can specify text to display for empty cells or error values. You can also specify the indent width for subsequent row fields when using the compact layout option.

- On the Totals & Filters tab, you can set the option to allow multiple filters per field.

- On the Display tab, you can change the display order of fields in the PivotTable Field List pane.

Formatting PivotTables

Formatting PivotTables is very much like formatting ranges as tables. You get a separate set of PivotTable Styles, which you can create and customize almost exactly as you can Table Styles in Excel. The only difference is that, with PivotTable Styles, you can create custom formatting for additional table elements, such as Subtotal and Grand Total rows and columns, as well as Page Field Labels and Values (which refer to fields added to the Report Filter area of the table).

Access PivotTable Styles on the PivotTable Tools Design tab. Notice also that this tab includes style options for displaying row and column headers as well as banded rows and columns, similar to Table Style options.

For more details on creating and working with these styles, see the section on formatting table styles in Chapter 13, "Data-Based Documents: Formatting and Managing Worksheets."

Using PivotCharts

A PivotChart is just a PivotTable in another form—it's also an Excel chart just like any Excel chart, but with additional functionality.

In fact, the column chart that follows, also shown earlier in this chapter as a comparison to a basic PivotTable, is actually a PivotChart. It's available for your perusal in the sample file(Pivot Tables.xlsx) referenced earlier.

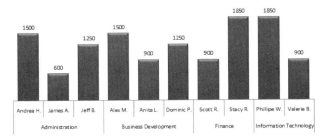

Yes, it looks exactly like a regular column chart, and you can use it as a regular column chart if you choose. The only difference, as shown in the image that follows, is that you get added functionality when you select this chart. Notice the contextual PivotChart Tools tabs that include the three Chart Tools tabs as well as an Analyze tab from which you can refresh or filter data. The PivotTable Field List pane is also available to Pivot-Charts, as you see here, for managing the fields included in your chart.

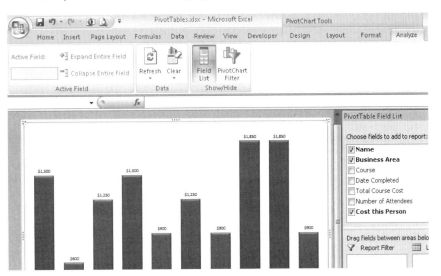

Using a PivotChart adds a visual dimension to working with PivotTable reports and can be an excellent solution when your PivotTable is to be included in a report or presentation. PivotCharts can also be a nice way to assess different charted configurations of your data when deciding what chart type to use or which elements of your data to present.

Creating and Using a PivotChart

A PivotChart is always based on a PivotTable because the chart is, essentially, just a visual representation of the table.

- If you create a PivotChart from an existing PivotTable, by clicking the PivotChart option on the PivotTable Tools Options tab, you select the chart type and then the PivotChart is inserted on the same sheet as the source PivotTable, displaying the options currently active in the source PivotTable.

- If you create a PivotChart directly from source data—that is, on the Insert tab, click to expand PivotTable options and then click PivotChart—a PivotTable and PivotChart are created together. To populate the chart, just populate the table with fields as needed.

When you first create the PivotChart, the PivotChart Filter Pane opens. This pane, shown in the following image for the sample chart presented earlier, provides additional access to the sort and filter options available for Row, Column, and Report Filter fields. Notice that, for a PivotChart, Row Labels are referred to as Axis Fields (Categories) and Column Labels are referred to as Legend Fields (Series).

It also gives you the option to show or hide the PivotTable Field List pane to save space if you only need to access the sort and filter options. The PivotChart Filter Pane can roll up to be very small (drag from the bottom or corner edges to change pane size), and it enables you to scroll through all available options when the pane size is reduced.

Because you have access to the PivotTable Field List pane, there's no reason to use the filter pane instead unless you want to reserve the space. Even when you move a Pivot-Chart onto its own sheet, the same options (including the PivotTable Field List pane) are available to it. Note that, if you close the filter pane and later want to use it, you can toggle that pane open or closed from the PivotChart Tools Analyze tab.

> **Note**
>
> When working with a PivotChart, you can actually click the field where it appears on the chart to select it for use with the Active Field group options on the PivotChart Tools Analyze tab. Even in the case of multiple row fields, as in the chart example shown earlier—if you click the Business Area labels where they appear on the chart x-axis, the Business Area field is selected. If you click the Name labels on the x-axis, that field is selected.

Keep in mind that you can format a PivotChart exactly as you format a regular chart. In earlier versions, much custom formatting was lost when the chart data was refreshed, but no more.

Managing the Connection Between PivotTable and PivotChart

The most important thing to remember about using a PivotChart is that it's always linked to its PivotTable. Delete, filter, or collapse a field on the PivotChart and the same will happen to the PivotTable on which the chart is based.

For best results when you need both a PivotTable and PivotChart, create a copy of the PivotTable before generating the PivotChart, so that you can manage each independently.

Quick Reference—Create and Format a PivotTable

For easy reference, once you have the concepts down, follow these steps to create and manage the basics of PivotTable and PivotChart reports.

1. Create your data in columns, with a single row of headings and a value in every cell of the range. For best results, format your data range as an Excel table.

2. Click in the table and then, on the Insert tab, click PivotTable.

3. Just click OK in the Create PivotTable dialog box to accept the defaults and create your PivotTable on a new sheet, with the selected table as your source data.

4. On the new sheet, click to select the fields in the PivotTable Field List pane that you want to include in your PivotTable.

5. After your fields are added to the PivotTable Row Labels and Values areas on the PivotTable Field List pane, drag field names to reorder them or to move fields to the Column Labels or Report Filter areas, if needed. Use the PivotTable areas as follows.

- ○ Each field in the Values area is the equivalent of a column chart data series.
- ○ Each field in the Row Labels or Column Labels area is the equivalent of the category axis labels or series names in a column chart.
- ○ A field placed in the Report Filter area is used as criteria by which to filter the row or column fields shown in your table.

6. To customize the way a field looks in the PivotTable, use the available settings on the PivotTable Tools contextual tabs or the shortcut menu available when you right-click. Or, to customize subtotals or set page breaks between field entries for printing, use the Field Settings dialog box. Find the dialog box among the available right-click options or on the PivotTable Tools Options tab.

7. If the PivotTable options you need are not available from the PivotTable Tools contextual tab, find a wide range of settings—from customizing the way error values are displayed to preserving cell formatting when the table is refreshed—in the PivotTable Options dialog box. This dialog box is available either when you right-click in the table or from the PivotTable Tools Options tab.

8. To format the PivotTable, on the PivotTable Tools Design tab, apply a PivotTable style. Similar to table styles, you can use a built-in style, create your own custom PivotTable style from scratch, or duplicate and customize a built-in style. You can also specify options and layout preferences on the PivotTable Tools Design tab, such as banded rows and columns, report layout, and subtotal display.

9. To create a PivotChart, click PivotChart on the PivotTable Tools Options tab and then select a chart type. Keep in mind that the PivotChart is linked to its PivotTable. To avoid losing PivotTable data when you remove or rearrange fields in the chart, create a copy of the PivotTable before creating the chart. You can format the chart just as you would a regular Excel chart—including moving the chart to its own sheet. See Chapter 15 for help formatting Excel charts.

The Excel–Visio Connection

Microsoft Visio is a powerful technical diagramming program. But, as demonstrated many times throughout this book, powerful doesn't have to mean complicated. This chapter on Microsoft Office Visio 2007 is included here because of the power you can get when you let data do the drawing for you. Unlike SmartArt or any Office Art capabilities in the core programs of the 2007 release, Office Visio 2007 diagrams can be created from, return, or otherwise interact with data.

So, what does that mean for you? First of all, you can automatically build some types of diagrams from data, no drawing required. Second, several types of diagrams can integrate with data sources so that they update automatically based on changes in your data—meaning that you get many more options for effective ways to graphically present data. And, finally, it means that you can use diagrams as a visual interface to help easily manage many types of data.

> **Note**
>
> Some of the functionality discussed in this chapter (including PivotDiagrams and the ability to link data to shapes) is specific to Visio Professional 2007 and is not available in Visio Standard 2007.

Visio can get far more technical than I have any intention of getting here. The purpose of this chapter is to give you an idea of what kind of power you can add to your presentations when you let Visio sink its teeth into your data. That said, I'm using Microsoft Office Excel 2007 as the example data source in all cases throughout this chapter, but Office Excel 2007 is not the only possible data source for any of these features. Depending on the type of graphic you're working with, other possible data sources can include Microsoft Access databases, Microsoft Windows SharePoint Services Lists, Microsoft Exchange Server files, XML files, or delimited text files. Possible data sources are specified in each applicable chapter section.

Because Visio is not part of the core Microsoft Office suite, I'm not making any assumptions about your experience with this program. The only assumptions made in this chapter are that you are an advanced Microsoft Office user, that you have some experience creating and working with shapes in Microsoft PowerPoint, and that you can create and work with basic Excel PivotTables. For a primer on PivotTables, check out Chapter 16, "Powerful Reporting, Easier Than You Think."

> **Note**
>
> If you don't already have a copy of Visio Professional 2007, you can download a free 60-day trial from Microsoft Office Online. Find a link to the Web page where you can access trial versions of any 2007 Office release program on the Extending Microsoft Office tab of this book's CD.

Visio Essentials—A Quick Reference Overview

Before jumping in to working with data, I think it's important to provide a framework for those who don't have much experience working in Visio. So, this section is organized to provide a quick reference guide for working with shapes and pages in Visio.

Creating a Diagram

When you begin to create a new diagram in Visio, you can start a few different ways, as follows.

- On the File menu, point to New, point to the category you want (such as Business or Engineering), and then click the diagram type you want to create. For example, take a look at the partial list of Business diagram types shown here.

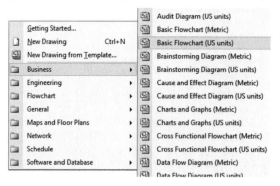

When you select a diagram type, Visio opens sets of appropriate shapes for you to use in creating your diagram. These sets of shapes are known as stencils. Depending on the diagram type, one or several stencils might be opened for you. For example, if you select a Workflow Diagram, six stencils are opened, as you see in the following image. Click the title of any stencil to reveal its shapes.

> **Note**
>
> As an alternative to using the New option on the File menu to access diagram categories, click the arrow that appears beside the New icon on the Standard toolbar.

- Press CTRL+N to create a blank new document with no open stencils when you first open a new instance of Visio, or to create another file using the most recent diagram type you selected.

  To open stencils if you start with a blank document, or to make additional stencils available to any diagram type, on the File menu, point to Shapes, point to the category you want, and then click to open individual stencils.

> **Note**
>
> Those with previous experience in Visio will notice many new types of shapes with greatly improved graphics, such as those on the Workflow Objects and Workflow Steps stencils.

- Start a diagram from one of many available templates that include both starter templates and recommended stencils for the diagram type. To start with a template, on the File menu, point to New and then click Getting Started.

Chapter 17

- Some diagram types, such as PivotDiagrams and Organizational Charts, can be created with wizards, which are discussed later in this chapter.

Working with Shapes

Once you have a new page and the stencils you want to use, follow these key tips to help you work with shapes and create your diagram.

- To add a shape to a page, drag it from the stencil to the sheet.

- To duplicate shapes, use CTRL+D or CTRL+Drag, as you can for AutoShapes in Microsoft PowerPoint.

- You can add text to virtually any shape, including lines and connectors. To do this, just select the shape and begin typing.

- Independent formatting options for shapes include Text, Line, Fill, Shadow, and even Corner Rounding (all of which are available from the Format menu). You can do quite a bit of customization with each of these—particularly Text formatting that offers options for all of the tab categories you see in the following image.

Note that Corner Rounding options are also available from the Line dialog box.

- Before you start to manually format shapes, however, notice that Visio has its own set of Themes. Visio Themes are separate from the Document Themes in the 2007 release programs Word, Excel, and PowerPoint. However, Visio Themes use the same core concepts—apply several formatting attributes at once throughout one or all pages in a Visio file. Theme Colors are also very much the same setup, providing a Theme Colors palette for fill, line, or text color options that includes the specified colors for the active theme along with several variations on each color.

  To use Themes, on the Format menu, click Theme to open the Theme Colors task pane. You can switch between Theme Colors and Theme Effects directly from the task pane.

  - Click a Theme to apply it to the active page, or click the arrow that appears on a theme option when you point to it and then select the option to apply the Theme to all pages in that file.

  - Theme Colors consists of a set of 12 colors with designations to different object types or elements, as you see in the New Theme Colors dialog box shown in the following image.

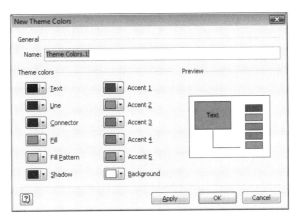

○ Visio Theme Effects are much more detailed than Theme Effects in Document Themes, including settings for text, line, fill, shadows, and connectors.

○ To create your own Theme Colors or Theme Effects, click the New option at the bottom of the applicable task pane, or click the arrow beside a built-in option and then click Duplicate, as you see here.

○ If shapes don't update when you apply Theme options, right-click the shape and then click Allow Themes. This is likely to be needed in particular with diagrams that were originally created in earlier versions.

● When you hover over many types of shapes, a ScreenTip automatically appears with the shape name. However, to add, edit, or delete ScreenTip text from any shape, on the Insert menu, click either Shape Screen Tip or Edit Shape Screen Tip (the latter option appears on the menu once a ScreenTip exists for the selected shape).

● Grouping, Order, and Rotation And Flip options for Visio shapes are virtually identical to PowerPoint and are available from the Shape menu or from the Shape options available on the shortcut menu when you right-click.

● Alignment options, also available on the Shape menu, appear to be identical to those in PowerPoint, but they work a bit differently. Instead of aligning to whichever shape is farthest in the direction to which you're aligning (such as aligning the tops of shapes by whichever shape is highest on the page), Visio shapes are aligned to whichever shape you select first. (You'll notice that the selection outline for the dominant shape is thicker than for other shapes in your selection.)

Chapter 17

> **Note**
>
> Grouping, Order, Rotation, Alignment, and other shape actions are available from the nicely organized Action toolbar.

- To resize shapes or place them at a particular position on the page, use the Size And Position Window, available from the View menu.

- If a shape won't do what you need it to do, such as allow resizing, protection is most likely in place. To change protection settings for selected shapes, on the Format menu, click Protection and then change the settings as needed.

- One of my favorite Visio tools is the Operations group of functions available on the Shape menu. Draw lines horizontally through a triangle (you can find a straight line on the Drawing toolbar), for example, and then use the Fragment tool for creating the perfect pyramid diagram. Just draw lines that completely cross the shape, then select the shape with all lines and click Fragment. The results will be similar to what you see in the following image.

From this: To this:

Note that shapes created using Operations become independent, fully functional shapes. So, you can add text to the new shapes or apply whatever formatting you need. Try out the various Operations with a few different shapes to see what you can do. A couple of the most useful are Intersect and Subtract, which you use to create a shape just from the overlapping portions of selected shapes.

> **Note**
>
> When creating typical flowcharts, one helpful option is the shape named Flowchart Shapes that appears on the Basic Flowchart Shapes stencil. After you drag the single Flowchart Shapes object (shown here) to a new page, you can right-click the shape for the option to change it between any of the four basic flowchart shapes (Process, Decision, Document, and Data).
>
>

INSIDE OUT   Hyperlink between shapes in a Visio file

You can add hyperlinks to Visio shapes to link to external files or Web addresses, or to link to other shapes within the same Visio diagram or file. This is particularly useful if, for example, you plan to publish your diagram on a Web page for use as an interactive tool. To add a hyperlink, select a shape and then, on the Insert menu, click Hyperlinks (or press CTRL+K).

External addresses are quite straightforward to add—just browse to or type the location, add a description (which appears as the hyperlink ScreenTip), and then click OK. Internal address, however, require a bit more information.

To add a link to another shape, you can type the page name, a forward slash, and then the shape name. Or, you can click Browse to select the sheet name, then type the shape name, and Visio sets up the syntax for you. Either way, however, you need to know the shape name.

If you only have one shape of a given type on the sheet, the shape name is the same as the shape name in the stencil. Otherwise, access the shape name from the Special dialog box. This dialog box used to appear by default on the Format menu, but no longer. To access the Special menu, you must be working in Developer Mode. Similar to the Developer tab on the Ribbon in other programs, Developer Mode in Visio just gives you additional options—you don't need to be a developer to use it. To enable this setting, on the Tools menu, click Options and then click Advanced. Select Run In Developer Mode and then click OK. After you enable Developer Mode, the Special dialog box becomes available on the Format menu, so that you can easily find shape names.

Alternately, you can get the shape name from the title bar on the Shape Sheet—and you can edit the hyperlink from the Shape Sheet as well. To access the Shape Sheet, on the Window menu, click Show Shape Sheet. Or, when Developer Mode is active, you'll also find the Shape Sheet option on the shortcut menu when you right-click a shape. Learn more about using Shape Sheets in the next Inside Out tip in this chapter.

TROUBLESHOOTING

How do you stop shapes from creating new shapes when clicked?

When creating a flowchart, the new AutoConnect functionality can be handy. AutoConnect is the feature that controls the Drop And Connect arrows you see on each side of a shape when you point to it, as shown here. (These arrows appear blue when you see them in Visio.)

The idea behind these shapes is that they can save you time on layout and drawing connectors. Just click a Drop And Connect arrow and a new shape is created in the direction of the arrow, with an equal distance between shapes and a connector leading to the new shape. The new shape created will be the currently selected shape in the active stencil. You can even click the same arrow a second or third time (depending on available space) to add additional shapes with connectors originating from the same point, such as for lateral positions in an organization chart.

However, if you're not creating a flowchart with a typical layout, Drop And Connect arrows can become annoying, to say the least. To disable this feature, on the Tools menu, click Options and then click General. Click to turn off Enable AutoConnect and then click OK.

INSIDE OUT   Manage a surprising array of settings from the Shape Sheet

Every shape and every page in a Visio file has its own Shape Sheet. This sheet is a collection of various settings available to the shape or page, ranging from height, width, and position, to rotation angle, fill color, and then some. There are many technical details on the Shape Sheet that you might not recognize, but you can edit anything you do recognize from that sheet instead of through individual dialog boxes.

The sheet is organized like a spreadsheet, as you see in the following image, so it's quite easy to move through. Click the heading of any section on the sheet to expand or collapse it. You can click into any cell to change a value. Or, use the Shape Sheet Formula Bar that becomes available in the toolbar area when your insertion point is in a Shape Sheet.

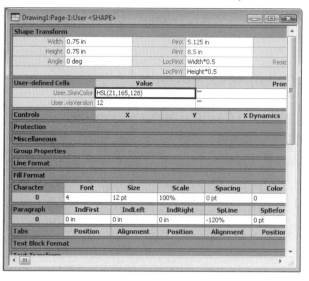

One interesting option that you won't find in a standard dialog box is that you can change the skin color appearance of any shapes that represent people, as you see in the preceding image. Colors are represented in the Shape Sheet using the HSL color model, but RGB values are also accepted.

Using Connectors

You can add connectors to your diagram by using the AutoConnect option discussed in the troubleshooting tip earlier in this chapter. But, you also have options for drawing connectors yourself, if you prefer.

- On the Standard toolbar, click the Connector tool. While active, your insertion point adds connectors whenever you drag between two shapes. Hover over a shape until you see a red box around it, then drag to the shape where you want the connector to end.

- Select a connector from a stencil. Many stencils offer the Dynamic Connector, which you can drag to the sheet and then drag each end over the shape where you want it to connect. When a red box appears highlighting the destination shape, release the mouse pointer.

- Some stencils offer multiple connector types. However, a Connector stencil also exists. On the File menu, point to Shapes and then point to Visio Extras to find this stencil. Note that not all connectors are dynamic. Those that are not won't provide the red box indicator to release the pointer.

  However, with any connectors—dynamic or not—you can take advantage of what Visio calls Snap To Geometry, which refers to the drawing grid. Snap To Geometry enables you to place a connector end virtually wherever you want it, and it will stay put.

- You can change connector types and set many options, from the number of sides of a connector to causing jumps to appear when connectors cross. To do this, select the connectors to format and then, on the Format menu, click Behavior and then click Connector.

TROUBLESHOOTING

Why do shapes jump around when I add other shapes to the diagram?

Visio offers extensive options for shape behavior, including how connectors route around shapes and whether shapes are allowed to overlap.

By default, many shape types will jump out of the way when you place another shape near them. Visio calls this Plowing. However, you can change this setting and many others to control the way shapes behave in your diagram.

You can turn shape plowing on or off for all shapes on the page at once. To do this, on the File menu, click Page Setup. On the Layout And Routing tab of that dialog box, click to enable or disable the setting Move Other Shapes Away On Drop, and then click OK.

To change this setting for just selected shapes, on the Format menu, click Behavior. I recommend reviewing all tabs of this dialog box for some really nice options like allowing a shape to split connectors or controlling how a shape behaves when grouped. However, you'll find the specific setting you're looking for on the Placement tab. On that tab, select Lay Out And Route Around from the Placement Behavior list. This will enable most tab options. From the list labeled Move Other Shapes Away On Drop, select Plow No Shapes and then click OK. Apply this setting to shapes to keep them from plowing other shapes, regardless of the page setting.

Formatting Pages

On the File menu, click Page Setup for several familiar page formatting options, such as Print Setup and Page Size. For some layout options, you can also set defaults for the page as well as the depth and position of shadows when applied to shapes.

However, in addition to the typical settings you'd expect to find in a Page Setup dialog box, and some Visio oddities such as the Shadow defaults, two items will especially come in handy, as follows.

- If you're creating a diagram to add to a document in another program, consider setting a custom page size to match the size allotted to the diagram in the destination document. Then, you can zoom in on the available space to ensure that you create your diagram to fit. For example, use the dimensions of a placeholder table cell in a Microsoft Office Word 2007 document.

  Alternately, once you've created your basic diagram, you can use the Size To Fit Drawing Contents option on the Paper Size tab, which fits the page to your diagram to help you control your available work area.

> **Note**
>
> To copy a Visio diagram for pasting into another program, you don't need to select the diagram unless you're only taking some content on the page. For best and most consistent results when you want to copy all page content for pasting into another program, just press CTRL+C to copy without first selecting anything. To paste Visio diagrams in Office Word 2007 or Office PowerPoint 2007, press CTRL+ALT+V in the destination program to open the Paste Special dialog box. Then, for best quality, select either Picture (Enhanced Metafile) or Device Independent Bitmap as the paste type. The Windows Metafile option does not provide good resolution for Visio graphics pasted into other Microsoft Office programs in most cases. (If you prefer a PNG picture, which may reduce file size, you can cut the picture after pasting it into Word or PowerPoint and then use Paste Special again, where you'll see PNG as a picture type option.)

- On the Page Properties tab, you can name the page, set unique measurement units to use for the page, identify a page as a background or foreground page, and apply a background page.

  Background pages in Visio are where you place content that you want to appear on one or more sheets but not be editable from those sheets. This is a nice place for template design elements, such as logos or headers and footers. Background pages are also the place to add a watermark. Once you set a page as a background page, it then becomes available to be applied to other pages.

In addition to Page Setup properties, keep the following in mind for working with Visio pages.

- Double-click a page tab to rename the page. Or, right-click the page tab for the options to add, delete, rename, or reorder pages.

- To add drawing guides to the page, hover over the bottom edge of the horizontal ruler or the right edge of the vertical ruler until you see a double-backed black arrow. The position of the guide appears on the Status bar as you drag the guide. To delete a guide, just select it and then press DELETE.

- As mentioned earlier, each page also has its own Shape Sheet that you can access when you right-click the page. On the Shape Sheet, you can set a number of properties, such as page size, margins, or grid density.

Creating a Visio Organization Chart from Worksheet Data

This feature is not new, but it is pretty impressive. Just type a list of names, titles, and managers in an Excel worksheet and Visio will create even the most extensive organization chart for you in a couple of clicks.

> **Note**
>
> Depending on your needs for an organization chart, you might want to use this feature or the new SmartArt diagrams discussed in Chapter 18, "Creating Professional Presentation Graphics." For large, intricate organization charts, Visio is the more flexible choice. But, when you create SmartArt diagrams in PowerPoint, you can convert a bulleted list to a diagram in two clicks and then add or revise diagram entries just by typing text.
>
> Visio is also a better choice when you want to store data in diagrams or create diagrams that are interactive, such as diagrams with hyperlinks published on a Web page. But, if you just need a high-quality, simple organization chart to add to a document without having to draw any shapes, consider whether a SmartArt diagram might not do the trick for you more easily. Also, unlike Visio diagrams, SmartArt diagrams use the Document Themes, Quick Styles, and graphic effects available across Word, Excel, and PowerPoint. So, your SmartArt organization chart can automatically coordinate with your document.

To create a Visio organization chart from data stored in Excel, do the following.

1. Set up your data in Excel in columns with a single row of headings. Headings will become field names for use in creating the organization chart. The only required fields are a field for the person's name and a field for the person to whom they report. Include other fields as needed for content you want to include in your chart, as you see in the following sample data.

Name ▾	Title ▾	Reports To ▾
John L.	CEO	
Ellen B.	VP, Marketing	John L.
Alex W.	VP, Finance	John L.
Josh B.	VP, Sales	John L.
Rick N.	Director of Marketing	Ellen B.
Juliette S.	Director of Client Development	Ellen B.
Michel T.	Director of Research	Ellen B.
Sheila B.	Senior Sales Manager	Josh B.
Julie K.	Global Sales Leadership Director	Josh B.
Baerd P.	Director of Finance	Alex W.

To use the sample data shown here, find the file named Visio org chart data.xlsx in the sample files you can install from the Welcome tab of this book's CD.

For the Organization Chart Wizard to map the diagram correctly, the name of the person reported to must be typed the same in the Reports To field as it is where it appears in the Name field. When you've finished setting up the data, close the Excel file. Visio will not be able to access the file if it's open in Excel.

2. In Visio, on the File menu, point to New, point to Business, and then click Organization Chart Wizard.

3. Click Next at the first screen to select data from an existing source file. Notice that data can be in an Excel file, a text file, a Microsoft Office Exchange Server directory, or a database. At the second screen, select the option that includes Excel File and then click Next again. Browse to and select your file, and then click Next once more.

> **Note**
>
> The first screen of the Organization Chart Wizard indicates that .xls files are the Excel file type to use. This screen simply hasn't been updated. Excel 2007 files (such as the sample data file provided) work fine.

4. Once Visio accesses your data, it will attempt to match field names (column headings) to the Name and Reports To fields for the organization chart. Confirm that Visio has selected the correct fields and then click Next.

At this point, you can just click Next until the Finish button becomes available and then click Finish to generate your chart. However, take note of the options at each wizard screen between. On the last wizard screens, you can specify fields from your data to display on the chart and the order in which to display them within shapes, select fields to store in shapes as Shape Data (see the section of this chapter titled "Using Shape Data and Data Graphics" for more on Shape Data), and specify layout requirements.

When the organization chart is generated from the sample data shown in the preceding steps, it looks like this.

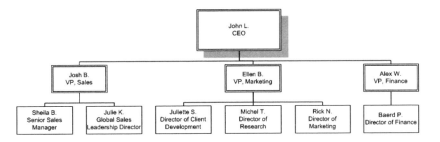

It takes just two more clicks to format this chart with Theme Colors and Theme Effects. You can then add shapes from the Organization Chart Shapes or any other stencil and format them as you would any Visio shape. You can also use options on the Organization Chart menu (this menu appears only for this diagram type), including the following.

- Select Options to globally apply format settings, such as shape size and text formatting for each visible field (such as italicizing titles).

- Change the position type (such as executive or manager) for selected shapes.

- Click Export Organization Data to export all data from your completed organization chart to a new Excel file. Just type a name for the new file and click Save.

  Note that this works just as well with organization charts you create from other sources or by drawing shapes. So, for example, if you create your organization chart from Excel data and then add shapes to the chart manually in Visio, when you export that data to Excel, it will include the shapes you've added as well as those that were automatically generated. Also note that, by default, the exported file is saved as an .xlsx file.

Creating a PivotDiagram

This is one of my top-ten favorite features in the 2007 Office release. A PivotDiagram is just what it sounds like—a diagram that displays data just like an Excel PivotTable or PivotChart. A PivotDiagram is a hierarchal diagram (similar to the structure of an organization chart) that remains connected to data, so that you can look at the data visually in as many different configurations as your data allows.

Generating a PivotDiagram

Note

This section uses the same sample data that was used for PivotTables in Chapter 16. Find the file Pivot Data.xlsx in the sample files you can install from the Welcome tab of this book's CD.

Chapter 17

To create your PivotDiagram, start with data setup in Excel as for a PivotTable (data in columns with a single row of headings and values in all cells) and then do one of the following.

- If your Excel data is formatted as a table, on the Table Tools Design tab, click the Export options and then click Export Table to Visio PivotDiagram.

- Whether your Excel data is formatted as a table or a range, you can also create your PivotDiagram from Visio. To do this, on the File menu, point to New, point to Business, and then click PivotDiagram. Follow the wizard to select your Excel file and, if necessary, select the specific sheet or range in that file. Then, just keep clicking Next until the Finish option appears. Click Finish to create your table.

  When you create the PivotDiagram using this wizard, source data can originate in an Excel workbook, an Access database, a Windows SharePoint Services list, a SQL Server Database, or another OLEBD (Object Linked Embedded Database) or ODBC (Open Database Connectivity) compatible data source.

CAUTION!

If your Excel file contains any charts on their own sheets, use the method provided here to generate the PivotDiagram from the Table Tools Design tab in Excel. Or, open the Excel file before starting the Visio PivotDiagram Wizard. The wizard is unable to access Excel files that contain chart sheets unless the file is currently open.

With either of the preceding methods, the PivotDiagram page is generated with a single shape to designate the top level of the diagram and a shape identifying the source data, last update, and any filters in place, as shown in the following image.

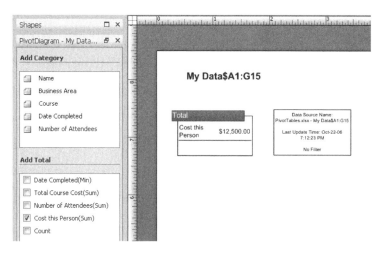

Notice that all available fields for the PivotDiagram are provided in the PivotDiagram pane, divided into Categories (the equivalent of Row or Column fields in a PivotTable) and Totals (the equivalent of Value fields in a PivotTable).

Formatting and Managing a PivotDiagram

Just click to apply a category from the PivotDiagram pane to the page and Visio will generate the applicable shapes. Also in the pane, select the totals you want to appear in each shape. In the following example, training cost per person is shown by business area.

Following are some key tips to help you create the PivotDiagram you need.

- The Total in the preceding PivotDiagram example is listed as cost per person because this is the name of the applicable column heading in the Excel data. But, because you're actually showing total training cost for the department in this case, you might want to change the field name. To change the name of any Category or Total field as it will appear in the diagram, click the arrow that appears when you point to the field in the PivotDiagram pane and then click Configure Column. Edit the name as needed and click OK. The field name will automatically change throughout the table.

- To break out the categories further, select the shapes representing the categories you want to break out and then click the category for which you want to see the detail. For example, to show cost per person in the business development department, select the Business Development shape that contains the total and then click Name in the PivotDiagram pane. The result looks like this.

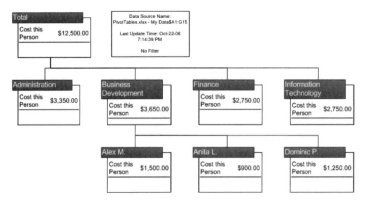

Because you can show detail for individual shapes, you must select all shapes in a category when you want to add a new subcategory for all. Be sure to select the part of the shape that contains the total and not the shape heading. To quickly select all shapes in the category, point to the category name in the PivotDiagram pane, click the drop-down arrow that appears, and then click Select All.

- You can format and resize shapes just as you would any shapes in a Visio diagram. To resize several shapes at once, select all shapes to be resized and then drag from the handles surrounding the selection to resize them as a group.

- To change the number format for totals, on the PivotDiagram menu, click Edit Data Graphic. Or, on the PivotDiagram pane, click Other Actions and then click Edit Data Graphic. Then, do the following.

  1. Select the Data Graphic that contains the field name for which you want to change the format and then click Edit Item.

  2. In the Value Format field, click the ellipsis to open a Data Format dialog box, where you can specify the number format you need.

For more detail on working with Data Graphics, see the next section of this chapter.

- The shapes in a PivotDiagram that contain the totals for each shape in a category are known as Pivot Nodes. You can apply more interesting shapes to Pivot Nodes by using the Apply Shape option on the PivotDiagram menu or pane. Just select the Pivot Nodes to which you want to apply a shape, and then in the Apply Shapes dialog box, click a shape and then click OK. Shapes from the Departments and Workflow Objects stencils are available automatically through this dialog box.

  To make other shapes available to your PivotDiagram, on the File menu, point to Shapes and then select the stencils you want. Once you open a new stencil, it becomes available from the Stencil dropdown list in the Apply Shape dialog box.

- To access filter options for any field in the diagram, click the arrow that appears when you point to a field in the PivotDiagram pane and then click Configure Column.

- From the PivotDiagram menu, you can manage the diagram layout, sort selected shapes in the diagram, merge selected shapes into a single shape (this can be a great way to save space when you want to break out several categories in a single diagram), and set a variety of options for your PivotDiagram.

  Use the PivotDiagram Options dialog box, available from the PivotDiagram menu, to change the name of the table, choose to show or hide diagram elements, and revise your data source, as you see in the image that follows.

TROUBLESHOOTING

How can I edit the ScreenTip of an applied shape in a PivotDiagram?

If you apply a shape to a Pivot Node, as discussed in the preceding list, you might want to change the ScreenTip that appears when you point to the shape. However, if you se- lect the shape and then click the Insert menu expecting to find the Edit Shape ScreenTip option, you might see the option Shape ScreenTip instead. The latter option indicates that no ScreenTip currently exists for the selection.

The reason you don't see the edit option is that your selection is actually a group of shapes. The applied shape is automatically grouped with the Pivot Node. To edit the existing ScreenTip for the applied shape, click once on the applied shape (this selects the group) and then click a second time (this is slower than a double-click) to select just the applied shape within the group. When the shape itself is selected, you'll see an x inside each of the shape handles. Once just the shape is selected, click the Insert menu and the Edit Shape ScreenTip option will be available.

Thanks to Support Engineer Jagadeesh Parameswaran, an intrepid member of the Visio 2007 test team, for this and a couple of other tips in this chapter.

Using Shape Data and Data Graphics

As in previous versions of Visio, you can store data in shapes. Known as Custom Prop- erties in earlier versions, this functionality is now referred to as Shape Data. You can create Shape Data directly in Visio or generate it automatically from a variety of sources. Additionally, you can now add Data Graphics to display this data directly on shapes.

> **Note**
>
> As mentioned earlier, the dynamic content in a PivotDiagram is created as Data Graphics. To edit a Data Graphic that appears in your PivotDiagram, on the PivotDiagram menu, or the Other Actions menu in the PivotDiagram pane, click Edit Data Graphic.

To create Shape Data from an external source, use data originating in an Excel work- book, an Access database, a Windows SharePoint Services list, a SQL Server Database, or another OLEBD or ODBC compatible data source.

Creating Shape Data

Shape Data is information you store in shapes on your diagram. For example, you might want to store serial number and location information for computer equipment that ap- pears in a floor plan diagram of your office.

In addition to displaying Shape Data in a Data Graphic, you can export data from shapes into a report generated as an Excel workbook, an HTML file, an XML file, or a shape on your active Visio page.

To create Shape Data, select one or more shapes to which you want to add data and then, on the Data menu, click Shape Data. Or, right-click, point to Data, and then click Shape Data. The first time you add data to the selected shapes, you'll be asked if you want to define Shape Data. After you click Yes, the Define Shape Data dialog box appears, as you see in the following image.

If Shape Data already exists for the selected shapes, the Shape Data dialog box appears showing the available data fields. Click Define in the dialog box to access Define Shape Data.

Note

Notice an option in the Define Shape Data dialog box labeled Ask On Drop. If you check this option for a Shape Data property, you'll be prompted to add or edit the value of that property when you duplicate the shape. You must enable this option separately for each property that you want to appear in the prompt.

Each field you add to Shape Data is called a property. To add more than one property for selected shapes, click New at the bottom of the Define Shape Data dialog box. If you need to edit existing Shape Data properties, select the item to edit from the Properties list in the Define Shape Data dialog box.

Chapter 17

> **Note**
>
> Some types of shapes, such as those in the Office Equipment stencil, come with built-in Shape Data properties. These properties work exactly the same as the Shape Data properties you create. If you don't want to use the built-in properties, in the Define Shape Data dialog box, select individual unwanted properties and then click Delete.

Generating a Data Report

To generate a report of all Shape Data in the active diagram or the entire workbook, first create a custom report and then run that report as needed. To do this, on the Data menu, click Reports and then click New. Then, do the following.

1. In the Report Definition Wizard, choose to create your report for all shapes on the current page, in the entire file, or just selected shapes and then click Next.

    You can also click Advanced on this first wizard screen to filter the shapes included in the report.

2. Built-in shape properties as well as the custom Shape Data properties you define are available on the second wizard screen. Select the properties to include in your report and then click Next to continue through the wizard. You'll have the opportunity to name the report and to set other properties such as subtotals or sorting options, as applicable, and then click Finish.

3. Once your custom report appears in the Reports dialog box, select it and then click Run. You'll be prompted to choose output as Excel, HTML, Visio Shape, or XML. When you choose Excel, HTML, or XML, the report is generated as a separate file.

Linking Data to Shapes

As an alternative to creating and editing Shape Data directly on shapes, you can import that data from another source, as mentioned earlier.

> **Note**
>
> External source data for linking to shapes should be arranged in columns with a single row of headings.

To import data, on the Data menu, click Link Data to Shapes. In the wizard that opens, locate and select your data source. Once you've specified the data source, you can simply click Finish to import the data, or follow the wizard through to specify data fields to import or a field to use as a unique identifier when refreshing data.

The data appears in the External Data pane, which opens below the page by default, as shown here.

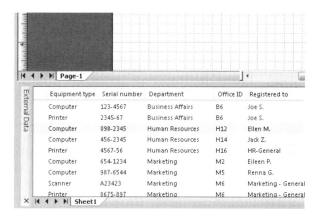

To link your imported data to shapes, do one of the following.

- Select the shape you want to use in the active stencil, but don't drag the shape to the page. Then, drag rows from your data onto the page. One shape will be generated for each row of data, and the linked data will be stored in the shapes as Shape Data.

- If shapes already exist to which you want to link data, drag a row of data to the shape that you want to link. A box will appear around the shape when the data is ready to be dropped. Just release the mouse button to link the data to the selected shape.

When a row is linked to a shape, a link icon appears at the beginning of the row in the External Data pane. You can double-click in a linked row to select its linked shape on the page. Or, right-click a shape containing linked data, then point to Data for the option Show Linked Row, which selects the linked row in the External Data pane.

> **Note**
>
> Right-click in the External Data pane and then click Configure Refresh to edit the source data range, set up automatic refresh, or set the data refresh to override changes users make to Shape Data.

INSIDE OUT   Automatically link imported data to shapes

Once you import data using Link Data To Shapes, as discussed in the preceding steps, you can use the Automatically Link feature to add that data to shapes on the sheet. Well, that's almost true.

The catch to the Automatically Link feature is that you must have a Shape Data property in each shape that matches one field name and a corresponding value in the imported data in order for Automatically Link to work. Of course, it's logical that Visio would need a field to match in order to know which data record to link to which shape. But, because there is some manual data entry involved in this method, decide based on your particular data and diagram whether Automatically Link or dragging records from imported data to specific shapes is going to be the more efficient option for your needs.

To use Automatically Link, first create a Shape Data property in the shapes to be linked that matches one of the fields in the imported data, and then enter the corresponding value from an imported data record into the Shape Data of each shape. Once you have a property value in the Shape Data that matches a field of the same name in a record of the imported data, on the Data menu, click Automatically Link, and then follow the prompts to automatically link all remaining fields from the imported data to your shapes.

Creating and Managing Data Graphics

Once your shapes contain Shape Data, you can add Data Graphics to them to display the data along with the shape. Data Graphics can display as text (this is the type of Data Graphic used to generate PivotDiagrams) or can be displayed as data bars, icon sets, or color bars (similar to the new Conditional Formatting options in Excel).

Note

When you link external data to shapes, text data graphics may be added to the shapes automatically. You can edit or delete these in the Edit Data Graphic dialog box as well. Or, to delete all Data Graphics from selected shapes, right-click, point to Data, and then click Remove Data Graphic.

To create a Data Graphic, select the shapes to which you want to add the graphic, right-click, point to Data, and then click Edit Data Graphic. In the Edit Data Graphic dialog box, do the following.

1. Click New Item and then select the type of Data Graphic you want. In the New <Graphic Type> dialog box, select the field that you want the graphic to display. Fields refer to the Shape Data properties available for the selected shape. Notice

also that you can click More Fields in the Data Fields drop-down list to select additional options for your data graphic, including creating a custom formula.

2. Specify the formatting details for the data graphic. Available options vary by graphic type, including the following.

   ○ Text, data bar, or icon set graphics appear as callouts that you can place on top of or adjacent to the shape by using the Callout Position options. Note that Color By Value Data Graphics change the color of the shape itself.

   ○ You can set the Value Format (such as a number format) for text or data bars. For icon sets and colors, assign specific values from the selected field to represent each available color or icon.

   ○ The callout display for text or data bars can take on a variety of graphic forms.

   Once you've applied all of the settings you want, click OK twice to apply the graphic.

Once you create a Data Graphic for shapes in a file containing linked data, new shapes created from that linked data will take on those graphics automatically. You can disable this option, Apply After Linking Data To Shapes, from the Data Graphics task pane. To access the task pane, on the Data menu, click Display Data On Shapes.

Also on the Data Graphics task pane, previews are available for all Data Graphics you've created in the active file. Just click a preview to apply the graphic to selected shapes. Or, for a variety of other options to help you manage your Data Graphics, click the arrow that appears when you hover over a preview (as you see here).

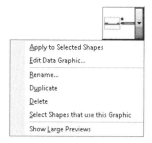

More Visio Data Connections

Several additional data integration options exist for Visio diagrams, in addition to those discussed in this chapter. For example, you can generate a Brainstorming diagram from XML data or export data from a Brainstorming diagram to Word, Excel, or an XML file.

Other common data integration options include creating a Gantt chart from project management data or a calendar from Microsoft Office Outlook data. Both of these are available from the Data menu under Insert Data Solutions.

To learn more about working with data connections in Visio, check out the book *Microsoft Office Visio 2007 Inside Out*.

Chapter 17

PART 4
PowerPoint

CHAPTER 18
Creating Professional Presentation Graphics

The best advice I can give to you on the subject of creating graphics for your documents is this:

The fact is that, good or bad, graphics get attention. No matter what the reason for a particular graphic, we all add graphics to documents to make a point or emphasize information—in short, to get the content noticed. A poorly crafted business graphic is like wearing sweaty gym clothes to walk the red carpet at the Academy Awards. You'll definitely get attention, but is that really the impression you want to make?

For example, take a look at the bulleted list in the following image.

- **President and CEO**
  - **Senior VP, Marketing**
    - **Director of Business Development**
  - **Senior VP, Finance**
    - **Director of Finance**
  - **Executive VP, Operations**
    - **VP, Human Resources**
    - **Director of Information Technology**

A graphic can certainly improve on this handful of boring bullets, such as the clean and simple organization chart you see here.

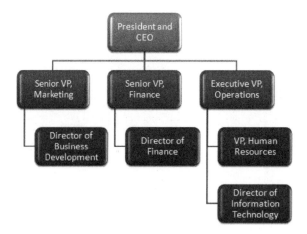

But, what about the graphic that follows?

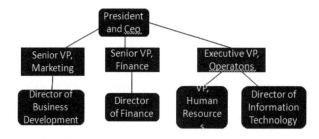

Personally, I'd take a boring bulleted list any day of the week over the type of attention this graphic would get.

So, am I telling you to stick to boring bulleted lists if you're not a graphic design whiz? Absolutely not. As a matter of fact, it took less than a minute (literally) to create the first organization chart shown in this section and about ten minutes to create the mess you see in the preceding image.

One of the best reasons to use Microsoft Office PowerPoint 2007 to create presentation graphics for your documents is that creating the perfect graphic is faster and easier than making a mess, even if you can't so much as draw a straight line. And, for those looking for something a bit more challenging, the new graphics engine in Office PowerPoint 2007 provides far more flexibility than ever before for creating precisely the graphic you need.

In this chapter, I'll introduce what you need to know before you create your presentation graphics—from determining the best type of graphic for your information to graphic formatting considerations by document type. Then, we'll take a dive into the new graphics engine with tips and best practices for creating the perfect business graphic every time.

Chapter Assumptions

This chapter assumes that you've created diagrams and worked with shapes in previous versions of PowerPoint, and that you've used diagrams or other graphics (from any source) in your Microsoft Word documents (or, you've at least thought about it). I also assume that you have enough experience creating diagrams or otherwise working with graphics in the Microsoft Office programs to appreciate the good news that the sad, old Diagram And Organization Chart tool is gone, whether or not you've ever been able to do a better job creating diagrams without it.

So, I won't take your time with basics here unless they're new or notable. Instead, we'll look at the underlying concepts that can help advanced users capitalize on the benefits of the new graphics engine. And, we'll explore best practices and techniques for creating truly professional business graphics with astonishingly little work.

In the introduction to this book, you can find a list of resources for those who want more basic-level information, in the section titled "Who Will Benefit Most from This Book."

What's New for Presentation Graphics in PowerPoint 2007?

Because of the new graphics engine in the 2007 release, it's fair to say that just about everything is new for PowerPoint presentation graphics. You still have AutoShapes, but they're just called shapes now and they're far more flexible. You still have WordArt, but it's available to text in any shape. And, you still have a diagramming tool, but it's like nothing you've seen before.

You can still use much of what you already know when working with graphics in PowerPoint—from shapes to connectors to the Align and Distribute tools. But there's something new in almost every feature you'll encounter, including the few I've just noted, so let's take a look at your options one at a time.

- The biggest news on the subject of business graphics, as introduced in Chapter 1, "Welcome to the 2007 Microsoft Office System," is surely the new SmartArt diagram tool. Completely unlike the tragic Diagram And Organization Chart tool that preceded it, SmartArt is powerful, flexible, and very easy to use (okay, well, that's mostly true).

  - SmartArt enables you to create absolutely beautiful diagrams with almost no effort, for any of dozens of available diagram layouts, from organization charts (such as the first organization chart you saw in this chapter) to process diagrams, relationship diagrams, and more.

  - The available formatting effects for these diagrams are simply terrific and provide a great range of options. And, when created in PowerPoint, you can even convert a bulleted list to a diagram in just one click.

  - Complications with SmartArt occur when you need to customize beyond the available SmartArt design, color, and layout styles. You'll most likely be able to get just what you need in almost all cases, but there are a few issues to note. Keep in mind that SmartArt is brand new functionality—there are still a few kinks in the system. I suggest that you think of SmartArt like a medical prescription for improving your diagrams. Can you live with a few side effects in order to get the cure?

  People accustomed to using the Align and Distribute tools may experience some temporary discomfort while adjusting to the alignment limitations of SmartArt. Side effects include the occasional accent shape that can't be deleted and unfriendly text resizing under certain circumstances. Most people who experience these symptoms are not bothered enough to stop using SmartArt.

  Puns aside, you're unlikely to encounter any complications serious enough to prevent you from using this impressive new tool—just don't expect it to be problem free under all conditions. Learn everything you need to know for successfully navigating the advantages and disadvantages of SmartArt in the section titled "Making Smart Choices with SmartArt" later in this chapter.

- Even though PowerPoint offers a handful of new shapes, you'll no longer need more shapes to choose from because you can turn any shape into anything you like. All shapes can now be converted to freeform drawings, after which you can edit individual points within the shape to get really creative or just to get precisely the shape you need. See the section of this chapter titled "Editing Shapes" to learn how to work with the new flexibility available to shapes.

  Note that, after being converted to a freeform drawing, a shape still maintains the properties of a built-in shape, including its internal text box and the ability to use the Change Shape feature to change it to another built-in shape. In fact, when you draw a new freeform shape, it now takes on the properties of built-in shapes that were not formerly available to freeform drawings (such as built-in text). The only downside to this new, expanded freeform drawing ability is that you can no longer constrain angles by holding the Shift key while drawing.

- If you never took WordArt seriously, you probably should have. What has always looked a bit like a feature that school children might use to create flyers for a bake sale, has actually been a deceptively effective tool for artistic text in professional diagrams and other business graphics (such as logos). In the past, WordArt essentially enabled you to insert a block of text that could be formatted like shapes by using features such as fill effects and the ability to change the shape of characters. Well, WordArt has changed.

  Instead of inserting a separate object, WordArt now provides a selection of formatting available to any PowerPoint text—from placeholders on slides to the text within a shape's text box. When you select text or a shape containing text, that text automatically is WordArt. From the Drawing Tools Format menu, you can apply WordArt fills, lines, or graphic effects, as well as a selection of Quick Styles. See the section titled "WordArt as a Powerful Design Tool" later in this chapter for more information.

- If you check out WordArt and are disappointed to find that the former character spacing feature is no longer available, just navigate over to the Home tab. Click the dialog launcher in the Font group for the enhanced Font dialog box, with long overdue new options (such as All Caps and Small Caps) and a new Character Spacing tab for the same expanded and condensed character spacing flexibility found in Microsoft Office Word 2007.

  If this dialog box looks familiar, remember that Excel charts are also part of the new graphics engine—so you might have already seen this new Font dialog box (along with several features of the new graphics engine) in Microsoft Office Excel 2007 when working with charts. For more on this topic, see Chapter 15, "Charts."

- As mentioned earlier, the available formatting effects that you see for SmartArt are just part of the new graphics engine, which encompasses a wide range of graphic types. High-quality, creative effects (such as reflections and 3-D rotation) are available to many types of objects, such as shapes and pictures. However, one of the most interesting changes among these new effects is the new approach to creating gradient fills for shapes.

  When you first look at the new gradient options, it may no longer seem possible to select the exact colors you want. But, look a bit closer and you'll find that it's not just possible, it's much more flexible. For the ins and outs of this new functionality, see the Troubleshooting tip in this chapter titled "How can I specify exactly the colors I want in a gradient?"

- The Selection And Visibility Pane (available from the Editing group on the Home tab or the Arrange group on the Drawing Tools Format tab) is another of my favorite new features, which you might also recognize from Office Excel 2007. (As mentioned in earlier chapters, keep in mind that Excel adopted much more of the new graphics engine functionality [most of which is PowerPoint-based] than did Office Word 2007.) The Selection And Visibility pane is one of those features

Chapter 18

you'll find in PowerPoint and Excel but not in Word. (Yet another reason to use PowerPoint to create the graphics you need in your Word documents.)

With the Selection And Visibility pane, you can easily select any object on the slide, even when you have several layers of shapes and objects in a graphic. You can also rename or even hide objects from this pane. See "Managing Shapes with the Selection And Visibility Pane" later in this chapter for more detail.

- It's worth noting that when you insert a line or a straight arrow from the Line options in the Shapes gallery, you now get a connector. Straight connectors have always been able to behave like lines when you're not hovering over a shape, so there's not much change here other than the naming.

  The only real issue with this is to note that the properties for what you know as Line and Arrow shapes have changed. For example, insert a line and then right-click. You won't see Edit Points among the options, but you will see the option to change connector type. If you happen to need a simple straight line for which you can enable Edit Points, just use the Freeform tool to draw the line.

Determining the Best Diagram for Your Content

In Chapter 17, "The Excel-Visio Connection," I introduced several new tools for dynamic, data-based diagrams. In this chapter, I'm talking about the new graphics capabilities in PowerPoint, including SmartArt diagrams and the new flexibility for shapes and WordArt. So, how do you know where to begin for the particular graphic you need?

When deciding how to create a new business graphic, you can determine the general graphic type you need and the best method to use for creating it by looking at the type of information as well as what you need to convey about that information.

- If your information is quantifiable data, it's likely that the best graphic is either an Excel chart or a dynamic Visio diagram. Ask yourself what you want to convey about your data. For example, to show impressive sales figures, you might want a line chart that displays changes in sales volume over time, or a column chart to compare sales across regions or against competitors. Or, you might want to use a PivotDiagram to enable recipients to look at the same sales figures broken out in multiple ways—such as by region, by product, or by quarter. See Chapters 15, 16 ("Powerful Reporting, Easier than You Think"), and 17 for help with Excel charts, PivotTables, and Visio PivotDiagrams, respectively.

- If your information is organizational or other hierarchical data for which you can use an organization chart, determine how much information needs to be included and what you need to do with that data.
  - If you have a reasonably limited amount of data (small enough to fit on one page), create a SmartArt organization chart in PowerPoint. Available formatting effects for SmartArt enable you to easily create a professional-looking

diagram. And, adding shapes, editing text, or changing hierarchy in a SmartArt organization chart is as easy as editing a bulleted list.

  ○ If you have an extensive amount of data that needs to be laid out across more than one page, if you need to use the same data in other programs, or even if the data is likely to change frequently, consider creating an organization chart from Excel data using the Visio Organization Chart Wizard. Visio can generate the shapes you need from a simple worksheet, break the chart across pages for you, and hyperlink between related shapes on pages. You can even change formatting throughout the diagram all at once (such as changing the formatting for all job titles shown in the chart) or export the data for use elsewhere. See Chapter 17 for more information on this topic.

● If your information is qualitative—such as laying out a timeline, defining relationships, or explaining a process—ask similar questions to those you ask when planning an organization chart.

  ○ If the information simply needs to be displayed in a high-quality, professional-looking diagram that coordinates with your document, use SmartArt.

  ○ If the information is highly technical, complex, or requires interactivity (such as hyperlinks between individual shapes in the diagram), consider using Visio.

  ○ If PowerPoint is more appropriate for your diagram type than Visio but SmartArt doesn't offer the diagram options you want, create your diagram using shapes. See the section of this chapter titled "Using Drawing Tools to Their Fullest" for help creating flawless business graphics using shapes and drawing tools in PowerPoint.

● If your information is a combination of qualitative and quantitative data, such as a workflow diagram in which you need to store cost and resource data or a floor plan in which you need to store data about equipment, use Visio to create your diagram and take advantage of the Shape Data and Data Graphics tools discussed in Chapter 17.

● If the business graphic you need isn't a diagram at all, such as when you need to create a logo or other branding elements, use shapes and drawing tools in PowerPoint.

If you think you need a vector graphics program or even a professional designer to create such a graphic, you might be right—but give PowerPoint a try before considering more complex or expensive alternatives. PowerPoint is a presentation graphics program, not graphic design software, but you may be able to take it quite a bit further than you think. Check out the section of this chapter titled "Using Drawing Tools to Their Fullest" to learn how to push the PowerPoint design envelope.

Making Smart Choices with SmartArt

SmartArt is nothing more than a tool for creating business diagrams. It just happens to create really beautiful diagrams, with extremely professional formatting effects, in almost no time—so it's probably worth a look.

In this section, we'll walk through creating, editing, and customizing SmartArt diagrams, and address common troubleshooting issues encountered when working with this new tool.

Creating a SmartArt Diagram

You have a few choices concerning where to start when using SmartArt diagrams.

- If you're creating a slide presentation, just click the SmartArt icon on any content layout (as you see in the following image) to add a diagram at the appropriate size. (See Chapter 19, "Slides and Presentations," to learn about what's new when working with slide layouts.)

- If you're creating a diagram for use in a Word document, Excel workbook, or other destination, start with a blank slide layout so that a layout placeholder doesn't control the size of your diagram. Then, on the Insert tab, click SmartArt.

> **Note**
>
> Of course, you can resize the content in a placeholder. The only issue with using a placeholder to create a diagram or other graphic for use in other programs is that, if you reset the slide layout, the placeholder will be resized automatically to fit the layout.

- If you already have a bulleted list on a PowerPoint slide—whether in a text placeholder or any custom text box—right-click in the text area and then point to Convert To SmartArt to see a gallery of options, as shown in the following image.

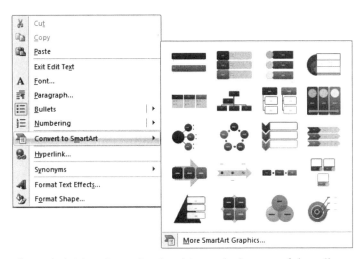

If you click More SmartArt Graphics at the bottom of the gallery, you get the same Choose A SmartArt Graphic dialog box (discussed under the next heading) that appears when you use either of the two preceding methods to create your diagram.

Selecting a Diagram Layout

The Choose A SmartArt Graphic dialog box is nicely organized, with tips to help you select the right layout, as you see in the image that follows.

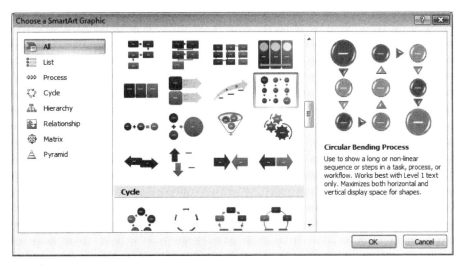

Similar to the way that Excel charts provide guidance on what type of data is best for the particular chart, SmartArt diagrams help you determine which diagram to use based on what you need to convey about the information in your diagram. The diagram types you see in the Choose A SmartArt Graphic dialog box are referred to as SmartArt

Chapter 18

layouts. They're considered layouts because they're largely interchangeable. That is, you can change the layout of an existing SmartArt diagram to any other layout that fits your content.

> **Note**
>
> There are dozens of SmartArt layouts. However, notice that some of the layouts in the Choose A SmartArt Graphic dialog box are repeated under more than one category.

In addition, as you see from the description of the selected diagram shown in the preceding image, several of the diagram types also provide direction about the amount and organization of text that's appropriate for the type of diagram and the best arrangement on the page for the particular diagram (that is, utilizing height or width).

One of the factors that makes SmartArt diagrams simple to use is that they think like multilevel bulleted lists, which you notice as soon as you begin to read the diagram descriptions. Some diagram types are intended for single-level lists only (note the mention of "Level 1 text only" in the sample diagram description shown earlier); others may accommodate more than one level of text but be better suited to a single-level, or they may be limited in the number of items they can have on a given level.

For example, as you saw at the beginning of the chapter, a three-level bulleted list converts to a three-level organization chart. To look at another example, think about a simple process. In bullet form, that process might look like the following list.

- Start process
- Process step 1
- Process step 2
- Process step 3
- Process step 4
- End process

To display this list as a diagram, you might select a Basic Chevron Process, as shown in the following image.

Or, you might choose a Basic Timeline, as you see in the next image.

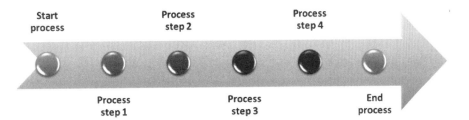

However, the layout named Vertical Chevron List (you can see the top of the diagram in the following image) doesn't work at all with a single-level list because most of the space in the shapes is reserved for lower-level bullets. In fact, the top level should have a much smaller amount of text to make it legible. A diagram of this sort would be far more effective, for example, with step numbers as the first level and a bulleted statement for the second level.

In the layout descriptions, it's also important to note that some layouts are limited as to how many levels (or how many total items) they're able to use in any configuration. For example, notice that the Upward Arrow layout can use only five Level 1 bullets, as stated in the description shown in the following image. You can, however, add a second level of bulleted text under the five items.

Upward Arrow

Use to show a progression or steps that trend upward in a task, process, or workflow. Each of the first five lines of Level 1 text corresponds to a point on the arrow. Works best with minimal text. Unused text does not appear, but remains available if you switch layouts.

Similarly, many of the radial diagram types can have just a single Level 1 bullet as the center of the radial and multiple Level 2 bullets beneath it that become the outer ring of circles, as explained in the following description.

Chapter 18

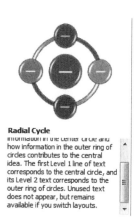

Radial Cycle

information in the center circle and how information in the outer ring of circles contributes to the central idea. The first Level 1 line of text corresponds to the central circle, and its Level 2 text corresponds to the outer ring of circles. Unused text does not appear, but remains available if you switch layouts.

Every SmartArt diagram has an attached text pane, as you see in the following image.

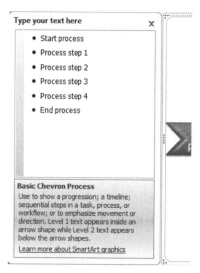

Type your text here X

- Start process
- Process step 1
- Process step 2
- Process step 3
- Process step 4
- End process

Basic Chevron Process

Use to show a progression; a timeline; sequential steps in a task, process, or workflow; or to emphasize movement or direction. Level 1 text appears inside an arrow shape while Level 2 text appears below the arrow shapes.

Learn more about SmartArt graphics

If you convert an existing list to a SmartArt diagram, your text will automatically appear in this list when you create the diagram. Otherwise, you can type the text in this list or in the shapes themselves, as you prefer.

If a red x appears in place of any bullet when adding a new bullet or changing bullet level, it means the layout you selected can't display that text. You might be able to change the level of the bullet to make it appear in the diagram (press TAB or SHIFT+TAB at the beginning of the paragraph to do this, just as in any multilevel list). Or, if changing the level is not appropriate for your content, select a different layout. Learn how to change SmartArt layouts under the next heading in this section. Also, learn about using the SmartArt text pane to do more than you might expect, under the heading "Editing SmartArt Diagram Content" later in this section.

Understanding and Using SmartArt Styles and Formatting

When you first create a SmartArt diagram, it may look a bit uninspired—plain shapes, solid fill, and no particular text formatting worth noting. It may perhaps look something like the following image.

However, using the two SmartArt Tools contextual tabs, you can progress from that simple diagram to the one that follows in just a few quick steps.

To go from the first to the second diagram in the preceding example, I selected just four options, as follows.

1. On the SmartArt Tools Design tab, I applied the SmartArt Styles gallery option named Polished.

2. While still on the SmartArt Tools Design tab, I applied the Change Colors setting named Colorful – Accent Colors.

3. On the SmartArt Tools Format tab, I applied the WordArt Styles gallery option named Fill, White, Warm Matte Bevel.

4. While still on the SmartArt Tools Format tab, I selected the four primary shapes and then applied the Shape Effects Reflection setting named Half Reflection, 4-Pt Offset.

Let's take a look at the two contextual tabs referred to in the preceding steps to discover what you can accomplish with them.

> **Note**
> When working with any of the Quick Styles or other formatting galleries on the two tabs discussed in this section, remember that Live Preview functionality is available. So, you can point to options in a gallery to see how each will look on your diagram. Then, just click to apply the one you like.

The SmartArt Tools Design tab that you see here contains three formatting galleries as well as a handful of tools for working with the diagram content.

- The SmartArt Styles gallery offers several Quick Styles, each of which applies a set of formatting effects to the entire diagram, such as Bevel and 3-D Rotation settings.

- The Change Colors option in the SmartArt Styles group provides another gallery, presenting color options for recoloring your entire diagram at once.

> **Note**
>
> Notice that both galleries in the SmartArt Styles group change to reflect your active Theme colors, active Theme effects, and active diagram layout.

- The Layouts group enables you to change the layout for an existing SmartArt diagram. The layouts from the same category as your active SmartArt layout appear in the Layouts gallery. You can also click More Layouts at the bottom of the gallery to access the dialog box from which you can select any SmartArt layout.

- The Create Graphic group contains the Right To Left tool, which you can click to change the direction of the diagram flow. In the case of the four-step Basic Process diagram shown earlier in this section, clicking Right To Left would put step one on the right, step four on the left, and would turn the arrows in the opposite direction. Layouts behave differently with this tool based on their content and organization. For example, an organization chart may change the order of subordinates that appear on the same level.

  Other than the Right To Left tool, most options in the Create Graphic group simply provide an additional method for accessing features available from the text pane or the diagram itself, as discussed under the "Editing SmartArt Diagram Content" heading in this section.

The SmartArt Tools Format tab contains most of the same formatting galleries and options that you'll see on the Drawing Tools Format tab, discussed later in this chapter, along with a selection of tools for editing individual shapes in your diagram.

- The Size and Arrange groups that are condensed in the preceding image contain the same size and arrange options that you're probably familiar with from working with other object types, such as pictures. All of the options available in the Arrange group are shown in the following graphic.

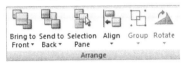

The Size group contains only height and width options. Note that proportions are not constrained by default when sizing SmartArt diagrams, so a change to either the height or width setting will not automatically cause a change in the other dimension. Also note that the Size group only sizes the entire diagram and not individual shapes within the diagram.

- The WordArt Styles group provides fill, line, and effects for formatting text within SmartArt diagram shapes, as well as a gallery of Quick Styles. You can select the entire diagram to apply formatting to all text at once, or select just specific shapes or even text within a specific shape.

> **Note**
>
> In the WordArt Styles gallery, which applies several formatting effects at once (as most Quick Styles do), note that some Quick Styles are specified as available to apply to selected text or only available to apply to all text in selected shapes. This distinction works as advertised in shapes that are not part of a SmartArt diagram. But, when working in SmartArt diagrams, this differentiation is irrelevant—any styles in the WordArt Styles gallery can be applied to as little as a single character in any SmartArt diagram shape.
>
> Also note that the Format Text Effects dialog box, available from the dialog launcher in the WordArt Styles group, will only open if one or more shapes are selected.

Get the scoop on working with the new WordArt styles later in this chapter, in the section titled "WordArt as a Powerful Design Tool."

- Similar to WordArt styles, the Shape Styles group offers fill, line, and graphic effects formatting, as well as a selection of Quick Styles. The options in this group format selected shapes in your diagram, and do not affect diagram text.

Chapter 18

Note that, if you select the diagram rather than the shapes within the diagram, the gallery of Shape Quick Styles are unavailable. However, Shape Fill, Shape Outline, and Shape Effects settings are available to be applied to the diagram area itself. Shapes within the diagram are not affected when you format the diagram area in this way—just as a chart data series is unaffected when you apply formatting to the chart area.

- In the Shapes group, you see the familiar Change Shape options that work precisely as they do for shapes that are not part of a diagram. That is, you can change the shapes within your diagram to other built-in shapes.

The Larger and Smaller options in this group proportionally change the size of selected shapes, just as if you were to drag the corner handles of selected shapes. Notice that, whether you use these buttons or drag to resize, other shapes in the diagram also resize proportionally to accommodate the size change of your selected shapes. For example, if you want the last shape in a process diagram to stand out as larger than the rest, increase the size of the last shape; all other shapes will become proportionally smaller to accommodate the larger shape without changing the diagram area.

The last option in this group, Edit In 2-D, is only available when your diagram contains 3-D Rotation settings. Edit In 2-D temporarily removes the appearance of 3-D rotation so that you can easily access shapes for editing (as well as the text within those shapes) without having to remove and reapply the 3-D Rotation setting. When you've finished editing, just click Edit In 2-D again to turn off this feature, and your 3-D Rotation settings (as well as any other formatting removed by the Edit In 2-D feature) are returned.

Note that Edit In 2-D is not available if only a bevel is applied to your graphic rather than a 3-D Rotation setting. The purpose of Edit In 2-D is not to remove any 3-D effects, but to flatten objects that are more difficult to edit while rotated.

Note

Notice the Reset Graphic option at the far right of the SmartArt Tools Design tab. When you experiment with the range of formatting available on both of the SmartArt Tools contextual tabs, and you don't like the result, click Reset Graphic to reset the diagram to the default settings and reapply the formatting you want. This can be a nice timesaver, particularly since it can be difficult to keep track of which settings are part of a Quick Style and which you've applied independently.

If you need to undo undesirable formatting for only specific shapes, however, don't cause yourself extra work by resetting the entire diagram. Just right-click the shapes in question and then click Reset Shape.

TROUBLESHOOTING

How can I custom-align content in a SmartArt diagram without Align tools?

As mentioned earlier in this chapter, the Align tools (including the Distribute options) are unavailable in SmartArt diagrams.

This isn't usually an issue, because SmartArt is smart enough to adjust the layout automatically for you as you add, remove, or change shapes. However, when you need to custom-align shapes in a diagram, the solution is one of the best reasons to create your SmartArt diagrams in PowerPoint regardless of where the diagram will end up. That is, use drawing guides.

To access the guides, right-click an empty area of the slide and then click Grid And Guides. Or, on the SmartArt Tools Format tab, in the Arrange group, click Arrange, click Align, and then click Grid Settings. (You can also access Grid Settings from the Align settings in the Arrange options available from the Drawing group on the Home tab.) In the Grid Settings dialog box, click Display Drawing Guides On Screen and then click OK.

You won't be able to select the part of the guides that fall within the SmartArt diagram area. However, remember that guides always cover the entire screen, so you can easily select and manage the guides from outside the diagram area. For help getting precise measurements with the guides or duplicating the guides, see "Using Drawing Guides" later in this chapter.

So, when might this come in handy in a SmartArt graphic? Take the following image as an example. I'm using the Basic Process diagram layout that places all shapes in a single row. When I move the shapes at an angle, the connector arrows change angles automatically. As you see in this example, I can use drawing guides to ensure that the spacing between my shapes is equal. Doing this also causes the connector arrows in this example to automatically adjust their size and position.

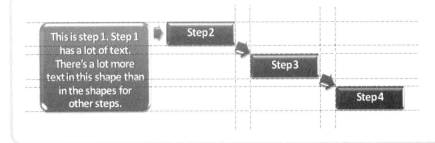

Editing SmartArt Diagram Content

My favorite thing about working with SmartArt diagrams is that the text pane and the diagram shapes are largely interchangeable for many tasks, as follows.

- Add and edit text in either the text pane or the shape itself.

- Apply text and shape formatting to selected shapes or text by selecting content in the text pane or selecting shapes.

- Add or remove shapes by taking actions in either the text pane or in the graphic itself.

Let's examine the options a bit more closely.

- By default, when you create any SmartArt diagram, the text pane automatically appears. To close the text pane at any time, click the X in the top-right corner of the pane. To open the pane when you don't see it, click the opposing arrows icon shown here, which appears on the left edge of the diagram frame.

Note that you can also drag the text pane (by its title bar) to any convenient place on the screen. To reattach the pane to the diagram frame, simply close it and then reopen it using the icon in the preceding image.

- Remember that the diagram is a visual representation of the outline in the text pane. So, to add a new shape to the diagram using the text pane, simply add a new bullet where you want that shape to appear. To do that, press ENTER from the end of the preceding paragraph, just as you would to add a bullet in any outline list.

Depending on the level of the bullets in question and the active diagram layout, keep in mind that adding a bullet might add a new shape or it might add another paragraph in the active shape.

For diagram layouts that use multiple outline levels, promote or demote bullets in the text pane to change either the shape type associated with the bullet or to change the level of the text as it appears in a shape. Take a look at the examples that follow.

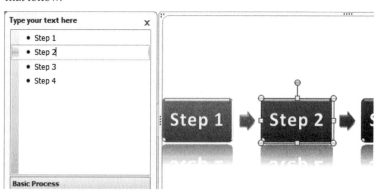

○ My insertion point in the preceding diagram is at the end of the Step 2 bullet in the text pane.

○ Because my insertion point is in the Step 2 bullet, the shape associated with that bullet is automatically selected.

○ If I press ENTER with my insertion point at its current location in the text pane, I'll add a new primary shape to the diagram, as you see here.

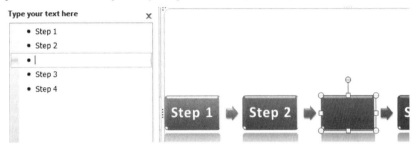

○ If, however, I press the TAB key at the start of this new bulleted paragraph to demote the bullet one level, the new shape goes away, and I add a lower-level bulleted paragraph inside my Step 2 shape, as you see in the following image.

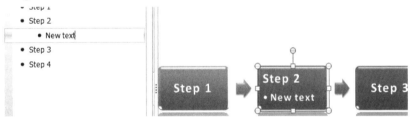

○ If I was using a different layout—such as the Hierarchy List diagram shown in the following image—that new second-level bullet would receive its own shape.

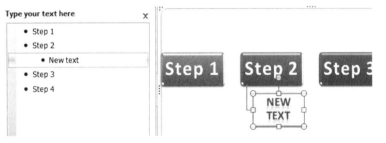

So, by using ENTER, TAB, and SHIFT+TAB to add and change the levels of bullets within your outline, you add or change the levels of shapes (or their text) in the corresponding diagram. Similarly, you can delete a bullet from the text pane to delete the associated shape or shape content from the diagram.

Chapter 18

- Notice that, as you add text to a diagram, the size of all text in the diagram adjusts to accommodate the smallest font size needed in the diagram.

TROUBLESHOOTING

The text reduces throughout my SmartArt diagram shapes when I resize one shape

It's usually helpful that your text resizes equally throughout your diagram as needed for your content, but that can sometimes get out of hand when you have one shape with too much text, want a single shape with smaller text, or reduce the size of a shape that contains a great deal of text. You might recognize this behavior as similar to the fortunately defunct Auto Scale feature for text in earlier versions of Excel charts. When the size of the diagram or its content changes, font size adjusts automatically.

When your text disappears into oblivion, don't worry. You can resize the font size for particular shapes simply by selecting those shapes and changing the font size manually. Change font size of selected shapes from either the Font group on the Home tab or by pressing CTRL+SHIFT+< or > to decrease or increase font size, respectively.

However, note that there are some potential complications with manually resizing the font for just specific shapes. Depending on the diagram layout you're using and on which shape you select, the text in other shapes within the same diagram may adjust automatically based on your changes. For example, resizing the text in the first shape of the Simple Process layout resizes the text in all subsequent shapes.

So, what do you do if you don't want font size to change automatically at all in your diagram? First, check the font size after you first create the diagram. Then, select the diagram frame (which means that all content inside the diagram will be affected) and manually apply the active font size on the Home tab. (For example, if the font size is set to 16, just click in the Font Size box on the Home tab, type **16**, and then press ENTER.) The appearance of the diagram won't change, but the Auto Scale functionality for text will be disabled. However, avoid doing this for the entire diagram at once in diagrams with more than one level, because it's common for different levels to use different text sizes. Also avoid doing this in diagrams where you plan to use the automatic layout, because automatic font resizing can help the diagram look consistent, which keeps it looking professional.

If you set font size manually and later want it to adjust automatically, you can either use Reset Graphic (on the SmartArt Tools Design tab) or Reset Shape (available on the shortcut menu when you right-click a shape). Keep in mind, however, that these options reset all formatting defaults for your selection. So, you might lose other formatting customizations as well.

- If you prefer to edit shapes directly, just click in a shape to add or edit text. Or, right-click a shape for the option to add a new shape before or after the selected shape (or above or below the selected shape in applicable diagram types).

> **Note**
>
> The Add Shape option, available when you right-click a shape or from the Create Graphic group on the SmartArt Tools Design tab, is the only way to add an Assistant shape in an organization chart diagram. An Assistant is the only shape in an organization chart that you can't add by demoting or promoting bullets in the text pane.

Note that, if demoting or promoting a bullet in the text pane will create a new shape, you can't demote or promote that same text directly in the shape where it currently exists. This is one of the reasons why editing the diagram directly in the text pane is easier, because when you do, the text moves into a new shape or a lower level within the same shape automatically, as appropriate for the layout.

- Notice that, because shapes are automatically selected when you select the corresponding bullet in the text pane, you can select text in the text pane to format the associated shape or text. Just click in a bullet to select the associated shape, and you can then apply any shape formatting that you would when selecting the shape itself. Or, select any text in the text pane to apply font or WordArt formatting.

  Note, however, that all formatting applied will be reflected in the diagram itself—the appearance of the text in the text pane is not affected.

It's also worth noting that you can copy any shape out of a SmartArt diagram and paste it onto a slide, where it will behave like any built-in shape.

TROUBLESHOOTING

I can't delete shapes in a SmartArt diagram

You can select and move any shape in a SmartArt diagram. However, accent shapes (such as connector arrows between the shapes that contain text) can't be deleted. You also don't have access to the Order commands when working in SmartArt diagrams, so you can't send a shape behind another to hide it. Additionally, the new Selection And Visibility pane recognizes a SmartArt diagram as a single object, so you can't use it to hide individual shapes in the diagram.

Okay, so what can you do? It's old fashioned and a bit of a hack, but it works—select the shapes you don't want to appear in the diagram and then, on the SmartArt Tools Format tab, in the Shape Styles group, change the Shape Fill and Shape Outline settings to None.

When you do this, however, remember that the shapes are still there. So, if you select the entire diagram to make changes or reset the graphic, those shapes might once again appear. Also, check the results when printing documents containing a graphic with shapes hidden in this way because some older printers may cause the shapes to appear on the page.

Using Drawing Tools to Their Fullest

I have long been a believer that the drawing tools in PowerPoint are very much under-valued. No, PowerPoint isn't a graphic design program. But, as mentioned earlier, when it comes to creating business graphics, this program can probably do quite a bit more for you than you think.

That statement is surely true today—consider the greatly improved graphic effects of the new graphics engine and the ability to convert shapes to freeform tools—but it applies equally as well to some longtime friends, from the Arrange tools, to Edit Points, to the ability to ungroup and customize Clip Art (yes, I said Clip Art).

In this section and the "Editing Shapes" section that follows, learn how to get creative with the drawing tools in PowerPoint and use some fairly simple tools to take your business graphics to a new level.

"Perfect" Is Easier than "Close Enough"

The less work you do, the better your results will be. That's my favorite theme for creating documents across the Microsoft Office programs, and nowhere is it more true than when creating business graphics in PowerPoint. In fact, so many easy ways are available to create graphics precisely that you have to work pretty hard to overcomplicate things. However, that's exactly what most people do.

I've seen this phenomenon in every PowerPoint class I've ever taught. For some reason, one of the hardest things for people to accept about a software program is that it's *not* hard. When you let PowerPoint be as easy as it can be, you might just impress yourself with what you can do.

Let's start by inserting a shape on a slide, and then we'll take a look at a few essential shortcuts. Because we're working with drawing objects and not creating a slide pre-sentation, start with a blank slide layout so that no placeholders get in the way. Simply right-click the slide, point to Layout, and then click Blank. (You can also find the Lay-out options in the Slides group on the Home tab or by right-clicking a slide thumbnail in the Slides pane.)

- You can insert shapes from the Shapes gallery available in the Drawing group on the Home tab, the Illustrations group on the Insert tab, or (when a drawing object is selected) from the Insert Shape group on the Drawing Tools Format tab.

- As always, after you click in the gallery to select the shape you want, you can either click on the slide to insert the shape at its default size, or you can drag to insert the shape at the size you need. If you choose to just click, note that this op-tion is highly sensitive in the 2007 release. If you drag even slightly when clicking to insert a shape, you'll get a very tiny version of that shape. Of course, if this hap-pens, you can just drag a corner handle to resize the shape as needed.

- Need to create multiple instances of the same type of shape? Right-click a shape in the Shapes gallery and then click Lock Drawing Mode. You can then insert the same shape multiple times, in different sizes or configurations as needed. Press ESC to turn off drawing mode.

CAUTION

Don't use Lock Drawing Mode when you need several identical shapes. In such cases, you'll do less work for better results if you insert and format one shape and then duplicate it to create the others.

Regardless of whether you prefer to work with the mouse or the keyboard, certain keystrokes are very important when working with shapes and objects. Let's take a look at what using the SHIFT, ALT, and CTRL keys can do for you when moving, resizing, and duplicating objects.

Key	Actions
SHIFT	• When dragging an object's corner handle to resize it, the SHIFT key constrains proportions. • When dragging an object to move it, the SHIFT key constrains angles so that the object stays on the same vertical or horizontal plane.
ALT	• When dragging any handle to resize an object, the ALT key enables you to resize in smaller increments than the grid. (By default, the grid is set to 0.083 inches [0.212 centimeters]. The ALT key enables you to move 0.01 inches [0.025 centimeters] at a time.) • When dragging an object to move it, the ALT key enables you to move in smaller increments than the grid.
CTRL	• When dragging any handle to resize an object, the CTRL key causes the object to resize from its center. • When dragging an object to move it, the CTRL key causes the object to be duplicated rather than moved. • When using the arrow keys on your keyboard to move an object, the CTRL key enables you to move objects in smaller increments than the grid (the same result as when you use the ALT key while dragging to move an object).
Key combinations	• Use ALT with either SHIFT or CTRL while dragging to resize an object in smaller increments than the grid while either constraining proportions or resizing from the center, respectively. • Use SHIFT and CTRL together while dragging a corner handle to resize an object proportionally from the center. (Add ALT as well to resize in smaller increments.) • Use SHIFT and CTRL together while dragging an object to duplicate it and keep the new object on the same vertical or horizontal plane as the original. (Add ALT as well to move the new object in smaller increments as you're dragging to create it.)

Chapter 18

Want to stick strictly with the keyboard for duplicating objects? Simply select the object and then press CTRL+D, but don't stop there. If you need to duplicate the object several times (such as to create a grid of shapes), don't touch the mouse after you duplicate the object. Instead, use the arrow keys to move the new object to the exact position you want. Then, press CTRL+D again—PowerPoint will remember the distance between the first two shapes and create the third at the exact same distance from the second.

How about sticking strictly to the mouse for duplicating objects? No problem. Right-drag an object (that is, hold the right mouse button while dragging), then release where you want the duplicated object to appear. When you release the right mouse button, you get the options to Move Here, Copy Here, or Cancel. Just click the option you need to complete the action.

> **Note**
>
> Terrific as CTRL+Z is to undo unwanted actions, the ESC key can help you avoid the need to undo when using the mouse to perform many actions in PowerPoint. Simply press ESC before releasing the mouse button to cancel resizing, moving, or duplicating of objects.

Knowing the standard shortcuts is a good first step in creating more precise graphics. But, hand in hand with the shortcuts, the most important tools you have for working precisely in PowerPoint are logic and organization. Take a moment before creating shapes to think through the steps that will require the least amount of work.

For example, say that you want to use shapes to create a diagram. Several shapes in the diagram will be the same type and size and use most of the same font formatting. How can you do the least work for the best result? Try the following steps.

1. Create and size the first shape, and then add the necessary text to that shape based on whatever shape will contain the *most* text. Using this technique allows you to apply font formatting that will work for all duplicated shapes without needing to resize text.

2. Apply all formatting to that first shape that will be identical in the duplicated shapes. Even if the new shapes will use different colors or have other formatting differences, save time by applying your fill, borders, and graphic effects before duplicating anything. For example, if you want different colored gradient fills, setting up the gradient in the first shape still saves you time because you can retain the type and direction of the gradient in subsequent shapes and merely change the color.

3. Duplicate the shapes. If your finished graphic needs to be constrained to a certain height or width, duplicate the shapes across or down to create the most shapes needed in a single row or column. Space the shapes and be sure that they fit before doing any further duplication or formatting, in case you need to resize them.

4. If you need to resize the objects, select them all and then use either the Size group on the Drawing Tools Format tab or drag a handle on one of the shapes in the selection.

> **Note**
>
> If you group the shapes before dragging to resize them, PowerPoint will maintain the same amount of space between shapes while resizing.

5. Before making any formatting changes to the shapes in a diagram, consider which shapes may need the same formatting and always select all applicable shapes to act on them at the same time.

As you can see in the preceding steps, by using your own powers of planning and organization, along with the simple timesaving tools provided by PowerPoint, perfect can indeed be much easier than "close enough."

Managing Shapes with the Selection And Visibility Pane

As mentioned earlier in "What's New for Presentation Graphics in PowerPoint 2007," the Selection And Visibility pane enables you to select an object on the slide, hide the object without deleting it from the slide, and rename an object. If that doesn't sound particularly important to you, look at an example of how it can simplify your work.

The larger of the two concentric boxes shown here is in front of the smaller one, so that the semitransparent gradient can partially mask the smaller shape.

Your only problem is that you need to change the shape or formatting of the smaller shape. How do you select it? If you have the space on the slide, you can drag around the smaller box, creating a selection area often called a marquee. When you release the mouse button, all objects fully contained within that marquee are selected. But, what if the slide is too crowded to give you a clear place from which to drag, or what if the shapes are grouped (as they are in this case)?

If you're a keyboard fan, you can select the group and the press TAB to cycle through selecting different shapes within the group. Note that pressing TAB will cycle through shapes included in the group first, and then will continue to select other shapes on the slide, one at a time.

Alternatively, on the Home tab, in the Editing group, click Select and then click Selection Pane. This opens the Selection And Visibility pane, where every shape and object is listed individually. As you see in the image that follows, just click the shape name to select it—despite the fact that the shape is behind another and they're grouped. (You can apply formatting or even add or edit text in individual shapes while they're grouped.)

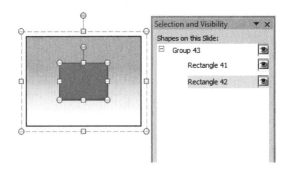

So, what if there are dozens of objects on the slide—how do you know which one you need? It takes just a minute to click through them. And, if your objects are grouped, notice that the group appears as an option at the top of the list of individual items, so you can narrow the field more quickly by clicking group names first to see which group fits your shape. But, once you find the shape you need, you can also rename it in the pane so that you can find it again more easily later. Simply click the shape name again after selecting it to access the text box for that shape name (just as you might do to edit a file name in a Windows Explorer). Then, replace the existing name with the shape name you want and press ENTER.

> **Note**
>
> Those of you who use Visual Basic for Applications (VBA) will be pleased to see this simple new access point for renaming objects on a slide. Keep in mind that the names you give to shapes or other objects here can also be used in your VBA macros. If you don't yet use VBA but would like to learn, don't forget to check Chapter 21 of this book, "VBA Primer."

Finally, the Selection And Visibility pane offers the ability to hide any object without deleting it. While designing diagrams or other slide content, this can be a handy tool to temporarily hide elements as you decide what you want for your final graphic. It can also be useful when working with stock content that you frequently reuse, to hide certain elements on a slide during a specific presentation.

CAUTION!

If you use the Selection And Visibility pane to hide slide content, remember that the content remains in the presentation and anyone who opens the presentation can easily unhide that content. Because this is one of the features that the Document Inspector searches for, it's a good idea to run the Document Inspector before sharing a PowerPoint file if there's a possibility that slide content has been hidden. Learn about the Document Inspector and other options for managing hidden document content in Chapter 2, "Understanding Electronic Documents."

Formatting Shapes Effectively

In Chapter 12, "Planning Your Documents," I referenced one of my favorite quotes when talking about designing document content. When it comes to formatting graphics for your documents, that quote warrants another mention.

> *"Dress sharply and they notice the dress. Dress impeccably and they notice the woman."*
>
> *—Coco Chanel*

Woman, man, or document, the same holds true. You have a far wider range of formatting effects available to your PowerPoint graphics in the 2007 release, and some of them are absolutely beautiful and extremely professional. But, use them wisely. Throwing every effect and the kitchen sink onto your shapes isn't going to help your information make an impact. Remember that the purpose of a business graphic is to get your important content noticed— nobody will give you their business simply because you know how to use gradients, shadows, and bevels.

That said, what type of formatting can you do with shapes in the 2007 release? Let's take a look.

For this topic, we'll focus on the Shape Styles group of the Drawing Tools Format tab. Notice that all of the features in this group are also available in the Drawing Group on the Home tab for easy access, as you see in the next image.

Chapter 18

When you use Shape Fill or Shape Outline options, remember that you must select a color from the Theme Colors portion of the palette (as discussed in the Themes sections of Chapter 5, "Styles") for the colors you apply to swap automatically if the applied Theme changes. The color you apply from the Theme Colors palette (shown in the Shape Fill options in the following image) is recorded by PowerPoint as the selected palette position rather than a particular color. So, if you change the active Theme or Theme Colors for the document, the color you apply will change automatically to whatever color is at that same palette position for the new Theme.

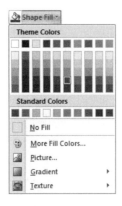

If you need a custom color that's not in your Theme (and you don't need it to be Theme-ready), click More Colors from the Shape Fill (or Shape Outline) options to type in any RGB or HSL color value. Also notice that fill effects have been moved to the Shape Fill options, including Picture, Gradient, and Texture fills. Gradient options have changed to provide more flexibility in the gradient style. See the Troubleshooting tip later in this section titled "How can I specify the exact colors I want in a gradient?" for help using this newly refined feature.

> **Note**
>
> If you have difficulty formatting the picture in a picture fill (such as when you need to lock the aspect ratio of a picture used as a fill), consider using the new Picture Shape feature available from the Picture Tools Format tab, in place of using a picture fill with your shape. As mentioned in Chapter 7, "Managing Graphics," you can now apply any shape to a picture. To do this, insert the picture and format as needed. Then, on the Picture Tools Format tab, in the Picture Styles group, click Picture Shape and then click to apply the shape you need. The shape is applied to fit the proportions of the selected picture.

You'll also notice that line weight, line style, and arrowhead options are now available from Shape Outline options. The Gradient and Texture options under Shape Fill and the Weight, Dashes, and Arrows options under Shape Outline each provides a gallery of preset choices, as well as a More <Feature> option that opens the appropriate tab of the Format Shape dialog box, where you can customize the formatting you need.

CAUTION !

Watch out for unexpected results in the new Gradient gallery available under Fill options. If you apply a gradient from either the gallery options or a custom gradient and then go back to the Gradient gallery and select No Gradient, the secondary color used to create the gradient is retained and not your original color. Instead, to remove a gradient and reset the shape to its original solid color fill, in the Format Shape dialog box, on the Fill tab, click Solid Fill. To access this dialog box, click either the dialog launcher in the Drawing group on the Home tab or the Shape Styles group on the Drawing Tools Format tab, or right-click the shape and then click Format Shape.

One other point worth noting about the Shape Fill and Shape Outline options is that, to the left of the Shape Fill or Shape Outline label, you'll find an icon that shows the most recently applied color. Click the icon to quickly apply that color to your selection.

Most of the new formatting options are available under Shape Effects, as you see here.

The Preset options are Quick Styles that combine a selection of formatting effects to give you an idea of the combinations you can create. For example, using the Preset gallery options, you can go from the plain teardrop shape shown on the left in the following image to either of the other versions in just one click. Not bad.

Chapter 18

(The middle shape uses Preset 11 and combines a shadow, bevel, and 3-D rotation. The shape on the right uses Preset 10. It adds an outline as well as a shadow, bevel, and 3-D rotation.)

Looking at the other Shape Effects options, note that Reflection and Soft Edges both offer preset gallery options only and don't have the ability to further customize your own settings. However, both of these effect types are extremely well done and worth checking out, and the presets offer a good range of choices. The Shadow gallery provides similar preset options to shadows found in earlier versions. However, when you click the option at the bottom of the gallery to customize your own shadow, the dialog box offers quite a bit more flexibility, as you can see in the image that follows.

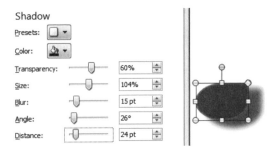

Don't be thrown by the additional options for these and other formatting settings. They don't need to complicate matters—they simply provide you with more options for getting the result you want. My suggestion with Shadow settings is to apply a preset that's close to what you want and then use the Shadow settings in the Format Shape dialog box to tweak the shadow until you see precisely what you want.

One of the nicest things about the formatting dialog boxes, such as the Format Shape dialog box shown here (or the Format <Element> dialog boxes available for Excel charts), is that much of the formatting you apply updates as you apply it, while the dialog box is still open. For example, you can adjust the sliders in the Shadow settings and watch the effect they have on your shape as you change them. It's a good way to become comfortable with the capabilities of those options.

The only downside to the new Format <Item> dialog boxes is that you must use CTRL+Z in place of the missing Cancel button to undo the last action if you apply formatting that you don't like. That is, there's no way to cancel your action in those dialog boxes. On another positive note, however, notice that the Format <Item> dialog boxes are modeless, meaning that you can click between the document and the dialog box without closing the dialog box. So, when you've finished formatting one shape, just click onto the slide and select other shapes to format without closing and reopening the dialog box.

INSIDE OUT   Save time applying the same formatting to additional shapes

One of my all-time favorite keyboard shortcuts—F4 to repeat your last action—works while the Format Shape dialog box is open. So, you can apply a setting and then, if another object outside of your selection needs that same formatting, you can just select it and press F4 without closing the dialog box. F4 used in this context will apply the set of formatting that you last applied. For example, if you set up a custom shadow (changing Transparency, Size, Blur, Angle, and Distance settings) and then select another shape and press F4, the full set of shadow settings is applied to the selected shape.

Additionally, because it can be a challenge to stay on top of each formatting effect applied to a given shape (particularly when you use Quick Style formatting to apply several settings at once), note that you don't need to spend time trying to recreate the same formatting for additional shapes. Use the Format Painter keyboard shortcuts to copy and paste formatting between shapes, text, or objects in PowerPoint just as you do between pieces of text in Word.

To do this, select the shape containing the formatting you want to copy and then press CTRL+SHIFT+C. Then, select the shapes to which you want to apply the same formatting and press CTRL+SHIFT+V. Just as in Word, these shortcuts act as a formatting clipboard. So, once you copy formatting on any PowerPoint slide, it's available to paste on any slide, in any presentation, until you copy another set of formatting or exit PowerPoint. Note, however, that the Format Painter keyboard shortcuts create separate formatting clipboards in PowerPoint and Word (and are not available in Excel)—you can't copy formatting from one program and paste it in the other.

Mouse users may also want to note that these keyboard shortcuts in PowerPoint are the equivalent of the Pick Up Style and Apply Style commands you may know from early versions of PowerPoint. Though Pick Up Style and Apply Style are not available on the Ribbon, you can add them to your Quick Access Toolbar through the Customize tab of the PowerPoint Options dialog box.

The last item in the Shape Styles group is the Shape Styles gallery of Quick Styles (referred to as Quick Styles in the Drawing group on the Home tab). These styles are fairly simple and straightforward sets of Theme-ready formatting, including fill, outline, shadows, and bevels.

When you use Quick Styles to format shapes, remember that you can use them in conjunction with other formatting. For example, apply a Quick Style that provides the color, gradient, and bevel you want, and then separately add a reflection. Just make sure that the formatting you select complements and emphasizes the content in your diagram. Avoid effects that obscure your content (such as 3-D Rotation that puts text at an extreme angle), and avoid using different combinations of complex effects in the same graphic, so that you don't overwhelm the reader with formatting. For example, if you use a reflection effect, use the same reflection setting for any shapes in the graphic that use that effect. The same best practice goes for gradients or other complex effects. Remember that you can use even complex effects consistently, such as applying the same custom gradient settings to shapes that have different color fills (simply apply a different color to the gradient stops while leaving the gradient type and stop settings the same). To learn how to work with the new gradient functionality, see the Troubleshooting tip that follows.

TROUBLESHOOTING

How can I specify the exact colors I want in a gradient?

So, the preset gradient options available under Shape Fill or Text Fill don't knock your socks off. But, you open the Format Shape or Format Text Effects dialog box to set your own custom gradient, and a color you don't want at all becomes the second color in your gradient (the Accent 1 Theme Color, by default).

Do you need to change your Theme Colors just to accommodate the secondary color in a gradient fill? Not at all. The new custom gradient options offer much more flexibility than you used to have with gradients, and they're easy to use. The only trouble is that there's nothing in that dialog box to help you understand how easy they are to use. So, let's do that here. To begin, select a shape and then open the Format Shape dialog box to the Fill tab. Click Gradient Fill, and your dialog box will look something like this.

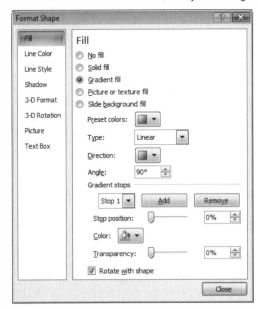

Ignore the Preset options for now. They're a bit garish for the most part, but you never know when a rainbow or a television test pattern can come in handy. The Type and Direction options work together to provide the options you're familiar with from previous versions (select a Type and then check out the available Direction options). When you select Linear as the type, you also get the Angle option that enables you to set the exact angle at which you want the light to hit your shape. (Remember that the settings will update in your shape as you apply them, so you can try out several and watch the results with the dialog box open.)

The key to setting a custom gradient is found under the heading Gradient Stops. The stops are the point at which the color changes in the gradient. When you select a new color (or shade of your color) for a stop, PowerPoint applies the graduated change between the colors to create the gradient effect. A gradient has three stops by default, but you can add stops for as many as 10 in total or remove stops for a minimum of two. For each stop, select the color you want and the Stop Position. The position is the percentage of the shape covered by that color. If you think of this in terms of the default, linear gradient, the stop is the distance from the left edge of the shape covered by that color. Notice that stops are cumulative, so if the first stop is at 33 percent and the second is at 66 percent, each of the first two stops cover 33 percent of the shape.

To create a typical gradient with the color of your choice, simply select progressively lighter or darker variations of your color for each stop. The Theme Colors palette makes this easy, providing several shades of each Theme Color. If you need a custom color or custom shade of your color, just click More Colors from the Color options and use the slider on the Custom tab of the Colors dialog box to select your shade.

Note that while using Transparency under Gradient Stops to lighten colors might seem like it accomplishes the same thing as choosing lighter shades, it doesn't really do so. It actually makes the gradient semitransparent. Also note that whatever gradient you set remains the gradient setting until you select a new seetting or exit PowerPoint. This is a nice touch because it enables you to quickly apply the same gradient setting to multiple shapes, even in multiple presentations, without having to remember your settings.

Thanks go to PowerPoint MVP Echo Swinford (http://echosvoice.com) for insight into this topic.

Using the Size And Position Options

To size any object quickly, you can use the Size group on the contextual Format tab for the selected object type. However, to scale (that is, to size as a percent of the original), change the setting to constrain proportions, crop pictures, position an object on the slide (from the top and left edges), or add alternative text when creating Web pages, use the Size And Position dialog box.

This dialog box is available from the dialog launcher in the Size group, except on the SmartArt Tools Format tab. However, as with most object types, you'll find Size And Position on the shortcut menu when you right-click the frame of a SmartArt diagram.

With SmartArt diagrams, you can only use the Size group or the Size And Position dialog box to resize the entire diagram. When you use the Size And Position dialog box with SmartArt diagrams, only size, scale, position, and alternate text options are available.

As in previous versions, PowerPoint doesn't constrain proportions when you change the height or width of any Office Art object other than Clip Art (that is, for SmartArt diagrams, shapes, and WordArt), but does constrain proportions by default for pictures and embedded objects (such as an embedded Word table). However, you can change that setting for any object using the Size And Position dialog box (by clicking the Lock Aspect Ratio option under the Scale settings) before changing height or width in either size or scale. Once that setting is applied to an object, you can resize the object using the Size group on the applicable Format contextual tab, and your setting to constrain or not constrain proportions will be honored.

Note that, on the Picture Tools Format tab, the Crop tool is also available from the Size group, so you can drag to crop rather than opening the dialog box to apply crop settings when you don't need specific crop values. To use the Crop tool, select the image to crop and you'll see the shape handles change to black lines. Hover over a handle until your mouse pointer changes to a T shape, with the horizontal line of the T facing the direction you can crop. Then, drag to crop as needed. Note that your insertion point will look like a crosshair while you're dragging to crop. Also note that you can hold the ALT key while dragging to crop in smaller increments than the grid setting.

> **Note**
> If you don't like your crop or size settings, in the Size And Position dialog box, on the Size tab, click Reset. You can click Reset in the Adjust group on the Picture Tools Format tab to do this as well, but that option will also reset any color adjustments you've made to your picture.

Organize Content Precisely with the Arrange Tools

Many of the options that you may know from the Draw menu in earlier versions are now combined in the Arrange group that appears on the Format contextual tab for most object types in PowerPoint (such as the Drawing Tools Format, Picture Tools Format, and SmartArt Tools Format tabs). The same Arrange options also appear in the Drawing group on the Home tab. These options include the following.

- Order actions, including Bring To Front, Send To Back, Bring Forward, and Send Backward.

- Grouping actions, including Group, Ungroup, and Regroup.

- Align actions, including both Align and Distribute options, as well as access to Grid Settings (which includes drawing guides).

- Rotation actions, which include Rotate and Flip presets as well as the ability to set custom rotation (which is another means to access the new Size And Position dialog box, discussed under the previous heading).

Note that you can also access the Selection And Visibility pane from the Arrange options on any tab where those options appear.

The only new functionality for these features in the 2007 release is the fact that Power-Point automatically recognizes whether you want to align multiple objects or align an object relative to the slide. When you select only one object and then click Align, you'll see that all of the Align actions are available to you and that Align To Slide has automatically been selected. When you next select multiple shapes and click Align, the setting Align Selected Objects will automatically be selected. The only time this automatic selection doesn't work is if you switch the setting manually. For example, if you select multiple shapes that you want to center relative to the slide, you need to click Align To Slide. Once you do that, you'll need to reselect Align Selected Objects if you need that option again during the same PowerPoint session. The automatic defaults are reset after you exit PowerPoint.

Okay, so the Align, Distribute, Order, and Group commands might not be new, but that doesn't make them less important.

Order and Group

The Order actions are an important precision formatting tool. For example, if you use a semitransparent fill on a shape, you can send other shapes behind it for interesting effects. You can also send one object behind another to hide part of the first object (such as when using freeform lines instead of connectors in a diagram, and you need to hide the end of the line behind the object it meets). To use the Order actions from any Format contextual tab, you can either click Bring To Front or Send To Back, or click the arrow beside one of those settings for the option to bring the selected content forward or backward by one layer.

Grouping objects is a good way to save yourself extra work. Once you've finished placing, aligning, distributing, and ordering objects, group them to keep your result precise. As discussed earlier under the heading "Managing Shapes with the Selection And Visibility Pane," you can still select and format individual objects in a group. Grouping simply keeps the elements of your graphic together, so that they can be managed as a single object.

CAUTION

It is now possible to drag or nudge selected shapes within a group to move them. They remain part of the group, but their position changes. Grouping still helps to maintain your alignment settings, because it does take a rather deliberate action to select an individual object within a group and then move it. However, since the purpose of grouping is often to keep alignment and other positioning settings intact, this is an important change to watch for.

Grouping (actually, ungrouping) also comes in handy when you want to customize Clip Art drawings, as discussed in the section titled "Ungrouping Clip Art to Create Custom Graphics" later in this chapter. Grouping can also be used as an editing tool, such as when temporarily grouping objects to align or distribute them, as discussed in the next section, "Using Drawing Guides."

Align and Distribute

If you're one of those people who nudges shapes until they look aligned, how long does it take you to get them just right? The answer to that question is probably less than it was a few versions back, because nudging objects moves them along the grid, so it's not terribly hard to align things precisely even with that workaround. But, don't you have something better to do with your time?

If you need several objects to be top-aligned, for example, select them all and then, in the Align options, click Top. That's it. No nudging, no guessing, no zooming to see if they're perfect. Just click and you know that they're perfect—done. If you need equal space between several objects, select them and then, in the Align options, click either Distribute Horizontally or Distribute Vertically. (Note that a minimum of three objects are required in the selection to enable the Distribute options.) Following are a few additional points to keep in mind to help you align objects more easily.

- When aligning selected objects, they will align to the object that's furthest in the direction you're aligning. For example, clicking Top will align all objects to the top of the object closest to the top of the slide.

> **Note**
> This is different in Visio, where shapes will align to the first shape you select if you click to select each shape. However, if you drag a marquee to select all shapes to be aligned, the alignment follows PowerPoint style and aligns to the furthest shape in the direction of the alignment.

- When aligning smaller and larger objects, if the larger object fully covers the distance of the smaller object in the direction you're aligning, the larger object doesn't move. For example, to align the middles of the two shapes in the following image (move them vertically so that their middle handles align), only the smaller shape would move.

However, the following two shapes would both move toward the center.

- When you use the Distribute options, the outermost objects don't move. Only the objects between the left and right, or top and bottom, shapes adjust to create equal space between all selected objects.

Once you align or distribute objects, be careful not to include some of the aligned objects in another Align or Distribute action, or you might throw off the first alignment. For example, though organization charts are easy to create with SmartArt diagrams, you might have occasion to want to create one using shapes. Look at the image that follows.

To align and distribute the shapes in the three rows, I would do the following.

1. Select the three VP shapes and apply Distribute Horizontally.

2. Group the three VP shapes so that I can center-align them as one item under the CEO shape.

3. If I then want to center the two Director shapes under the VP, Sales & Marketing shape, I can't group the Director shapes and center them under the VP shape, nor can I distribute the three shapes horizontally, because either action will move the VP shape so that it's no longer equally distributed with the other VP shapes.

So, what do you do? That's where the drawing guides come in.

Using Drawing Guides

The drawing guides have two primary functions.

- Specify page layout when you need objects that aren't inside placeholders to be aligned precisely or in the same position across slides.

- Align objects when the Align or Distribute tools can't be used, as in SmartArt diagrams or in situations such as the organization chart example provided immediately before the preceding heading.

When you show drawing guides on screen, you start with one vertical and one horizontal guide that cross in the center of the slide. When you drag a guide, it shows you the distance you move the guide, measured from the center of the slide (guides display measurements in your default unit of measure, such as inches or centimeters). Drawing guides don't print and aren't selected when you drag a marquee to select objects, so they're a very handy tool for creating the layout you need. Use the following guidelines to get the most out of drawing guides.

- To show drawing guides, right-click a blank area of the slide and then click Grid And Guides. Or, in the Arrange group on the applicable Format contextual tab for your objects (or the Arrange options in the Drawing group on the Home tab), click Align and then click Grid Settings. In the dialog box that opens, click Show Drawing Guides On Screen and then click OK.

> **Note**
>
> With the exception of the right-click option, this feature is badly hidden for something so frequently useful (it used to be available from the CTRL+G shortcut, but is no longer). So, remember that you can add Grid Settings to your Quick Access Toolbar.
>
> To do this, just right-click Grid Settings where it appears on the Align options and then click Add To Quick Access Toolbar. If you miss the CTRL+G shortcut, also remember that once something is on your Quick Access Toolbar, it has an easy shortcut—ALT + the Quick Access Toolbar position. For example, I access Grid Settings by pressing ALT+5, because it's the fifth item to the right on my toolbar.

- You get one set of drawing guides per presentation. So, if you add, move, or delete drawing guides on a slide, those changes will be reflected regardless of the active slide in the presentation. However, drawing guide settings are independent for each presentation. Drawing guide settings are also saved with the document, so if you hide the guides and turn them on in a separate work session days later, your last guide settings in that presentation will have been retained.

- To drag a guide in smaller increments than the grid, hold the ALT key while dragging.

- To measure the distance from the current location when you drag, hold the SHIFT key while dragging. The SHIFT key resets the position indicator on the guide to zero at the point of origin.

- To duplicate a guide, hold the CTRL key while dragging.

- As with shapes and other objects, you can use the preceding keyboard shortcuts together to get exactly the measurement you need. For example, if you need a second guide 0.25 inches from the first, hold the CTRL, SHIFT, and ALT keys while you drag to duplicate while showing the distance from the point of origin and moving in precise increments.

- If you no longer need duplicate guides, drag vertical guides off the right edge of the screen to delete them and horizontal guides off the bottom edge of the screen to delete them. Note that you can't delete the default guides in this way.

So, how would I align the two Director shapes under their VP in the preceding sample diagram by using drawing guides?

1. Select the VP shape and then position a vertical drawing guide over the center handles of that shape.

2. Group the two Director shapes so that they can be positioned as a single shape, and then move them so that the center handles of the group are directly on the guide, as you see in the image that follows.

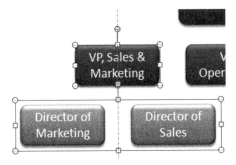

> **Note**
>
> There's often more than one way to go about the alignment of a graphic—it depends on where you start. If you take a moment to think through and plan your actions, you might be able to simplify even further that which seemed like a simple approach to begin with.
>
> For example, in the case of the organization chart created with shapes (shown in this section), you could have used Align and Distribute tools exclusively (and not drawing guides) if you'd worked upward from the bottom of the diagram. In that case, you would have centered the VP, Sales & Marketing shapes between the two Director shapes, then distributed the three VP shapes horizontally and grouped them, and finally centered the CEO shape over the group of VP shapes.

Editing Shapes

For a human being to change can take years of study, education, or travel. Or, we might undertake more materialistic types of change, such as going under a plastic surgeon's knife.

Shapes, on the other hand, have it easy. If you were a shape, you could change and grow practically at will. In some cases, shapes can morph into different forms just by moving their yellow diamond reshape tool. Most shapes can use the Change Shape tool to become different shapes, and all shapes can use the new Convert To Freeform tool to become anything they want to be.

Okay, so shapes don't have it quite that easy. They need a human being with a mouse pointer to change their characteristics. But, while your shapes aren't self actualized, they do make your work easier when you need custom graphics.

Change your shapes whenever and however you please. No plastic surgery, no Botox, not even a trip to the dermatologist—and certainly no need to recreate your graphics from scratch just to change shapes. Remake your shapes in just a few clicks.

Changing Shapes

There are three ways to change the shape of a built-in shape.

- Many shapes have one or more reshape tools (the yellow diamond that appears on the perimeter of the shape when selected) that you can drag to alter the shape.

  Some reshape tools handle fairly basic changes, such as the depth or thickness of an arrow or the size of a pie slice. Others can dramatically change shapes. For example, look at the new Teardrop shape in three different forms. On the left is the default shape, and the other two options are created by dragging the reshape tool in opposite directions.

Similarly, the 4-Part Star becomes an octagon when its reshape tool is moved as far as it can go.

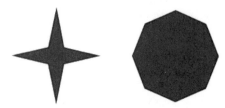

Some reshape tools also provide useful details that you might not know are available to you. For example, the two reshape tools on the Right Brace shown in the following image change the curve of the brace and the position of the pointer on the brace, respectively, as you see here.

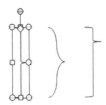

- You can change any shape (other than connectors) to other built-in shapes by using the Change Shape tool, such as if you want all of the rectangles in a SmartArt organization chart to be diamonds instead (or, if you just want one of the shapes to be different from the rest). You can even change your own shapes that you create with the Freeform tool into built-in shapes.

  To access the Change Shape tool, first select the shapes you want to change. Then, on the Drawing Tools Format tab, in the Insert Shapes group, click to expand the Edit Shape options, point to Change Shape and then click to select the shape you want. (Change Shape is also available on the SmartArt Tools Format tab, in the Shapes group.)

  One of the best things about this tool is the fact that it doesn't work on connectors. So, you can select an entire diagram or other graphic at one time and change the shape of all of the primary shapes without worrying about any connectors included in your selection.

- For those times when there is no built-in shape to suit your needs, and the reshape tool doesn't give you enough flexibility, you can now convert any built-in shape (other than connectors) to freeform objects and then use Edit Points (discussed under the next heading) to create absolutely anything you want.

  To do this, select one or more shapes to convert and then, on the Drawing Tools Format tab, in the Insert Shapes group, click Edit Shapes and then click Convert To Freeform. The shape doesn't visibly change when you do this, but it becomes a freeform drawing. So, when you use Edit Points, you can literally turn that shape into any type of drawing you need. Also, as mentioned earlier in this chapter, you now have the ability to format freeform shapes just like built-in shapes, such as adding text to a freeform shape—so you don't lose functionality when you make this change.

  The only oddity you're likely to encounter when changing your shape to a freeform shape is that the internal text area gets larger. So, formatting of text already in the shape when you make this change might be altered. See the Troubleshooting tip "The text area changed when I converted a shape to a freeform drawing," which is located under the WordArt topic in this chapter because the difference is most dramatic when your text uses certain types of WordArt formatting.

Chapter 18

Edit Points to Create Virtually Anything

Okay, so you've converted your shape to a freeform drawing. Now what? When you enable Edit Points, you can literally edit each point in the shape independently. For example, look at the rectangle in the following image. This is how a selected shape looks when Edit Points is enabled. Each black square is a point that you can manipulate.

After a few clicks, that rectangle now looks like the image that follows.

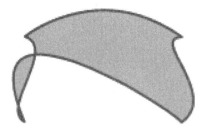

Using Edit Points is quite easy to learn, but if you've used it in the past, there are some changes in behavior. Following are key points to help you master this feature and even have some fun with it.

- To enable Edit Points, right-click any freeform drawing and then click Edit Points. Or, on the Drawing Tools Format tab, in the Insert Shapes group, click Edit Shape and then click Edit Points.

- If you click anywhere on the slide outside of the shape being edited, Edit Points automatically turns off.

- Edit Points is one of very few features for which most elements are exclusively available when you right-click.

- When hovering over an object in Edit Points mode, if your insertion point looks like a box inside a cross, your insertion point is over a line segment. If it looks like a box surrounded by four triangles, your insertion point is over a point. Right-click for the options available in either case.

- If you see the insertion point that indicates a line segment, you can drag to add a new point to the shape. Alternately, you can right-click anywhere on the perimeter of a shape and then click Add Point.

- To delete a point, right-click the point and then click Delete Point.

- When you right-click anywhere on the shape perimeter, you see the option Open Path. Or, if you right-click on a freeform drawing that's an open line, you'll see Close Path. Open path separates segments to form a line; close path joins segments to turn a line into a shape. Note, however, that your freeform drawings can use Shape Fill and Shape Effects whether or not the path is closed.

- When you click a point, you see two blue handles with white boxes on the end. These handles control the curve of the segments on either side of the point. If you change the type of point (available when you right-click a point), the appearance of the segments on either side of the point may change, but the behavior of the point handles does not.

  This is a change in the 2007 release. For example, in the previous version, smooth points would cause a change to the segment on one side of the point to affect the segment on the other side of the same point. This is no longer the case. Segments on either side of the point operate independently regardless of the type of point you choose.

  Instead, when you change the point type, the segments on either side adjust (if applicable) to match the point type you've requested. For example, if you have a corner that looks like this:

  and you change the point to a straight or smooth point, it will look like this:

  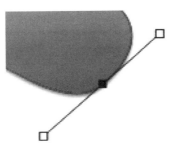

  However, once you begin to move the handles again, they behave exactly the same and allow you to create whatever shape you need.

- Similarly, you can right-click a segment and then click Straight Segment to immediately remove the curve from a segment. However, you are still free to manipulate the handles on the points adjacent to that segment to once again add a curve if needed.

- To control the size of the curve in a segment, drag the white box at the end of a point handle closer to or further from the point. The shorter the handle, the tighter the curve; the longer the handle, the looser the curve can be.

- Each handle only controls half of a given segment. Use the handles on either side of a segment to control the full bend of a curve.

  To get a feel for the angles you can create with the handles on any point, drag a handle in a variety of directions to see how the curve changes. Remember that you can press ESC before releasing your drag on the handle to cancel the action.

- In addition to using Edit Points to create custom drawings, it can be a very useful editing tool. When you use single or multi-segment freeform lines (instead of connectors), you can enable Edit Points to shorten, lengthen, or change the angle of a given line segment.

Note

If you want to create your own freeform drawing (or multi-segment line) from scratch instead of converting a shape to a freeform, start with the Freeform option under the Lines category in the Shape gallery. To use this tool, don't drag to draw. Instead, just click each time you want to turn a corner and then double-click to end the drawing. Remember that you can turn corners into curves later by using Edit Points.

WordArt as a Powerful Design Tool

If you've read the section of this chapter on formatting shapes, you already know most of what you can do with WordArt. As mentioned earlier, WordArt is functionality that enables you to format text as you do shapes—with fills, outlines, and graphic effects. However, with WordArt, you can use Font formatting (such as the Character Spacing functionality that's new to PowerPoint) along with WordArt formatting for even more flexibility.

The beauty of WordArt is that the ability to format text as shapes adds tremendously to your options for using PowerPoint to create the types of business graphics you might never have imagined you could do on your own, such as creating your own logo.

You can apply WordArt formatting to any editable text in a PowerPoint object by using the WordArt Styles group on the Drawing Tools Format tab or the SmartArt Tools Format tab. Or, you can insert a WordArt object—which is now just a text box that comes with placeholder text.

Take a look at a few options for what you can do very simply with WordArt effects and Font formatting combined.

   Your Text Here

Note

When you apply WordArt formatting or Shape formatting to a shape and don't seem to be getting what you need, check to make sure that you're using options from the correct tab group. The Shape Styles and WordArt Styles options look very similar. But, Shape Styles affect the shape area and not the text; WordArt Styles affect only the text (so that, if your shape contains no text, it won't appear altered).

The Text Effects for WordArt don't include the Soft Edges options available to Shape Effects. However, WordArt also offers the unique Transform set of effects that are not available to shapes. Transform effects curve or warp the appearance of the text. When using Transform settings, notice that the curve or warp will change based on the size of the text area and the amount of text. See the Troubleshooting tip in this section for information on how Transform is affected by converting shapes to freeform drawings.

Overall, the range of effects for WordArt has increased over previous versions. But the biggest change is surely the fact that you can apply WordArt formatting to any text and no longer need a separate object to use these effects.

Notice that the Text Fill and Text Outline options in the WordArt Styles group have the same range of options as Shape Fill and Shape Outline, including the ability to use picture, gradient, or texture fills for text. Also notice that WordArt Styles have their own set of Quick Styles. And remember, when you want to use the new font formatting options (such as Small Caps or Character Spacing) along with WordArt, on the Home tab, in the Font group, click the dialog launcher.

TROUBLESHOOTING

The text area changed when I converted a shape to a freeform drawing

When you convert a built-in shape to freeform, the internal text box area typically becomes a bit larger, so the text wrap on existing text in the shape may change when you make the conversion. With basic text formatting, the primary difference you'll see is where the text wraps, because the text box will be wider.

However, when you use WordArt Transform settings (curving text within the shape), you might see a much more significant change (such as between the two shapes shown side by side in the image that follows).

WordArt text with applied Transform settings doesn't behave the same with internal text box margins as standard text. And, changing the size of the text box relative to the amount of text can dramatically alter the way a Transform setting affects your text. When the conversion to a freeform object changes the size of the text area, the WordArt Transform setting adjusts to use the new, larger text area.

Changing text box margins when this happens isn't likely to give you the result you want. For the easiest, best results when this happens, change the Transform setting to No Transform and then use Live Preview with the Transform options to see which setting works best with the new text area.

Ungrouping Clip Art to Create Custom Graphics

I'll be the first person to tell you that, when you want professional business graphics, you probably don't want to use a Clip Art drawing. But, you can save a lot of time and reap a lot of benefits by taking advantage of Clip Art to create your own custom graphics.

At last count, there were over 150,000 pieces of Clip Art (across a variety of media) available for free on Office Online. With that type of selection, it's likely that you might find something you can use on some occasion. Rather than starting from scratch when you need a drawing (especially if, like me, you're not much of an artist), find a Clip Art drawing that contains either elements you need or something similar to what you need. Then, ungroup it and either edit it or extract the pieces you need.

Let's take a look at an example. I needed a drawing of an elegant woman at a country club reception. So, I found the Clip Art drawing you see in the following image by using the Clip Art gallery available on the Insert tab. But, this lady looks a bit too much like a Hollywood starlet for my country club set.

So, I ungrouped the drawing, deleted the pieces I didn't need, and made a few simple adjustments. I used Edit Points to make both her hair and dress more conservative, and changed colors to soften her makeup. Then, I deleted existing jewelry and created a dainty pearl choker from a few small, white ovals. It took about five minutes to make these changes, and my country club hostess is in perfect form as you see here.

Most drawings that you find in Clip Art can be ungrouped. To do this, insert the Clip Art image onto your slide and then right-click the drawing, point to Group, and then click Ungroup. You'll be prompted to confirm whether you want to convert the picture to a Microsoft Office drawing object. Click Yes to confirm and nothing seems to happen, but it has. Right click, point to Group, and click Ungroup once more, and you'll get something like this.

Chapter 18

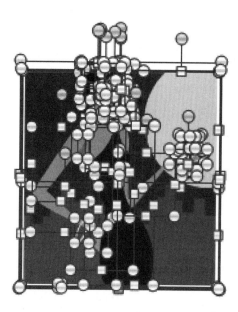

You can press ESC to deselect the shapes and then click or drag a marquee to select any elements you want to delete. Remember also that you can zoom in more tightly on the drawing to see the pieces more clearly.

Getting Your Graphic into Other Programs

As mentioned in Chapter 7, PNG is the picture format that provides the best resolution for graphics you create with SmartArt or drawing tools in PowerPoint. In fact, PNG provides by far the clearest image when you use many of the new formatting effects.

To copy your graphic into another 2007 release program, just select and copy it in PowerPoint and then, in the destination program, choose the PNG picture format in the Paste Special dialog box.

To use your graphic in documents you create outside of the 2007 release programs, or to share just the graphic itself, you can save your graphic as a picture. To do this, right-click the graphic and then click Save As Picture. The Save As Picture dialog box will open, where you can select a location and name for your new picture file. In most cases, PowerPoint selects the best picture format for your object. But, if you need to save your graphic in a different picture format, just change the Save As Type setting in the dialog box before saving the picture.

> **Note**
>
> Also keep in mind that, if you need a picture in a different format than the file you have handy, you can use the Microsoft Office Picture Manager to export it to another file format. To access Microsoft Office Picture Manager, on the Start menu, click All Programs, then click Microsoft Office, and then click Microsoft Office Tools. Also note that, when you right-click a picture file in a Windows Explorer and then point to Open With, Microsoft Office Picture Manager should be one of the available options.

Slides and Presentations

Microsoft Office PowerPoint 2007 is a program that's finally come into its own. Most of the limitations that you ran into in earlier versions are gone. As you saw in the previous chapter, the sad little diagram tool has been replaced with beautiful SmartArt graphics, and the range of available shapes is now only limited by your imagination. But, the story gets even better here: No more clumsy charts, no more layout limitations, and the new design capabilities are cool enough to make earlier versions downright ashamed of themselves.

So, why are you frustrated? Well, don't worry, it's not just you. Big changes have occurred, and they're not all intuitive when you first begin working with them, no matter how much experience you have. But, simple solutions exist for learning to capitalize on the new functionality and new methods, as well as easy workarounds for the occasional unfortunate change (like the cruelly butchered Recolor Picture feature). This chapter will help you surmount frustration, overcome ambivalence, and fall head over heels in blissful productivity with the *very* new Office PowerPoint 2007.

Chapter Assumptions

You've created slides, used masters, and at least played around with animation. You know what slide layouts are and how to apply them. You know that if you apply colors from a PowerPoint color scheme and then change the active scheme in your presentation, the applied colors will change. You've presented a PowerPoint slide show before, even if the only audience member was your cat. In short, you're pretty comfortable with the basics of creating and formatting presentations in at least a recent version of Power-Point.

In this chapter, I won't take your time explaining core basics such as what placeholders are, or the basic differences between adding something to a slide or slide master. Instead, we'll focus on bringing those basics together to create effective, custom presentations. And, we'll explore ways to take advantage of everything this new version has to

Chapter 19

offer. We'll also look at some common advanced tasks and how they've changed, such as editing embedded Microsoft Word tables.

In the introduction to this book, you can find a list of resources for those who want more basic-level information, in the section titled "Who Will Benefit Most from This Book."

What's New for Slide Presentations in PowerPoint 2007

For all of the preceding references to how much is new, the list doesn't seem very long. The changes in PowerPoint slide presentations are large in impact rather than large in number.

- First on the list of big news is the new custom slide layout functionality. Finally! You can now customize any built-in slide layout and create your own. This major improvement changes the way slide masters think and the number of masters you're likely to need in a presentation. Title masters, for example, are no longer needed, because you can customize the Title slide layout. Find everything you need to know to manage this new capability effectively in the section of this chapter titled "Working with Masters, Layouts, and Designs."

- The other major news is Themes. Think you've got Themes down cold and covered because you know how to work with them in Microsoft Office Word 2007 and Microsoft Office Excel 2007? Not quite. Themes can do everything in PowerPoint that they can do in the other programs. But, as mentioned in Chapter 5, "Styles," Themes are PowerPoint-based functionality. Evolved from PowerPoint design masters, you receive additional functionality for Themes in PowerPoint, including formatting for slide masters, layouts, and backgrounds. Get the information you need to make the most of Themes in the section of this chapter titled "The Themes—PowerPoint Connection."

- If you work in a company that runs Microsoft Office SharePoint Server 2007 and you're using one of the 2007 release suites that supports enterprise content management, you have access to the new Slide Library feature for sharing and reusing slides.

  It's a very cool feature, but if you don't have it, don't fret. You, too, can reuse slides from existing presentations. Yes, you've been able to insert slides from other presentations in the past. That feature is now a bit reorganized and easier to access. Learn about both enterprise and individual capabilities for reusing slides under the heading "Reusing Slides" later in this chapter.

- New text formatting options make working with text far friendlier than before. Included are new Font formatting options (discussed in Chapter 18, "Creating Professional Presentation Graphics") and new paragraph formatting, such as having up to nine levels of bulleted text, text columns inside an individual text box, and improved indents, spacing, and tab options. For details, see the heading "Working with Text" later in this chapter.

- One small change is worth noting for a big benefit. A new feature named Reset now does what reapplying a slide layout did in the previous version. But, you can now reapply the active layout instead of resetting the slide to move your place-holders back into position without losing custom formatting. For details, see "Control the Layout—Don't Let it Control You" in the section of this chapter titled "Effective Document Setup."

- A couple of features are gone—one of them with good riddance and the other with a few tears.

  - Had I known that Fast Saves was going away, I would have thrown a bon voyage party. This antiquated feature hasn't done much for some time except to risk the sharing of private information. Fortunately, it's no longer around in any 2007 release program and won't be missed.

  - On the other side of the spectrum is the dearly departed Recolor Picture feature. Yes, there is a Recolor Picture option on the Picture Tools Format tab and in the Format Picture dialog box. But, if you've used Recolor Picture in the past, trust me, the functionality that you know is gone. The new in-carnation of Recolor Picture is only available to pictures, and it's a shadow of its former self. (The Recolor button you still see on the Picture tab of the Format Object dialog box was an accidental leave-behind and doesn't do anything.)

If, like me, you relied on this feature for tasks such as recoloring embedded Word tables, your immediate reaction to this news might be rather intense. Well, don't head for the fainting couch just yet—there's a workaround so simple that you're sure to recover without the need for smelling salts. Get the scoop in the Troubleshooting tip titled "How can I easily edit an embedded Word table without Recolor Picture?"

- The new Photo Album feature is slicker than you might expect. It's simple to use and definitely a timesaver when you want to share pictures. Because it's so simple and straightforward, and because this is an advanced book, there's not much to say about it here other than to point out the feature and provide a few tips so that you don't miss giving it a try.

Chapter 19

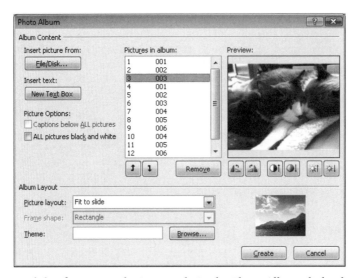

Find this feature on the Insert tab. In the Photo Album dialog box, shown in the preceding image, you can select files from multiple sources to add them to a single photo album, reorder them, perform basic picture editing (such as rotating a picture or changing its brightness setting), set up a layout with anything from one to four photos per slide, and add captions below the pictures. Note that the option to insert a text box inserts a slide containing only a text box and no photos (so as to act as a section divider). Instead, to get editable text box captions on each slide, choose any layout other than Fit To Slide and the Captions Below ALL Pictures option will become available. Note that photo albums are always created as a separate presentation. When a PowerPoint photo album is open on your screen, the Photo Album options on the Insert tab include the option to edit that album.

Beyond the preceding list, the answer to the question of what's new for PowerPoint presentations includes the occasional detail (such as the fact that you can now select Footer, Date, and Slide Number placeholders directly on any slide) as well as the same answer that you've encountered about topics throughout this book—the new organization of features with the introduction of the Ribbon, and new or changed shortcut options. All of these will be addressed, as applicable, throughout the chapter.

When Your Document Lives in PowerPoint

The secret to PowerPoint presentations that are easy to create, edit, and manage is this: PowerPoint is easy. Really, that's it. PowerPoint provides the tools to make your work simple and straightforward. Just use the available tools, and the time you spend in PowerPoint will be downright pleasant—quick, simple, and painless—and the presentations you create may be far better than you expect.

But, there's a catch (c'mon, you knew there would be). If you don't use the available features—if you insist on using workarounds and overcomplicated solutions rather than learning to use the tools that PowerPoint benevolently provides—it just might smite your presentation. It may even seem as if PowerPoint is laughing while your work goes up in smoke.

So, my advice is, don't tempt it. Even with its shiny new capabilities, PowerPoint is set in its ways. Use the features the way they're designed to be used, and you and your presentation will get along swimmingly. So, how do you bow to the will of PowerPoint?

First and foremost, your document should only live in PowerPoint when it's going to be a slide presentation, or a similar document type that requires the use of masters and layouts. If you need a lot of text on many pages (such as for a report), or need many complex pages with text and graphics (such as a print pitch book), your document will almost certainly be easier to create in Office Word 2007. Just create the graphics for that document in PowerPoint (and other programs, as applicable). See Chapter 4, "Building Easy-to-Manage, Robust Documents," and Chapter 12, "Planning Your Documents," for more on creating hearty and great-looking complex Word documents.

As a rule of thumb, I suggest that you use PowerPoint as a home for your document when you can answer *yes* to at least one of these questions.

1. Will the document be delivered as an on-screen presentation?

2. Do you need to use slide masters for any purpose other than what you can do with paragraph styles and the header\footer layer in a Word document?

3. Do you need to use slide layouts for any type of page layout that you can't accomplish with paragraph formatting or tables in a Word document?

Once you determine that your document belongs in PowerPoint, consider the following.

- With few exceptions, if the slide layout you're using doesn't fit the layout you need, don't use that layout. Either customize a layout or, for single-use layouts, use the Blank or Title Only slide layouts and do your own thing.

  However, the layouts are there for a reason and can substantially reduce your work. What's more, a presentation full of slides that don't use layouts with place-holders is sure to be a struggle, at best—so, please don't misinterpret the preceding bulleted paragraph as instructing you to disregard layouts.

- Use Theme-ready elements, including colors, fonts, and slide backgrounds, unless you intentionally want specific formatting to remain even if the Theme changes.

- Use slide masters. If you have to place the same item on more than one slide, ask yourself whether you could use a master instead (or, in PowerPoint 2007, a slide layout) to accomplish what you need in one step rather than many.

- Use the Align, Distribute, and Order tools (addressed in Chapter 18) to position content precisely. Nudging and guesswork defeats the purpose of using Power-Point and will never give you the best results. When you use the available drawing tools, it takes almost no time to positioning content perfectly.

- Watch file size carefully. PowerPoint provides features to help you minimize file size even when you need a wealth of graphics in your presentation, such as the ability to compress pictures or to paste pictures in a variety of formats (using Paste Special). One of the most common causes of PowerPoint document corruption is bloated file size. See Chapter 7, "Managing Graphics," for information about using Microsoft Windows Paint or Microsoft Office Picture Manager to convert pictures to other formats to reduce file size without losing quality. Also, see Chapter 18 for information on working with pictures in PowerPoint.

- If a task feels like a lot of work, stop doing it. Take a moment to consider if there's a way to make it easier, because there probably is. And, because making it easier means using the right tool for the task, it's also likely to improve your results.

  For example, pay attention to AutoCorrect actions (such as automatically fitting text to a placeholder), and set your defaults to the result you most often want (such as turning off AutoFit for body text). You have many options for working effectively with AutoFit, so don't continually fight with it—you won't win. For help with this example, see the Troubleshooting tip later in this chapter titled "What can I do to stop font size from automatically changing?"

If you're thinking that the preceding list isn't much help if you don't know whether you're using the referenced features effectively, you're absolutely right. But the information you need to answer those questions is all here, so read on.

Effective Document Setup

It's common to forget that a PowerPoint presentation is a document, but that it is. So, understanding the elements that can appear on the page, and how a given element may appear under different circumstances (such as on screen or in print), can simplify your work considerably.

In this section, we'll look at how slide layout and page setup can affect your presentation.

Control the Layout—Don't Let It Control You

This heading refers to the way that placeholders behave in slide layouts. The idea behind placeholders (such as the title and subtitle placeholders on a title slide) is to provide the size and positioning (and in some cases, the formatting) for slide content so that all you have to do is drop the content into place.

The problem that arises is that people often use slide layouts that don't really fit the content or layout they need, and they adjust the size or formatting of placeholders on individual slides. Of course, the entire purpose of placeholders is to enable you to keep layout and formatting consistent. So, when the layout is reset, all of your customizations are lost—such as the size and positioning of objects, and formatting of text.

Working with placeholders is much easier in the 2007 release, since you can now customize slide layouts and create your own to get exactly the size and position you need for any placeholder. The important thing is to use the capability that's provided and take the extra step to go into the slide layout to make your change, rather than making the change on each individual slide. Learn when to customize the master versus the individual layout, and how to customize layouts, in the section of this chapter titled "Working with Masters, Layouts, and Designs."

Of course, there are exceptions to what can be set up on the slide layout or in the slide master. When you need custom formatting, such as direct font formatting on just a few words in a text placeholder or a border around a content placeholder, how can you avoid losing those customizations? The answer used to be that you needed to avoid re-applying the layout, but that's no longer true.

When you need to reset a placeholder position on a slide, you can use either the new Reset option or reapply the active layout from the Layout gallery. Reset behaves the way that reapplying a layout used to behave—that is, all customizations are lost and the slide is reset to use only the positioning and formatting that appear on the slide layout. However, if you instead simply reselect the active layout (just click the thumbnail for the layout you need in the Layout gallery), your placeholders return to their prescribed size and position, and all custom formatting remains. Find both the Reset option and the Layout gallery in the Slides group on the Home tab, or when you right-click either a slide or a thumbnail in the Slide pane.

So, what happens when you need text or objects to have a custom size or position on just one individual slide? Don't move or resize placeholders on individual slides—use custom objects.

- When you insert a text box (either a traditional text box or a WordArt text box) from the Insert tab, rather than using an existing text or content placeholder, you get a custom object that isn't affected by changes in slide layout. Keep in mind, however, that custom text boxes don't have the formatting that's preset in place-holders (such as several levels of bulleted text)—so you're on your own in terms of formatting your custom text.

- When you place other object types (such as a picture, table, diagram, or chart) from the Insert tab onto a slide that has an empty placeholder designed for that content type, your new object is automatically placed in that empty placeholder and sized accordingly. (If the slide contains similar placeholders, but they already have content, using the Insert tab to insert an object will insert the custom object you need without attaching it to a placeholder.)

- Of course, when you need a custom object, the goal is to not attach it to a place-holder so that it isn't affected by changing, reapplying, or resetting the layout. So, when you need objects to be independent of placeholders, usually the easiest thing to do is use the Blank or Title Only layout, as mentioned earlier. However, if you need a custom object on a slide that has empty placeholders, there is an easy workaround, as follows.

  Insert the object into the empty placeholder. Then, select and cut the object (CTRL+X), and then paste (CTRL+V). The object will be pasted back on the slide, but it will sit on top of the placeholder rather than using the placeholder. If you move the pasted object, you'll see that the empty placeholder remains.

TROUBLESHOOTING

What can I do to stop font size from automatically changing?

The AutoFormat As You Type options that AutoFit body or heading text to placeholders are enabled by default. But, when AutoFit takes action, a SmartTag appears outside the bottom-left corner of the text box, where you can disable the action. Click the arrow to expand the SmartTag options, and you'll see something like the following image.

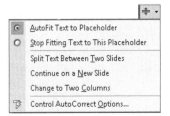

The options you see in the AutoCorrect SmartTag depend on the type of placeholder, the slide layout, and your AutoCorrect settings. The options to split text between slides, continue on a new slide, or set the placeholder to two columns are only available in built-in layouts with a single body content placeholder (such as Title And Content)—but are available whether or not you have AutoFit enabled for body text.

You can turn off AutoFit from this SmartTag, or choose another appropriate action, for the individual placeholder only. Or, click Control AutoCorrect Options and then click AutoFormat As You Type for a list of options, including (at the bottom of the list) the options to AutoFit title text and body text to placeholders. You can also access the Auto-Correct Options dialog box from the Proofing tab of the PowerPoint Options dialog box.

Once you turn off AutoFit for title or body text, the AutoFit SmartTags for applicable placeholders will no longer contain the options to AutoFit text to the placeholder or stop fitting text to the placeholder. However, you'll still see the SmartTags that provide access to the AutoCorrect Options dialog box.

It's a good idea to keep these settings enabled and use the SmartTags to disable the setting where needed. Even if you don't want AutoFit to change your font size, seeing the changes made by AutoFit is a good heads-up that your slide contains too much text or needs a different type of layout. See the heading "Creating Effective Slides and Layouts" later in this chapter for more on the subject of using the right layout for your content and the types of content that make effective slides.

Page Setup Considerations

On the Design tab, in the Page Setup group, you have access to the familiar Page Setup dialog box, as well as quick access to changing the page orientation between portrait and landscape.

As with earlier versions, you can't have both portrait and landscape slides in the same presentation. For text slides in print presentations, however, you can create custom layouts with rotated text (and rearrange other placeholders, such as footer and page number) to approximate the look of opposite orientation pages. Or, for on-screen presentations, link slides between presentations to have both landscape and portrait slides appear in an on-screen show. See the Troubleshooting tip in this section for help linking slides between presentations.

In the Page Setup dialog box, you'll notice two new preset size options (shown in the following image), both of which are for widescreen shows. The default slide size is a standard (4:3 ratio) On-Screen Show.

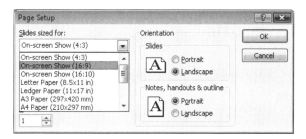

When formatting presentations for print, pay particular attention to the width and height measurements in this dialog box, shown below.

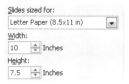

Notice that, when set to letter-sized paper (8.5 by 11 inches), the page width and height are each one inch smaller than the indicated slide size. The difference between width and height settings versus the slide size setting happens regardless of the size you select. PowerPoint builds the margins into the page size, so what you see on screen doesn't include page margins.

This is important if you're using PowerPoint for a document that will be delivered in print, because what you see on screen is not actually the full paper size. In part, this is useful, because if you have objects that bleed to the edge of a slide, they'll still print on printers that can't accommodate bleeds. However, when you need to print a true bleed or otherwise need to use the full paper size, you have two options.

- In the Page Setup dialog box, change the Height and Width settings to the paper size you need. For example, for a landscape, letter-sized page, type 11 as the Width setting and 8.5 for the Height setting. (If your default unit of measure is something other than inches, adjust the preceding measurements accordingly.) The Slide Sized For setting will change to Custom when you do this.

- Alternately, if you just want to use more of the page when printing, but want to retain the standard slide size setting for on-screen use, in Print Preview, click Options and then click Scale To Fit Paper.

Typically, it's not necessary to use these two options together. If you change the slide size to the full paper size and place objects that bleed to the edge of the slide, but Print Preview still doesn't show the slide bleeding to the edge, the most likely reason is that your active printer can't accommodate bleeds from PowerPoint or you may need to change the printer's settings to print a bleed. You can, however, always change the active printer to a virtual printer (such as Send To OneNote 2007 or Adobe Acrobat (PDF)) to preview the full bleed.

> **Note**
>
> To access Print Preview, click the Microsoft Office Button and then point to Print. (Remember that you can right-click Print Preview for the option to add it to your Quick Access Toolbar.) You can also click the Preview button in the Print dialog box to access Print Preview—which is a good way to preview any changes you make to printer settings. To change settings for your active printer, in the Print dialog box, beside the name of the active printer, click Properties. Printer properties depend on your printer's driver and are not part of the Microsoft Office programs.

TROUBLESHOOTING

I need to show portrait and landscape slides in the same presentation

As discussed in this section, all slides in a single presentation must use either portrait or landscape orientation. So, when you need portrait slides in an on-screen, landscape presentation, what do you do? Use hyperlinks to get this done in a snap.

Each slide in a presentation behaves like a bookmark within that file. So, you can simply apply a hyperlink from a slide in the landscape presentation to the slide you need in the portrait presentation. Then, add a hyperlink in the portrait presentation to return to the correct slide in the landscape presentation.

Hyperlinks in PowerPoint can be applied to any object—so you can apply the hyperlink to an existing object on the slide or insert a shape to use for the link. (Remember that, if you don't want the shape you're using for the link to appear on screen during your show, you can set both the shape fill and outline to None. If you do that, just be sure to remember where the shape is located when you need to click it during your show. Don't click the link until you see the insertion point change to the hand icon that indicates you're hovering over a hyperlink. Clicking a slide in a slide show when you see the default arrow insertion point advances your active file to the next slide.)

To add a hyperlink to a slide in another presentation, just select the object to which you want to add the link and then, on the Insert tab, in the Links group, click Hyperlink. In the Insert Hyperlink dialog box (shown here), select Existing File or Web Page in the Link To options, then use the Look In options to locate the file to which you want to link.

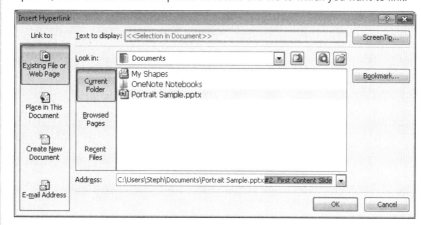

To link to a specific slide in that file, click Bookmark. Each slide title in the selected presentation is listed in the Bookmarks dialog box. Notice that, once you select a bookmark, it appears after a pound sign in the Address bar of this dialog box, as highlighted in the preceding image. Then, in the portrait presentation, just add another hyperlink back to the next slide you need in your main presentation.

Alternately, if you need text slides in a print presentation to have opposite orientation, use slide layouts with rotated text objects so that you can create all of your slides in the same document.

Understanding Headers and Footers

Headers and footers seems pretty straightforward in PowerPoint, but there are some important considerations to keep in mind. The list that follows provides you with key points on using headers and footers in PowerPoint, including how-to tips and what to avoid.

- Slides have footer, date, and slide number areas available from the Header And Footer dialog box (on the Insert tab). Notes and handouts have a separate set of footer, date, and page number settings, and they also have an available header.

- You can, potentially, have a separate footer on every slide in the presentation, or on each master and each slide layout. However, you only have one set of header and footer options for all Notes and Handouts in the presentation.

- Be careful applying footers to slide layouts. Though existing slides that use that layout update automatically to take on the new footer, when you apply that layout to new slides or change the layout of existing slides, the footer will not update automatically. Of course, there is a workaround—see the Troubleshooting tip in this section titled "Footer doesn't update when I change slide layouts" for more information.

- If you turn off a footer, but don't delete the content from the footer text box, it used to be strictly true that the content remained in your document. So, if you share that document and a recipient opens the Header And Footer dialog box, they would still see the content even if it's set to not appear on the slide.

  In PowerPoint 2007, this has changed somewhat. If you have a footer that is applied only to an individual slide, when you turn off that footer and apply the new setting to the slide, the footer content is deleted from the dialog box. However, if you apply a footer to a slide master or slide layout, the footer is retained in the Header And Footer dialog box as before, whether you turn it off on an individual slide or on the master or layout where you applied it. This is an important consideration to watch for when sharing files electronically. It's a good idea to ensure that no private or otherwise inappropriate information remains in the Header And Footer dialog box, even if it doesn't appear on slides. To remove this content, just delete the content in the Footer text box and then click Apply To All.

- If you use the Fixed option under Date And Time in the Header And Footer dialog box, the privacy issues discussed for footers in preceding paragraphs hold true as well, because you can type anything into the Fixed box that you can type into the Footer box. In fact, if you're not showing the date and time on your slides but you do need both a header and a footer, using the Fixed option under Date And Time for your header text is an easy workaround, as it works exactly the same as the Footer.

> **Note**
> Keep an eye on Date And Time when using handouts, because the date appears on handouts by default. To remove the date from handouts, either delete the Date placeholder from the handout master or take these steps: In the Header And Footer dialog box, on the Notes And Handouts tab, select Date And Time, select Fixed, clear the text in the Fixed textbox, and then click Apply To All.

- Remember that the Footer, Date, and Slide Number text boxes are just placeholder text boxes that you can format and move as needed. For example, if you need a header but no footer, place the Footer text box at the top of the appropriate layout or master. However, if you edit the text of the footer directly in the placeholder, the results might not be what you expect. Editing the placeholder won't turn on the footer, and the text may not update as expected if you edit the placeholder on a master. For the most consistent results, format the placeholder as needed, but edit its content in the Header And Footer dialog box.

- To create a footer for all slides that use a given layout or master in a presentation, create that footer when the desired master or layout is active and use the Apply setting in the Header And Footer dialog box to apply it, just as you would when applying a footer to individual slides. Only use Apply To All if you want all slides, regardless of layout or master, to take on those settings.

- You can apply Header And Footer dialog box settings to multiple selected slides, regardless of their layout or master. To do this, select the slides in Slide Sorter view and then, on the Insert tab, click Header And Footer. Access Slide Sorter view from the View tab or from the view shortcuts on the Status bar.

- You can now access the Footer, Date, and Slide Number placeholder text boxes directly on any slide. So, you can delete them from just one slide without having to go through the Header And Footer dialog box. Note that, if you use the Header And Footer dialog box to reapply the footer, date, or slide number to a slide for which you deleted the applicable placeholder, the placeholder is automatically returned.

TROUBLESHOOTING

Footer doesn't update when I change slide layouts

Though you can now apply unique footers to different slide layouts, their behavior isn't perfect. In fact, you'll get more consistent results (with less room for error) when you stick to adding footers to masters or slides. When you apply a footer to a slide layout using the Header And Footer dialog box, that footer appears automatically on any slides to which that layout is already attached. However, when you apply that layout to additional slides, the footer won't update automatically.

To update the footer on the slide with the newly applied layout, with the slide active, on the Insert tab, click Header And Footer. Turn off the Footer option and then click Apply. Reopen that dialog box and you'll see the new layout's footer information in the Footer box. Click to enable the footer and then click Apply again.

Working with Masters, Layouts, and Designs

So, here's the start of the really big news. First, the role of the slide master has changed somewhat with the introduction of both custom layouts and Themes. Additionally, the new layout functionality—though long awaited and most welcome—does require attention to a few subtleties to manage your layouts effectively.

In this section, we'll take a look at what's new for masters and layouts, and then take a brief tangent into creative best practices to address what goes into creating effective slides and layouts.

The New Master-Layout Relationship

As in the previous version of PowerPoint, you can still have multiple slide masters in a presentation. Each master appears in your Themes gallery on the Design tab as an active Theme in the current presentation, similar to the way that they used to appear on the Slide Design task pane. (Learn more about this topic later in the chapter under the heading "The Master–Theme Relationship.")

The primary difference for masters in PowerPoint 2007 is that each slide layout is a separate entity attached to its master, as you see in the following image.

To easily differentiate between a slide master and a layout, notice in the preceding image that the thumbnail for the master is larger than those of the layouts and it's numbered. So, for example, if you have two masters in the presentation, you'll have two Title layouts, two Title And Content layouts, and so on. Each layout is also separately accessible for editing, so that you can use master formatting and content on all layouts or create custom content and formatting for any layout. Also, because of the ability to customize an individual layout with features such as its own background and background graphics, you're likely to have much less need for multiple masters than in the past.

Also as in previous versions, you can copy masters between presentations, or copy and change them within the same presentation. In PowerPoint 2007, you can also do this with any individual layout.

Managing Masters and Layouts

Use the following guidelines and best practices to access and manage slide masters and layouts in your presentations.

- When using multiple masters in a presentation or template, be sure that Preserve Master is enabled for each master. Without enabling Preserve Master, masters are automatically deleted from a presentation when unused. This is particularly important for templates in which users may need to access different masters for new presentations or to change masters (such as to change the presentation for different brands within the same company).

  This setting is enabled automatically when you add multiple masters to a presentation or template, but it is not enabled automatically for the first master in the default PowerPoint template. To enable this setting for any master, right-click the master in the Slide pane (where you see the slide master and layout thumbnails) and then click Preserve Master. Or, on the Slide Master tab, in the Edit Master group, click Preserve.

> **Note**
>
> When you open Slide Master view, if you don't see the Slide pane (containing thumbnails of the slide masters and layouts) on the left side of the screen, move your insertion point to the very left edge of the screen and then drag to the right. Your insertion point will turn into a double-backed black arrow when hovering over the edge of the pane. The Slide pane is visible by default both in Normal view and in Slide Master view. However, if you close the Slide pane in Normal view, the thumbnails won't appear in Slide Master view. You can open this pane in either view by dragging it from the left side of the screen.

- You can copy, duplicate, or rename any master or layout from the options available when you right-click the thumbnail for that master or layout in the Slide pane. Once you copy a layout or master, you can paste it into the Slide pane in the same or another PowerPoint presentation or template.

- When you add a new master to a presentation or template, it contains the default set of slide layouts, regardless of which layouts are attached to other masters in the file.

- If you select a new Theme from the Edit Theme group on the Slide Master tab, a new slide master will be added by default with the new Theme attached. To apply a new Theme to the selected master instead of adding a new master, right-click the Theme you want from the Themes gallery and then click Apply To Selected Slide Master. (Note that if you select a new Theme from the Themes gallery on the Design tab when not working in the master, a new master will be added for the new Theme if the master applied to the active slide is set to Preserve.)

  However, if you apply different Theme Colors, Theme Fonts, or Theme Effects from the Edit Theme group on the Slide Master tab, the change will be applied to the selected master. To apply the new colors, font, or effects to all masters in the presentation, right-click the option you want in the Theme Colors, Theme Fonts, or Theme Effects gallery, and then select Apply To All Slide Masters.

- Though the Page Setup group that appears on the Design tab also appears on the Slide Master tab, don't be fooled. Paper size, orientation, and slide number start at value can only be set once for the presentation.

- Be careful to edit either the master or the layout, as needed. Changes made to the master will affect all of its layouts *until an element on a layout is customized*. Once you customize any element on a given layout, that element will no longer update when the same element on the master is changed. For example, if you change the format of bulleted text on an individual layout and then change the format for all bulleted text in the presentation on the master, the text levels you edited on the customized layout will not change to reflect those changes from the master.

CAUTION !

When you open Slide Master view, pay attention to what's selected before you begin editing. Though it may look like the slide master is in front of you, it's not! When you open Slide Master view, your active view becomes the layout attached to the active slide. This is important because, if you make changes to the layout that you intended to make to the master, not only won't those changes be part of the master, but the layout you edited will then be detached from the master for future changes to the customized elements.

- You can rename any layout and delete layouts that are not in use. If a layout is applied to any slide in the presentation, it can't be deleted. If you delete a built-in layout that you later need, there are a few ways to replace it. As with most tasks for managing slide masters and layouts, the first two options that follow use the Slide pane in Slide Master view.

    - Create a new, blank presentation and copy the layout from that presentation. To paste the copied layout, click anywhere in the Slide pane and then paste (CTRL+V).

    - Insert a new master into the same presentation, copy the layout you need, and then paste it under the master you're using. Then, delete the unwanted master.

    For either of the preceding options, if you select a master or layout in the Slide pane before pasting, the pasted layout will appear immediately after the selected thumbnail. Or, you can click between thumbnails before pasting to indicate the exact paste location you want.

    - If you use Visual Basic for Applications (VBA), you can easily get the deleted built-in layouts back by applying them to a slide from the Immediate Window in the Visual Basic Editor. See the Inside Out tip that follows for more information.

INSIDE OUT   Replace deleted or changed layouts using VBA

You can apply any built-in layout to a slide easily by using a single line of code in the Immediate Window of the Visual Basic Editor, as you see here.

```
☒ ppLayoutLargeObject
☒ ppLayoutMediaClipAndText
☒ ppLayoutMixed
☒ ppLayoutObject
☒ ppLayoutObjectAndText
☒ ppLayoutObjectAndTwoObjects
☒ ppLayoutObjectOverText
```

```
ActivePresentation.Slides(1).Layout =
```

(If you're not familiar with VBA fundamentals or how to use the Immediate Window, see Chapter 21, "VBA Primer.")

If the layout you apply when using this method doesn't currently exist in your presentation, it will be added as a slide layout attached to the active slide master. So, you can use this method to quickly replace a built-in, default slide layout that you deleted. So, if you customize a built-in layout and want to reset it to the default, one easy option is to delete your customized version and then use this method to replace the default version of that layout.

You can also add additional built-in layouts to your presentation using this method. Notice that there are more layouts in the list of available ppLayout constants than appear in a new, default presentation. Most of the layouts in this list that don't appear in a default presentation are holdovers from the previous version of PowerPoint. When used in a PowerPoint 2007 presentation, they'll automatically update for new content types as appropriate (such as, an organization chart layout will become a SmartArt layout).

The only layouts from this list of constants that may not remain in the Layout gallery after you apply them (if they don't stay applied to at least one slide in the presentation) are the two built-in text-only layouts containing vertical text. If they don't remain, it's because those layouts are intended for use when using Japanese as an editing language. See the related Troubleshooting tip later in this chapter for more about working with the built-in vertical text layouts.

- New layouts that you add to the master, whether you create a new layout or paste it from another master or presentation, take on the current formatting of the master layout for any applicable placeholders.

- In previous versions, the main text placeholder on the master layout was the object area for all layouts. This is no longer the case. Customizing the size of the text placeholder in the master layout will only affect slides formatted with a single text and content area (such as the Title And Content layout).

- Notice that the text and content layouts have been combined. For example, a Title And Content layout can contain either text or objects, such as a table, chart, or diagram. When a content layout is applied to the active slide, either start typing text and the placeholder will behave like a typical text placeholder, or click the appropriate icon in the center of the content placeholder (as shown here) to add the type of content you want. Content type options in addition to text include tables, charts, SmartArt diagrams, pictures, Clip Art, and media clips (such as video).

Note that, if you delete all content from a content placeholder, it again becomes accessible for text or any of the six available object types.

- Eleven built-in slide layouts appear in a new, default presentation. All of these can be customized. You may notice, however, that only nine of the layouts appear in the Layouts gallery. The two layouts that contain vertical text are, as mentioned earlier, intended for use when editing in Japanese. If Japanese is not an enabled editing language in your copy of the 2007 Office release, these layouts won't appear in the gallery. For help accessing these layouts, see the Troubleshooting tip "How can I use the vertical text layouts in my presentation?" later in this section.

Customizing Slide Masters

As in previous versions, when you want content or formatting to appear on every slide that uses a given slide master, add that content or formatting to the slide master and it's automatically added to all slides that use that master.

However, because of customized slide layouts, there are now exceptions to the way in which changes to the slide master may affect slides. If an element on a slide layout is customized (such as a placeholder from the master layout), that element becomes disconnected from the master and won't be affected by future changes to that element on the master.

However, in the interest of doing the least work possible, it's still best practice to add any formatting that you want to apply to all, or even most, layouts to the master. You can then remove unwanted additions from any layouts that shouldn't use them. For example, if you want nine of 11 layouts to use certain title text formatting, apply it to the master and then just change the formatting of the title on the two remaining layouts.

However, when you add graphic elements to the master (such as a logo), those can't be accessed from individual layouts. Only the master layout placeholders can be edited for individual layouts. But, you don't necessarily need to add the item separately to each applicable layout simply because you don't want it to appear on others. If a graphic needs to appear in the same size and position on several layouts, you can still insert it on the master. Then, for layouts that shouldn't take on the graphics from the master, you can hide background graphics for the individual layout. See the next heading in this section for helping getting that done.

Use the following guidelines to help edit and manage the formatting of your slide masters.

- Each slide master contains five placeholders, including the title, text, date, footer, and slide number. These are known as the master layout. If you delete any of these placeholders, they become available to reapply from the Master Layout dialog box on the Slide Master tab.

CAUTION

If you delete a placeholder from the master layout and then reapply it, it will be added back at its original size and position, but any custom formatting you added to the content in that placeholder will have been retained. However, if you customize a master layout placeholder and then delete it, any layouts that use that placeholder will retain the customized version of the placeholder and the placeholder on those layouts will be detached from the master for future editing.

- The main text placeholder defines the main content area for the Title And Content layout, but it no longer defines the content area for all layouts.

- Though five levels of bulleted text appear in the text placeholder of the master layout, you can now have up to nine levels. For help adding the additional levels and formatting the text and bullets in your master layout (or in any slide or layout), see the heading "Working with Text" in the section titled "Managing Slide Elements" later in this chapter.

- Remember that placeholders are not text boxes, even though they look like them. If you add text to the master layout placeholders on the slide master, that text will be ignored. You can't change placeholder text on the master layout. You can, however, change placeholder text in a slide layout—see the next heading in this section for details.

- When you apply a Background to the master from the Background Styles gallery on the Slide Master tab, it's applied to all layouts attached to that master—even overwriting any custom backgrounds applied to individual layouts. However, any slides that have individual background settings will retain those settings.

  With the slide master active, if you select the Format Background option from the Background Styles gallery and customize the background through the Format Background dialog box, the new background will be applied to all layouts attached to the master *except* those that have customized backgrounds. To apply a background that you customize in the Format Background dialog box to all layouts, including overwriting any custom backgrounds, click Apply To All. Note, however, that this action won't override custom backgrounds applied to individual slides. To reset individual slides so that they take on the master background, with the slide active, on the Design tab, click Background Styles, and then click Reset Slide Background.

Customizing and Creating Slide Layouts

Much of what you need to know about customizing layouts is covered under the preceding heading about editing masters, because it's essential to know how masters affect layouts before you begin to customize or create your own layouts. The following list provides additional guidelines, how-to instructions, and best practice tips for customizing and creating your own layouts.

- To customize a layout, you must be in Slide Master view. To customize any individual layout, just select that layout from the thumbnails in Slide Master view and then customize the layout as you would customize a slide master.

- You can move, resize, or delete any placeholder on any layout. But the really big news is that you can also add your own placeholders to any layout. To do this, on the Slide Master tab, click Insert Placeholder, then click the placeholder type you want from the options you see here.

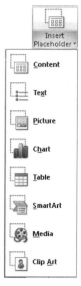

Your insertion point will change to a cross-hair. You can then drag to insert the new placeholder at the exact size and position you want.

- Text and content placeholders come with five levels of default-formatted bulleted text—so don't be concerned if you insert one of those placeholder types and get what looks like much more text than you bargained for. Just format the text as appropriate for your new placeholder, exactly as you'd format text in the master layout. All other placeholders come with a title that indicates the type of placeholder, such as the chart placeholder shown here.

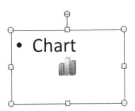

Note that you can delete the text in a text or content placeholder, but you'll still be able to add text (up to nine levels of text) in that placeholder on slides using that layout. And, if you customize the formatting of that text before deleting it, your customizations will be retained when you use that placeholder on a slide.

You can also edit or format the text in other placeholder types. For example, you can change the bulleted title "Chart" in the preceding image to "Click to add a chart" and format it in small, red font. You'll see the edited text appear with the edited formatting in the placeholder on slides that use that layout. However, that text won't appear in print or in a slide show (just like master layout placeholder text) and it can't be edited from a slide.

> **Note**
>
> A quick way to reduce font size when you insert a placeholder that's too small for the default text formatting is to select the placeholder and then press CTRL+SHIFT+<. As you may recall, this keyboard shortcut reduces font size in Word as well as in PowerPoint text boxes. It also works perfectly in PowerPoint on the text in any selected object.

- As mentioned earlier, notice that there is no longer a title master for each slide master because you have access to the Title slide layout (which is, essentially, the same thing). Also notice that one of the new built-in layouts is called Section Header. This is a nice addition and worth pointing out because Title masters were often used in the past for both title and section divider slides, even when the two slide types required different formatting.

- If a layout needs different graphic elements than the master, you can hide all of the master graphics (such as accent shapes or logos) and add your own to the specific layout. To do this, select the layout to customize and then, on the Slide Master tab, in the Background group, click Hide Background Graphics. You're probably already familiar with using this feature to hide background graphics on individual slides. Having it available to layouts as well is a nice touch. (Note that using Hide Background Graphics on a slide layout applies to the graphics on the layout's master, whereas using this option on a slide refers to the graphics on that slide's layout.)

  When you apply this setting to a layout, any graphic objects from the slide master (other than the five master layout placeholders) will be hidden on that layout.

However, if the layout shares a background style with the master, that will be retained. To hide only certain graphics from the master layout on an individual layout, apply Hide Background Graphics and then copy the graphics you do want from the master onto the applicable layout.

- By default, new layouts that you add will be named Custom Layout, then 1_Custom Layout, 2_Custom Layout, and so on. Remember that you can change the name of any layout—which is a good idea for ease of use, particularly if others will be using the presentation or template. To do this, right-click the layout thumbnail and then click Rename. Or, on the Slide Master tab, in the Edit Master group, click Rename.

- Custom layouts that you add become available automatically in the Layout gallery for the presentation or template in which you create them. If you save a custom Theme from the active presentation, your custom layouts will also be available as part of that Theme. See "The Themes—PowerPoint Connection" later in this chapter for more details on saving custom Themes in PowerPoint.

TROUBLESHOOTING

How can I use the vertical text layouts in my presentation?

The two new built-in layouts named Vertical Title And Text and Title And Vertical Text are only available in the Layout gallery if Japanese is an enabled editing language for the 2007 Office release programs on your computer. However, if you want to use these layouts but don't need to edit presentations in Japanese, you can just update the placeholders on the layout and they'll work perfectly.

To do this, in Slide Master view, select the vertical text layout that you want to add to the Layout gallery. Click on the layout itself (as opposed to its thumbnail in the Slide pane) and then select either the Title or Text placeholder. Cut the selected placeholder (CTRL+X) and then immediately paste it back (CTRL+V). The layout will then show up in the Layout gallery.

If you want these layouts to continue to show up in all new presentations, after you use this workaround to add the layouts to the gallery, just save the active presentation as a custom Theme and then set that custom Theme as your default for new presentations. Learn about working with default Themes in the section of this chapter titled "The Themes—PowerPoint Connection."

Thanks go to this book's technical reviewer, Microsoft Office System MVP Beth Melton, for snatching this simple solution out of the jaws of such an odd little glitch.

Creating Effective Slides and Layouts

Up to this point, this section has addressed the mechanics of creating and customizing slide masters and layouts. But, before moving on, let's spend a bit of time on the subject of what makes an effective slide from a design perspective. If you use PowerPoint as the home for documents other than slide presentations, this topic doesn't apply (instead, see Chapter 12 for some design best practices). This section is about creating slides that capture and keep your audience's attention and help get your points across effectively.

When planning your slides, consider the following.

- If you're delivering the slide in person or adding a voice-over, only key points should be displayed on the slide.

  Avoid having slides that repeat the same text you'll be saying or that will be included in any voice-over. The audience doesn't need you to read the slides to them, and doing so will usually lose their attention. Instead, use the slides to guide the audience, provide a framework for your presentation, and highlight important information that you want to emphasize.

- Keep slides clean and accessible, with text or graphics that are large enough to be seen clearly. Crowded slides are hard to read and lose the audience's attention.

  For example, if you think you need eight charts on a slide, stop and think about it. Is the audience really going to look at those eight charts? If they do, how much are they going to absorb from all that information? Similarly, if you have so much text on a slide that you have to reduce font size, consider splitting the content onto multiple slides or displaying some of the text content in graphics.

- Bullets are boring and they don't grab attention. So, should you avoid them completely? Perhaps not, but you can do better than bullets without extra work.

  - If you need your text slides to be text slides, consider using different text formatting for different levels (such as a unique font color) instead of bullets, to give your presentation a cleaner feel.

> **Note**
> Note that, if a text level doesn't use a bullet, TAB and SHIFT+TAB won't work to change the active paragraph to a different level. Instead, use ALT+SHIFT+left or right arrow to change text levels or the Increase and Decrease Indent buttons on the Home tab.

  - Are you sure you need text slides to be text slides? Remember that you can convert a bulleted list to a SmartArt diagram in just one click. And, a simple diagram can often make a much clearer statement with more impact than bulleted text—even if it contains the same content. In fact, if you want a more professional-looking slide, but can't part with your bullets, notice that many SmartArt diagrams are designed to display bulleted text.

    Diagrams help organize your content and enable you to emphasize information more effectively. See Chapter 18 for the full scoop on working with SmartArt.

- With all of the great design elements at your disposal in the 2007 release, be careful not to let design overwhelm content. As discussed in Chapter 18, when you use formatting effects, use them consistently (such as using the same type of gradient across all shapes in a diagram, even if colors in each shape are different).

  This also applies to the master and slide design. For example, just because ten colors (and several shades of each) are available in your active Theme doesn't mean that you need to use all of them in the presentation (and certainly not all together on one slide). Use designs for on-screen presentations that are clean and make it easy for the audience to see the slide content clearly.

See Chapter 18 for more on using the many new formatting effects available in this version, and see Chapter 12 for tips on effective document design that can apply to PowerPoint presentations as well.

Managing Slides and Slide Elements

In this section, we'll look at slide elements for use when creating presentations, including considerations for charts and diagrams, new text formatting options, the much-improved PowerPoint tables feature, and tips for working with embedded objects. We'll also look at some tools for managing slides, including sharing slides (and their associated designs) between presentations and options for reusing slides.

For help creating presentation graphics with SmartArt diagrams, shapes, pictures, WordArt, or Clip Art, see Chapter 18.

A Note About Legacy Presentations

Remember that new functionality, such as SmartArt diagrams, new graphic effects, and native Office Excel 2007 charts in PowerPoint presentations are not available to documents saved in the legacy file formats.

Also keep in mind that, if you save an Office Open XML Format file that contains new functionality down to the legacy file format, objects created with the new graphics engine (such as SmartArt) will be bitmap images when opened in a version of PowerPoint earlier than the 2007 release. Because of this, file size also increases significantly when saving a presentation with many graphics down to the legacy format.

Working with Charts

When you create a chart on a PowerPoint 2007 slide, you now get an Excel chart (provided that Excel 2007 is installed on your computer). What's even better is that the Excel chart isn't an embedded object, but a live, editable object on your PowerPoint slide. Select a chart element, and you'll get the same Chart Tools contextual tabs that you get in Excel. And, because the chart becomes an active slide element, it automatically takes on the active Theme and related formatting.

> **Note**
>
> If Excel is not installed on your system, charts that you create on your PowerPoint slides will still use the MS Graph add-in program used to create charts in earlier versions of Excel.

If you paste a chart from Excel into PowerPoint using the default paste method (CTRL+V), you'll now get the same result as if you created the chart in PowerPoint. However, watch out for two issues.

- If your Excel chart is a PivotChart, it will become a regular chart when pasted into PowerPoint. PivotChart functionality is not supported in PowerPoint. However, the chart will retain all other formatting and layout settings and remain fully functional.

- When you paste a chart from Excel into PowerPoint, you get a linked chart by default. So, if you don't save the source workbook or it becomes unavailable, the source data will be inaccessible.

  When you first paste the chart from Excel into PowerPoint using CTRL+V, you'll see a paste SmartTag at the bottom-right corner of the chart. You can click that SmartTag for the option to embed the data in the chart, so that you don't need the source workbook. Alternately, if you paste the chart as a linked chart and accidentally lose the data, you can paste the chart back into Excel to retrieve that data. For help doing this, see the Troubleshooting tip titled "How can I retrieve lost chart data?" in Chapter 15, "Charts."

CAUTION

> Take care when embedding an Excel chart into PowerPoint (or any program), because the *entire* source workbook (not just the chart data) is embedded when you do this and will be accessible to any recipients of your PowerPoint file who select the chart source data. For this reason, if you need to paste your chart from Excel rather than creating it in PowerPoint, consider creating a copy of the workbook before embedding the chart in PowerPoint, so that you can delete all content other than the chart and its source data.

For help working with the new Excel charting tools, see Chapter 15.

Working with Text

As mentioned earlier in this chapter (and addressed, to some extent, in Chapter 18), there are quite a few new options for font and paragraph formatting on PowerPoint slides. The list that follows addresses the new options along with tips to help you make the most of them.

Font Formatting

New font formatting options include the long awaited All Caps and Small Caps font attributes, as well as Character Spacing, as you see in the dialog box shown here.

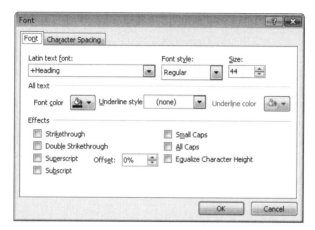

To access this dialog box, click the dialog launcher in the Font group on the Home tab.

Notice the new Clear All Formatting command in the Font group on the Home tab, which clears font formatting (including WordArt Text Fill, Text Outline, and the Shadow, Reflection, and Glow Text Effects) from selected text objects. Alternately, you can use the keyboard shortcut CTRL+SPACEBAR for the same results. Note that this keyboard shortcut (also available in Word) is not new to PowerPoint 2007. The main difference in PowerPoint 2007 is that, because WordArt is now available on native PowerPoint text objects, this shortcut or its Home tab icon equivalent will now clear quite a bit of WordArt formatting as well.

Note that the options to expand or condense character spacing work exactly as they do in Word. Though you can change spacing by as little as one-tenth of a point, it usually requires a full point or two to see a significant difference in text spacing (this varies based on point size and selected font). So, condensing font by just one or two tenths of a point can be a good way to fit text without reducing font size, and won't create much of a visible difference in most cases. However, also keep in mind that some WordArt formatting can have a dramatic effect on text, which might cause character spacing to look different than you expect.

On the subject of WordArt, remember that you can now apply WordArt formatting to any text object or any selected text on a PowerPoint slide. Some WordArt Quick Styles can only be applied to the entire object—this is because some WordArt Text Effects (such as 3-D Rotation or Bevel) can only be applied to the entire object. However, you can select just some text in a text object (such as a text placeholder or a custom text box) and apply Text Fill and Text Outline settings, as well as some Text Effects and WordArt styles. For more on using WordArt, see Chapter 18.

Paragraph Formatting

The primary changes for paragraph formatting are the ability to add multiple columns to a single text box, the ability to add up to nine outline levels in a single text box, and improved indents and spacing formatting.

Before you add additional outline levels, however, ask yourself if the document belongs in PowerPoint. Documents with enough text on the page to require more than five outline levels (or, in many cases, to benefit from the use of text columns) will usually be easier to create in Word and offer more text formatting flexibility.

If, indeed, the document does belong in PowerPoint, use the following guidelines to keep your work as simple as possible when working with any PowerPoint paragraph formatting.

- Text columns are available in any text placeholder or custom text box. To apply a multiple-column setting, on the Home tab, in the Paragraph group, click the Columns button and then click the number of columns you want, as shown here.

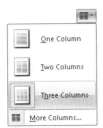

  However, columns in PowerPoint have no space between them by default. So, for better results, select the More Columns option that you see in the preceding image, where you can set the number of columns and specify space between columns. Even though you're not likely to have a reason for many columns in one text box, any text box can have a maximum of 16 columns.

  Also notice that columns in PowerPoint are newspaper columns, meaning that content automatically wraps from one column to the next as you add content. There are no column breaks in PowerPoint, so use this feature only where it makes sense for your text to automatically wrap to new columns as needed.

- To add more than five outline levels to a slide layout or the master layout text placeholder, place your insertion point at the end of the level-five paragraph and then press ENTER, followed by TAB to demote the new paragraph to the next level. (As mentioned earlier, if the active text level isn't bulleted, you can't use TAB and SHIFT+TAB to change the paragraph to another level. In that case, use ALT+SHIFT+left and right arrow, or the Increase and Decrease Indent buttons on the Home tab, to change text levels.) You can repeat this action for up to nine levels.

Format any outline level as you did in the previous version. That is, make changes to outline formatting on the layout or the slide master, as applicable.

- ○ Avoid changing the outline on the slide itself to avoid having inconsistent formatting between slides.

- ○ To apply formatting to all levels (such as font or font size), select the bullet for the top level to select all text in the placeholder, or select the placeholder object itself.

- ○ To apply formatting to an individual level, such as changing bullets or indents, just click in that level. You can also select the entire paragraph for a level in a placeholder to apply font formatting to that level.

- ○ If you change font color for a text level, but want the bullet or number attached to that level to remain the original color, set the bullet or number color separately. To do this, click in the level for which you want to set the bullet or number color. Then, on the Home tab, in the Paragraph group, click to expand the bullet or number options and then click Bullets And Numbering. (You can also find this option when you right-click and then point to either Bullets or Numbering.) Change the color on the appropriate tab of the Bullets And Numbering dialog box. Note that, regardless of the bullet or number color you want, do not leave the color palette setting at Automatic if you want the color to be different from the paragraph text color—select the specific color from the palette instead.

- On the Home tab, in the Paragraph group, click the dialog launcher to open the new Paragraph dialog box. This dialog box, shown in the following image, looks quite a bit like the Indents And Spacing tab of the Paragraph dialog box in Word, with options for paragraph alignment; left, hanging, or first-line indents; spacing before or after the paragraph; and line spacing settings including single, double, exact, and multiple options.

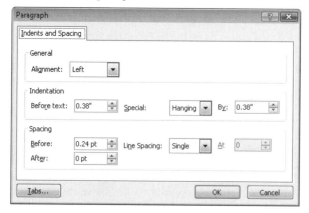

Note that the Before Text indent is the left indent and will behave like a left indent if you set the Special indent setting to None. As in Word, First-Line and Hanging are the options available as Special indents. Paragraph and Line Spacing options work here exactly as they do in Word.

> **Note**
>
> When setting paragraph formatting in PowerPoint, think of the slide master and slide layouts as you think of paragraph styles in Word. To keep paragraph formatting (such as line and paragraph spacing) consistent from slide to slide, set all paragraph formatting that you can on the slide master. For paragraph formatting that applies only to slides using a specific layout, set that formatting on the slide layout. Only apply paragraph formatting directly to an individual text box on a slide when you specifically need unique formatting for that one instance—just like applying direct formatting to paragraphs in Word.

- In the new Paragraph dialog box, also notice that you have a Tabs button, which opens a new Tabs dialog box. Using that dialog box, shown here, you can now set default tab stops (the measurement of 1 shown in this example refers to one inch—tab stops are set in your default unit of measure), set or clear individual tabs, or clear all tabs in the active text box or placeholder.

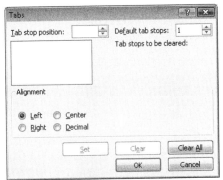

  All of these options work as they do in Word, including the fact that you can only edit the default tab stops from the dialog box (and not on the ruler).

- Despite the addition of the new Paragraph and Tabs dialog boxes, you can still change indents and set or move tab stops on the ruler. To show the rulers (horizontal and vertical), on the View tab, in the Show\Hide group, click Ruler.

  - To move an indent or tab stop on the ruler, drag it just as you would on the ruler in Word. However, to drag an indent or tab in smaller increments than your grid setting (0.083 inches by default), hold the CTRL key while dragging (as opposed to the ALT key in Word).

  - Notice that, fortunately, each outline level's indents now show up separately instead of being crunched together on the ruler at the same time. This makes it easier to adjust indents for individual levels, because you don't have to use the CTRL key to drag the indent from one level over another.

  - When you drag a tab to move it on the ruler, the tab stop icon appears below your insertion point while you drag. This doesn't mean that you're dragging the tab stop off the ruler—the tab stop will still appear in the new location when you release the mouse pointer. However, to remove a tab stop from the ruler, drag the tab stop down off the ruler as you have in the past.

PowerPoint Tables

Native PowerPoint tables are much improved. So much, in fact, that you're likely to need to embed Word tables less often.

However, you can't apply or edit paragraph formatting on multiple selected cells at once, and decimal tabs don't work like alignment in PowerPoint tables (meaning that you have to place a tab character before the text to use them), so you're still likely to want to embed a Word table when you need complex financial tables in your Power-Point presentations. See the next heading in this section for tips on working with embedded Word tables.

But, when it comes to basic text tables, native PowerPoint tables now have everything you need. In fact, because tables in PowerPoint have access to the new graphics engine for formatting, such as WordArt or gradient fills, native PowerPoint tables are now an easier approach (with more flexible formatting) than embedding that table from Word unless you need formatting for complex financials.

Also note that, if you copy a table from Word or Excel and use the default paste method (CTRL+V) to paste it into PowerPoint, it will paste as a native PowerPoint table.

CAUTION !

If you want a table from Word or Excel to paste into PowerPoint as a table, don't select anything on the slide before pasting. If your insertion point is in a text box on the slide, PowerPoint will (logically) assume that you want to paste the table content as text within the active text box.

When you insert a table onto a PowerPoint slide, either from a content placeholder, from the Insert tab, or by pasting it from Word or Excel, you get the Table Tools Design and Layout contextual tabs. The Table Tools Design tab has familiar features—similar to options in Word or Excel—including Table Styles and Table Style Options. On the Table Tools Layout tab, shown here, you get several new formatting options that finally make native PowerPoint tables a serious tool, including cell sizing and cell margin capabilities (and notice the nice Lock Aspect Ratio option when sizing the table).

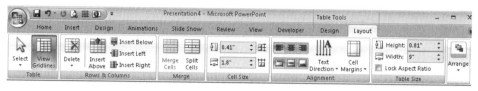

Working with Embedded Objects

Though embedded Excel charts on PowerPoint slides behave very much like native, editable PowerPoint objects (as discussed earlier in this chapter), the same is not true for embedded objects from other programs. When you need to embed an object (so that it remains editable in its original program), use the following best practice guidelines to help simplify your work. Note that this list focuses primarily on embedded Word tables and Microsoft Office Visio 2007 diagrams.

- When you use the default paste method (CTRL+V) to paste text or tables from Word, they paste as native PowerPoint text boxes or tables (respectively). When you use CTRL+V to paste a diagram from Office Visio 2007, it pastes as a picture. To paste these elements instead as embedded objects, so that you can continue to edit them as needed in their source program, use Paste Special. You can access the Paste Special dialog box from the Paste options on the Home tab, or with the keyboard shortcut CTRL+ALT+V.

  When the object you've copied is text or a table from Word, in the Paste Special dialog box, select Microsoft Office Word Document Object. When the object originated in Visio, the Paste Special option to select is Microsoft Visio Drawing Object.

- The embedded object is selected when it's pasted on the slide, and the non-printing, light blue selection box that you also see on diagrams and charts in the 2007 release is visible, as you see in the example shown here.

	Q1	Q2	Q3	Q4
Product A	157.1	72.5	169.2	196.2
Product B	102.0	86.4	120.6	171.6
Product C	179.5	105.5	145.4	168.7
Product D	171.6	102.1	142.7	145.1

- If you paste an embedded Word table that doesn't use the full width (between margins) of the page from which you copied it, you're likely to get extra white space when you paste, as shown in the following example.

	Q1	Q2	Q3	Q4
Product A	157.1	72.5	169.2	196.2
Product B	102.0	86.4	120.6	171.6
Product C	179.5	105.5	145.4	168.7
Product D	171.6	102.1	142.7	145.1

If this happens, you can edit the size of the embedded object. To do this, right-click the object, point to Document Object, and then click Edit. The object will open in editing mode, as shown here.

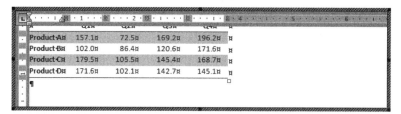

Drag the black handles of the object frame when in edit mode to change the size of the embedded object. You can simply drag in from the bottom-right corner handle to remove most of the white space from around the table.

CAUTION!

Before you drag to resize the frame of an embedded Word table, make sure the table's AutoFit setting is set to Fixed Column Width, or dragging to resize the embedded object may resize your table as well (and Undo won't work on this action). You can apply Fixed Column Width from PowerPoint while editing the Word table in edit mode, as this mode actually opens a Word window. Just click in the table and then, on the Table Tools Layout tab, in the Cell Size group, click AutoFit and then click Fixed Column Width.

- Other than changing the size of the overall embedded object window, to make any changes to embedded objects, use the Open option instead of the Edit option. (To access these options, right-click the object and then point to <Object Type> Object.) The Open option opens the object in a full-size window in its source program rather than in the embedded object area, making it easier to access and edit. In the case of Visio, the Open option also provides full access to the Visio menus, while the Edit option doesn't. (In Word, you get the Word Ribbon with either the Edit or Open option.) When you've finished editing the object in Open mode, you can click the X in the top-right corner of the window to close the object and return to the PowerPoint slide. Or, on the File menu in Visio (or the Microsoft Office Button options in Word), you'll see an option to close and return to the presentation.

TROUBLESHOOTING

How can I easily edit an embedded Word table without Recolor Picture?

If you've had experience using embedded Word tables in the past, you may have depended on Recolor Picture when pasting a table onto a PowerPoint slide with a dark background. The premise was that you could recolor the object for the way it appears in PowerPoint only, but still see the text normally on the plain white Word page when you open the object to edit the table.

Recolor Picture, however, no longer works for embedded objects. But, don't start looking for cumbersome workarounds—you don't need them. Instead, when you open the object to edit it in Word, you can apply a dark page color from the Page Background options on the Page Layout tab. Page Backgrounds don't print by default, so it won't appear on the slide in PowerPoint. But, using a dark page background will allow you to recolor the table so that it looks correct on the dark background in PowerPoint. And, since the Page Background from Word doesn't show up in PowerPoint, you don't have to worry about matching the background color of the slides. For example, to get a table on a PowerPoint slide that looks something like the following image, apply any dark page color from the Page Background settings in Word and recolor the table as you'll need it to appear in PowerPoint.

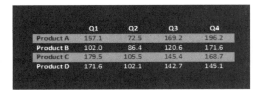

All of the table and text formatting that you apply to the object will show up when you return to the PowerPoint slide, but the page color will not, so that the table will appear exactly as you need it to on your slide background. (Remember to use None as the fill or outline color setting for table elements if you want them to take on the slide background color in PowerPoint.)

Managing Slides

This topic focuses on using the thumbnails in the Slides pane and the Slide Sorter view to access and organize slides, or to share slides between presentations.

The Slide pane and Slide Sorter view are interchangeable for many slide management tasks, including moving quickly to a specific slide or reordering slides by dragging them. You can also paste a slide from one presentation into another in either of these locations. Use the following tips to help you work more efficiently when using the Slide pane and Slide Sorter view.

- The Slide pane is open by default in Normal view. If you don't see this pane, place your insertion point over the left edge of the screen until you see a double-backed black arrow and then drag to the right to expand the pane. This pane includes a tab for slide thumbnails and a tab for an outline of slide titles and any text in text placeholder outline levels. And, as mentioned earlier in this chapter, when you work in Slide Master view, this pane shows thumbnails for slide masters and layouts.

- To open Slide Sorter view, on the View tab, click Slide Sorter. Or, click the Slide Sorter button in the view shortcuts on the Status bar.

- To move to any slide in the presentation, just click that slide in the Slide pane or double-click the slide in Slide Sorter view.

- To delete a slide from the presentation, just select the slide in either the Slide pane or Slide Sorter view, and then press DELETE.

- To add a slide at a specific location, in either Slide Sorter view or the Slide pane, click between slides where you want the new slide to appear, and then press CTRL+M, or right-click and then click New Slide. If you select a slide before inserting a new slide, the new slide will appear after the selected slide.

- To copy or move a slide from one presentation to another, select the slide in either the Slide pane or Slide Sorter view and then copy (CTRL+C). Then, in the new presentation, click in the Slide pane or Slide Sorter view at the location where you want the new slide to appear and then paste (CTRL+V). By default, the slide will take on the destination formatting. However, to retain source formatting, click the paste SmartTag that appears immediately after you paste the slide and then click Keep Source Formatting.

> **Note**
>
> When you select Keep Source Formatting for a slide pasted from another presentation, PowerPoint adds the applicable slide master from the source presentation, along with its associated slide layouts and its applied Theme. When a slide master is added in this way, note that Preserve Master is not turned on; if you delete all slides that use this master, it will be automatically removed from the presentation. To keep the new master even if slides are removed, select the master in Slide Master view and then, on the Slide Master tab, in the Edit Master group, click Preserve.

- Notice that you can perform several actions from the options available when you right-click a slide in either the Slide pane or the Slide Sorter, such as adding a slide, deleting or copying the slide, or changing the slide background. However, from the Slide pane, you also have access to the Layout gallery.

- For most actions in either the Slide pane or the Slide Sorter view, you can select multiple slides at once. As with most selection actions, hold the SHIFT key to select multiple neighboring items and the CTRL key to select noncontiguous items.

- One of the most important features to point out for managing slides is the fact that, because you can have multiple Themes in a PowerPoint presentation (as discussed in the next section of this chapter), you can apply a Theme to any slide or group of slides. To apply a unique Theme to an active slide in Normal view, simply right-click the Theme you want from the Themes gallery on the Design tab and then click Apply To Selected Slides. If the selected Theme isn't already active in your presentation, a new slide master will be added to accommodate this Theme.

You can also select multiple slides in the Slide pane or Slide Sorter to apply a Theme to selected slides. When multiple slides are selected in either of these locations, just click the Theme you want in the Themes gallery to apply it to only the selected slides.

Reusing Slides

As discussed in the What's New section of this chapter, the options for reusing slides depend on the specific edition of the 2007 Office release that you own and whether or not your company uses Office SharePoint Server 2007.

- If you use the Microsoft Office 2007 Ultimate, Professional Plus, or Enterprise editions, a Publish Slides option is available that enables you to save selected slides out of a presentation for later use. Note that, if you purchased your 2007 release suite at retail, the only suite that includes the Publish Slides feature is Ultimate. Professional Plus and Enterprise are both sold only under enterprise licensing agreements.

- The new Publish Slides feature is designed for use with the new Slide Library feature, which is a feature of SharePoint Server 2007. (If you're not sure if your company runs SharePoint Server 2007, check with your IT department.)

- If you're running an edition of the 2007 release that doesn't include Publish Slides, you can still use the new Reuse Slides pane to easily reuse slides from other presentations.

Let's first look at Reuse Slides. On the Home tab, click New Slide, and then click Reuse Slides to access the Reuse Slides pane shown here.

Notice that the Browse options do the same thing as the hyperlinked options Open A Slide Library and Open A PowerPoint File. Whichever one of these you use, available slides appear listed as thumbnails (with their titles as labels) in the Reuse Slides pane. You can point to any slide for a magnified preview, as you see in the following example.

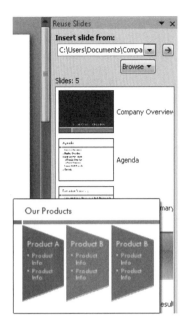

Just click a slide in this pane to insert it in the presentation. To insert the slide at a location in the presentation other than after your active slide, click in the Slide pane where you want the new slide to be added and then click the slide in the Reuse Slides pane to insert it.

To retain source formatting when you insert slides, select Keep Source Formatting in the Reuse Slides pane before clicking the slides you want to insert. Or, if you realize that you want the source formatting after inserting the slides, just right-click the slide in the Reuse Slide pane and then click Apply Theme To Selected Slides.

> **Note**
>
> When using the Reuse Slides pane, if you use either the Keep Source Formatting option or the option Apply Theme To Selected Slides option from that pane, the master associated with the source slide is added to your presentation, but only the slide layouts attached to the inserted slides are included with the master. If you then add other slides with different layouts that use the same master from the same presentation, the new layouts will be added to the appropriate master.

If you aren't using Slide Libraries, the features discussed to this point in the section are all you need for effectively reusing slides. If you use an edition of the 2007 release that supports the Slide Libraries feature, you'll see a Publish Slides option when you right-click a slide in Normal view, the Slide pane, or Slide Sorter view. When you select this option, the Publish Slides dialog box opens, displaying all slides in your presentation. Click to select the slides you want to publish (if you select slides before selecting Publish Slides, your selected slides will appear selected when the dialog box opens), specify a publish location, and then click Publish.

There are three principal benefits to publishing slides to a Slide Library.

- Slide Libraries are designed for enterprise use, meaning that users across your group, department, or organization (depending on permissions assigned in the particular library) can share slides.

- You can add slides from multiple presentations to the same library and later search through that library by topic or simply browse the entire library at once.

- Slide Libraries have revision history capabilities, so that you can update your edited slides in the Slide Library and confirm that you have the most recent version of slides in your presentation. To do this, right-click a slide in the Slide pane or Slide Sorter view and then point to Check For Updates.

If you have the Publish Slides feature but are not using SharePoint Server 2007, publishing slides is not particularly useful. This feature will let you select a location and will behave as if it's publishing your slides to a library, but here's the catch. Each slide is published as a separate PowerPoint file when you use the Publish Slide feature. So, if you don't actually have access to Slide Libraries, when you try to access published files through the Reuse Slides pane, you'll need to use the option to open a PowerPoint *file* rather than a library and then open and view one slide at a time. Yuck. This might occasionally be handy when you have a specific slide or two that you'll need to use often or that you want to share with others as individual slides. Otherwise, just use Reuse Slides with your existing presentations for a more productive experience.

The Themes—PowerPoint Connection

Themes and PowerPoint have a special relationship because Themes are PowerPoint-based functionality, evolved from Slide Designs in earlier versions.

As mentioned earlier in this chapter, Themes in PowerPoint have the same capabilities that they have in Word and Excel. However, in PowerPoint, Themes have additional functionality as well.

> **Note**
>
> For the basics of working with Themes, including understanding the concept and core components of Themes and Theme templates, see Chapter 5 before continuing here. This section assumes that you're already familiar with the Theme basics covered in that chapter.

Why Create Themes in PowerPoint?

Regardless of whether you save a custom Theme in Word, Excel, or PowerPoint, that Theme becomes available automatically to all three programs. However, if you save the Theme in PowerPoint, all slide masters and their slide layouts (built-in and custom, including customizations to built-in layouts) in the active file are saved with that custom Theme.

When you apply a built-in Theme from the Themes gallery in PowerPoint, notice that the Theme contains slide master content and formatting. These are the same built-in Themes found in Word and Excel, but they also carry the slide design with them for use in PowerPoint.

> **Note**
>
> Because Themes are PowerPoint-based functionality and Theme files (.thmx format files) store slide master content, if you right-click a .thmx file in a Windows Explorer and then click New, you'll get a new PowerPoint presentation based on that Theme.

The same behavior holds true for the custom Themes you save, so when you save them from PowerPoint, you get the slide design built in to your custom Theme, as well as the Theme functionality you need for Word and Excel. Keep in mind that you can overwrite an existing custom Theme. So, if you save a Theme from Word or Excel, you can apply it to a PowerPoint presentation, add the slide master and layout customizations you need, and then resave the custom Theme to add those components.

The Master—Theme Relationship

When you open the Themes gallery on the Design tab, notice that you have three categories—This Presentation, Custom, and Built-In—as shown in the following image.

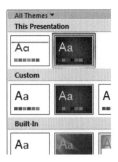

The items listed under This Presentation are the available slide masters in that presentation. When you apply a Theme that contains multiple masters, each master becomes an option in the This Presentation list.

To apply any item from any category in the Themes gallery to only some slides in the presentation, right-click the gallery entry and then select the applicable option from those shown here.

Note that the Apply To Matching Slides option refers to all slides currently using the same master. This option only appears in presentations with more than one slide master. Also note that the Set As Default Theme option, discussed under the heading that follows, does not appear when you right-click a Theme that appears in the This Presentation options.

> **Note**
>
> Remember that, if a slide uses a different Theme, it takes on that Theme's colors, fonts, and graphic effects as well as slide master formatting (just as Slide Designs in the previous version could have their own color schemes). This is an important point to acknowledge when applying multiple Themes in the same document to ensure that you obtain the consistency you want from slide to slide.

Setting a Default Theme

The default Theme is the Theme applied to new, blank presentations that you create without specifying a PowerPoint template. To set a default Theme, right-click the Theme you want in the Themes gallery on the Design tab and then click Set As Default Theme (as you see in the preceding image). Nothing will appear to happen, but the default will have been changed. To test your new setting, press CTRL+N to create a new presentation, and check the Themes gallery to confirm that the This Presentation options are the masters from the Theme you set as default.

Putting on a Show—Slide Show Setup and Animation

Slide Show functionality is largely the same as it was in the previous version, other than being reorganized onto two tabs—the Slide Show tab and the Animations tab, both shown here.

However, some features are worth noting, even if you've used them before. You'll find a summary of notable features under the headings that follow, along with tips for effective slide show setup, slide animations, and slide transitions.

Slide Show Setup

Other than providing additional options under Resolution (which is normally best to set on Use Current Resolution), the Slide Show tab offers nothing new. However, several of these features might seem new simply because they're nicely organized and easily accessible here.

Note that the Setup Slide Show dialog box is virtually identical to the previous version, but you won't need to use it as often because several of the features in that dialog box are now accessible on the Slide Show tab, such as the Monitors group of options. But, the dialog box still has some good options, such as the ability to suppress narration or animation during the show.

A small detail worth noting if you use the pen while presenting a slide show is that, when you choose a pen color from the Setup Slide Show dialog box, you get your primary Theme colors along with the legacy Microsoft Office color palette. However, if you choose your pen type and pen color from the pen options in the slide show, shown in the following image, you can select from the full Theme colors palette.

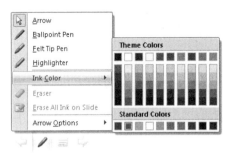

Another change that warrants noting is that you no longer have the option to show speaker notes in a separate window on the same screen within an active slide show. Of course, when delivering a show from a computer attached to both a monitor and a projector (or multiple monitors), you can use Presenter View to have your notes (or anything else you need to access) on one screen and the show on another.

However, you can control the show from the Slide options (shown in the following image) on the presenter panel during the show, whether or not you use Presenter View.

Two additional features that deserve mention are Custom Slide Show and Hide Slide, both available on the Slide Show tab. When you hide slides (which you can also do when you right-click a slide in the Slide pane or Slide Sorter view), the slide doesn't appear when you deliver the slide show on screen. (Note, however, that hidden slides are available in the Go To Slide list on the Slide options shown in the preceding image.) In the Slide pane, you see a box with a line across it over the slide number for a hidden slide and, to help you recognize hidden slides more easily, they now appeared faded in the Slide pane as well. However, it's easy to forget that slides are hidden if you want to skip them sometimes and use them at other times. So, if you haven't tried Custom Shows, I recommend giving that feature a try instead of using the Hide Slide feature.

When you create a custom show, you can specify which slides to include and in what order. And, custom shows are saved with your presentation. To create a custom show, on the Slide Show tab, click Custom Slide Show and then click Custom Shows. In the Custom Shows dialog box, you can click New to define a new show, or edit, delete, or duplicate existing custom shows. You can also select a custom show in this dialog box and then click Show to start the slide show. Once custom shows exist in your presentation, when you click Custom Slide Show on the Slide Show tab, the custom shows will be listed. Just click one of the entries in that list to start the show. (Note that slides you exclude from a custom show are not available in the Go To Slide list in the Slide options when in Slide Show view.)

> **Note**
>
> Remember that many keyboard commands are available while you're in a slide show to help you navigate and manage the show more easily. That list, shown in the dialog box image that follows, is available by pressing F1 while in Slide Show view.
>
>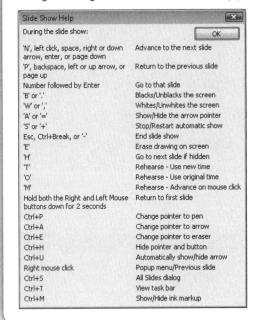

Animations and Transitions

The Animations tab is also primarily a reorganization, but it does offer some welcome easy access to commonly used features. And, there are a few nice changes in Animations simply because certain object types (such as charts) are now editable, accessible objects (so PowerPoint can animate them one element at a time).

Notice the Animate list in the Animations group, where you can select from common animation options, which vary as available to different object types. For example, if you select a title placeholder on a slide, you'll see the following quick-access Animate options.

If, on the other hand, you select a chart, the following Animate options are available.

Of course, you can also click Custom Animation on the Animations tab to open the Custom Animation pane, where you can apply a wide range of animation options to each slide element. The Custom Animation pane is unchanged from the previous version, as you see in the following image.

Just select a slide element and then click Add Effect, where you can select from a variety of Entrance, Emphasis, Exit, or Motion Path animation options. Notice that you also get options for each effect, such as how the effect starts (by mouse click, or during or after the previous animation) as well as the speed and (if applicable) direction of the effect. You can change the order of effect execution, and you can click the drop-down arrow that appears next to each applied effect to view several options, including an Effect Options dialog box with settings that vary based on both the effect type and the object type (such as animating a chart by series, category, or individual elements within each). Finally, notice the double chevron icon below the second effect in the Custom Animation pane shown earlier. That icon is an expander, which is available when one animation contains several sub-steps. In the image shown earlier, the animation with an expander is a chart animated by series. When you click the expander, you see and can individually access the sub-steps for that effect.

> **Note**
>
> For the occasional presentation that warrants some whimsy, check out custom paths if you've not tried them before. When you click Add Effect, point to Motion Paths, then point to Draw A Custom Path and click to select a tool to use for drawing (Line, Curve, Freeform, or Scribble). Try the Freeform tool, using it exactly as you would if you were drawing a freeform object (see Chapter 18 for help with that tool).
>
> Your freeform drawing won't appear on the slide, because you're just drawing a path for the selected object to follow. When you preview the animation for your custom motion path, you'll see that the object to which you applied that animation will dance around the screen, following the path of your freeform drawing like a buzzing bumble bee. It's not the most practical tool for the typical business presentation, but it's quite a bit of fun.

As for Slide Transitions, the functionality is actually the same as in the previous version, but transition effects are now available from a gallery instead of a task pane. As with most galleries, just point to an option to see a Live Preview of the effect on your active slide. Also notice that the same additional settings are available in the Transition To This Slide group that were formerly available on the Slide Transitions task pane, including Speed, Sound, Advance Slide options, and the option to apply a single transition effect to all slides. (Note that the Apply To All option applies the transition effect, sound, speed, and advance slide settings.)

Using Animation Effectively

Be consistent and use animation sparingly. As is the case with slide formatting, slide animations and transitions can overwhelm or distract your audience from your content if used either inconsistently or too liberally.

It's usually a good idea to use the same or similar transitions from one slide to the next (unless you have content that specifically warrants a unique introduction). When it comes to using animation effectively, best practice normally dictates the use of consistent, simple animation (if any) to introduce points as you address them. Then, add more unique or flamboyant animation *only* for major announcements or key hot buttons. Think of it from the audience's perspective—if your information needs that much dressing up, what's wrong with your information?

Additionally, always consider who your audience is when deciding what transitions and animation to use. For example, if you're presenting to your manager's conservative boss or an unknown potential client, silly sounds and charts that explode across the screen are probably not the best way to go.

As with any type of formatting for any document, remember that the point of your presentation isn't to demonstrate how many cool software features you know; it's about conveying your important information.

Chapter 19

PART 5

Templates, Automation, and Customization

The Many Faces of Microsoft Office Templates

A re you ready to take it to the next level? You're about to begin the part of this book where you have an opportunity to do just that.

Actually, the question isn't really whether you want to take it to the next level, but how far you want to go. Templates in the Microsoft Office programs can mean everything from a simple document that you reuse to custom functionality that automates the process of creating or customizing documents. In fact, templates now can even mean individual document components, such as Quick Style Sets in Microsoft Office Word 2007 or Themes that work across multiple programs in the 2007 Microsoft Office release.

In this first chapter of the templates, automation, and customization part of the book, we're examining the options—the types of templates you can create using Office Word 2007, Microsoft Office Excel 2007, and Microsoft Office PowerPoint 2007, and what you need to know to get them done.

> **Note**
>
> Programming coverage actually begins in the next chapter, but programming options for automating templates are discussed here. Note that the terms *automation*, *extensibility*, and *programming* all refer to using a programming language, such as Microsoft Visual Basic for Applications (VBA) and XML that are addressed in later chapters. Also note that the term *code* is used in this and subsequent chapters to refer to programming code— that is, commands written using a programming language such as VBA or XML.

Chapter Assumptions

For this chapter, I assume you know the basics of what a template is and how to create a new document based on a template, and that you're at least somewhat familiar with template file extensions from a recent version of Microsoft Office. I also assume that you're familiar with many of the features discussed throughout the Word, Office Excel 2007, and Office PowerPoint 2007 parts of this book. For example, you'll find instructions for creating a Building Block template in this chapter, but you'll need to be familiar with Building Blocks to be able to use those instructions.

For help with that particular example, see Chapter 9, "Quick Parts." For help with any unfamiliar feature that I mention in this chapter, see the applicable Word, Excel, or PowerPoint chapter for the topic. I won't assume you're familiar with any feature unless it's covered in this book.

In the introduction to this book, you can find a list of resources for those who want more basic-level information, in the section titled "Who Will Benefit Most from This Book."

What's New for Templates in the 2007 Release

Templates take on a wider role in the 2007 release than they play in earlier versions. You can still create templates for the same purposes as you've used them in the past, but you can now also create and share a variety of custom content and custom formatting types as templates. In addition to saving documents as templates in Word, Excel, and PowerPoint, you can save Quick Style Sets or Building Blocks to their own templates in Word, custom charts to their own individual templates in Excel, and your own custom Themes for use in all three programs.

For some new template types, such as Themes and Excel charts, there are new, unique file extensions. For others, such as Building Blocks and Quick Style sets, the type of template you get is determined simply by where you save the file.

As for adding automation to templates, you'll learn a bit about the possibilities in this chapter, but how to get it done is addressed in the three chapters that follow. One of the most significant changes regarding automation relates to what you can and can't customize in the user interface. You used to be able to create toolbars and menus for Word, Excel, or PowerPoint, directly from the user interface or using VBA. Now, though you can save a custom Quick Access Toolbar right from the <Program> Options dialog box for any Office Open XML Format document or template, customizing the Ribbon requires the use of XML. Ribbon customizations can, however, be stored in individual templates, providing more flexibility for some programs than toolbar and menu customizations could in the past. Learn the basics for customizing the Ribbon in Chapter 22, "Office Open XML Essentials."

> **Note**
>
> Remember that the term Office Open XML Formats refers to all 2007 release files that use the new four-character file extensions. For the core file types in Word, Excel, and PowerPoint, the Office Open XML Formats are those that append the three-character file extensions you know (such as .dot or .xlt) with an *x* for macro-free templates or an *m* for macro-enabled templates. For a review of essentials for using the Office Open XML Formats, see Chapter 1, "Welcome to the 2007 Microsoft Office System."

What Type of Template Do You Need?

Do you just want to create a simple template with some content or formatting to use as the basis for new documents? If so, here's what you need to know.

1. Start with the document that you are going to save as a template and add whatever content and formatting you want to include in the template.

2. Click the Microsoft Office Button and then click Save As (or press ALT+F, A). Select the template type you want from the Save As Type drop-down list (such as .dotx for a Word template, .xltx for an Excel template, or .potx for a PowerPoint template), name your file, and then click Save.

   In Excel and PowerPoint, notice that your Save In location is automatically moved to the designated user Templates folder when you select a template file type. This occurs so that your new template will automatically be available from the New Workbook or New Presentation dialog box (depending on the program).

   In Word, because the default template type (.dotx) can be used for content templates as well as for Building Block or Quick Styles templates that reside in different locations, your folder location isn't changed automatically when you select a template file type. Instead, if you're running the 2007 release on Windows Vista, click Templates in the Favorite Links pane, as you see here.

If you're running Microsoft Windows XP, click Trusted Templates in the My Places bar.

> **Note**
>
> The Templates option in Favorite Links or My Places is available only when you're working in Word, and can be found in both the Open and Save As dialog boxes.

You now have a template that can be used as a basis for new documents. Just click the Microsoft Office Button and then click New (or press ALT+F, N) to open the New <Document Type> dialog box. Then, to access your custom templates, click My Templates in the list of template sources on the left side of the dialog box. That's all there is to it.

Wait a minute. That's not really all there is to it. Though you can create a template that way and be done with it, and you'd be far from alone in doing so, I don't advise it.

Technically speaking, all it takes to create a template is to save your file in a template file format. But, whether you create templates to simplify document creation, save time, standardize content, or standardize appearance, take a bit of time to consider how the template will be used and by whom, and put some best practices in place. After all, if the template is not well-crafted or intuitive for others to use, it won't simplify, save time, or standardize anything.

The subsections that follow explain the types of templates available in Word, Excel, and PowerPoint, along with some best practice recommendations. Then, the program-specific sections later in this chapter help you identify elements to consider when planning whatever type of template you need.

INSIDE OUT   Do you really need a template?

If you're creating a template just to reuse the same content, do you need a template at all? When you just want to reuse one document as the basis for another, you can use the feature New From Existing <Document Type> in Word, Excel, or PowerPoint to create a new document that is an exact copy of your selected document. Find this option among the template sources listed in the New <Document Type> dialog box (ALT+F, N). Or, right-click a document in a Windows Explorer and choose New to accomplish the same result.

So, is there a difference between using the New From Existing feature and creating a template, when all you need is to reuse content? In some cases, templates can store information that documents can't—such as Building Block entries in Word (which is the case for AutoText entries in earlier versions as well). But, when the physical content on the page and a bit of formatting (such as a set of styles) are all you need, the main difference between using a template or a base document is conceptual, not functional.

The benefit of using a template just for reusing content is to avoid losing or overwriting existing document content. For example, when a document is saved as a template for reuse, double-clicking that template file from a Windows Explorer automatically creates a new document instead of opening the existing document.

However, though you can save templates to your user Templates location to access them from My Templates when creating new documents, you can save documents, workbooks, and presentations in that folder as well, and they'll also appear in My Templates for the applicable program.

If you are the only person who will be reusing this document and you don't need to re-use it often, using New From Existing or saving a document to your user Templates location is every bit as good as creating a template, and you can always save it as a template later if the need arises. But, when you need to create similar documents frequently, or you're creating a template for others to use, saving the file as a template helps keep the file's purpose clear and intuitive regardless of what content the template requires.

Also keep in mind that, when Word documents are attached to a template, you may be able to make your changes just to the template in order to apply them to all documents attached to that template. See the section titled "Considerations for Word Templates" later in this chapter for more information.

Content Templates

The most common types of templates, by far, are content templates. A content template simply means a template that contains content you want to reuse. Templates of this kind might contain boilerplate text, graphics, page layouts, and a variety of Building Block types (such as cover pages and tables of contents), or they might be complete documents that you often need to copy and change. Consider the following examples.

- Templates for fax cover sheets, memos, or similar basic business documents may contain your company letterhead and contact information, as well as the heading table in which you enter fax or memo data such as to, from, and subject.

- A template for a report that you submit periodically may contain page layouts set up for the types of content required in your report, as well as some boilerplate text for items that remain largely the same from one report to the next.

- A template for a new client presentation may contain several complete slides that you use as-is or customize for each new business pitch.

- A project budget template is likely to contain a list of line items to help ensure that you remember to plan for all possible costs. And, it may be organized into tables with formulas so that you can just add the new numbers for each new project and get your calculations automatically.

Design Templates

The idea of design templates is most closely associated with PowerPoint, where a .pot file created in previous versions contains slide masters and color schemes that can be applied to any presentation. However, a design template actually means any template you use for the purpose of keeping appearance consistent from one document to the next, such as a template that provides custom font or color formatting to match your company's branding.

For example, a Word template containing letterhead formatting, a logo, and a set of styles might be considered a design template—even though the letterhead information and logo make that a content template as well. Similarly, an Excel design template might include a company logo along with custom table and cell styles.

However, design templates have been redefined in the 2007 release with the introduction of Themes. Instead of storing a set of colors or font preferences in an individual template, you now store them in a Theme template—a .thmx file—from which you can apply them to any Word, Excel, or PowerPoint document or template. Other design elements, such as logos, letterhead, and styles, still belong in your individual templates.

For more information on Theme template components, see the section of this chapter titled "Sharing Themes." For help working with Themes in each program, see the following.

- See Chapter 5, "Styles," for the basics of using and creating Themes in Word.

- See Chapter 13, "Data-Based Documents: Formatting and Managing Worksheets," for information on using Themes in Excel (which is extremely similar to using them in Word).

- See Chapter 19, "Slides and Presentations," for an overview of the Themes–PowerPoint connection, including additional elements of Themes created in PowerPoint, as well as how Themes relate to PowerPoint templates and masters.

INSIDE OUT   Apply a PowerPoint design template from previous versions

In previous versions, you can apply a design template (.pot or any PowerPoint file from which you want to use just the design) to a PowerPoint presentation by using the Browse option on the Slide Design task pane (or the Apply Design Template dialog box, depending on the version). To use a template for slide design in PowerPoint 2007, you apply that template as a Theme.

To do this, on the Design tab, in the Themes group, click to expand the Themes gallery and then click Browse For Themes. In the Choose Theme Or Themed Document dialog box, select your design template and then click Open. Each master in the template you select will be added to your current presentation as its own custom Theme. For more on this topic, see Chapter 19.

Form Templates

Creating templates for forms that others complete and return is a bit different from creating a typical content template, because the purpose of the form is to collect information. Forms contain unique layout requirements and might require other settings, such as Document Protection in a Word-based form template.

If you're like most people, you probably think of form templates as being created in Word, or perhaps in Excel. But, there is a logic to which program is the best for the form-related task.

Forms can do more than provide a static document into which users can enter information. Before creating your form, think about how that form will be used, such as how the form is delivered to the intended recipient and where the information in that form needs to go (such as into a database). That information can help you determine the best program and best approach for the particular form.

For any form from which the data doesn't need to be entered into another system, it's fine to treat the form like a content template and just create it without much concern about how the form data is structured. You might use a basic table with cells as form fields, for example, or use Content Controls in Word or ActiveX controls in Excel or PowerPoint, without worrying much about the properties or behavior of those controls beyond what you need the user to see on the screen.

However, before you say that the data doesn't need to be entered anywhere else, think twice. If a form is returned on paper, such as a checklist of services required that someone might complete when dropping off a document in the copy department—you're probably correct that the form data doesn't need to be entered anywhere else. But, for just about any form that's delivered electronically, something gets done with the data in that form. Even if you're only compiling a list from the returned forms, would it save time for that list to be automatically compiled from the form data?

Also remember that, just because you're not creating the form with the intention of putting the returned data into an electronic receptacle, doesn't mean that information from that form will never need to be electronically entered somewhere else. Consider human resources (HR) performance review forms, for example. Perhaps the HR department simply prints the performance reviews when they receive them and places a hard copy in the employee's paper file. Is there no information from the form that gets added to an electronic employee record? What if employee records that are currently on paper become electronic in the future? Wouldn't it be more efficient and cost-effective to create the form in a way that could be easily adapted to extract that information if the need arises?

When you want to be able to extract data from a form automatically, you have a few choices. First of all, the Office Open XML file formats make it much easier than ever to extract data from documents through a few methods. My favorite of these is using Content Controls in Word, where you can bind the control to custom XML data. Then, when the form is returned by the user, it just takes some simple code to extract that custom XML into whatever format you need, such as an Excel table. To learn about using Content Controls in Word, including an explanation of data binding, see Chapter 11, "Content Controls: Creating Forms and Then Some." To learn the basics of how to bind Content Controls to custom XML data, see Chapter 22.

Chapter 20

> **Note**
>
> If you're creating a form template in Word that you don't believe needs to return data automatically, using Content Controls to structure the form is still a good idea, both for ease of completion by the user and to make it easier in the future to adapt those forms for dynamic data if the need arises. Learn more about structural considerations for Word templates in the Word-specific section later in this chapter.

No question about it, XML is the easier way to go, and data binding with Content Controls in Word makes that about as easy as it can be. But, if you must, you can still use the legacy form controls in Word, or the Form or ActiveX controls in Excel (or even ActiveX controls in PowerPoint) to create forms. Then, use VBA or more advanced programming techniques (such as managed code written in Microsoft Visual Studio Tools for Office) as necessary to enable the behavior you want from the form controls or to extract data from the completed form.

Because easier and more dynamic options are available in the 2007 release, the legacy form control approach isn't addressed specifically in this book. Of course, if the simplicity of data binding in Word leaves you pining for the overcomplicated solutions of the past, keep in mind that you can use what you'll learn in this book's VBA Primer as a jumping off point for anything you want to learn to do with VBA in Microsoft Office.

> **Note**
>
> If your company needs several forms that return data for use in other systems, think about whether a form-specific solution might be a better way to go than just creating individual forms in Word, Excel, or PowerPoint. Microsoft Office InfoPath 2007 is an XML-based program used specifically for creating forms as part of a workflow process. With an InfoPath form, a user can click a button to submit the form, and data from that form can be parsed into several locations (such as databases or e-mail messages) as needed.
>
> Office InfoPath 2007 integrates with Word and Excel, so that you can create InfoPath forms in Word or Excel (if you prefer) when both programs are installed on your system. InfoPath can also integrate with Excel as well as Microsoft Office Access 2007 and Microsoft Windows SharePoint Services, for both creating the data source and returning data. Additionally, if dynamic forms are a substantial requirement for your company (such as for a market research firm or an insurance company), check out Microsoft Office Forms Server 2007 for an enterprise-level form-management solution.
>
> Find links to more information about InfoPath and Office Forms Server 2007 on the Resources tab of this book's CD, along with a link to free trial versions of InfoPath or any 2007 release program. Also on the Resources tab, find an article titled "Always in Good Form: Collect and Share Information Easily with Office InfoPath 2007 and the 2007 Office System" by Beth Melton, a Microsoft Office System MVP and this book's technical reviewer.

Feature-Specific Templates

Document Themes, discussed both earlier and later in this chapter, are the most wide-reaching of template types in the 2007 release—storing PowerPoint master content as well as sets of colors, fonts, and graphic effects for use in Word, Excel, and PowerPoint documents.

On the other side of that spectrum, you also get three new, very specific template types that apply to individual features—Document Building Blocks, Quick Style Sets, and Excel charts.

Document Building Blocks

You can save a template of Building Block entries to be available to any Word document. Document Building Blocks are one of two new types of global templates available in Word. (See the section titled "Differentiating Between Automated Templates, Global Templates and Add-Ins" later in this chapter for more on global templates.)

Building Blocks can be saved in any Word template that uses the new Office Open XML Formats (.dotx or .dotm). However, when they're saved to a document template that you use to create new documents, the Building Block entries stored in that template are only available to the documents attached to that template. Instead, if you save that template in the Document Building Blocks folder, any content in that template other than Building Block entries is ignored, but the Building Block entries saved in that template become globally available. Additionally, Building Block entries stored in any global template (such as those stored in the Startup folder for Word) are available to all documents as long as that global template is loaded.

To create a Building Block template, do the following.

1. Save a blank Word document as a Word template, using the .dotx file extension. In the Save As dialog box, choose the Document Building Blocks folder as the Save In location.

   By default, assuming that C is the drive letter where you have Microsoft Office installed, this folder is located in Windows Vista at C:\Users*your name*\AppData\Roaming\Microsoft\Document Building Blocks. In Windows XP, the path is C:\Documents and Settings*your name*\Application Data\Microsoft\Document Building Blocks. (You can also save Building Block templates to the numbered subfolder inside the Document Building Blocks folder, which is the location of your Building Block.dotx template, discussed later in this section.)

> **Note**
> The numbered folder used in this and other default file paths provided in this chapter differs by locale, corresponding to language settings. For example, the folder number for US-English installations is 1033.

Chapter 20

Remember that, to store Building Block entries, the file must be saved as a template. You can use the .dotm file extension instead of the .dotx extension, but there's no reason to allow macros in a template used only for Building Block entries. Also keep in mind that, if you save Building Block entries to a legacy format template (.dot), those entries can only be added to the AutoText gallery (which doesn't appear on the Ribbon by default).

2. Add Building Block entries to the new template, in one of the following ways.

  o Select your new template as the Save In location when saving the Building Block entry, as you see in the following dialog box.

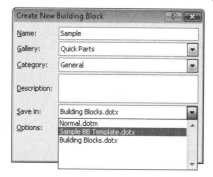

  o Move the entry to the new template by editing the properties of that entry. To access the properties of a Building Block entry, right-click the entry in the gallery where it appears and then click Edit Properties. Or, select the entry in the Building Blocks Organizer and then click Edit Properties.

> **Note**
>
> For a template to be an available Save In option when you save a new Building Block entry or edit the properties of an existing entry, it must be open in your current Word session, attached to the active document, or installed as a global template.

3. Once you have the Building Block entries you want, save the file and exit Word. When you next open a new Word session, the Building Block entries saved in your new template should appear in their assigned galleries, available to all of your documents.

   Alternatively, if you don't want to exit your Word session, you can just save and close the template and then load it through the Templates And Add-Ins dialog box, to make its entries available during your current Word session. When you next start Word, the template will load normally on its own. To load a template manually, on the Developer tab, in the Templates group, click Document Template. Then, click the Add button, browse to and select your new template, and then click Open, followed by OK to close the Templates And Add-Ins dialog box.

> **Note**
>
> Once you've saved a template in the Document Building Blocks folder or loaded it as a global template, that template becomes a global Building Block template, available as a Save In location for any new Building Block entries. Whenever you add Building Block entries to a global template, keep in mind that you will be prompted to save changes to that template when you next exit Word.

TROUBLESHOOTING

How can I reset Building Blocks.dotx to its original state?

Similar to Normal.dotm, the global template in which many of your Word settings are saved, if you delete Building Blocks.dotx when Word is not running (you can't do this while it is running), a new Building Blocks.dotx will be generated when you next open Word.

Find your Building Blocks.dotx file, by default, in a numbered folder that resides inside your Document Building Blocks folder. Be sure that this is the location from which you delete Building Blocks.dotx. As discussed in the remainder of this tip, there is also a master Building Blocks.dotx file that you should never delete. Also, take note of the instruction here to delete the Building Blocks.dotx file rather than to rename or move it. Unlike Normal.dotm (or Normal.dot in earlier versions), renaming or moving Building Blocks.dotx will not necessarily keep its settings from loading. If you want to save the entries from the Building Blocks.dotx file that you need to replace, you can rename it, but you must also move it to a location where you know that it won't automatically load as a global template (such as to one of your document folders).

Each time a new Building Blocks.dotx is generated, the file returns to its original state without your custom entries. Of course, that original state has to come from somewhere as well—and that's the master Building Blocks template. So, for example, if you're working in a company where you need to customize everyone's Building Block galleries, you can customize the master Building Blocks.dotx so that deleting the Building Blocks.dotx that appears in the user's folder will replace it with your customized version.

Find the master Building Blocks.dotx file in the numbered folder that appears in C:\Program Files\Microsoft Office\Office 12\Document Parts. (This file path is the same regardless of your operating system.) However, be aware that damaging this file will cause Building Blocks to be unable to regenerate itself. So, it's a good idea to make a backup copy before making changes to the master Building Blocks file. For more on master files, see the section titled "Understanding Template Locations" later in this chapter.

Quick Style Sets

You can save the set of styles included in the Quick Style list for any active document or template as a Quick Style Set template. To do this, customize the Quick Style gallery as you want it to appear for the Quick Style Set template (keep in mind that styles added to the Quick Style list will be included whether or not they appear in the gallery), and then do the following.

1. On the Home tab, in the Styles group, click Change Styles, point to Style Set, and then click Save Quick Style Set.

2. In the Save Quick Style Set dialog box, name your new template and then click Save. The template is automatically saved using the .dotx file format and is placed in the Quick Styles folder.

By default, your Quick Styles folder is located in the same path as the Document Building Blocks folder (which varies based on your operating system), as indicated in the preceding section.

Even though you can save Quick Style Sets from any active document through the Change Styles option, you can also save any .dotx file as a Quick Style Set template. Similar to the way Building Block templates work, when you save a .dotx file in the Quick Styles folder, the Quick Style gallery saved in that template automatically becomes a Quick Style Set available to all documents.

When you do this, the name of the template becomes the name of the Quick Style Set, and is added to your Style Set list the next time you start a new Word session. Find the Style Set list on the Home tab, under the Change Styles options. To learn more about Quick Style sets, including how to create them by adding or removing styles in the Quick Style gallery, see Chapter 5.

> **Note**
>
> Technically, you can save a .dotm or .dot file as a Quick Style Set template as well as a .dotx file, just by saving it in the Quick Styles folder. However, similar to the reasons for saving Building Block templates as .dotx files, there is no need to enable macros in a Quick Style Set template (making .dotm files unnecessary). In addition, a .dot file (the legacy template format) will be missing some functionality essential to styles, such as the ability for styles to be Theme-ready.

Excel Chart Templates

In earlier versions of Excel, you can save user-defined custom chart types . All of your user-defined charts are saved to the same file, which you can then share with others. You can even create new charts in that file and they appear as user-defined custom chart options. (User-defined charts in the previous version of Excel are stored in the file Xlusrgal.xls.)

The new Chart templates in Excel have very similar principles to the previous user-defined chart types, such as the fact that all format and layout settings are saved as part of the Chart template (including such potentially tricky settings as customized axes, discussed later in this section). However, with Chart templates, each chart you save as a template is saved as a separate file, which you can individually share with other users or other computers.

To save a chart as a template, select the chart and then, on the Chart Tools Design tab, click Save As Template. The file is saved in the new Chart Template File format (.crtx) to the Charts folder that's located inside the main user Templates folder. Unlike the feature-specific templates in Word, Chart templates do not use a template format that you can select through the Save As dialog box. To save Chart templates, always use the Chart Tools Design tab option.

When saving a chart as a template, it's important to keep in mind that literally all settings will be stored. (Some formatting, however, may not behave as expected when you use your chart template. For details, see the Troubleshooting tip later in this section titled "Charts based on my custom template don't respond to Theme changes.") So, as mentioned earlier, if you customize an axis scale to match the data of your current chart, the template you save based on that chart will have that customized scale. If you then use that template to create a new chart containing different data, the data might not appear correctly on the chart. For example, if your template contains a value axis scale set to a maximum of 100, and you use that template to create a chart with values ranging from 200 to 300, none of your values will appear on the new chart until you correct the axis scale.

> **Note**
>
> Though all settings in your chart are stored in the template, including which titles appear on the chart, text you add to the chart title or axis titles is not stored in the template. New charts based on that template show placeholder text for any titles that were included on the template's base chart.

Note that Chart templates might not work seamlessly for some complex chart types. For example, if you save a template based on a combination chart for which the different series use different types of x-axes (such as a price/volume chart, discussed in Chapter 15, "Charts"), you might need to correct for some confusion in charts based on that template, such as applying the correct chart type to the correct series, or changing the axis on which a series is plotted. When you save a Chart template, particularly if others will be using it, try it out on sample data to ensure that it will be easier to use than creating that chart from scratch.

Chapter 20

TROUBLESHOOTING

Charts based on my custom template don't respond to Theme changes

Even if you use Theme-ready formatting (such as colors from the Theme Colors palette) when formatting the chart you save as a Chart template, charts based on that template won't automatically respond to Theme changes.

When you create a chart based on a Chart template and want that chart to update to reflect the Theme in the current workbook, either reset the chart to match the applied style, or select a different style from the Chart Styles gallery on the Chart Tools Design tab. To reset the chart, select the Chart Area and then, on the Chart Tools Layout tab, in the Current Selection group, click Reset To Match Style. Depending on the formatting applied to your chart, keep in mind that you may lose some customizations when you reset the chart to match the applied style.

Differentiating Between Automated Templates, Global Templates, and Add-Ins

You can add automation, such as macros or custom Ribbon groups, to any document template in Word, Excel, or PowerPoint. Learn more about doing this in Chapters 21 ("VBA Primer") and 22.

In addition to automation for document templates, you can also create global templates in Word—or add-ins in Word, Excel, or PowerPoint—containing automation or customizations that can be available to any document in the applicable program.

A global template in Word, as mentioned earlier, is a template with content that's available to you in Word regardless of the template attached to the active document. Normal.dotm is the default global template for Word, in which many of your defaults and settings are stored, and it serves as the default template for new documents. If you customize Normal.dotm and later want to reset it to the default, just delete Normal.dotm from your user templates folder (identified in the section that follows) or rename that file, and a new Normal.dotm will be generated the next time you start Word.

You can add other global templates to Word, such as to save custom macros containing company-specific information, or to save a set of timesaving document production macros for yourself to be available when you work on any document. When you save a template in your Word startup folder, it automatically becomes an available global template when you next open Word, provided that your macro security is set to allow global templates and add-ins to be added. You can also save templates to any trusted location and then add them as global templates through the Templates And Add-Ins dialog box. As mentioned earlier, to access this dialog box, on the Developer tab, click Document Template. To add a template as a global template, on the Templates tab of that dialog box, click Add.

If your template is not saved in a Trusted Location for global templates, such as your Startup folder for Word, you will need to manually load it on subsequent sessions. The way in which global templates load also depends to some degree on your Trust Center settings, discussed in Chapter 23, "Using VBA and XML Together to Create Add-Ins."

In Excel or PowerPoint, automation must be saved in an add-in file format, and stored in the Add-Ins folder, in order to make automation or customizations stored in that file available when you work on any document in the applicable program. You can save Excel or PowerPoint add-in files directly from the Save As dialog box in either program. Learn how to create global templates as add-ins for Word, as well as simple add-ins for Excel and PowerPoint, in Chapter 23.

Add-ins can also be created for Word, Excel, or PowerPoint by using managed code. Professional developers can take automation and customization further by working in a professional development platform, such as Visual Studio Tools for Office, and packaging programs to install as add-ins to your Microsoft Office programs.

 Using developer tools that require software beyond the Microsoft Office programs or Windows utility programs is beyond the scope of this book. However, if you find yourself itching for more after the VBA and Office Open XML introductions in this book, find additional resources (including resources for learning about Visual Studio Tools for Office) available on this book's CD.

Understanding Template Locations

Several references have been made throughout this chapter to folder locations for accessing or saving templates. Following, for quick reference, is a summary of template locations and some key points for working with them.

User templates

- Your primary Templates folder, which also contains the Chart templates folder, can be found in the same location as your Document Building Blocks and Quick Styles folders.

    - By default, on Windows XP, this location is:
      C:\Documents and Settings*user name*\Application Data\Microsoft

    - By default, on Windows Vista, this location is:
      C:\Users*user name*\AppData\Roaming\Microsoft

Built-in and master templates

- Master Building Blocks.dotx as well as the built-in templates (including Themes) for several Microsoft Office programs can be found by default in C:\Program Files\Microsoft Office, regardless of your operating system.

    - Find most built-in document templates in the numbered folder that appears at: C:\Program Files\Microsoft Office\Templates

    - Find the built-in Document Theme files at:
      C:\Program Files\Microsoft Office\Document Themes 12

    - Find the master Building Blocks template in the numbered folder that appears at: C:\Program Files\Microsoft Office\Office12\Document Parts

If you explore these folders, please do so carefully. C:\Program Files\Microsoft Office is also the location where, by default, the actual executable program files and supporting system files are stored for your Microsoft Office programs.

You can edit or add to your trusted locations, such as changing the destination folder for user templates, through the Trusted Locations tab in the Trust Center. To access this dialog box, click the Microsoft Office Button and then click <Program> Options. Click Trust Center, then click Trust Center Settings, and then click Trusted Locations. You'll see the options to add, modify, or remove trusted locations.

Considerations for Word Templates

When creating content templates for Word, keep the following best practices in mind.

- Use the Manage Styles dialog box to hide any styles you don't want users of the template to access, as well as to prioritize the order in which styles appear in the Styles pane. If your template is set to use a Theme or Quick Style Set specific to your company branding, remember that you can disable Theme or Quick Style Set switching in the Manage Styles dialog box.

- Make sure any components that you want to use the applied Document Theme, such as styles or existing template content, are Theme-ready.

- Also, to help keep the correct styles easy to identify and use, add styles you want users to access to the Quick Style gallery, and remove any styles from the gallery that are not used in the template.

- Be sure that all styles are updated to include all formatting you need in those styles. To make the styles and formatting as intuitive as possible for others to use, avoid leaving direct formatting on top of paragraphs in your template content.

- Remember that you can set up headers and footers for more pages than your template contains. For example, if you use a Different First Page header and footer for a letter template, but the template you save will only contain a single page, you can add a page break while creating the template in order to add content to the regular header and footer that will appear when a user's letter exceeds one page. To save the template with only the first page, just delete the page break once you're done. Once you add header or footer content to a document, that content remains until you remove it, even when it doesn't appear on the page.

- If your template includes tables, particularly if users will need to add tables, create or customize table styles and set the table style you want to be used for most tables in the template as the default table style for that template. Also take the time to add details, such as Repeat Header Rows, on tables as needed.

- If your template includes some elements that you want to be sure are not edited, you can protect the document so that only specified portions of the document body can be edited. To do this, on the Review tab or the Developer tab, click Protect Document and then click Restrict Formatting And Editing. Check the option

Allow Only This Type Of Editing In The Document and then select No Changes (Read Only) from the list. Once you do this, you can select parts of the document and then choose to allow all or specified users to freely edit those portions, as you see in the following task pane.

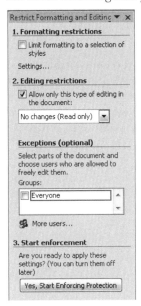

Note that headers and footers can't be made editable in a protected document, but footnotes or endnotes can be edited when the reference appears in an editable part of the document.

When you click the option to start enforcing protection, you can add a password if desired. Editable portions of protected documents are highlighted on screen by default, and a pane appears to users of the document through which they can turn off highlighting or browse through editable portions of the document.

Because documents based on a template remain attached to that template, keep a few things in mind when using documents created from custom templates.

- To reset the styles that are part of the template, use one of the following options.

  ○ Use the new option Reset To Quick Styles From <template name> Template. To find this option, on the Home tab, in the Styles, group, click Change Styles and then point to Style Set. Reset To Quick Styles From <template name> Template appears below your list of available Quick Style Sets. This option will reset any styles that exist both in the active document and the attached template's Quick Style list, and will add any styles in the template's Quick Style list that don't appear in the active document. Custom styles saved only in the document will remain intact.

  ○ Use the option Automatically Update Document Styles. To access this option, on the Developer tab, click Document Template. Once you select this option, the styles from the attached template are added to your active document, replacing existing styles of the same names. However, any additional styles you've added to your document that are not in the attached template will not be affected.

It's a good idea to avoid leaving this setting enabled, so that you don't accidentally delete customizations or lose your custom styles if the attached template becomes unavailable.

- If you make changes to the styles or formatting defaults through the Manage Styles dialog box that you want to be available to all documents based on the same template, select the New Documents Based On This Template option at the bottom of the Manage Styles dialog box. As that option indicates, only new documents based on that template will be affected. However, if the changes you save are style definitions, those can be updated in existing documents attached to the same template by using one of the methods mentioned earlier in this list.

- If the template attached to a document contains Building Block entries, macros, Ribbon, or Quick Access Toolbar customizations, those are available to any document based on the template as long as the attached template is accessible. So, if you make changes to Building Block entries, macros, Ribbon, or toolbar customizations in the template, those will apply to existing documents based on that template as well as to new documents.

> **Note**
>
> Find a set of basic Word templates in the sample files you can install from the Welcome tab of this book's CD, that you can use as an example of some of the preceding best practices. This template set includes coordinated letter, fax, memo, and report content templates, along with related Building Block (Custom BB Sample.dotx) and Quick Style Set (Custom QSS Sample.dotx) templates.

Considerations for Excel Templates

Keep the following best practices in mind when creating Excel templates.

- Custom Cell Styles and Table Styles will be available to any workbooks based on the template. So, be sure that custom styles are Theme-ready if you want to allow Theme-switching. Also, consider details to simplify working with styles, such as setting your preferred default table style.

- Watch for potential user complications in workbooks saved as templates. For example, avoid hidden rows, columns, or sheets in your template unless they're intentional, to avoid leaving unwanted content in the workbooks created from the template. Also, remove any print area settings or frozen panes, unless they're intuitive and would be applicable to any use of that template. You might also want to delete any unused sheets in content templates, to avoid user confusion and keep workbooks looking consistent.

- Avoid linking cell content to external content unless that content will be available to any workbook created that's based on the template.

- When you name ranges, tables, charts, or PivotTables in a template, consider if the names will be intuitive for others to recognize and use effectively.

- If you reduce the data range from its original state, take a moment to reset the used range on any worksheets in the template. See the Troubleshooting tip on this topic in Chapter 14, "Working with Data," for help getting that done.

- Remember that Excel workbooks, like Word documents, can now use different headers and footers for the first page or for odd and even pages, and format your template accordingly. As in Word, header and footer content that you add to the template is retained even if it doesn't appear in the workbook.

- As mentioned earlier, when saving Chart templates, avoid customizing scales on axes. Also, as mentioned previously, test out your Chart template for possible complications, particularly if it's for a complex chart type, to ensure that using it to create new charts will be easier than creating those charts from the built-in chart types.

> **Note**
>
> Remember that you can add the sheets from any Excel template saved in your user Templates folder to your active workbook. To do this, right-click a sheet tab in the active workbook and then click Insert. From the Insert dialog box that opens, select the template to apply and then click OK. All sheets in the template (as well as any custom cell styles saved in that template) are added to your active workbook.

Considerations for PowerPoint Templates

When creating PowerPoint templates, consider the following.

- PowerPoint templates (.potx or .potm files) are now similar to Word and Excel templates in that they should be used as content templates. Themes are now the better way to save design content, as discussed in Chapter 19.

- Any formatting that should be global to all slides, or all slides that use a particular layout, should be set up on the applicable master or layout for consistency and ease of use. See Chapter 19 to learn about the relationship between Themes, masters, and layouts.

- Remove any layouts from the slide masters that you don't want to be available to users. And, be sure to use intuitive naming conventions for any custom slide layouts you create.

- Be sure that any slide content that you want to update with changes to the Theme is applied using Theme-ready formatting, such as colors or fonts from the Theme options.

- If your template is for a slide show, remove any animation, transition, or timings applied to slides unless those settings should always be used for the particular slide, regardless of the presentation. If such settings are used on slides, consider adding notes about this in the notes pane for the slide or in a comment on the slide, to avoid unexpected complications for users.

Sharing Themes

To share a custom Theme with another computer, keep in mind that a Theme consists of four files.

- The .thmx file, which is the main Theme file
- An XML file for the Theme colors
- An XML file for the Theme fonts
- An XML file for the Theme effects

If you copy just the .thmx file to another computer, that Theme will be available from the Themes galleries in Word, Excel, and PowerPoint on that computer. However, Theme font, color, and effects will not be visible on those galleries as separate entities unless the XML files related to those fonts, colors, or effects also exist on the destination computer (such as when built-in options are used).

Similarly, you can copy just a set of custom Theme colors to another computer without taking its related custom Theme. Find your custom .thmx files and XML files for custom Theme fonts, colors, or effects, in a Themes folder within your user Templates folder, the location of which is referenced earlier in this chapter.

To share a custom Theme with all of its components, copy all four files to the matching folders on the destination computer. Note that, typically, you'll only need to copy the .thmx file and the XML files for fonts and colors. This is because Theme Effects can't be customized from the user interface in Word, Excel, or PowerPoint, so most of your custom Themes will use a built-in Theme Effects set (unless you have created custom Theme Effects XML files) that would be available on the destination computer by default.

Also keep in mind, as mentioned earlier, that you can share a custom Theme with another computer by opening a file that uses that Theme through the Browse For Themes feature. Just save the custom Theme, as well as custom Theme colors, fonts, and effects, from the active document to create that custom Theme on the destination computer.

The Office 2007 Automation Story

When you want to create macros to save yourself time while working in Word, Excel, or PowerPoint, use VBA. To add macros for any purpose to the Ribbon, or to customize the Ribbon in other ways (such as creating a tab with some of your favorite features), use XML. VBA or XML can be used, depending on the specific functionality you need, to automate actions in your documents. And, the two can be used together to create add-ins for Word, Excel, or PowerPoint.

In the next chapter, learn the basics of VBA programming. Following that, get the essentials of Office Open XML, including how to edit Office Open XML Format files directly in the XML, how to bind data to Word Content Controls, and the basics of how to customize the Ribbon. Finally, in Chapter 23, learn how to begin using VBA and XML together to create simple add-ins for Word, Excel, and PowerPoint.

Chapter 20

If you have any concerns about venturing into this chapter, take a deep breath and relax. You'll be perfectly comfortable here. This is the first thorough primer on Microsoft Visual Basic for Applications (VBA) written for advanced Microsoft Office users, and not for programmers.

I'm not a programmer, so I won't treat you like one. The fact is that you don't have to be a programmer to make effective use of VBA (or XML, as discussed in the next chapter). Yes, I use VBA and XML to develop solutions for clients, but that just means I'm taking advantage of all the tools that Microsoft Word, Microsoft Excel, and Microsoft PowerPoint have to offer for creating documents. If you can learn to format a table, create styles, or create fields in Microsoft Word; to write formulas or generate charts in Microsoft Excel; or to customize masters in Microsoft PowerPoint, you can learn VBA.

After years of avoiding VBA because it seemed technical and scary, I fell head over heels one day after I had no choice but to venture into the Visual Basic Editor for a client. I discovered both how easy it is and how much you can do with VBA even with just a basic level of knowledge. But, the most important thing I discovered was how much of the VBA language I already knew just from being an advanced Microsoft Office user. Nearly all elements of VBA that are specific to each program are the names of features and tasks you already know from using the program. Keep in mind that VBA is just an additional way to work with, and expand the capabilities of, the programs you already know.

Outside of the program-specific feature and task names, most VBA language and structure is virtually identical across Word, Excel, and PowerPoint. So, the majority of what you'll learn in this primer will apply to macros you may want to write in any of these programs. However, because I assume that this is your first introduction to writing VBA (or writing any programming language, for that matter), I use one program for most examples, to avoid the confusion of trying to cover too much too fast. Because Word is the primary document production program for Microsoft Office, most examples throughout this primer use Word VBA. Just keep in mind that, once you're comfortable with Word VBA, you can apply all of the basics you learn to VBA tasks in Excel and PowerPoint as well.

When and Why to Use VBA

One of my favorite examples of both when and why to use VBA if you're not a programmer, came up one evening at dinner with a friend. She had been up until 3 A.M. the night before cleaning up tables for a report that was due that day. It was a Word document containing 50 tables copied from Excel that needed to be cleaned up and reformatted. The task took her, a power user, about six hours—which, at just over seven minutes per table, isn't bad.

But, she wanted to know if there was a quicker way for her to have gotten it done. She had created a few table styles and even recorded a macro for some of the formatting, but still had click into each table to apply them and then manually take care of any unique elements for each table.

In reply to her question, I asked if she knew any VBA, and she looked at me as if I had to be insane. But, then I told her that if she had known some basic VBA (just part of what you'll learn in this primer, by the way) she could have accounted for most of the differences between her tables in one macro and then formatted all of those tables at once. The task would have taken about six minutes instead of six hours. As you can imagine, learning VBA no longer seemed like a crazy idea.

Of course, this timesaving example is just one of several types of situations where you can benefit from VBA. As you saw in a couple of simple examples in the Excel chapters of this book, you can often use a single line of code to save substantial time or even do things you can't do through the features in the user interface. Or, to take things further, you might also use VBA to create customizations or automation for your documents and templates, such as with custom dialog boxes that can help users complete form documents.

In general, the answer to the question of when to use VBA is the same as when to use any feature in the Microsoft Office programs—use it when it's the simplest solution for the task at hand. In the case of VBA, however, you may also be able to use it when there doesn't appear to be a solution for the task. VBA expands the capabilities of Word, Excel, and PowerPoint, so that you might find yourself with easy answers to tasks that you didn't even know were possible.

In the 2007 release, however, it's important to ask yourself if VBA is still the simplest solution before you embark on a complex project. With the introduction of the Office Open XML Formats, you can do some things in the 2007 release more easily today with XML—such as automatically populating document content with data from other sources. Also, some functionality that would have required automation in the past can now be done with built-in features, such as using a Content Control to display a custom Building Block gallery when you need a selection of boilerplate text options that can't be deleted. However, VBA macros are still almost exclusively the way to go when you want to use automation to save time on repetitive or cumbersome tasks.

Introduction to the VBA Language and Code Structure

The easiest way to begin learning VBA is to record macros and then look at what you've recorded in the Visual Basic Editor. In the subsections that follow, we'll use this method to help you become acquainted with how to read VBA code.

> **Note**
>
> Macros can no longer be recorded in PowerPoint (which has always been the most limited of the three programs in terms of VBA capabilities), but you can still write VBA macros in PowerPoint. Macros can be recorded and written in Word and Excel.

So, what is a macro? A macro is simply a set of commands that can be executed together, similar to a paragraph style. However, where a style is a collection of settings that you can apply at once, a macro is a collection of actions.

Recording Macros

When you record a macro, literally every step you take is recorded, including moving your insertion point up or down or making a selection. Note that, while recording a macro, your insertion point can't be used as a selection tool. Use the arrows on your keyboard, along with the SHIFT key, to make selections as needed while recording a macro.

> **Note**
>
> Experienced users of VBA continue to find macro recording useful for learning how to accomplish new tasks in VBA. One thing we all run into at some point, however, is the fact that a handful of commands can't be recorded. For example, if you record a macro while adding items to the Quick Access Toolbar or the Quick Styles gallery, your steps won't be recorded. In some cases, a macro that can't be recorded means that you can't accomplish the task through VBA, but it doesn't always. You can do a great many things when writing VBA that can't be done by recording macros, such as applying a document Theme. Learn more about this later in this chapter, as well as how to get help for finding commands that can't be recorded.

 To begin recording a macro, on the Developer tab, in the Code group, click Record Macro. Or, on the Status bar, click the Record Macro icon shown beside this paragraph.

Once you click Record Macro, the icon changes to a blue Stop Recording box. Click Stop Recording on either the Developer tab or the Status bar when you've finished recording your macro.

Let's try one together, as an example. Say that you're starting a new, long presentation document. Each page of the document needs to begin with Headings 1, 2, and 3, consecutively, followed by a paragraph of body text. The first several pages of that document will each begin with the text *Company Overview–* in the Heading 1 paragraph, which will be followed after the em dash by different text on each page.

To save a bit of time, let's record a macro for setting up these pages.

> ### Setting up the sample document
>
> Before recording the macro, I set up the document in the interest of using the simplest method for any task. I set Style For Following Paragraph for Headings 1, 2, and 3 to the style that follows each heading at the top of every page. I also added Page Break Before formatting to the Heading 1 style, so that my new pages are started automatically when I apply Heading 1. Even so, I can still save time on setting up these pages by using a macro.
>
> If you'd like to save time on this document setup, you can find the file First Recording.docx in the sample files you can install from the Welcome tab of the book's CD. The document contains no text, just styles Heading 1 through Heading 3 customized as indicated in this sidebar.

With your insertion point at the top of the empty document, click Record Macro and then do the following.

1. In the Record Macro dialog box, type a name for your new macro. Macro names must start with a letter and can include letters, numbers, and the underscore character, but can't include spaces or most special characters.

   Notice in the Record Macro dialog box, shown in the following image, that recorded macros are stored, by default, in the global template Normal.dotm.

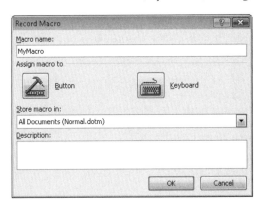

In the Save In drop-down list, you have the option to select any open document or template, including currently loaded global document templates (Building Block and Quick Style Set templates won't be available here). For now, leave the default Save In setting and click OK to begin recording.

2. Apply Heading 1 style to the active paragraph.

3. Type **Company Overview–** (To add the em dash, you can use the keyboard shortcut CTRL+ALT+(keypad)-.)

4. Press ENTER four times.

Because Style For Following Paragraph has been set for the first three heading styles, these four hard returns add paragraphs with the styles Heading 2, Heading 3, and Body Text, consecutively, followed by an additional Body Text paragraph. That additional Body Text paragraph is where your insertion point will be when the macro starts to run again, so it will become Heading 1 style in the first step of the macro.

5. Click Stop Recording.

To run that macro, on the Developer tab, click Macros, select the macro you just recorded, and then click Run.

With this particular macro, you could run it each time you need to set up a page, or run it as many times as you'll need identical pages. Or, you could edit it to add functionality that enables it to do even more for you, such as automatically adding the number of pages you need. But, for the moment, let's just look at this macro as an example to demonstrate how to read VBA code.

How to Read VBA Code

To view the macro you just recorded, on the Developer tab, click Macros. Then, select your macro from the Macro Name list and click Edit. This will open the Visual Basic Editor with your macro open on screen. Your screen should look something like the following image.

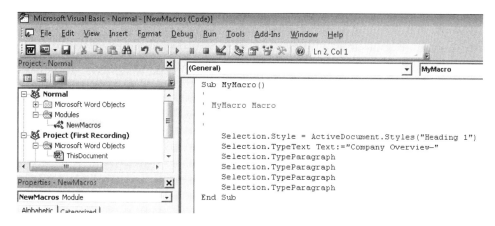

For now, focus on the macro itself—we'll look at the different elements of the Visual Basic Editor shortly.

- Sub stands for subroutine, which is basically just another term for macro. Every macro begins with **Sub** and ends with **End Sub**, as you see in the preceding example.

- The first few lines below **Sub** in the preceding example have an apostrophe at the beginning of the line. Those are comments. An apostrophe at the beginning of a line of VBA code means that there is no code to run on that line. When you record macros, VBA automatically adds some comment lines, one of which includes the name of the macro, as you see in the preceding image.

  You can delete any line that begins with an apostrophe without damaging the macro. Be sure, however, not to delete the apostrophe and leave other text on the line that you don't want to run as a VBA command. The apostrophe is what causes the line to be skipped when the macro runs.

- After the comment text, you see the commands that comprise the steps of this macro. If you tried this for yourself and you see more lines of code in your macro than in my sample, ask yourself if you took other steps. If, for example, you made a typo in the *Company Overview* text and went back to correct it, that could have been recorded as a collection of several steps. Remember that when a macro is recorded, every keystroke is recorded. So, each time you use a different arrow key to move your insertion point, for example, you'll get another line of code. Take a look again at the commands from the preceding macro.

```
Selection.Style = ActiveDocument.Styles("Heading 1")
Selection.TypeText Text:="Company Overview-"
Selection.TypeParagraph
Selection.TypeParagraph
Selection.TypeParagraph
Selection.TypeParagraph
```

Notice that this code doesn't include any unfamiliar terms, even if you've never seen a line of VBA code before. Selection, style, active document, type text, and type paragraph all refer to extremely basic Word tasks. The majority of program-specific terms in VBA will be similarly familiar, just from your experience with the program.

As you progress through this primer, you'll come to understand how to construct the lines of code you see above and how you can write your own macros that are even simpler than recorded macros for accomplishing the same tasks.

TROUBLESHOOTING

Why does my recorded macro have so many lines of code, when I only did one thing?

As mentioned earlier, when you record a macro, every keystroke is recorded. So, you often end up with much more code for a simple action than you would if you wrote the macro yourself.

In particular, if you use a dialog box to execute an action while recording a macro, you're likely to get far more code than you may expect. The reason for this is that, when you click OK to accept the settings in a dialog box, you're accepting all settings in that dialog box. VBA doesn't record your keystrokes while you're in most dialog boxes, so it must record every setting you accepted when you clicked OK.

For example, if one step in my macro was to bold a selected word, and I used the bold icon in the Font group on the Home tab, the code for that command would look like this:

```
Selection.Font.Bold = wdToggle
```

If, on the other hand, I opened the Font dialog box to apply bold and then clicked OK to close the dialog box, the code for that command would include all of this:

```
With Selection.Font
.Name = "+Body"
.Size = 11
.Bold = True
.Italic = False
.Underline = wdUnderlineNone
.UnderlineColor = wdColorAutomatic
.StrikeThrough = False
.DoubleStrikeThrough = False
.Outline = False
.Emboss = False
.Shadow = False
.Hidden = False
.SmallCaps = False
.AllCaps = False
.Color = wdColorAutomatic
.Engrave = False
.Superscript = False
.Subscript = False
.Spacing = 0
.Scaling = 100
.Position = 0
.Kerning = 0
.Animation = wdAnimationNone
End With
```

Notice that what VBA did was record a setting for every option in the Font dialog box. This is because of the limitations related to recording macros with dialog box commands.

Chapter 21

If you write a macro, or edit your recorded macro, you don't need to specify any setting unless you want the macro to execute that setting. In this example, if you were to delete everything between the lines that begin `With` and `End With`, except the `Bold` setting, you'd still get the result you need. (Learn about the `With...End With` syntax later in this primer, in the section titled "Grouping Statements.")

Statements, Procedures, Modules, and Projects

To begin to work in the Visual Basic Editor, one of the most important things to understand is how files work in VBA—that is, how macros are organized and stored. The following common items are the principal components you need to know.

- A **statement** is a single command or action in a macro—that is, it's a line of code. For example, `Selection.Font.Bold = wdToggle` is a statement. As you'll see in the section titled "Writing, Editing, and Sharing Simple Macros" later in this chapter, when you think of VBA as a language, think of a statement as a sentence.

- A **procedure** is, essentially, another way of referring to a macro, although there are other types of procedures as well, such as **functions**. A function is a procedure that returns a result.

- A **module** is a collection of code. Think of a module as a code document. A module can contain several procedures. And, like documents, modules can be saved as files, copied, and shared.

- A **project** is the collection of all modules and related VBA objects in your document, template, or add-in. A project might have one or several modules, as well as other elements such as UserForms (dialog boxes).

Understanding and Using the Visual Basic Editor

Before you start working with VBA code, take a few minutes to settle in to your surroundings. To help you work more comfortably, the subsections that follow tell you a bit about each of the components of the Visual Basic Editor that are identified in the following diagram.

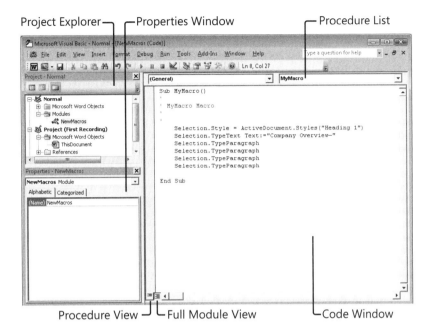

Project Explorer — Properties Window — Procedure List

Procedure View — Full Module View — Code Window

The Code Window

The code window is where your procedures appear. This is where you type macros when writing code and where you find the macros you've recorded. Notice that the Procedure list is at the top-right of the code window. From this list, you can quickly move to any procedure in the active module.

Also notice the view options at the bottom of the screen. When you have several macros in a module, it can be helpful to view them one at a time. Full Module view is the default, but you can change this setting and many others through the Options dialog box, discussed under the heading "Setting Up Your Workspace" later in this section.

Project Explorer

Project Explorer is where you see the list of all VBA projects that are currently open or loaded. All open documents, as well as open or loaded document templates, appear here, whether or not they contain macros. You can collapse or expand a project to view the modules and objects that it contains.

Chapter 21

> **Note**
>
> Documents appear in this list whether or not they're macro-enabled file formats. This is important to keep in mind because, if you add code to a document using an Open XML Format that ends with the letter *x*, you won't be able to save the document with its code. Save the document with the equivalent file format that ends in the letter *m* to enable your code to be saved along with the document or template.

- A project only has a Modules or Forms folder if it contains code modules or User-Forms. However, in Word and Excel, each project contains an Objects folder, such as the Microsoft Word Objects folder you see under each of the projects visible in the preceding image.

  In Word, the Objects folder contains a document object referred to as ThisDocument. In Excel, it contains both a ThisWorkbook object and a sheet object for each existing sheet in the workbook. Some types of code (such as a type of procedure known as a document-level event) are added directly in the code window for the document object rather than in a module. However, you will often have projects that have no code added to the document objects. Learn more about using the document objects in the section titled "Introduction to Using Events" later in this chapter.

The Properties Window

The Properties Window shown in the preceding image doesn't look like much, but don't be fooled. For modules, the Properties Window is generally used only to edit the module name. However, for some object types (such as UserForms), the Properties window becomes extremely important because it's populated with many settings that you can edit directly in that window, ranging from the height and width of a UserForm to the value to display on a form control (such as a text box or an option button).

To edit the name of a module in the Properties Window, click into the name where it appears on either the Alphabetic or Categorized tabs, edit it as you would document text, and then press ENTER to set it. Module naming rules are the same as macro naming rules—no spaces or special characters, and the name must begin with a letter.

> **Note**
>
> All names in VBA subscribe to a similar set of rules. Names must always start with a letter, and can't include spaces or most special characters. Most names are limited to 255 characters in length. However, module names can't exceed 31 characters, and macro names added in the Record Macro dialog box are limited to 80 characters.

Note that, when you record macros, they're always added to a module named NewMacros. You can rename that module if you like, but the next time you record a macro, a new module will be created with the name NewMacros.

Setting Up Your Workspace

You'll find many settings that can be customized in the Options dialog box, available on the Tools menu in the Visual Basic Editor. I don't recommend spending much time in this dialog box just yet, because you might not be familiar with many of the settings. But, it's good to know that it's there, because you will need it. I'll point out, throughout this primer, when settings can be customized in this dialog box.

Possible settings in the Options dialog box include default behavior for a number of programming actions (such as the way you're notified about errors in your code), the formatting for each type of text or notification you see in the code window (such as comment text or errors), and the way the window itself is arranged.

In addition to settings in the Options dialog box, notice that you can drag to resize docked panes in the Visual Basic Editor window (such as the Project Explorer or Properties Window), or close those you don't need. Use the View menu to access any windows you've closed. If you're unable to dock any window in the Visual Basic Editor, you can change the setting for that window on the Docking tab of the Options dialog box.

Chapter 21

Writing, Editing, and Sharing Simple Macros

> Note
>
> All code samples shown throughout the headings in this section are available in procedures in a module named PrimerSamples.bas, which you can find in the sample files you can install from the Welcome tab of this book's CD. See the heading "Saving and Sharing Macros" later in this section for help importing a module into your Visual Basic Editor.
>
> Most of the features you'll learn about in this section are programming basics. They're written here specifically for VBA. However, it might be useful to know, should you ever want to learn another programming language, that many of the concepts and terms used throughout this section are fairly standard across common programming languages.

One of the most important differences between macros you record and macros you write is that, when you record a macro, you need to select an object to act on it. But, when you write macros, you can usually identify items to act on instead of selecting them. That apparently simple difference gives you tremendous power and flexibility. For example, you can write a macro to act on all tables in your document automatically, rather than recording a macro that you run from each table.

The section you're beginning is the core of this primer. From creating a macro to reading and understanding essential VBA language constructs, the headings in this section progress in a logical order to help you learn in a way that you can immediately put your knowledge into practice. I recommend reviewing the content under each heading and trying examples for yourself in the Visual Basic Editor. Be sure that you understand the content covered under each heading before progressing, and you'll be using VBA comfortably before you know it.

Creating Modules and Starting Procedures

To create a module, start by selecting the project (in Project Explorer) to which you want to add the module. Note that you can click any element contained in the project, such as the project name or the Modules folder (if one exists). Then, on the Insert menu, click Module.

> **Note**
>
> You can also insert a module from the Insert icon on the standard toolbar. Notice that this icon defaults to what you last inserted (such as a module or a UserForm). Click the arrow beside the icon to select a different item from the available options, as you see here.
>
> - UserForm
> - Module
> - Class Module
> - Procedure...

To rename the module, click into the name field in the Properties Window, as mentioned earlier. Type the new module name and then press ENTER.

Once you have a module in which to create your macros, you can just click in the code window and begin typing to create a macro. As you saw in the sample recorded macro, every macro begins with the term **Sub**, followed by the name of the macro, and then followed by a pair of parentheses. Those parentheses can be used to hold instructions for the macro or information about references in the macro, but it's rarely necessary to type anything between the parentheses for basic document production macros. Even if you type nothing between the parentheses, however, you must include the parentheses in this line.

Notice as well that every macro ends with the line **End Sub**. Many types of instructions you'll learn throughout this section are paired (such as **With** and **End With**, demonstrated under the heading "Grouping Statements" later in this section). When you type the first line of a macro (beginning with **Sub** and ending with the pair of parentheses) and then press ENTER, VBA adds the **End Sub** line automatically. (If you prefer, you can omit the parentheses when you type the first line and VBA will add them as well.)

Chapter 21

But, with most paired terms, the end term isn't added for you. It's good practice to always type both ends of a paired structure at the same time, so that you don't forget to later. When macros become longer or more complex, finding the missing end portion of a paired structure can be a frustrating use of time.

So, to start a macro in your new module, type the following.

```
Sub MacroName()
End Sub
```

The statements that comprise your macro will go between these two lines.

> **Note**
>
> Throughout the next several headings in this section, code samples are provided that show only the relevant code for the particular topic. Remember that, to run that code in the Visual Basic Editor, it needs to appear within a procedure, so you need to add the surrounding **Sub** and **End Sub** statements discussed here.

Objects, Properties, and Methods

Just as the languages you speak are comprised of nouns, verbs, adjectives, and other parts of speech, VBA is comprised of objects, properties, and methods. Think of objects as nouns, properties as adjectives, and methods as verbs.

- An object is just that—it's a thing that can be acted on.

- A property is a characteristic of an object—something that describes the object, such as its size or style.

- A method is an action you can perform on an object. For example, **Save** and **Close** are both available methods for the **ActiveDocument** object.

The only difference between the sentence structure in a spoken language and in VBA is that, though you need a noun and a verb in any sentence, you need an object in every statement, but either a property or a method might be used to complete the statement. Let's take a look at a few examples.

- In the following statement, **ActiveDocument** is an object and **Save** is a method.

  ```
  ActiveDocument.Save
  ```

- In the following statement, **Selection** is the object (referring to the location of the insertion point—the actively selected content) and **Style** is a property of that selection. **Body Text**, in this case, is the setting for the indicated property.

  ```
  Selection.Style = "Body Text"
  ```

- Objects are often used as both objects and as properties of other objects, depending on where they're placed in a statement. In the following statement, `Tables(1)` refers to the first table in the active document. Though a table is an object, it's also used here as a property of the active document. `Style`, in this statement, is a property of the specified table.

```
ActiveDocument.Tables(1).Style = "Table Normal"
```

  Even though `Tables(1)` in this case is a property of `ActiveDocument`, it's still an object. Notice that the style being set is a property of the specified table.

  You typically don't need to think about whether an object is being used as an object or a property, similar to distinguishing whether an *-ing* verb (such as *creating*, *editing*, or *dancing*) is being used in a given sentence as a noun or a verb. What's important is to see that many objects, such as a table, require a higher-level object to make the reference specific enough for VBA to understand. For example, you can't write simply `Tables(1).Style` to indicate the style of the first table, because VBA needs to know what range you're referring to when you tell it to act on the first table. Otherwise, you might be referring to the first table in the document, the first table in the selection, or a number of other possible ranges. Just keep the distinction in mind that many objects can also be used as properties of other objects, because this will come in handy when you reach the heading "Getting Help" at the end of this section.

Looking at the preceding list of examples, you might be wondering how you're possibly supposed to memorize every possible object, property, and method name for each program in which you need to learn VBA. Well, relax. You hardly need to memorize anything at all when it comes to program-specific terms. When you understand the concept of using objects, properties, and methods to create statements, and you remember what you already know (the features of the program you're automating), you'll learn the names of the particular objects, properties, and methods the same way you learn vocabulary in a spoken language—simply by using it.

Object Models

The set of VBA vocabulary that's specific to a given program is known as the program's object model. The Visual Basic Editor in each program also contains a "dictionary" of sorts for that object model, known as the Object Browser. You can use the Object Browser (available from the View menu or by pressing F2) to search for the correct terminology to use for a given feature, or to see what properties or methods are available to a given object. For example, take a look at the range of results you get when you use the Object Browser in the Word Visual Basic Editor to search for the term *table*.

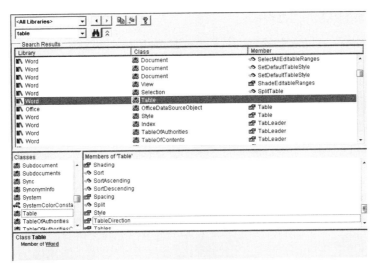

Notice in the preceding image that the selected item in the search results is the table object. The heading *Classes* refers to items in an object model that can have an available set of members—such as objects or modules. Properties and methods are members of a specified class. Notice the headings *Classes* and *Member Of 'Table'* in the bottom panes of the Object Browser.

> ### Note
>
> When searching for terms in the Object Browser, remember that terms don't get spaces between multiple words in VBA. Separate words in a single term are denoted by initial capital letters, such as the `ActiveDocument` object or the `PageSetup` property. Searching in the Object Browser isn't case-sensitive, but the Object Browser won't recognize multiple words as a single term. For example, searching for *page setup* in the Object Browser will return no results, but searching for *pagesetup* will return several.

In the following list, also notice the icons used in the Object Browser to denote objects, properties, methods, or library. These will also be seen while you're writing code, as explained under the next heading.

- Object
- Property
- Method
- Library (An object model is a type of library. For example, results shown in the earlier image of the Object Browser were members of the Word library, which is the same as saying the Word object model.)

TROUBLESHOOTING

Why do I get an error when I try to set some properties?

The key to this question is to remember that you sometimes need to use VBA statements to get information about the document as well as to apply settings or execute actions. Many properties are read-only, meaning that you can only use them to return information and not to apply a setting.

For example, `ActiveDocument.Name` is a read-only property to tell you the name of the active document. You can't set the name using this property, but that doesn't mean you can't name a document using VBA. Using this example, to change the name of the document, you'd use the `SaveAs` method (that is, `ActiveDocument.SaveAs`). With this method, it's possible to specify several settings for how you want the document saved, including its name.

To learn whether a property is read-only, select that property in the Object Browser. At the bottom of the Object Browser is a pane where you see the hierarchy for the selected item (what class and library it belongs to). This pane also indicates when a property is read-only, as you see in the example that follows.

```
Property Name As String
    read-only
    Default member of Word.Document
```

In the example shown here, Word is the library, and Document is the object to which the read-only property `Name` belongs. Learn more about ways to use read-only properties as this primer progresses.

Using Auto Lists

One of the main reasons you don't have to memorize the object model for the program you're automating is that the Visual Basic Editor often gives you the available options as you write. When you type an object, for example, followed by a period, you automatically see a list of properties and methods available to that object, as shown in the following image.

Notice the icons, shown earlier, that appear in this Auto List to indicate properties or methods. All the members of a given object (that is, all properties and methods available to that object) appear in the Auto List.

To scroll through an Auto List, you can use the up or down arrows as well as the Page Up and Page Down keys. You can also begin to type the item you need, if you know at least the first character, to move to that position in the Auto List. For example, if you type the letter *t* immediately after the period that follows **ActiveDocument**, the Auto List would move to the image you see here.

When you select the item you need in the Auto List, press the TAB key to add the item to your statement. (You can also press the spacebar instead of using the TAB key. However, doing so will add a space in your code after the selected item.) Note that, if you press ENTER once an item is selected in an Auto List, you'll get an error unless the selected item was the last required term in the statement.

Variables

In addition to objects, properties, and methods, most macros use other types of terms as well, including variables and constants (the latter of which are discussed under the next heading in this section).

Variables are types of data used to represent objects, statements, or other elements required in your code. They're often used to save time and make code more efficient, such as by using a single term in place of a statement that you have to reference several times. They are also often used when you need to refer to any instance of a given object type, rather than specifying an instance of an object. Consider the following examples.

- If you need to refer to the full name (the **FullName** property includes the file path) of the active document in a few places within your macro, you might want to declare a variable to represent the full name of the document, as you see in the following statement.

  ```
  myName = ActiveDocument.FullName
  ```

  The name of the variable in this case is **myName**. Once you've typed this statement in your macro, you can use the term **myName** in place of **ActiveDocument.FullName** wherever you need to use the full name of the document.

- When you use loops (discussed later in this section) to execute a command for several instances of an object (such as if you want to apply the table style named Table Contemporary to even-numbered tables in the document), you might use a variable as a counter, to help you accomplish that.

  ```
  Dim myInt as Integer
  For myInt = 2 To ActiveDocument.Tables.Count
     ActiveDocument.Tables(myInt).Style = "Table Contemporary"
  Next
  ```

The code above uses a **For...Next** loop, explained under the heading "Loops" later in this section. However, notice how the variable **myInt** is used here.

- First, you declare the variable as an integer.
- Then, the start of the loop (the line that begins with the word **For**), tells the code to begin executing with the variable equal to the number 2 and run until the variable equals the number of tables in the document. Each time the loop executes, the number is automatically increased by 1.
- Next, notice that the variable is used to denote the table number in the statement that applies the style to the table.

Using variables in place of a complete statement, or as counters, are common, useful tools. Other uses of variables are demonstrated under applicable headings later in this chapter, including "Conditional Structures" as well as "Loops."

> **Note**
>
> For code that's easier to read, follow, and edit, use intuitive variable names. Variable names can't contain spaces and can't be a VBA term used for any other purpose (such as the name of an object, property, or method). Keeping those requirements in mind, make your variable names as short as possible, just to save yourself work.

Introducing Variable Data Types

As you saw in the preceding examples, variables can be used to represent different types of information, such as numbers, text strings, or objects. Several variable data types are available, and you can even create your own. However, to keep things simple as you begin using variables, following are commonly used variable data types.

> **Note**
>
> For a complete list of data types supported in VBA and their definitions, search the topic "Data Type Summary" in Visual Basic Help, available from the menu bar in any Visual Basic Editor.

Data Type	Possible Values
Boolean	True or False
Integer	An integer, ranging between –32,768 and 32,767
Long	A long integer, ranging between –2,147,483,648 and 2,147,483,647

Data Type	Possible Values
Currency	A scaled integer, ranging from –922,337,203,685,477.5808 to 922,337,203,685,477.5807
String	A text string, such as a VBA statement (text strings are relatively unlimited—they can be up to approximately two billion characters in length)
Variant	A variant can be a number or a text string (if you don't specify the data type for a variable, it is a variant by default)

> **Note**
>
> You can also declare variables as specific types of objects (such as a table, a style, or a document). Variables declared as a specific object type are called *object variables*, and they offer additional benefits, discussed under the heading that follows. Note that this is *not* the same as the object *data type* that you'll see in complete lists of possible variable data types. The object *data type* was omitted from the preceding list because it's not recommended. On the other hand, *object variables* are an invaluable tool.

Declaring Variables

When you specify a variable type, which is called declaring the variable, you can save time and reduce errors. For more complex macros, declaring variables is also important because undeclared variables default to the variant data type, which uses more storage space than other data types, creating more work for the program running your macro.

Additionally, when you require that variables be declared in your modules, VBA lets you know while you're still working on your code if variables contain spelling errors that could cause an error when users run your macro. See "Running Macros and Compiling Projects" later in this section for more on this subject.

When you declare an object variable—that is, a variable declared as a specific type of object—VBA recognizes the object so that you get Auto Lists for completing statements that include the variable.

> **CAUTION**
>
> When you declare a variable as a particular data type, you must use it as that data type. For example, if I declare `myInt` as a string, VBA won't understand if I use it in a statement as if it was a number (such as `For myInt = 2 to ActiveDocument.Tables.Count`, as demonstrated earlier). Variables you want to use as numbers must be declared with an appropriate numeric data type (see the preceding table for the possible values available to different numeric data types). Similarly, to use a variable as a text string, the information after the equal sign when you set the value of that variable must either be a VBA statement or a text string enclosed in quotation marks.

To declare a variable, use a **Dim** statement. For example:

```
Dim myInt as Integer
Dim myName as String
```

Once you type the word *as* in a **Dim** statement, you get an Auto List of available options to help you complete the statement, such as you see in the following image.

INSIDE OUT Declare multiple variables in one statement

You can declare multiple variables on the same line; just be sure that you specify a data type for each. For example, the statement that follows does *not* declare all three variables as strings.

```
Dim myName, myPath, myStyle as String
```

The preceding code will seem to work, and you'll not get any errors as a result, as long as **myStyle** is used as a string data type. That's because **myName** and **myPath** are declared as variants—no data type is specified for them. The correct statement to declare all three variables as strings would read as follows.

```
Dim myName as String, myPath as String, myStyle as String
```

To require variable declaration in a module, click in the very top of the module, type the words **Option Explicit**, and then press ENTER. That statement is one of several you can place at the top of a module to apply to all procedures in your module. Notice that, when you press ENTER after typing this statement, a line appears beneath it, just as a line automatically appears between macros. This section of the module is known as the General Declarations section.

Note

You can set the Visual Basic Editor to require variable declaration automatically whenever you create a new module, through the Options dialog box available on the Tools menu. On the Editor tab of that dialog box, check Require Variable Declaration.

Sharing Variables Throughout a Project

If you have multiple macros that need to refer to the same variables, you can declare them publicly for the entire project, so that you don't need to type out the declarations in each applicable macro.

To do this, type your variable declarations in the General Declarations section of any module in the project, and use the word **Public** instead of the word **Dim** to begin the statement. For example, the following statement makes **myName** a string variable, and **myIn** an integer variable, available to all procedures in the project.

```
Public myName as String, myIn as Integer
```

Note, however, that you must be in a procedure to assign a value to a variable. For example, you can declare **myIn** as an integer variable for use throughout the project, but the statement **myIn = 1** must appear inside a procedure. The way to use one set of variable values for multiple macros across all modules in your project is to put all value assignments for public variables in one macro, and then access that macro from any procedure where you need to use those values. To learn how to get that done, see the heading "Running One Macro from Another" later in this section.

Chapter 21

> **Note**
>
> You can also use the General Declarations area at the top of a module to declare variables so that they're available to all macros in the same module, but not other modules. To do this, use **Private** or **Dim** instead of **Public** to start the variable declaration.

INSIDE OUT   Never write the same code twice

One of the best pieces of advice I received when I first started learning VBA was that, if you have to type the same statement twice, ask yourself if there's a faster way. For example, consider the steps discussed in this section for declaring public variables to use the same set of declarations in all procedures throughout your project. Using grouping structures as well as loops (both discussed later in this section) are other ways to avoid doing the same work twice.

Keep in mind that writing efficient code isn't just about typing less. Just as in documents, the less work you do, the better your results will be every time—and the easier job you'll have when that content needs editing. What's more, efficient code also makes it easier for the program to run your macros, so you get macros that are easier to write, easier to edit, and easier to run.

TROUBLESHOOTING

What do I do when the variable type doesn't work?

If you don't know the variable type you need, can't find the variable type you think you need in the Auto List that appears in your `Dim` statement, or you get a "Type Mismatch" error, which means the variable type declared doesn't match the way you've used the variable, there is an easy way out.

Though it's not good practice to do this regularly, particularly in long or complex code, you can simply type `Dim <variable name>` and not specify it as a particular type. When you do this, VBA classifies the variable as a variant data type, so you won't get Auto Lists when using the variable in statements. But, even if you have `Option Explicit` set for the module, as I hope you do, you can declare a variable in this way and continue on. (Alternatively, to avoid other editors of the code thinking that you've accidentally omitted the data type, you can declare the variable as a variant.)

It's a bit of a sloppy workaround—what programmers refer to as a *hack*—but if you're writing simple macros just for your own use, there's really no harm in doing it occasionally, and it can save you time while you're still learning about variable types. Just try not to make it a habit.

Document Variables

In addition to the variables that you use in your macros, there is an object type named *Variable* in the Word object model. These are known as document variables, because you use them to store information in the document that's collected or created by your macros, rather than as a place to store data just while the macro is running—such as when you need the document to remember information from one use of a given macro to the next.

For example, in template automation projects I do for clients, I sometimes add document variables to store user preferences that are specific to the individual document, such as which of a selection of design choices the user wants for the active document. The document needs to store that information after the macro runs, so that the user's preferences are remembered the next time they use the design macros.

In Word, information of this sort can be stored using either a document variable or a custom document property (which you're most likely familiar with from the Document Properties dialog box). However, Excel and PowerPoint don't offer a document variable object, so custom document properties are the way to go for storing document-level data in your workbooks and presentations.

In addition to document-level data, there are several ways to store data on the application or system level—that is, so that data can be accessed by your macros for use by more than an individual document. One of the most common and easiest of these methods is storing data in the Windows Registry.

As you can imagine, there are many uses for storing data in variables, document properties, or system-level resources such as the Registry. To explore this topic, use the

Object Browser in your Visual Basic Editor to look up the **Variable** object, the property named **CustomDocumentProperties**, and the **GetSetting** and **SaveSetting** functions (these functions are used for storing information in the Windows Registry).

Object Model Member Arguments

In addition to the variables that you can declare for use in your procedures, many items in the VBA object models include elements that use the same data types as variables to specify settings for that item. The elements, known as arguments (similar to arguments in an Excel formula), can be required or optional, and are most commonly seen for methods. Take a look at a few examples.

- When you use the **SaveAs** method of the **Document** object in a statement, you get the following options in the Quick Info ScreenTip that appears after you type the open parenthesis following **SaveAs**.

```
Documents(1).SaveAs (
         SaveAs([FileName], [FileFormat], [LockComments], [Password], [AddToRecentFiles], [WritePassword],
         [ReadOnlyRecommended], [EmbedTrueTypeFonts], [SaveNativePictureFormat], [SaveFormsData],
         [SaveAsAOCELetter], [Encoding], [InsertLineBreaks], [AllowSubstitutions], [LineEnding], [AddBiDiMarks])
```

  Most of the arguments shown in the preceding graphic are optional. Notice that optional arguments appear in the Quick Info inside brackets. Also notice that it's common for optional arguments not to specify a data type in the Quick Info.

- When you use the **Add** method for a **Table** object, you get the following arguments.

```
Documents(1).Tables.Add(
         Add(Range As Range, NumRows As Long, NumColumns As Long, [DefaultTableBehavior],
         [AutoFitBehavior]) As Table
```

  The **Add** method is used for many objects in Word, Excel, and PowerPoint. It has different arguments, of course, for each, based on the type of object being added. For the **Table** object, the range argument (location where you want the new table to appear), number of rows, and number of columns are required. The range is an object variable (referring to the **Range** object), and the number of rows and columns both use the long data type (as noted in the Quick Info). Note that the optional AutoFit behavior setting is a variant data type, but it requires a value from an available set of constants. Learn about constants under the next heading in this section.

- The **HomeKey** method, shown in the following image, is used with the **Selection** object. It's the VBA equivalent of using the Home key on your keyboard.

```
Selection.HomeKey(
         HomeKey([Unit], [Extend]) As Long
```

  The two available arguments used here—both optional and both using the variant data type—determine how far your insertion point moves (Unit) and whether the selection is extended (equivalent of holding the SHIFT key when you press the Home key) or your insertion point is simply moved to the new location. Both of these arguments require selections from a set of available constants, discussed under the next heading in this section.

Chapter 21

There are two ways to specify most arguments in statements such as those in the preceding list of examples. The first approach is to type the values for the arguments between parentheses immediately following the method (as you saw in the preceding images showing Quick Info ScreenTips for three sample methods). When you use that approach, type a comma after each value you add. You'll see that the active argument (the one for which you can add a value at your insertion point) is shown as bold in the *ScreenTip. If you don't intend to include a value for each argument, type consecutive commas until the argument you want to specify is bolded. If you place an argument in the wrong position between parentheses, the method won't work correctly. Notice, however, that this approach can be confusing and difficult to read when you need to edit or troubleshoot a macro.

> **Note**
>
> Note that some types of arguments can be specified simply in quotation marks after the statement name.

Instead, for methods that take more than a single argument, specify each by typing the argument name, followed by a colon and an equal sign, followed by the value you want to assign. Separate each argument you specify with a single comma, and note that argument order doesn't matter when you use this approach. Take a look at the following two examples.

```
ActiveDocument.SaveAs FileName:="Sample.docx", WritePassword:="example"
Selection.HomeKey Unit:=wdStory, Extend:=wdExtend
```

Using the explicit approach shown here helps to keep your code easy to read, edit, and troubleshoot.

INSIDE OUT How much do you really need to know about arguments?

It's important to know the syntax for specifying arguments, but in most cases, you don't need to worry about the data type or whether the argument is required.

Of course, you typically see the data type for required arguments in the Quick Info. But, for optional arguments as well, you'll often know the type of information that needs to go there just from using the program. Because you're an experienced user of the program you're automating, you're likely to go looking for an argument that should be available for a given method (such as specifying a file type or setting a password for the file when you save a new document) more often than you'll need help to understand the ones you happen to find.

In the case of SaveAs, for example, not even the file name is a required argument because the Save As dialog box, as you've surely seen, always provides a default name. Word and PowerPoint either default to the first phrase in the document or, for blank documents, to the document or presentation number assigned when a new document was generated. In Excel, the Save As dialog box always defaults to the Book number assigned when the workbook was generated.

Always remember that one of the most important tools you have for working in VBA is your knowledge of the program you're automating. As an advanced user, VBA is likely to be easier for you to learn than it is for a professional developer who doesn't use the programs. Think of it this way—if you're already a pretty good skier, you're likely to learn how to snowboard much faster than someone who designs snowboards for a living but has never stepped foot on a mountain.

However, there will still be times when you'll need help determining what data type to use for an argument's value or knowing when an argument is required. You can find a description of each argument for most applicable object model members, along with its data type and whether it's optional or required, in the help topic for that item. Learn how to find the help you need easily under the heading "Getting Help" later in this section.

Constants

As mentioned under the preceding heading, many items in VBA require the use of another data type, known as a constant. Unlike variables that can change as needed, constants are used when a defined set of options exists for the feature. Most constants in VBA are either specific to the individual program object model or are available in VBA for any Microsoft Office program.

Chapter 21

Note

It's possible to define your own constants in VBA as well. However, the discussion of constants in this chapter is limited to built-in constants, generally referred to as *intrinsic* constants.

Constants specific to the Word object model start with the letters *wd*; those specific to the Excel object model start with the letters *xl*; those specific to PowerPoint start with *pp*; and those for use across the Microsoft Office programs start with *mso*. There are also sets of constants that are specific to Visual Basic language and available to VBA in all of the Microsoft Office programs—these constants begin with the letters *vb*.

Because constants are defined members of an object model, you can search for them in the Object Browser. For the purposes of searching the Object Browser, note that a set of constants is considered a class and the constants within that set are the members of that class. Sets of available constants for a given argument are also usually easy to find through VBA help. Additionally, Auto Lists are available for many constant sets, particularly object and property constants. Take a look at a few examples.

- The **Type** property of the **Field** object is available as a set of constants, provided in an Auto List when you type a valid statement for using this property. The example shown here is the beginning of a conditional statement.

```
If Selection.Fields(1).Type = |
```

Learn about conditional statements under the heading "Conditional Structures" later in this section.

- Because different header or footer types are available in each section, the **Header** and **Footer** objects have a set of constants from which to select when you use those objects, as you see here.

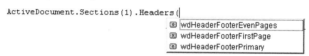

```
ActiveDocument.Sections(1).Headers(|
```

- The first macro you saw in this primer recorded four consecutive statements for adding four paragraphs to the document. If you had written that macro instead, you could have used the constant **vbCr**, which is the VBA constant to indicate a carriage return. In that case, that first macro could have been written with the following code, in just two statements instead of six.

```
Selection.Style = ActiveDocument.Styles("Heading 1")
Selection.TypeText("Company Overview—" & vbCr & vbCr & vbCr & vbCr)
```

> **Note**
>
> The ampersand is used to combine the text and constant portions of the text string, just as you can do to combine text, functions, and cell references into a text string in Excel. Learn more about using operators in VBA under the heading "Operators" later in this section.

- Many arguments for different methods use the same sets of constants, which often are not available in Auto Lists, but are easy enough to find. For example, the **HomeKey** method shown earlier uses constants for both of its arguments. The Unit argument uses the **wdUnits** set of constants; the Extend argument uses the **wdMovementType** set of constants.

The easiest way to learn the constant set you need is to use the Type A Question For Help box in the Visual Basic Editor to look up the applicable method. This is because, in some cases, not all members of a constant set are available to all methods that use those constants. For example, **wdUnits** includes 16 constants, but only four of these are available when used with the **HomeKey** method. (The four available in this case are **wdLine** [the default if you don't specify the argument], **wdStory**, **wdRow**, and **wdColumn**—the last two of which apply only when your selection is in a table.) If you searched for the **HomeKey** method in VBA help, you'd see information about the available constants for both arguments. (Note that the heading later in this section that covers getting help shows you how to use the Object Browser and VBA help reference together to save time.)

Collection Objects

Objects for which there can be many of the object type within a given scope are available as both an object and a collection object. A collection is the entire collection of all of a given object type within the specified scope. This distinction is important because the object and its collection object can have very different members (that is, a very different set of available properties and methods). For example, compare the two statements that follow.

```
Documents(1).Tables.Count
Documents(1).Tables(1).AllowAutoFit = True
```

The first of the two preceding statements uses the **Tables** collection object. The second uses the **Table** object, specifying the first table in the collection. Both statements also use the **Document** object, specifying the first document in the **Documents** collection. (Note that the **Documents** collection in the Word object model refers to all currently open documents. The first document in the collection refers to the most recently opened document.)

The **Table** object has a very broad set of members, as you see in the following image. It's used whenever a single object is being referenced from the collection. Notice that only a fraction of this object's member list is visible in a single screen.

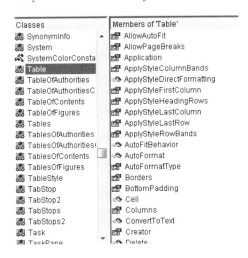

In contrast, the **Tables** collection object has very few members (shown in the following image), including only those items that can apply to the entire collection at once.

Chapter 21

INSIDE OUT To toggle or not to toggle

When you record some formatting options, such as applying bold or italic text formatting, you see the constant wdToggle set as the property's value. That's because, as you've likely noticed when using some types of font formatting, these settings toggle on and off—so you could, for example, apply a style that contains bold formatting to un-bold text that was previously bolded.

However, when you write VBA macros, you can set toggle commands to absolute values where you need them, instead of using the wdToggle constant. To do that, instead of using wdToggle as the value, simply use either True or False.

Selection.Bold = True, for example, will result in bold text whether or not the selection was bolded before the macro ran.

TROUBLESHOOTING

I can't find properties or methods that should clearly be available to my object

If you look for a member of an object that you just know has to be there but it's not, the problem isn't a limitation in VBA, it's just syntax. And, more often than not, the **Range** object is the solution.

For example, if you want to act on all cells in a specific table, you might be looking for the following:

```
Documents(1).Tables(1).Cells…
```

However, when you get the Auto List after you type the C for the word *Cells*, you see that Cell is an option, but the Cells collection is not. Does this mean that VBA can't act on all cells in a table at once? Of course not. What VBA is looking for is the following.

```
Documents(1).Tables(1).Range.Cells…
```

The **Range** object is often used to specify that you're identifying the preceding object as the active scope of your statement. So, before you decide that you can't do what you need to do with a given object, try using range in your statement as you see in the preceding example, and see what options you get in the Auto List that follows that range.

The **Range** object is also an important one to know because it can give you added flexibility. People new to VBA often use the **Selection** object frequently because they don't know how to identify objects in the document without first selecting them, but that slows down your code and often limits what you can do. You can use the **Range** object to identify any element in your document—which lets you take action without having to first select the item in the document. So, it's less code for you to write and less code for the program to execute.

For example, the following statement identifies the page number on which the first table in the document ends, without having to first select that table.

```
ActiveDocument.Tables(1).Range.Information(wdActiveEndPageNumber)
```

Grouping Statements

Say that you're in a restaurant and you need three things from the waiter. If you ask for some ketchup, then ask for a glass of wine when the waiter drops off your ketchup, and then ask for a glass for your friend when the waiter returns with your wine, that's a lot of work for the waiter (not to mention that he might be tempted to sneeze in your soup).

Instead, if you say to the waiter, "I need some ketchup, please. I'd also like another glass of wine, and my friend will have one as well," you've given the waiter three tasks that he can execute together. That is, you've just grouped a set of statements (not to mention saving yourself from a possible cold).

Though VBA won't sneeze in your soup, macros do run more slowly when you force the program to execute several related tasks independently. Instead, grouping related statements together helps make your code more efficient (and saves you time writing code, because you'll be writing less).

Statements can be grouped using the **With…End With** structure, as you saw in the recorded macro example in the earlier Troubleshooting tip titled "Why does my recorded macro have so many lines of code…" You can use **With…End With** anywhere that two or more statements apply to the same object, or the same combination of objects, properties, and methods. For example, the very first macro looked at in this chapter contains six statements, all of which apply to the **Selection** object. So, if you had written that macro instead of recording it, you could have typed the following:

```
With Selection
    .Style = ActiveDocument.Styles("Heading 1")
    .TypeText "Company Overview-" & vbCr & vbCr & vbCr & vbCr
End With
```

Though you might not be saving much when the macro is just two lines long, imagine something a bit more lengthy. For example, say that you wanted to do several things to the first table in the document. Instead of starting each line with **ActiveDocument.Tables(1)**, you can group the statements using a **With…End With** structure, as follows.

```
With ActiveDocument.Tables(1)
    .Style = "Table Contemporary"
    .Range.Style = "Table text"
    .Columns(4).Shading.ForegroundPatternColor = wdColorLavender
    .Rows(1).Range.Style = "Table heading"
    .Rows(1).HeadingFormat = True
End With
```

In fact, you can take that grouping a step further. Notice that the first row of the table is referred to more than once. You can add a nested **With…End With** structure for those rows, as follows.

```
With ActiveDocument.Tables(1)
    .Style = "Table Contemporary"
    .Range.Style = "Table text"
    .Columns(4).Shading.ForegroundPatternColor = wdColorLavender
    With .Rows(1)
        .Range.Style = "Table heading"
        .HeadingFormat = True
    End With
End With
```

The thing to remember with grouping structures is that all items in the **With** statement must apply to all statements between **With** and **End With**, if the statement starts with a period (indicating that it uses the object referred to in the **With** statement). For example, you can do some things directly to the **Row** object that you can't do directly to the **Column** object, such as applying a style. In that case, you might want to first select the column for which you need to apply a paragraph style, as you see here.

```
With ActiveDocument.Tables(1)
    .Style = "Table Contemporary"
    .Range.Style = "Table text"
    With .Columns(4)
        .Shading.ForegroundPatternColor = wdColorLavender
        .Select
    End With
    Selection.Style = "Table Subheading"
    With .Rows(1)
        .Range.Style = "Table heading"
        .HeadingFormat = True
    End With
End With
```

In the preceding code, **Selection.Style** doesn't have to refer to the object in the **With** statement, because it isn't using that object.

Chapter 21

CAUTION

As mentioned earlier in this chapter, remember that `With...End With` structures (as well as the code structures that follow under the next two headings) require a pair of statements. For ease of editing and to reduce errors, whenever you type the first part of the structure (the `With` statement in this case), type its paired closing statement (`End With`) as well, so that you don't forget to do so later.

TROUBLESHOOTING

How can I apply Theme fonts and colors with Word VBA?

In the preceding examples of grouping structures, you may have noticed that I used an intrinsic constant to apply a shading color. The set of constants you get when you apply colors in Word VBA code are from the standard Microsoft Office color palette that was available in earlier versions. These are not Theme colors.

However, if you find and try to use the **wdThemeColor**... constants, you'll find that they don't work as expected. (Note that in Excel VBA, the **xlThemeColor**... set of constants do work as expected.) So, how do you apply colors that will update if the document Theme changes?

If you record a macro in Word to apply a color from the Theme colors palette, you'll see a numeric value in the resulting code that appears to represent the color you selected. That value actually represents the position you selected in the Theme Colors palette. So, using that value in your own macros will consistently apply the Theme color at that palette position.

For example, in the preceding grouping structure code sample, if you wanted to apply the Theme Color palette position for the Accent 1 color instead of the standard color lavender, the line of code to apply the color would read as follows.

```
.Shading.ForegroundPatternColor = -738131969
```

But, you don't have to take the time to discover the 60 values that comprise the 10 Theme colors in the palette and their variations. I've done it for you. Find a macro named ThemeColorReferenceTable in the file named Sample Macros.dotm that's available from the practice files you can install from this book's CD. That macro (available from the SampleMacros module in the referenced file) will generate a new document with a table representing the Theme Colors palette. The color and associated value number for each position in the palette are applied to the table, so that you can save that table and use it as a reference tool whenever you need it.

Applying Theme fonts in Word VBA is much simpler. Wherever you would specify the font name, you simply specify that name as "+Headings" or "+Body" to apply the Theme heading or body font, rather than using the name of a specific font. For example, the first line of code that follows applies the font "Cambria." The second line applies the active Theme's heading font.

```
ActiveDocument.Paragraphs(1).Range.Font.Name = "Cambria"
ActiveDocument.Paragraphs(1).Range.Font.Name = "+Headings"
```

Loops

If I had to pick one feature of VBA that's the most useful on a daily basis for document production and document troubleshooting, it would be loops. Loops enable you to act on several instances of a given object within one macro. Fortunately, as much as loops can do for you, they're also extremely easy to use.

In this primer, we're going to look at variations on two of the most common types of loops, **For** loops and **Do** loops.

For Each...Next and For...Next Loops

A **For Each...Next** loop enables you to act on all instances of a given object within a specified range. For example, you might use this type of loop to format all tables in your document at once or to change the fill color of all text boxes in your document to a particular Theme color. Similarly, a **For...Next** loop enables you to specify a range of instances of the given object on which you want to act. For example, say that all tables in your document other than the first five need to have the same formatting. You can use a **For...Next** loop to specify that the formatting apply to only the tables you want.

To use a **For Each...Next** loop, start by declaring a variable of the object type upon which to act and then use that variable in your loop. Take a look at the code for the two examples given in the preceding paragraph.

- Apply the style Table Contemporary to all tables in your document.

```
Dim atb as Table
For Each atb in ActiveDocument.Tables
    atb.Style = "Table Contemporary"
Next atb
```

  The use of **atb** as the variable name for the table object is just a personal choice. As mentioned earlier in this chapter, you can use any name for a variable that meets VBA naming requirements (such as no spaces and a letter for the first character) and isn't the name of any member of an available object model.

- Remove any user-defined styles from the active document.

```
Dim ast as Style
For Each ast in ActiveDocument.Styles
    If ast.BuiltIn = False Then
        ast.Delete
    End If
Next ast
```

  Specifying the variable in the **Next** statement, as I do in both preceding examples, is optional. But, it's good practice to do this to avoid confusing the statements you need to keep or alter when you edit a macro, particularly when you use multiple loops in the same procedure.

To use a **For...Next** loop, start by declaring a numeric variable data type to use for counting the instances upon which you want to act. The code for the example given earlier—formatting all but the first five tables in the document—follows.

```
Dim myI as Integer
For myI = 6 to ActiveDocument.Tables.Count
   ActiveDocument.Tables(myI).Style = "Table Contemporary"
Next
```

Notice that I could have used a **With…End With** structure instead of retyping **Acti-veDocument** each time I needed it. Of course, that would be more helpful if I was doing more than just applying a table style, as you see in the following example.

```
Dim myI as Integer
With ActiveDocument
   For myI = 6 to .Tables.Count
      With .Tables(myI)
         .Style = "Table Contemporary"
         .AutoFitBehavior (wdAutoFitWindow)
      End With
   Next myI
End With
```

In the preceding code, notice that I use the **For…Next** loop with nested **With…End With** structures to make this macro as efficient as possible to write, and as efficient as possible for Word to execute.

Do Loops

A Do loop, aside from being fun to say, can be another useful way of creating a loop for specified instances of an object. (Note that this type of loop is usually referred to as a **Do…Loop** structure, which helps to clarify the fact that, like **For…Next** loops or **With…End With** structures, a **Do…Loop** actually requires a pair of statements.)

Do…Loop structures can either be executed while a qualification is true or until a qualification becomes true. Similar to **For…Next** loops, **Do While…Loops** are usually used with a numeric variable. **Do Until…Loops** may be used with a numeric variable or until a given condition is true. Take a look at a couple of examples.

- Say that you're troubleshooting a document. Using Open And Repair, you find that a floating object is causing the unstable document behavior. But, you don't see any floating objects in the document (this would happen if floating objects were off the page or hidden behind opaque document elements because of the Behind Text wrapping style). Using a **Do…Loop**, you can delete all floating objects in the body of the document, as follows.

```
With ActiveDocument
   Do Until .Shapes.Count = 0
         .Shapes(1).Delete
   Loop
End With
```

In the preceding code, notice that **ActiveDocument.Shapes(1)** refers to the first shape in the document. I wouldn't use a **For…Next loop** in this case with a counter, because each time a shape is deleted, the shape object reference **.Shapes(myI)** would refer to a different object. Instead, if I continually delete the first shape until there are no more shapes, I don't need to be concerned with the way VBA counts the shapes in the document as their number is being reduced.

> **Note**
>
> In the case of deleting all shapes in a document, you may wonder why I didn't use a **For Each…Next** loop for this, since I want to act on all instances of shapes in the document. **For Each…Next** loops are an easy solution in most cases that require acting on all instances of an object type. However, there are two reasons why the **Do…Loop** was the better choice here. First, there's less code with a **Do…Loop** in this case because you don't need to declare the object variable before executing the loop. Second, there's an anomaly when you use a **For Each…Next** loop specifically to delete floating graphics (that is, members of the **Shapes** collection object) and one or more shapes may be left behind. Using the **Do…Loop** structure instead ensures that all shapes are deleted.

- The following code uses a **Do While…Loop** instead of a **For…Next** loop for formatting all tables with the Table Contemporary style and AutoFit To Window behavior.

```
Dim myI as Integer

myI = 6
With ActiveDocument
    Do While myI <=.Tables.Count
        With .Tables(myI)
            .Style = "Table Contemporary"
            .AutoFitBehavior (wdAutoFitWindow)
        End With
        myI = myI + 1
    Loop
End With
```

Notice in the preceding code that the integer variable was set to start counting at six, so the first five tables in the document would be ignored. The **Do While** statement says to execute the code in the loop while the integer value is less than or equal to the number of tables in the active document. Then, at the bottom of the commands that fall within the loop, I've added a counter for the integer variable to increase the number by one on each iteration of the loop.

In the first of the two preceding examples, a **Do…Loop** structure is a better choice than a **For…Next** loop (as explained in the text that follows that sample code). However, in the second of the preceding examples, a **For…Next** loop would have been the more efficient choice. Notice that, in the second example, if you use a **For…Next** loop, you don't need a separate statement for the counter—the **For** statement is a built-in counter.

So, how do you decide whether to use a **For…Next** loop or a **Do…Loop** structure? You just need to ask yourself a few simple questions, as follows.

> **Note**
>
> I wish I had conceived the questions that follow, but I can't take the credit. Many thanks to Beth Melton, this book's technical reviewer, for sharing her clear and concise approach to this topic (and others).

- Do you know the number of repetitions you need in the loop?

   As demonstrated by the preceding code samples in this section, if the answer is yes, use a **For**...**Next** loop. If the answer is no, use a **Do**...**Loop**.

- If using a **Do**...Loop structure, is the condition initially true?

   If the condition is initially true, you need a **Do While** statement to begin your loop. If, on the other hand, the loop needs to execute until the condition becomes true, start your loop with a **Do Until** statement.

There's one more variable to consider when deciding on the loop type you need. You can evaluate the condition specified in a **Do**...**Loop** structure either at the top of the loop (as shown in the earlier example of a **Do While**...**Loop** structure) or at the bottom of the loop (with a **Do**...**Loop Until** or **Do**...**Loop While** structure).

A top evaluation loop is structured as follows.

```
Do While <condition>
    <statements>
Loop
```

A bottom evaluation loop, on the other hand, looks like the following.

```
Do
    <statements>
Loop While <condition>
```

(Remember, in the preceding structures, to substitute **Until** for **While** if you need to execute the code *until* the condition becomes true.)

So, to determine whether you need a top or bottom evaluation loop, ask the following question: Must the code execute at least once?

If the code must run at least once for your macro to do what you need, use a bottom evaluation loop so that the condition isn't evaluated until after the first time the code runs. If the code doesn't have to run at least once, use a top evaluation loop so that the condition is evaluated before the first time the code runs. For example, in the sample **Do**...**Loop** structure shown earlier, in which case the loop is used to delete all shapes from the active document, a top evaluation loop is appropriate because the code doesn't need to run if the document contains no shapes from the outset.

The following diagram summarizes the decision process for selecting the best type of loop for your macro.

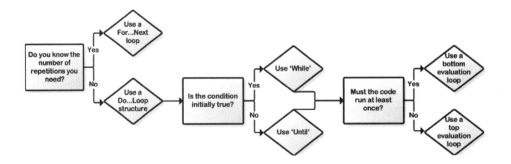

TROUBLESHOOTING

Using a loop to delete objects from a Word document leaves behind objects in the header and footer

If you press CTRL+A to select the entire Word document and then press CTRL+SHIFT+N to apply Normal paragraph style to everything selected, content in headers, footers, footnotes, endnotes, comments, or floating text boxes remains unaffected. This is because Select All really means selecting everything in the active Word story. See Chapter 4, "Building Easy-to-Manage, Robust Documents," for an explanation of Word stories.

Similarly, when you work in VBA, some commands require that you execute them separately for each story in which you want to take action. For example, deleting all floating objects from the active document, as shown in this section of the primer, won't delete those objects in the header or footer stories. To do that, you need to access the particular story you need. To delete floating objects in the main header of section 1, for example, instead of `ActiveDocument.Shapes`, you would specify `ActiveDocument.Sections(1).Headers(wdHeaderFooterPrimary).Shapes`.

Keep in mind that you can nest multiple loops inside one another. For example, say that you want to apply a paragraph style to every header in the document. You need to loop through each header, in each section, which requires two loops, as follows.

```
Dim asc As Section
Dim hft As HeaderFooter
For Each asc In ActiveDocument.Sections
    For Each hft In asc.Headers
        hft.Range.Style = "Heading 1"
    Next hft
Next asc
```

Note that some actions require that you access the story in which you want to act before executing actions, rather than just identifying the story. Also, before you try to loop through all story ranges in a document, be sure that the type of object upon which you're acting is accessible to all story ranges, or you'll get an error. For example, floating objects aren't allowed in footnotes, endnotes, comments, or other floating objects, so including those ranges in your loop to delete shapes will throw an error.

Conditional Structures

As demonstrated with **For...Next** and **Do...Loop** structures, there are several ways to apply conditions to the commands you want to execute with VBA. Frequently, however, the condition you need may be something other than the instances of an object. Conditional structures in VBA, other than loops, are formed using the paired **If** and **End If** statements. Much like the IF function in Excel and the IF field in Word, **If...End If** structures in VBA are used for executing actions only when specified criteria are met. Take a look at the following examples.

- Say that you're creating automation to help format new business presentation documents. Your branding specifies that any presentation of longer than three pages should use landscape orientation. If the user clicks the button to use your formatting macro, you may want the macro to first check the length of the document and then set the orientation to landscape if the document exceeds three pages.

```
With ActiveDocument
  If .RangeInformation(wdActiveEndPageNumber) > 3 Then
    .PageSetup.Orientation = wdOrientLandscape
  End If
End With
```

- Say that you're applying a template to a document that uses only built-in Word styles, such as Body Text and Heading 1–9. Once you've reformatted the document content as needed, you may want to clean up the document styles to help ensure that the document continues to be formatted with the styles you want. The following code removes any styles from the document that are not built-in styles.

```
Dim ast As Style
For Each ast In ActiveDocument.Styles
  If ast.BuiltIn = False Then
      ast.Delete
  End If
Next ast
```

If...End If structures are often used with multiple conditions, such as when you want to set one value if the condition is true and another if it's false, as you see in the following example.

```
With ActiveDocument
  If .RangeInformation(wdActiveEndPageNumber) > 3 Then
    .PageSetup.Orientation = wdOrientLandscape
  Else
    .PageSetup.Orientation = wdOrientPortrait
  End If
End With
```

The preceding example adds an additional qualifier to the similar code shown earlier, so that if the document is three pages or shorter, your macro ensures that the document uses portrait orientation.

Chapter 21

If statements can also include multiple conditions by including **ElseIf** statements. For example, say that you have many tables in your document with different layouts, but all financial tables have either four or six columns. Those financial tables with four columns should use the custom table style named Table Financial 4, those with six columns should use the style named Table Financial 6, and all other tables in the document should be formatted using Table Normal style.

```
Dim atb As Table
For Each atb In ActiveDocument.Tables
   With atb
        If .Columns.Count = 4 Then
             .Style = "Table Financial 4"
        ElseIf .Columns.Count = 6 Then
             .Style = "Table Financial 6"
        Else
             .Style = "Table Normal"
        End If
   End With
Next atb
```

Notice that both **If** and **ElseIf** statements require **Then** at the end of the line. Also notice that, regardless of the number of conditions in an **If** statement, **End If** is still required at the end of the complete structure.

Note

See the heading "Trapping Individual Errors" in the section titled "Creating Error Handlers" later in this chapter for an example of another type of conditional structure known as **Select Case**. Though **If** structures are more common, **Select Case** can be an extremely efficient alternative and is definitely worth a look.

INSIDE OUT   **The value of indenting code**

As you can see throughout the code samples in this chapter, code is indented to indicate statements within a group, loop, or condition. And, where multiple structures are nested, code is indented a bit further for each level of nesting.

Though VBA doesn't require indenting code, it's fairly standard practice to do so, because it makes the code and the logic of the macro's progression much easier to read.

For example, consider that when structures are nested, it's essential that the end statements of paired structures fall in the correct order. For example, if you nest an `If...End If` structure inside a `For...Next` loop, the `End If` statement needs to appear above `Next` (that is, if the `If` structure starts inside the loop, it has to end inside the loop). Indenting phrases can make it much easier to diagnose this type of hierarchy issue.

To indent a line of code, press the TAB key at the beginning of the line. Your indent will be kept when you press ENTER. Backspace to remove the indent. Note that you can customize the indent width on the Editor tab of the Options dialog box. Tab Width is set to four characters by default.

To indent several lines of existing text, select those lines and then press TAB. Similar to behavior with outline numbered lists, using TAB and SHIFT+TAB with one or more paragraphs selected will demote or promote the text rather than deleting it. However, if only one statement is selected, you must be sure to select the entire statement or pressing a keystroke will replace the existing text.

Operators

VBA uses both symbols (such as &, <, >, =, +, -, /, *) and terms (such as And, Or) for operators, depending on the usage. In all cases, however, operators follow standard mathematical syntax rules. Take a look at a few examples.

- When I finish writing a chapter of this book, I need to copy all of the Heading 1 and Heading 2 paragraphs to update the table of contents. To do that, I make a copy of the document from which I delete any paragraphs that don't have those two styles applied.

```
Dim apr as Paragraph
For each apr in ActiveDocument.Paragraphs
    If apr.Style <> "Heading 1" And apr.Style <> "Heading 2" Then
            apr.Range.Delete
    End If
Next apr
```

Notice that the less than and greater than operators can be used together to mean "is not equal to."

- If, instead, I wanted to delete all paragraphs that match either of those criteria, I would have written the following code.

```
Dim apr as Paragraph
For each apr in ActiveDocument.Paragraphs
    If apr.Style = "Heading 1" Or apr.Style = "Heading 2" Then
            apr.Range.Delete
    End If
Next apr
```

- What if I wanted to delete all paragraphs that use Heading 1 or Heading 2 style, but only if they don't appear in a table?

```
Dim apr as Paragraph
For each apr in ActiveDocument.Paragraphs
    If (apr.Style = "Heading 1" Or apr.Style = "Heading 2") And _
    apr.Range.Information(wdWithinTable) = False Then
            apr.Range.Delete
    End If
Next apr
```

In the first line of the **If** structure, the space followed by an underscore at the end of the line is used to allow a single statement of code to break to a second line. Breaking the line is not required, but is used when the line of code is too wide to read in a single screen.

Notice in the preceding code that the conditions that use the logical operator **Or** are grouped in parentheses, with the **And** operator outside of the parentheses. Just as in a mathematical equation, that phrasing ensures that the condition within the parentheses is evaluated first.

As you've seen in examples throughout the primer to this point, an ampersand is used to combine arguments into a text string, and typical arithmetic operators can be used on numeric values as they are in Excel formulas, including +, - ,*, and /. The plus sign can be used in some cases to combine text strings, but when you want to mix different types of variables in a text string, the plus sign can cause a "Type Mismatch" error, because it tries to calculate a result rather than combine the strings. So, using the ampersand to combine arguments into a string is always a good practice.

Notice also throughout these examples that comparison operators can be used either individually or together, such as < to indicate "less than" or <= to mean "less than or equal to."

The operators mentioned in this section are likely to be all that you need, but this isn't an exhaustive list of every operator available in VBA. To learn about others, search for the topic Operator Summary in VBA help.

Message Boxes and Input Boxes

When creating macros for others to use, you're likely to need to either give the user information or have the user specify information. Use message boxes to share information and input boxes to collect it.

Message Boxes

A message box might just provide information, or it might require a response, such as Yes, No, Cancel, Abort, Retry, or Ignore.

The **MsgBox** command is one of several in VBA that can be used both as a statement and as a function. Use a **MsgBox** statement to provide information; use **MsgBox** as a function when you need a response from the user.

- To create a message box statement, type **MsgBox** with the string of text you want the user to see. For example, take a look at the following message box statement and the message box it produces when run in Word.

```
MsgBox "You're an unstoppable VBA genius!"
```

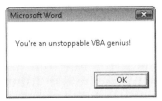

Even if your message box doesn't require a reply, however, you might want to get a bit more creative with it. The **MsgBox** command includes optional arguments that let you customize the title bar and add an information icon, such as in the following example.

```
MsgBox "You're an unstoppable VBA genius!",vbInformation,"My Message Box"
```

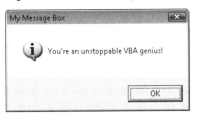

The intrinsic constant **vbInformation** is one of a set of options in the buttons argument that enables you to add both an icon (as you see here) and response buttons. The third argument customizes the title of the message box.

> **Note**
>
> Note that both message box and input box functions also include optional arguments for adding help files to those boxes. To learn about creating help files for use with your VBA automation, see the MSDN Library. MSDN (Microsoft Developer Network) offers a free library resource at http://msdn.microsoft.com/library, which provides a number of tools for those who want to continue learning about Microsoft Office programming capabilities. See the last section in this chapter for more information on additional resources.

- To use **MsgBox** as a function (that is, to require a response from the user), first declare an integer variable for your message box, so that you can use the response in the macro, as you see in the following example.

```
Dim myRes As Integer
myRes = Msgbox("Are you an unstoppable VBA genius?", vbQuestion _
+ vbYesNo, "My Message Box")
```

Chapter 21

```
If myRes = vbYes Then
    Msgbox "I knew it!", vbExclamation, "My Message Box"
Else
    Msgbox "Hang in there.", vbCritical, "My Message Box"
End If
```

The first message box in the preceding code looks like this:

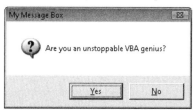

Depending upon your response, you then get one of the following two message boxes.

Notice the constant **vbYes** used to represent the response to the first message box. If you look up **vbYes** in the Object Browser, you find the set of constants that are available (shown in the following image) depending on the buttons you include in your message box.

Members of 'VbMsgBoxResult'
- vbAbort
- vbCancel
- vbIgnore
- vbNo
- vbOK
- vbRetry
- vbYes

Note

If you're thinking that you don't have to be a math whiz to know that a term comprised of several letters (such as **vbYes**) is not an integer, guess again. The seven constants that comprise the possible return values for a message box translate to the integers 1 through 7. So, you'll get the same result if you use the integer value instead of the constant. Use Quick Info to find the integer value you want. For example, if you have a macro that includes the constant **vbYes**, right-click in that constant and then click Quick Info to see its value.

Input Boxes

Input boxes are similar to messages boxes, except that they're always used as a function because they always require a response. Take a look at the following example.

```
Dim myInp As String
myInp = InputBox("How would you score on a basic VBA exam?", _
"My Input Box", "Perfect")
Msgbox myInp & " is pretty good!", vbExclamation, "My Input Box"
```

The input box from the previous example looks like this:

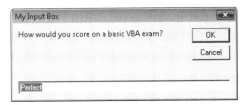

The text of the preceding message box is referred to as the prompt, the title bar text is the title argument (as in a message box) and the value you see in this image is the default value of "Perfect" specified in the third argument. Note that input boxes also include optional arguments for vertical and horizontal position on the screen (not shown here), if you don't want the box to automatically appear in the center of the screen.

Because the input box was declared as a string variable, notice that the response is used as part of a text string in a message box that looks like this:

If, instead, you need to use a response as a numeric value, declare the variable accordingly. In the following example, the input box asks for the number of columns to include in a new table being created by the macro. The variable defined as the input box reply is declared as an integer. (Notice that the input box in this case has only a prompt and a title bar—no default value is set, so the text box within the input box appears blank to the user.)

```
Dim myInp As Integer
myInp = InputBox("How many columns would you like?", "My Input Box")
With Selection
.Tables.Add Range:=.Range, NumRows:=5, NumColumns:=myInp
End With
```

> **Note**
>
> There is a possible problem, however, with the preceding code sample. If the response is not an integer (including if the user cancels the input box without adding a reply), the macro will end in an error. You can, however, add what's known as an *error handler* to correct for any error that may occur. Error handlers are an important part of writing macros effectively. Learn to work with basic error handlers later in this chapter, under the heading "Creating Error Handlers." You'll find an example in that section of an error handler created specifically for the preceding macro.

Running One Macro from Another

When you create a solution, such as developing a set of document production macros for yourself or creating a set of macros to help users format a template, you're likely to have some of the same commands repeat in multiple macros. When those duplicated commands run to more than a few lines of code, it can be helpful to put the duplicated code into its own macro and run it as part of each of the macros that need it. That way, you don't have to write that code out in every macro where you need it.

Running one macro from another is also commonly done when several macros use the same variable definitions. For example, say that you declare the following public variables in the General Declarations section of the module.

```
Public myName as String, myComp as String, myIn as Integer
```

If several macros need to use the same values for that information, create a procedure just to store the values of those variables. That entire macro might look something like this:

```
Public Sub VarDefs()
myName = Application.UserName
myComp = ActiveDocument.BuiltinDocumentProperties("Company").Value
myIn = 1
End Sub
```

To then use these variable definitions in any macro in the project, just call the macro that includes the definitions. The statement to call a macro is just the word **Call** plus the macro name. If the macro exists in a different module from the macro where you're calling it, also specify the module name.

For example, to call the preceding macro from a macro in the same module, I would type the following statement.

```
Call VarDefs
```

If the macro from which I want to call **VarDefs** is in a different module, the statement would look like the following (assuming that **VarDefs** is in a module named **myMod**).

```
Call myMod.VarDefs
```

Note that, as long as the variables are declared as public, you don't actually have to specify Public in the Sub statement of the preceding macro to make the contents of that procedure available to other macros in the project. However, if you want to allow the contents of that procedure to be shared only by other macros in the same module (such as in cases where macros in a different module might need to share a different set of values for the same variables), use `Private Sub <procedurename>()` to start the macro. Keep in mind also that private procedures don't appear in the Macros dialog box available from the Developer tab, so identifying a procedure as private is also a good way to keep it hidden from the user.

CAUTION!

> When you call one macro from another for the purpose of using variable definitions, make sure the call to the source macro appears prior to where you use those variables in the destination macro.

Note

Your macros might share many types of variables in a given project. I've presented the preceding variable example to point out one place where the 2007 release may offer you a simpler solution than VBA, depending on your particular needs. For adding document property information to your documents and templates, you can use the built-in Document Property Quick Parts (see Chapter 9, "Quick Parts," for more information) that have information already bound to Content Controls. For other types of information not available in the Document Property set of Quick Parts, see the next chapter of this book to learn how to bind Content Controls to your own custom XML data.

Setting Macros to Conditionally Stop Executing Commands

You can add a statement to end the macro under specified conditions or to exit just a part of the macro.

To end code execution entirely, just type **End** on its own line. For example, say that you want to stop a macro from running if no document is open. That code would look like this:

```
If Documents.Count = 0 Then
End
End If
```

To exit a loop when a condition is met, use an **Exit** statement specifically for the loop type, such as **Exit For** or **Exit Do.** Following is an example of an **Exit For** statement.

```
Dim ast as Style
For each ast in ActiveDocument.Styles
   If ast.NameLocal = "Sample" Then
      ast.Delete
      Exit For
   End If
Next
```

When you run one macro from another, you might also want to exit just the individual macro under certain conditions and not stop executing code altogether. For example, if you call one macro from another but only want to run the called macro under certain conditions, you can tell the code to exit that called macro with an **Exit Sub** statement, as you see in the following example.

```
If ActiveDocument.Tables.Count = 0 Then
Exit Sub
End if
```

Running Macros and Compiling Projects

You can run a macro directly from the Visual Basic Editor, or you can add it to the user interface to run it from the Quick Access Toolbar (or, in Word, from a keyboard short-cut). To learn how to add macros to the Ribbon, see Chapter 23, "Using VBA and XML Together to Create Add-Ins."

Running Macros

To run a macro directly from the Visual Basic Editor (as I do frequently with on-the-fly document production macros), just click in the macro (anywhere between the **Sub** and **End Sub** lines will do) and then click the green Run Sub\User Form arrow icon on the Standard toolbar. This option is also available from the Run menu, or by pressing the F5 key.

To add a macro to the Quick Access Toolbar, click the arrow at the end of your Quick Access Toolbar and then click More Commands to open the Customization tab of the <Program> Options dialog box. Then, do the following.

1. In the Choose Commands From list, select Macros.

2. If you want to add the macro to the toolbar just for a specific document or template, select that document or template from the Customize Quick Access Toolbar list.

   To be available in this list, the document or template must use an Open XML Format and must be open at the time.

3. Select the macro to add from the list at the left and then click Add.

4. To customize the appearance of the macro on the Quick Access Toolbar, select it in the list on the right, and then click Modify. In the Modify Button dialog box, you can select a different icon and edit the way the name appears in the ScreenTip for that macro.

To add a macro to a keyboard shortcut in Word, open the Word Options dialog box to the Customize tab and then click the Customize button to open the Customize Keyboard dialog box. As you see in the following image, select Macros in the list on the left and then select the macro you want to assign to a shortcut on the right.

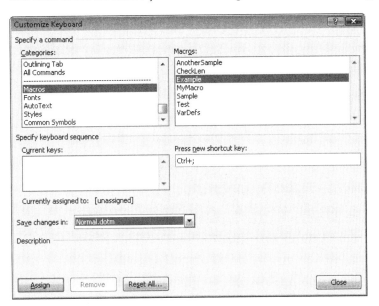

Press the keystroke combination you want to use—such as CTRL+; shown in this example. A notice appears to let you know if the combination is already assigned. You can select it even if it's already assigned to another action, as long as you don't need the shortcut for that other action. Notice that you need to select the document or template in which to save the shortcut. Keyboard shortcuts can be saved in both Open XML Format and legacy format Word documents and templates.

> **Note**
>
> For many actions, you might want to run just one line of code at a time—such as to get information about your document or to execute a single action. In this case, you can run the code from the Immediate Window in the Visual Basic Editor. This is an extremely handy option that you're likely to use regularly once you become accustomed to using VBA as a document production tool. Learn how to use the Immediate Window later in this chapter.

Chapter 21

Compiling Projects

As you're writing lengthy macros, or when you're ready to use your macros, compiling the project is an important step. Compilers are actually used to translate source code to executable code, which isn't strictly necessary for typical VBA macros. But, using the compiler in the Visual Basic Editor is an essential way to help ensure that your code works properly.

To compile a project, just select a module or click into a procedure in the project and then, on the Debug menu, click Compile <Project>. Depending on the size of the VBA project, compiling might be instantaneous or it might take a few moments. If VBA recognizes errors in your code, it will select the code containing the error and display a message box telling you the type of error. Learn about recognizing, fixing, and managing errors under the heading that follows.

Understanding Errors

Errors can occur when you compile a project or when you attempt to run a macro. Following are a few of the most common error types, along with their corresponding error numbers.

- "Type Mismatch" (error number 13) indicates that you're trying to act on an item in an unavailable way, such as if you define an integer variable for the response to an input box that requires a text string response. Note that the absence of this error doesn't guarantee that you've assigned the correct data type to your variable because VBA can automatically allow for incorrect data types under some circumstances.

- "Method or Data Member Not Found" (error number 461) usually indicates that you either misspelled a term or you referenced an item that doesn't exist.

- "Requested Member of the Collection Does Not Exist" (error number 5941) appears when you run a macro on a range that doesn't include the object you specified to act on. For example, this would occur if your macro includes the statement `ActiveDocument.Tables(3).Delete` and two or fewer tables are in the active document.

- "Object Required" (error 424) indicates that you need to specify an object upon which to act. This error might occur, for example, in a **For Each...Next** loop when you don't correctly define the collection of objects upon which you want to act. A similar error may appear as "Object Doesn't Support This Property or Method."

> **Note**
>
> Error numbers are provided in the preceding list because it is possible to correct for individual errors—that is, to write code that enables your macro to respond differently to different errors. When you do this, you need to identify the error by number, as discussed later in this section, under the heading "Creating Error Handlers."

When an error occurs while you're compiling a project, the error statement is selected and a message box appears telling you the type of error and offering help. If you click the help option, an article explaining the error type is opened in most cases.

If an error occurs when you run a macro, a similar message box appears to indicate the error type, but it provides the options End, Debug, and Help. Just as with compile errors, the help option usually provides an article with more information on the error type. (Note also that clicking the help option doesn't close the error message for either compile or runtime errors.) Click End to dismiss a runtime error message if you're familiar with the error and know where to find it. Or, click Debug for guidance in correcting a runtime error.

When you click Debug, the statement that caused the error is highlighted. (Note that, by default, the statement is highlighted in yellow with a yellow arrow at the margin indicator bar, but you can customize this formatting in the Options dialog box.) This also puts the program into Break Mode, which stops code from executing. When this occurs, "[break]" appears in the title bar after the project name. To exit Break Mode, which removes the highlight from the error statement, click the Reset button on either the Standard toolbar or the Run menu. (Note that Break Mode also restricts many actions in the application window. So, resolve the error and turn off Break Mode before you return to working in the applicable program.)

If a compile error occurs at runtime (meaning that you didn't compile the code, but ran a macro that contains a compile error), the project goes into Break Mode when you click OK to dismiss the error message. The title line of the macro that caused the error is highlighted and the error statement is selected.

Testing Your Macros and Debugging Errors

When you're not sure of the cause of an error, there are several ways to go about finding it efficiently. Some of these options can also be used when you want to see the results of just a portion of your code at a time, even if errors don't occur. A few of the easiest options for testing or debugging code are described in the following list.

- You can step into a macro to execute one line at a time and see the results as you go. To do this, click in the macro and then press F8 to start executing the macro one line at a time. Press F8 again each time you want to run the next statement.

  You can also click in a specific line in the macro and then press CTRL+F8 to execute the macro up to the line where your insertion point appears.

- Use a breakpoint to run a macro using a traditional method (such as by pressing F5 from the Visual Basic Editor or running the macro from the Quick Access Toolbar) but execute statements only up to a specified line of code. To add a breakpoint, click the margin indicator bar to the left of the line of code. A circle appears on the window edge where you clicked, and the statement is shaded (in burgundy, by default), as you see in the following image.

If you're not sure where to click, you can right-click in the statement instead, point to Toggle, and then click Breakpoint. To remove a breakpoint, just click the circle that appears to the left of the statement. (As with error notifications, you can customize the formatting of breakpoints in the Options dialog box.)

- You can comment out a block of code, so that it gets skipped when a macro runs. This is a great tool to use when you want to try running just part of your macro, especially if you have lines of code that aren't finished (which would otherwise throw an error when you run the macro). To do this, right-click the toolbar area and then click Edit to open the Edit toolbar. On that toolbar, you'll find Comment Block and Uncomment Block buttons as shown below, which add or remove an apostrophe from in front of each selected line of code.

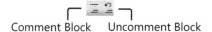

Comment Block   Uncomment Block

Creating Error Handlers

When you write macros, particularly for others to use, it's a good idea to try to account for any errors you can control. You can account for many possible errors with conditional structures to protect the macro from conditions you know would cause an error. For example, if the macro acts on the active document, you can set the macro to end without taking any action if no documents are open, as shown under the earlier heading "Setting Macros to Conditionally Stop Executing Commands."

However, you might also want to set up error handlers to manage what the user sees if an unexpected error occurs. In some cases, you might even know that certain conditions could cause an error, but find it more efficient to add an error handler than to write code to account for every possibility.

The two most common types of error handlers are the statements `On Error Resume Next` and `On Error GoTo ErrorHandler`. Let's look at those one at a time.

Use `On Error Resume Next` when a given instance of a loop, for example, might throw an error under certain conditions, but you'd still want the loop to continue running after it encounters an error. To do this, type `On Error Resume Next` on its own line early in the macro, before any code that could possibly throw the error for which you want the handler to correct. Then, if the possible error occurs, the user won't be notified—the code will just skip the instance it couldn't act on and continue on its merry way.

Use **On Error GoTo...** when you want to control what happens when an error occurs. For example, you might write an error handler that contains a message box telling the user that an error has occurred and what to do to correct it. Take a look at the following example.

```
Sub Sample()
On Error GoTo MyHandler
<code statements>
End
MyHandler:
MsgBox "Please place your insertion point in the table you want to copy before run-
ning this macro.", vbExclamation, "Please Try Again"
End Sub
```

Notice that this handler consists of an **On Error GoTo...** statement as well as another statement with the name of the handler followed by a colon (both in bold in the preceding sample). You can name the handler anything you like, within VBA naming conventions. Notice also the **End** statement that precedes the error handler, so that a macro that doesn't throw an error ends before the error handler is executed. If you call one macro from another, use **Exit Sub** in place of the **End** statement shown in the preceding example. The **End** statement ends all code execution. **Exit Sub** exits the active macro and returns to the macro from which it was called.

What this error handler indicates is that, if an error occurs, the code stops executing and moves to the line following **MyHandler:** to continue executing code from that point. In this case, the handler just displays a message box giving the user information on why they couldn't run the macro.

> **Note**
>
> A term followed by a colon is known as a Line Label. It's simply a way of naming a position in your code. If you weren't using an error handler, you could just type **GoTo SampleName** where you want the code to pick up at another position in the macro and then precede the new position with a line that reads **SampleName:**.

CAUTION

> If you add an error handler of any kind to your macro, be sure to comment that line out (add an apostrophe in front of the statement) when you test the macro. Otherwise, any errors might be ignored, causing you not to see the reason for an unexpected result. Also remember that an error handler can't account for code that comes before it. So, be sure to place an error handler before any code that might cause the error you want to address.

When deciding on how to handle errors for a particular macro, consider whether accounting for possible conditions or adding an error handler is the more effective way to go. For example, in the preceding code sample, if you just need the user to click in a table before running the macro, you might have added the following code at the beginning of the macro instead of an error handler.

```
If Selection.Information(wdWithinTable) = False Then
MsgBox "Please place your insertion point in the table you want to copy  before run-
ning this macro.", vbExclamation, "Please Try Again"
End If
```

Trapping Individual Errors

As mentioned earlier in this chapter, you can identify different actions to take in an error handler based on the type of error. One way to do this is to use another type of conditional structure referred to as **Select Case**.

Similar to an **If...Else...End If** structure, the **Select Case...End Select** structure enables you to specify different actions based on conditions you identify. Select Case is not at all strictly for error handlers, but it's mentioned here because trapping individual errors offers a good example of using this type of structure.

While **If...End If** structures evaluate each **If**, **Else If**, or **Else** expression independently, you can use a **Select Case** structure when you want to compare several possible results to a single expression. Take a look at the following code, for example, that uses one of the input box macro examples from earlier in this chapter.

```
Dim myInp As Integer
ResumeInputBox:
On Error GoTo ErrorHandler
myInp = InputBox("How many columns would you like?", "My Input Box")
With Selection
    .Tables.Add Range:=.Range, NumRows:=5, NumColumns:=myInp
End With
End
ErrorHandler:
Select Case Err.Number
    Case 13
        MsgBox "Please enter a numeric value to continue.", vbInformation
        Resume ResumeInputBox
    Case Else
        Msgbox Err.Description
End Select
```

Similar to an **If...End If** structure, you can identify several cases with the **Select Case** structure and provide for all cases not specified with a **Case Else** statement. As with all paired structures, remember to add **End Select** at the end of the structure, or your code will return an error.

Getting Help

Of course, you can search for help using the Type A Question For Help box on the Visual Basic Editor menu bar. But, there are often faster ways to get to exactly what you need.

In the case of error messages, remember that the Help button in those message boxes takes you directly to a help article on that specific error message. If, however, you need information on an error message any time other than right when it occurs, search for the topic Trappable Errors—available from the Visual Basic Editor in Word, Excel, and PowerPoint. You can then use CTRL+F for the find feature, to quickly locate the name or number of the particular error you need. The Trappable Errors article lists each error with a hyperlink to its article.

In the case of any object model member, right-click the name of the item where it appears in the code and then click Definition. This opens the Object Browser to the selected item—which might be enough information if you just need, for example, to see the available members of a selected object.

However, in the Object Browser, you can right-click any item and then click Help to open the help topic on that article. Note that some items, such as individual constants, might not have help articles—but articles are available for most members of the active object model.

Saving and Sharing Macros

You can export a module of code (as well as some other project elements, discussed later in this chapter), which is the equivalent of saving a copy of the file. To do this, right-click the module in the Project Explorer pane and then click Export. Choose a location and name the file, following file naming conventions. The file name doesn't need to match the module name. Notice also that VBA modules have the file extension .bas.

To import a module of code, such as the samples available on this book's CD (discussed in the next section), right-click the project in Project Explorer and then click Import. Browse to and select the .bas file you need, just as if you were opening a document.

> **CAUTION**
>
> If you export or import modules, remember that some modules refer to code outside of the module itself, such as when the project contains a UserForm (discussed in the section titled "Creating UserForms" later in this chapter) or when one macro calls another from a different module in the project. Be sure that you're aware of the project components that need to work together, so that you export or make note of everything you'll need when you or someone else imports that content later.

Because you can share an entire VBA project by sharing the Word, Excel, or PowerPoint file in which the project is stored, exporting is more often used as backup. This is often a good idea, because if you lose a document or template, you of course lose any code it contained.

In particular, if you store a module of document production macros, for example, in Normal.dotm, exporting that module periodically for backup is an important safety measure, considering that you might solve some Word performance issues by deleting Normal.dotm and allowing Word to regenerate a new default template, in which case your macros would be lost.

Sharing Projects

To share an entire project, just compile the project, save the file, and share it as you would any file. Keep in mind, of course, that some networks block Microsoft Office files that contain macros—so you might want to either compress the file into a zip container (though, keep in mind that many networks search compressed files for prohibited file types) or arrange another method of safely sharing the project with others.

Some macro projects need to be saved as particular file types, such as for Excel and PowerPoint add-ins. Additionally, signing projects can help to avoid systems or programs blocking your macros. Get information on how to accomplish both of these tasks in Chapter 23.

You can also protect your code when sharing projects—such as when you want others to be able to use the macros, but not to be able to see or copy your source code. To do this, select the project in Project Explorer. Then, on the Tools menu, click <Project> Properties.

In this dialog box, you can rename the project (following VBA naming conventions), which does not affect the file name of the document, template, or add-in where the project resides. You can also click the Protection tab to require a password to view the code. You must enable the Lock Project For Viewing option and provide a password for this to work. When you do, double-clicking the project in Project Explorer will display a box where you can type the password. Without the correct password, the macros can still be run from the user interface, but their code can't be viewed.

> **Note**
> Password protection will start the next time the project is opened.

> **CAUTION!**
> Be sure to keep a record of the name of the password you choose. Lost passwords might render your code permanently locked.

Using VBA to Save Time on Document Production and Troubleshooting

Once you understand the elements addressed in the preceding section of this chapter, you're ready to start using VBA. As mentioned earlier in this chapter, find a file named Sample Macros.dotm in the practice files you can install from this book's CD. That file contains two modules. One of those modules (named SampleMacros) includes a few of my favorite simple document production and troubleshooting macros. The other module (named AutomateUserForms) includes a couple of basic dialog boxes with related automation for use with some of the sample templates referenced in Chapter 20, "The Many Faces of Microsoft Office Templates." (Note that dialog boxes are known in VBA as UserForms and are introduced later in this chapter.) Check out these macros and UserForms as examples, or use them as jumping off points for creating your own automation.

Before you go to it, however, there is one important tool in the Visual Basic Editor that can sometimes save you even more time than writing a macro. As mentioned earlier, when you just need to execute a single line of code, you don't need to write a macro at all—you just need the Immediate Window.

Using the Immediate Window

To open the Immediate Window in the Visual Basic Editor, press CTRL+G. Note that this is not a toggle command. So, to close the Immediate Window, click the X at the top-right corner of the window.

To execute a command in the Immediate Window, type the command and then press ENTER. Note that, because code executed from this window can only be one line long, you can press ENTER from anywhere in the line, and it will not push text to a new line.

I use the Immediate Window frequently for a few different purposes. Take a look at some examples.

- Use the Immediate Window to get information about your document when troubleshooting problems, or to interact with your document in ways you can't from the user interface. For example, if Open And Repair tells you that a floating object is causing an error in the document, but you see no floating objects, you might want to go ahead and delete them all—as demonstrated earlier in the chapter under the heading "Loops"—or you might want to check first to see how many you're dealing with and then try to select them to know what they are before removing them.

  To ask a question in the Immediate Window, start with a question mark. For example, to see how many shapes exist in the main document body, type the following.

  ```
  ?ActiveDocument.Shapes.Count
  ```

  When you press ENTER from this line, you'll see the answer in the Immediate Window. If any shapes exist, you might want to use the Immediate Window to select one at a time and see what each is. To execute an action in the Immediate

Window, no leading character is necessary. Just type the statement and press EN-TER. In this case, type the following.

```
ActiveDocument.Shapes(1).Select
```

Though you can only execute one line at a time in the Immediate Window, you can type several lines if you need them, so that you don't have to keep retyping the same thing. You can't run individual lines of the same macro consecutively—the Immediate Window doesn't work like running a procedure. Each time you execute a line, it's an entire procedure. So, things like loops or conditional statements that require more than one line can't be done here. But, you could leave the line `?ActiveDocument.Shapes.Count` and type `ActiveDocument.Shapes(1).Select` below it. You can continue to type lines as you need to in that window, placing your insertion point in the statement you want to execute before you press ENTER.

> ### Note
>
> When you press ENTER from the line that reads `ActiveDocument.Shapes(1).Select`, the first floating object in the document is selected. But, because it might be off the page or hidden, you might not see it immediately. So, just remember what you already know. That is, VBA isn't a foreign program—it's an extension of the program you're using (Word, Excel, or PowerPoint).
>
> What does that mean? In this example, it means to use the methods you already know for getting to that object once you've used VBA to select it for you. For example, after telling VBA to select the shape, switch back to the document window (ALT+F11), press CTRL+X to cut the selection from the document (if you're not able to see it), create a new document, and then paste (CTRL+V) to see what the object is.

- In Chapters 14, "Working with Data," and Chapter 15, "Charts," I gave examples of using the Immediate Window to execute tasks that aren't possible from the document window, as follows.

  - To reset the used range for the active worksheet (that is, the last used cell that is selected when you press CTRL+END in a worksheet), use the following statement.

    ```
    ActiveSheet.UsedRange
    ```

  - To apply the setting to connect chart lines where empty cells exist in the data, you can use the Hidden And Empty Cells dialog box available from Select Data Source. However, if your chart is a combination chart that contains one or more series that aren't line series, that option is unavailable. In that case, use the Immediate Window and type the following statement.

    ```
    ActiveChart.DisplayBlanksAs = xlInterpolated
    ```

- The Immediate Window is also a good place to execute simple or repetitive actions that aren't available from the user interface. For example, say that you want to add a few hidden bookmarks to the document. Create hidden bookmarks by starting the bookmark name with an underscore, which can't be done from the Bookmark dialog box. Instead of writing a procedure that you have to run to add each bookmark after you select the range where you want the bookmark to appear, use the Immediate Window to do this. Type the following statement.

```
Selection.Bookmarks.Add("_name")
```

  In the above statement, substitute the name of your bookmark for *name*. Just place your insertion point where you want that bookmark to appear, then use ALT+F11 to switch back to the Visual Basic Editor and press ENTER from this statement to add the hidden bookmark.

> **Note**
>
> Hidden bookmarks are often used in documents or templates as markers for where you want a macro to insert specified content (such as a user's reply in a dialog box).

- When you're not sure of the phrasing for an action that only requires a single statement, the Immediate Window is a great way to test the code you think you need. You get the same Auto Lists and ScreenTips in the Immediate Window that you get in a code module, so it's a good way to try out your syntax. Note, however, that the Immediate Window is automatically cleared whenever you exit Word. So, if you want to reuse anything you figure out using the Immediate Window, copy it into a module and save the module before ending your Word session.

Introduction to Using Events

> **Note**
>
> This and the remaining sections of this chapter are intended to provide a taste of some additional capabilities of VBA beyond the basic macro, for those who feel confident with the primer content to this point and would like to try something a bit more complex. These sections assume you've already mastered everything included in the primer to this point.

Events in VBA are procedures that run automatically when a specified event occurs. There are several types of events in VBA, such as those that occur with a specific document action (such as opening a document), an application-specific action (such as exiting the program), or an action taken in a dialog box (such as clicking a command

Chapter 21

button). In this section, the concept of events is introduced using document-level events.

The method shown here for adding document-level events to a project is available in Word and Excel. This is where we get to use the **ThisDocument** or **ThisWorkbook** object that you see attached to any project in the Project Explorer.

Most of the work to create the event is done for you using the drop-down lists at the top of the code window. When you select Document (or Workbook in Excel) from the Object list at the top-left of the Window, as shown in the following image, the Procedure list at the top-right of the window is populated with the available events.

Many more events are available in Excel than in Word, but the basics (such as open, save, close, and print) are available in both.

Document-level events can be simple or complex, just as any macro. At the simplest, say that you're working on an important, complex document with other document editors, and it's essential that all editors are aware of certain formatting requirements. The particular requirements involve table layout or other specifications that can't be controlled through document protection or any other built-in features. Adding a comment in the document would be fine, but this document keeps getting messed up, the deadline is looming, and so you want those formatting requirements to pop out at anyone who opens the document. Just create an event that displays a message box with your instructions, whenever the document is open.

To do this, take the following steps.

1. In the Word Visual Basic Editor, double-click the **ThisDocument** object and then select Document from the Object list.

   When you do this, a **Document_New** event is created for you because this is the default event type. If you don't want a **Document_New** event, you can delete it later.

2. To create a **Document_Open** event, select Open from the Procedure list.

   Notice that the **Sub** and **End Sub** statements are automatically created for you, along with the procedure name. Don't change the procedure name, because the name is what tells VBA this is a procedure to be run automatically under the specified circumstance.

3. Type the code for your macro. In this case, it's just a message box. Then, save and close the document.

The code for the event you just created would look something like this:

```
Sub Document_Open()
MsgBox "<text of your instructions>", vbCritical, "IMPORTANT!"
End Sub
```

Then, the next time that document is opened (and each subsequent time), a message box similar to the following image appears automatically.

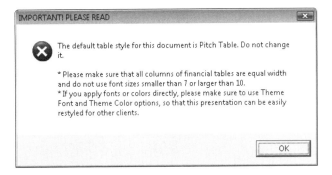

> **Note**
>
> To create line breaks and space between lines in a message box, as you see here, an easy option is to use the **vbCr** constant for adding a carriage return. Just place text portions of the string in quotation marks and separate each phrase with an ampersand. So, for example, to make a single line break, you would write "**<message text>**" & **vbCr** & "**<message text>**". To create two consecutive line breaks (space between lines), you would put two **vbCr** constants, each between separate ampersands, between the text phrases in quotation marks (such as ..." & **vbCr** & **vbCr** & "...). Remember that constants, being VBA terms, are never surrounded by quotation marks, even when they appear as part of a text string.

Note that some document-level events require arguments between the parentheses in the **Sub** statement. When they do, those arguments are provided for you. For general macros of the type discussed in this primer, you don't need to be concerned at all with those declarations.

In Excel, notice that you can create document-level events for the workbook or for an individual sheet. To create an event procedure for a specific sheet, or just to view what events are available to worksheets, double-click a sheet object in Project Explorer instead of the **ThisWorkbook** object. When you select Worksheet from the Object list, you can see the available worksheet procedures in the Procedure list.

If you don't see an event you want in Word, you might be able to accomplish what you need using Word VBA to write procedures for controlling built-in Word commands. For example, Excel workbooks have an available event named BeforePrint, but Word documents do not. However, in Word, you can use VBA to control the built-in Word print command. For information on where you can learn how to use VBA to control built-in Word commands or to get information about application-level events, see the last section of this chapter, "Next Steps for Working with Automation in Microsoft Office."

Creating UserForms (Dialog Boxes)

When you want to create automation to interact with the user in ways that a message box or input box can't do, create a dialog box (known in VBA as a UserForm). You can create a custom dialog box in VBA that looks very much like any built-in dialog box you see in Word, Excel, or PowerPoint.

If you've ever created form controls in a document or created and formatted AutoShapes on a PowerPoint slide, you already know most of what you need to know to create a custom dialog box. The following subsections walk you through steps to create and use a simple UserForm.

Designing a UserForm

To begin creating your dialog box, select the project (in Project Explorer) to which you want to add your dialog box. Then, on the Insert menu, click UserForm (or select User-Form from the Insert button on the Standard toolbar). When you do, an empty dialog box is created at a default size, as you see here.

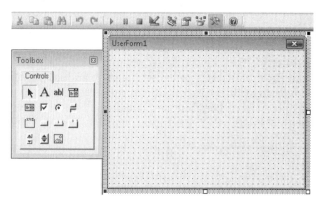

If the toolbox that you see in the preceding image doesn't appear automatically when the form is created, click the Toolbox icon that you see highlighted on the Standard toolbar in this image. The toolbox contains all of the controls you'll need for creating your form.

Before you start to add controls, take a look at the Properties Window. You'll see a long list of available settings here (as you see in the following image), some of which you might want to customize immediately.

Following are some basic settings in this window that can be particularly helpful.

- Name—change the name of the dialog box, using VBA naming rules. This is the name that appears in the Project Explorer and that you'll use to refer to the dialog box in macros. It's common, though not required, to start UserForm names with the letters frm. For example, name this form **frmSample**.

- Caption—the caption is the text that appears in the title bar of the form. This can be any text string and is limited only by the width of the dialog box as to how much text can appear in the title bar.

- Height and Width—these settings control the size of the dialog box. You can also drag the handles on the form to resize it. However, using these options to set a precise size can come in handy for a few reasons, such as if you have a large dialog box that needs to fit within the user's window at low resolution.

- Left and Top—these settings control where the dialog box appears on the screen. If you set these measurements, remember to account for any users who might use a lower resolution setting for their screen.

Notice that you can also customize font, borders, and fill color for the form.

To add controls to the dialog box, in the Toolbox, click the control type you want and then either click or drag to create that control on the form, just as you would do with shapes on a PowerPoint slide. Point to each option in the Toolbox for a ScreenTip indicating the type of control.

In the steps that follow, we'll create the dialog box you see here.

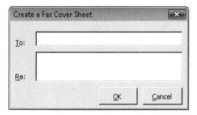

To create this dialog box, we'll add the following controls.

- Two labels, containing the text To: and Re:.

- Two text boxes, one allowing for a single line of text in the To field, and the other allowing for text to wrap in the Re field.

- Two command buttons—one for OK and one for Cancel.

To create these controls, do the following.

1. Click the Label button in the Toolbox (the capital letter A), and then click the form, approximately where you want the label to appear. A label is similar to a text box in a document, so just click into it and replace the text with the text you want (To: for the first label).

CAUTION

Unlike many programs where you can edit graphic objects, such as text boxes, don't double-click on a UserForm to edit a control. If you do, you're likely to accidentally open the Code window for that UserForm and automatically add the default event for the control you double-clicked. Meanwhile, If this happens, just delete the structure for the unwanted event and then double-click the UserForm name in the Project Explorer to return to the form. Control events are discussed later in this section.

2. Select the label and then, in the Properties Window, change its name to something easy to access in a macro. I named this first label labTo. To specify the accelerator keystroke, as you see in the preceding image, type **T** in the Accelerator field in the Properties Window. Remember to press ENTER to apply a value after typing in any field in this window.

3. To size the label to fit the text, with the label selected, click Format and then click Size To Fit. This will help you align the controls when you have them all on the form.

4. CTRL+drag to duplicate the label and then set up the other two labels you need, using the same actions in steps 1–3.

5. Click the TextBox button in the Toolbox and then click the form. Just as you would with any shape, drag to size it as needed.

6. In the Properties Window, name this text box. For ease of reference, I usually give text boxes the same name as their labels, but with a different prefix. So, for example, if I have a label named labTo, I would name the accompanying text box txtTo.

7. Press CTRL+drag to duplicate the text box, then rename and resize as needed.

   For the second (Re:) text box, notice that you need it to accept multiple lines. By default, a TextBox control only accepts a single line. To allow text to wrap to multiple lines, in the Properties Window, set the MultiLine field to True. If you want to allow the user to add hard returns (by pressing ENTER) in that field to start a new line, also change the EnterKeyBehavior field value to True.

8. Use the same procedure to create and name the two CommandButton controls.

   Note that the text that appears on the command buttons (OK or Cancel) is typed as you would on a text box. Just click in the default text, then delete and replace it with the text you need. Also notice that the text in a label or on a command button is the text in the Caption field in the Properties Window, so you can replace the text in that window if you prefer.

9. Notice that, on the Format menu, you have Align tools as well as Horizontal Spacing and Vertical Spacing options. Select controls as you would shapes on a slide and use these formatting tools to align the controls, as you see in the preceding sample.

   It's worth noting that the Align options here work similarly to the way they work in Microsoft Visio (as discussed in Chapter 17, "The Excel-Visio Connection") and not as you may be familiar with from PowerPoint. That is, controls align to the first control you select. The dominant control has white handles when selected, so that you can easily identify the direction in which selected controls will align. (However, holding the SHIFT key while selecting constrains which controls you can select. If you hold the CTRL key instead, you can select any controls on the form in any order, and the last object you select will be the dominant control.)

10. Right-click the form and then click Tab Order. In the Tab Order dialog box, move control names up or down as needed so that an applicable label appears immediately before its related text or combo box control, and so that the controls appear in the order in which you'd want to access them if you were tabbing through the dialog box. For the sample form, my completed Tab Order dialog box looks like this:

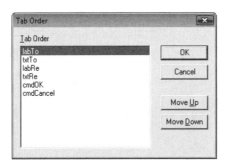

Note that, if a label doesn't precede its related field, using the accelerator key on the label won't access that field.

Once your controls are named and positioned, you're ready to add the automation you'll need to use this form.

Automating a UserForm

There are two parts to automating a dialog box, as follows.

- The code you add directly to the control, to manage its behavior in the dialog box.

- The code you write in a module to display the form and use it to interact with the user.

Depending on the types of controls that your dialog box includes, the code in your UserForm might get rather complex. For our sample dialog box, however, all we need is code to manage what happens when a command button is clicked. To do this, start by double-clicking the OK button.

When you double-click a control, the code for that control appears with a procedure created for you, using that control's default event Similar to document-level events (discussed earlier in this chapter), the name of the procedure connects it to a specific event. For command buttons, the default event is the one you'll usually want. For others, however, you might want to change the default event (for example, the default event for a check box is click, but you might need an event to occur when the value changes rather than when the box is clicked). As with document-level events, the available events in the Procedure list are those available to the type of control you're automating (the control selected in the Object list).

For the OK button, all you need to do is set it to hide the form. The macro that runs the form will continue to run after the form is hidden by the user. For the Cancel button, however, you'll want to unload the form and then end code execution (in two separate procedures), so that the macro doesn't continue to run.

You can refer to a UserForm as **Me** in code contained in that UserForm. Though you can also refer to the form by name, using **Me** is handy because you won't need to change the references if you change the form name. The code for the OK and Cancel buttons would look like this:

Chapter 21

```
Private Sub cmdOK_Click()
Me.Hide
End Sub

Private Sub cmdCancel_Click()
Unload Me
End Sub
```

You can end code execution from the preceding event for the Cancel button. However, if you instead add a separate event—the **Terminate** event for the UserForm—you'll also account for the user clicking the close button in the title bar of the UserForm instead of using your Cancel command button. This additional event looks like the following.

```
Private Sub UserForm_Terminate()
    End
End Sub
```

To create this event, you can simply type it beneath the other events in the Code window for your UserForm. Or, select UserForm from the Objects list at the top of that code window and then select Terminate from the Procedures list. Note that, when you select UserForm, its default event (Click) will be added to your code. You can simply delete that if you don't need it.

> **Note**
>
> To toggle between a UserForm and its code, right-click the form name in Project Explorer and then click View Code or View Object, as needed.

To automate the form in a procedure that you'll run from a module, set up anything you want to specify about how controls look when the dialog box is launched, then show the dialog box (using the **Show** method you see in the following sample) and then execute any commands you want for using the information the user adds in a dialog box. Take a look at one possible sample macro for automating the preceding dialog box.

```
Sub Fax()
    With frmSample
        .txtTo.Value = ""
        .txtRe.Value = ""
        .Show
        With ActiveDocument.Tables(1)
            .Cell(1, 2).Range.Text = frmSample.txtTo.Value
            .Cell(2, 2).Range.Text = frmSample.txtRe.Value
        End With
    End With
End Sub
```

Let's take a walk through this code.

- First, I set up a `With…End With` structure using my UserForm, which I named `frmSample`, as the object.

- Within that grouping structure, all controls that I added to the form are members of the `frmSample` object. So, when I start a new line inside that `With…End With` structure by typing a period, I get an Auto List that includes the control names I added to the form. In the preceding code, I set the values of the To and Re text boxes to nothing, so that the last value the user set wouldn't be accidentally left behind.

- The **Show** statement appears on a line by itself. This action displays the dialog box to the user.

  I added another `With…End With` structure here because typing `ActiveDocument.Tables(1)` is longer than typing `frmSample`, and I need to reference the first table in the document on each line where I'm placing the text the user adds to each text box in the dialog box into a specified table cell in the document. (Note that bookmarks, hidden bookmarks in particular, are another common method of identifying where in a document to place information collected in a dialog box.)

  Because `frmSample` and `ActiveDocument.Tables(1)` are completely separate objects, when my insertion point is inside the `ActiveDocument.Tables(1)` `With…End With` structure, notice that I can't use the `frmSample` `With…End With` structure that surrounds it. In a procedure this short, the second `With…End With` structure is used only to demonstrate placing one independent grouping structure within another—but where you have more dialog box controls, with more actions to take, doing this might save you some code.

To learn about adding and automating more complex controls on a dialog box (such as combo box or multipage controls) or to learn other options for automating your User-Forms (including what types of procedures you can do directly from the UserForm's code), see the additional resources recommended in the next section of this chapter.

> **Note**
> Because the macros provided in the preceding section reference UserForms, this code is not included in the sample file PrimerMacros.bas. Instead, find similar examples of basic UserForms and automation for those forms in the sample file Sample Macros.dotm, also referenced earlier.

Next Steps for Working with Automation in Microsoft Office

Once you've mastered the basics in this primer, you're likely to find more complex VBA to be quite easy. As mentioned earlier, Microsoft provides the MSDN Library, a free on-line resource, where you can find instructions and samples for quite a bit of VBA code.

Are you thinking, perhaps, that you might want to go even further? Now that you're writing macros, can VBA take you far enough, or does your work warrant a foray into professional development tools like Microsoft Visual Studio?

Tristan Davis, a Program Manager on the 2007 Office release product team and programmability guru, has this to say about how to set the goals that are right for you when it comes to automating Microsoft Office.

"There are three big steps I see in working programmatically with Office:

- First, people typically get into recording macros to automate their own common tasks, which ends up being a huge time saver when they find out they can do XYZ once and have it automatically repeated when they press a key combination. Relatively easy to do, but not a lot of power.

- Then, you can graduate to VBA. Usually, you want to change a macro you've recorded and somehow end up in the Visual Basic Editor to do it, ushering you into that new world. A lot more power once you figure it out, but more complex.

- Then, there's the big step up to the world of managed code: You're into Microsoft Visual Studio now using Visual Studio Tools for Office to do it. Another leap in available functionality, but now it's 'real' coding."

Tristan adds the graphs that follow, to help you look at the cost/benefit of automating Microsoft Office from two perspectives.

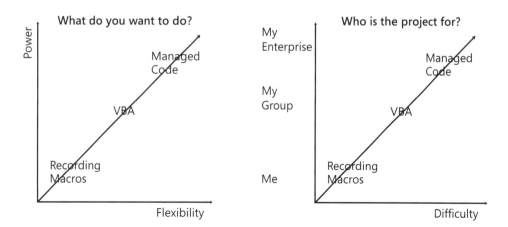

Note

Find links to a range of developer resources, from select MSDN pages to blogs from both members of the 2007 Office release product team and MVP experts, on the Resources and Expert Tips tabs of this book's CD.

Before you go, however, the next chapter in this book provides a similar primer on the basics of using the Open XML Formats to edit documents, binding data to Content Controls in Word, and beginning to customize the Ribbon. After you check that out, see Chapter 23 to learn how to use XML and VBA together to begin creating simple add-ins.

In my favorite novel, Alexandre Dumas' *The Count of Monte Cristo*, the imprisoned Abbe Faria wrote a book without access to paper or writing implements. A 19th century genius resourceful enough to turn MacGyver green with envy, the good Abbe fashioned a pen out of a fishbone, ink out of soot and wine, and 12 rolls of parchment from two shirts. Not bad for an old man who was locked away in a dungeon.

In previous versions of Microsoft Office, the idea of editing a document without first opening the program in which it's created is much like writing a book in a 19th century dungeon. Without the know-how of an Abbe Faria (or, in this case, a software engineer of equal talent), you're probably out of luck.

Well, thanks to the ingenuity of some talented software engineers, you no longer need to be a fictional genius (or hold an advanced computer science degree) to understand every bit of a document's structure well enough even to create one from scratch (if you're so inclined). Though you never have to know a thing about the XML behind your documents to use the 2007 release programs, the benefits of getting to know the Office Open XML Formats can be great. Using the XML content for these new file formats, advanced Microsoft Office users can see and understand literally everything that goes into a 2007 release document.

As discussed at several points throughout this book, the transparency of the new file formats can save time, add flexibility, improve integration with external content, and simplify essential tasks such as protecting the private content in your documents or troubleshooting document problems. But, my favorite thing about these new formats is just the fact that you don't have to be a programmer to reap many of the aforementioned benefits.

It's important to reinforce that this is not an introduction to the XML programming language, but to the Office Open XML Formats. That said, in this primer, you'll learn to understand the structure of an Office Open XML Format document and how to edit documents directly in their XML. You will also learn the basics of how to customize the Ribbon and how to create custom XML for binding data to document content.

Chapter Assumptions

As with the preceding Microsoft Visual Basic for Applications (VBA) primer, this chapter assumes that this may be the first time you've ever seen a line of programming code, but also that you're an advanced Microsoft Office user and comfortable with the features covered throughout this book.

Though this primer is written for Microsoft Office users and not for programmers, you might have noticed that I've already specified *advanced* users more than once. That's because incorrectly editing a document's XML can break a document faster than you can blink.

That statement isn't meant to scare you away. If you're an advanced user, learning to edit your documents' XML can be easy, and you can just as easily learn to quickly fix anything you may inadvertently break. Rather, I mention this primarily for the trainers or tech support professionals among you who might consider sending basic or intermediate users into a document's XML.

You'll gain tremendous power and flexibility by being able to edit a document's XML, but please don't consider it just another method for accomplishing document tasks—such as just one more option you'd teach in a Microsoft Word course for how to edit the definition of a paragraph style. This is an avenue for those with the skill to take document production and troubleshooting to a new level.

Consider this: If a document were a car, then the document's XML would be the tools of an auto mechanic. Before you can begin to understand what's going on under the hood, you need to know how to drive. That said, experienced drivers are going to have a great time with the tools in this chapter.

> **Note**
>
> As with the VBA primer in this book, much of what you'll learn in this chapter can be applied to any program that uses the Office Open XML Formats. However, because I assume that you're new to any use of XML, all examples in this chapter use Microsoft Office Word 2007 documents and tasks for consistency.

XML Basics for Reading Your Documents

XML is a language used to contain and describe data. In the case of Office Open XML, the data is your document content, and the description includes the settings required for that document to function in the applicable program as well as the settings you apply to the document.

Before you begin to explore a document's XML, the subsections that follow provide a bit of background and basics to help you prepare for the task.

Reading a Markup Language

XML is a markup language. Just as you mark up a document while reviewing it—with comments, corrections, or margin notes—a markup language marks up data with descriptive information about that data.

If you've ever looked at the HTML source code of a Web page, you already have some experience with the type of language you'll see throughout this primer. However, instead of paired formatting codes wrapped around text that you see in HTML (such as **text** to turn bold formatting on and then off), the Office Open XML Formats use paired codes nested in a hierarchy that compartmentalizes, organizes, and defines everything you need to know about your document.

The following example shows the word *text* along with its formatting definition. This word is part of a paragraph but is separated out in the source code (the markup) because it contains unique formatting. The bullets that follow the code sample explain in detail how to read this sample.

```
<w:r>
    <w:rPr>
            <w:b />
    </w:rPr>
    <w:t>text</w:t>
</w:r>
```

- The **w:** that begins each line indicates that this information is describing an Office Word 2007 document. You will see different prefixes in your Microsoft Office Excel 2007 and Microsoft Office PowerPoint 2007 documents. Also notice that each code is surrounded by angle brackets (<>).

- As with HTML source code, XML code used to describe content is usually paired, and the second of the pair (the end code) begins with a slash character.

- The section of code shown in the preceding sample is known as a *run*, noted by the **w:r** that introduces the first line of code. A run is a region of document content that contains similar properties.

  To complete the structure, the entire content of the paragraph to which the word *text* belongs is stored between the two ends of a higher-level paired code, not shown here, that indicates the start and end of the paragraph (**<w:p>** and **</w:p>**). The collection of paragraphs (and any other content) in the body of the document is in turn positioned within another paired code (**<w:body>** and **</w:body>**).

- The second and fourth lines in the sample comprise a paired code containing the formatting for the specified text. Notice that between those lines, the third line simply indicates that the specified text is bolded **<w:b />**.

Because formatting information in Office Open XML is stored in a structure that defines where the formatting is to be applied, the specific formatting itself doesn't need a paired code. If the text for this sample were also italicized, for example, the code `<w:i />` would appear on its own line, also between the lines of the same paired code that contains the bold statement. Also notice that, because the bold (or italicized) statements stand on their own, they include a slash at the end of the single code to indicate that there is no end code for this statement. You'll see the slash at the end of other codes throughout this primer, wherever the item is not paired.

- The specified paragraph text appears on the fifth line, between a pair of codes (`<w:t>` and `</w:t>`) that indicate it's the text being described.

- The last line in the preceding example is the end code that indicates the end of the description for this specified text.

If the preceding example seems to be quite a lot of work for one word, don't lose heart. It's just an example of how you see Word formatting applied to text in the XML markup, used here to demonstrate how code in the Office Open XML Formats is spelled out. Though it also serves to demonstrate why working in the XML wouldn't be considered an equal alternative to the built-in program features for many document editing needs, that's not the reason for this example. Understanding how to read XML structure will help you work more easily when you begin to use a document's XML in ways that can simplify your work and expand the possibilities.

Don't worry about trying to memorize any specific codes used in the preceding example. The important thing to take away from this is the general concept of how the XML code is structured. Everything in XML is organized and spelled out, like driving directions that take no turn for granted. So, though the example given might seem like a lot of code for very little content, the fact that it's organized explicitly is the very thing that will make the tasks throughout this primer easy to understand even to those who are new to XML.

Chapter 22

> **Note**
>
> If you look at the markup for one of your own documents, you may see code similar to the preceding example along with additional codes labeled `w:rsidR` and `rsidRPr`, each followed by a set of numbers. Those codes and their corresponding numbers are a result of the feature Store Random Number To Improve Combine Accuracy, which you can find on the Privacy Options tab of the Trust Center. (See Chapter 23, "Using VBA and XML Together to Create Add-Ins," for more on using the Trust Center.)
>
> Unless you intend to use the Combine feature (available from the Compare options on the Review tab) with a particular document, there's no benefit to enabling this option (but it is on by default). For the sake of simplicity, since these codes are not essential to your documents, they're not included in any XML samples throughout this chapter.

Understanding Key Terms

I'll introduce terms as they arise for each task, but there are a few terms that can be useful to note up front.

- As mentioned in Chapter 1, "Welcome to the 2007 Microsoft Office System," the Office Open XML Formats are actually compressed folders containing a set of files that work together. ZIP technology (the .zip file extension) is the method used to compress the files into a single unit, and the set of files that comprise an Office Open XML Format document is referred to as the ZIP **package**.

- Each file within the package is referred to as a **document part**.

- When you read about XML, you often come across the word **schema**. An XML schema is a set of standards and rules that define a given XML structure. For example, multiple schemas are available for defining different components of Office Open XML, and you'll see reference to some of these in the document parts used for the tasks throughout this chapter. Anyone can freely use the schemas for the Office Open XML formats. Developers can also create their own custom schemas for custom document solutions. (Note, however, that creating schemas is an advanced XML skill that is beyond the scope of this chapter.)

   On the Resources tab of this book's CD, find the schema for customizing the user interface in the 2007 release programs that use the Office Open XML Formats. You can open this file, named customUI.xsd, in the Microsoft Windows utility program Notepad to view its content and give yourself an idea of the type of information contained in an XML schema.

XML Editing Options

Most professional developers use Microsoft Visual Studio for editing XML, but you certainly don't need to do that. You can use Notepad for the same purpose, or any of a wide range of programs from Microsoft Office SharePoint Designer 2007 to a number of freeware, shareware, and retail XML editors.

Many people who don't need a professional development platform for their work will use a freeware or shareware XML editor to see the XML hierarchy in a tree structure that's easy to read. When you edit XML in Notepad, it typically looks like running text with no manual line breaks.

For those who don't want to install another program for this purpose, you can use Microsoft Internet Explorer to view the XML in a hierarchical tree structure and easily find what you need, and then use Notepad to edit the XML. This is the approach I use for the examples throughout this primer.

> **Note**
>
> Find a link to the download page for XML Notepad 2007, a free XML editing tool from Microsoft, on the Resources tab of this book's CD. XML Notepad provides both an editor and a viewer, along with features such as drag-and-drop editing and error checking. However, using the editor in XML Notepad requires some knowledge of XML language structure. So, for those who are seeing XML for the first time in this chapter, start with the Microsoft Windows Notepad utility and consider moving up to XML Notepad once you get your bearings, if you find yourself yearning for a more structured editing environment.
>
> That said, even if you're not using XML Notepad 2007 regularly to edit your code, it can be a handy tool for understanding the structure of your code and troubleshooting syntax errors, as discussed later in this chapter. So, you might want to download it sooner than later.

When you open an XML file in Internet Explorer, you're likely to see a bar across the top of the screen indicating that active content was disabled. Right-click that bar and activate content to be able to expand and collapse sections of your code by using the minus signs you see beside each level of code that contains sublevels. For example, here's what the code shown earlier looks like when viewed in Internet Explorer.

```
- <w:r>
  - <w:rPr>
      <w:b />
    </w:rPr>
    <w:t>text</w:t>
  </w:r>
```

The same text in Notepad looks like this:

```
<w:r><w:rPr><w:b/></w:rPr><w:t>text</w:t></w:r>
```

TROUBLESHOOTING

The document won't open after I edit an XML file, but I know my code is correct

Remember that a small syntax error (such as leaving off one of the angle brackets around a code) in one XML file within a document can cause that document to be unreadable. However, if you know that the code you typed is correct, there may be another reason that's just as easy to resolve.

Some XML editors that display the XML code in an easily readable tree structure may add formatting marks (such as tabs or line breaks) when you add code to that XML structure. When this happens, these formatting marks can be interpreted as a syntax error (just like a missing bracket) and cause the document to which that XML file belongs to become unreadable in its native program.

If you don't know how to recognize unwanted formatting marks in your XML editor or if the file won't open in your XML editor, see the Inside Out tip titled "Using XML Notepad and Word to help find syntax errors" later in this chapter for steps to help you locate the error.

Getting to Know the Office Open XML Formats

This section will show you how to access the ZIP package for an Office Open XML Format document and how to begin to make sense of what you find there. For the best results, I suggest that you take each subsection that follows step by step and be sure you understand and feel comfortable with the content before continuing onto the next.

Breaking into Your Document

Because each of your 2007 Office release Word, Excel, and PowerPoint documents is actually a ZIP package in disguise, you can just change the file extension to .zip to access all of the files in the package. There are a few ways to go about this.

CAUTION

If you have software installed that extracts files from a ZIP package, you might be able to look at the files in the ZIP package by using that extraction software, without first changing the file extension. However, you're unlikely to see the folder structure of the package when you do this, which is an essential part of the package integrity. Changing the extension takes just a second and enables you to view and manage your files in Windows Explorer, for familiar file access options.

- Append the .zip file extension to the existing file name. To do this in a Windows Explorer, or on the Windows Desktop, just click to select the file and then click again on the file name (this is slower than a double-click) to enter editing mode for the file name. For the same result, you can also press F2 once you select the file. Leave the existing file name and extension intact and just add .zip, so that you can open the package in a Windows Explorer to see its content.

  When you change the file extension in a Windows Explorer or from the Windows Desktop, you'll see a warning that changing the file extension may make the file unusable. Just disregard this message and click Yes to confirm that you want to continue. (However, to protect your files, it's a good idea to save a copy of the document with its original file extension before appending the .zip extension or beginning to make changes in the XML.)

Note

Renaming the file to a .zip extension is easier to do if you are viewing file extensions. If you don't see the extension for your Office Open XML Format file (such as .docx), change your setting in Windows Explorer to view all file extensions. To do this in Windows Vista, in any Windows Explorer window, click the Organize button and then click Folder And Search Options. On the View tab, turn off the option Hide Extensions Of Known File Types and then click OK. To find the same option when working in Windows XP, in a Windows Explorer, on the Tools menu, click Folder Options and then click View.

Chapter 22

- You can save a copy of your file with the .zip extension, while it's open in its source program, to bypass the step of changing the extension later. In the Save As dialog box, type the entire file name followed by .zip inside quotation marks. The file is still saved in whatever format is listed (so you still need to choose a macro-free or macro-enabled file format, for example, as needed), just as if you saved it first and appended the zip extension later. The only difference is that the file's ZIP package is immediately available to you without taking an additional step after you close the file. For example, to save a file named *sample.docx* as *sample.zip*, type "**sample.zip**" in the File Name box of the Save As dialog box.

INSIDE OUT   That ZIP package is still a document

When you're editing the files in the ZIP package, you might not want to spend the time switching back and forth between the Office Open XML file extension (such as .docx) and the .zip extension. Well, you don't have to!

From the Open file dialog box in Word, Excel, or PowerPoint, you can open documents that belong to the applicable program even when they're using the .zip file extension. To see your ZIP package file, just select All Files from the file type drop-down list beside the File Name text box and then select and open the file as you would when using its original extension. There's nothing else to it. Word, Excel, and PowerPoint know that the Office Open XML Formats are ZIP packages and read the XML within those packages whether the file is saved using .zip or a file extension that belongs to the program.

Note that you can also open the ZIP package in the appropriate program through the Open With options available when you right-click the ZIP package on the Windows Desktop or in a Windows Explorer. If you do this, just be careful not to accidentally set the applicable program as the default for opening this file type, or you'll add an extra step for yourself every time you want to access the document parts in the ZIP package.

However, for ease of use as well as for sharing documents with Microsoft Office users of all experience levels, it's a good idea to make sure the file extension is changed back to its original state once you've finished editing the files in the ZIP package.

The Office Open XML File Structure

Once you change the file name to have the .zip extension, open the file in a Windows Explorer. The example that follows walks you through the ZIP package of a simple Word document, originally saved with the .docx extension..

When you first view the ZIP package for a Word document in a Windows Explorer, it will look something like this.

Note that, at the top level of the ZIP package that you see in the preceding example, Excel and PowerPoint files look very similar except that the folder named **word** in the example is named **xl** or **ppt**, respectively, for the applicable program.

- The **docProps** folder is exactly what it sounds like—it contains the files for the document properties and application properties, ranging from author name to word count and software version.

- The **_rels** folder contains a file named *.rels*, which defines the top-level relationships between the folders in the package. Note that additional relationship files may exist, depending on the document content, for files within a specific folder of the package (explained later in this section).

  The relationship files are among the most important in the package because, without them, the various document parts in the package don't know how to work together.

- The file *[Content_Types].xml* also exists at the top level of every document's ZIP package. This file identifies the content types included in the document. For example, in a Word document, this list typically includes such things as the main document, the fonts, styles, Theme, document properties, and application properties. Files with additional content types, such as diagrams or other graphics, will have additional content types identified.

Exploring a bit further, when you open the folder named **word**, you see something similar to the following image.

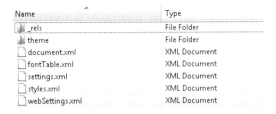

- A new Word document contains XML files for the fonts, styles, settings (such as the saved zoom setting and default tab stops), and Web settings, whether or not formatting related to these items has been applied in the document. If headers, footers, footnotes, graphics, comments, or other content types have been added, each of them will have its own XML document part as well.

  In the ZIP packages for Excel and PowerPoint files, you'll see a similar organization, with xml document parts for file components (such as *styles.xml* in Excel or *tableStyles.xml* in PowerPoint). Additionally, the **xl** folder in an Excel ZIP package

Chapter 22

contains a **worksheets** folder by default, because there is a separate xml document part for each sheet in the workbook. The **ppt** folder in a PowerPoint ZIP package also contains folders named **slides**, **slideLayouts**, and **slideMasters**, by default.

- In addition to the XML document parts you see in the preceding image, notice the **theme** folder—which exists in the program-specific folder (**word**, **xl**, or **ppt**) for Word, Excel, and PowerPoint ZIP packages. The file contained in this **theme** folder contains all document Theme settings applied in the document. It is because of this file that you're able to share custom Themes by sharing documents, using the Browse For Themes feature at the bottom of each Themes gallery.

- The **_rels** folder inside the program-specific folder defines the relationships between the parts inside the program-specific folder. The relationship file contained in this _rels folder is called *document.xml.rels* for Word documents, *presentation.xml.rels* for PowerPoint documents, and *workbook.xml.rels* for Excel documents.

  Depending on the content in a given folder, its **_rels** folder might contain more than one file. For example, if a header exists in a Word document, the **word** folder contains a part named *header.xml,* and its **_rels** folder contains a file named *header.xml.rels.*

- Content in your document from other sources (such as embedded objects, media files, or macros) are either stored in their original format (as is the case for picture files) or as a binary file (.bin file extension). Because of this, you can save time on many tasks related to working with media files (such as pictures), as discussed in the section "Editing and Managing Documents Through XML," later in this chapter.

- As mentioned at the beginning of this section, the ZIP package shown in the two preceding images is for a docx file. Remember that the *x* at the end of the file extension indicates that it's a macro-free file format. If this were, instead, the package for a docm file, you would also see a file named *vbaData.xml* and one named *vbaProject.bin.*

If you return to the top level of the ZIP package and then open the **docProps** folder, the following is what you'll see.

Name	Type
app.xml	XML Document
core.xml	XML Document
thumbnail.wmf	WMF Image

By default, this folder contains the files *app.xml* (for application properties such as word count and program version) and *core.xml* (for document properties such as the Document Properties summary information like author and subject). Additionally, if you use the options to save a preview picture or a thumbnail for your document, you see a thumbnail image file in the docProps folder. For Word and Excel, this will be a wmf file and for PowerPoint it will be a jpeg file.

> **Note**
>
> If you're running the 2007 Office release on Windows Vista, you'll find an option in the Save As dialog box in Word or Excel to save a thumbnail image of your document. In PowerPoint, or in all three programs when running Windows XP, you'll see the option Save Preview Picture in the Document Properties dialog box.

Taking a Closer Look at Key Document Parts

Let's take a look at the XML contained in a few of the essential document parts, to help accustom you to reading this file content.

The image you see below is the *[Content_Types].xml* file for the sample ZIP package shown under the preceding heading, as seen in a Windows Explorer.

```xml
<?xml version="1.0" encoding="UTF-8" standalone="yes" ?>
- <Types xmlns="http://schemas.openxmlformats.org/package/2006/content-types">
    <Default Extension="wmf" ContentType="image/x-wmf" />
    <Default Extension="rels" ContentType="application/vnd.openxmlformats-
      package.relationships+xml" />
    <Default Extension="xml" ContentType="application/xml" />
    <Override PartName="/word/document.xml" ContentType="application/vnd.openxmlformats-
      officedocument.wordprocessingml.document.main+xml" />
    <Override PartName="/word/styles.xml" ContentType="application/vnd.openxmlformats-
      officedocument.wordprocessingml.styles+xml" />
    <Override PartName="/docProps/app.xml" ContentType="application/vnd.openxmlformats-
      officedocument.extended-properties+xml" />
    <Override PartName="/word/settings.xml" ContentType="application/vnd.openxmlformats-
      officedocument.wordprocessingml.settings+xml" />
    <Override PartName="/word/theme/theme1.xml"
      ContentType="application/vnd.openxmlformats-officedocument.theme+xml" />
    <Override PartName="/word/fontTable.xml" ContentType="application/vnd.openxmlformats-
      officedocument.wordprocessingml.fontTable+xml" />
    <Override PartName="/word/webSettings.xml" ContentType="application/vnd.openxmlformats-
      officedocument.wordprocessingml.webSettings+xml" />
    <Override PartName="/docProps/core.xml" ContentType="application/vnd.openxmlformats-
      package.core-properties+xml" />
  </Types>
```

- The first line that you see in this or any XML file in an Office Open XML Format ZIP package will look very much like the first line in the preceding image. This line simply defines the type of XML structure being used.

- Notice that the second line, which begins **<Types**..., is the first half of a paired code for which the end code is at the bottom of this document. All other lines in this file are the definitions of the content types in this document.

   ○ On the second line, inside the **Types** code, you see **xmlns** followed by a URL. The reference **xmlns** refers to an XML **namespace**, which is a re-quired component in several document parts. Technical though this term might sound, a namespace is nothing more than a way to uniquely identify a specified item. The reason for this is that there can be no ambiguous names in the ZIP package (that is, the same name can't be used to refer to more than one item). So, the namespace essentially attaches itself to the content it identifies to become part of that content's name.

It's standard to use a Web address as the namespace, but note that the file doesn't attempt to read any data from the specified address. In fact, if you try to access some of the URLs you see in the files of an Office Open XML ZIP package, you'll find that some are not even valid addresses. Typically, the address in a namespace identifies the location of the source schema or other definitions used to define the structure of the items assigned to that namespace, and the Web page associated with that address may actually contain those definitions. But, any URL can be used as a namespace—the address itself is actually irrelevant to the code.

- For the lines between the paired **Types** codes, notice that each defines one of the document parts you saw in the images of this sample ZIP package, under the preceding heading.

  - ○ The first three lines in that group define the three file extensions included in this particular package, rels (the relationship files), wmf (the Windows metafile picture used for the document thumbnail), and xml.

  - ○ The remaining lines in that group, each named `Override PartName`, define the content type for each of the XML document parts that you saw in the **word** and **docProps** folders for this ZIP package. Take a look at just the first of the `Override PartName` lines, shown below. This one is for the main document content—the file *document.xml* that resides in the word folder.

    ```
    <Override PartName="/word/document.xml" ContentType="application/vnd.openxmlformats-officedocument.wordprocessingml.document.main+xml" />
    ```

    Notice that the definition of the `Override PartName` that appears in quotation marks is actually the path to the specified file within the ZIP package. The content type definition that appears in quotation marks as the second half of that line of code is a reference to the content type definition defined in the applicable schema.

The following image shows you the content of the *.rels* file in the top-level **_rels** folder shown earlier for the sample ZIP package.

```
<?xml version="1.0" encoding="UTF-8" standalone="yes" ?>
- <Relationships xmlns="http://schemas.openxmlformats.org/package/2006/relationships">
    <Relationship Id="rId3"
      Type="http://schemas.openxmlformats.org/package/2006/relationships/metadata/core-
      properties" Target="docProps/core.xml" />
    <Relationship Id="rId2"
      Type="http://schemas.openxmlformats.org/package/2006/relationships/metadata/thumbnail"
      Target="docProps/thumbnail.wmf" />
    <Relationship Id="rId1"
      Type="http://schemas.openxmlformats.org/officeDocument/2006/relationships/officeDocument"
      Target="word/document.xml" />
    <Relationship Id="rId4"
      Type="http://schemas.openxmlformats.org/officeDocument/2006/relationships/extended-
      properties" Target="docProps/app.xml" />
  </Relationships>
```

> **Note**
>
> The *.rels* file should open without issue in Internet Explorer. But, if this doesn't work for you, append the .xml file extension to a copy of the *.rels* file, just for viewing purposes. Also note that, when in the ZIP package, files will only open in their default assigned program. To be able to open a document part in both Internet Explorer and Notepad, as needed, copy the file out of the ZIP package. Then, right-click the file and point to Open With to select the program you need.

- Notice that, although the content of the *.rels* file is very different from the content of the *[Content_Types].xml* file, the concept of the structure is the same. That is, the first line defines the XML standard being used, and the second line opens the paired code that stores the core file content and specifies a namespace for the content that appears between the lines of the paired code.

- Take a look at one of the relationship definitions from the *.rels* file—the one for the main *document.xml* document part. Notice that each relationship contains three parts—the **ID**, the **Type**, and the **Target**.

```
<Relationship Id="rId1"
  Type="http://schemas.openxmlformats.org/officeDocument/2006/relationships/officeDocument"
  Target="word/document.xml" />
```

  - An **ID** is typically named **rID#**. This structure is not required, however, so you might occasionally see relationships with different IDs.

  - The **Type** uses a type defined in the applicable schema, which appears as a Web address. As with an XML namespace, the document doesn't need to read data from that address. However, in this case, the **Type** is a specified element of the applicable schema and does need to be a content type recognized by the Office Open XML structure.

  - The **Target**, as you likely recognize, is the address within the package, where the referenced file appears. When you create a relationship yourself, it's essential that this be correct, because the relationship will do no good if it can't find the specified file.

Depending on the content in your files, you might run across defined relationships in your *.rels* files that aren't used to specify files in the ZIP package and therefore might take on a slightly different structure for the relationship target. For example, notice the following relationship from a *document.xml.rels* file for a document that contains a hyperlink to the Microsoft home page.

```
<Relationship Id="rId4"
  Type="http://schemas.openxmlformats.org/officeDocument/2006/relationships/hyperlink"
  Target="http://www.microsoft.com" TargetMode="External" />
```

Though the relationship ID and Type have the same structure as a relationship to a document part, notice that the target in this case is to an external hyperlink instead of a file in the package.

Chapter 22

When you open a file in its originating program (Word, Excel, or PowerPoint), keep in mind that the *.rels* files are the first place the program looks to know how to put the pieces together for the purpose of opening that file.

Building a Basic Word Document from Scratch

The document shown in the preceding portions of this section is a simple Word document with all the defaults you get when you use Word to create a new document in the docx file format. Now, it's time to build a docx file yourself, without using Word.

If you're thinking about skipping over the rest of this section because it sounds either too complicated or unnecessary for your needs, please wait. This exercise is important for three reasons.

1. You might be amazed at how easy this is to do. And, discovering the simplicity for yourself can help you master the tasks in this chapter that you want to learn.

2. You can find all the XML code you need for this section in a provided sample file (explained in a note that precedes the first part of the following exercise), if you prefer not to type out the XML for yourself.

3. This exercise is included early in the primer because doing a similar exercise when I was first learning about the Office Open XML Formats was the most helpful thing I did toward understanding the basics of how the parts in an Office Open XML ZIP package work and fit together.

That said, the exercise that follows walks you through creating a simple, essentials-only Word document. Though it's good practice for anyone creating Office Open XML Format documents through code to include all of the defaults that the source program (Word, Excel, or PowerPoint) includes when it creates a new document, only a few of those files are actually required for the source program (Word in our example) to be able to recognize and open the file. If you create a file that only contains the required bare basics, Word will recognize the missing pieces and add the document parts and relationships needed as you begin to use Word features in your document.

Every Office Open XML document requires *[Content_Types].xml* as well as a top-level **_rels** folder containing the *.rels* file. Each file also requires its program-specific folder with the main program-specific content file that goes in that folder (*document.xml* in a folder named **word**, in the case of a Word document). For a Word document, such as we're about to build, these are the only three files you must have in your ZIP package to create a docx file that Word will recognize and open without an error. In Excel and PowerPoint, a few other files are required.

- An Excel xlsx file also requires the **sheets** folder inside the **xl** folder, with an xml document part for at least one sheet. This is because an Excel workbook must contain at least one worksheet. Because of that **sheets** folder, the **xl** folder also needs its own **_rels** folder containing a workbook-level *.rels* file that defines the relationship between worksheets and workbook.

● A PowerPoint pptx file also requires the **slideLayouts**, **slideMasters**, and **theme** folders (each of which contain required files), because a presentation must contain a Theme, at least one slide master, and at least one slide layout. These folders, all of which reside in the **ppt** folder, also require a **_rels** folder in that **ppt** folder to define the relationships between the presentation, slide master, and Theme. Note that the master and layout folders contain their own **_rels** folders, which is why there is no reference to the slide layouts in the presentation-level relationships file.

To create your first Word document from scratch, you'll need to create *[Content_Types].xml*, *.rels*, and *document.xml*, and place them in the correct folder structure. The steps that follow will walk you through getting this done.

> **Note**
>
> In the sample files you can install from the Welcome tab on this book's CD, find the Copy XML.txt file, which contains all of the code in this and subsequent sections of this chapter, that you can copy into the files you create in Notepad if you prefer not to type the XML yourself.

Create the Folder Structure

On your Windows Desktop, or in any convenient location, create a folder named **First Document** (or any name you like; this name is for identification purposes in this exercise only). This folder will store the structure for your new docx file. In that folder, create two subfolders, one named **_rels** and the other named **word**. It is essential that these two folders are correctly named. When you're done with this step, your folder structure should look like the following image.

Create the Main Document File

The main document file, *document.xml*, needs to reside in the **word** folder you just created. To create this file, do the following.

1. Open Notepad and save a new file as *document.xml*, inside the **word** folder you created. Be sure to type the .xml file extension as part of the file name, so that Notepad doesn't save the file in the .txt file format. (Notepad will save the file correctly when you type *document.xml* in the File Name box, even though the Save As Type list indicates a .txt file.)

2. In Notepad, add the following code to the *document.xml* file. This code is shown below first in Internet Explorer, so that you can see the organization of it, and then in Notepad, to see how it looks without the tree structure applied.

If you're typing this text from scratch, it's easier to copy from the version shown in the tree structure. If you do, note that you need a space between each xml namespace (**xmlns** definition) because those definitions all appear together inside the same code (the same pair of angle brackets). However, you don't need spaces between any codes that are enclosed in their own pair of angle brackets. Remember, however, that you can copy this code from the sample file Copy XML. txt, if you prefer.

```
<?xml version="1.0" encoding="UTF-8" standalone="yes" ?>
- <w:document xmlns:ve="http://schemas.openxmlformats.org/markup-compatibility/2006"
    xmlns:o="urn:schemas-microsoft-com:office:office"
    xmlns:r="http://schemas.openxmlformats.org/officeDocument/2006/relationships"
    xmlns:m="http://schemas.openxmlformats.org/officeDocument/2006/math"
    xmlns:v="urn:schemas-microsoft-com:vml"
    xmlns:wp="http://schemas.openxmlformats.org/drawingml/2006/wordprocessingDrawing"
    xmlns:w10="urn:schemas-microsoft-com:office:word"
    xmlns:w="http://schemas.openxmlformats.org/wordprocessingml/2006/main"
    xmlns:wne="http://schemas.microsoft.com/office/word/2006/wordml">
  - <w:body>
    - <w:p>
      - <w:r>
          <w:t>This is the first Word document I've created from scratch.</w:t>
        </w:r>
      </w:p>
    - <w:sectPr>
        <w:pgSz w:w="12240" w:h="15840" />
        <w:pgMar w:top="1440" w:right="1440" w:bottom="1440" w:left="1440" w:header="720"
          w:footer="720" w:gutter="0" />
        <w:cols w:space="720" />
        <w:docGrid w:linePitch="360" />
      </w:sectPr>
    </w:body>
  </w:document>
```

CAUTION

To accommodate the page layout for the book, code in the unstructured XML samples throughout this chapter may break to a new line in the middle of a term or use a hyphen to start a new line. When you view code in Notepad, it might appear to break in the middle of a word as well, but it won't use hyphens. Remember that all of the code between a single paired code (such as the <document> code shown here) is considered a single line and should not get manual line breaks when you type the code.

If you are typing this code yourself, double-check your syntax against the structured version of the same code that appears along with each unstructured sample. If copying the code instead of typing it, do so from the sample file named Copy XML.txt referenced earlier.

```
<?xml version="1.0" encoding="UTF-8" standalone="yes"?>

<w:document xmlns:ve="http://schemas.openxmlformats.org/markup-compatibil-
ity/2006" xmlns:o="urn:schemas-microsoft-com:office:office" xmlns:r="http://
schemas.openxmlformats.org/officeDocument/2006/relationships" xmlns:m="http://
schemas.openxmlformats.org/officeDocument/2006/math" xmlns:v="urn:schemas-mi-
crosoft-com:vml" xmlns:wp="http://schemas.openxmlformats.org/drawingml/2006/
wordprocessingDrawing" xmlns:w10="urn:schemas-microsoft-com:office:word" xmlns:
w="http://schemas.openxmlformats.org/wordprocessingml/2006/main" xmlns:
wne="http://schemas.microsoft.com/office/word/2006/wordml"><w:body><w:p><w:
r><w:t>This is the first Word document I've created from scratch.</w:t></w:
r></w:p><w:sectPr><w:pgSz w:w="12240" w:h="15840"/><w:pgMar w:top="1440" w:
right="1440" w:bottom="1440" w:left="1440" w:header="720" w:footer="720" w:
gutter="0"/><w:cols w:space="720"/><w:docGrid w:linePitch="360"/></w:sectPr></
w:body></w:document>
```

Once you're satisfied that your code is accurate, you can save and close this file. Notice that this code contains items you saw in the example from the preceding chapter section.

- The first line of code provides the XML version definition.

- The second line is the open code for the overall document content, where the namespaces are defined. Notice that a document file contains multiple namespaces to cover different content types.

- The document content in this file is the single-line paragraph of text contained inside the paired **<body>** code.

- The last piece of content is the paired **<w:sectPr>** code, which you can see stores the basic section formatting (page setup) information. You can omit this information and the document will open in Word using default settings. Note that the formatting settings and values you see here are explained in the next section of this chapter.

Let's look at that document in one more format to help clarify the content. The image below shows the same *document.xml* file opened on the Tree View tab of the XML Notepad editor.

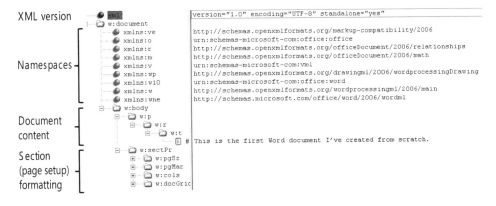

Create the Content_Types File

In Notepad, save a file named exactly *[Content_Types].xml* to the root of your **First Document** folder. As with the *document.xml* file, following are two versions of the code that you need to add to this file, first shown in Internet Explorer so that you can clearly see the tree structure, and next shown as run-of-text, similar to the way code appears in Notepad.

```
<?xml version="1.0" encoding="UTF-8" standalone="yes" ?>
- <Types xmlns="http://schemas.openxmlformats.org/package/2006/content-types">
    <Default Extension="rels" ContentType="application/vnd.openxmlformats-package.relationships+xml" />
    <Default Extension="xml" ContentType="application/xml" />
    <Override PartName="/word/document.xml" ContentType="application/vnd.openxmlformats-
      officedocument.wordprocessingml.document.main+xml" />
  </Types>
```

```
<?xml version="1.0" encoding="UTF-8" standalone="yes"?>
<Types xmlns="http://schemas.openxmlformats.org/package/2006/content-types"><Default
Extension="rels" ContentType="application/vnd.openxmlformats-package.
relationships+xml"/><Default Extension="xml" ContentType="application/xml"/><Override
PartName="/word/document.xml" ContentType="application/vnd.openxmlformats-officedocu-
ment.wordprocessingml.document.main+xml"/></Types>
```

As you see, this is a very simple file, containing the XML version statement at the top as well as the open code named **Types** that is the code in which all codes in the file are nested and where the namespace for the content types is defined. After that, you see the following.

- The only file extensions present in your basic Word document are .xml and .rels, so they are the only file extensions that require definition here.

- The only part name that requires definition as a content type is the main document (*document.xml*) because that is the only document part currently included, aside from the two structure-related files *[Content_Types].xml* and *.rels*.

Create the .rels File

The relationship file for this new document is the simplest of the three you need to create. In Notepad, create a new file and save it as *.rels*, inside the **_rels** subfolder you created within the **First Document** folder. Then, add the following content to that file (shown in both structured format and in Notepad run-of-text format).

```
<?xml version="1.0" encoding="UTF-8" standalone="yes" ?>
- <Relationships xmlns="http://schemas.openxmlformats.org/package/2006/relationships">
    <Relationship Id="rId1"
      Type="http://schemas.openxmlformats.org/officeDocument/2006/relationships/officeDocument"
      Target="word/document.xml" />
  </Relationships>
```

```
<?xml version="1.0" encoding="UTF-8" standalone="yes"?>
<Relationships xmlns="http://schemas.openxmlformats.org/package/2006/relationships">
<Relationship Id="rId1" Type="http://schemas.openxmlformats.org/officeDocument/2006/
relationships/officeDocument" Target="word/document.xml"/></Relationships>
```

In the preceding code, the XML version is defined (as it is in every .xml or .rels format file within the package); followed by the open code for the relationships content along with its namespace definition; followed by the single required relationship in this case, which is to the part named *document.xml*. See "The Office Open XML File Structure" earlier in this chapter for details on the three-part structure (ID, Type, and Target) of a relationship definition.

Compile and Open Your New Document

Once you save and close the *.rels* file, you can exit Notepad. You're now ready to put your ZIP package together and open the file in Word, using the following steps.

1. Open the **First Document** folder in a Windows Explorer.

2. Select the file *[Content_Types.xml]* as well as the two subfolders (_**rels** and **word**).

3. Right-click, point to Send To, and then click Compressed (zipped) Folder.

4. When the .zip folder is created, change the name (including the file extension) to **First document.docx**. Then, press ENTER to set the new name and click Yes to confirm when you see the warning about changing file extensions.

Double-click to open your new Word document. It should open in Word without error. If it does not, see the Troubleshooting and Inside Out tips at the end of this section for help finding the problem.

Add More Content Types, Document Parts, and Relationships

Even though you didn't add all of the default content types and relationships that Word adds to a new document, all Word functionality is available to your new file. Make any edit (you can even type just a space if you like) and then save the file while it's open in Word. Then, close it, change the file extension to .zip, and take a look at what Word did to your files.

What you'll find is that Word added the default files it provides when it creates a new docx file, and it added the necessary content type and relationship definitions to go along with them. Review the changes that Word made to your file. Once you're comfortable with the ZIP package content, you're ready to start working directly with the XML behind your Office Open XML documents.

TROUBLESHOOTING

How can I find the error when my ZIP package won't open in Word, Excel, or PowerPoint?

When an Office Open XML Format document won't open in Word, Excel, or PowerPoint, the problem can be as simple as a missing space, angle bracket, or another single character. But, when you have ZIP packages with multiple long files, how do you even begin to find the problem? Actually, in most cases you don't have to—Word, Excel, or PowerPoint will do it for you.

When you try to open the file and an error message appears, click the Details button on the error message. In most cases, the precise location of the error will be listed, and the error type might be included as well. Take a look at the following example.

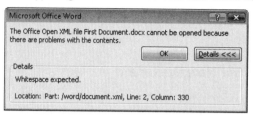

In this example, I left the quotation mark off following one of the namespace definitions in the *document.xml* part. Notice that the detail here shows you the document part, the line within that part, and the location in that line where the error occurs. See the Inside Out tip that follows for more on interpreting the location references.

Note that, if you're using Internet Explorer to view and Notepad to edit your XML document parts, if there's an error in one of the parts, Internet Explorer will most likely be unable to open it in the tree structure. Because of this, if you use the error detail to lead you to the error location and try to correct it in Notepad, you can confirm that the error is corrected before returning the file to the ZIP package and changing the file extension back to its original state, just by trying to open it in Internet Explorer.

See the Inside Out tip that follows for some help on how to locate the error in your code without any wasted time or effort.

INSIDE OUT   Using XML Notepad and Word to help find syntax errors

Perhaps you tried to open a file in Word, as discussed in the preceding Troubleshooting tip, and got an error. Or, maybe you just created one of the XML parts for a new document, such as a *document.xml* file, and then tried to open it in Internet Explorer only to get a syntax error at that point.

The error message you see may indicate a line and position number, or it may indicate a line and column number. Note that column and position are not the same thing. Position is the easier of the two to identify, as it corresponds to characters.

One easy way to find the line and position number of the error is to try to open the file in XML Notepad, the free utility program mentioned earlier in this chapter (this is not the same as the Windows Notepad utility). So, if the Word error message tells you that the error occurred in the *document.xml* part, for example—or the error occurred in Internet Explorer when trying to open an individual XML part—you can try opening that document part in XML Notepad to instantly see the line and position number where the problem exists.

Keep in mind that everything within a paired code is considered a line of code. So, for example, in *document.xml*, line 2 refers to everything inside the paired `<w:document...>` code. Line 1 is the code that indicates the XML version. If then, for example, the XML Notepad error tells you that the error is located at line 2 and position 645, you're looking for character 645 in the second line of code. Copy that line of code (you can open it in Windows Notepad to do this) and paste it into a blank Word document. Then, open the Visual Basic Editor (ALT+F11), press CTRL+G to open the Immediate Window, and type the following code in that window. (You may want to turn off Word Wrap from the Format menu in Notepad before copying text to Word, to avoid copying unwanted formatting marks.)

```
ActiveDocument.Characters(645).Select
```

Substitute 645, of course, for the position of the error in your code. Press ENTER from that line of code and then switch back to the document (ALT+F11), and you'll see the character causing the error selected on screen. No fuss, no muss, and no tearing your hair out because you can't find the error when you look at the amorphous blob of code that appears in Windows Notepad.

Editing and Managing Documents Through XML

Under each of the headings within this section, you'll find a different exercise for editing the document parts in the XML package. These exercises include editing text, formatting, and style definitions; replacing a picture; and removing comments from a document.

Note

The purpose of these exercises is to familiarize you with the structure and rules of a ZIP package and how to work with the XML syntax in the document parts to manage and troubleshoot documents. Some of the specific tasks in these exercises are not tasks that you would likely use the ZIP package for on a daily basis when working with individual documents (such as editing text or deleting comments from a document), because doing this in Word is faster and easier than doing it in the ZIP package for just one file.

However, another benefit of being able to edit documents through the ZIP package is that developers can create automation to batch edit files without ever opening the source program. For example, a developer might create a program to remove comments from all files in a given folder. In that case, doing so through the ZIP package, without having to open the files in Word, greatly simplifies the automation.

Before You Begin Editing a Document Part

A couple of important points warrant noting before you begin editing Office Open XML Format ZIP packages.

- Most document measurements that appear in a document part for an Excel file will appear as the measurement you enter. For example, 16-point font appears as the number 16; a one-inch margin appears as the number 1. Though this might seem like stating the obvious, I mention this because point size measurements do not appear as set in the document parts of a PowerPoint or Word ZIP package.

  - In Word, point size measurement for font sizes is doubled in the document part. So, for example, 12-point font appears as the number 24. All other point size measurements are multiplied by twenty (that is, they use a unit of measure known as a *twip*, which is 1/20th of a point or 1/1440th of an inch). So, 12-point spacing after a paragraph appears as 240 in the *document.xml* part (if it's applied as direct formatting) or in the applicable custom style definition in *styles.xml*.

  - In PowerPoint, point size measurements are multiplied by 100. So, 12-point spacing after a paragraph or 12-point font size applied to text would appear as the number 1200.

- Built-in, default style definitions are not stored in the XML for a Word document. Only the definitions for user-defined styles as well as any built-in styles that have been customized are accessible in *styles.xml*. Learn more about *styles.xml* in the Style editing exercise that follows later in this section.

Editing Text and Formatting

You can edit any document content or formatting directly in the ZIP package. In this sample exercise, we'll walk through editing text, adding text, changing the settings in a paragraph style, and adding direct formatting to specified text.

> **Note**
>
> To try the exercises in this section, you can either create your own sample document to work with or open one provided on this book's CD. To create your own sample file, create a new Word document containing one line of text, such as *This is my sample text*. Then, create a custom paragraph style but don't apply it to any text. To match the exercise in this section on editing styles, your custom style should include 12 point Arial font, 12 points spacing after the paragraph, and the Theme Color Accent 1 for the font color. When you've finished this setup, save the file using the .docx format in a location where you can easily access it (such as the Windows Desktop) and then close the file.
>
> To use the sample file provided, find the file Text editing.docx in the sample files you can install from the Welcome tab of this book's CD.

To edit the ZIP package, change the file extension for *Text editing.docx* (or your own sample file) from .docx to .zip. (Remember that you can do this by appending the .zip file extension if you like, rather than replacing the .docx extension, to save a bit of time when you're ready to change the file extension back to.docx.) Once you've opened the ZIP package, give the following exercises a try.

Edit Text and Settings in document.xml

To begin editing any document part, as mentioned at the start of this section, first copy it out of the ZIP package (for example, paste a copy on the Windows Desktop). Do this with the *document.xml* file inside the **word** folder for your sample document, and then do the following.

1. Open *document.xml* in Internet Explorer. If you're using the sample document provided, the document content following the namespace definitions will look like the image that follows.

   ```
   - <w:body>
     - <w:p>
       - <w:r>
           <w:t>This is my sample text.</w:t>
         </w:r>
       </w:p>
     - <w:sectPr>
         <w:pgSz w:w="12240" w:h="15840" />
         <w:pgMar w:top="1440" w:right="1440" w:bottom="1440" w:left="1440" w:header="720"
           w:footer="720" w:gutter="0" />
         <w:cols w:space="720" />
         <w:docGrid w:linePitch="360" />
       </w:sectPr>
     </w:body>
   ```

   Notice the construction of the text. There is one paragraph of text, nested within the paired code `<w:p></w:p>`, followed by some document settings, including paper size and page margins. (If you're using your own file for this exercise and you see additional codes in document.xml labeled `rsidR` and `rsidPr`, see the note earlier in this chapter at the end of the section titled "Reading a Markup Language" for information about those codes and why they appear.)

> **Note**
>
> Most XML coding uses characters or abbreviations that are logical and easy to interpret by anyone who knows the program, such as `<w:p>` to refer to a Word paragraph, `pgSz` to refer to the size of the page, or `pgMar` to refer to page margins. In the comprehensive documentation for Office Open XML that you can learn more about in the last section of this chapter, you can find each and every one of these codes. However, you can see how, just using logic and what you know about the program, it's very easy to decipher an XML document part without having to memorize the XML language details.

Chapter 22

2. Leave the document open in Internet Explorer, for easy reference, and open it in Notepad as well.

   You can save changes to the document in Notepad even while it's open in Internet Explorer, and you can then refresh the Internet Explorer page to view your saved changes.

3. Find the text *This is my sample text.* in Notepad, and then delete the word *sample*.

4. Copy the codes for that entire paragraph, starting with **<w:p>** and ending with **</w:p>**. Then, paste what you've copied immediately after the existing **</w:p>** code.

   You've just added a second paragraph to your document. You can now change the text that appears between the **<w:t>** and **</w:t>** codes that denote the paragraph text. I chose to have that new paragraph read *This is fun. I'm editing a Word document without opening Word.*

5. Change the left and right page margins to 0.75 inches each. Remember that you'll need to calculate the values in twips for *document.xml* to understand the values you add. Because there are 72 points to an inch, three-quarters of an inch is 54 points. To convert that number to twips so that *document.xml* understands it, multiply the number by twenty. (Or, since a twip is 1/1440th of an inch, multiply 1440 * 0.75.) So, you'll enter **1080** as the left and the right margin values. Be sure to leave quotation marks and related codes intact when you change the numbers.

6. Save *document.xml* and then close Notepad. In Internet Explorer, refresh the page and check your changes.

   Following is what the body portion of document.xml looks like in my file after these changes.

```
- <w:body>
  - <w:p>
    - <w:r>
        <w:t>This is my text.</w:t>
      </w:r>
    </w:p>
  - <w:p>
    - <w:r>
        <w:t>This is fun. I'm editing my Word document without opening Word.</w:t>
      </w:r>
    </w:p>
  - <w:sectPr>
      <w:pgSz w:w="12240" w:h="15840" />
      <w:pgMar w:top="1440" w:right="1080" w:bottom="1440" w:left="1080" w:header="720"
        w:footer="720" w:gutter="0" />
      <w:cols w:space="720" />
      <w:docGrid w:linePitch="360" />
    </w:sectPr>
  </w:body>
</w:document>
```

7. When you're happy with your changes, copy *document.xml* back into the ZIP package, overwriting the existing *document.xml* file.

8. Open the document in Word.

Because the next exercise also requires editing this ZIP package, save time by opening the zip file in Word instead of changing the file extension back and forth. To do this, open Word and then press CTRL+O for the Open file dialog box. Browse to the location of your ZIP package, change the file type list setting to All Files, and then select and open your ZIP package. As mentioned earlier, it will open like a regular Word document.

If you're happy with the changes and additions to your text, and the changes to your page margins, continue to the next exercise.

Add Formatting to Text in document.xml

In this exercise, you'll add some direct formatting to one paragraph in the sample document *Text editing.docx* and then add direct formatting to just part of the second paragraph. To do this, if you still have the copy of *document.xml* that you edited in the last exercise, continue using that file. If not, copy *document.xml* out of the ZIP package again. Then, do the following.

1. Open *document.xml* in both Internet Explorer (for reference) and Notepad (for editing).

2. Add direct formatting of bold and italics to the first paragraph in the document. To do this, in Notepad, take the following steps.

Place your insertion point immediately before the <w:t> code for the first paragraph of text and then type the following code.

```
<w:rPr><w:b /><w:i /></w:rPr>
```

As you might recognize from the first code sample in this chapter, you've just added bold and italic formatting to the first paragraph in the document.

3. Save and close the file in Notepad. Then, return to the Internet Explorer window where *document.xml* is open, and refresh the page to check your changes. The paragraph you edited should look something like this:

```
- <w:p>
  - <w:r>
    - <w:rPr>
        <w:b />
        <w:i />
      </w:rPr>
      <w:t>This is my text.</w:t>
    </w:r>
  </w:p>
```

4. When you're happy with your edits, copy *document.xml* back into the ZIP package, overwriting the version that exists. Then, in Word, press CTRL+O for the Open file dialog box, and then select and open the ZIP package as you did in the previous exercise.

When you confirm that you completed the preceding steps correctly, the next exercise is to add direct formatting (14-point font in this example) to just part of the second paragraph in the document. Close the document when you're ready to continue, and then take the following steps.

1. Open *document.xml* in both Internet Explorer and Notepad. (Use the most recent copy of *document.xml* that you updated for the preceding exercise, if you still have it available. Otherwise, copy the file out of the ZIP package again.)

   If you're using Text editing.docx or a version of the same document that you created, the second paragraph contains the text *This is fun. I'm editing my Word document without opening Word.* The steps that follow will add 14-point font size to just the first sentence in that paragraph.

2. Since you'll be adding formatting to just part of the paragraph, you first need to separate the parts of the paragraph that will have different formatting. To do this, take the following substeps.

   First, place your insertion point between the two sentences of the second paragraph. (If you've been following along with the preceding exercises, your insertion point will be after the period that follows the text *This is fun.*) Type the following code between those two sentences, and then type a space (so that a space separates the new codes and the sentence they precede).

   ```
   </w:t></w:r><w:r><w:t>
   ```

   The first two codes in the preceding structure end the text and the text of the run and then end the run of code. The next two codes begin a new run of code, followed by a new text string. The space you added after the four new codes is the space that will appear between the two sentences of text in the document.

   Inside the new **<w:t>** code (the last of the four codes you just typed), add a space after the letter *t* (and before the closing angle bracket), followed by **xml:space="preserve"**. That code should now look like the following.

   ```
   <w:t xml:space="preserve">
   ```

   This "preserve" statement tells the XML to preserve the space you added at the beginning of the second sentence, so that spacing between the separated sentences is retained. Following is the way the code for this paragraph should look at this point.

   ```
   - <w:p>
     - <w:r>
         <w:t>This is fun.</w:t>
       </w:r>
     - <w:r>
         <w:t xml:space="preserve">I'm editing my Word document without opening
           Word.</w:t>
       </w:r>
     </w:p>
   ```

3. Now, it's time to add the 14-point font formatting to just the first sentence in the paragraph. In Notepad, place your insertion point immediately before the **<w:t>**

code that precedes the first sentence in the second paragraph (the one for which you intend to add the formatting). Then type the following.

```
<w:rPr><w:sz w:val="28" /></w:rPr>
```

4. In Notepad, save and close the document. Then, in Internet Explorer, refresh the page to check your code. Code for the paragraph being edited should now look like this:

```
- <w:p>
  - <w:r>
    - <w:rPr>
        <w:sz w:val="28" />
      </w:rPr>
      <w:t>This is fun.</w:t>
    </w:r>
  - <w:r>
      <w:t xml:space="preserve">I'm editing my Word document without opening
        Word.</w:t>
    </w:r>
  </w:p>
```

Notice that you used 28 to represent 14-point font size, as discussed earlier in this section. The paired `<w:rPr></w:rPr>` codes that you also used in the preceding exercise are the codes inside which you store any unique formatting for the specified text. As with the preceding exercise, you could add additional lines of code to represent other font formatting after `<w:sz w:val="28" />`, such as the bold or italic codes you used earlier.

When you're happy with the code you see in Internet Explorer, copy document.xml back into the ZIP package and once again, from Word, open the ZIP package file to check your results. If your results are successful, close the file and continue on to the next exercise.

Edit Custom Styles in styles.xml

This is the last exercise using the file *Text editing.docx*. In this exercise, you will edit a custom style that's saved in this document. To begin, copy the file *styles.xml* out of the **word** folder in the ZIP package for the sample file.

Open the file *styles.xml* in Internet Explorer. This is a long file that contains a list of every built-in style available to the document, other than those that are used by built-in features not used in the active document. The list includes the style visibility and priority settings that correspond to the settings on the Recommend tab of the Manage Styles dialog box (see Chapter 5, "Styles," for information on the new Manage Style settings). For example, the styles Header and Footer are used by the document header and footer. If you've not yet accessed the header and footer layer in the document, those styles won't appear in this *styles.xml* list.

However, only definitions of your own custom (user-defined) styles, or any built-in styles that have been customized, appear in *styles.xml* at all. The definitions of any built-in styles that are not customized do not appear anywhere in the ZIP package, because Word "knows" these settings, so it doesn't need to record them in the file's XML. If you see exceptions to this, they are most likely for styles new to Word 2007, because Word records these style definitions when the document is opened in an earlier version.

To begin this exercise, scroll to the bottom of *styles.xml* in Internet Explorer, where you'll see the custom style named MyStyle, which I created in the sample document. If you're using a similar sample document instead that you created by following the instructions at the start of this section, look for your own custom style name at the end of *styles.xml*. The code for the definition of MyStyle looks like this:

```
- <w:style w:type="paragraph" w:customStyle="1" w:styleId="MyStyle">
    <w:name w:val="MyStyle" />
    <w:basedOn w:val="Normal" />
    <w:qFormat />
  - <w:pPr>
      <w:spacing w:after="240" />
    </w:pPr>
  - <w:rPr>
      <w:rFonts w:ascii="Arial" w:hAnsi="Arial" />
      <w:color w:val="4F81BD" w:themeColor="accent1" />
      <w:sz w:val="24" />
    </w:rPr>
  </w:style>
```

Now, open *styles.xml* in Notepad. The following steps walk you through changing the paragraph spacing and the font included in this custom style.

1. Scroll to the bottom of the document and find the definition for the custom style that you just reviewed in Internet Explorer.

2. Notice that the paragraph spacing is set to 12 points after (which is written as the value 240 in the XML). Change this setting to 6 points after the paragraph by replacing 240 with 120. Then, add six points before the paragraph as well, by adding the following code immediately before or after the spacing after code.

   ```
   <w:spacing w:before="120"/>
   ```

3. Now, change the font. Notice that the font is listed twice, once in a code specifying ANSI text and one in a code specifying ASCII text. This is because Word styles can carry a separate font for those languages that don't use Latin text. To avoid having a separate setting added to your style (unless you deliberately want one), change the font in both of those settings from Arial to Times New Roman. Be sure to leave the quotation marks and all other code syntax intact. (Note that, if you have multiple editing languages enabled, you may see additional font definitions in your documents as well.) Then, save and close the file.

4. If you'd like to refresh the page in Internet Explorer to check your work, do so. Then, copy *styles.xml* back into the ZIP package, overwriting the existing version of the same file.

5. You're now done editing the ZIP package, so you can change the file extension back to .docx, and then double-click to open the file in Word. Check to confirm that the changes you made to the style look correct, either by checking the style definition in the Styles pane or by applying the style to an existing paragraph.

Congratulations! Now that you can edit text and formatting for your documents through the ZIP package, try two other exercises that follow for editing document content through the XML. These exercises include programmatically changing a picture in a Word document and removing the comments from a Word document.

Editing Pictures

> ### Note
>
> For the exercises titled "Editing Pictures" and "Removing a Document Part," use the files Content edit.docx and Fearless logo.png that you'll find in the sample files you can install from the Welcome tab of this book's CD. The second of these is a logo image that you'll use in the first of the two exercises.
>
> If you prefer to create your own sample file, create a file that uses one picture in two places (such as in the body of the page and in a header) and add two comments to the document, using the Comments feature on the Review tab. For the picture, use a picture saved in the .png file format.

The sample file *Content edit.docx* is a simple starter document containing a few lines of text on two pages, as well as a placeholder picture for a logo on the front page and in the header of the second page (which is a new section). The file also includes two comments that will be used in the exercise that follows.

For this exercise, you'll use the ZIP package to replace the placeholder logo file. First, however, open the file *Content edit.docx* in Word, so that you can take note of the picture (the logo placeholder) that appears in both the second section header and in the body text of the first page. Notice that the picture has different sizing in the two positions and that it has a picture style applied where it appears on the first page of the document. Once you've noted this, close the file and then, in a Windows Explorer (or on the Windows Desktop if that is where you've placed this file), change the file extension to .zip.

1. Open the ZIP package, and then open the **word** folder. Notice that this folder contains a **media** folder. The picture that appears in the document is stored in this folder.

2. Open the **media** folder. Notice that the picture is actually saved as a picture file. If you're using the sample files provided, the file name in the **media** folder is *image1.png*, as you see in the following image.

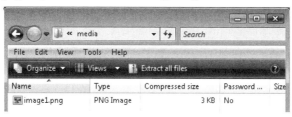

In fact, any pictures pasted or inserted into your document are saved as complete picture files in the media folder within the ZIP package, which is one of my favorite timesavers for using the ZIP packages in daily document production work. If you need to use a picture from an Office Open XML document in another document or another location, and you don't have the original picture file, simply copy the complete picture file out of the ZIP package and use or share it as needed.

3. To replace the placeholder image with the logo image, just rename the file *Fearless logo.png* to *image1.png*. Then, copy it into the ZIP package, replacing the existing *image1.png* in that package.

4. Open the file in Word.

   The placeholder logo has been replaced with the Fearless logo.png image in both locations, and all picture size, placement, and other formatting remains intact.

INSIDE OUT   Replace an image file with a different file type

In the "Editing Pictures" exercise, you replaced one .png file with another just by changing the file name and copying the new picture. But, what if you need to replace a .png picture with a .bmp or a .jpg, or you don't want to change the file name?

Changing the file name to match the existing image file allows you to replace the file without having to edit any relationships. However, you can replace the image file with another image of a different name and file type, as long as you edit the relationships and content types in the ZIP package accordingly.

To do this, open the **_rels** folder located in the **word** folder. In the case of the sample file, there are *.rels* files for both the document and the header. Copy both of these out of the ZIP package and then open each in Notepad. Find the reference to the file *image1.png* and change it to the name of your new image file, such as *Northwind.tif*. Then, copy the files back into the ZIP package, overwriting the existing files of the same names.

 Note that the file Northwind.tif is available in the sample files you can install from the Welcome tab on this book's CD, if you'd like to try this for yourself.

Next, copy *[Content_Types].xml* out of the ZIP package. and open that file in Notepad. Notice that there is a `Default Extension` definition near the top of the file for the .png format. You can either copy this entire definition string to add one for the .tif format, or (if there are no other png images in your document) replace the two references to png in that string with tif, so that the string looks like the this:

```
<Default Extension="tif" ContentType="image/tif"/>
```

Save and close the file and copy it back into the ZIP package, overwriting the existing file of the same name. That's it. Just change the file extension back to .docx and open the file in Word to see your new image. If you've used *Northwind.tif*, the image will look exactly like *Fearless Logo.png* in the preceding exercise, because these files use the same logo.

You know that the exercise in this sidebar worked, however, because the file wouldn't open and display the new image if you had not correctly revised the relationships and content type definitions.

Removing a Document Part

In this exercise, you'll remove all comments from the ZIP package. Doing this requires the following changes.

- Delete the *comments.xml* document part that resides in the **word** folder.

- Delete the relationship for the comments document part.

- Remove the comment placeholders from the *document.xml* file.

Take the following steps to do this.

1. Open the ZIP package for the sample file used in the preceding image exercise.

2. In the **word** folder, select and delete *comments.xml*.

3. In the **word** folder, open the **_rels** folder and copy the file *document.xml.rels* out of the ZIP package.

4. Open *document.xml.rels* in Notepad and delete the relationship to the comments part. Be sure to delete the entire relationship and nothing else. Though the relationship ID might vary if you're using a file other than the sample provided (indicated by the pound sign in the ID shown in the sample that follows), the content to delete should look like this.

   ```
   <Relationship Id="rId#" Type="http://schemas.openxmlformats.org/officeDocu-
   ment/2006/relationships/comments" Target="comments.xml"/>
   ```

5. Save and close the file. Then, copy the file back into the ZIP package, overwriting the existing file of the same name.

6. From the **word** folder, copy the file *document.xml* out of the ZIP package and then open that file in both Internet Explorer and Notepad.

7. In Internet Explorer, look for two comment references. Each one should look very much like the following image.

   ```
    - <w:r>
      - <w:rPr>
          <w:rStyle w:val="CommentReference" />
          <w:rFonts w:asciiTheme="minorHAnsi" w:eastAsiaTheme="minorHAnsi"
            w:hAnsiTheme="minorHAnsi" w:cstheme="minorBidi" />
          <w:color w:val="auto" />
          <w:spacing w:val="0" />
          <w:kern w:val="0" />
        </w:rPr>
        <w:commentReference w:id="0" />
      </w:r>
   ```

   Notice that the reference begins with the open code **<w:r>** (the reference to a run, or a portion of related content) and ends with the matching end code **</w:r>**. Most of the content between is similar to code you've worked with before. Notice that everything except the next-to-last line of this sample is information about formatting for the comment. The next-to-last line of the sample is the comment placeholder itself.

Just above the second comment reference, you'll see two lines of code that read `<w:commentRangeStart`... and `<w:commentRangeEnd`...., separated by a few other lines, as you see in the following image.

```
<w:commentRangeStart w:id="1" />
- <w:r>
    <w:lastRenderedPageBreak />
    <w:t>My document text will start here.</w:t>
  </w:r>
  <w:commentRangeEnd w:id="1" />
```

These appear here because the second comment in this document was inserted with text selected, rather than being inserted at a blinking insertion point.

8. In Notepad, delete both complete comment references, including all lines of code shown in the first image in the preceding step, as well as the comment range start and end lines of code shown in the second image in the preceding step. Do *not* delete the lines between the comment range start and end statement, as those are part of the document text. Save and close the file when done, and then refresh the page in Internet Explorer to check your work.

9. Copy *document.xml* back into the ZIP package and change the file extension back to .docx. Open the file and you should see no sign of the two comments that previously existed.

> **Note**
>
> The content types file in a document containing comments includes a content type definition for comments. However, it's not necessary to delete a content type definition from this file when deleting a document part. As you noticed earlier in this chapter, when we first looked at the ZIP package content of a new, default Word file, several content types are included by default even if they're not used in the document. It's essential to remove the relationship for a deleted document part, but content types can remain without causing any problems.
>
> Also note that, if you didn't delete the comment placeholders from *document.xml*, the document still would have opened. The comment text would have been gone (you only need to delete the document part and its relationship to accomplish that), but the comment placeholders would remain.

Customizing the Ribbon

This is my favorite part of working with the new Office Open XML Formats. You can customize the Ribbon for any document or template in Word, Excel, or PowerPoint.

What's the catch? XML is the only way to get this done. Should that bother you? Not at all. If you successfully completed the preceding exercises and you feel comfortable with the basic components of an Office Open XML Format ZIP package, this is going to be a breeze.

For Excel and PowerPoint fans, the toolbar and menu customizations you can make from the Customize dialog box in earlier versions aren't stored in the document or template—you have to generate those from VBA if you want to share them with other computers. So, this new approach in the 2007 release provides more flexibility.

However, the Word devotees among you might be troubled by the fact that you can't customize the Ribbon from something like a Customize dialog box, because those customizations are saved in documents or templates in earlier versions. All I can say is this: Give XML a chance and you just might be delighted with the flexibility and simplicity of the new approach.

In this section, I'll take you through the required structure and basic syntax for customizing the user interface (referred to as the UI for the remainder of this section). Then, we'll walk through exercises to add a custom tab to the Ribbon and add a custom group to a built-in tab.

The Basic Components of Ribbon Customization

As with comments or images, or even the main document text, when you customize the UI for a document, template, or add-in, you need to add the appropriate relationship. However, there's not much more to it than that. UI customization requires the following components.

- A folder stored in the root of the ZIP package, named **customUI**.

- A document part inside the customUI folder named *customUI.xml*. (This is where the specific custom settings are stored.)

- A relationship for the customUI file in the top-level *.rels* file, located in the **_rels** folder in the root of the ZIP package. The syntax of that relationship is as follows (where **value** refers to a unique ID value, such as **"rID5"**):

```
<Relationship Type="http://schemas.microsoft.com/office/2006/relationships/ui/
extensibility" Target="/customUI/customUI.xml" Id="value" />
```

> **Note**
> You can change the order of the three elements included in a relationship definition without causing an error. For example, you might see the ID appear before the Type definition in some instances.

Adding a Ribbon Tab

When you add a custom tab to the Ribbon, you can choose to add that tab to the built-in Ribbon, or to use only your custom tabs. You specify the name for your custom tab

Chapter 22

and the name for each group on that tab, and then identify each item to be included. Custom tabs can contain built-in features, including custom Building Block galleries, and can also contain your own VBA macros.

The following image shows the content of a *customUI.xml* file that suppresses all built-in tabs and adds a custom tab named My Tab, with one custom group in which three built-in features are displayed, two of which have been given unique labels.

```
- <customUI xmlns="http://schemas.microsoft.com/office/2006/01/customui">
  - <ribbon startFromScratch="true">
    - <tabs>
      - <tab id="customTab" label="My Tab">
        - <group id="customGroup" label="My Sample Group">
            <button idMso="PasteSpecialDialog" visible="true" size="large" label="Choose a Paste
              Option" />
            <gallery idMso="TableInsertGallery" visible="true" size="large" label="Add Table" />
            <button idMso="FileSave" visible="true" size="large" />
          </group>
        </tab>
      </tabs>
    </ribbon>
  </customUI>
```

The resulting Ribbon for the preceding automation looks like this:

Note that, if you were to omit **startFromScratch** from the **<ribbon...** code, the custom tab would appear at the end of the Ribbon, following the built-in tabs. Notice a few things in particular about the preceding code.

- The hierarchy is very straightforward. The code referencing the Ribbon is the outermost code, inside that is the tabs collection, inside that is the individual tab, then the group, then within the group is each individual item you want to add to that group.

- The term **idMso** refers to a built-in item and the term **id** refers to a custom item.

- If you omit a label value from a built-in item, the built-in label is used. But, you can add a custom label to custom or built-in items.

> **Note**
> You can add custom images to buttons, just as you are able to do with toolbar and menu items in earlier versions. That is not done in the preceding sample code, but it is done in the second Ribbon customization exercise in this chapter, under the heading "Add a Group to a Built-In Ribbon Tab."

After this code is added in *customUI.xml*, and that file is added to the **customUI** folder in the root of the ZIP package, all you need to do is add the relationship provided at the start of this section to the *.rels* file in the top-level **_rels** folder.

INSIDE OUT **Watch out for the Microsoft Office Button when using** *startFromScratch*

When you use the *startFromScratch* command referenced earlier in this section to re-place the built-in Ribbon tabs with your custom tabs, don't forget about the Microsoft Office Button, which is a part of the Ribbon and can (for the most part) be customized as well.

When you start from scratch, the Microsoft Office Button still appears, but the only op-tions that remain accessible by default through that button are New, Open, Save, Recent Documents, <Program> Options, and Exit. (To see an example of this, open the file **Gen-erate GUID.docm,** available in the practice files you can install from the Welcome tab on this book's CD. This file is used for the data binding exercise later in this chapter.)

Ready to give it a try? The following exercise walks you through creating a custom tab for your document at the end of the built-in Ribbon in Word, with one custom group containing a selection of built-in commands.

Note

You don't need a sample file to execute this exercise. However, you can see a completed example of the exercise in the file named My tab.docx, in the samples files you can install from this book's CD.

1. In Word, create a new, blank document. Save your file to the Windows Desktop as a docx with a .zip file extension. As explained earlier in this chapter, under the heading "Breaking Into Your Document," type the entire file name (including extension) in quotation marks when in the Save As dialog box to save using the .zip file extension. Name the file *First tab.zip* and save it to your Windows Desktop, for ease when following the remaining instructions. You can add content to the document if you like, but it's not necessary to do so. Close the file once it's saved.

2. On the Windows Desktop, create a new folder named **customUI**. Note that this folder name is case sensitive, as are most XML commands.

3. Open Notepad and save a new file, named *customUI.xml*, into the **customUI** folder you just created.

4. In Notepad, add the following code to the file you just saved. This code matches the sample shown earlier in this section. (As with earlier exercises that require significant amounts of code, you can find this code in the sample file named Copy XML.txt, if you prefer to copy it rather than typing it yourself. For those who prefer to type it, see the image that follows showing the code structured as it appears in Internet Explorer, for ease of reference.)

```
<customUI xmlns="http://schemas.microsoft.com/office/2006/01/customui">
<ribbon><tabs><tab id="customTab" label="My Tab"><group id="customGroup"
label="My Sample Group"><button idMso="PasteSpecialDialog" visible="true"
size="large" label="Choose a Paste Option" /><gallery idMso="TableInsertGalle
ry" visible="true" size="large" label="Add Table" /> <button idMso="FileSave"
visible="true" size="large" /></group></tab></tabs></ribbon></customUI>
```

```
- <customUI xmlns="http://schemas.microsoft.com/office/2006/01/customui">
  - <ribbon>
    - <tabs>
      - <tab id="customTab" label="My Tab">
        - <group id="customGroup" label="My Sample Group">
            <button idMso="PasteSpecialDialog" visible="true" size="large" label="Choose a Paste
              Option" />
            <gallery idMso="TableInsertGallery" visible="true" size="large" label="Add Table" />
            <button idMso="FileSave" visible="true" size="large" />
        </group>
      </tab>
    </tabs>
  </ribbon>
</customUI>
```

Once you add this code to customUI.xml, save and close the file. You might want to open the file in Internet Explorer to check your code against the preceding image.

5. Open *First tab.zip*. Drag the folder **customUI** and drop it into the root of the ZIP package, so that the top level of the ZIP package looks like the following image. (You can, of course, also cut or copy the folder and paste it into the ZIP package, instead of dragging it.)

Name	Type
_rels	File Folder
customUI	File Folder
docProps	File Folder
word	File Folder
[Content_Types].xml	XML Document

6. Open the **_rels** folder in the root of the ZIP package. Then, copy the *.rels* file out of the ZIP package.

7. Open *.rels* in Notepad and add the following code before the **</Relationships>** code. Be sure not to place this code in the middle of another relationship definition. (Note that # in the following code represents a number not already used for a relationship in this file.)

```
<Relationship Type="http://schemas.microsoft.com/office/2006/relationships/ui/
extensibility" Target="/customUI/customUI.xml" Id="rId#" />
```

8. Save and close *.rels* and then copy it back into the ZIP package, overwriting the existing *.rels* file.

That's all there is to it. Time to open your file and check out the results.

To get comfortable with this code, I strongly recommend editing *customUI.xml* a few times with different settings. Try small buttons instead of large (just remove the `size="large"` reference to change the button size to small), add or remove a custom label for one of the commands, try adding a second group (just give the new group a unique name, such as `customGroup2`), or try using different commands. See the note that follows for help finding the correct syntax for the command you need.

> **Note**
>
> Find files that contain control IDs for every Word, Excel, and PowerPoint command in the sample files you can install from the Welcome tab on this book's CD. Control IDs refer to the `idMso` values in the preceding exercise.
>
> The files, named *WordRibbonControls.xlsx*, *ExcelRibbonControls.xlsx*, and *PowerPointRibbonControls.xlsx*, as well as the icon gallery workbook and *customUI* schema file (discussed in the next section) are available on the CD thanks to the 2007 release product team.

Add a Group to a Built-In Ribbon Tab

Adding a group to a built-in tab is an almost identical process to the preceding exercise. The difference is simply in how you reference the tab name. So, in the following exercise, you'll edit the *customUI.xml* file you created in that exercise to add your new custom group to the Home tab instead of a custom tab, and then specify the position on the Home tab where you want your new group to appear. And, because making this change requires just a minor edit to your existing *customUI.xml* file, we'll also customize the image for one of the buttons in this same exercise.

> **Note**
>
> In the file named Office2007IconGallery.xlsm, located in the sample files you can install from the Welcome tab on the this book's CD, you can find the idMso values for every available built-in button image. As with the control ID files mentioned earlier, this file was created by the 2007 release product team. Instructions for using this file are available directly in the file.

To begin, if you don't still have a copy (outside of the ZIP package) of the *customUI.xml* file you just created, copy this file out of the ZIP. Open the file in Notepad, and then do the following.

1. Find the code **<tab id=**... and edit that code to read as follows.

   ```
   <tab idMso="TabHome">
   ```

   Note that the label definition has been removed from this code. If you leave the label in the code when you change the tab id reference to the idMso reference to the Home tab, you'll rename the Home tab with the label value. (If you want to use a different built-in tab for this exercise, you can find the correct control ID for the tab names along with the control ID for feature names in the <Program>RibbonControls workbooks mentioned in the preceding section.)

2. Change the **<group**... code as follows.

   ```
   <group id="customGroup" label="My Sample Group" insertAfterMso = "GroupFont">
   ```

   All you've done here is add **insertAfterMso** and set its value to **"GroupFont"**. As you'll find in the WordRibbonControls workbook, **GroupFont** is the control ID for the built-in Font group that appears on the Home tab. The **insertAfter-Mso** setting specifies the position on the tab where you want your new group to appear. If you omit this setting, your group will appear at the end of the tab.

3. The last edit you'll make in this file is to add an idMso value for a custom image setting to appear in place of the built-in Paste Special image. To do this, edit the button code for the Paste Special dialog box to look like the following.

   ```
   <button idMso="PasteSpecialDialog" visible="true" size="large" imageMso = "Cre-
   ateReportFromWizard" label="Choose a Paste Option" />
   ```

   Notice that all you need to do here is add the **imageMso** statement with its value of **CreateReportFromWizard**. The **imageMso** IDs are available in the Office-2007IconGallery workbook mentioned earlier in this section. The icon I chose appears in Gallery 1 in that file, in the second column of the fourth row. You can choose any ID from any of those galleries provided in place of the one I selected. Just point to an icon in one of those galleries to find the correct syntax for referencing that icon.

4. When you've finished making changes, save and close the file and then copy it back into the ZIP package, overwriting the existing *customUI.xml* file. Change the file back to the .docx extension if you want to do so, and then open the file to see your new custom group added to the Home tab, following the Font group, as you see in the following image.

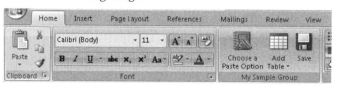

Chapter 22

Having fun yet? I certainly hope so. When you feel comfortable customizing the built-in Ribbon tabs and creating your own tabs, check out the next chapter, "Using VBA and XML Together to Create Add-Ins," to learn how to add your own macros to the Ribbon. But, don't go there quite yet—first check out the next section of this chapter to learn how to bind Word Content Controls to custom XML data.

> **Note**
>
> Want the full skinny on customizing the UI? Find customUI.xsd (the schema for UI customization) on the Resources tab of this book's CD. Remember that you can open and review the text of .xsd format files in Notepad, where you can scan through all available syntax for UI customization.

TROUBLESHOOTING

My UI customization doesn't appear when I open the file in Word, Excel, or PowerPoint

As shown earlier in this chapter, when you have a syntax or structural error in any document part in a ZIP package, the file might not open in the applicable program, but may instead display an error message. When you make errors in customUI syntax, this isn't always the case.

If your *customUI.xml* file contains an error, such as specifying a control ID that doesn't exist, the document or template will open without displaying any errors. However, the Ribbon customization you added won't appear.

When this happens, check the *customUI.xml* file for errors, such as referring to a gallery as a button or using an incorrect control ID. Remember also that most XML is case sensitive, so check for details such as the spelling and capitalization throughout your *customUI.xml* code.

Binding Data to Content Controls

The ability to bind external data to Content Controls in a Word document means that you can use XML to populate parts of a document with information that's stored in other sources. For example, use data binding to automatically populate the user's contact information in a typical business document or to populate fields in a boilerplate contract form. You can use any data source for this purpose that can be translated by XML—from data stored directly in the custom XML in the document's ZIP package, to data in an Exchange Server directory or a Microsoft Windows SharePoint Services list.

In this section, we'll look at the required elements of a bound control and then I'll walk you through the process of binding Content Controls to a custom XML document part.

> ### Note
>
> Keep in mind that binding data is a two-way street. That is, when you have a Content Control bound to custom XML data, content added to that control in the document is added to your custom XML. One of the nicest benefits of this is that, for example, if you have the client's name as custom XML bound to several controls in your document, you can change the name in any one of those bound controls and all controls bound to the same data will automatically update.
>
> For a simple example of this, insert a couple of instances of the same Document Property Quick Part into your document and then edit the value in one of them. Then, for further examination, open the ZIP package for that document and check out its *document.xml* file to view the data binding code for those Quick Parts. Document Property Quick Parts are discussed in both Chapter 9, "Quick Parts," and Chapter 11, "Content Controls: Creating Forms and Then Some."

The Components of a Bound Content Control

There are a few more elements to data binding than you've encountered for previous tasks covered in this chapter. However, most of the components required here are similar to those you've already used, as follows.

- A folder stored in the root of the ZIP package, named **customXML**.

- Three elements inside the **customXML** folder, including the following.

    - One or more files containing the custom XML data (that is, the data to be bound to controls in the document). In the exercise that follows, this file is named *item1.xml*.

    - A file that defines the properties used (specifically, the referenced namespaces) for each custom XML file. In the exercise that follows, this file is named *itemProps1.xml*.

    - A **_rels** folder in which you'll create a relationship file for the custom XML. That relationship file in the following exercise is named *item1.xml.rels*.

- One Content Control in *document.xml* for each piece of custom XML data that you want to bind to a control.

- A relationship in the file *document.xml.rels* for the bound custom XML data.

The section that follows walks you through the process of binding two Content Controls to custom XML stored in the document's ZIP package. For working through the exercises that follow, you can use the file named Data Binding.docx, located in the sample files you can install from the Welcome tab of this book's CD. If you prefer to create your own file, you can base it on Data Binding.docx, which is simply a Word document containing two lines of text and two plain text Content Controls. If you're not familiar with the new Content Controls or how to add them to your documents, see Chapter 11 before continuing here.

> **CAUTION**
>
> When binding data to Content Controls, use only plain text types of Content Controls, such as the Text , Drop-Down list, or Date Picker controls. Data binding doesn't support rich text content, such as tables and graphics, so attempting to bind data to a control that supports rich text leaves your document open to possible errors. (Remember that plain text controls do allow font and paragraph formatting, so you don't have to lose any formatting customization in the document when you want to bind controls to custom XML data.)

Binding a Control to Custom XML

To begin, save the file *Data Binding.docx* (mentioned in the preceding note), or your own comparable file, to the Windows Desktop and change the file extension to .zip. Then, follow the steps under each of the subheadings that follow.

Create the Custom XML Files

1. On your Windows Desktop, create a folder named exactly **customXML**. Then, inside that folder, create another folder named exactly **_rels**.

2. In Notepad, create a new file and save it in the root of your new **customXML** folder, as *item1.xml*. Add the following code to this new file and then save and close the file.

```
<?xml version="1.0" encoding="UTF-8" standalone="yes"?><myinfo xmlns="http://
www.arouet.net/AMOD/CustomXML.htm"><email>My e-mail address</email><motto>Add a
favorite saying here.</motto></myinfo>
```

For ease of reference, here's the way the preceding code looks in Internet Explorer.

```
  <?xml version="1.0" encoding="UTF-8" standalone="yes" ?>
- <myinfo xmlns="http://www.arouet.net/AMOD/CustomXML.htm">
    <email>My e-mail address</email>
    <motto>Add a favorite saying here.</motto>
  </myinfo>
```

Notice what's included in the preceding code. After defining the XML version, you identify a namespace for the set of fields you want to use as your custom XML items. The set of items in this sample is referred to as **myinfo**. The two fields included, which you'll map to Content Controls in this exercise, are **email** and

motto. If you choose to do so, you can replace the placeholder text between the paired code with your own text for each of these fields.

3. In Notepad, create a new file and save it in the root of your new **customXML** folder, as *itemProps1.xml*. Add the following code to this new file and then save and close the file.

```
<?xml version="1.0" encoding="UTF-8" standalone="no"?>

<ds:datastoreItem ds:itemID="{462820BB-4D2B-41C2-812E-F3CA7850A5A9}" xmlns:
ds="http://schemas.openxmlformats.org/officedocument/2006/2/customXml"><ds:
schemaRefs><ds:schema Ref="http://www.arouet.net/AMOD/CustomXML.htm"/></ds:
schemaRefs></ds:datastoreItem>
```

For ease of reference, the following is the same code viewed in Internet Explorer.

```
  <?xml version="1.0" encoding="UTF-8" standalone="no" ?>
- <ds:datastoreItem ds:itemID="{462820BB-4D2B-41C2-812E-F3CA7850A5A9}"
    xmlns:ds="http://schemas.openxmlformats.org/officedocument/2006/2/customXml">
  - <ds:schemaRefs>
      <ds:schema Ref="http://www.arouet.net/AMOD/CustomXML.htm" />
    </ds:schemaRefs>
  </ds:datastoreItem>
```

This code in this file provides information about the namespace used in the file where you store the custom XML items. Note that the data store item ID is used to identify the custom XML where you bind the data to controls in document.xml. The **datastoreItem** ID shown in the preceding code is what's referred to as a GUID (Globally Unique Identifier). GUIDs are used in many places in programming to provide unique identification for a particular item being referenced in the code. For example, if you've ever explored the Windows Registry, you've probably seen many GUIDs.

> **Note**
>
> Many professional development platforms, such as Visual Studio, provide tools for generating GUIDs. You can also find free tools on the Web for generating GUIDs. However, it takes just a fairly simple macro in VBA to get this done as well.
>
> So, to save you some time when you need to generate your own GUIDs, I created a file named Generate GUID.docm, that you can find in the Practice Library on this book's CD. When you open this file, enable macros and then click the single button available on the Ribbon.
>
> As mentioned in the Inside Out tip earlier in this chapter about the **startFrom-Scratch** UI customization command, you can also check out Generate GUID.docm to see an example of a **startFromScratch** Ribbon. The only tab available in that file is the one containing the GUID macro button. For those interested in the macro to generate GUIDs, you can also find that in the Visual Basic Editor once you open this file.

4. Once again, in Notepad, create a new file. This time, save the file into the **_rels** subfolder in the **customXML** folder you created, naming it *item1.xml.rels*. Add the following code to this new file and then save and close the file.

```
<?xml version="1.0" encoding="UTF-8" standalone="yes"?>

<Relationships xmlns="http://schemas.openxmlformats.org/package/2006/relationsh
ips"><Relationship Id="rId1" Type="http://schemas.openxmlformats.org/officeDocu-
ment/2006/relationships/customXmlProps" Target="itemProps1.xml"/></Relation-
ships>
```

Following, for ease of reference, is a look at this code in structured format, as shown in Internet Explorer.

```
  <?xml version="1.0" encoding="UTF-8" standalone="yes" ?>
 -<Relationships>
   <Relationship Id="rId1"
      Type="http://schemas.openxmlformats.org/officeDocument/2006/relationships/customXmlProps"
      Target="itemProps1.xml"/>
  </Relationships>
```

Notice that this file simply creates a relationship to the custom XML properties file.

5. Open the ZIP package for the file *Data Binding.docx* (or your own similar file that you created for this exercise) and copy the entire **customXML** folder you created in the preceding steps into that ZIP package.

Once you've done this, it's time to bind that custom XML to controls in your document.

Binding Custom XML to Content Controls

To bind Content Controls to the custom XML you just created, you'll need to add just one statement in *document.xml* for each control that you want to bind, as well as one statement in the *document.xml.rels* file to create a relationship to the custom XML. To begin, copy both of these files out of the ZIP package.

> **Note**
> As you may recall from earlier exercises in this chapter, *document.xml* is located in the **word** folder in the ZIP package, and *document.xml.rels* is located in the **_rels** folder within the **word** folder.

Start by adding the data binding statements to *document.xml*. To do this, let's take a look at what the code looks like for the paragraph containing the first Content Control. That paragraph, including the control, looks like this when opened in Word:

My·e-mail·address·is:·Click·here·to·enter·text.¶

Following is the way that same paragraph looks in *document.xml*.

```
- <w:p>
  - <w:pPr>
     <w:pStyle w:val="BodyText" />
    </w:pPr>
  - <w:r>
     <w:t xml:space="preserve">My e-mail address is:</w:t>
    </w:r>
  - <w:sdt>
    - <w:sdtPr>
       <w:id w:val="29485172" />
      - <w:placeholder>
         <w:docPart w:val="DefaultPlaceholder_22610167" />
        </w:placeholder>
       <w:showingPlcHdr />
       <w:text />
      </w:sdtPr>
    - <w:sdtContent>
      - <w:r>
        - <w:rPr>
           <w:rStyle w:val="PlaceholderText" />
          </w:rPr>
         <w:t>Click here to enter text.</w:t>
        </w:r>
      </w:sdtContent>
    </w:sdt>
  </w:p>
- <w:p>
```

The code representing the Content Control in this paragraph begins with the line `<w:sdt>` in the preceding code. The data binding statement needs to be placed two lines beneath that, between `<w:stdPr>` and `<w:id...>`. Following is the statement to add to *document.xml* for binding the first control in the document to the email field from the custom XML file.

```
<w:dataBinding w:prefixMappings="xmlns:ns0='http://www.arouet.net/AMOD/CustomXML.
htm'" w:xpath="/ns0:myinfo[1]/ns0:email[1]" w:storeItemID="{462820BB-4D2B-41C2-812E-
F3CA7850A5A9}" />
```

For ease of reference, take a look at the same statement in Internet Explorer, shown with the immediately surrounding statements referenced earlier.

```
- <w:sdtPr>
   <w:dataBinding
     w:prefixMappings="xmlns:ns0='http://www.arouet.net/AMOD/CustomXML.htm'"
     w:xpath="/ns0:myinfo[1]/ns0:email[1]" w:storeItemID="{462820BB-4D2B-41C2-
     812E-F3CA7850A5A9}" />
   <w:id w:val="29485172" />
```

The `w:dataBinding` statement includes the following.

- `w:prefixMappings` is the namespace identified in *item1.xml*. Notice that this namespace is identified as `ns0`.

- `w:xpath` provides the path inside *item1.xml* where you can find the particular field being bound. In this case, the **email** field is within the group of fields named **myinfo**.

- `w:storeItemID` is the same GUID used in the *itemProp1.xml* file.

This statement will be identical, other than the **xpath**, for each control in this document that's mapped to the same data source. In fact, the only difference in the statement that you need to add to map the second control to the motto field is to change the word **email** to **motto** in the preceding statement, after you copy and paste that statement to the proper position for the Content Control that appears in the second paragraph.

Once you've finished adding these two statements to *document.xml*, save and close the file in Notepad. At this point, you might want to check the file in Internet Explorer to be sure you've added the code correctly. Remember that, if you made a structural error in adding the new XML, the code won't open in Internet Explorer.

Copy your updated *document.xml* file back into the ZIP package, overwriting the existing file of the same name. Once you do, the last step is just to add the relationship to the custom XML in *document.xml.rels*. Open that file in Notepad, and add the following relationship before the **</Relationships>** code.

```
<Relationship Id="rId#" Type="http://schemas.openxmlformats.org/officeDocument/2006/
relationships/customXml" Target="../customXML/item1.xml" />
```

CAUTION !

As with previous relationship statement samples in this chapter, be sure to replace the pound sign in the preceding statement with a number that is not already used in *document.xml.rels*.

Save and close the document and then copy it back into the ZIP package, overwriting the existing file of the same name. That's it! You've bound your Content Controls to custom data. Open the file in Word to check out your results.

To try out your bound controls, modify the content inside the controls while the document is open in Word. Then, save and close the file, change the extension back to .zip, and view your changes in the custom XML.

Note

Want to save yourself the steps of writing out the code to bind your custom XML data to each control in the document? Tristan Davis, the Word 2007 Program Manager who has generously shared his knowledge and insights at the end of Chapter 21, turned me on to a tool that I highly recommend checking out. Matt Scott, a Software Design Engineer in Microsoft Research and former member of the Microsoft Office Word team, created the "Word 2007 Content Control Toolkit," which is free to download and available through a link you'll find on the Resources tab of this book's CD. Using this tool, which runs as a separate program outside of Word, you can simply drag a custom XML field and drop it on the control you want to bind to that data. It's a very cool timesaver and a good resource as well for helping you to understand how the data is mapped to the controls.

INSIDE OUT   **Convert control types between plain text and rich text**

In the code shown in this section for the first paragraph in the sample file *Data binding. docx*, notice the `<w:text />` code that appears near the middle of the XML that represents the first Content Control. This text code is used to identify the control as a plain text control. If you were to insert a Rich Text control into a document and then view the XML, you'd see that this code (or anything like it) doesn't appear. In fact, this text code is the thing that separates rich text and plain text controls.

To turn any plain text control into a rich text control, all you need to do is delete the `<w:text />` code from the XML representing that control in *document.xml*. Similarly, if you want to bind data to controls in your document, but you've used the Rich Text control type, you can add the `<w:text />` code in the same position relative to those controls where they appear in *document.xml* to turn those controls into plain text controls, rather than spending extra time to replace the controls throughout your document.

Next Steps for Working with the Office Open XML Formats

The Office Open XML Formats have come about as the result of an enormous amount of work by an international committee of experts, working through a standards organization named Ecma International. Because this is an open standard, Ecma International makes the complete documentation of the language and standards related to these formats freely, publicly available.

The complete documentation is about 6,500 pages, broken into five core documents and several supporting documents, which are all available for download from Ecma International. For ease of reference, the final drafts of those documents (the most recent versions available as of press time for this book) are also available in PDF format on the Resources tab of this book's CD. Assuming, however, that you may not have the time or inclination to read several thousand pages on this subject, following is a brief summary of what you can expect to find in a few of these documents that I believe will be the most useful for those who want to go further with Office Open XML.

First, note that much of the content in these files is written for developers and assumes knowledge of XML. So, I definitely recommend getting comfortable with the content in this chapter before venturing too far into the standards documentation.

- *Office Open XML Part 1: Fundamentals* provides extensive technical detail for the structure of the ZIP packages and parts within them. However, it also provides one item in particular that might be of interest—an overview of the different types of Office Open XML used for documents from each of the applicable programs (such as WordprocessingML for Word or SpreadsheetML for Excel). Following the overview, the further you dive into this document, the more you'll find of the structural requirements for each type of Office Open XML.

- *Office Open XML Part 3: Primer* is an extensive primer, written for developers, on working with the features of the new formats. It provides quite a bit in the way of detailed examples and illustrations, and is a great place to go to continue learning once you have your bearings with the information provided in this chapter.

- *Office Open XML Part 4: Markup Language Reference* is a whopping 5,219 pages. It's a complete, detailed reference to the Office Open XML language, including the storage of custom XML data. As of the final draft, most of the first 32 pages of this PDF are tables of contents that break down the available terminology for use with documents from each program. I wouldn't recommend this resource to someone new to the Office Open XML Formats because its depth and breadth could easily be overwhelming. But, once you have the basics down, it's the ultimate reference tool if you decide to take your work with the XML formats to another level and, particularly, if you want to move toward projects in which you would create ZIP packages for complete documents through code.

But, before you go anywhere, check out the next and final chapter of this book, and learn how to put your VBA and XML knowledge together to build your own Word, Excel, and PowerPoint add-ins.

Chapter 22

Using VBA and XML Together to Create Add-Ins

You can write a macro and you can customize the Ribbon. But, what do you need to know to put those skills together and start creating add-ins for the 2007 Microsoft Office release programs Word, Excel, and PowerPoint? You might be surprised at how much of the process you've already got covered.

Getting your macros onto a customized Ribbon tab takes just two more steps than adding a built-in command to the tab. Once you've got that down, you just need to decide how to share the particular automation in question and what (if any) security measures to take before sharing the file. For example, does your automation belong in an individual document or template, or do you want it to be available to all documents in the applicable program? Are you sharing this automation with others and, if so, should you digitally sign the file?

In this chapter, we'll look at key considerations for creating simple add-ins and help you get started with sharing the automation you create.

Chapter Assumptions

This chapter assumes that you're familiar with everything covered to this point in Part 5, "Templates, Automation, and Customization." In particular, you'll be much more comfortable with the content in this chapter if you understand the following.

- When a template is needed, the different types of available templates, and unique considerations for creating templates in each program (Chapter 20, "The Many Faces of Microsoft Office Templates)

- How to write a Microsoft Visual Basic for Applications (VBA) macro and how to declare variables (Chapter 21, "VBA Primer")

- How to create a custom Ribbon tab as well as how to customize built-in tabs (Chapter 22, "Office Open XML Essentials")

Adding Your Macros to the Ribbon

To add a macro to a tab, you need to declare the macro as a Ribbon control, and then create a button definition in *customUI.xml* that includes an **onAction** command. As you might know from creating custom toolbars or menus through VBA in previous Microsoft Office versions, you use **onAction** to identify the macro that runs when the specified button is clicked.

Examine, for example, the sample file *Generate GUID.docm* used in Chapter 22. This file contains one macro and uses a single Ribbon tab with a single button for running that macro.

The following image shows the contents of *customUI.xml* for this file.

```xml
<?xml version="1.0" encoding="utf-8" ?>
- <customUI xmlns="http://schemas.microsoft.com/office/2006/01/customui">
  - <ribbon startFromScratch="true">
    - <tabs>
      - <tab id="customTab" label="GUID">
        - <group id="customGroup" label="Generate a GUID">
            <button id="GUIDgen" visible="true" size="large" label="New GUID" onAction="GUIDgen"
              imageMso="HappyFace" />
          </group>
        </tab>
      </tabs>
    </ribbon>
  </customUI>
```

Take note of the following items in the preceding code sample.

- This code uses the **startFromScratch** command in the **<ribbon** ... statement. This replaces the built-in Ribbon and shows only your custom tabs. As demonstrated in Chapter 22, you can omit that command to add your tab at the end of the Ribbon, following the built-in tabs. Or, add your custom buttons to a built-in tab.

- In the **<button** ... statement, you use **id** instead of **idMso** when adding your own custom content. (Keep in mind that **idMso** refers to built-in commands that have a control ID identified for use with the customUI schema. The complete list of control IDs for the 2007 release programs Word, Excel, and PowerPoint are available in Microsoft Office Excel 2007 workbooks provided in the practice files for Chapter 22.)

- Also in the **<button** ... statement, the only other difference from a reference to a built-in command is the inclusion of the **onAction** command, which identifies the name of the macro.

> **Note**
> Remember that this file (just like any file containing a **customUI** folder) also needs a relationship for the custom content in the top-level *.rels* file. The structure of that relationship, provided in Chapter 22, is the same for any file containing Ribbon customization.

Now, take a look at the first line of the macro to which that **onAction** command refers.

```
Sub GUIDgen(ByVal control As IRibbonControl)
```

The only thing you need to add to your VBA code is the argument declaration you see in the **Sub** statement that introduces the macro.

As you probably recognize from the syntax of the **ByVal** declaration, adding an argument for your procedure is very similar to declaring a variable as a particular object type in a macro (see Chapter 21 for more information on declaring object variables). In this case, an argument for the macro is being declared as another type of object (a Ribbon control).

The **ByVal** statement is used with many procedure types in VBA to essentially make a copy of the argument's value available to a procedure as opposed to making the actual value available, so that the actual value can't be changed within that procedure. (For more information on **ByVal** references as well as where and how to use them, search for **ByVal** in the Visual Basic Language Reference available through Help in any Visual Basic Editor.)

However, all you really need to know to make use of this statement is that the exact statement **ByVal control as IRibbonControl** is used between the parentheses in the **Sub** statement for any macro you want to assign to a button on a Ribbon tab.

Want to give it a try? In the following exercise, you'll add a very simple macro to a new Microsoft Office Word 2007 document and then add that macro to a control on the View tab.

1. Create a new Office Word 2007 document and save it to your Windows Desktop as a .docm file. Name the file anything you like.

2. Press ALT+F11 to open the Visual Basic Editor, add a module to the new document, and then add the following macro.

```
Sub Sample(ByVal control as IRibbonControl)

    Msgbox "Hello!"

End Sub
```

CAUTION!

If you use a different name for your macro, be sure to make the appropriate adjustment in the XML code provided in step 5.

3. Save and close the document and then change the file extension to.zip.

4. On the Windows Desktop, create a folder named **customUI**. Then, open the Microsoft Windows Notepad accessory program and create a new document, saving it to the **customUI** folder as *customUI.xml*.

5. In *customUI.xml*, add the following code and then save and close the file. (This code is shown structured as it appears when viewed in Microsoft Internet Explorer. As explained in Chapter 22, the structure is created for you when you type the correct syntax in Notepad. To copy this code and paste it into your new customUI.xml file, instead of typing it yourself, find it at the end of the file Copy XML.txt that's available in the practice files that you can install from the Welcome tab of this book's CD. This file is part of the practice files provided for Chapter 22.)

```xml
<?xml version="1.0" encoding="utf-8" ?>
- <customUI xmlns="http://schemas.microsoft.com/office/2006/01/customui">
  - <ribbon>
    - <tabs>
      - <tab idMso="TabView">
        - <group id="myGroup" label="Say Hello" insertAfterMso="GroupZoom">
            <button id="Sample" visible="true" size="large" label="Click Me" onAction="Sample"
              imageMso="QueryBuilder" />
          </group>
        </tab>
      </tabs>
    </ribbon>
  </customUI>
```

6. Copy the folder **customUI** into the ZIP package for the .docm file you just created.

7. Copy the file *.rels* out of the top-level **_rels** folder of the ZIP package to edit it. Then, open the file in Notepad and add the following relationship before the **</Relationships>** code. (Be sure to replace # in the following code with a number not already in use in this file for a relationship ID.)

```
<Relationship Type="http://schemas.microsoft.com/office/2006/relationships/ui/
extensibility" Target="/customUI/customUI.xml" Id="rID#" />
```

8. Save and close *.rels* and then copy the file back into the ZIP package, overwriting the existing file of the same name.

That's it! Just change the file extension back to .docm and open your file. When you look at the View tab, you should see a new group after the Zoom group, as you see in the following image. (Depending on your macro security settings, keep in mind that you may need to enable macros when you open the file in order for the Click Me button to work.)

Though this example added the macro to a tab in a Word document, note that the steps are the same to add macros to the Ribbon for any macro-enabled Office Open XML Format file in the 2007 release programs Word, Excel, or PowerPoint—including (as applicable to the program) document, template, and add-in files.

TROUBLESHOOTING

A macro I added to the Ribbon is no longer available in the Macros dialog box

Once you declare arguments for any procedure, the procedure no longer appears in the Macros list on the Customize tab of the <Program> Options dialog box, the Macros dialog box, or (in Word) the Customize Keyboard dialog box. In fact, if you click into the procedure in the Visual Basic Editor and press F5, the macro won't run. This is because after you add an argument for the macro (such as to declare it as a Ribbon control), VBA assumes that this procedure will be called from another procedure or that it otherwise requires additional input you can't add when running the procedure independently.

However, although your procedure no longer behaves like a macro in several ways, it is still a macro and so it's affected by your macro security settings. See "Using the Trust Center," later in this chapter, for information on macro security in the 2007 release.

Note also that you can still add your macro to the Quick Access Toolbar (or to a keyboard shortcut in Word) if you've added it to a button on the Ribbon. Once your macro, or any customization, is added to a Ribbon tab, it becomes available (listed by the item label, such as a button or a group name) from the Choose Commands From list on the Customize tab of the <Program> Options dialog box. If your items are on a custom tab, that tab name will be listed in the Choose Commands From list. Otherwise, select All Commands from that list and locate your items alphabetically.

Creating Simple Add-Ins for Word, Excel, or PowerPoint

An add-in is functionality outside of the built-in program features that's made available from within a program, and is not part of an individual document or template. Many different types of add-ins are available to the 2007 release programs, as summarized in the list that follows, and as you see when you view the Manage list on the Add-Ins tab of the <Program> Options dialog box.

Chapter 23

Note

A handful of add-ins are built in to the programs and loaded when you first install the program (such as some types of SmartTags in Word or Office Excel 2007, and some parts of the Document Inspector in Word, Excel, and Microsoft Office PowerPoint 2007). So, unless you view the Add-Ins tab of the <Program> Options dialog box, you'd simply think they're built-in functionality. The interesting thing about this is that the features that have such add-ins are extensible, meaning that you can create your own add-ins for them. For example, add components to the Document Inspector to have it search for and remove the types of content you specify. Or, add your own custom SmartTags. This type of extensibility requires the use of a professional developer's platform like Microsoft Visual Studio and is more complex than the type of customization and automation you're learning in this book. However, if you're interested in venturing there, see "Next Steps" at the end of this chapter for additional resources.

- Excel provides a number of optional add-ins that come with the program but are not loaded by default, as you see in the Add-Ins dialog box shown here.

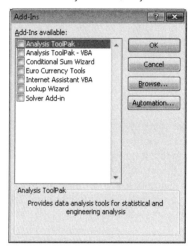

  To access this list of available Excel add-ins, in the Excel Options dialog box, click the Add-Ins tab. Then, select Excel Add-Ins from the Manage list and click Go. To load any of the add-ins you see in the preceding dialog box, just check the box beside the add-in name and then click OK.

- COM add-ins are created using the Component Object Model (COM), a Microsoft technology for creating software components that can interact with one another, across different programming languages and technologies. Most Microsoft Office add-ins that are packaged as executable files are COM add-ins (though add-ins created directly in the program can also be packaged using software that creates installer files, such as files with the .msi extension). COM add-ins are always created as managed code, through a professional developer's platform such as Visual Studio.

- Add-ins created in the program itself are saved in Excel or Office PowerPoint 2007 as add-in files, and in Word as templates. This is the category of add-in, discussed in the next section of this chapter, that you can create using VBA along with the customUI schema of the Office Open XML Formats.

Note that selecting either Word Add-Ins or Templates from the Manage list on the Add-Ins tab of the Word Options dialog box (shown here) will take you to the Templates tab of the Templates And Add-Ins dialog box.

> ### Note
>
> XML Expansion Packs (a group of files that defines the rules of an XML structure) and XML Schemas are shown as add-in types in the Manage list on the Add-Ins tab of the Word Options dialog box. Similarly, the XML Expansion Packs option is available on a similar list in the Excel Options dialog box. Such types of XML content aren't add-ins in the same sense as the other add-in types being discussed, because they don't independently provide functionality to the user.
>
> Also note that XML schemas used in the Office Open XML formats, as discussed in Chapter 22, don't appear when you select the XML Schemas option from the Add-Ins tab of the <Program> Options dialog box, because those schemas are inherently known by the 2007 release programs. XML developers can create and load custom schemas and expansion packs for use with documents and templates, but they're less commonly needed in the 2007 release because of the new file formats.
>
> Schemas and expansion packs were always installed to Office Word 2003 or Office Excel 2003 for use with Smart Documents (a somewhat cumbersome ancestor to the Office Open XML Formats).

Do You Need an Add-In?

Before creating an add-in, think about your needs for the particular project. If you create automation in VBA to be used with documents based on a particular template, it might be easier and cleaner to store that automation in the template itself, so that it only appears in documents based on that template.

When you store macros in a Word template, remember that the macros are actually in that template, so the documents based on that template can still be macro-free. What's more, the macros only appear as available to the document when its template is available, so that you can share the document without any concern of sharing your custom macros.

This is not the case, however, with macros stored in Excel or PowerPoint templates. Though Ribbon customization can travel with any Office Open XML Format document,

Chapter 23

macros can only travel with macro-enabled file types. Unlike in Word, where the document and template remain linked, an Excel or PowerPoint document is not linked to its source template after creation. Documents based on those templates must be saved in macro-enabled file formats so that the macros can travel with the document, or the macros will not be available to the document.

TROUBLESHOOTING

Template-specific macros aren't available in my document

As discussed in this section, one of the benefits of storing macros in a Word template is to keep your documents macro-free while having unique macros available only to the documents based on that template. If the template is moved from the location where it appeared when the document in question was created, or if the document is moved to another computer that has no access to the template location, the template becomes unavailable, so that Ribbon customizations and macros in that template don't appear when the document is open.

To confirm if this is the case with your document, on the Developer tab, click Document Template. On the Templates tab of the Templates And Add-Ins dialog box, the full path and file name of the attached template appear in the Document Template box. Click OK to confirm that the template is available. If a message appears indicating that the template doesn't exist, this means it doesn't exist in the specified path. Notice the Attach option on the Templates tab of this dialog box, where you can reselect the template in its current location. When you do, the template customizations will again appear in the document. Similarly, if you want to detach a document from its template so that the customizations never appear, delete the template path and file name from this dialog box and then click OK.

If the document in question is an Excel or PowerPoint file, remember that (as discussed in this section) Excel and PowerPoint documents don't remain attached to their source templates after creation. So, for macros to remain available to the document, save the document in a macro-enabled file format. Also keep in mind that this means any Ribbon customization and related macros will be available to that document whenever it's opened on any computer in the 2007 release version of the applicable program.

If you want your automation to generate documents (such as a set of formatted letters, memos, and invoices for your company) instead of creating automation that applies to a specific document type, create an add-in. This type of automation belongs in an add-in because you'll want to be able to access the automation before creating the related document. Automation that provides additional functionality for use with more than one document type (such as document production macros for tasks like removing excess paragraph marks in a document, or turning off Link To Previous for all headers in a document) also belongs in an add-in, so that it can be available to you regardless of the document or template in which you're working.

INSIDE OUT   **Making a macro available to most, but not all, documents**

You can set conditions and error handlers in your macros (as demonstrated in Chapter 21), so that making a macro available to many types of documents doesn't require making it available to every document. For example, if you have a macro to clean up formatting for tables pasted from the Web, you might write a conditional statement at the beginning of the macro to confirm that tables exist in the document and end the macro with notification if no tables are present.

```
If ActiveDocument.Tables.Count = 0 Then

    Msgbox "This macro is for use with documents containing at least one table.", _

    vbInformation,"My Macros"

    End

End If
```

Because the **End** statement appears inside the conditional statement, it will only be executed if the condition is true.

One of the most commonly required conditional statements when saving document production macros in an add-in is ensuring that at least one document is open. (That is, using the same structure as the preceding sample macro, **If Documents.Count = 0 Then**...) In general, when structuring your conditions and error handlers for any macros—particularly those in an add-in—make sure that any variables required for the macro to function correctly are considered, such as what view or story is active, or whether a referenced object exists in the active document.

What about storing macros directly in a document itself? Certainly, you can do this—and can add it to a custom Quick Access Toolbar or a customized Ribbon that travels with the document in Word, Excel, or PowerPoint—but consider carefully before you do so. Macros such as custom functions in Excel that apply to a specific workbook, or a custom series of cleanup steps for a particularly complex Word document, make sense to store in the document. However, when you need a substantial amount of custom functionality for a document—such as a complex form with multiple dialog boxes used for completing the form—storing that code in the document is a cumbersome approach that is likely to create a cumbersome experience (at best) for the users.

Remember that a document is not intended to store complex code for additional functionality—you have the capability to create add-ins for exactly this purpose. It might seem more complicated to install the functionality to each user's machine, but saving and loading an add-in takes just a minute and only has to be done once. Then, the functionality you need the user to have will be available whenever they need it. In contrast, a document that stores a mass of code might run slowly or even crash when the user's system resources are limited, and it's certain to take longer to save or share than the document would if the code were stored separately.

Chapter 23

So, when an add-in is the thing you need, the following three subheadings summarize what you need to know to get that add-in saved and loaded in Word, Excel, or PowerPoint.

Word: Global Templates

A global template in Word is a template that's available regardless of the document in which you're working. That is, a global template is an add-in.

To create a global template for custom functionality, save the file containing your macros and related Ribbon customization as a .dotm file (a macro-enabled Word template), either in your Word **Startup** folder (recommended), or another trusted location (see Chapter 20 for information about file locations and trusted locations).

If you save the template in a **Startup** folder, it loads automatically the next time you start Word and every time thereafter. If you save it in another location, you'll need to manually load it each time you start Word.

If your template doesn't load automatically the first time you start Word after saving the template, take the following steps to get that done. (However, if you've saved the template to the **Startup** folder and it still doesn't load automatically on the next Word instance, see the Troubleshooting tip "My add-in doesn't load automatically" later in this chapter.)

1. On the Developer tab, click Document Template. Or, on the Add-Ins tab of the Word Options dialog box, select Word Add-Ins from the Manage list and then click Go. This opens the Templates And Add-Ins dialog box.

2. If you see your template in the Global Templates And Add-Ins list on the Templates tab of this dialog box, simply check the box beside it to load the template and then click OK.

   If you don't see your template in this list, click Add, browse to and select your template, and then click Open. It will be added to the list and loaded in the same step. Click OK to close the dialog box. Remember that, if the template is not stored in a startup location, you'll need to repeat this process for subsequent Word sessions.

That's all there is to it. Any Ribbon customizations and macros saved in that template should now be available to you, as well as other globally available elements stored in that template (such as Building Block entries).

CAUTION!

Although Normal.dotm is the default global template and thus stores a variety of your settings and preferences, it behaves just like any other global template in terms of customizations and automation that you store in the template. This is good news and provides a simple solution when you want to customize defaults for yourself or your company, but it's a good idea to consider storing your customization (such as a custom Ribbon or a set of macros) in a separate global template.

Remember that, when Word exhibits unstable behavior that isn't specific to a document, a common troubleshooting step is to delete Normal.dotm as it regenerates a clean copy of itself the next time you open Word. So, when you store your customizations and automation in a separate global template, you protect both your customization and Word by keeping customization separate from program defaults. (I can't count how many modules of timesaving macros I lost to this purpose because I'd saved them in Normal.dot for ease of access and not backed them up.)

Notice, for example, how built-in Building Blocks are stored in Building Blocks.dotx—a global template that can contain only Building Block entries because of the location where it's saved—even though you can save Building Block entries in any template. For ease of use and troubleshooting, use this same best practice and save your custom add-ins as their own custom global templates.

Excel Add-Ins

To save an Excel workbook as an add-in, use the .xlam file extension (the Excel Add-In file format). When you save a file in this format, your Save In location will automatically be moved to the **AddIns** folder.

As soon as you save the add-in, Excel closes the file. Though you can reopen the file from the **AddIns** folder to edit the VBA project saved in the file, note that only the VBA project is accessible when you do this (an add-in contains no worksheets and won't appear to be open unless you're working in the Visual Basic Editor). Also note that the VBA project remains accessible and editable (unless you lock it and set a password, which is covered in Chapter 21) once you load the add-in, so there's no need to separately open the add-in file to edit the VBA project.

Once you save an add-in file, however, it is an Office Open XML file. So, you can still change the file extension to expose the ZIP package and add or edit Ribbon customization.

When you start your next Excel session after saving the add-in, the add-in will appear in the Add-Ins dialog box, but it won't be loaded. To load the add-in, select Excel Add-Ins from the Manage list on the Add-Ins tab of the Excel Options dialog box, then check the box beside that add-in and click OK. Once the add-in is initially loaded, it will continue to load automatically for subsequent Excel sessions.

PowerPoint Add-Ins

Similar to Excel add-ins, PowerPoint add-ins use an add-in file format (.ppam). When you save a presentation as a PowerPoint add-in, your Save In location is automatically moved to the **AddIns** folder. And, as in Excel, the add-in file is closed when you save it.

However, it's essential to save a complete copy of your automation in a PowerPoint presentation file format (such as .pptm) before saving it as an add-in, because the VBA project contained in a PowerPoint add-in file is not available in the Visual Basic Editor. So, to create an add-in with custom automation in VBA, make your updates to the add-in content in a presentation file and then resave the updated content as the add-in.

Chapter 23

TROUBLESHOOTING

How can I access macros that are only saved in a PowerPoint add-in?

So, you created a PowerPoint add-in without first saving it as a presentation or template file, right? Don't panic—you're using the new Office Open XML Formats.

In previous versions, you're pretty much out of luck if you have code stored in a Power-Point add-in and not backed up anywhere else. But, this is an excellent example of the benefits you get from the modularity of the new file formats.

To extract macros from a PowerPoint add-in, copy the add-in and then change the file extension to .zip. In the **ppt** folder inside the ZIP package, you'll see the VBA project file. It's a .bin (binary) file, as mentioned in Chapter 22.

You can copy this, along with its relationship and content type definition, to a new presentation and retrieve your macros for editing in that presentation. To do this, copy the following from the ZIP package for the add-in to the ZIP package for a new, macro-enabled presentation document (a .pptm file).

- The file *vbaProject.bin*, which resides in the **ppt** folder (copy it to the same location in the destination ZIP package)

- The relationship for the VBA project from the file *presentation.xml.rels*, located in the **_rels** folder that resides inside the the **ppt** folder. (Be sure to change the relationship ID to one not already used in the *presentation.xml.rels* file for the .destination document.)

- The default extension definition for the .bin file format, from *[Content_Types].xml*

When you change the presentation file format back to .pptm and open it in PowerPoint, the presentation will open with your macros intact and accessible for editing.

The other essential difference between a PowerPoint add-in and an Excel add-in is that the PowerPoint add-in isn't automatically added to the Add-Ins dialog box. Once you save an add-in, do the following to load it for the first time. As with Excel and Power-Point, the add-in will load automatically on subsequent PowerPoint sessions after you initially load it.

1. In the PowerPoint Options dialog box, on the Add-Ins tab, select PowerPoint Add-Ins from the Manage list and then click Go.

2. In the Add-Ins dialog box, click Add. Then, select your add-in file and click Open. If your macro security is set to disable macros with notification (recommended), you'll be prompted with the option to enable or disable the macros. Click Enable Macros and your add-in will load.

> **Note**
>
> In Word and Excel, add-ins saved in a trusted location are immune to your macro security settings, meaning that you can load add-ins containing macros from these locations, regardless of macro security. However, even though the macro security settings (discussed in the next section of this chapter) indicate in all three programs that trusted locations are exempt, that's not the case in PowerPoint. When you select the macro security setting to disable all macros without notification, your PowerPoint add-in files (.ppam) will not load. However, once a PowerPoint add-in is loaded from a trusted location, if macro security is changed to the highest level, previously loaded add-ins will continue to function correctly and to load automatically.

TROUBLESHOOTING

I can't edit the Quick Access Toolbar for my Excel or PowerPoint add-In

As discussed in this section, once you save an Excel add-in, the only element of that add-in that you can access through Excel is the VBA project. Customizing the Ribbon, of course, is always done through the ZIP package. But, if you've already saved your add-in file and don't have a backup copy of that file as an Excel workbook or template, the same goes for the Quick Access Toolbar.

If you open the ZIP package of any Office Open XML file containing a customized Quick Access Toolbar, you'll see a folder named **userCustomization.** This folder contains a file named *customUI.xml*, which includes automation similar to Ribbon customization. The syntax is a bit different, as you see in the following image, but the same control IDs are used for both Ribbon and Quick Access Toolbar customizations.

```
- <mso:customUI xmlns:mso="http://schemas.microsoft.com/office/2006/01/customui">
  - <mso:ribbon>
    - <mso:qat>
      - <mso:documentControls>
          <mso:control idQ="mso:PivotTableInsert" visible="true" />
        </mso:documentControls>
      </mso:qat>
    </mso:ribbon>
  </mso:customUI>
```

An applicable relationship is also added in the top-level *.rels* file. This relationship looks identical to the one used for Ribbon customization, with just a different path to represent the **userCustomization** folder name, as you see here.

```
<Relationship Id="rId#" Type="http://schemas.microsoft.com/office/2006/
relationships/ui/userCustomization" Target="userCustomization/customUI.xml" />
```

So, just as you do with the Ribbon, you can add Quick Access Toolbar customization to your add-in file through the ZIP package. (In fact, to save yourself work, copy the **userCustomization** folder and applicable relationship statement from a file that contains these items and edit it to add the control IDs you need, rather than starting from scratch.)

Chapter 23

Using the Trust Center

I love the name Trust Center. It sounds so imposing, as if you have a personal security system (or, perhaps, a tiny but powerful Doberman Pinscher) stored directly in the 2007 Office release programs, ready to protect your documents at any cost.

The fact is, though there are a few new options, the Trust Center is really just a reorganization of security settings, bringing together related options you already know from earlier versions. Essentially, you can find the following types of settings in the Trust Center.

- Preferences for trusted file locations (includes default file locations, such as User Templates)

- Permissions and related behavior for non-native functionality, such as macros and ActiveX controls

- Permissions for features that require accessing the Internet, such as translation options or participation in Microsoft's Customer Experience Improvement Program

- Document security preferences, such as warning before you print, save, or send a Word document that contains tracked changes and comments

- Permissions for external content (Excel), including workbook links and data connections

> ### Note
> Most of the programs in the 2007 Office system have a Trust Center, though the available tabs and options vary based on what's applicable to the individual program. For those programs that have a Trust Center but don't use the new user interface (such as Microsoft Office Visio 2007), find the Trust Center on the Tools menu. Note that though parts of Office Outlook 2007 do use the new interface, you'll still find the Trust Center in Outlook via the Tools menu and not through the Editor Options dialog box.

To access the Trust Center in Word, Excel, or PowerPoint, in the <Program> Options dialog box, click the Trust Center tab and then click Trust Center Settings. As you can see in the following example from Word, the Trust Center is organized very much like the <Program> Options dialog box, with its own set of tabs.

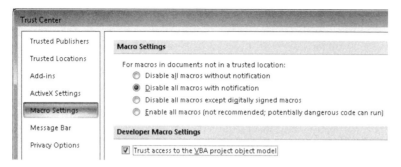

- To add a publisher to the Trusted Publisher's list, the add-in or template containing automation must be digitally signed and verified by a certification authority. When this is the case, the dialog box that provides the option to enable functionality offers the option to trust all content from this publisher. (See the next section of this chapter for more on digital signatures.)

- As mentioned in Chapter 20, select the Trusted Locations tab to add or edit file locations.

- Note that the Trust Center has an Add-ins tab. This is different from the Add-Ins tab in the <Program> Options dialog box, and not just because of the difference in capitalization of the tab name. This tab in the Trust Center does not provide access to managing add-ins. It only offers preferences for enabling or disabling certain types of add-ins (such as enabling only add-ins electronically signed by a publisher in your Trusted Publishers list).

- The ActiveX Settings and Macro Settings tabs provide security options for their respective types of automation. As you saw in the image that precedes this list, the names of the macro security options have changed. Instead of a range from low to very high, the options in the 2007 release are now simply descriptive. The option Disable All Macros With Notification is the equivalent of the Medium setting in earlier versions, and it is a good setting to recommend in most cases. This option will prompt you to enable macros in any documents or templates that are not saved in trusted locations, every time you open the file. However, note that you will not usually be prompted with a dialog box when macros require enabling, but with the Message Bar discussed in the next bullet. Click the Options button on the Message Bar for the Microsoft Office Security Options dialog box, where you can enable your automation.

- Beware of the Message Bar tab in the Trust Center! That is, beware of changing the default setting available there. This tab provides just two options. The default is to show the message bar when content has been blocked. That message bar appears below the Ribbon and looks similar to the image you see in the following image.

If you change this option to never show information about blocked content, you do the same as selecting the highest security level for macros and ActiveX controls—that is, disabling all content not saved in trusted locations. This is because if you don't see the Message Bar, you can't access the Microsoft Security Options dialog box, where you are able to enable this content.

- The Privacy Options tab, shown in the following image for Word, contains a set of options at the top that are consistent across Word, Excel, PowerPoint, and several other 2007 release programs. Setting these options in any program sets them for all (similar to many options on the Popular tab of the <Program> Options dialog box). So, for example, if you opt in to the Microsoft Customer Experience Improvement Program in Word, you've opted in for all programs.

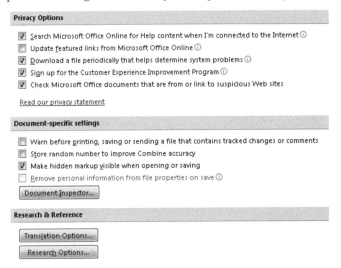

The Document-Specific Settings (shown here for Word) include the familiar option to Remove Personal Information From File Properties On Save. This option is usually disabled because the new Document Inspector feature (available through this dialog box or through the Prepare options under the Microsoft Office Button) handles this and more in terms of helping you avoid sharing personal or proprietary information in your documents. In Word, Excel, and PowerPoint—where this option appears—it's enabled in documents created in previous versions if the option was previously enabled. It's also enabled for a document after you use the Document Inspector to remove personal informaiton from that document. (Note that this option and the accompanying Document Inspector access point are the only document-specific settings available in the Excel and PowerPoint Trust Centers.)

The Research & Reference options are available in all programs that offer the Research task pane. As with the Privacy Options, setting the Research & Reference options in any program sets them in all applicable programs.

> **Note**
>
> For some good insight on the Customer Experience Improvement Program, see the Resources tab of this book's CD for an article by Microsoft Office System MVP Beth Melton, who (as mentioned a few times in earlier chapters) is also this book's talented technical reviewer. The article is titled "What Every User Should Know" and includes some other cool tips as well for getting yourself set up to work comfortably in the 2007 release.

TROUBLESHOOTING

My add-in or global template doesn't load automatically

As discussed earlier in this chapter, if you follow specified conditions, your add-ins should automatically load each time you open the program. These conditions include the following.

- For Word, save the template to the Word **Startup** folder or the **Startup** folder located at C:\Program Files\Microsoft Office\Office 12.

- For Excel, load the add-in the first time you start Excel after saving the file. If you've saved it to the **AddIns** folder, it will appear in the Add-Ins dialog box automatically and you just need to check the box beside the add-in name to load it. It will load automatically for subsequent Excel sessions.

- For PowerPoint, the process is the same as for Excel, with two exceptions. You need to click Add in the Add-Ins dialog box to add your add-in to the list and load it. It will then load automatically for subsequent sessions. However, if your macro security is at the highest setting, a new add-in can't be added to the Add-Ins dialog box.

If you've met these conditions and your add-in still doesn't load automatically on subsequent sessions of the applicable program, check for three possibilities.

- Check to see that the location where you saved the file is indeed a recognized **Startup** folder for Word. If you saved the Excel or PowerPoint add-in to an **AddIns** folder that the Save As dialog box automatically browsed to when you selected the file type, you can be sure that this is the correct location. However, for Word, if you use the Word **Startup** folder, rather than the Office 12**Startup** folder, check the Trusted Locations tab in the Trust Center to ensure that the folder you used is the folder Word recognizes as the startup location.

- If you've used a location other than the Word **Startup** folder, the Office 12**Startup** folder, or the **AddIns** folder, confirm that your location is listed on the Trusted Locations tab of the Trust Center.

- If you unload an Excel or PowerPoint add-in at any time, it will stop automatically loading. All it takes to unload an add-in is to remove the check from the box beside the add-in's name in the Add-Ins dialog box.

Chapter 23

Understanding Digital Signatures

A digital signature is a way to verify the authorship of content or to protect a document from changes by unauthorized authors. They're more and more commonly used in any content that contains code, as a way to help reassure the user of the integrity of the content.

You can set up a digital signature directly in the 2007 Office release programs. However, that signature will only be verifiable on your own computer, and it applies to the document rather than to the code. So, for example, you might want to do this if sending a document for review. Once edits are made to a document after you sign it, the signature becomes invalid and needs to be reapplied. So, if the document comes back to you with an invalid signature, you know to check it for changes.

However, if you need a signature that can be verified by others, that signature needs to be set up through a certification authority. Many companies offer this service (usually at a fee). You can sign up with some of these companies through the Microsoft Office Marketplace, accessible when you select the option to add a digital signature in a 2007 release document. Additionally, some companies have their own digital signature servers and thus can act as their own certification authority. (If you work for a large company, you might want to check with your IT department before purchasing a digital signature account on your own.)

CAUTION!

> Some of the vendors available as certification authorities through the Microsoft Office Marketplace offer signatures that are only compatible with Word. Make sure you can do what you need with your signature before purchasing one. (Note that a certificate that can be used for document signing is likely to be different from a certificate for code signing.) In fact, most vendors of this service offer a free trial period, and it's a good idea to use that option to make sure the signature works as you need. Just keep in mind that you can't use the free trial, for example, to sign a macro project and then let the trial expire. Recipients of that document or macro project won't be able to verify the signature if your account is expired.

Once you acquire your digital signature and install it on your computer, or once you set up a signature with the built-in digital signature tool, you can digitally sign 2007 release documents. To digitally sign a document, click the Microsoft Office Button, point to Prepare, and then click Add A Digital Signature. Then, after making changes to a previously signed file, remember to update the signature. To sign a VBA project, in the Visual Basic Editor, click the Tools menu, and then click Digital Signature.

> **Note**
>
> For more information and additional resource links about digital signatures, find a link to a Microsoft Office Online help article titled "About Digital Signatures" on the Resources tab of this book's CD.

Next Steps

With the information in this and the preceding chapters on VBA and XML, you might be amazed at how far you can take the customization capabilities of the 2007 release program. However, if you want to take your work with Microsoft Office programmability further, find links to some next-step resources (such as the Office Developer Center on the Microsoft Web site) on the Resources tab of this book's CD.

Also, keep in mind the additional resources on this CD that were referenced in the two preceding chapters, including the following.

- Links to the Developers Reference documentation for Word, Excel, and Power-Point VBA, which can help you build on the VBA essentials taught in this book.

- The complete Office Open XML documentation published by Ecma International, which can help you go from the basics in Chapter 22 and this chapter to fighter-pilot-cool Office Open XML expert, with access to everything there is to know about the new file formats and how to customize them.

Regardless of where you choose to go with Microsoft Office development capabilities, remember that much functionality is already built in to the programs, and how much more can be done simply with VBA or by just editing the XML in the document's ZIP package. The capabilities across the 2007 release, from the most basic to the absolutely astounding, are all about helping you find the simplest solution possible for creating the documents you need. Or, to quote a favorite proverb (from Confucius), "Don't use a cannon to kill a mosquito."

Essentially, when it comes to automating and customizing your documents (just as with everything you do in your Microsoft Office documents), keep in mind that the less work you do, the better your documents will be—every time.

Chapter 23

Index to Troubleshooting Topics

This index covers the topics addressed in Troubleshooting sidebars throughout the book. If you don't find what you're looking for here, try the fully searchable eBook available from the Welcome tab of this book's companion CD-ROM.

Index

A

Accelerator keys, 15–16. *See also* Keyboard shortcut;
  KeyTips
Active Field group, 356
Active paragraph, 255–256
Active window, defined, 118
ActiveX controls, in Excel and PowerPoint, 495–496
ActiveX Settings, 641
Add-in
  conditions for automatic loading, 643
  create, 627–645
  defined, 631
  differentiating between automated templates, global
    templates, and, 502–503
  Excel, 632, 637–639, 643
  need for, 633–636
  PowerPoint, 637–639, 643
  Word, 632–633, 643
Add-Ins dialog box, 632, 638
AddIns folder, 637–639
Add method, 533
Add Shape option, 411
Add To Quick Style List option, 72
Add Web Parts dialog box, 46
Adjust group, 156–157
Advanced chart types
  bubble chart, 335–337
  price/volume chart, 337–342
Advanced Web Part Gallery And Options, 46
Align actions and tools, 424–429, 445
Aligned At setting, 99–100
Alignment
  cell, 114–115
  custom-align content in SmartArt diagram, 407
  decimally align numbers and currency symbols,
    132–135
  Horizontal Alignment option, 325
  paragraph, 94–95, 115, 132–133
  of shapes, 369
  Vertical Alignment option, 325
  See also AutoFit; Bullets and numbering; Lists
Alignment group, 321
Alignment Tab, 174
Align tools, 573
All Caps, 466
Allow Only This Type Of Editing In The Document, 505
Allow Users To Edit Range, 37
All style behavior, 272–273

Alternate Text area, 151
ALT key, 413
Anchor, object, 153–154
And operator, 550
Angle option, 423
Animation, 484–485
Animations tab, 482–485
Apply Formatting To list, 102
Apply Shapes dialog box, 381
Apply Style, 421
Apply Styles pane, 73
Apply To list, 170–171, 173
Apply To Matching Slides, 479
Arguments, 533–535
Arrange feature, 138
Arrange group, 158, 282, 405, 407, 424–428
Arrow shape, 396
Arrows option, 419
As Shown On Screen, 344
Assistant shape, 411
AutoCaption, 220
AutoComplete, 288–289, 294, 301
AutoConnect, 371–373
AutoCorrect actions, 446
AutoCorrect dialog box, 19
AutoCorrect Options dialog box, 448
AutoCorrect SmartTag, 448
AutoFilter, 306–307
AutoFit, 108, 120–121, 125, 533
AutoFit setting, 472
AutoFit SmartTags, 448
AutoFit To Contents, 121
AutoFit To Window, 121, 128–129
AutoFormat As You Type, 448
Auto List, 526–527
AutoMark file, create index from, 222–223
Automated template, 502–503
Automatically Link feature, 386
Automatically Resize To Fit Contents, 121
Automatically Update Document Styles, 505–506
Automatic numbering, aligned incorrectly, 100
Automatic Updates, 26
Automation
  Content Controls and, 242–243
  next steps, 577–578
  and programming language, 489
  See also Macro(s)
Auto Scale setting, 321

About the Author

Stephanie Krieger Stephanie Krieger is a Microsoft Office System MVP and author of the book *Microsoft Office Document Designer*. A New York City-based consultant, she has helped many global companies develop enterprise solutions for Microsoft Office and taught numerous professionals and professional software trainers to build great documents by understanding the way that Microsoft Office programs "think." Stephanie writes regularly for several Microsoft Web pages and frequently delivers Microsoft webcasts.

When not glued to her computer, Stephanie spends much of her time studying her favorite hobbies—wine and Enlightenment-era history. You can reach Stephanie through her Web site, *www.arouet.net*.

Additional Resources for Home and Business

Breakthrough Windows Vista™: Find Your Favorite Features and Discover the Possibilities

Joli Ballew and Sally Slack
ISBN 9780735623620

Jump in for the topics or features that interest you most! This colorful guide brings Windows Vista to life—from setting up your new system; accessing the Windows Vista Sidebar; customizing it for your favorite gadgets; recording live television with Media Center; organizing photos, music, and videos; making movies; and more.

So That's How! 2007 Microsoft® Office System: Timesavers, Breakthroughs, & Everyday Genius

Evan Archilla and Tiffany Songvilay
ISBN 9780735622746

From vanquishing an overstuffed inbox to breezing through complex spreadsheets, discover smarter ways to do everyday things with Microsoft Office. Based on a popular course delivered to more than 70,000 students, this guide delivers the tips and revelations that help you work more effectively with Microsoft Office Outlook®, Excel®, Word, and other programs. Also includes 'webinars' on CD.

Look Both Ways: Help Protect Your Family on the Internet

Linda Criddle
ISBN 9780735623477

You look both ways before crossing the street. Now, learn the new rules of the road—and help protect yourself online with Internet child-safety authority Linda Criddle. Using real-life examples, Linda teaches the simple steps you and your family can take to help avoid Internet dangers—and still enjoy your time online.

The Microsoft Crabby Office Lady Tells It Like It Is: Secrets to Surviving Office Life

Annik Stahl
ISBN 9780735622722

From cubicle to corner office, learn the secrets for getting more done on the job—so you can really enjoy your time off the job! The Crabby Office Lady shares her no-nonsense advice for succeeding at work, as well as tricks for using Microsoft Office programs to help simplify your life. She'll give you the straight scoop—so pay attention!

Microsoft Office Excel 2007: Data Analysis and Business Modeling

Wayne L. Winston
ISBN 9780735623965

Beyond Bullet Points: Using Microsoft Office PowerPoint® 2007 to Create Presentations That Inform, Motivate, and Inspire

Cliff Atkinson
ISBN 9780735623873

Take Back Your Life! Using Microsoft Office Outlook 2007 to Get Organized and Stay Organized

Sally McGhee
ISBN 9780735623439

See more resources at **microsoft.com/mspress**
and **microsoft.com/learning**

Microsoft Press® products are available worldwide wherever quality computer books are sold. For more information, contact your bookseller, computer retailer, software reseller, or local Microsoft Sales Office, or visit our Web site at **microsoft.com/mspress**. To locate a source near you, or to order directly, call 1-800-MSPRESS in the United States. (In Canada, call **1-800-268-2222**.)

Additional Resources for Business and Home Users

Published and Forthcoming Titles from Microsoft Press

Beyond Bullet Points: Using Microsoft® PowerPoint® to Create Presentations That Inform, Motivate, and Inspire
Cliff Atkinson • ISBN 0-7356-2052-0

Improve your presentations—and increase your impact—with 50 powerful, practical, and easy-to-apply techniques for Microsoft PowerPoint. With *Beyond Bullet Points*, you'll take your presentation skills to the next level—learning innovative ways to design and deliver your message. Organized into five sections, including Distill Your Ideas, Structure Your Story, Visualize Your Message, Create a Conversation, and Maintain Engagement—the book uses clear, concise language and just the right visuals to help you understand concepts and start getting better results.

Take Back Your Life! Special Edition: Using Microsoft Outlook® to Get Organized and Stay Organized
Sally McGhee • ISBN 0-7356-2215-9

Unrelenting e-mail. Conflicting commitments. Endless interruptions. In this book, productivity expert Sally McGhee shows you how to take control and reclaim something that you'd thought you'd lost forever—your work-life balance. Now you can benefit from Sally's popular and highly regarded corporate education programs, learning simple but powerful techniques for rebalancing your personal and professional commitments using the productivity features in Outlook. When you change your approach, you can change your results. So learn what thousands of Sally's clients worldwide have discovered about taking control of their everyday productivity—and start transforming your own life today!

On Time! On Track! On Target! Managing Your Projects Successfully with Microsoft Project
Bonnie Biafore • ISBN 0-7356-2256-6

This book focuses on the core skills you need to successfully manage any project, giving you a practical education in project management and how-to instruction for using Microsoft Office Project Professional 2003 and other Microsoft Office Professional Edition 2003 programs, such as Excel® 2003, Outlook 2003, and Word 2003. Learn the essentials of project management, including creating successful project plans, tracking and evaluating performance, and controlling project costs. Whether you're a beginner just learning how to manage projects or a project manager already working on a project, this book has something for you. Includes a companion CD with sample Project templates.

Design to Sell: Using Microsoft Publisher to Inform, Motivate, and Persuade
Roger C. Parker • ISBN 0-7356-2260-4

Design to Sell relates the basics of effective message creation and formatting to the specific capabilities built into Microsoft Publisher—the powerful page layout program found on hundreds of thousands of computers around the world. Many Microsoft Office users already have Publisher on their computers but don't use it because they don't think of themselves as writers or designers. Here is a one-stop guide to marketing that even those without big budgets or previous design or writing experience can use to create compelling, easy-to-read marketing materials. Each chapter has an interactive exercise as well as questions with answers on the author's Web site. Also on the Web site are downloadable worksheets and templates, book updates, more illustrations of the projects in the book, and additional before-and-after project makeovers.

Microsoft Windows® XP Networking and Security Inside Out: Also Covers Windows 2000
Ed Bott and Carl Siechert • ISBN 0-7356-2042-3

Configure and manage your PC network—and help combat privacy and security threats—from the inside out! Written by the authors of the immensely popular *Microsoft Windows XP Inside Out*, this book packs hundreds of timesaving solutions, troubleshooting tips, and work-arounds for networking and security topics—all in concise, fast-answer format.

Dig into the tools and techniques for configuring workgroup, domain, Internet, and remote networking, and all the network components and features in between. Get the answers you need to use Windows XP Service Pack 2 and other tools, tactics, and features to help defend your personal computer and network against spyware, pop-up ads, viruses, hackers, spam, denial-of-service attacks, and other threats. Learn how to help secure your Virtual Private Networks (VPNs), remote access, and wireless networking services, and take ultimate control with advanced solutions such as file encryption, port blocking, IPSec, group policies, and tamper-proofing tactics for the registry. Get up to date on hot topics such as peer-to-peer networks, public wireless access points, smart cards, handheld computers, wireless LANs, and more. Plus, the CD includes bonus resources that make it easy for you to share your new security and networking expertise with your colleagues, friends, and family.

For more information about Microsoft Press® books and other learning products, visit: **www.microsoft.com/mspress** *and* **www.microsoft.com/learning**

Microsoft Press products are available worldwide wherever quality computer books are sold. For more information, contact your book or computer retailer, software reseller, or local Microsoft Sales Office, or visit our Web site at **www.microsoft.com/mspress**. To locate your nearest source for Microsoft Press products, or to order directly, call 1-800-MSPRESS in the United States. (In Canada, call **1-800-268-2222**.)

2007 Microsoft® Office System Resources for Developers and Administrators

Microsoft Office SharePoint® Server 2007 Administrator's Companion

Bill English with the Microsoft SharePoint Community Experts
ISBN 9780735622821

Get your mission-critical collaboration and information management systems up and running. This comprehensive, single-volume reference details features and capabilities of SharePoint Server 2007. It delivers easy-to-follow procedures, practical workarounds, and key troubleshooting tactics—for on-the-job results.

Microsoft Windows SharePoint Services Version 3.0 Inside Out

Jim Buyens
ISBN 9780735623231

Conquer Microsoft Windows SharePoint Services—from the inside out! This ultimate, in-depth reference packs hundreds of time-saving solutions, troubleshooting tips, and workarounds. You're beyond the basics, so now learn how the experts tackle information sharing and team collaboration—and challenge yourself to new levels of mastery!

Microsoft SharePoint Products and Technologies Administrator's Pocket Consultant

Ben Curry
ISBN 9780735623828

Portable and precise, this pocket-sized guide delivers immediate answers for the day-to-day administration of Sharepoint Products and Technologies. Featuring easy-to-scan tables, step-by-step instructions, and handy lists, this book offers the straightforward information you need to get the job done—whether you're at your desk or in the field!

Inside Microsoft Windows® SharePoint Services Version 3

Ted Pattison and Daniel Larson
ISBN 9780735623200

Get in-depth insights on Microsoft Windows SharePoint Services with this hands-on guide. You get a bottom-up view of the platform architecture, code samples, and task-oriented guidance for developing custom applications with Microsoft Visual Studio® 2005 and Collaborative Application Markup Language (CAML).

Inside Microsoft Office SharePoint Server 2007

Patrick Tisseghem
ISBN 9780735623682

Dig deep—and master the intricacies of Office SharePoint Server 2007. A bottom-up view of the platform architecture shows you how to manage and customize key components and how to integrate with Office programs—helping you create custom enterprise content management solutions.

Microsoft Office Communications Server 2007 Resource Kit

Microsoft Office Communications Server Team
ISBN 9780735624061

Your definitive reference to Office Communications Server 2007—direct from the experts who know the technology best. This comprehensive guide offers in-depth technical information and best practices for planning, designing, deploying, managing, and optimizing your systems. Includes a toolkit of valuable resources on CD.

Programming Applications for Microsoft Office Outlook® 2007

Randy Byrne and Ryan Gregg
ISBN 9780735622494

Microsoft Office Visio® 2007 Programming Step by Step

David A. Edson
ISBN 9780735623798

See more resources at **microsoft.com/mspress**
and **microsoft.com/learning**

Microsoft Press® products are available worldwide wherever quality computer books are sold. For more information, contact your bookseller, computer retailer, software reseller, or local Microsoft Sales Office, or visit our Web site at **microsoft.com/mspress**. To locate a source near you, or to order directly, call 1-800-MSPRESS in the United States. (In Canada, call **1-800-268-2222**.)

Windows Vista™ Resources for Administrators

Windows Vista Administrator's Pocket Consultant
William Stanek
ISBN 9780735622968

Portable and precise, this pocket-sized guide delivers immediate answers for the day-to-day administration of Windows Vista. Featuring easy-to-scan tables, step-by-step instructions, and handy lists, this book offers the straightforward information you need to solve problems and get the job done—whether you're at your desk or in the field!

Windows Vista Resource Kit
Mitch Tulloch, Tony Northrup, Jerry Honeycutt, Ed Wilson, Ralph Ramos, and the Windows Vista Team
ISBN 9780735622838

Get the definitive reference for deploying, configuring, and supporting Windows Vista—from the experts who know the technology best. This guide offers in-depth, comprehensive technical guidance on automating deployment; implementing security enhancements; administering group policy, files folders, and programs; and troubleshooting. Includes an essential toolkit of resources on DVD.

MCTS Self-Paced Training Kit (Exam 70-620): Configuring Windows Vista Client
Ian McLean and Orin Thomas
ISBN 9780735623903

Get in-depth preparation plus practice for Exam 70-620, the required exam for the new Microsoft Certified Technology Specialist (MCTS): Windows Vista Client certification. This 2-in-1 kit focuses on installing client software and configuring system settings, security features, network connectivity, media applications, and mobile devices. Ace your exam prep—and build real-world job skills—with lessons, practice tests, evaluation software, and more.

MCITP Self-Paced Training Kit (Exam 70-622): Installing, Maintaining, Supporting, and Troubleshooting Applications on the Windows Vista Client – Enterprise
Tony Northrup and J.C. Mackin
ISBN 9780735624085

Maximize your performance on Exam 70-622, the required exam for the new Microsoft® Certified IT Professional (MCITP): Enterprise Support Technician certification. Comprehensive and in-depth, this 2-in-1 kit covers managing security, configuring networking, and optimizing performance for Windows Vista clients in an enterprise environment. Ace your exam prep—and build real-world job skills—with lessons, practice tests, evaluation software, and more.

MCITP Self-Paced Training Kit (Exam 70-623): Installing, Maintaining, Supporting, and Troubleshooting Applications on the Windows Vista Client – Consumer
Anil Desai with Chris McCain of GrandMasters
ISBN 9780735624238

Get the 2-in-1 training kit for Exam 70-623, the required exam for the new Microsoft Certified IT Professional (MCITP): Consumer Support Technician certification. This comprehensive kit focuses on supporting Windows Vista clients for consumer PCs and devices, including configuring security settings, networking, troubleshooting, and removing malware. Ace your exam prep—and build real-world job skills—with lessons, practice tests, evaluation software, and more.

See more resources at **microsoft.com/mspress**
and **microsoft.com/learning**

Microsoft Press® products are available worldwide wherever quality computer books are sold. For more information, contact your bookseller, computer retailer, software reseller, or local Microsoft Sales Office, or visit our Web site at **microsoft.com/mspress**. To locate a source near you, or to order directly, call 1-800-MSPRESS in the United States. (In Canada, call **1-800-268-2222**.)

What do you think of this book?

We want to hear from you!

Do you have a few minutes to participate in a brief online survey?

Microsoft is interested in hearing your feedback so we can continually improve our books and learning resources for you.

To participate in our survey, please visit:

www.microsoft.com/learning/booksurvey/

...and enter this book's ISBN-10 number (appears above barcode on back cover*).
As a thank-you to survey participants in the United States and Canada, each month we'll randomly select five respondents to win one of five $100 gift certificates from a leading online merchant. At the conclusion of the survey, you can enter the drawing by providing your e-mail address, which will be used for prize notification only.

Thanks in advance for your input. Your opinion counts!

*Where to find the ISBN-10 on back cover

ISBN-13: 000-0-0000-00000-0
ISBN-10: 0-0000-00000

00000

0 000000 000000

Example only. Each book has unique ISBN.

Microsoft Press

No purchase necessary. Void where prohibited. Open only to residents of the 50 United States (includes District of Columbia) and Canada (void in Quebec). For official rules and entry dates see:

www.microsoft.com/learning/booksurvey/